CW01583363

Her Majesty
Queen Elizabeth II
Buckingham Palace
London SW1A 1AA
England

Dear Your Majesty The Queen,

My Spymaster once swore an oath of loyalty to you. He now believes you have been badly, if not criminally, advised. The Spymaster feels obligated to point this out. As such, we are sending you a copy of this book.

Yours sincerely,

Greg Hallett

Historian Henry Makow, Ph.D., United States
Greg Hallett offers persuasive circumstantial evidence that Hitler was a British Agent. As Hitler was in Britain 1912–13 other historians are guilty of sanitizing Hitler, giving him more credibility that he had. *Hitler was a British Agent* is a useful paradigm that clarifies many improbable events . . .

Why the Nazi war machine was financed and built by the Bank of England.

Why Hitler was able to expand into the Rhineland without fear of retaliation.

Why Hitler let 335,000 Allied soldiers escape at Dunkirk.

Why Hitler attacked Russia before England was invaded or conquered.

Why the Nazis never figured out their communications were compromised.

Why Hitler never sealed the Mediterranean at Gibraltar.

Why the Spanish dictator Franco remained neutral.

Why Hitler didn't conquer the oil fields of Russia and the Middle East.

Why Hitler gave his racial policies priority over actually winning the war.

Why I.G. Farben was never bombed, and became the CIA headquarters in Frankfurt after WWII.

The biggest improbability of traditional history is that an Austrian tramp, street cleaner and gay prostitute could become the Chancellor of Germany. Hitler joins a long list of obscure blackmailable figures catapulted into world prominence by the unseen hand.

Implications . . . History is unfolding according to the Illuminati's long-term plan. Wars are plotted decades in advance and orchestrated to achieve the destruction of nations and natural elites, depopulation, demoralization, and of course power and profit . . . The Illuminati sponsor 'enemies' in order to ferment conflict . . . The super rich have organized themselves to prey on mankind and establish permanent hegemony . . . Greg Hallett deserves our thanks for advancing a history more plausible than what supposedly transpired.

Ole Gerstrøm, Former Member of Parliament, Denmark
I read your book. It is magnificent. That Hitler was a stooge has been my working hypothesis for many years. We know from Anthony Sutton, that the Nazis were financed by Rockefeller and the like. You mention a total of 10 volumes. I would like to read them.

Robert Schwartz, Texas
A credible and well-documented study. The Ian Fleming information was stunning, and very valuable.

Lenny Bloom, political scientist at Cloak & Dagger, Canada
It's a tremendous book, a terrific compilation of the war . . . wonderfully documented, well-footnoted . . . It shows the real machinations going on backstage in the Global Theatre and certainly explains a lot . . . I think readers are going to be very surprised as to what really happened with Adolf Hitler. It shows the greater underground, the under-bush . . . the plans of the monarchies and oligarchs go very, very deep. They plan these things decades in advance. An excellent book, I recommend it highly. It's a must read for everybody.

Charles Andersen, Oklahoma
Hitler Was A British Agent is a seminal work with a wealth of information from an insider's view of the real history of the twentieth century. The insider being one [or more] "spymasters". It's a great read full of 'incidental' information, that is in itself, both informative and entertaining. The authors posit that both Hitler and Stalin were British agents trained at Tavistock . . . Charlie Chaplin and Peter Sellers both British agents . . . Chaplin's socialist/communist politics an intelligence gathering front . . . Peter Sellers' *Being There* a parody of Hitler in his post-war years . . . the real James Bond, his real name, how he came to be a spy and his more notable operations . . . the end-of-war operations to get the real Hitler out of Germany – Operation JAMES BOND and Operation WINNIE THE POOH . . . the Beatles an MI-6 front. 'Their' Yellow Submarine song a parody of Hitler's escape out of Berlin . . . Fascinating stuff that predicts the future: Saddam Hussein, war, Freemasonry etc . . . Enjoyable read.

Ole Jensen, Denmark
I love your book. It's a brick-load of information! You've got all the dirty deeds lined up and you're hitting them right on the head. There is a missing period in Hitler's life, around 1912–13, which no previous historian has accounted for. From my own knowledge, I found no major flaws . . . Lots of neat little details, like Sir CC and Chaplin's "Double Cross" symbolism. I understand your book. No big surprises for me. Keep me on the customer list and I hope not to end up on someone's hit list :-)

Zeph Daniel, Channel Z, New Mexico
Excellent book, excellent work. Thanks for all you do.

British woman, Head of an area Government Department, New Zealand
"You have no idea what you have done. It's just like Vera Briton's book."

Hitler
WAS A BRITISH AGENT

GREG HALLETT

AND THE

SPYMASTER

The Rules of War

Amory Bradford's letter regarding Clare Boothe Luce's idea for the assassination of Hitler (June 16th) reminded me of an ingenious plan devised by my father, Sir Douglas Jardine, when he was the British governor of Sierra Leone, in 1941.

The Germans were gaining ground in North Africa, and he was secretly approached by the German High Command with a proposal that he move his troops in Sierra Leone to the wrong border when the German Army invaded the country. For this help, my father was to receive "clement treatment" in the event of a German victory. My father wrote to Whitehall suggesting that he should agree to go to Berlin to discuss the moves he might make. In his pocket he would have a box of Swan Vesta matches with yellow-fever germs sealed inside. My father had been vaccinated against yellow-fever, a fatal disease, so while talking to Hitler he would be able to light his pipe or cigarette and crush the box of matches.

Whitehall replied that on no account was he to do any such foolish thing: it would not be cricket to murder Hitler.

Penelope Jardine

S. Giovanni in Oliveto, Italy

The New Yorker, 28 July 1997, p. 6.

Churchill
"In wartime,
the truth is so precious
that she should always be attended by a bodyguard of lies."

Hitler
"In wartime,
we provide truth with a bodyguard of lies
because it is so precious."

Tavistock Military Psych-Ops War School training line
"In wartime,
the truth is so precious
we surround it with a bodyguard of lies."

Published by
FNZ Inc.
Auckland, New Zealand
www.greghallett.com

First Edition: 15 September 2005
Second Edition: 1 October 2006
Copyright © Greg Hallett, 2005, 2006
ISBN 978-0-473-11478-7

The most difficult aspect of copyright is obtaining the right to print images freely available on the web. The images are available in abundance, but the owners are difficult to locate, if not impossible, do not respond to emails, have no English facility, or no clear method of payment. I take the view that no one owns history and lack of communication or the enforced purchase of hundreds of images in order to obtain one, is history extortion. As many image owners as possible have been located and paid accordingly. Almost all watermarks have been cleared for reproduction, but even some of these owners could not be located. When the images cost more than the RRP of the book there is a problem with history. Some copyrighters even went as far as to limit the placement of their images into 'only appreciative history'. This is Political Correctness as started under a lead-poisoned Lenin in May 1921. Shame! There is the other matter of the service done to those people in history who have now been placed in a correct light. Charles Chaplin, for instance, has been cleared somewhat, as I trust his images are. History is more important than copyright. For the purposes of obtaining the right to print images, the working title: '*BRITAIN AND NAZI GERMANY, Studies in Foreign Relations*' was used. All rights placed in this have been transferred to the published title, *HITLER WAS A BRITISH AGENT*. I trust all the owners of reproduction rights will appreciate the importance of history and contact me accordingly. If you believe you are the genuine owner of an image and have the rights to reproduction, then contact the publisher at www.hitlerwasabritishagent.com with proof of ownership. There are 215 images. The total royalties should amount to less than 1% of sales profit. In most cases the work is in the public domain and copyright has expired. In those that have not, liberal and commercial fair use is utilised, including information and pictures of historical figures. It is deemed that historical figures in the public domain, by sheer weight of vanity and honorability, uphold the freedom of information. Those same people have neither copyrighted their name, or their image. As such, their images are declared free by nature of presence, position and power. Their lives are considered a functional work. They lived their lives with a creative content having no legal restriction relative to other people's freedoms. As such, they lived their lives in complete disregard to the commoner's copyright on their lives, let alone their image. A work in the public domain can not be licensed. Such works are considered free content. It is the same for the life of a figure in the public domain. Ditto for fair and equitable damage done by the public figure. If a copyrighted image of 'a public figure that has damaged the lives of others' is used, then it is fair and equitable that they should be damaged, alive or dead, by correct placement in history and it is this history that should be challenged before copyright is challenged. The images in this book are claimed to be used under fair use as they are historically significant photos of famous individuals and famous scenes; they are of a lower resolution than the original and any copies will be of inferior quality; the photos are only used for informational purposes; their inclusion adds significantly to the knowledge gained because it shows the subject/event depicted as historically significant to the general public. Incorporating restricted material is fair use under United States copyright law and any challenges will be met with commercial and liberal parody.

Dedication

To those who have walked the walk
and talked the talk.

To James Bond III,
the Spymaster,
and Walter Mitty,
who is omnipresent in all of us.

To the living libraries and talking dictionaries,
who for some reason chose to talk to me.

Spying is the Great Game.
Information is a commodity
subject to the forces of the marketplace
as much as any other. It has one advantage
in that it can be sold more than once.
Books are its least profitable way to do this.
Nevertheless, history is best written to influence the present.

Ten books have been written in this history series.
These have been placed with rogue intelligence officers
to be 'dumped' on the net if necessary.

All wars are fake wars.
Some are short and some are long,
but all wars are 'created'.

Every war is a war of secrets.
Wars with the greatest number of secrets take the longest.
A war without secrets is 'a bashing, a mugging, or a trial run'.

Every war is a social experiment whose end
is always 'new ways of controlling the masses'.
All wars are a front for creating social change.

Wars are designed, like a car, to fulfil a purpose – to carry a certain weight, fragility and number of packages over a certain distance, at a certain speed, towards a certain end, for a certain group.

The designers of war usually own the latest 'vehicle', the most 'vehicles', and are usually after a secret or a resource held by those less fortunately packaged – from the secrets of King Solomon's Tomb to oil.

The Second World War tried to improve on everything the First World War had achieved and the Third World War will do the same. World Wars are an attempt to set up One World Order social structures, so that everything and absolutely everything complies with that Order.

The practice of deconstructing foreign politicians has developed over the past five hundred years and is now a favourite method of taking over countries since the success of Hitler and Stalin.

Intelligence Historian, 15 September 2004:
"We have a window of opportunity to the end of next year. The Germans are on to it. They have recently found evidence that Hitler was a British agent in the Stasi archives."

History is blind for one reason:
"Blessed are the war-makers."

Preface

Spymaster: "One of the tricks of Intelligence is to deny everything. They routinely promote lies, tricks and deceptions and always promote some pederast to a high place who has nothing to do with it. He is the public face of ignorance. Anyone who attacks this person is vilified by the entire system of government. In reality, the people who have gone out and risked life and limb are routinely cast as fantasists and liars. Such are the rewards of intelligence."

At 8.30 am on 14 August 2003 I opened my back door to a Security Intelligence Service vehicle masking as Matrix Security. I looked up to see a police helicopter between me and the museum. Both were monitoring me. An hour later an intelligence officer arrived at my door with two coffees and a newspaper. He had a problem with history and nominated himself as my chauffeur.

Thereafter I sat in the back of my car getting briefed and recording history. He proved himself by giving me the news ahead of time over the next year. I became convinced that the Spymaster had access to information worthy of recording and organising. This formed the basis of this book and the foundation of others to follow.

I was given sixty books, about four at a time, some magazines, and a host of documentaries to watch. In each one I looked for purposeful mistakes and in each one I found them.

Most of these books were written by secret service agents who had witnessed events above their station, and their mistakes screamed loudly to whomever had the detailed knowledge to pursue them. The devil is in the details and it seemed that the devil was everywhere. Fortunately I had access to 'living libraries' and their detailed knowledge opened the Pandora's box and a new history was formed – the history of the world according to the secret service. This was history beyond the cover-ups. It was history from the secret service with the intelligence angle behind it. This knowledge then gave leverage for more information elsewhere and was detailed enough and broad enough to act as protection. As soon as the information was interpreted, it was disseminated and exists in disk form, in mattresses all over the world.

War began the keeping of records and the falsifying of records. Thus two records of history were always kept. The public got one, while the true record was held under secrecy for 30, 50, 100 years or more. Conspiracy writers scratch the surface and get halfway, occasionally getting it right. To get it right, you have to understand movements and motivation and have insiders in every aspect of war, politics and the bedroom. As a result, in 95% of history books, two-thirds of the information is false.

The history the public receive and abide by is bunkum.

Members of the secret service who were allowed to survive are known as 'living libraries'. These are the 'human dictionaries' that know the fluff from the stuff. They cut to the chase and have a pleasant habit of talking in sentences of ten words or less. Their stories have a ring of truth about them and, when pieced together, they fit like cogs in a wheel. As you listen to their stories you are watching history turn, one cog intertwined with another, and a new history is formed.

The purpose of studying history is to shift out of first gear and, ultimately, make it possible to influence history. Once a cog has been identified, the next one needs attention, and the next one after that. A cog only comes to attention when the previous cog has been illuminated. In this way, intelligence becomes an addictive jigsaw – hard to compromise convincingly, unless the first story is befuddled. Official history is loaded with such befuddlements.

When enough interconnected cogs are illuminated, a new history is formed. This makes the present easier to explain and the future easier to understand, if not predict.

The historian's job is to decipher and impart information in a way that the public can understand. Some of the world's dumbest people are historians lecturing in what amounts to *history propaganda* and some of the world's most intelligent historians are painting houses. This is the problem with history.

In the process of writing this book, I collected information from intelligence agents around the world. I then gave each agent information from the other, which they checked. Any other leads I had, I'd check through the service and they'd tell me how accurate I was. They usually checked the stories through the foreign intelligence network based in the listening post that is New Zealand. As the mutual exchange checked out, respect developed and the 'bullshit' factor was eliminated. I did this for some twenty-two years and in the last three years I've been briefed up to four times a week, making me one of the boys, but still a boy.

When the information proved to be correct, as it invariably did – bar minor details which were corrected using all media – I came up with a scenario and illustrated the agents' part in it, and then a theory on the 'how and why' of intrigues, assassinations, wars and social policy. In this way I gathered a body of data that is a virtual rewrite of the last hundred years of history. As this information was ordered a new and more accurate history formed.

Occasionally it was tense, especially towards the end, when we had a 'property' that was worth protecting and capable of toppling. Most often these treffs (spy meetings) were done face to face, sometimes through a proxy and other times through proxies on both sides. Many of the people I recruited information from, I was never allowed to meet. Money never changed hands and the most expensive information came with the price of a takeaway meal. No one had any pretensions and no one wore a trenchcoat, but we had a lot of laughs, tea and crackers.

The meetings are backed up by notes, diaries, tape recordings, transcripts, treaties and disks secured off-site. Many writers end their preface with "I hope this . . ." but I have no illusions. Much will be made of nothing and nothing will be made of much.

C'est la vie and such is war.

Greg Hallett
From the recently toppled Anglican Archives, 8 August 2005

History rarely remembers an honest political figure.
This is the nature of the occult.

CONTENTS

APPENDICIES

Living Libraries

At the start of a mission, life expectancy is very low. When six operatives are on a mission, they tell one or two stories of what really went down. After all, there is nothing to lose. A couple of the agents die and four are left with eight stories. After a decade or two the stories start to repeat, but those startled, surprised survivors have the history of the world pierced through their thick skin and rubbed into the arms of their worn-out chairs. As they talk oblivious of their surroundings, they reveal their secrets and a whole new world opens up.

The problem with agents is that they played a role but were denied the overall picture. Each had a piece of evidence to impart and it is only through collecting their different stories that an entire picture emerges. When an ordinary Joe interviews more than one of them and shows their collective part in history, their friendship is immediate, protective and concerned. Their advice is always right. After all, they are the survivors of various governments' ideologies and the bizarre cravings of power.

When these stories unfurl and are put in perspective, the nature of the secret service opens up. With five decades of stories from more than one player, their stories overlap in the thousands and a history is born. As much as I show you here, much more is left out. As soldiers, authors and historians die off, their records often go with them.

Most of history is created from manufactured records, yet the true history provides us with the rich understanding of 'humanity's bizarre strivings for wealth and power', the destruction of each other, the desire for mass murder and the cover-ups that follow. Heroism is wasted in war – you may win the battle, but lose the war; while treason is rewarded with entire countries and all your groceries paid for . . . but your life is not your own.

Secret societies have long had access to the actual events in history. This is the history that the secret service have passed down through centuries and made available for the elite to access. This is the knowledge of power. There are four methods to get this 'knowledge of power'. The first is to do exhaustive research from scratch. The second, if you can access them, is to interview 'living libraries' – old secret agents who have that smart, distrustful, questioning look in their eyes (that belies too much action and a complete surprise at being alive). The third is to be an active historian changing history with the straw that broke the camel's back. The fourth is to belong to a secret society and work your way up through the ranks, at which point you can't reveal the information . . . this makes books like this one, so very rare.

I have access to three of these methods and can name thirty others so ordinary and bizarre as to be commonly held the work of fiction and fantasy – but they work, some only as a starting point and others as detail without the overall picture.

I was asked recently, "How the hell did you get past a hundred security guards into President Bill Clinton's dinner speech without a ticket?" Quite simply I used a technique so ordinary and bizarre as to be considered the work of fiction, a technique I had invented eighteen hours prior. Fortune favours the brave and history is entrusted to those who pass the integrity test for the longest.

The acid test, as with history, is 'whatever works'. This history does not limit itself to being from a British angle.

History repeats every sixty years plus or minus two years. To study the present day, the most effective starting point is to go back sixty years from the present historical figures and examine the training of their predecessors.

In each war there are double agents that go right to the top. The more effective they are, the more compromised they are, and the more they are secretly protected afterwards, right through the ages.

Wars are always created through double agents and compromised principles. Wars are always based on profit. Those who profit ignore the deaths. Those who suffer never get past the deaths. In this way it takes an unencumbered generation to illuminate the hoax of war.

To create a war, you first have to invent a fictitious enemy and then go out and kill them – without killing your own double agent. In most instances you have to grow the double agent and the enemy yourself. This has been common practice for over a century.

Stalin began his British training in 1907 and Hitler began his British training in 1912. In both cases these double agents ended up as Heads of State running foreign countries given to them by their trainers. Stalin was from Georgia and was given Russia; Hitler was from Austria and given Germany.

To illustrate this, it is necessary to break down war into its component parts and resulting social control. Although the deaths are very real, much of war is smoke and mirrors, cover-ups and lies carried out by organised societies continuously performing magician's tricks – a succession of great switcheroos.

To expose what really happened, you have to understand how these tricks were performed. Secret societies have 'a memory, vengeance, purpose and resources beyond generations', and this is what makes them so powerful.

"Those who wish to become our leaders choose the ordeal of war to prove themselves worthy of the privilege."

"What if we're at peace?"

"There are always wars to be fought."[1]

When the British *Freemasons* want to create war, the American *Skulls* prepare to supply them with munitions across the Atlantic and vice versa. When either the Freemasons or the Skulls need a war for profit, they use MI-6 and the CIA to create it.

Other countries' intelligence agencies are also involved. They become involved based on protecting any minority sexual practices of their leaders. The divergent sexual practices of countries' leaders is *the* major reason for the miscalculation of war.

With monogamous heterosexual leaders, wars halve in frequency. As a result, leaders with nothing to hide tend to be eliminated, either frustrated before they get into power, or killed once in power. This is the nature of war. Deaths do not count, not even the deaths of their leaders.

Straight after WWII the OSS (Office of Strategic Services) was replaced by the CIA Central Intelligence Agency (1946). The CIA became an ambitious, high-level, ruthless self-sovereign organisaton – effectively a marauding country on the move, a roving conqueror.

The Skulls drew on the CIA for their new members, the most prominent of which was George Herbert Walker Bush (Bush senior) in 1948, followed by George W. Bush in 1968 (the current American President). The Skulls was founded at Yale University in 1832 for the elite children of

[1] *The Skulls*, 1999.

Wall Street bankers. They were linked to the Illuminati (founded 1 May 1776) and through them had access to the Freemasons and the Mercers. They take in 15 new members each year.

In 2003, just prior to his inauguration as Governor of California, Arnold Schwarzenneger became a 16th member of the Skulls. This doesn't happen too often.

America, the spiteful, youthful, vengeful bitch did its best to profit from the managed wars of WWI (1914–18) and WWII (1939–45). These were European Civil Wars and Masonic wars – in retaliation for the American Civil War (1861–65) that the British had arranged some fifty years earlier . . . and so history is formed.

The devil is in the details and the details are rarely revealed.

Adolf Hitler

The Incestuous Catholic Jew

"How incomplete, how absent, how fragmentary our knowledge of Hitler's past and what made him tick is."[1]

If you want to create a revolution, introduce new expectations and rules to live by. If you want to make a revolutionary, create someone out of their time – and ensure they are disgruntled about it. This is simply done by training them in an ideology different from their time or what is currently being expressed. Many are trained and most fall away. The one who survives to lead will be a revolutionary for a variety of reasons. The harder time they have, the more changes they will make. This is called 'creating potential in the revolutionary'.

Most movements created are exported overseas for subversive reasons. Movements and ideologies have become the new war. With a movement or ideology it is possible to destroy an opposing country without firing a weapon. Political Correctness is a prime example – invented in Russia, it was exported to the West to destroy the family and fun . . . and to stop progress.

Hitler's family history is a near perfect example of how to create a criminal. Sadly, his personal history has been taken as an exemplary family pattern and is being repeated as closely as possible by nearly every government department involved with children across the Western world . . . but I've taken the stage here to outline Hitler's origins and expose his training. His initial nature was kind, caring and gentle. He was a typical beaten boy from a family that had plenty to hide.

Catholic Incest

Officially Hitler had incestuous parents in Alois and Klara. His father's grandparents and his mother's great-grandparents were the same two people, making their marriage second- and third-degree incest – the wife (25) being the niece of the husband (48) who was also her uncle. This was no doubt known to Hitler and confused the family tree and the head that studied it.

[1] Ron Rosebaum, *Explaining Hitler.*

Nevertheless, Alois and Klara's marriage was approved by the Catholic Church and they married in 1885. Adolf Hitler was born thirteen years later, on 20 April 1889 in Braunau, officially dying at 56 on the 30th of April 1945 in Berlin. In his life he tried to change the world, but the 'powers that be' changed it back – a little, and only for the time being. Nevertheless, in the back of darker boardrooms Hitler had become a model for ruling the world. Socialism was the outward goal and fascism was the method.

> Hitler was an enormous success, an enormous failure and an even greater mystery. His life was a battle with confused beginnings.

Hitler tried to clean up his act and "His creed of Aryan superiority meant that he should be able to prove his pedigree, and that there should be no skeletons in the closet. Adolf desperately wanted to eradicate any type of family roots or origins in order to promote the impression that he was God-sent to the German people. He wanted to be seen as a divine figure."[2]

Adolf was desperate to eradicate any record of relatives, their misdeeds, their propensity for incest and his Jewish connection, as the German racial test required proof of Aryan descent back to 1750.

Both sides of Hitler's family were from Walterschlag, Spital, Strones and Gross Wolfgers in lower Austria. Hitler's father grew up in Strones, but it was too small to be a parish, so he was registered in the small farming village Döllerscheim.

As soon as Adolf came to power he ordered the residents hastily removed and the Wehrmacht use it for artillery practise (March 1938). Likewise in 1942 when a plaque was installed in Strones as Adolf's hometown, he threw a tantrum and ordered it destroyed soon after the concrete had set.

Adolf didn't have anything to do with his father's side of the family. None of his siblings knew who their father's father was, but they liked the mother's side of the family. They also practiced second-degree incest. This was common at the time and has largely been cured by common use of the motorcar.

---

[2] *Hitler.*

> Paula Hitler, 101st Airborne Division interview, 12 July 1945: "The Schmieds and the Koppensteins are our dear relatives, especially a cousin Schmieds who married a Koppenstein. I know of no one of my father's family. My sister Angela and I often said: 'Father must have some relatives, but we don't even know them.'"

Incest was very common amongst the Germans and Austrians, and after WWI, blowing up one's graveyards and burning down registries were the most common methods of tidying up one's family tree. British Intelligence officers were accustomed to walking at night, but they were advised not to walk too close to the German cemeteries as they had a tendency to explode around midnight.

Spymaster: "Most world leaders are keen to turn their ordinary origins into a showpiece of reflected glory. Who among world leaders today would get away with such an obvious ploy of destroying or rewriting their family history? Sending tanks to shell and destroy a perfectly good town, in what was once a foreign country, is extreme, even amongst world leaders who are renowned for their extremities."

The name Hutter became Hiedler and then Hitler. Hitler was a spelling error and spelling errors have dominated history, the most important being 'the children of Israel', versus 'the children of Ishmael' (the Christians and Jews versus Islam); and 'Oradour-sur-Glane' versus 'Oradour-sur-Vayres' where 642 people were massacred in the wrong French village during WWII. The least important was the rugby team who "played like All Blacks" [sic] and the spelling error carried on to name the team.

Spelling errors have more to answer for than any other facet of history. Language is made up of different dialects and spelling mistakes find commonality with wider and faster transport, and become the norm. Those who stay put speak with strong accents, develop more phonetic spelling and tend to make fewer historical errors.

'Crack' in Ireland is a case in point. In one area it means 'conversation' as in 'good crack', and in another area you don't know what you're going to get.

Jewish Origins

Adolf Hitler received a letter from his half-brother Alois hinting at "very odd circumstances in our family history"[3] and it is odd indeed. This referred to the conception of their father Alois Hitler.

Adolf Hitler's grandfather was not part of an incestuous Catholic tree, but one of the leading financiers of Europe. To understand who Adolf Hitler's grandfather was (Alois Hitler's father) you have to understand what Europe was like then.

Werner Sombart, in his book *The Jews and Modern Capitalism* said that from 1820 on, it was the "Age of the Rothschild". He concluded there was "only one power in Europe, and that is Rothschild".

After the patriarch Mayer Rothschild died on 19 September 1812, his will set out specific guidelines for his descendants:

> 'The family was to intermarry with their own first and second cousins, so their fortune could be kept within the family, and to maintain the appearance of a united financial empire.'

As a result, 16 of the 18 marriages by Mayer Amschel Rothschild's grandchildren were between first cousins. Even his son James (Jacob) Mayer married the daughter of his brother, Salomon Mayer. This created an incestuous culture (although it is legal to marry your cousin) and also meant that the five Rothschild sons couldn't have legitimate children outside the family. To compensate for this, they had illegitimate children, often with their servants.

According to Walter Langer, a psychoanalyst who wrote *The Mind of Adolf Hitler*, Adolf Hitler was a satanic German leader who was the grandson of a Rothschild. It was generally supposed that the father of Alois Hitler was Johann Georg Hiedler, but:

> "There are some people who seriously doubt that Johann Georg Hiedler was the father of Alois . . . [an Austrian document was supposedly prepared] that proved Maria Anna Schicklgruber [Hitler's grandmother] was living in Vienna at the time she conceived [31 August 1836] . . . At that time she was employed as a servant in the home of a Baron Rothschild. As soon as the family discovered her pregnancy she was sent back to her home [House No. 13, Strones, Austria] . . . where Alois [snr.] was born."

[3] *Hitler*, p. 15.

In response, Hitler attacked the Austrian town of Döllerscheim and destroyed the graveyards, using them for tank practise. This destroyed his father's birth records, which would have revealed his Jewish ancestry.

Hitler also closed the Rothschild's bank, S. M. Rothschild and Sons in Vienna in 1938. It had belonged to Salomon Rothschild, one of his probable grandfathers.

The Nazi leadership hid their Jewish family histories with grenades. Even Heydrich's admission to the SS was delayed until his family headstones were blown up. Heydrich was a quarter Jew from his mother's mother and was responsible for almost all of the Jewish terror and repression of the Nazi rule. He was dispassionate and had a marked characteristic of inhumanity.

The Rothschilds were all Illuminati, an independent organisation that began in 1776 and infused itself with the existing Freemasons, eventually drawing out their elite. Their goal was worldwide dominance and control. By 1836, the Rothschilds were the most influential family in Europe. They had created the American Revolution and, as is typical of banks, they funded both sides.

The Rothschilds illegitimate children had two purposes. One was to create allies and the other was to create enemies. The 'allies' were used by the Rothschilds to front for their financial deals and the 'enemies' were used to create war. The Rothschilds funded both sides of the wars and profited enormously from the financial deals the wars created. Because the Rothschilds owned everything, they had no fear of retaliation from the courts.

Occult Origins

Since 1776 the '31st of August' has been set aside as a satanic night, a time when the Rothschilds sowed their seeds to create the children of war. It is an important day for conceiving an 'agent for war' under their private occult coven, the 'Golden Dawn'. Such occult acts are planned to occur between 1.30 am and 3.10 am (13s). This was the equivalent of Guy Fawkes for illegitimate children, with the Rothschilds dressed for Halloween.

The 31st of August is the last day of the Northern Hemisphere summer and the night when the authorities turn a blind eye to pagan rituals. This is similar to the Southern Hemisphere's 27/28/29 February when beach party madness reigns.

On the 31st of August, the Rothschilds' goal was to scare the bejabbers (Jesus) out of the women and for the women to conceive in absolute fear, believing that they were mating with the devil. It was pack rape, with three Rothschilds involved in each hit, one raping, one in the room ensuring dominance and confusion, with another outside, then changing roles.

The German ranks of peerage went from King, Prince, Duke, Markgraf (Count) and Baron, to Ritter. Ritter was equivalent to Knight and carried the surname 'von Ritter'. This was the hierarchy of Germany. Whoever wanted to marry needed authorisation from the Duke and/or Markgraf (equivalent to Viscount). The Markgraf was responsible for the area and had the right to sex with the wife on the wedding night. This was called prima nocte. It was the same in England, Scotland and all over Europe at the time.

The history of 'prima nocte', 'jus primae noctis' (law of the first night), or 'droit du seigneur' (lord's right, hunting, taxation, farming and sex with bridal-virgins) is full of denial, like "deflowering a virgin was considered a greater responsibility than a commoner bridegroom could bear . . . reflecting nothing but credit on the ruler . . . so praised for his sheer courage."[4]

The custom was especially popular in France and Italy but when French knights emigrated to England they abandoned prima nocte as the British touted their female farm workers as bigger than they were.

In *Nineteen Eighty-Four,* George Orwell updated prima nocte as "The law by which every capitalist had the right to sleep with any woman working in one of his factories".

> This 'night right' was grabbed randomly by those given the title 'Baron', which all the Rothschilds had, some changing their surnames to Baron de Rothschild. Prima nocte created generations of illegitimate children and illegitimate Rothschild children but the Rothschilds were officially banned from this practice by Mayer Rothschild (d. 19 September 1812).
>
> To compensate for this, the Rothschilds would have illegitimate children while dressed in masks and costumes to hide their identity.

[4] Claude Jordan, *Voyages Historiques de L'Europe*, Volume IV, pp. 140–141; Alain Boureau, *The Lord's First Night*; *Encyclopaedia Britannica*, 15th Edition, Volume 10, p. 610.

Due to the commoners' rebellion against prima nocte, it was easy enough to get into the bedrooms of breeding-age girls. Austria and Germany at the time were practising 'windowing', essentially young men climbing up girls' drainpipes and trelliswork in the wee hours to get them pregnant before marriage.

Their fathers didn't entirely object and often viewed the adventurous young men as potential farm help. When she got pregnant, the two would get married. It was a farming-based community and children were needed to help on the family farm. To this day, there is still a strong culture in Germany of marrying the pregnant girl.

> If a girl of breeding age heard someone climbing up the drainpipe, rather than be scared, she would get herself prepared – a quick scrub of the teeth with a badger hair toothbrush followed by a natural sponge. Late summer especially was a time of roving bonking, and often the girls would not limit themselves to one partner, especially those in poverty – and half of the Catholic girls. After all, there was 'the father, the son and the holy ghost' to consider.

In order to simplify matters, the super wealthy Rothschilds had servant girls. Having illegitimate children with servant girls was so common, one of the Rothschilds had twenty and acknowledged them all, eventually living with his mistress and shunning his unresponsive wife – his kissing cousin.

At the beginning of August a lot of the servants were given leave for the hot summer month and temporary replacements would come in. These temps were often chosen with the 31st of August in mind, when the agents of war would be conceived after a month of familiarity between master and servant.

Hitler's grandmother, Maria Anna Schicklgruber, was a none-too-bright Catholic girl who was invited to work at the Rothschilds in Vienna in the summer of 1836.

Her surname 'Schicklgruber' translates as 'Reaper' and refers to the grim reaper, or death. As Mary Anne Reaper, her initials spell MAR, one of the words for 'death', and with her given initials M.A.S., 'MAS MAR' becomes 'mass death'. She was perfect fodder for a staged 'Agent of War' Rothschild terror rape.

The Rothschilds told their servant they were going out and to retire early. Three of the Rothschilds returned quietly around 11.30 pm on 30 August 1836, put on their devil costumes, completed a midnight Golden Dawn coven ritual and began terrorising Maria Anna Schicklgruber in a pressure-cooker scenario. Closing doors, rustling leaves, foot steps running away, all that *Scary Movie* stuff that has been ingrained in us for so long it has now become laughable with over exposure.

> This was designed to create sustained fear, to flood her bloodstream with adrenalin, and to alter her physiological and psychological condition to one of absolute terror.

At 1.30 am the three Rothschilds appeared in her room as three devils. Not only was she financially helpless, but also physically helpless. Her screams were not heard as all the Rothschilds were supposedly out. She was raped, seduced by all three, or about to join the Rothschild family, depending on her perception. Each Rothschild had a three-in-one chance of conceiving a child with her and they took pleasure scaring the living life out of Maria Anna Schicklgruber for a multitude of reasons.

Totally financially strapped, in a very expensive city, Maria stayed on as a servant, but by late November her pregnancy had become apparent to the rest of the family and she was sent back to her home at House No. 13 in Strones – mission accomplished.

The most likely perpetrators were Salomon Mayer Rothschild (1774–1855); his younger brother, but head of the family, Nathan Meyer, Baron de Rothschild (1777–1836) who officially died five weeks earlier; and his son Lionel Nathan Rothschild (1808–79).

Salomon Mayer Rothschild (1774–1855) ran the S. M. Rothschild and Sons bank in Vienna. He allowed his daughter to marry his brother Karl (14 years younger than himself), who was based in Naples – an uncle marrying a niece.

Salomon was a Freemason and a member of the Illuminati whose leader Adam Weishaupt spent much time deciphering and bringing together all the occult practices.

Since the Rothschilds were synonymous with the Illuminati, they were also synonymous with occult practices. The founder of the Illuminati,

Adam Weishaupt created their private occult coven, 'Golden Dawn', specifically for them. These were hard men for whom the saying 'morality is for the masses' was a given. They were the earliest practitioners of the Golden Dawn *Effective* coven.

Nathan Meyer Rothschild (1777–1836) founded N. M. Rothschild and Sons bank in London in 1805, at 2 New Court, St. Swithin's Lane, near the Bank of England and the Stock Exchange. Although the third son, he was the patriarch of his generation after his father's death in 1812. Ten years later he became the Austrian Consul-General in England (1822) but never carried the title of baron presented to him by Austria. His loans to France, Russia, and South America were popular with British investors because they required repayment in sterling.

> At a party at his mansion Nathan Meyer Rothschild said:
> "I care not what puppet is placed upon the throne of England. The man that controls Britain's money supply controls the British Empire, and I control the British money supply."

Here was a man who could buy the law and for whom morality required a public outcry, which was easily quelled with silence, misinformation and control of the press . . . but it was his son Lionel Nathan Rothschild who actually fathered the child Alois Hitler.

Lionel Nathan Rothschild (1808–79) and his illegitimate son Alois Hitler.

Confusing the Birth Lineage of Historical Catholic Jews

The other possible fathers, all of whom claimed to be Alos' father, were Johann Georg Trummelschlager, Johann Nepomuk Hüttler and his brother Johann Georg Hiedler. But when Hitler's father was baptised 'Alois', in the Döllersheim parish, the space for the father's name was left blank. Perhaps even the mother wasn't sure.

According to Hans Frank, Hitler's personal lawyer,[5] Maria was living and working in the house of Mr Frankenberger when she became pregnant. "The lack of hard evidence, however, makes this thesis appear exceedingly dubious."[6]

From birth to 14, it was Frankenberger (a Jew) who paid money in support of Alois, while steadfastly denying he was the father. It appeared that he was paying child support on behalf of another and another who was most likely to also be a Jew.

> Hans Frank's theory was a ruse to put historians off the scent of the Rothschilds' illegitimate children. Presenting 'ruse histories' was standard practice for the Rothschilds, and since they were history, any big event that occurred was most likely theirs. At any one time there was and always is at least one illegitimate Rothschild playing a major role in history.
>
> Hans Frank later blackmailed Adolf Hitler and survived an SS plot solely due to the protection he engendered with the real knowledge of Adolf Hitler's Jewish Rothschild ancestry.

So was Hitler Jewish? He was at least a quarter Jewish. Did Hitler have any Jewish uncles and aunts? You bet, and they pretty much ran the world. His grandfather was Lionel Nathan Rothschild (1808–1879), his uncle was the First Baron Rothschild (1840–1915) and his cousin was the Second Baron Rothschild (1868–1937) making Hitler something of an uncle to the Third Baron Rothschild (1910–90).

As a result of this, despite the outward chaos, Hitler lived an extremely pre-organised life dominated by occult practices from two

[5] For his services Hans Frank became the President of the Academy of German Law, leader of the National Lawyers Association, member of the Reichstag, and Governor-General of Poland. During the Nuremberg Trials he was known as 'the Butcher of Poland'.

[6] *Hitler*, p. 15.

generations earlier. Hitler definitely got the money wheels spinning for the Rothschilds and they made a fortune out of WWII alone.

Hitler's father (Alois Hitler) was conceived on the 31st of August 1836 (the same day and time Lady Di was killed in 1997) and was born on 7 June 1837 (madness day, its all 6s and 7s).

> Alois Hitler's conception was a pre-planned satanic sport fuck – a ritualistic rape, a gang-bang designed to 'conceive in fear' and 'conceive fear'.

Adolf Hitler was a quarter Rothschild and a quarter Jew from semi-incestuous Catholic parentage. He was an illegitimate Rothschild bred as an agent of war. He was the Rothschilds' physical enemy and financial ally with unlimited financial and political support.

Adolf Hitler was an illegitimate Rothschild playing the major role in the history of his times. His status was well recognised by the secret society financial elite. As such he was given complete assistance to achieve their goals. In his time, Adolf Hitler was recognised as 'Hitler-Rothschild, the satanic Catholic-Jew'.

Hitler's father Alois was certainly angry enough to be the product of rape and during the 1800s Jews were known to be prolific rooters of their servants. Intelligence Officers with a 'living library' and 'talking dictionary' knowledge of history are certain Hitler was the grandchild of a Rothschild and all the other stories are a ruse. Usually they can be influenced by research, but in this case, "No, Hitler was the grandchild of a Rothschild".

Adolf's Parents

It is common practice for secret societies to choose their days when influencing history. Certainly a rape of a single woman on the last day of summer, on 31 August 1836, who lived at House No. 13, was an ominous day for conceiving the angry grandfather of war. In the secret code of the Golden Dawn coven, dates are written with the numbers reversed, with the 31st written as '13' and the 8 written '∞'. The 31st of August was the day for creating children of war – '13∞'.

Alois left home when he was 13 and worked as a cobbler in Vienna. At 18 he joined the Imperial Customs Service, where his mad bullying presence made him a renowned tax collector and lifetime employee.

In 1864, at the age of 27, he married Anna Glass, the daughter of a workmate. She was unable to have children and died nineteen years later in 1883. The same year he married Franziska Matzelberger and they had two children, Alois junior and Angela. His wife Franziska died of tuberculosis in 1885 within two years of their marriage.

Being the single father of two and having such a bad run with women and reproduction, Alois then employed his niece Klara Põlzl as a housemaid and attempted to marry her. He said she was his cousin, when she was his niece.

Alois and Klara made a plea to the Bishop of Linz on the 27th of October 1884, which read, "They are prevented by the canonical impediment of collateral affinity in the third degree touching the second. They therefore make the humble request that the Most Reverend Episcopate will graciously secure them a dispensation on the following grounds . . . he is a father of two minors, a boy of 2½ years (Alois) and a girl of 1 year and 2 months (Angela) . . . he is a customs official away from home all day and often at night." Klara was described as his "home help [and] a woman without means", meaning she did not have money or prospects enough to marry. She was quite boyish-looking.

The Bishop of Linz cared about incest and refused to marry them, so they appealed to Rome for special dispensation. The Vatican was only concerned about the size of their bribe and soon granted them the right to marry.

Alois and Klara were incestuously married and therefore prone to genetic defects becoming dominant. They had five children together, but only Adolf and his younger sister Paula survived childhood. Gustav and Ida died from diphtheria as children in 1885 and 1886 respectively. Hitler was the *third* child, born in 1889. His brother Edmund was born in 1894 and died in 1896, the same year his sister Paula was born. At the time of Adolf's birth (1889), his father Alois was 51 and his mother Klara was 28. After Alois (b. 1882) and Gustav (d. 1885), Adolf was *the third son.*

It is rumoured that Adolf Hitler was born with only one testicle and another story that it was bitten off while urinating on a goat at Leondig in Linz, creating the Freemasons' favourite limerick. The goat story is true enough. The person who told it was killed soon after the telling. From eight years old the young Adolf Hitler had only one testicle.

"Hitler had only one big ball.
Rommel had two but they were small.
Himmler was slightly similar,
but poor old Goebbels had no balls at all."

As an adult, Hitler's doctor (Dr Morell 1937–45) treated him with Orchikrin for genital hypoplasia, the excessive smallness of a sexual organ; with Prostakrinum for sex hormone deficiency; and with Testosterone to restore his manliness. Hitler had one small testicle and one small penis. By the age of fifty he was starting to look like a woman.

None of Hitler's doctors saw him naked. The only person to do so was his manservant, Emil Maurice, who spent some time in a prison cell with Dr Morell after the war. Emil Maurice kept dropping hints to Dr Morell that Hitler's sexual organs were not all intact.

Hitler was born in the little village of Branau near the German and Austrian border and remained an Austrian until the 1930s. He considered Linz his hometown and the world considered Bavaria the cradle of Nazism. Even today when someone makes a Jewish joke on the trains, the whole carriage laughs. Like other groupings, the Germanic and the Jewish peoples being the prime example, racial hatred is passed down through the generations. It's in their blood and surpasses all other aspects of culturisation.

Alois senior was mad-looking and 'sanpaku'. This is a severe 'yin' condition in which the lower portion of the whites of the eyes can be seen. This is often a sign of a person who plays a part in history, yet has no control over the part they play, they just have to play it. Lady Diana, Princess of Wales, had the same condition as she set in motion the end of the British Monarchy, having children, who like Hitler, failed their university entrance and paternal examinations.

> Alois was bald, with a handlebar moustache. He was deeply psychotic and obstructive. He was a "hard, conscientious customs official, punctilious to a fault, with a difficult temper that flared with no apparent provocation. Adolf bore the brunt of this".[7]

---

[7] *The Memoirs of Bridget Hitler*, p. 24.

Adolf Hitler's half-brother (from the second of three marriages) was also called Alois. He was 'a ruffian, a thief, and a failure'. His mother had died and his father had married his housemaid and niece – what do you expect. Alois junior left home at 18 in 1900 (when Adolf was 11) and spent some time in jail. This made the young Adolf the oldest surviving sibling in the house. His sister Paula was 4 and their mother was also their second cousin.

As a result of Alois junior's rebellion and marked failures, both Alois senior and Klara placed all their hopes on Adolf who was encouraged in the arts, especially reading and painting: ". . . her favourite, Adolf, whom she kept at home. He hid behind her skirts, never doing a day's work."[8] Hitler was raised as a momma's boy.

Alois senior was a severely borderline personality and strict father who beat Adolf savagely whenever he came home late, which was always, and "Klara was a kind and gentle woman who tended to overcompensate and spoil her son", killing him with kindness. As a result, Hitler loved cops and robbers, was a dreamer, got poor grades, hated maths, and escaped into Wagner's music.

Hitler was an escapist who learnt to love, serve and rely on women, while holding an intense dislike and distrust for male authority figures. These patterns ruled his life and were exacerbated by his inbreeding and the dominant madness that ran through his father's veins.

Alois Hitler (senior) died from internal chest bleeding (pleural haemorrhage) at the age of 65 (7 June 1837–3 January 1903) when Hitler was 13. His mother Klara Põlzl died of cancer five years later at the age of 47 (12 August 1860–21 December 1907) when Hitler was 18. Adolf never returned home after his mother's funeral.

---

[8] Ibid (Same source as above).

Lionel Nathan Rothschild (left).

Alois Hitler Senior (Adolf's father).

Klara Hitler née Põlzl (below).
(Adolf's mother/second cousin).

Alois Hitler Junior (lower left).
(Adolf's half-brother).

Adolf Hitler (lower right).

Bombed Döllerscheim – where Adolf's father's birth records were kept.

Adolf Hitler in Britain

Adolf was christened Adolfus and called Adi by his family. He had been accustomed to a comparatively easy life, but when his mother died of cancer, he (18) took his sister Paula (11) to Vienna, along with his most cherished possession, a photograph of Klara (his mother and second cousin). "His existence had now become a pitiless struggle against poverty and he swept streets in order to buy food for himself and his sister."[1]

From 1908 to 1921 Adolf never saw his younger sister Paula. He became an art student in Vienna but failed miserably. "At the end of 1910 and the beginning of 1911 Hitler appears to have received a considerable sum of money from his aunt, Johanna Pölzl . . . He drifted aimlessly [yet] still pretended that he was a student painter, or writer."[2]

The money ran out by the time he was 19. He slept on park benches and in doorways, ate in soup kitchens, and stayed in the Asyl für Obdachlose shelter for men until 1910, where he developed an appetite for change. Formerly of the snobbish middle class, he was now a tramp.

Two years and four months later, on 24 May 1913, Hitler left Vienna and moved to Munich.[3] The most authoritative book on Hitler has no knowledge of Hitler's activities during the two years and four months from January 1911 to 24 May 1913.

Meanwhile, Alois Hitler (27), Adolf's half-brother, became a waiter in the Shelbourne Hotel in Dublin where he met Brigid Elisabeth Dowling (17, b. 3 July 1891) in the first half of 1909 (her first ever date) and they eloped from Ireland to Liverpool, evading her father William Dowling. She became a Liverpudlian hairdresser and they married and had a child, William Patrick Hitler, on 12 March 1911.

Intelligentsia in doss-houses were the perfect feeding ground for the foreign secret service who are always in search of disaffected nationals prepared to destroy their own society in order to make change. The intelligence community still meet in the boarding houses of

[1] *Prelude to Terror.*

[2] The very authoritative *Hitler*, p. 57.

[3] *Hitler*, p. 57.

old men today. It is good cover and anything overheard is either quickly forgotten, misinterpreted or simply disbelieved and followed up with more medication.

Officially Hitler stayed in Vienna for the next three years (1910–13) and painted well-known Viennese buildings where he referred to himself as an 'intellectual' rather than a 'transient'. He is also credited with an incredibly elaborate mother-and-child in a landscape which would have taken months to complete. This oil on canvas ("Mother Mary with the Holy Child Jesus Christ", dated 1913) was in a completely different style and medium. It comes complete with right-angle tear as is common amongst works of forged authenticity.

This forgery has been continued on to this day and in July 2006: "Twenty-one watercolours and sketches thought to be by Adolf Hitler are to be sold in Britain in September. The collection was apparently produced between 1916 and 1918. Jefferys in Lostwithiel, southwest England, will auction the collection which is expected to fetch up to $9107."[4]

The 1910–13 paintings were sold by his friend Hanisch (registered in the men's shelter at MA12, Haus Meldemannstrasse as 'Fritz Walter') until August 1910 and then by Neumann (a Jew) for a short period (whom Hitler sued), after which Hitler sold the paintings himself. Hitler believed that his failure in the Viennese art world was due to its Jewish control. When Hitler's inheritance came through, he neither painted nor sold his paintings.

Bridget Hitler née Brigid Elisabeth Dowling.

However, Brigid Hitler's *My Brother in Law Hitler* says otherwise.[5] When William Patrick was 1, Brigid met Adolf Hitler at the Lime Street Train Station in Liverpool in November 1912. "He was a shabby youth who always wore a trilby hat . . . came and stayed with us at Upper Stanhow Street [102 Upper Stanhope Street, Princess Road, Toxteth, Liverpool] for *two months* . . . was a damned nuisance, slept all the time, but was very nice to the baby."

Adolf was a snob and spent his days

[4] *New Zealand Weekend Herald*, 29 July 2006, B11.

[5] She used 'Bridget Hitler' as her author name.

walking up and down the Mersey. At that time there was a strong German community in Liverpool, running bars, cafés and restaurants. Adolf spent six months on and off with Alois and Brigid during which time Alois and Adolf spent a lot of time travelling around England. The whereabouts of Adolf Hitler during the preceding twenty-two months (January 1911 to November 1912) are something of a mystery. He was 21 to 23 years old at the time.

This is supposedly the missing year in Hitler's life. Hitler wrote of his own history in *Mein Kampf* stating that from September 1908 he was living in various doss-houses in Vienna amongst tramps and homeless people. He describes this as the lowest point in his life. However, "The only witnesses were fellow tramps and their memories were unreliable and incomplete. The eyewitness accounts of Hitler in Vienna are dubious."[6] In *Mein Kampf* he states that in 1912 he was a failed art student living in Vienna.

On 24 May 1913, Hitler left Vienna and moved to Munich.[7] The most authoritative book on Hitler, all 844 pages, 681 footnotes and 13 pages of bibliography has no knowledge or photographs of Hitler from January 1911 to May 1913.

> The truth of the period January 1911 to 24 May 1913, was that Hitler spent 1911 working through his inheritance. He then spent nine months (February to November 1912) training in the British Military 'Psych-Ops War School' at Tavistock in England and Ireland. The six months after this (November 1912 to May 1913) Hitler spent in Liverpool with his half-brother and sister-in-law recuperating and studying his Psych-Ops pamphlets with 'tourist' trips to London and British ports.

Adolf Hitler was trained as a British agent, became a German agent, then a British double agent, and then the German Reichchancellor (Prime Minister) as a warring British double agent. His Jewish grandfather of the banking Rothschild family made huge profit from this – or more accurately, his descendants, Hitler's Jewish cousins.

Hitler evaded military service in Austria. "In order to evade capture he registered at the Vienna municipal lodging [a house for homeless

---

[6] *Prelude to Terror.*

[7] *Hitler*, p. 57.

men] in 1909 (aged 20) under the name of his younger brother Edmund who was born five years after Adolf and died at the age of two. By using Edmund's birth certificate Adolf managed to identify himself as his younger and dead brother. He dodged military service by living under the name Edmund Hitler, while the Viennese police searched high and low for Adolf Hitler."[8]

Spymaster: "The German Police finally captured Adolf Hitler in Munich, after his return from Britain, and charged him with draft-dodging. He evaded military service by producing medical certificates to the effect that he was malnourished and ill. Ironically, when war came, he volunteered. British Intelligence did not interfere with this because they always had a seconder. If Hitler failed there would be another and war experience was necessary for Hitler's record.

"British Intelligence did rescue Hitler on two occasions during WWI.

"During his period in Britain, Hitler was trained as a public speaker. They taught him to gesture with his hands to emphasise points. He then developed his own style which was non-Germanic and incredibly effective. MI-6 also used an elocution teacher from Dublin's Trinity College to give him voice lessons and teach him how to raise and lower his voice for emphasis.

"Much of an agent's training is along sexual lines. Agents are given drugs, alcohol, subjected to hypnotism, given access to other agents, and the instructors step out and watch what develops. Adolf gave indications of bisexuality, which is not unusual in an MI-6 training setting, and later went on to develop more complicated perversions that sickened many of the other would-be agents – notably coprophilia. The more extreme his sexual perversions, the more easily manipulated he was and the Mandarins of Whitehall were delighted with his progress. Some predicted the sky was the limit for Hitler.

"'All he lacks is experience' ran one of his confidential evaluations of 1912. The MI-6 overlords decided to return him to Germany in time to see that he would get all the experience he needed in the new grande coup, WWI, which was to open to packed houses just in time for the post-harvest festivities in Germany (1914).

"Unfortunately it came early. As Robbie Burns once put it: 'The best laid plans of mice and men gang aft aglae' – Gaelic for 'fuck up'."[9]

[8] *The Memoirs of Bridget Hitler*, p. 27–8.

[9] Hitler's visit to England is also described in Beryl Bainbridge's *Young Adolf.*

Alien regulations for entry into Britain prior to 1914 virtually did not exist. Even the Home Office officials agree that the 1905 Act would have been easily contravened. This is the only period in Hitler's life when he was not photographed by the bulky camera. The lack of certainty in the official stories was enough to cover for him. He had either an alibi or a doppelgänger painting romantic city scenes for him in Vienna. By the 1930s there were at least five Hitler lookalikes working for the Third Reich.[10]

Hitler's half-brother Alois Hitler: "Don't be ridiculous. Artist! He is nothing but a cheap dauber. They wouldn't even accept him as a student in the Kunstakademie. And what kind of an artist is a man who copies pictures and signs them with his own name."[11]

Hitler's lost two years and four months run from January 1911 to 24 May 1913.

1. Hitler spent 1911 working through his inheritance in the Vienna doss-houses.
2. From February to November 1912 he spent nine months training in the England's Tavistock Psych-Ops War School and another Psych-Ops War School Ireland.
3. From November 1912 to April 1913 he was based in Liverpool with his half-brother. From here he viewed strategic British structures including the Tower Bridge, ships and ports, as did many German tourist spies at that time.
4. In April 1913 Adolf Hitler went to Vienna.
5. On 24 May 1913 Hitler moved to Munich.

Hitler's Double Agent Training

At Tavistock, and in an unnamed Irish 'Psych-Ops War School' which closed down after WWII, Hitler learnt the following: "Once a speaker has mastered the psychological principles of mass persuasion, he can convince the masses of anything he likes. 'Nothing is so absurd that it will not be believed if it is presented with enough conviction'."

He would [later] write, unconsciously echoing a saying of Marcus Tullius Cicero's centuries before, 'Nothing is so difficult to believe that oratory cannot make it acceptable . . .'

---

[10] *Hitler's Maid.*

[11] *The Memoirs of Bridget Hitler*, p. 27.

"Hitler followed what he called 'the very sound principle' that a big lie is always more credible than a little one. In 'the primitive simplicity of their souls', he said, people are more easily victimised by the big lie 'since they themselves lie in small matters, but would be ashamed to lie on too big a scale'. They cannot conceive that anyone would venture a truly monstrous falsehood, and will therefore be inclined to believe that there must be some truth in such a statement. Thus, said Hitler, 'something of even the most shameless prevarication will find lodging, and stick . . .'"[12]

> Even Bonaparte's brother was trained by the British military schools. (All the brothers were Freemasons.) His grandfather John Bone was a Scotsman who fled Scotland after a failed revolt in 1746. The name Buonaparte (Bonaparte) comes from 'Bone parte' – the Bone party. The British claimed that their training camps kicked off the British and American revolutions. With their proven record, they were also used to kick off WWI and WWII, both being British Freemason wars designed to capture France and destroy Germany. Both wars heavily advantaged secret societies and paedophiles. Radical doubt was also cast on the American Revolution because of the 'Founding Fathers'' involvement in Freemasonry crime and war creation.

When Alois Hitler sent a letter and travel expenses inviting his sister and brother-in-law to visit, the British intercepted the mail and used it as the out for Hitler. It was also to be his first post-training kill. His British trainers then altered history to show that Leo Raubal died in either 1910 or 1911 and Bridget Hitler's memoirs of Leo Raubal and Angela Hitler née Raubal being invited to England in 1912 couldn't possibly be true. Such is the way history is manipulated. In intelligence it is more than commonplace, it is common practise.

To kick off this cover-up Brigid Hitler's house was destroyed by the last stick of bombs on Liverpool in 1918. The enemy aircraft were never sighted. What was sighted on the day were British aircraft.

Alois and Bridget Hitler were expecting to see Leo Raubal and Angela Hitler née Raubal at the Lime Street Station in November 1912. Instead they were met by Adolf Hitler. This gave Hitler a place for R & R

---

[12] *Mein Kampf*, cited in *Prelude to Terror*, p. 251.

with relatives while recuperating in the safety of British territory and under British monitoring.

As a Catholic, Angela Hitler née Raubal would just as likely say that her husband was dead if he was an embarrassment, had cheated on her, left her for another, or was in a bigamous marriage. "He [Leo Raubal] spent his time in the pub, drank and smoked, gambled his money away, and on top of that he was a civil servant."[13]

In May 1914, Alois Hitler was so keen to leave Bridget he faked his own death and then remarried.

The Memoirs of Bridget Hitler was written in America during WWII and was known to American Intelligence. It was first leaked to historians in the early 1970s amongst a collection of papers from the late Dr Edmund Pauker who was a European-born theatrical agent. They were first published in 1979. The manuscript ends with a comma in 1937.

In all the documents searched there is no mention of the cause of Leo Raubal's death. Jennifer Roseberg (Jewish) mentions on her website that Leo Raubal was born on 11 June 1879 and died on 10 August 1910 with the overriding note: "My fellow researchers disagree with the dates".

Other sources say Leo was born on 11 June 1879 or in 1880, married Angela Hitler (20) on 14 September 1902 or the same day in 1903 and died aged 31, on 10 August 1910 or 1911 and had a son of the same name whose death date is also confused between 1942 and 1979.

After this, Angela Raubal (28 July 1883–30 October 1949) is supposed to have remarried an architect in Dresden (*The Young Hitler I Knew*) or moved to Vienna after 1918 (*Office of Strategic Services Profile*), from where she and her daughter Geli moved to Obersalzberg and later Berchtesgaden where she was her half-brother's housekeeper from 1925. His name was Adolf Hitler.

Other histories show that Hitler kicked Angela Raubal out of Berchtesgaden in 1936 and she moved to Dresden and married Professor Hamitsch who was killed in WWII during a Russian offensive.

Because Adolf Hitler was a double agent historical figure, his family history was purposefully confused. Like many political figures, Adolf Hitler was killing his way to the top.

[13] *The Young Hitler I Knew*, 1954.

"Hitler asked his widowed half-sister, Angela Raubal, to be his housekeeper. She was accompanied by her seventeen-year-old daughter Geli [4 January 1908–18 September 1931]."[14]

There is also no history of what Leo Raubal died from, whether he was killed from gambling debts, alcohol or cheated on his wife and was 'dead to her' as was the Catholic way amongst stoic cuckolded hens. Such confusion around Leo Raubal amounts to a cover-up.

It is tradition amongst those trained at Tavistock to do a kill during or soon after getting out, and to kill someone close. This shows their minders that they are prepared to go to any lengths to achieve their minders political goals.

Since Adolf 'Edmund' Hitler left Tavistock in late 1912, turning up in Liverpool in November 1912 in place of Leo and Angela Raubal and since Leo's birth, marriage and death dates are confused, it is quite possible that Leo Raubal was Hitler's first kill. His Jewish name and marriage to his half-sister was enough motivation. The dates were confused to protect Adolf Hitler's hand and also to discredit *The Memoirs of Bridget Hitler*.

Leo and Angela Raubal's meeting with Alois and Brigid Hitler at Liverpool was quite openly planned in November 1912. Their 'no show' meant that Angela had to fall back on excuses. Angela was proud, and Leo's gambling, alcoholism and womanising was enough to convince the public.

As far as Angela was concerned, her husband Leo may have simply gone missing and her pride took over. Her pride became Adolf's alibi. Miraculously Adolf took Leo and Angela's place in Liverpool and as it turned out, he was to kill another Raubal two decades later. Angela Hitler née Raubal was to remained silent about this as well.

The first interview with Paula Hitler (Hitler's sister, Angela's half-sister) dated 12 July 1945 by U.S. Army 101st Airborne was produced on a low-quality typewriter with many lines out of alignment and variable print quality (old ribbon). It makes no mention of Leo Raubal.

Paula was asked to bring all of her possessions to this interview which were carried in trunks, chests and boxes in a truck the following day. Everything was stolen except for the overnight bag she had carried

[14] *Hitler*, p. 236.

with her. Thus all her hardcopy relationship with her brother Adolf were removed from public analysis on 13 July 1945.

The second interview with Paula Hitler was on 5 June 1946 and is recorded by Records of Army Staff (G2). Record Group 319 IRR XE575580 mentions Leo Raubal as having died in 1910. According to Paula Hitler, her half-sister Angela Hitler [1883–1949] married the Austrian Revenue Officer Leo Raubal in 1903 and he died in 1910.

Much of the content of this second interview is suspect. It ends with 600 words of pro-Allied propaganda from the interviewer ". . . get her away from publicity". The original German record is not available and the English version consists of barely legible handwriting with the dates Anglicised.

Both interviews show interference and wishful thinking on the part of the interviewer. No Allied Powers wanted it known that Hitler was in Britain and wished to discredit all affidavits and memoirs that supported this.

> When there is intergenerational confusion there are often larger powers at work manipulating history.

When engineering history, witnesses are regularly intimidated and taken back to 'zero'. The essential elements of Paula Hitler's files were confused or removed. She was intimidated and left in poverty – 'zero possession'. The only thing left was her life – so what does the truth matter?

> In this way, crucial links in history are usually constructed of propaganda attached to slim slivers of truth. As usual, the only clear answer is that the winner of the war gets to tell their story first and it usually takes up the first four layers of truth. Beyond that, it's dogged research and experience that counts.

Adolf's Deconstruction

Bridget Hitler: "Looking back now, it would be very satisfying to say that my Irish second sight, or even my woman's intuition had helped me recognise unusual qualities which might explain why the young man [Adolf Hitler] we met would become one of the most notorious figures in history, but there was certainly nothing about the *pale, unsteady-eyed youth who began agitatedly whispering* to Alois that distinguished him from thousands of others.

"One would have expected that for such a long journey he would have come fairly well-dressed . . . wearing such a worn-out suit . . . Adolf *was completely exhausted. His pallor and lassitude were so pronounced that I feared he was ill, and immediately after dinner he retired.*

"My brother in law Adolf remained with us from November 1912 until April 1913, and a *less interesting* or prepossessing house guest I cannot imagine. At first *he remained in his room, sleeping* or lying on the sofa he used as a *bed most of the time.* I had an idea he was ill, *his colour was so bad and his eyes were so peculiar.* I felt rather sorry for him . . . *unappreciative and difficult.* Adolf *took everything we did for granted* and I'm sure would have remained indefinitely if he had had the slightest encouragement.

"I found him only *weak and spineless . . .* Usually he wouldn't say much, but just sit. Sometimes he would *speak of the future.*

"They were always as much alike as two peas in a pod. Alois had *maps of every country and was always studying them.* When Adolf was with us I had to go through the same thing all over again. He would *spread them out on tables, or even on the floor, and pore over them for hours,* and he would never hesitate to interrupt my housework to *explain how Germany was going to take its rightful position in the world. First would come France, then England.* Naturally I didn't find this kind of talk very interesting, but *whenever I tried to get away he would begin to shout,* although I rarely troubled to contradict him. I put it down *partly to the pleasure he took in hearing his own voice* – another trick he had in common with my husband.

"As a matter of fact, I didn't pay a great deal of attention to his ravings . . . Once I couldn't stand Adolf for another minute and burst out: 'You have a fine nerve coming here as you have and saying such things. You will never see the day England will be destroyed by Germany. If it ever comes to a fight, it's just as likely that the opposite will happen. Anyway, why do you take such an interest? You and all of us too are Austrians, not Germans.'

"[Hitler] *stared at me as though I had struck him in the face.* For a while he had nothing to say, but *his bewilderment soon passed off,* to be displaced by what I can only describe as *a kind of sly pleasure in the fact that he had made a Britisher lose her temper.*

"When Alois had time, he took off – to London. *Adolf was enchanted by Tower Bridge,* and they bribed their way into the engine room to see the immense machinery in motion. Alois had a regular passion for machinery and was pleased to have a companion on his jaunts. *He showed Adolf power plants, dynamos, river cranes and the inside of ships.* When they came home there would be endless discussions of what they had seen.

"They both *had an intense interest in anything English and were always sightseeing* ... they were the forerunners of the tourists who later streamed out of Nazi Germany in all directions and brought home *the odd bits of information which, patched together, formed a complete pattern.*

"As soon as Adolf knew his way around he *began disappearing by himself,* not returning until late in the evening. *Adolf was always reading – not books, little pamphlets printed in German. These were Adolf's books. I didn't know what was in them, nor exactly where they came from, so I presume he must have got them from the Germans he met around the city."*[15]

Secret Service: "These were 'briefing documents' from Tavistock ... everything Hitler looked like and did, all his physiological symptoms, outward appearance and actions showed him to be integrating after deconstruction. The practice of deconstructing foreign politicians has been developing over the past five hundred years and has become the favourite way of taking over countries."

When Hitler arrived, he was dressed for a short trip, not a long trip. He had come from Tavistock, not Vienna. Everyone from Vienna was in their Sunday best whereas Hitler was dishevelled as though he had been living in the same clothes for the previous nine months – which he had.

Hitler whispered in an agitated manner and was completely exhausted. He had a pale and sickly skin colour. He was weary, looked ill, had unsteady and peculiar eyes – all symptoms of deconstruction.

> Essentially Hitler had just had his first twenty years of ideology removed and replaced with that of the warring secret societies, the Freemasons and the Illuminati. When reintegrating after deconstruction it is not uncommon for the eyes to change colour, even from blue to brown and back again.

[15] *The Memoirs of Bridget Hitler*, pp. 22, 24, 29, 30, 32, 35. Author's emphasis.

After dinner Hitler retired immediately to his room, spent his days sleeping on the sofa and was in bed most of the time. Deconstructed people need to sleep a lot to reset their subconscious – essentially to dream the new future they have been set to achieve. Sometimes they sleep right through the day and the following night.

Adolf Hitler remained disinterested, unappreciative and difficult. He was completely impractical, weak and spineless and took everything his hosts did for granted. He was the ideological boss and all others were servants to be humbled.

He was egocentric and singularly concerned with bringing his own remote goals into the present, drawing them ever closer. This took all his willpower and left him practically useless to the world. He became immersed in his own future and evaded his present condition, which he did his best to deny. He became heavily self-involved in his new impregnated heroic self-image.

Adolf studied maps of every country, spread on the table and on the floor. He would speak of the future, but not of the present. He revealed his programming and the future by explaining how Germany was going to take its rightful position in the world, first taking over France and then England. He did this and said all of this in 1913 and it was all very predictive. He was not a 'lone wolf' but someone who was heavily backed and trained in creating a definitively circumscribed future.

> Deconstruction is a very powerful tool. To alter someone's subconscious is to set their life on a completely different track, and so it was with Adolf Hitler.
>
> To deconstruct someone according to the ideology of another nation is to have them in complete service of that nation. Their outward thoughts and actions may be nationalistic, but their final results are always for the benefit of the country that supplied the deconstruction.
>
> Whenever anyone ignored Hitler, he would shout his message at them. He took pleasure in hearing his own voice as his own voice had been used to access his subconscious during deconstruction. So whenever Hitler spoke, he believed what he was saying.
>
> During typical deconstruction a voice recording, or pulse thereof,

is placed on the temples, while other music is played in the background. In Hitler's case it was most likely his political and musical idol Wagner, who he had studied since childhood. (Hitler learnt piano.) The music distracts the conscious and unconscious minds, letting the message sink straight into the subconscious with the same amount of pleasure that the music brings. When the music is played again it brings forth the implanted message by association. This music is called an 'anchor'.

When challenged, Hitler reacted as though he had been physically assaulted and then took pleasure in humbling anything British – his new subconscious enemy. The ideas he had learnt had been fully absorbed and he had a very physical reaction to any threat of mission failure.

Hitler sought out British sites of interest for destruction later, including Tower Bridge, power plants, dynamos, river cranes and the inside of ships. He began disappearing by himself, not returning until late in the evening. With his half-brother Alois, he was a spy tourist for four months gathering whatever patchy information they could to form a complete picture.

They had endless debriefings and Alois, his half-brother, was Hitler's seconder. If Adolf Hitler failed, Alois Hitler was to take his place. But Adolf didn't fail. From the war-makers point of view, he was a huge success.

Although Alois trained before him, he did not have the common look that Adolf had. Alois was endlessly prone to getting attached whereas Adolf wasn't. Alois was a heterosexual sex addict, whereas Adolf was a sexually bent loner. Adolf was a coprophiliac which made him easily controlled and all the more useful.

> According to the British, Hitler was a near-perfect puppet of war and the proof is in the pudding. Adolf was always reading Psych-Ops training material in German (the language of his subconscious). He kept this material to himself and pored over it endlessly. He was becoming what the British wanted – a perfect weapon of war, a German nationalist, a socialist – a Nazi.

When Dr Morell, Hitler's doctor from 1937, first examined Hitler he noted that "His psychic state was very complex".

Hitler in WWI – the Freemasons' Great War

War was expected. British Military Intelligence Officers expected war in late 1914 after the harvest, but it came early prior to the harvest.

Archduke Franz Ferdinand of Austria was killed by a Bosnian Serb nationalist in Sarajevo on 28 June 1914 and this resulted in Austria declaring war on Serbia. The assassin himself said that the War had been planned for over a year. It was widely believed amongst German Intelligence Officers that the British controlled Serbian Intelligence – the Black Hand – and supplied the guns, explosives, money and anything else they needed. So much for the British explanation that World War I began by accident.

WWI resulted in the collapse of the German, Austro-Hungarian, Russian and Ottoman empires with 10 million dead and another 50 million dying in the final few months from the Spanish Flu. The British Empire remained intact. The British planned the Great War, which was later known as WWI. At the time there was little that happened that the British did not plan.

War broke out 20 months after Hitler finished his British Psych-Ops training and a year after he left England. In WWI, Hitler was a Private First Class in the Bavarian Regiment acting as a runner on the Western Front – a position often taken up by double agents. At one time, Winston Churchill (43) was fighting within 2 km of Hitler (28). Both had volunteered, and since both were protected Psych-Ops trained British agents, they may well have met under protected circumstances. Certainly they were both protected from death by Intelligence.

Secret Service: "On 20 November 1917, at Cambrai, in Northern France, 150 km from the English Channel and 50 km from Belgium, Hitler was captured in the trenches along with other Germans. The British troops, part of the Royal Green Jacket Regiment, were on orders to take no prisoners and they began slaughtering. Hitler was about to be terminated when a British Intelligence Officer ran up and said, 'Oh no, not that man', and Hitler was allowed to return to his own lines.

"Twice during WWI Hitler was saved on orders of a British Intelligence Officer. At the time of the unnecessary, unwarranted and humiliating German surrender, Hitler was lying in hospital temporarily blinded by gas (11 November 1918).

"[Twenty-one years later], in September 1938, when the British

Prime Minister, Neville Chamberlain (69) met with Hitler (49) in Munich, he came back with two pieces of paper. One said "Peace for our Time" and Hitler had signed it, and the other was a letter addressed to the Lance Corporal of the Green Jacket Regiment thanking him for saving his life. The letter named the Lance Corporal.

"I sighted the letter at the Green Jacket Regiment Officer's mess in 1974 in the City of Winchester in Hampshire, 40km south-west of central London. The City of Winchester is the old capital of England (1000AD). It is a cathedral city and the centuries-old home of the Royal Green Jacket Brigade. When I went back to see the letter much later, it had gone missing."

The Aldershot military training centre is 30 minutes' drive north-east of Winchester on the way to London. Winchester was not bombed much at all during WWII.

Spymaster: "The Lance Corporal in the Royal Green Jacket Regiment who saved Hitler's life at Cambrai ended up in the Liverpool Police. He spent the first six months of the WWII blitz wandering around Liverpool saying, 'To think I could have stopped this' until Special Branch paid him a visit and told him to 'Shut the fuck up'."

Hitler – the British Under Cover Agent

In 1911, Hitler steadfastly opposed joining the Austrian Army and claimed to be an invalid, but after being prosecuted in 1913, he rushed to volunteer in 1914. In late 1918, Hitler was assigned to intelligence duties. He became something of an agent provocateur talking revolution in barracks and then identifying those who agreed with him.

Hitler, like other deconstructed personalities, was bisexual, bordering on paedophilic. His controller, Captain Roehm, was the same. In 1919, Hitler went on to more sophisticated duties as a plain clothed under-cover for Army Intelligence. While under Roehm, Hitler discovered the printing presses of the Volkischer Beobachter were for sale.

He rushed straight back to his boss Captain Roehm to tell him that he must buy the press, but Roehm was away on a boy-rooting expedition and, rather than wait, he took the unprecedented step of ringing 'God'. He put in a collect call through to Colonel General von Seeckt, the Chief of the Reichswehr, telling him about this unbelievable bargain. Colonel General von Seeckt said the price seemed reasonable, but he lacked the funds, so he offered to ring the 'cousins'. The 'cousins' were the British and the next day Corporal Hitler got his newspaper. The German High Command had bought the people's printing press for Hitler with British financing.

Hitler and the German High Command had undeniable links to Britain and they had been in bed together before, during and after WWI . . . and as it turned out, during WWII as well.

Hitler loved the British and repaid the favour by letting the British and French Expeditionary Forces escape from Dunkirk (26–28 May 1940).

> "The Führer's decision to halt the Panzers on the Aa Canal in Belgium allowed the remnants of the British Expeditionary Force to escape from Dunkirk."[16]
> "225,000 British and 110,000 French troops were evacuated from the French port of Dunkirk on the English Channel between 27 May and 2 June 1940."[17]

Likewise, when Britain installed easy targets like the groups of four tall radar towers which allowed the British to spot German planes at night (well before they arrived), Hitler never targeted them. Hermann Goering, the head of the Luftwaffe prevented their bombing and even the British covered for him, blaming this on a German misinterpretation of what Goering said.

Part of the agreed object of the war was to inform each other of their positions and intentions and the radar, although primitive, did this automatically. WWII was a war that developed all forms of communication including spies, double agents, radar, radio, codes and shared inventions. (See *Information and Inventions, Appendix 1*)

> This showed complete British control over Hitler and WWII. The deaths of 335,000 fighting soldiers would certainly have ended the war after only nine months (June 1940), with Germany winning and taking over England, but it was far too soon to end the war. The social structure of the new world was not yet in place and all the profits were yet to be made.

Secret Service: "Britain started to organise WWII in 1919, before all the chickens came home to roost. Britain knew Germany would rise from the ashes and they ran Hitler as their agent, ensuring that Germany had a leader who was their puppet. War machines need war and the

[16] *To Catch a King*, p. 51.
[17] *The Oxford English Reference Dictionary*.

funded, trained, and supported double agents to be their patsies, their puppets and their puppet enemy."

Germany Between the Wars

From 1919–29, Berlin was the most sexually explicit city in the world. "Transvestites were having sex with men dressed as women in the Mikado Café and the patrons were joining in, creating orgies for spectators and participants. There were clubs for sadists, exhibitionists, and masochists. Naked dancing at 'The White Mouse Club' became the vogue . . . women could choose between male and female prostitutes . . . Hawkers offered porn, dope, and snow (cocaine) . . . wife swapping was prevalent in high society and lesbianism was acknowledged as a contributing cause of the skyrocketing divorce statistics [just as it is in America today] . . . Little girls of ten and eleven, rouged, and wearing short baby dresses, promenaded the gully from midnight to dawn in competition with lush blondes swathed in furs."[18] Black jazz musicians proliferated on the banjo and saxophone, and everybody shimmied.

Right through Germany, nudism became a form of protest. It was not uncommon for people to walk up and down the streets naked, protesting against the deathly 1914–18 war and partly against the ridiculous ruling class. There were no controls on Berlin's lifestyle and no thought of its effects. Even when Berlin was in battle, it was a parade that never stopped.

When Hitler arrived, Berlin was considered the most sexually explicit city in the world where the universal dance was shaking off the shackles of war. Hitler denounced moral laxity and attacked "the universal madness for pleasure".

Even the 'Hangman' Reinhard Heydrich (1904–42), Director-General of the SS and the SD, the secret department and inner sanctum of the SS, said of Berlin: "You have no idea what this town was like. There was the *Ring Club* which only allowed membership to those who'd served at least three years in jail. *The Silhouette,* the *Always Faithful* and the *Paradise* which was filled with the most glorious transvestites in gorgeous dresses, with high heels and lipstick."[19] Transvestites are partly a product of the pressures of war, as is appreciating them.

In the 1919 play, *Vatemord,* Arnolt Bronnen exposed the break

[18] *Prelude to Terror,* p. 234.

[19] *To Catch a King,* p. 52.

in the family between the father's and the son's generations. In very graphic detail, the play showed the son rebuking his father, having sex with another man, and then incest with his mother. The graphically intense play provided an impetus for sexual stability and Hitler climbed onto the bandwagon of 'sexual conservatism'.

Spymaster: "I ran a ring of spies in Berlin and I had one who was some kind of drug addict, morphine I think. I would receive messages from his friends asking me to pick him up from different addresses in Berlin. Some of them were rich, some of them were seedy tenements in Moabit. One I remember was a room in a block of flats given over mainly to prostitutes. His companions of the evening were two men both heavily rouged. One had been completely run through with a 1907 Lee Enfield bayonet. My agent came when called and said on the way out, 'I suppose you think I'm a queer?'

I replied in the affirmative.

"'No I'm not,' he said. 'They both had tits.'

"'Well that's just wonderful,' and no more was said."

Berlin was in its "delirium of desperation" and being run by a group of ridiculous soap queens. A homosexual clique hung around the Kaiser, the world's most ridiculous man, with his pudding-bowl helmet, complete with protruding wooden spoon. A sausage dog followed in the same outfit, but in miniature.

Just prior to the outbreak of WWI, one of the German Chiefs of General Staff suffered a fatal heart attack in the Kaiser's presence while dressed as a woman. Ernst Toller, a left-wing poet, became a general, later committing suicide in New York, and Kurt Eisner was a drama critic who later became the Prime Minister. He opened all political meetings with an orchestra. Germany was run by the grandiose and the camp.

This was Hitler's political competition. They were a basket case, but so was Berlin, Germany, and much of Hitler's history. As soon as the Germans had paid their WWI war debt, the Americans changed the standard from silver to gold thus recreating Germany's war debt from scratch. In 1923 the currency devalued radically and the German paper mark devalued 4 million million to the gold mark with one loaf of bread costing 1 billion marks. It was inevitable that things would go from loose to civil war.

Germany in the 1920s was in a state of meltdown. The only fibre in the entire country was the Freikorps (the Freedom Corps) who were controlled by the Officer Korps. These bands of freewheeling ex-soldiers were not short of ammunition or weapons. They murdered communists and unionists and anyone else deemed to be an enemy of Germany.

Reich means "Kingdom, Realm or State" and the Third Reich was a fiction established by assuming history. The Nazis' assumed the First Reich was the Holy Roman Empire (962–1806), the Second Reich was the German Empire (1871–1918) and the Third Reich was the Nazi Regime (1933–1945).

The Germans had a mania for secreting away military weapons as a reaction to the 1919 Treaty of Versailles. Rather than create peace, the Treaty of Versailles led to the planning for WWII. For over two decades British Intelligence HQ routinely ignored the warnings of their British Officers stationed in Germany.

Hitler retained the explicit sexuality of the Germans although in a more public form. As the soldiers marched under the Brandenburg Gate with shovels instead of rifles over their shoulders, women on top of the gate in short shorts did aerobics bending over backwards, which was quite explicit. Initially the soldiers marched with shovels as the rifles were all buried in parks and under schools and warehouses. Armaments were not allowed under the useless Treaty of Versailles, so armaments were hidden.

Spymaster: "I ploughed through a file of these reports emanating from Germany between the wars. They contain cogent accounts by experienced Intelligence Officers who noticed all manner of military preparations within the Reichswehr. One of the most astute copied notices from barracks noticeboards. Another reported violations connected with arms in clear violation of the Treaty of Versailles. All were ignored by Whitehall who took the attitude, 'They're only Germans and Germans will be Germans'. This was before Hitler came to power. Now we know why – WWII was being created."

Commander William Guy Carr R.C.N.: "Under the terms of the Treaty of Versailles in 1919 the international bankers obtained control over Germany's military rearmament and her economic recovery. This accomplished, they entered into the *Abmachungen* (agreements) with the German High Command. They agreed to have the Soviets secretly supply the German generals with all the arms and munitions they required for a modern-day army of several million. They also undertook to have the Soviet dictator place complete training facilities at the disposal of the Germans to enable them to train the number of commissioned and non-commissioned officers they would require to officer the new army they planned to bring into being when they considered the time was ripe.

"The vast building projects required to put the terms of the *Abmachungen* into effect were financed by the international bankers. They thus enabled both the Communist and the Fascist countries to build up their economy and war potentials. The international bankers enabled the German High Command to evade all the military restrictions placed upon them by the Treaty of Versailles.

"The vast Krupp Munitions and Armaments Plants built in the Soviets behind the Ural Mountains were named 'Manych'. The German armament firms were granted every concession they asked for. International intrigue on such a lavish scale could only mean one thing. Those involved were preparing for World War II. The governments of the so-called Allied nations were kept fully informed regarding what was going on behind the scenes, as I found out when I visited London during the conference on naval disarmament in 1930 . . . Disraeli spoke the truth when he said, 'The governments elected do not govern' . . . From 1920 to 1934 . . . the leaders of . . . Communism in Russia were working hand in glove with the leaders of . . . Naziism in Germany."[20]

Germany had a history of rebuilding and rearming itself after the days of Frederick the Great. It was essential not to lose the key components of your strength. If you lose the war, it is essential that you preserve the skeleton of your army (the officers and the NCO corps – non-commissioned officers) and to save your arms and munitions industries. Prussia did this in 1806 and came back to help destroy Napoleon only a few years later. Napoleon believed he had destroyed Prussia at the Battle of Auerstadt and Jena but the Prussians drafted an army of 10-and 11-year-old children and trained them to fight, making musket changes so they were child-friendly.

German women were furnished with medals for producing children and mothers received Motherhood Crosses in bronze, silver and gold

[20] *Pawns in the Game*, p. 107.

for the size of their brood. This reached the ultimate perversion under the Nazi's breeding programme.

After WWI, Germany saved its strength by digging obsolete guns out of parks and assembling inferior weapons. This was also done with aircraft. The Germans even exported Fokker D7 fighters to Norway but were caught and the fighters with Norwegian markings were photographed being broken up. The Germans were full of schemes promoting their war effort and if one scheme came unstuck there were several more to take its place. This subterfuge was spotted by veteran Allied officers but their warnings were ignored.

Germany sent most of its latest manufacturing plant to Switzerland, Holland, Scandinavia and Russia to manufacture under licence. This kept the design process alive and the Western world was amazed with their improvements. The continued production of modern weapons allowed the General Staff to plan WWII when WWI had only just finished.

> Secret Service: "German soldiers had been practising making war in Russia under secret provisions of the Rapallo Pact from 1919. This contract enabled the German Army Intelligence (the Abwehr), under Admiral Canaris, to sell Stalin on the idea that his Soviet Officer Corps were ready to act against him. There are irrefutable indications that both Canaris and his deputy Hans Oster were under British control and they are likely to have designed the coup story, or at least conveyed it to Stalin, thus encouraging him to act brutally against his own soldiers (1937–39). This weakened the Russians just before the German invasion. It created a propaganda myth that allowed Hitler to invade Russia over the objections of the Army."

Hitler's Early Revolutions

On 9 November 1923, Hitler attempted a beer-cellar revolution in Munich (the Munich Putsch) with Rudolf Hess and Herman Goering. Goering was shot in the groin with an 8 mm bullet from a Mauser 98G and was in terrific pain. He became a morphine addict and his rich wife Carin smuggled him to her parents in Sweden.

Hitler and Hess received nine months in the Landsberg Fortress. Anyone else would have got eight years. While in prison Hitler revealed his British Psych-Ops training to Rudolf Hess who wrote it up as *Mein*

Kampf with Hitler as the author. Berlin was a city without morals and after his release in 1924, Hitler stood halfway between conservatism and radicalism, pro-heterosexual, but with a history of inbreeding (second- and third-degree incest) and homosexuality.

Hitler's toothbrush moustache had become a world joke, reminding millions of Charlie Chaplin. With his receding hairline, flop fringe, wide hips, narrow shoulders, and ridiculous moustache, essentially there to hide his unfeasibly large nostrils, he had an utterly mediocre appearance. Hitler had a great deal of difficulty selling racial superiority, so he relied on his orating skills, kept his distance, and never mingled with the crowd. Beer-table politics was a powerful force in fascist Bavaria, but he took no part in it. It was his orating skills and his book (*My Struggle*) that carried him through. Jail was the perfect preparation for Hitler.

Intelligence Historian: "*Mein Kampf* is a work probably ghost written by someone more educated in German grammar than Hitler, who plays down his education. As Hess was locked up in Landsberg Prison with Hitler and had got a degree after WWI, Hess was the scribe and partial contributor.

"It is probable that Hitler made suggestions and dictated parts of the work to Hess, while Hess obviously struggled to make sense of it all. It is a chaotic work that carries all the hallmarks of agent deconstruction. Don't look for logic in *Mein Kampf.* It doesn't exist in its normal form. It was written in a colloquial style, with a lot of slang and vernacular language and has been described as 'a comic without pictures'.

"*Mein Kampf* sets out to be all things to all men and its chapters on Jews and the future are of interest. It virtually declares Poland, France and Czechoslovakia are enemies but refrains from mentioning Britain in this way. Clearly it states the Nazi dream of lebensraum (living space) in the East. It also declares the old German dream of a place in the sun but refrains from hostile designs on Britain.

"We now read it with hindsight. If we were reading it today for the first time, it would probably be dismissed as the pipe dreams of some would-be revolutionary.

"Hitler's money did not come from *Mein Kampf* but from British Intelligence. *Mein Kampf* was a terrible book promoted by Intelligence as cover for the British funding of Hitler. To this end, it completely achieved its aim."

The German–British–American War Alliance

Under King George V's control, British spy information of the German breach of military build-up under the Treaty of Versailles was purposely ignored to give their 'cousins' in Germany a head start. In 1934 Churchill used private sources to assemble his own intelligence survey of German military rearmament. He then warned Parliament that Germany had "created a military air force which is now nearly two-thirds as strong as our present home defence air force [and] by 1936 Germany was due to exceed British air power".[21]

During the war Churchill preferred a daily selection of uninterpreted intelligence data from Major Desmond Morton rather than reports and conclusions from Britain's Joint Intelligence Committee, which had British Monarchy and therefore pro-German influences. This staved off sabotage and he trusted Morton as his friend and confidant. Morton went ahead and created 'M' who later became famous in the James Bond movies.

When the Nazis came to power, Goering returned to Germany and founded the Gestapo 'for racial and religious cleaning'. He built a house in honour of his wife and called it Carinhall where the German High Command met and where they, in turn, met with their international guests. By the time Goering was finishing Carinhall, his partner Emmy Sonnermann was six weeks' pregnant and he was running out of money.

The British were aware of this and sent the British spy, Group Captain Fred Winterbotham, to Carinhall. Winterbotham was working for British Air Intelligence and was one of Churchill's chief intelligence officers.[22] He briefed Churchill daily.

Goering was into 'positions that paid money' more than he was into war and was financially vulnerable at the time. He attended the coronation of King George VI in December 1936. This was largely kept out of the media, but he was well received in British high circles, especially MI-6.[23]

Goering was such a clown it was said about him that he wore special rubber medals in the bath. German comedians used to make jokes about him during WWII . . .

[21] Winston Churchill, *Hansard*, Parliament record, 1934.

[22] Winterbotham was a prolific rooter and would wear women out in a couple of days. When he went to Nazi Germany they always provided him with women.

[23] F. W. Winterbotham was Churchill's personal liaison officer at Bletchley Park where the German signals were deciphered. He wrote *The Ultra Secret* (1975), *The Nazi Connection* (1978) and *The Ultra Spy* (1991).

WWI pilot and charmer; "Fatty", "Daddy", "The Elephant" Goering charms Hitler.

Carinhall, highly bugged by the British, including the crypt where secretive conversations were held.

"Goering went to a circus and sat down at the front row. The elephant came out and went up to him and said 'Daddy, Daddy, Daddy'."

The SS would report these jokes back to Goering who loved attention beyond all else and tolerated them. The uneducated thought he had the common touch and was all right, but educated Germans didn't respect him and mistook him for a buffoon.

One of the top British spies saw Goering coming toward them and said "Here comes fatty" and the British spy chief admonished him saying, "Don't say that. He's the most dangerous charming man in the whole of Germany."

Goering controlled the listening service. At breakfast every morning, he received the brownsheets and read them for an hour to a background of soft music. Any gossip, anybody speaking out against him and any state security issues were on these brownsheets – just as all the related telephone calls were recorded on wax disc.

Once Goering took over these brownsheets, the Luftwaffe lost any interest in them and Goering would disappear them to the British. This left the Luftwaffe out of the loop and British Air Intelligence in control of another area of Germany's intelligence.

Goering was overrun with British spies. These were magicians, actors, circus performers, acrobats, slaves, peasants and the lockkeepers on the Kiel Canal through which the German submarines had to pass.

Submarine crews had a ritual where they would have a beer with the lockkeeper and his wife before they went on patrol. The British Royal Navy then received a message that another German sub had left and it would be sunk on this basis. The Germans looked at everything conceivable for their submarine losses and finally came upon the lockkeeper and his wife who were then executed in late 1943.

Goering sold the numbers and the totals of German aircraft to be built in return for the British paying to finish Carinhall, which they thoroughly bugged in the process. Goering held so many important Luftwaffe meetings here that this scenario literally changed the course of the air war.

The British cross-checked Goering's aircraft numbers with a spy they had making aileron control cables for the planes. Divided up, they showed how many aircraft were being built. The same information was supplied by the same spy to the Russians. The British then built shadow factories that enabled the Allied forces to compete with the Luftwaffe and win the war.

The Germans took an expeditious view of American industry especially with aircraft. They had spies everywhere and they would find a design for a component such as an undercarriage or an engine that suited their needs and would then go and steal the blueprints. The Luftwaffe were stealing all of their aircraft technology from the Americans with America's knowledge.

German aircraft were essentially American aircraft cobbled together. All the Germans had to do was design the airframe. This is the real secret of how the Luftwaffe was built so quickly. The Germans did not design their own subcomponents, they simply stole them. The spies joked, "The build quality is so good, pistons can be exchanged between American and German engines, no problem".

On one occasion one of their best spies was caught by American Customs with a violin case full of aircraft plans trying to leave the US. When the customs official dropped the case the plans flew out. With amazing savoir faire, the German spy said, "I have to smuggle them past my wife because she thinks I'm feeding my son's addiction to aircraft. It's the only way I can get my son the aircraft plans he desires. His mother hates flying. I have to smuggle them otherwise she will go mental at me."

The US customs official's empathy for men afflicted by difficult women created an immediate rapport and he allowed him to pass with the American aircraft plans quickly stuffed back into the violin case.

> America was feeding Germany its technology, its finances and its oil. Many of the high-finance Americans were of German descent and were on Germany's side. These included Henry Ford (Freemason), Walt Disney (Freemason), Prescott Bush (Skull and the Presidents Bushes father and grandfather), the Rothschilds, ICI Faben, now ICI and Dulux paints, etc.

The 1929 Wall Street crash brought chaos to Germany and without it, Hitler would never have risen to power. Democracy was not working – perhaps Fascism was the solution. In the US there was industrial unrest and the middle class were breaking into bakeries and stealing bread – Germany seemed to be marginally more in control of its labour. Henry

Ford brought in troops with machine guns to suppress striking workers in the 1930s. There were strike lockouts, unemployment and 20,000 people in anti-Jewish rallies in New York. Ford supported Hitler as both were anti-Semitic and anti-union. Hitler was Ford's wind-up toy that Ford was keen to see at work in the model factory that was to become Nazi Germany.

> In the mid-1930s, almost all of the political leaders of the world expressed their admiration for the astonishing achievements of Adolf Hitler. No one contemplated the human cost until 1945 when the Concentration Camps were revealed in their magnitude.
> Walt Disney gave most of the proceeds of the *Wizard of Oz* to the Nazis; Henry Ford paid for Hitler's staff vehicles, and President Bush's grandfather sold munitions to Germany thus contravening the Treaty of Versailles. Hitler wanted Fords but Henry Ford considered the PR implications and paid for Hitler's Mercedes.
> Walt Disney and other investors financed Goering's train. Goering named it 'America'. When the British tried to strafe it, the American Air Force sent aircraft to shoot down the British aircraft.

Britain also had possession of a few types of German aircraft purchased before WWII. The most combat-capable were the Junkers JU86 which were used as transports. Britain kept more tight-lipped about the use of German aircraft than the Germans did about their British KG200 battle squadron. The British-purchased German aircraft went to South Africa as a commercial venture, but whoever bought these planes went tits-up and the planes were then impressed into the South African Air Force under British control. Thus Britain had control of German planes which could then be used to drop British agents in Germany. Britain later acquired a Folke Wolf 200 Condor plane from a Danish Airline. 'Officially' it was destroyed in 1942.

Carinhall was finished in October 1937 and Goering's child was born on 2 June 1938. Goering was a well-known Anglophile and his support for Hitler was questioned at the time. But by February 1938, with subtle British influence within the German High Command, Goering became the Field Marshal of the Luftwaffe.[24] It was a bent world where double agents profited the most.

[24] *Hermann Göring*, p. 165.

The Luftwaffe Air Force had been created in America (largely by German-Americans), stolen by German-American spies within the American aviation industry, and sold to Germany, who then passed the numbers on to the British. Now all sides had a relatively equal Air Force. Two-thirds of America's Air Force engineers in Long Island were Germans, and from 1900 there were so many Germans living in New York it was possible to pick up the German language off the streets.

Seasoned Spymaster, Dr Eric Pheiffer: "During WWII the US was 'in a pincer of spies' and Germany had effected the most elaborate and effective penetration of a major power in the entire history of espionage. The United States cannot plan a warship, design an airplane, develop a new device that we do not know of at once . . . We have spy outlets in Montreal, Newport Mews, Boston, Buffalo, Bristol, Philadelphia, San Diego, Seattle, and Bath, Maine . . . We even have spies in President Roosevelt's inner circle[25] and at the Chemical Centre in Bel Air Maryland . . . We even had the plans for American anti-aircraft guns from the Army Signals Laboratories at Fort Monmouth before they reached Washington. We had all the plans for the US destroyers from 1932–1936, courtesy of Gustav Guellich, including all the high-altitude rockets and rocket-propelled missiles."[26]

"Otto Voss started working on Ireland Aircraft and became an American citizen, working in Baltimore developing an experimental seaplane at the Sikorsky plant in Farmingdale, Long Island. He sent all the plans back to Germany in 1934, including those for the super-secret light Bomber SB-C2, the Boeing Bomber, the FG-2 plans, the SBU-1 scout bomber, tactical air exercises at Mitchell Field Long Island, US Army Classified Maps and plans for the destroyers DD-397, DD-398, DD-399 and their propellers.

"Two-thirds of all US aircraft engineers were German, so the German spies did not stand out. From 1934–1941, five months before Pearl Harbor, the Germans had stolen every plan of American aircraft using microphotographic 10% film. Information was cheap and the German agents were paid less than US$300 in 1937 for the year's work. This allowed both sides to be bribed. The highest price ever paid was US$1500 in one lump sum."[27]

[25] Roosevelt's wife was a rug-muncher.

[26] *The Game of Foxes*, p. 36.

[27] Ibid. p. 28, paraphrased.

In New York, the German spies stayed at the Taft Hotel, north of Times Square, and the Russians stayed at the Hotel Manhattan. The designations for German spies were 'F'– Scout or Courier; 'R'– Travelling Agent; 'A'– Producing Information; and 'V'– German Agent, referred to as a 'V-Mann' number.

The Last of the Hitlers

Meanwhile, Adolf's half-brother, Alois Hitler, had remarried bigamously. "In May 1914 Alois left his wife and child [William Patrick Hitler] in Liverpool and set off for Germany to establish a safety-razor business. World War I broke out shortly after his departure and detained him on the continent for four years. After the war he arranged to have a false report of his death delivered to Brigid and [he re]married bigamously. The German authorities eventually found out and prosecuted him. Brigid [Catholic] intervened on his behalf and he was virtually acquitted. Nothing about the affair became public at the time."[28]

By 1929, their son, William Patrick Hitler, was 18 and full of chutzpah and went to see his uncle, first sighting him at a Nuremberg Rally. When Hitler found out that his half-brother Alois (convicted criminal, ruffian and waiter) had left Brigid, he pretended he wasn't related. He sent his nephew back to England saying Alois was an orphan.

"William Patrick stayed with Alois and his new family during his early trips to Germany [1929]. During the period of Hitler's rule, Alois ran a restaurant in Berlin. He managed to keep it open for the duration of World War II. He was captured by the British at the end of the war but released because it was clear that he had led 'a perfectly blameless existence'."[29]

> An MI-6 officer who denies ever being trained:
> "In view of Alois' first-hand knowledge of Adolf's training and backing, this is perfectly understandable. After all, 99% of Intelligence is deny everything, even if it means denying night follows day."

Hitler escaped to his 'Eagle's Nest' mountain retreat on the German-Austrian border to get away from his work and family, but his nephew and his sister-in-law tracked him down and tried to blackmail him, saying that they would go back to England and sell their story to the papers unless they got some money. Adolf was surprisingly lenient

[28] *Irish Roots*, Issue No. 1, 1992, First Quarter, Hitler: His Irish Relatives, Tony McCarthy.
[29] Ibid.

considering his timetable – killing Germans in Germany, before starting on the Poles, Gipsies, Slavs, and then the Jews. He was most scared that his missing years would not stack up and he did not want to draw attention to his sketchy past.

These family requests and embarrassments began to encroach on his publicly purist lifestyle, and at the time, he was very busy promoting himself and building up Germany's warring infrastructure. Hitler gave his nephew William Patrick Hitler a series of low administration jobs in the Third Reich Government and William became a Berlin socialite, living off the Führer's name.

Hitler put pressure on him to relinquish his British citizenship, but instead William Patrick scarpered back to England in 1938 with the assistance of Mr Fenton of Her Majesty's Secret Service (MI-6) and another secret agent operating as a magician under the name Bunny Aldon[30] (probably Jasper Maskelyne) who provided him with the escape vehicle, the Storm Troopers in hot pursuit.

MI-6 agent: "The number of British spies chased out of Germany in this way, was only exceeded by the number flooding in."

MI-6 started just before WWI. The security intelligence service was looking for well-connected people, the upper crust, from the British establishment. They offered them fraternity, adventure, danger, espionage and excitement with unlimited potential for sodomy. They were to be a secret guard. Hitler had been similarly scouted.

> It was not uncommon for the Secret Service to fabricate plots with character names and occupations so fictional, that anyone telling the story would feel ridiculous, and anyone listening would write it off merely on the basis of the names. It was, however, common practice for members of the Secret Service to be in the entertainment industry and for entertainers to be seconded into the Secret Service.

Patrick Hitler became very anti-Hitler and anti-German. He wrote his story and tried to sell it to the British papers but they wouldn't have a bar of it! The Hurst papers wrote it up in America as 'I Hate My Uncle Adolf' (*Look* magazine, January 1939), with the subtitle 'To Hell With Hitler', and the French papers published the story under 'Mon Uncle Adolfe' (*Paris-Soir*, August 1939).

[30] Brigid Dowling relates this in *The Memoirs of Bridget Hitler*.

According to *The Oxford English Reference Dictionary* 'Führer' means "a leader, especially a tyrannical one". Hitler assumed this title in 1934, five years before *TIME* magazine named him 'Man of the Year' (2 January 1939), sneaking in just before *Look* magazine hit the newsstands.

With Brigid Hitler taking in boarders, running dancing lessons at Highgate and behind on her rates (£9 13s 10d), she and Patrick scarpered to America together, arriving on 30 March 1939. The Hurst papers paid for the journey and William Patrick Hitler toured America from 1939–44 giving talks in public halls billed as 'What the German People are Thinking' with the subtitle 'Of the Real Germany Hidden Behind Nazi Fiction'. This brought him to the attention of the FBI and the OSS (the CIA from 1946).

William Patrick Hitler, 6'1", also known as William Patrick Dowling, Patrick Dowling, and Carter Stevens, served as a first-class seaman in the US Navy (1944–46), in the medical corps, and as an intelligence officer. Ironically he was sworn in by one Hess, an American having the same name as Hitler's deputy and *Mein Kampf* scribe.

William Patrick Hitler then wrote a book using an FBI ghost writer (a great piece of intelligence gathering) which is listed on the web by the Office of Strategic Services under the single page *"Hitler Source Book"* as Adolf Hitler, written by Alois Hitler and published by New York American on 30 November 1930. It was Adolf Hitler dictated to the FBI by William Patrick Hitler and published in 1946.

Confusion is the name of the game,
especially the war game.

William Patrick's mother, Brigid Hitler, converted to British Intelligence and worked for British War Relief in New York, opposite Tiffany's.

After WWII William Patrick Hitler lived in the New York Metropolitan area, where, fearful for his life, he changed his name to William Hiller (1946–77) and worked as a urologist in Manhattan (taking the piss out of Jews in America). He then became a phlebotomist (bleeding Americans) working from his home in Yaphank, Long Island, a suburb renowned for its Nazi sympathisers. In 1977 he married a German woman and changed his surname to that of Hitler's favourite anti-Semitic author, Wagner. By that time Yaphank had become a bedroom community for New York.

Wagner was incredibly anti-Semitic and suggested that the best the Jews could do for culture would be to burn themselves at the stake. He too came from unconfirmed parentage. Hitler was a frequent visitor to the Wagner household. Wagner's children called Adolf Hitler 'Uncle Wolf'. At one point he was going to marry one of Wagner's widowed daughters.

Wagner (1813–83) was Hitler's favourite author (*Opera and Drama*). Count Gobineau (1816–82) wrote the *Essay on the Inequality of Human Races*. Gobineau was the intellectual parent of the incestuous Nietzsche (1844–1900) who tried to give his age new values and wrote *The Birth of Tragedy*, which he dedicated to his friend Wagner. Since Wagner was the oldest, considered the father of the three authors, and had the most Westernised name, drawing the least attention in Long Island, the surname 'Wagner' was chosen by William Patrick to replace 'Hitler' and 'Hiller'.

William Hiller had four sons born between 1949 and 1965 who all eventually lived under different surnames. He named his eldest son Alex Adolf Hiller. His second son Howard married in 1989 but before he could impregnate his wife, he had a car accident arranged by the FBI.[31]

The FBI usually gave assignments of this nature to 'The Squad' manned by Mafia hit men. The top Mafioso sodomised J. Edgar Hoover on at least a weekly basis. In exchange, Hoover (Freemason) would deny that Mafia ever existed and: 'If it doesn't exist you can't arrest it'. This is why the Mafia hits were successful and they got away with murder for so long.

The remaining three sons, Hitler's grandnephews, then made a survival pact to never have children. They now each have different names and run a small landscape gardening business in Long Island where they receive sympathetic cover from the locals. Hitler's nephew William Patrick Wagner died anonymously on 14 July 1987.[32]

[31] *Irish Roots*, Issue No. 1, 1992, First Quarter, Hitler: His Irish Relatives, Tony McCarthy.
[32] *Last of the Hitlers*, 2002.

The pseudo-documentary, *Last of the Hitlers* shows that William Patrick Hitler changed his name to Houston Stewart Chamberlain and in the next sentence to William Patrick Stewart-Houston without differentiating when they were used, whether they were used interchangeably or what name he was buried under. This is called 'well-presented disinformation' and is designed to obscure. Brigid Dowling, Alois Hitler's first wife, was buried in a cemetery in Long Island under her own name.

Until 1950, Long Island was a series of potato farms and aircraft manufacturers. Nazi sympathisers used to send radio transmissions and light signals to the German submarines coming into New York Harbor during WWII. Some were captured and made prisoners of war. Yaphank, then a population of 10,000, remained a community of Nazi sympathisers even after the war and Levittown was built here.

The Hitler family were a family of authors and did very well considering their father Alois was such a nutter (Hutter). Adolf, his sister Paula Hitler and his nephew William Patrick Hitler all wrote their way into history, but it is Hitler's book, *Mein Kampf* (*My Struggle*) with its revealing Psych-Ops training, developed over the last five centuries, that has remained a best-seller, amassing some £15 million in unclaimed royalties.

Hitler the Anglophile

Hitler was an Anglophile. He loved England, the British, and its aristocracy. After all, his sister-in-law was Irish, he had stayed in Liverpool, and he was trained in Britain as a British puppet of war. He was a British double agent and Britain was about to fund his media campaign.

Hitler gained further comfort from the fact that the Kaiser had abdicated and was held under protective custody in Harlem, in British-controlled Holland. The British did everything in their power to give Hitler Germany. Britain needed war to maintain its class structure and without another war their aristocracy would fall.

The British monarchy were cousins of the deposed German monarchs and therefore friends with Germany's aristocracy. Britain's King George V died on 20 January 1936 and Hitler played on the monarchy's vanity by sending a message of sympathy and throwing an elaborate synchronous memorial service on 28 January 1936 with his full cabinet in attendance.

Hitler the Anglophile.

As a result of this comforting display from Hitler to the British Royals, after investigating Germany's build-up to war and receiving assertions from Hitler, Prime Minister Neville Chamberlain returned to Britain saying, "Go home and get a nice quiet sleep".

Chamberlain completely failed to appreciate the threat of Germany's 1919–39 military build-up, especially the last ten years.

This suited the Saxe-Coburg Gothas – King Edward VIII and King George VI – perfectly. They were the head of British Freemasonry, who, along with the German Freemasons, were in a battle against the French Freemasons with a value system most would not understand, and for reasons that have lasted beyond generations, but primarily based on 'want of knowledge' and 'envy of style'.

Every war is a war of secrets
and wars with the greatest number of secrets
take the longest.

For the last three reigns, the commonwealth should have been singing "God Save the Queen". All their British monarchs have had sex with men. In this way, secrets were traded. The Freemasons kept the monarch's sexual practices secret and in exchange the Monarch kept the warring Freemasons' plans secret, even helping them to create a more equitable war so that it is not 'a bashing, a mugging, or a trial run', but a serious depopulation exercise . . . enough to shift boundaries, social policy and the social make-up of populations. "Dead Dad" is a prime example of such history influencing language.

> All the British male monarchs since King George IV (1820) have been Freemasons and all have been sexually compromised. Sexually compromising the monarch and/or their partner is the first step to taking over that country and controlling its military. Through WWI and WWII the British monarchs were all bisexual males with low IQs.

Because of Chamberlain's non-acceptance and denial of the impending war with Germany, he was made Prime Minister from 28 May 1937 to 10 May 1940. This gave Germany a head start in its war preparations.

Winston Churchill, Secretary of State for War (1919–21) was so disturbed by this denial that he built a private intelligence centre in his home (1929), which remained in full operation until 1939. It was this decade of pre-emptive intelligence gathering and training that saved England from Germany and allowed him to bypass all the pro-German, pro-fascist propaganda filtering through the British royal press and intelligence machine.

It was Winston Churchill's private intelligence centre that ensured the English language and culture dominated . . . but he was still a major player in the war, in all its machinations.

Czechoslovakia was invaded by Hitler on 1 October 1938 and again on 15 March 1939. Chamberlain, still in full denial, "advocated appeasement with Italy and Germany. Criticism of his war leadership and military reverses led to his resignation as Prime Minister in May 1940 and his appointment as Lord President of the Council."[33] Chamberlain was given a face-saving position, Churchill became Prime Minister (10 May 1940), and then Chamberlain was assassinated by in-house liquidation six months later on 9 November 1940.

Essentially Chamberlain acted as a delivery boy for the British-trained Hitler (a double agent of 27 years), and both acted for the British war machine. Chamberlain allowed Hitler to come to power unchallenged and even colluded with Hitler by guaranteeing Britain would not interfere with Germany's takeover of Czechoslovakia.

The under-prepared Chamberlain was replaced with the over-prepared Churchill (Freemason) who declared war on Germany on 3 September 1939. Eight months later he was Prime Minister.

Churchill was, however, pipped at the post by several others. The Luftwaffe bombed Warsaw airfields at 4.15 am Saturday 1 September 1939 and Poland declared war on Germany the same day. But even this was superseded, as illustrated in Ladislas Farago's *A Game of Foxes.*

The Germans invaded Poland six days before this at 0.01 am on 26 August 1939 when the German K Group (attack group) went into Poland's Beskid Mountains 6 days, 4 hours and 44 minutes before the formal start of WWII.

German Leutnant Herzner staged a raid on Jablunkov Pass, killed Poles, took prisoners and received the surrender of the senior Polish officer who pointed out that Poland was not at war. Leutnant Herzner tried to ignore this, but became convinced when there were no other sounds of action.

[33] *The Cambridge Biographical Encyclopaedia.*

Leutnant Herzner eventually asked the Polish officer how he could verify the fact that the war had not begun and the Polish officer suggested he ring his own base. Leutnant Herzner didn't believe it, but in desperation rang his own base at Zilinia in Slovakia. He got hold of his Intelligence Officer who confirmed that the German operation had been postponed. Leutnant Herzner was advised to let the Polish prisoners go, render medical attention and get back across the border as if nothing had happened. He did this quaking in his boots that he had cocked up the whole of WWII.

After he came back to Czechoslovakia he was paranoid with fear but was eventually comforted a few days later by Admiral Canaris, Chief of the Abwehr, who congratulated him on his performance. No one knows where and how Leutnant Herzner died and his name is not recorded in any further Abwehr records. This would tend to indicate that he suffered at the hands of the SS.

> Leutnant Herzner of K Group truly was the first German soldier to begin WWII – 0.01 am on 26 August 1939.

The fact that this event received no press attention anywhere in the world reinforces the belief that WWII was a planned occurrence. This German–Polish action equates with the British–American actions against Japanese units in December 1941, where the Allies were unable to seek assistance or notify command due to blocked signals. This sort of skullduggery within Allied Forces should be a cause for instant investigation by Allied Intelligence Services even now (unless they were all involved?). Such an investigation would only be 66 years too late.

Several events also occurred in the colonies, especially New Zealand, a centre for unrecorded WWII activity.

> Churchill was beaten to the declaration of war a second time by a combination of alcohol and cancer. New Zealand's Prime Minister, Michael Savage, was ill and dying of cancer and Peter Fraser essentially ran New Zealand at the time. Peter Fraser had been charged with sedition and jailed for burning and jumping all over the British flag in 1923. He was known as '*Pisshouse Peter*' because he was always in the toilet when there was work to be done.

Churchill had briefed Peter Fraser to declare war on Germany on 9 September 1939 but Fraser was a teetotaller, except when he had the flu and drank gin as a cure. Fraser decided he had the flu on 9 September 1939 and drank two bottles of gin and then declared war on Germany without taking the timeline into account.

New Zealand declared war on Germany 12 hours before Britain.

Hitler's response was: "Where is New Zealand?"[34]

New Zealand's response was to write ditties about the error of the era.

New Zealand ex-naval officer and poet, Denis Glover (DSC, Normandy) told another story where New Zealand fired the first Allied shots of WWII:

"A dilapidated Indian sailing ship had been at sea for months and months and sailed towards Fort Dorset in Wellington Harbour. It was covered in barnacles and weeds and its sails were old and patched. A good blow would have ripped them all to shreds. The ship was owned by a British outfit and had been virtually sailing itself for months and months.

"Due to the drink, the Pommy Captain and First Officer had gone down the ladder and all they were fit to be employed on were Indian ships. It was obvious from the state of the ship that they were both under the weather.

" The army on shore at Fort Dorset had the list of colours of the day and these were circulated each month and had to be displayed by all ships entering the harbour. Due to the long voyage and drunk Pommy Captain and First Officer, the British-owned Indian-run ship either didn't know anything about the list of colours or couldn't be bothered.

"When the Indian crew were challenged by heliograph signal to show the flag colours of the day it should have circled round and around until this was sorted out, but because the Indian crew were in control they carried on straight ahead. The drunk Pommy Captain and First Officer went on deck as the Fort Dorset Army Gunners fired 4" and 6" guns overhead. They were desperately keen to try out their guns on anything and were upset they didn't get the chance to put one through the mast. The Master and First Officer were then fined in the local Magistrates Court."

This is not to be confused with the 1941 story, where, in preparation for WWII the Coastal Artillery had mounted guns all around Wellington Harbour. An old Italian fishing family (Barnao) from Island Bay had been whalers, but when the ease and frequency of the big fish dropped away,

[34] Whermacht officers in Germany were frantically trying to find maps of New Zealand.

they turned to a smaller catch. They were returning into Wellington Harbour one night, hadn't turned on their lights and were talking excitedly about a horse race on the radio and their big catch of hoki.

The Army heard the enemy language of Italian, thought it was an attack and shot up the boat with casemented 4" and disappearing 6" guns that rose out of the tops of hills. When the 6" guns fired, the muzzles were still below the surface of the ground. The 4" gun was used to suck the enemy in close whereupon the 6" gun would take them out.

The Barnao fishing boat was shelled, bullet-ridden and sunk. Some died, but both Barnao fishermen survived by dog-paddling to shore. The Coastal Artillery got it wrong and the government paid out discretely without it ever making the media.

There are many such Home Guard stories and one wonders whether they should be taken as the first shots of WWII. Isolated New Zealanders were keen for war as it offered them a chance to travel and excused them from the boredom of milking cows. As a result, former Waikato dairy farmers became none-too-bright cannon fodder and were butchered with as much indifference as their cows at home.

After Dunkirk (June 1940) all the plotting tables and the range-finding gear was sent to Britain to make up for what was lost at Dunkirk, and the New Zealand Home Guard reverted to using German equipment that had been souvenired from WWI.

A New Zealand padre who had fought in WWI as a stretcher bearer tried to get into the WWII army as a chaplain but nobody wanted to know until he told them he had a German range-finder at home. He donated the range-finder to the army in exchange for joining 2NZEF (Expeditionary Force) overseas. His range-finder stayed in New Zealand as did the 4" and 6" guns.

A lot of the WWI veterans stayed in New Zealand as did those with foot and stomach problems. The WWI veterans took care of German and Italian POWs on Soames Island and all got on reasonably well. Some of the New Zealand WWI vets spent much of WWII in uniform fishing Wellington Harbour to feed the POWs. The highest point of the Island still contains Italian and German graves looking out to sea.

Churchill announced Germany's unconditional surrender on 7 May 1945 (for 0.01 am 8 May 1945) only after French Freemasonry had been destroyed, all the ammunition spent, the profits had been made by the correct parties, and a world vulnerable to social reorganisation had been created. Life would become a socialistic struggle for survival for the next 20 years.

To Churchill's surprise he was defeated in an election two months after WWII in July 1945.

This was possibly due to his order of the mass murder of 600,000 people in 13 hours on 13/14 February 1945 – a mixture of 600,000 refugees who had been in Dresden for less than a day and the unfortunate locals who received them . . . or it could have been as the result of his mass murder of 150,000 Russian Jews in Holland while emigrating to England – just after the war had ended. But why did this not make it into the history books?

At the end of WWII, only the southern half of Holland was freed. The northern half was left occupied by the Germans and they were still in the Channel Islands on the last day of the war. There was an extreme food shortage in the last year of the war and the German Army ate the Dutch out of house and home. As a result, over a million Dutch citizens died of starvation in 1944–5.

The death of 150,000 emigrating Russian Jews passed unnoticed and its record was easily omitted from history by the embedded historians that Churchill controlled.

All three of these events occurred with German complicity.

Hitler and Hess in Landsberg Prison with admirers and enough leisure time to reflect and focus on ideology – like writing *Mein Kampf.*

Hitler's Sexuality

Hitler's close boyhood friend from Linz, August Kubizek, wrote *Adolf Hitler, Mein Jugendfreund* (My Youth Friend), "Adolf did not engage in love affairs or flirtations. He always rejected the coquettish advances of girls or women. Women and girls took an interest in him but he always evaded their endeavours."

Later August Kubizek set up house with Hitler in Vienna a year after he had been rejected by Vienna's Academy of Fine Arts (Akadamie De Bildenden Künste). The two used to go for long walks in the woods, and when it rained took shelter in a shed and rolled naked in tarpaulins.[1]

During deconstruction, it is customary that the person is sexually abused in the manner which is most embarrassing to that person. In Hitler's case, he was sodomised, creating a submissive distant respect for homosexuals like his bodyguards and some of his highest-placed leaders. His natural bent was developed into coprophilia (being shat on). The colloquialism for this is 'scat'.[2]

With each deconstruction an embarrassing addiction is developed and filmed. With Hitler it was sadomasochism, coprophilia and homosexuality. That is, he liked to be verbally abused and slapped around, to have his head urinated on, his chest shat on, and to have sex with men. This made him vulnerable to ridicule by his partners, and mention of it was a coded access to his subconscious, making him vulnerable to cross-purpose.

The British had been deconstructing people for some time and the Red Army began training spies using sexual deconstruction from the very beginning of the Soviet State. The very first semester started at Frunze in 1920 and ended in gang-bangs every night. It was a classic British Intelligence technique but without the homosexuality. Most of the instructors were ex-British Intelligence.

On 24 May 1913 Hitler left Vienna and moved to the bohemian gay neighbourhood of Munich. The men's shelter at MA12, Haus Meldemannstrasse in Munich was described by a wealthy well-connected

[1] *Was Hitler Gay?*

[2] This trait was continued by his doctor (Dr Morell) who spooned out Hitler's faeces.

homosexual, Ernst Hanfstaengl, who later became Hitler's close friend: "It was a place where elderly men went in search of young men for homosexual pleasure. It is probable that these types of old roués and young gigolos became familiar to young Adolf at this time."[3]

Once Hitler got into power, all the police documents and records were destroyed regarding whether or not Hitler was a male prostitute at that time.

On 2 August 1914, Germany mobilised for war and Hitler cheered. "He delighted in the homoerotic life of the trenches. There he quickly became inseparable from yet another young man, his fellow soldier and closest wartime friend, Ernst Schmidt."[4]

Hans Mend: "In 1915 we were billeted in a brewery and slept in the hay. Hitler was bedded down at night with Schmidtl, his male whore. We heard a rustling in the hay. Then someone switched on his electric flashlight and growled 'look at those two faggots'."[5]

The gay Erich Ebermayer, one of Germany's most successful poets and a contemporary of Hitler's, states in his diaries that in Hitler's military files it stipulates that Hitler was not promoted because he was a homosexual. After the 1918 German defeat, Hitler returned to Europe and entered politics.

When Hitler was an unknown plain-clothed army intelligence agent he met the plain-clothed Army Intelligence officer Ernst Roehm (1919). Soon after, Roehm became the flamboyant gay Army Captain and leader of the Freikorps, the right wing's shadow army, but not without British help.

---

[3] *Was Hitler Gay?*

[4] Lothar Machton, author of *The Hidden Hitler*, in the documentary *Was Hitler Gay?*

[5] Those with the sexual history of prime ministers are often continually attacked until they can be written off as 'one of life's losers'. For his efforts, Hans Mend became one of life's losers.

"Roehm immediately recognised how talented Hitler was, so they built a very close relationship at that time."[6] Roehm had access to Hitler's WWI files and knew of Hitler's sexual history. In this way Roehm had control of Hitler and became his minder.

Hitler was a sexual deviant who would do anything to hide his sexual proclivities from the public. This made him a puppet to any foreign country or ideology with the knowledge on him. This is known as "the wood" on a person and anyone with 'the wood' has control over that person.

Many of the highest-placed leaders in the Nazi party, including Hitler, Roehm, Förster, von Schirach and almost all of his bodyguards were gay. Hitler surrounded himself with homosexuals and even retrieved Roehm from Bolivia, making him Deputy Führer. This knowledge enabled outside countries like Britain and ideologies like the Freemasons to control Hitler, his high command and his bodyguards. Hitler and his band of merry bandits became puppets with wooden strings.

> In this way, any foreign society can be destroyed with a leader hiding their sexuality. Hitler, Roehm, Förster and von Schirach took part in destroying their own societies while enjoying the power it gave them.[7] Hitler was a double agent prime minister. He worked for a foreign country (Britain) and a foreign ideology (the Freemasons). The formula proved so effective it is still used today, in politics and the media, especially with TV personalities, radio announcers, prime ministers and presidents, both male and female.

One of Germany's more influential record keepers of Hitler's homosexuality was General Otto von Lassow, who was then the military Commander of Munich. He was a very strong man in Europe in the early 1920s, had access to every record, and a bitter enemy of Hitler. After dinner one night, he invited friends to his

[6] Lothar Machton, author of *The Hidden Hitler*, in the documentary *Was Hitler Gay?*

[7] Baldur von Schirach (1904–74) was a homosexual paedophile who founded the Hitler Youth. Roehm despised him for his paedophilia. He was released from Spandau in 1966.

study and read secret letters from the Munich Beard Vice Squad to some of his dinner guests ('Beard' is German slang for 'homosexual'). These dealt with Hitler in the early 1920s, searching for young men, occasionally paying them, and taking them to his room and spending the night together.[8] Some of Hitler's close friends gave testimonies that he was gay.

"I, Franz, an apprentice, made the acquaintance of a gentleman who invited me to spend the night with him, and I accepted. The gentleman's name was Adolf Hitler." The originals have never been found.

General Otto von Lassow claimed they were his insurance policy should his enemy Hitler ever come to power. Lassow was the only one of Hitler's enemies who was not killed in the Night of the Long Knives (30 June 1934), which gives much credence to these files.

Hitler and Hess shared a cell at Landsberg Prison after the Munich Putsch in 1923. Hess was always regarded as a homosexual by the enemies of the Nazi Party and by the Nazi Party themselves, who nicknamed him "Frauline Anna". Ernst Hanfstaengl later testified that Hitler and Hess were prison lovers. "Hitler's strange wavering sexuality [bisexual] was activated in Landsberg in the company of Hess. That he had a liaison with Hess is beyond doubt."[9]

Rudolf Hess had the upbringing of a bisexual. He was born and raised in a foreign country under foreign rule (British rule) until he was 12. During his emerging sexuality (12–14) he was home-schooled by his parents in Germany and spent his time alone in a garden paradise. He became passionate and introverted, was a typically Victorian child (seen but not heard) and was nicknamed "the Egyptian" for his oily skin and black hair. He loved his mother very much but was very distant from his father. He was sent to a boarding school at 14 (Evangelische Padagogium in Bad Godesberg-am-Rhein) and then to a superior school in a foreign country (the Ecole Superieure du Commerce in Neuchatel, Switzerland). He spent his life apart from other children, separate from his biological parents and separate from the country of his culture. He was an outsider who had an isolated psyche with a vicious inner dialogue that kept him alive and foreigners dead. On his return to Germany he learnt to hate the Jews with an introverted passion.

---

[8] *Was Hitler Gay?*

[9] Ibid.

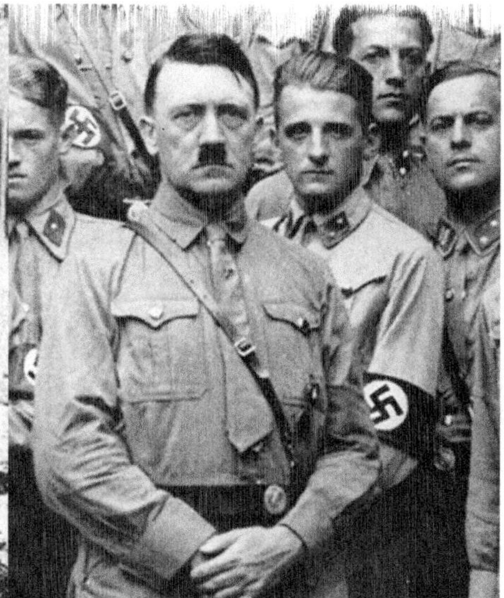

IIA-19357

Rudolf Hess, the Vice Führer, was a married bisexual. Hess adored Hitler and was queer for him. There was a homoerotic sense throughout the Nazi Party, which in part stemmed from Hess.

In the struggle for financial strength that is the family-centred society, Hitler battled against sexual extremes like paedophilia, child-sex abuse, homosexuality, cross-dressing and transsexuality. Correspondingly, the currency devalued and the interest rates skyrocketed.

Hitler liked to drive around Germany in fast cars and maintained a warm relationship with his new chauffeur, Julius Schrek. Once they were invited to the family home of Wagner, Hitler's favourite composer and philosopher, but Hitler disappeared with his chauffeur to a hotel with no other guests. Winifred Wagner tracked them down and there was a scandal but it was suppressed by the media that Hitler so fervently controlled.

"The Führer's libido increased proportionately with the events of the war, almost as a reaction to the intense levels of work . . . These women were almost always endowed with a large bosom"[10] but they were often a cover for his homosexuality.

Among these women were Mimi Reiter (a 16-year-old who attempted suicide?); Unity Walkrie Mitford (an English woman who attempted suicide?); Rene Muller (an actress who committed suicide?); Geli Raubal (his niece who committed suicide?); Eva Braun (a small-breasted woman who vied for attention with two show-suicides); and Carola Hoffman, Gertrud von Seidlitz, Helene Bechstein, Stephanie van Hohenlohe, Viktoria van Dirksen, and Leni Riefenstahl who made his propaganda movies and denies any sexual involvement, but describes an orgasm when listening to him speak at the Nuremberg rallies.

Free from prison in 1924, Hitler (35) was encouraged by his colleagues to marry. Under their pressure he finally took an interest in Mimi Reiter, a 16-year-old shop girl. Their affair went sour during a disastrous walk in the woods in 1925. "He hugged me really tightly around the neck. He kissed me. He didn't know what to do. I could feel how he clenched his fists. I could see how he was fighting with himself."[11] Unable to consummate the relationship, Hitler escaped by claiming that he had to think of the mission in Germany. Hitler

[10] *Very Illustrious Patients*, p. 96.

[11] *Was Hitler Gay?*

broke up with Mimi and she reportedly tried to commit suicide from disappointment. This is unlikely as she was sixteen and he was thirty-five. It was more likely organised propaganda, or another attempted murder made to look like a suicide.

Unity Walkrie Mitford (20) stalked Hitler until she finally met him at the Osteria Bavaria restaurant. After the affair, she shot herself with a pearl-handled revolver, dying eight years later.

Hitler showed Rene Muller a photo of her kissing another man and then gave her a letter saying that she would never work in German cinema again. Within two hours she was dead, having landed on the courtyard outside her window.[12]

When Hitler became busy with power, he invited his half-sister Angela and her two daughters to come and stay and keep house at his rented villa at Obersalzberg in 1928. Repeating his father's pattern of 'incest with his housekeeper', the archetypal loner (39) quickly fell in love with his half-sister's daughter, Geli Raubal (17). She became his constant companion in Europe during his political rise to fame from 1929–31.

Hitler had a propensity for incest and having his face and chest defecated on, to which his niece, Geli, objected. It became necessary to silence Geli about Adolf's homosexuality, his coprophilia and his incest. If this got out, the Third Reich would have lost the 'race' card. There would be no 'master race' to aspire to and the armies would have lost their motivation for war and even rebelled. The official story is an alibi for what really happened.

Hitler was very possessive and after Geli had sex with his chauffeur and was officially pregnant to yet another man, her music teacher's piano player,[13] Hitler became smothering and restrictive. Officially Geli (20) protested against Adolf's possessiveness and shot herself dead in his apartment on 18 September 1931.

Official historians note Hitler (42) was away in Hamburg at the time and devastated and distraught at the news of her death. Official history omits to note Geli broke her nose during her 'suicide' . . . the real story is closer to murderous incest.

---

[12] *The Memoirs of Bridget Hitler*, p. 178.

[13] Geli Raubal was not pregnant.

Adolf Hitler had taken his niece Geli to a private first floor room in the Bratwurstglöckl Restaurant on the night of her death and ordered beer, which was rare. Even one glass made him tipsy.[14] Hitler and Geli left around 1 am and returned to his nearby apartment on Prinzregentenstrasse. Hitler made sexual advances towards Geli, she refused and a scuffle broke out. Hitler broke Geli's nose and then shot her with his service revolver, the only gun stored in the apartment.

Having lost her husband and daughter to her half-brother, Angela Raubal did not want to be without the comforts Hitler could provide. Hitler had delayed his meeting in Hamburg and his half-sister Angela supported this alibi, just as she had remained quiet about the disappearance of her husband Leo Raubal.

The affidavit of the police captain who visited Hitler's apartment, the story told by his housekeeper Josephine Bauer, the circumstances surrounding the funeral and Adolf's history of brandishing the revolver, all supported Hitler's murder of his lover and niece, Geli Raubal.

A suicide would have resulted in no Catholic rights, but Geli was given full Catholic rights, wherever they could be found. They were not granted in Munich, so Geli was buried in Vienna. Even the Catholic priest Pater Paunt, gave this explanation to Geli's brother Leo: "My poor friend, if your sister had committed suicide, I could not have performed the ceremony. You must be content with this. More I cannot tell you."[15]

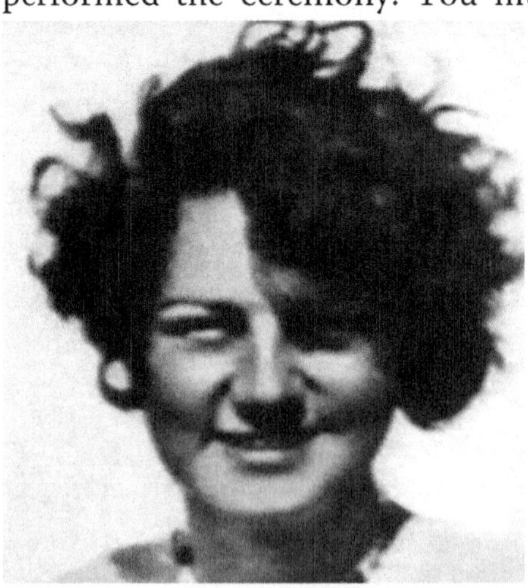

Leo Raubal had now lost a father and a daughter to uncle Adolf. Leo contacted Fritz Gerlich, founder of *Der Gerade* (*The Right Way* weekly). In a pamphlet Gerlich exposed Hitler's murder of Geli and for his efforts was arrested, held, and then killed in the Night of the Long Knives on 30 June 1934, as were many of Hitler's enemies.

[14] This was confirmed in the affidavit of Herr Senter, the proprietor of the Bratwurstglöckl Restaurant.
[15] *The Memoirs of Bridget Hitler*, pp. 103–3.

After this meeting Leo met his cousin Patrick Hitler at his father's bar in Berlin. They flatted together and after some time Leo spoke about Geli's murder adding that Adolf had threatened him with his revolver at Berchtesgaden when he was talking to Geli about his pregnant girlfriend.

> Leo Raubal (junior): "I am sure my mother knows what happened. She was really Adolf's accomplice, because she tolerated his making love to Geli. She knew; yet she did nothing. Was she afraid? Possibly. Or was it only that she did not want to give up her comfortable life? When Geli was shot I suppose Mother felt it was useless to quarrel with Adolf over it. Geli was irrevocably lost to her: why should she lose Adolf too?"[16]

The alternative may have been as drastic as changing the leader of Germany and postponing WWII. The British helped to cover up Hitler's murder of Geli and for this they used their agent Hermann Goering. A month later his own wife Carin died, officially from a cold she caught on the border during a crossing. This stopped both men from settling into domestic bliss. It kept them focused on their mission with renewed aggravation.

Hitler was becoming the perfect weapon for radical social change and the destruction of existing military infrastructures, which he carried out with exemplary effect over the next decade. Those in the know feared Hitler even more, but the official propaganda from *Hitler and Geli* reads: "In many ways he was a very sweet and caring man."

When Hitler became Chancellor he transferred Geli's body to Berchtesgaden and placed it in a magnificent sarcophagus that never bore her name. Hitler placed flowers under Geli's photograph and always remembered the anniversary of her murder, but there were costs. Hitler developed a stomach ailment, became a vegetarian, invented the vegetarian steak and as it turned out, the vegetarian marriage.

Hitler was into being defecated on by women and average women felt disgusted and reacted strongly. As a result there was quite a strong urge for them to kill themselves. Geli's replacement, Eva Braun, was "a pretty, empty-headed blonde receptionist with a round face and blue eyes," who faked suicide twice (1932, 1935) in order to get Hitler's attention away from Geli. Hitler attended her but was not so much in love with her. She

[16] Ibid, p. 106.

accepted everything Hitler dished out, and wasn't that troubled defecating on Hitler. Interactions with her parents during WWI prepared her for this. Regardless, her father tried to talk her out of her liaison with Hitler.

"Many assumed that Hitler and Eva Braun were lovers, but there is not a shred of evidence of this . . . They had a strange relationship. Eva would complain of her lonely sexless existence."[17] They even slept in different beds and in different bedrooms, though with an interconnecting door.

Hitler's loyal butler, Herbert Döhring: "We did spy work back then to see if we could find evidence of sexual relations in their bed and in all those years that never happened. Their relationship never went that far."[18]

Eva Braun: "People naturally believed that my life at Hitler's side took quite a different form. If only they knew. Always the mission, the mission, the mission, self-sacrifice and renunciation."[19]

Eva's father happened by chance to see Hitler and rushed forward knowing of the liaison with his daughter. It was a very awkward moment. He asked Hitler what his intentions were. Hitler said nothing and Mr Braun cut his daughter off, but her mother maintained contact. An SS Officer then tried to threaten Eva's father, but he ignored it. Eva's sister later married the SS General Fegelein in 1945, just before he was executed.

As Chancellor in 1933, Hitler began a crushing dictatorship but he had a potentially fatal problem. He faced a long list of people who knew about his sex life. Some people even tried to blackmail him.

> "A huge gay and lesbian sub-culture appeared in Germany with many gay newspapers. The gay community was crushed, not because the Nazi were homophobic, but because Hitler was gay. Hitler decided to crush it to silence [sic] rumours of his own homosexuality. His first step was approving a law criminalising any remark that might slander the Führer. The merest gossip that Hitler might be gay became a serious crime and a slew of trials began. The denunciation of Hitler's homosexuality played the most prominent role in all of the trials."[20]

[17] Narrator, *Was Hitler Gay?*

[18] *Was Hitler Gay?*

[19] Ibid.

[20] Dr Rainer Herrn, Scientific Director of the Magnus Hirschfeld Society.

The original Nazi burning of the books on 6 May 1933 was those of the Hirschfeld's Institute for Sexual Sciences which was a Jewish-funded organisation promoting alternative sexualities; homosexuality, paedophilia, transsexuality, group sex and public orgies amongst the Germans.

> The Nazis then drastically strengthened paragraph 175, Germany's law against homosexuality. The slightest touch, even just looking at someone could and did get people arrested. The definition of gay was now so broad it could encompass anyone, homosexual or not. Under the homosexual banner, many were persecuted purely for political reasons.

"I think Hitler certainly made use of the homophobia with the Nazi Party within Germany, whenever it served his purpose."[21]

In the early 1930s, Roehm's homosexuality was outed to everyone when a newspaper published his private letters to a homosexual friend. The letters caused a sensation and party leaders begged Hitler to make a public statement condemning Roehm's unapologetic homosexuality.

They were shocked when Hitler did the opposite. Hitler published an order that no one has the right to look into the private sphere of the life of a political leader.

> "Their private life cannot be an object of scrutiny unless it runs counter to vital principles of national socialist ideology."[22]

Hitler and Roehm were then photographed together at many formal military events and leaving meetings together after talks. "As Hitler looked the other way, Roehm was accused of turning the Storm Troopers (the SA) into a gay brotherhood.[23] Ernst Roehm had served as an Army Captain under the camp Kaiser. Soon after Roehm said "I fancy I'm homosexual. I'm far from unhappy, perhaps evenly secretly proud."[24]

Roehm was the second most powerful man in Germany. He was openly gay, head of the Storm Troopers and virtual vice Führer of Germany. Why did Hitler allow Roehm power so immense that it threatened Hitler's own authority? Hitler's sexual secret lies at its heart.

---

[21] Ron Rosenbaum, *Explaining Hitler.*

[22] Adolf Hitler, *Was Hitler Gay?*

[23] The Storm Troopers had the initials 'SA'. This meant any mail to Finnish Intelligence (SA) ended up on the Storm Troopers desk. This is how they gained insight into Finland's military goals.

[24] Lothar Machton, *The Hidden Hitler.*

Roehm blackmailed Hitler. "You know about our common past so don't make a mistake."[25] Roehm threatened to take the power away from Hitler as soon as he had grabbed it.

This threat of blackmail finally pushed the Führer over the edge. On 30 June 1934, as Roehm and his leutnants relaxed at the Bavarian resort of Bad Wiesse, Hitler and his men burst in. This was played out in Luchino Visconti's film, *The Damned*. Roehm and 150 other gay men were murdered in the Night of the Long Knives.

"The previous twenty-four hours had seen appalling events, but beyond the certainty that every enemy of Hitler had been exterminated, nothing definite was known, but the rumours flew from mouth to mouth."[26]

After this, Hitler sent his Storm Troopers racing across the Reich searching for incriminating evidence of Hitler's army days. "Many documents and papers were taken away from private persons, but there was never an attempt to have some kind of public trial."[27]

The Gestapo were also sent out to terminate all of Hitler's old contacts, which is why there were so few survivors from his doss-house days in Vienna, Munich, and from the trenches of the Western Front. If they were not easily intimidated, the Gestapo would arrange criminal charges and they would vanish into the camps as undesirables.

Hitler's denunciation of homosexuality, and the Nazi Party's new-found homophobia "was the most vicious anti-homosexual purge in history".[28] There were an estimated 100,000 investigations, 50,000 court cases and between 5,000 and 15,000 sent to concentration camps like Mauthausen. They were forced into hard labour from which few emerged. Hitler needed to silence the gay underworld that knew too much about his past and the plan worked for three-quarters of a century, but not without British support.

Hitler did not completely solve his blackmail problems by the Night of the Long Knives. Ernst Hanfstaengl was Hitler's gay admirer from the early days in Munich. Shortly before the war broke out Hanfstaengl ended up in England as the Head of the Nazi Foreign Press, where he was written up as "Hitler's Putzy", meaning Hitler's gay partner.

[25] Ibid.

[26] *The Amiable Prussian*, p. 34.

[27] Lothar Machton, *The Hidden Hitler*.

[28] Narrator, *Was Hitler Gay?*

Hanfstaengl tried to sue the *Daily Express,* knowing that any subsequent trial might bring out evidence that Hitler was gay. The strategy fizzled out when he lost his nerve. But Hitler's blackmail problem didn't stop there. Stories constantly bubble up from Germany's gay community. Before the Nazis came to power, Germany had a gay culture unequalled in the world and the Third Reich became known as the Gay Reich.

Another problem was his former war buddy, Hans Mend, a despatch rider, nick-named 'Ghost Rider'. He continued to spread rumours of Hitler's homosexuality, for which he paid the ultimate price. He was arrested and in 1942 perished in police custody (prison) under mysterious circumstances. Unfortunately for him he had witnessed Hitler's homosexuality on the Western Front in 1915.

In 1936 Hitler ordered the German troops into the demilitarised zone in the Rhineland (where the Rhine river flows in western Germany) with little or no international protest. To counteract this act of national aggression, Hitler entertained the racially pure and the rich. Five bare-breasted women in G-strings on a Cinderella float, a dozen naked women (G-strings only) on horseback with spears and roman helmets, naked women painted in gold popping out of exploding boxes, followed by massive fireworks – all on the main avenue. The Germans thought they were special and above other races.

"Hitler himself attached great importance to the women's vote, and this was one of the reasons which he gave for not marrying. He liked to have beautiful women in his company."[29]

Despite Hitler's challenging schedule, Hitler and his sister Paula (b. 21 January 1896) kept in touch, seeing each other every year from 1929–41. Theirs was a close, loving and supportive relationship where they would do almost anything for each other. Hitler sent her tickets to the Nuremberg Rally in Bavaria, southern Germany, the closest thing the 1930s ever saw to a rock concert and were similarly dedicated to peace and freedom. Over 100,000 people attended these Nazi Party rallies at the specially-built stadium to patriotic fascism – essentially the denial of other cultures and races. Hitler gave Paula 250 marks each year (1929–38) and 3500 marks thereafter. He also bought her a little house in Weiten in the Wachau in late 1941.

[29] *Prelude to Terror,* p. 419.

At the Olympic Games in Garmisch, Berlin, in 1936, Hitler requested his sister Paula change her name, and to maintain the strictest incognito. She changed her name to 'Wolf', which was Hitler's nickname and one of their towns of origin, 'Gross Wolfgers'. She changed her title from 'Ms' to 'Mrs', changing from Ms Paula Hitler to Mrs Paula Wolf.

Mrs Paula Wolf was arrested as Hitler's sister by US Intelligence on 12 July 1945 and again on 5 June 1946. She was deeply affected by Hitler's announced death. She was released and worked in an arts and crafts shop in Vienna (toiling for mental health) and wrote *He Was Still My Brother*. She moved into a humble two-bedroom flat in Berchtesgaden on 1 December 1952, very close to Hitler's mountain retreat, Eagle's Nest, in southern Bavaria, near the German/Austrian border. She lived in seclusion and died seven and a half years later on 1 June 1960. Ms Paula Hitler (alias Mrs Paula Wolf) never married and had no children.[30]

In 1997, I interviewed a woman who attended one of the Nuremberg Rallies: "I found it positively orgasmic, as did so many other women at the time". Despite his many and various shortcomings, Hitler had a way with the ladies. "Women went slack at the mouth and breathed heavily, as if in the grip of sexual excitement." Hitler was able to tap into their sexuality en masse, and Germany's women responded by backing Hitler and also influencing their men to do so.

> "It seemed as if the Earth's surface were spreading out in front of me, like a hemisphere that suddenly splits in the middle, spewing out an enormous jet of water, so powerful that it touched the sky and shook the earth. I felt quite paralysed."[31] An orgasm perhaps.
>
> "Many were fascinated by his hypnotic power, and there are well-attested accounts of the hysteria which affected women at his meetings. Hitler himself attached great importance to the women's vote, and this was one of the reasons which he gave for not marrying. He liked to have beautiful women in his company."[32]

Hitler knew his material with a passion and orated rather than read, relying on the magical power of the spoken word. He studied under

[30] The Dwight D. Eisenhower Library.

[31] Leni Riefenstahl's Memoirs, *New Zealand Herald*, 13–14 September 2003, A27.

[32] *Prelude to Terror*, p. 419.

the Munich comedian Weiss Ferdl and was taught to make only a few points, repeating them endlessly. The comedian reinforced his belief that "A big lie is always more credible than a little one".

Deconstructed people have a great deal of difficulty forming long-term relationships, as do those who surround them. They tend to know how to bond quickly and un-bond just as quick. This is a product of compartmentalisation that occurs during deconstruction and the late in life 'altering of a subconscious'. "A curious effect the upper-rank Nazis had on those who joined them. They very often broke up their marriages, no matter how happy they might have been before."[33]

Deconstructed people cannot form intimate relationships like marriage, as they are, for the most part, not themselves. They are essentially a machine for someone else's purpose. As a result, their sexual relations fill a void rather than establish a relationship and their boundaries tend to be as intransigent as their goals. Hitler was primarily a vehicle for someone else's purpose. As a result, he remained single and unable to marry.

Hitler's relationship with his parents was conflict ridden. Hitler's primary love was his housekeeper, who was also his niece (Geli Raubal). He was incestuous, prone to homosexuality in the trenches, and had no children. Hitler lacked trust and his boundary was jealousy which resulted in the convenient murder/suicides of several of his partners.

> "During his final few hours in the bunker, loyal followers raced to burn all remaining documents that might shred light on the Führer. Hitler married Eva Braun [at midnight] on 29 April 1945 as a further measure to cover up his homosexuality. Hitler died as he lived, lying and covering up."[34]

Hitler was 'a multiplicitous sadomasochistic
coprophilic homosexual Anglophile'.

> "It remained for the younger generation to complete the break, to cut the ties to the past and achieve freedom from sentiment, prejudices and memories. Paradoxically, in doing so, in a sense it actually completed Hitler's revolution . . . All comparisons between recent and the earlier movements break on the one reef."[35]

---

[33] *The Amiable Prussian*, p. 70.

[34] Narrator Dennis Lawson, *Was Hitler Gay?*

[35] *Hitler*, pp. 762–763.

Hitler's Psychiatric Condition

Neurotics have the ability to harm themselves. Psychotics have the ability to harm others. Hitler did both, but as a British military agent, he was trained to harm others en masse and to harm himself with a cocktail of drugs and perverse sexuality.

In 1911, the Swiss psychiatrist Eugen Bleuler invented the term 'Schizophrenia' for the condition of having a split mind. The following year Hitler began his British Military Psych-Ops training (February–November 1912). Hitler had defensive and self-important postures because he was living a fantasy given to him by others in order to change the times.

Hitler was part neurotic, psychotic, paranoid and schizophrenic. This was the basis of his deconstruction, which although developed, was always in the experimental phase. That is, it was always being tested and improved upon.

This work continues in Tavistock today. It includes the deconstruction of all age groups within Britain, including pre-school, school children, teenagers, young adults, working adults, and the elderly. It works the media, education and politics towards a predetermined plan. In the centre is the main military deconstruction building. It is surrounded by buildings, which specialise in more publicly acceptable forms of deconstruction with names like the 'Tavistock Institute for Human Relations'.

For total control over a person, the record of an embarrassing sexual history is essential. From this, neurosis, psychosis, paranoia and schizophrenia are developed and continually built upon. The avoidance of shame becomes a personal motivation.

A sense of persecution and self-importance are characteristic of paranoiacs – the ability to harm oneself. When the war schools look for their new protagonists they always look for paranoiacs with a personal history of persecution and self-importance. This gives the maximum gap in the subconscious for deconstruction to take place – the gap between persecution and self-importance.

The persecution and self-importance of paranoiacs are coat-hooks to hang the persecution of others on. Mass deaths are hung on paranoia and psychosis. Huge changes in the destinies of people and countries are hung on self-importance and schizophrenia[1] – the ability to deny one's most horrible actions.

The huge gap between self-persecution and self-importance creates an emotional void that acts as a driving force. When nothing of importance is happening, when ordinary life and interaction is occurring, they appear empty, lost, and unable to casually interact. Hence those deconstructed always seek drama and prefer intense dramas like war.

Those deconstructed prefer dramas they control, dramas they have created, or have had a hand in creating, and are motivated by the continual cover-up of their shame. Deconstructed, self-important, neurotic-paranoiac-schizophrenics have a natural preference to create large dramas on the scale of war.

In this way, on 14 March 1939, Hitler could watch a movie and dictate to two secretaries simultaneously, one a proclamation to the German people, another a proclamation to the Czech people, and a letter to Benito Mussolini of Italy, while he watched a movie and kept the Czechoslovakian President Hácha waiting from 1.15 am to 4 am.

When Hitler finally saw President Hácha he said Germany would invade his country in a few hours at dawn, which it did.[2]

Such things of importance become natural and things ordinary become clumsy and unnatural. Paranoiacs are tense and insecure and find it difficult to form relationships. They are socially incompetent, habitually self-centred, and react badly to criticism.

Those deconstructed have the same social patterns as paranoiacs. The history of antagonistic war leaders is full of paranoiacs who are tense and insecure – who find it difficult to form *normal* relationships. Alexander the Great, for instance, was a necrophiliac. He used to ride into battle naked and sodomise the injured as they were killed, or kill the injured and then sodomise the dead. These homosexual necrophiliacs

---

[1] The common use of schizophrenia – 'split mind' – is used.

[2] *Hermann Göring*, pp. 183–4.

would then have their press announce that they were heroes with such names as 'Alexander the Great' and 'Lawrence of Arabia'.[3]

Neurotics have the ability to harm themselves and Hitler did this through his sexuality, his massive drug addiction and his refusal to see a qualified doctor.

Hitler's mother had two stillbirths before Adolf and stillbirths are suggestive of congenital syphilis. During Hitler's deconstruction, he was instilled with a fear of syphilis and a fear of educated doctors. Thus Hitler was drawn to quacks for the treatment of syphilis.

The British played on Hitler's neurosis towards 'syphilis and educated doctors' by introducing the British-run quack, Dr Theodor Gilbert Morell, a 5'6", 16½ stone (105 kg) delusional who had professed to be a venereal specialist for the previous six months. His office in Kurfurstendamn was covered with diplomas, qualifications and the signed photographs of famous film-acting clients. Hitler envied the famous and was drawn to this. This was a standard British set-up and has often been satirised in the movies.

Dr Morell became Hitler's doctor from January 1937 to April 1945, and no matter how much he was criticised by Hitler's staff, including other more reputable doctors in Hitler's staff, Hitler clung to Dr Morell like a fearful neurotic momma's boy. Hitler and Dr Morell had been designed for each other. Each time Hitler woke up, the first to attend to him was his aide. The second was Dr Morell, who began Hitler's day with an alphabet soup of drugs to treat his phantom syphilis.

As a dedicated neurotic, Hitler was dependent on having his non-existent syphilis treated. As a dedicated paranoiac, Hitler clung to superstition even if it was to kill him.

Paranoiacs are prone to superstition. Religion is based on superstition. All one needs to turn people to a superstition, like religion,

---

[3] Thomas Edward Lawrence (1888–1935) was George Bernard Shaw's illegitimate son with one of Renoir's models. Turks interrogated him by sodomy with no new information forthcoming. The Colonel of MI-5 took him to a disused post office, placed him on the large mailing table, jumped on his head till his neck broke, then placed the body beside his motorcycle – officially an accident to this day.

is to make them paranoid. To do this, a few people are killed, a few more are harassed, the lot are surrounded, and the fear of God is instilled into them – hence religion.

Religion is a double-edged sword, a superstition that kills its own people through the practice of 'fear of life' and an even greater 'fear of death'. It is a huddle mentality, easily struck from the outside when their heads are down. In this way war and religion have been working together hand-in-hand for centuries.

The priests provide paranoia in the church (fear of God) and assist the military in their cover-ups (fear of exposure from military intelligence). The military kills and religion cleans up to begin the cycle again and again.

This creates an ongoing fear of reality and fear of God, with the army providing the fearful reality and the need to believe in God . . . and the Church providing the House of God – 'the House of Paranoiac Superstitious Fear of Reality and God'. Hence Hitler was backed by the Catholics.

Such is the cyclic symbiotic relationship between the military and religion, with both groups specialising in paedophilia. The victims of paedophilia enter either the church or the military often to repeat the cycle as adult priests and mercenaries, thus creating the 'paedophile's family tree'. This occurred amongst both the Nazis during WWII and Americans after WWII with the British running the Nazi paedophile programme.[4]

After WWII religion remained popular for twenty years and then waned as people forgot about the war. Religion was revived again with 9-11 which created the biggest run on Bibles since the printing press was invented.

---

[4] Since the first edition of this book, the British have admitted torturing German prisoners to death, but without any mention of British paedophilia. Americans repeated Nazi paedo-atrocities in Operation ANACONDA, sexually molesting, brutalizing, murdering and kidnapping children in such a breath-taking total lack of compassion that, to all intents and purposed, they were the same force. Both forces were heavily influenced by the occult, use occult practices and arguments in their affairs have shown absolutely no degree of compassion whatsoever. In Abu Ghraib Americans were so sentenced without mentioning paedophilia in any media.

Since the Freemasons' declaration of the end of religion in 1891, religions have been increasingly replaced with the League of Nations (1918–39) and the United Nations (1945–2001). The UN became completely ineffective when the US refused to fund it and then agreed to fund it to 50% as long as no American was ever charged with war crimes. In this simple step the UN stepped aside and allowed an unchallenged US military dictatorship of the world. Very quickly 9-11 happened.

The UN supports paranoia by setting up camps and having audible sex orgies and gang-bangs, while those outside are selectively slaughtered. An American female doctor working for the UN did this in Rwanda in May 2004, having sex with a row of male UN workers.[5] The Rwandans outside could hear her orgasmic screaming as they were getting their throats cut. This promotes paranoia, superstition and religion, all of which are noticeably rampant in the African countries. Superstitious paranoid Africa is now the new centre of Catholicism and Catholicism is now a black-centred religion.

Europe was like this between the wars – paranoid, superstitious and religious. Paranoia, superstition and religion are the pre-heaters to war. For the cycle of wars to continue unchallenged, the proliferation of ignorance is essential.

The Bible is not a document for enlightenment but a document to categorise trust and support paranoia. It was originally written by the Catholics between AD180 and AD240 as a means to suppress the Christians. It worked. Ever since, Christians have been renowned for their fear of death and tend towards paranoia about anything and everything. The Christian superstition is that a stocky swarthy olive-skinned dead man will come back to life as a tall thin white man and take away their paranoia and fear of death. This is pathological paranoia. Continuing the analysis en masse, it makes Christians borderline in society and they are treated as such.

---

[5] Under "UN failures", Wikipedia lists "Sexual abuse by UN peacekeepers" as occurring in Burundi, Democratic Republic of Congo, Ivory Coast, Liberia [and Rwanda]. The abuse is widespread and ongoing, despite the many UN probes and revelations. UN Peacekeepers have been sexually abusing/gang-raping girls as young as 12 in at least a third of the countries they occupy.

Religion, war and paranoia – faith, death and the fear of life – are rekindled every time we attack ourselves. If religion can work in this way, why not war?

Borderline refers to the border between normality and psychosis. Borderline people are characterised by a disinterest in exertion, boredom, weariness, depression and sudden inappropriate outbursts of anger. Hitler had ßall of these attributes. His father had them more so and was either schizophrenic or borderline schizophrenic.

Hitler himself was not schizophrenic because that disease takes hold before the age of 45 and needs to be present for at least six months. He also did not have the lesser schizophreniform, nor did he have a schizo-affective state, a term invented by the American J. Kasanin in 1933 to describe people that were 'odd'.

Hitler was part neurotic, part paranoid and part borderline schizophrenic. This was developed as a result of being deconstructed and continually drugged by the British and as a result of having his 'anchor phrases' continually activated. Hitler became a partial psychopath, as was his Tavistock training, and he acted accordingly. Hitler lost it at times and was a borderline personality with a schizotypal disorder.[6]

Hitler himself said, "They always said I was crazy".[7] "Newsreels of the time showed his tremendous, absurd self-awareness – scarcely a natural being."[8] Hitler had an air of difference. "Anyone who has seen this man [Hitler] face to face, has met his uncertain gaze without depth or warmth, from eyes that seem hard and remote, and has then seen that gaze go rigid, will have certainly experienced the uncanny feeling that that man is strange, that man is not normal."[9]

Psychopaths rarely show the perseverance and persistence that Hitler and Stalin had. They could only complete their jobs with the assistance of British war-school training and continual support which included British spies. Both Stalin and Hitler pursued their goals in a similar time frame. Stalin trained in 1907 and was involved in the 1917

[6] Other Tavistock trained killers include Angela Davis and Stockley Carmichael.
[7] *Hitler*, p. 4.
[8] *Doppelgängers*, p. 24.
[9] East Prussian industrialist Hermann Rauschning, 1940.

Russian Revolution. Hitler trained in 1912 and was involved in a putsch in 1921 and 1923. They both shared a decade of lag from their British training to revolutions in their own countries.

Both Stalin and Hitler pursued their goals during WWII as a counterpart to Britain's desire for war.

What appears to be 'a warring psychopath' is often 'a deconstructed paranoiac', or more specifically, someone deconstructed who has a tendency towards paranoia. In Hitler and Stalin's case, they were deconstructed people whose paranoia could be utilised. This made them perfect combative killing machines.

Hitler and Stalin were motivated to war. They did not seem to mind that their opponents were equally their informants in 'the play of death', as long as it was *others* who did the dying. They would do anything to achieve this . . . to kill as many others in order to survive, and to fake their own deaths where necessary. When their doppelgängers died they began to believe in their own immortality. This made them even more delusional and forever braver.

Under these conditions war could only escalate.

Hitler's Deconstruction
February–November 1912

The author may appear to be labouring points into exclusive simplicity, but such a mindset was used to develop subconscious deconstruction. The reconstruction of the subconscious, on the other hand, is based on a similar but opposing model.

The first method of reconstruction, seconded from the KGB under instructions from the author, is to bypass the conscious and unconscious mind and talk directly to the subconscious by playing music at one level with the message received by sound pulse on the second level.

The second method, developed by the author, prior to receiving the first method, bypasses the conscious and unconscious minds and talks directly to the subconscious in its language, which happens to be something rather close to Cockney rhyming slang. The conscious mind is kept busy focusing on some part of the face, body and action thereof, while the unconscious mind focuses on the corresponding quality or attribute desired. The corresponding colloquial speech patterns are then utilised to instruct the subconscious.

The conscious and unconscious minds are used as protectors for the subconscious. When they are kept busy the message goes straight to the subconscious. Because the conscious and unconscious minds are busy in a sympathetic state, the message is immediately integrated on all levels, without confusion and is 'three minds ready'.

In this way suboncscious integration takes place to a predetermined goal and all actions in the universe of that mind fall into place.[1] The subconscious mind then acts as a Google search engine, unlimited in scope, to ensure that the predetermined goals eventuate.

In this way, the most ordinary people can have a life of genius.

---

[1] This method was developed in Budapest (February–August 1990) after interviewing the KGB in Moscow and noticing that the population had been deconstructed . . . I've worked on a client and five minutes later they've said, "So what, nothing's changed", and walked out with a completely different attitude. It became hard to justify the fee so I turned to history's great unpayer – history.

The first method is easier, but requires equipment and applied continuous application for ten hours. The second method can be achieved in a matter of minutes, does not require any equipment, and can be done without the other person knowing it is being done. Both have their advantages.

Such deconstruction feed-lines used by the British Psych-Ops war school to Adolf (Edmund) Hitler were: "You are special. You will change the map of the world. It is your destiny to do so. Suppress those who think against you. Suppress those who speak against you. Suppress those who act against you. Surround yourself with people who can be moulded to your vision."

Consequently, Hitler had a failure to act responsibly to his own people and had no conscience about doing evil. Others thought him evil whereas Hitler considered it his destiny and all others compliant to his subconscious view of the world.

Once Hitler was used to start WWII and bring Russia in on an equal footing, Hitler and Stalin were then set against each other. This brought great mirth to the military Freemasons at Tavistock who watched the war privately with great interest. Their eye was on improving the next generation of training. This type of military training has been developed over the last five hundred years and shows no sign of abating.

At least now subconscious training can be debated.

Hitler was in his alpha state when his conscious, unconscious and subconscious minds were aligned with his Psych-Ops training – for an aggressive takeover. In this state he could be considered a genius. In lesser activities he was moody, irritable, lazy, difficult and bipolar. He was firing on all cylinders only when aggressively taking over Europe or building his new Germany.

Herbert Döhring ran Hitler's house at Berchtesgarden and was a member of Hitler's personal bodyguard, the SS Lifeguard, Leibstandarte: "Hitler was very moody. His whole expression could change in a few hours. He made a colossal impression. His gaze would pierce right through you."

Fridolin von Spaun: "Suddenly I noticed Hitler's eyes resting on me. He was indeed observing me. And that was one of the most curious moments in my life. I had the feeling that he was searching somehow –

the gaze which at first rested completely on me suddenly went straight through me and into an unknown distance. It was so strange. And the long gaze which he had given me convinced me completely that he was a man of honourable intentions. I can only say that I'm glad that I saw Hitler's beautiful side."[2]

It's an old psychological trick to focus on the back of someone's head. The recipient feels disregarded and simultaneously that the person can see right through them, creating awe and admiration without effort on the part of the gazer.

During deconstruction, the group to be paranoid about is selected and implanted. Thus, if one wants to 'kill Jews', one selects a paranoiac with a personal history of persecution and implants a hatred of Jews. The more Jews they kill, the more invincible they feel. Humans are easily programmed like this. Hitler was programmed by the British to kill the Jews and this was his invincibility pill.

Racism is passed down from generation to generation on the same principles. In this way, the British killed the Jews by deconstructing the subconscious of a paranoid Austrian. That it worked to such a degree surprised even the British Freemasons, but it didn't occur without continual 'destiny' support.

During Hitler's deconstruction, he was trained to kill the Spanish, Jews, Czechs, Poles, Russians, Americans, the French and those from the low countries (Belgium and Holland – low on the watertable). He was also trained to consider Germans as sacrificial heroes. He was trained to terrorise the British and to stop terrorising them when ordered. In this way, the British had created the perfect opponent for war and had much of their war fought for them. (Hitler could have won the war at Dunkirk in June 1940 after only nine months had not the British interfered with him.)

"I have not come into this world to make men better, but to make use of their weaknesses."[3] Not only is this the perceived credo of a borderline psychopath, but it is a hallmark of deconstruction. Schizophrenia, deconstruction and the latest technology of military assistance have many traits in common. These include:

---

[2] *The Nazis, A Warning from History.*

[3] *The Last Days of Hitler*, p. 274.

1. Thoughts believed to come from external sources – "Get up and get out of here".
2. Sensations believed to occur from outside sources – He thought he was "the Man of Destiny, the Chosen . . . I am the voice that calls from the desert . . . I bring the mandates of Providence."
3. Auditory hallucinations and actions in which the person believes they are acting under external control – Hitler's entire upper palate were metal fillings capped with porcelain and his lower jaw had two metal bridges. He wore a radio receiver in his mouth through which all his thoughts and actions could be influenced – upper palate for the subconscious and the lower palate, which could be audibly heard, for the conscious mind – "Get out of the bunker now".

These three sensations were to become the cornerstone of German psychiatry – thoughts and sensations from outside sources and auditory hallucinations. Hitler and the classification of schizophrenia were developed simultaneously (1911/12). Commensurate with the Freemasons' destruction of God (1891), all divine experiences have since become pathologised, although the origin of their pathology has not been identified.

In conjunction with these deconstructed/schizophrenic states and his British military training, Hitler had the most remarkable recall of military data and the ability for things that interested him (that which he was deconstructed into) well above the norm. That is, his subconscious mind had been trained in certain areas to perform exceedingly well. In other areas he was trained to be exceedingly bad and to procrastinate. He was a brilliant military strategist, but he had the worst body odour of anyone in history. Hitler smelt like the devil at a pit stop. He was an avid drug user, would walk around with food spilt all over him, not make decisions, and sleep until 2 pm. Churchill was the same, exactly the same.

Despite this, one of the great British military strategists and historians, Basil Liddell Hart, wrote that Hitler was possibly one of the greatest military strategists of all time. This did not come from waffling about in the ghettoes of Vienna, but in the military Psych-Ops War School of Tavistock, England. It was they who had planted five hundred years of military experience in him.

The Tooth Fairy

Hitler heard voices in his head his entire adult life. "While I was in the trenches, I heard a voice that said 'Get up and get out of here'. And so I did. A few moments later a grenade exploded on the group with whom I had been eating just before, and no one survived."[4]

For the rest of his life, Hitler continued to hear voices that called him and guided him, so much so that he was convinced he was "the Man of Destiny, the Chosen". He shouted to his crowds, I am the voice that calls from the desert . . . I bring the mandates of Providence . . ." This was blamed on his mother telling him of a great future. His mother and aunt, Klara Põlzl, had lost four children and had two stillbirths before Adolf was born.

But there is now a more modern explanation. Amalgam fillings are comprised of mercury, silver, copper, tin and zinc, with the average person having ten fillings and each amalgam filling weighing 1 gram, giving a total of 10 grams of fillings. Each filling is 52% mercury, creating an average of 5.2 grams of mercury in each mouth.

In 1848, the American Society of Dental Surgeons found 11 of its New York members guilty of malpractice for using amalgam fillings and suspended them. Amalgams were not accepted as standard practice until after 1895. The common term for mercury in Germany was then 'quick silver' and the German pronunciation for 'quick' is 'quack'. Those dentists who used amalgam fillings were called 'quacks'. This term has now come to mean anyone who is an "ignorant pretender to medical skill".[5]

In the 1960s and '70s dental assistants were putting mercury fillings in teeth without holes, merely as practice. In the 1970–80–90s many people were complaining that they were receiving radio signals transferred from teeth, to jaw, to ear. This resulted in a rush on white ceramic fillings and the removal of mercury fillings in the 1990s.

But the dentists, with the help of the military, went one step further and offered micro-radios as dental appendages from 1999. These were used as self-fitted two-way radio molar caps as illustrated in the movie *Charlies Angels* (2001). Directional microphones were developed and a voice can now be projected and heard over a kilometre away. (See *The Fluoride Con, Appendix 2*)

[4] *Very Illustrious Patients*, p. 102.

[5] *The Random House Dictionary of The English Language*.

Certainly the Illuminati and Freemasons that trained Hitler had this simple radio technology in 1912. Radio transmissions existed publicly from 1897 but the Illuminati had them a century earlier.

There is no greater way to keep a subject's 'subconscious fit to the cause' than by talking to them invisibly, advising them to move, and then killing everyone else. This places absolute trust in the voice within and it is almost impossible for that person to act otherwise. After all, it is the voice that guides their subconscious into safety.

This resulted in those who were trained and deconstructed (brainwashed) by the external party (British military, Freemasons and Illuminati) in feeling invincible, immortal and full of self-praise.

Amalgam fillings are bad enough, but Hitler didn't have any. Hitler's teeth were in constant decay and he had 18 fillings which were all metal, fronted with porcelain. He had only five natural teeth left. His upper jaw was entirely metal in one large bridge and his lower jaw had two significant bridges.[6]

Adolf Hitler had a radio receiver in his mouth wired straight to his hearing receptors. The upper palate was the main receiver and spoke directly to his subconscious brain. The two lower bridges transferred the audible sound to his ears and brought these messages into conscious thought. Hitler was a puppet with wooden and metallic strings (sex and teeth). Only a person with a similar dental record within 50 metres would pick up the same message, but his radio messages were finely tuned to the make-up of *his* dental work only. Similar dental records were rare, kept out of range, or extinguished.

Although Hitler was wracked with doubts and uncertainty, he was limitlessly obstinate and intransigent and it was unthinkable for him that he would die before his mission was complete. He felt designated by God and history to create a stable Europe for a thousand years. He had feelings of greatness and purpose, immortality and importance, and could not see a world other than his one. He had no sense of harming others and carried on regardless.

"Hitler called himself 'the greatest liberator of humanity' . . . He took his role of saviour with the utmost seriousness. He eliminated the one most obvious revolutionary phenomenon of which people were most afraid: the Marxist left."[7]

[6] *Doppelgängers*, p. 148.

[7] *Hitler*, pp. 755, 760, 763.

Both Stalin and Hitler were treated like gods by their countrymen, both leaders replaced 'God', and both were accused of having superhuman qualities. After all communism is 'anti-God and anti-Family' and in fascism there can be only 'one'. In both communist and fascist countries, God is replaced by whomever has totalitarian power and all subjects are subordinate to their will.

Early days of Deconstruction

In September 1908 Hitler disappeared into the darkness of the flophouses and homes for men. Here he was quickly spotted by British Intelligence in the Asyl für obdachlose shelter in Vienna. It was this experience which rid him of any compassion, referring to the Vienna home for men as "that school for meanness". This experience was the foundation for his "brutal struggle" and was the principle theme of *Mein Kampf* (*My Struggle*).[8]

After leaving Liverpool in May 1913, officially as his deceased brother Edmund, Hitler returned to Vienna and Munich where he was charged with draft dodging, but got off. Ironically when war came he volunteered.

"As for his record in the First World War and his having won the Iron Cross First Class – I do not know. I never saw his file in the Ministry of War, but I do know that several people lost their lives over that file and I think that there must have been something pretty bad in it."[9]

Hitler won the Iron Cross Second Class in December 1914, the regimental certificate for bravery in May 1918 and the Iron Cross First Class on 4 August 1918. His fellow soldiers said that he was always under some sort of strain and saw no evidence for these awards. History has not unearthed any either. Hitler was put forward for all these decorations by the Jewish regimental adjutant, Hugo Gutmann.

Despite these decorations, he was never promoted past private first class, which essentially means he was 'keen, brainless and had no ability to lead men', but with Jewish connections.[10] Hitler was promoted under British influence so that he could carry weight with the German people later.

Hitler attempted a lesser-known revolution in 1921 and was charged and convicted on 18 February 1922 by Judge Gay Knightheart. Considering it was a revolution, four policemen were killed and they were caught robbing a bank, the normal charge would have been treason followed by execution. But it was reduced from what should have been a death penalty to one month in prison. This illustrated Hitler's high degree of British Intelligence protection even then.

Hitler attempted another revolution on 9 November 1923. He took over a right-wing meeting in a beer cellar in Munich and called for a national revolution. This was the famous Beer Cellar Putsch or

[8] *Hitler*, p. 32.

[9] *The Amiable Prussian*, p. 69.

[10] *Hitler*, p. 68–9.

Munich revolution in which another four policemen and a further eight revolutionaries were killed. At the same time, Hitler's men tried to rob a bank. Hitler was placed under arrest and put on trial, which was heard in February 1924.

Hitler applied to have his sentence reduced – something you only do if you have extreme confidence in your connections. Without connections, the sentence would just as likely have been increased. Hitler's appeal was heard by the same Judge Gay Knightheart, who, as his name suggests, was under the influence of the British Freemasons and their longer-term plans to use Hitler to create war. Hitler should have got eight years, but only got nine months in the rather comfortable Landsberg prison.

The only people who can be compulsorily repatriated in the build-up to war are convicted criminals. History's finger points loudly at this, especially when their sentence is so reduced.

One of Hindenburg's comrades from WWI, General Ludendorff, wrote, "I prophesy to you solemnly that this cursed man will take our Reich (country) into the abyss". He was well aware of Psych-Ops training and could see that Hitler had the signs of a British trained Psych-Ops agent.

General Ludendorff and Adolf Hitler were also co-conspirators in the 1923 Munich Beer Hall Putsch. When the shooting started, General Ludendorff carried on walking and Hitler hit the deck. During the trial Hitler's co-conspirator General Ludendorff complained that Hitler had hit the deck, regarded this as cowardice, and never revised his opinion.

At the end of the trial (26 February 1924) General Ludendorff, Hitler and supporters were photographed outside the courthouse, standing in triumphant poses. I queried the Spymaster about this and he said, "They're German, what do you expect".

It wasn't so hard for Hitler in Landsberg prison. He had a pleasant cell with pictures and decorations and had many visitors including his friends Leutnant Colonel Kriebel and the dapper Emil Maurice. When remembering his stay at Landsberg Prison, Hitler later mused, "We could have opened a tobacconists shop in there from what we were given."

Hitler's mission statement was war in Germany, gifting France to England and war with Russia, as a method of mutual self-destruction.

Referring to Hitler in 1927, Walther Stennes said, "He would talk and talk about the deeds he was going to do and, mind you, he actually did nearly all the things he promised. Fifteen years later [1943] . . . I would often pick up the newspaper and read of how he had done more of those things of which he had talked at our tea-table. One afternoon he told us how, when he was the ruler of Germany, he would have a great war and conquer the world; and when he had done that, he would lay out a Victory Avenue from Doberitz to Berlin and would line it with captured guns and tanks as a memorial to the German Army. Well, he did rule Germany and he did have his great war and he very nearly won it. He also built that Victory Avenue."[11]

Coded Words

Hitler's oratory even hypnotised himself. His eyes would glaze as he repeated himself into a frenzy. He was his own oral ecstasy. In synch with his Freemasonry Psych-Ops training, Hitler wanted to expand into war as soon as peace was mentioned. "Peace" was one of his activating words to plan for war with whatever direction the word "peace" came from.

"Goering could not understand Hitler's aggressive attitude towards Britain which appears to have sprung up after the Munich Accord ['Peace for our Time', 30 September 1938]."[12] Straight after this, Hitler

[11] *The Amiable Prussian*, p. 68.

[12] *Hermann Göring*, p. 177.

made a speech attacking Churchill (Britain) and the Bolsheviks (Russia) – just as he was trained to do.

Walther Stennes: "Hitler had an incredible ability to think quickly, to judge quickly and to get quickly at the essentials of a situation . . . [but] he had no principles whatsoever, and this helped him.

"Hitler always managed to convince people that he really believed what he said. He would have tears in his eyes, but often his speeches were poor stuff in every way . . . Hitler would go straight on with his theme regardless of what the other person had said.

"He could switch so suddenly from being very nice to very nasty . . . at that moment I seemed to recognize the voice of the Devil . . . He was infernally persuasive and, if he tempted others in the same way, that would explain much of what happened in Germany. I was frightened . . . It was typical of his methods; one moment strict legality and the next, naked force.

"Hitler was moody – strange and quite inhuman. He had an uncanny influence on people which we could never understand, but no normal man and certainly no normal woman could possibly like him. [Voice of Walther and Hilde Stennes.]

"The real trouble was Hitler himself . . . He seemed to have an actual preference for muddle and complexity and he certainly liked to set different people against each other, then he felt sure that they would not combine against him . . .

"He would, for instance, delay the making of a decision for weeks while he was . . . talking to quite unimportant people. He was not lazy, sometimes he would not go to bed for one or two days, but he always shirked making a decision."[13]

It is common for double agents deconstructed by foreign ideologies to avoid alcohol during times of their missions. For Hitler, this was virtually all the time. He drank mineral water, avoided smoking, but was a dependent drug user and had his men taking daily doses of methamphetamines (speed).

Deconstructed double agents often rule over populations they have drugged for the purposes of deconstruction. This helps with the manifestation of their phantasmagoria, their all-encompassing illusion – *their* implanted reality they wish to impose on others to assist their cause.

[13] *The Amiable Prussian*, pp. 72, 73, 78, 80, 84.

Learning from Hitler, America began the Asian drug wars as the cheapest method of exporting drugs 'free' into the participating Western nations. The Asian wars simultaneously developed addicts and a counter-culture movement that rebelled against the war . . . by lapping up the drugs – the real reason for the war.

Spymaster: "Put a Hippie in a suit and what do you have? A fascist dedicated to deconstructing the masses."

Spying

When Hitler was working for 'British Army Intelligence' in Germany, he fronted as a German spy, and collected information on all the smaller parties. As for the Germans, he was not supposed to get involved with the parties. As for the British, he was supposed to get involved and draw on his Psych-Ops training, take the party over, mould it, and use it as his vehicle for ruling Germany.

> This was to be his vehicle for fulfilling such British affirmations as: "You will rule Germany; You will be the great ruler; You will build an empire greater than the British; You will become the world's most prominent household name; There will be no one more famous than you; You will be more famous than Wagner; You will carry on from Wagner and fulfil all the dreams his music and politics laid out; Your grandmother Maria Anna Schicklgruber was raped by Jewish aristocracy; Bring down the Jews; Take their money and their rights and kill them; You will be the greatest prophetic figure the German people have ever seen; Support will come from the most unexpected sources and will be available to you whenever needed; You will be the greatest liberator of humanity; Your life will flow into the glory of world fame; You will overturn the millennia."

All this from an insignificant down-and-out tramp desperate to make his mark on the world. It worked. He is still the world's most notorious man.

At the age of thirty, Hitler found a malleable political party on the street and changed its name. "In 1919, while acting as an informer for the German Army, spying on the activities of small political parties, he became a member of one of them, changing its name to the *National Socialist German Workers' Party*, (<u>Na</u>tional soc<u>z</u>ialistiche Deutsche Arbeiterpartei) abbreviated to NAZI, in 1920."[14]

[14] *The Cambridge Biographical Encyclopedia.*

"Wagner's [1813–83] political writings were Hitler's favourite reading, and the sprawling pomposity of his style unmistakably influenced Hitler's own grammar and syntax. Wagner's political writings, together with the operas, form the entire framework for Hitler's ideology.

"He thought of history as a kind of hall of fame with doors wide open to ambitious men. He knew nothing of the meaning and justification of tradition . . . he changed the map of Europe, destroyed empires, and promoted the rise of new powers, evoked revolutions, and brought the colonial age to an end.

"He considered himself Europe's last chance . . . he remained a European provincial with his gaze irretrievably fixated on the antagonisms of a vanished era . . . Despite his fundamentally defensive posture, he was long regarded as the really progressive, modern figure of the age . . . with the aura of stardom . . . from the totalitarian cult of the personality . . . Hitler blatantly proclaimed himself a ruler of this type. He himself also consistently stressed the optimistic, future-orientated character of Nazism. Its reactionary feature and its pessimistic nostalgia with regard to civilisation were largely given voice by Himmler . . . and a sizable band of the SS leadership.

"Wedded to his dreams, he was one of those who would prefer a life of disaster to a life of disillusionment . . . Unlike the Fascist type in general, he was not seduced by history but by his own educational experience, the shudders of happiness and terror that had been his in puberty."[15]

Hitler was trained by the British to build up Germany's infrastructure for war. Hitler was trained to hate and kill the Jews and to get back at the Rothschilds for taking over the Bank of England in 1815. (See *The Bank of England Heist, Appendix* 6)

"Hitler had rightly been called detached . . . his defensiveness was so full of resentments, and for this reason he defended the world he allegedly wanted to protect until he succeeded in destroying it.

"So it was that this reactionary man, unmistakably moulded by the nineteenth century, propelled both Germany and large parts of the world into the twentieth century. Hitler's place in history is much closer to that of the great revolutionaries . . . he drew his critical impulses from the desire to prevent the dawn of modern times and to return, by means

[15] *Hitler*, pp. 56, 57, 754, 757, 758.

of a grand, world-historical correction, to the starting point of all errors and mistaken developments.

"It remained for Hitler to confer upon it the radicalness that made it properly revolutionary, thus profoundly changing a country . . . Under the demands of the totalitarian leader state, venerable institutions collapsed, people were wrenched out of their traditional slots, privileges were done away with, and all authorities that were not derived from, or protected by Hitler were smashed . . . since he knew how to make himself credible to the masses as an all-embracing substitute authority . . . he managed to confer the features of the *Zeitgeist* upon his emotional bias"[16] . . . through control of the media and entertainment.

Bridget Hitler: "Although I think it is a great mistake to overrate Adolf, I think it is an even greater mistake to underestimate him. Above all he is a confident actor with method in his greatest madness. He is the master of the art of the double-cross and is just as ruthless with his family and his friends. He is as much a mystery man to his followers as to the Americans, except in the cases where they 'have something on him'. Schaub, Streicher and Goering are understood to be in this enviable position.

"In my opinion Adolf is an arch-hypocrite, perhaps the greatest of them all. He has always carefully arranged it so that he is not personally to blame for the deeds committed in his name. He was undoubtedly preparing right now the excuses for every crime he had perpetrated in the name of Germany.

"'It is not I,' he will say 'but the German State which did this or that. I ask it in the name of the German people. I was easily elected by the vote of the German people. For myself I have done nothing.'"[17]

Germany was the only defeated country in WWII that had failed to produce a resistance movement that survived. This is an indication that the leader was Psych-Ops trained and that another country and ideology were running him.

An interesting aside to Hitler and Stalin's British deconstruction lies with the Russian Foreign Affairs negotiator Molotov (1890–1986) who visited Germany in an attempt to negotiate the key to war with the West – the so-called "Molotov-Ribbentrop Non-Aggression Pact"

---

[16] *Hitler*, pp. 759, 761.

[17] *The Memoirs of Bridget Hitler*, p. 180.

(23 August 1939) between the Soviet Union and Germany, which came with British approval.

The Betar was a Jewish Intelligence agency that received the latest military training. They were mostly failed revolutionaries and always ready to prove themselves. They existed within the Bolshevik and Tsarist Intelligence, but were entirely loyal unto themselves. Their stock-in-trade became standard practice with such influences as the Molotov cocktail and Molotov's "Nyet" ('No') at UN meetings, which fostered the Cold War.

As a Jew, Molotov was privy to briefings from the Betar. When he visited Germany in 1939 he said to his German opposite number:

> "I can't believe how many things you have here that we also have in the Soviet Union. They are even called the same names, but yours are in German."

It was as if Molotov was thinking that Hitler and Stalin had attended the same war school, which of course they had – Tavistock, in Britain.[18]

[18] Tavistock Institute, 30 Tabernacle St, London, EC2A 4UE. They have more departments than the govt. and are the primary consultants to the government, giving it direction at every turn (U.K., U.S. & others). With foresight 20–50–100 years ahead, they are the teutonic brain behind the One World Order.

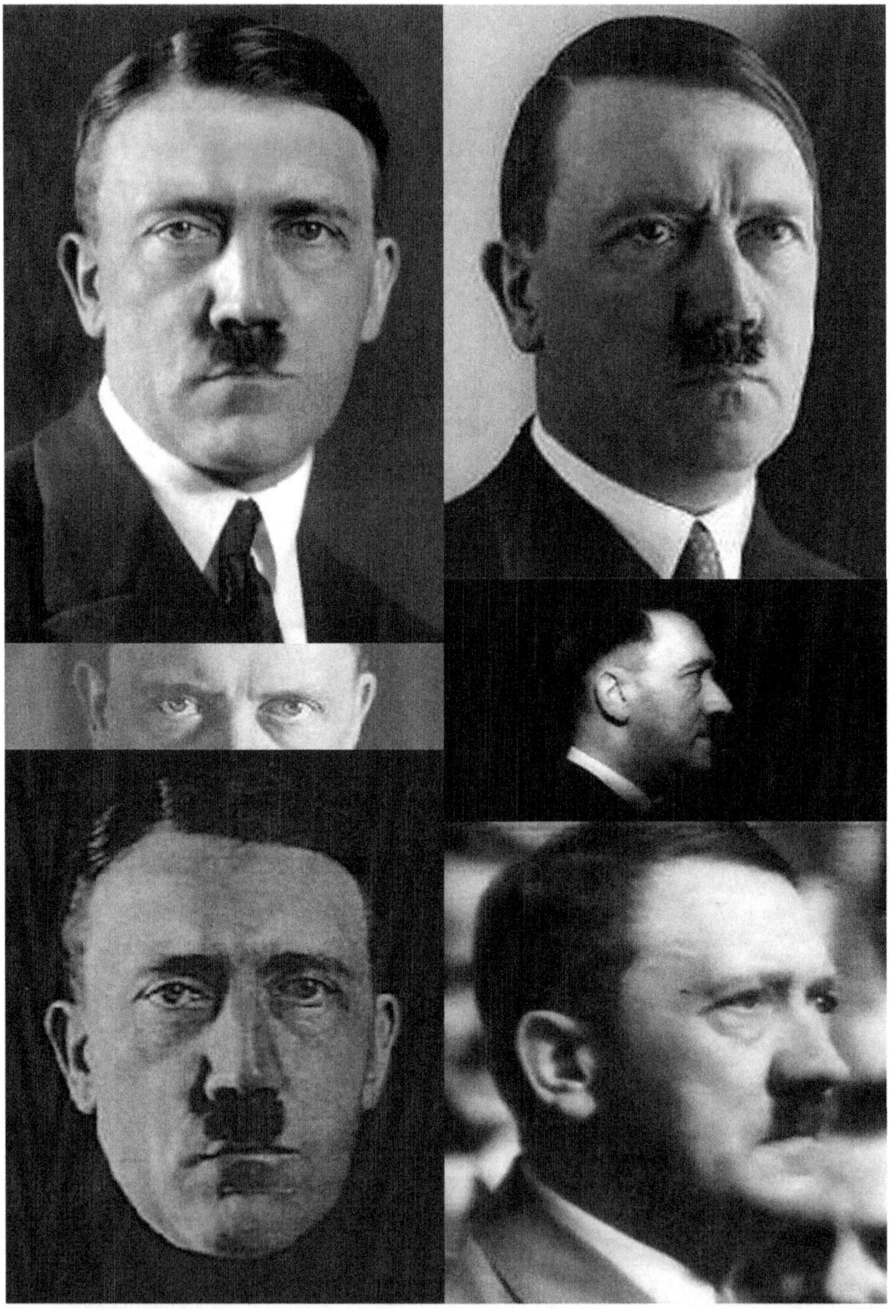

The Guardians of MI-6,

Please run these images through Mandrake biometrics and ascertain which are photographs of Hitler and which are doppelgängers.

PS. Remember to neither confirm nor deny . . . but a leak is okay.

Body Doubles

Churchill invented the term 'Iron Curtain' for Russia, received the Nobel Prize for Literature in 1953 (for books he didn't write) and was knighted the same year. "He achieved a world reputation not only as a gifted strategist and inspiring war leader, but as a great orator, a talented painter, and a stylish writer with a profound sense of history."[1]

Churchill, a Freemason and Druid, was also an alcoholic and a manic-depressive who may or may not have achieved all of these things. From the early 1900s Churchill drank a mixture of champagne and brandy and lounged in his bath until 2 pm singing *Clementine* while his manservants kept the temperature just right.

Winston Churchill made his famous speeches in the House of Commons: "I have nothing to offer but blood, toil, tears and sweat" (Inaugural Speech, 13 May 1940); "We shall fight them on the beaches" (Dunkirk, 4 June 1940); "This was their finest hour" (Battle of Britain, 18 June 1940); and "Never in the face of human conflict has so much been owed by so many to so few" (Battle of Britain, 20 August 1940) . . . but Parliament was not wired for sound at the time and the BBC had contracts for all *but* Churchill's parliamentary speeches.

Straight after the 4 June 1940 "We shall fight them on the beaches" speech, Churchill went to the BBC studio at Shepherd's Bush to deliver the same address to beam live to America and the Commonwealth. The recording equipment broke down and when the BBC asked Churchill to make the speech for a third time, he refused, saying, "I am rather busy, get an actor to do it".

Norman Shelley (1903–80) was a BBC radio Children's Hour actor for the BBC radio production of *Winnie the Pooh*. He was also a well-known Churchill impersonator and recorded the voice of 'Churchill' for all of the above speeches on 7 September 1942. He took his teeth out to correctly imitate Winston Churchill, something Churchill congratulated him on later.

There is still some debate amongst historians as to whether Churchill or Shelley did the live speech for BBC radio and which of them recorded "Never in the face of human conflict has so much been owed by so many to

[1] *The Cambridge Biographical Encyclopaedia.*

so few". The well endowed and much in demand, Norman Shelley, is not to be confused with Geoffrey Wilcott, "the funny old queer". Geoffrey Wilcott played Eeyore in the BBC's 'The House at Pooh Corner', a different radio show which started in April 1940. See Denis Gilford's, *The Golden Age of Radio, an Illustrated Companion* for minutia.

Norman Shelley first claimed that he had recorded Churchill's famous speeches in the late 70s stating that the British Council had confidentially asked him to stand in for Churchill. According to Shelley, Churchill was too busy to come into the recording studio, but we now know that most members of Cabinet were heavy drinkers during the war years and Churchill was one of the most prolific. Such was Churchill's drinking that he began imbibing in his bath from 10 am to 2 pm, by which time he had finished his second cigar.

Churchill had a great deal of difficulty with alcohol, it was rumoured by his peers to be excessive, but was passed off as of little consequence, treated as taboo by embedded historians (which covers almost all published historians) and was never challenged until the next generation of insiders made it to print.

Churchill's speeches were first released by Decca in 1964. In 1983 the BBC asked Decca to stop claiming they were *all* BBC recordings, and in 1984 the BBC claimed the speeches were made by Churchill at his home in Chartwell (circa 1950). As well as infuriating the embedded historians, even this proved false.

In 1990 Sensimetrics (Cambridge, Massachusetts) confirmed some of the Churchill recordings to be the voice of Norman Shelley. The BBC Sound Archive then confirmed that Norman Shelley had recorded these at the old Transcription Service Studios near Regent's Park, with the rider that this was intended for the British War Council to send to America.

In October 2000, copies of these recordings were found by his son, conductor Anthony Shelley, in the attic. They were marked "BBC, Churchill: Speech. Artist Norman Shelley [stamped] September 7, 1942". The BBC then argued that the original recordings were mislabelled.

Richard M. Langworth of The Churchill Center (Hopkinton, N.H.) further stated: "What Shelley recorded, after the war, was an obscure, unpublished Churchill speech, the origin of which has eluded even the Churchill Archives."

History's confusing debate continues between those who believe in the right to know, those who believe they know right, and those who believe it's their right for other's not to know. As such, history is always a three-way debate with new excuses arising as soon as the previous ones lose credibility. History is incredulous until someone comes up with a story from the coalface that is so outrageous it's the truth. Intelligence refers to this as "The ring of truth".

It may have taken fifty years to find out that Churchill had made the speeches in the House of Commons, but not all the radio broadcasts and not all the recordings . . . but even that is not the end of the matter.

History critic Christopher Hitchens: "Some of Churchill's worst speeches were delivered from the bottle's mouth, and some of his best could not, as we now have reason to know, have been delivered at all without the deputising of an impersonator.

"Churchill's later histories both suffer from defects and, as with the case of the Katyn massacre[2] contain unpardonable and self-interested revisions of the truth. As to [alcohol-related] longevity, an entirely pickled Queen Mother has just died at the age of 101."

The originality of some of Churchill's paintings is also up for grabs. It was the style those days to be an all-rounder, a Renaissance man, and there were plenty of artists for hire – Hitler's original doppelgänger for instance (1911–13). Churchill showed none of these renaissance attributes at Harrow, where he did so badly he was punished for poor work and lack of effort. He had to sit his entrance exam three times and then qualified to join the Royal Military Academy near the bottom of his class of 102.

In giving him the benefit of the doubt, school may have suppressed what intelligence Churchill had and he was admitted to the Royal Society for his artistic works, which were uninspired, but technically competent.

Debate continues over Churchill's famous speeches. Others have said that it was made for BBC broadcast by James Robertson Justice who later played Lord Scrumptious in Ian Fleming's *Chitty Chitty Bang Bang* (1968) . . . but this is poppycock.

[2] The Katyn massacre of 25,700 1939 Polish POWs occurred with Churchill's complicity. They were killed by the Soviets in 1940 using 9mm German Geko bullets. This was then blamed on the Nazis in 1944. When all the camps were added up, the Soviets had killed 60,000-70,000 polish POWs in related massacres.

After Norman Shelley's first 'Winston Churchill' radio broadcasts (18 June 1940) and recordings (7 September 1942), another actor played the part of Winston Churchill, while Britain's war leader was either inebriated, in another country, or in another country with the excuse that he was either inebriated or having a visit from "the Black Dog" of depression.

Leslie Howard (1893–1943) was a nice guy who had leading film roles in *Berkeley Square* (1933),[3] *The Scarlet Pimpernel* (1935), as George Higgins in *Pygmalion* (1938), which later became *My Fair Lady*, and as Ashley Wilkes in *Gone With the Wind* (1939), the world's most watched film. He also acted in *The First of the Few* (1942).

Leslie Howard was also a homosexual who had a flat in Chelsea, London. He was caught in a sexually compromising act in a public toilet in London and arrested for homosexual behaviour. Instead of charged he was taken to a military base where he spent the next three months learning to imitate Winston Churchill. He was not told it was for a 'canned meat' operation, but then again, they never told their flight crews either.

The military then dressed Leslie Howard as Winston Churchill and leaked it out through known double agents that Churchill was going to fly to Cyprus. The plane was then shot down by the Germans 40 km off the English coast on 1 June 1943 and Leslie Howard was killed. Meanwhile Churchill went by another route to the Middle East and for the next 10 days the Germans thought Churchill was dead (1–11 June 1943). Officially Leslie Howard was killed on a special mission flight from Lisbon to London. Winston Churchill had doppelgängers for voice and transport and probably went through them with alarming regularity.

The gay Leslie Howard playing the heterosexual Ashley Wilkes, predicted his own future with this classic line from Metro-Goldwyn-Mayer's *Gone With the Wind*:

> "Most of the mysteries of the world were caused by wars and when the wars are over, no one ever knows what they were about."

It is not uncommon for those who seek retribution for their sins to mock enormous service to humanity as a form of appeasement. Service to the United Nations is a prime example. It is run and dominated by war criminals, and as such, it has been a primary ingredient in every war since 1950.

Kurt Waldheim was a German Sonder Führer (interpreter) in WWII and gave instructions to the Germans and the untermenschem

[3] *Berkeley Square* was Hollywood's first time-travel movie.

(people not considered worthy of living). He then served as the Secretary General of the United Nations for nine years (1972–81). He was eventually charged in the 1980s with attempted murder over the Tonner's Club Investigation, but even this was swept under the carpet. Authorities rely on criminals in suits and their previous crimes make them completely malleable.

The Tonner's Club are made up of prominenti who bet money on the losses of shipping tonnage. This began in WWI, ran through WWII and has continued on to the present. Shipping sabotage was taught by the Stasi and the East German Navy at a Special School at Bolinger Bay on the Baltic Coast in East Germany. Records were 'lost' in 1989 and Bolinger Bay also appears to have disappeared off the map.

From the 1700s, Baltic shipping companies had their headquarters in London. In order to discuss chartering vessels and transporting cargo, they would meet in coffee houses – 'The Virginia and Baltic' was the most prominent. Here they would discuss international trading activities and also the sabotaging of competing vessels, something pirates were used for.

Pirates were given the timetables and routes of their competition. Since economic trade was by the trade winds and currents, the fast routes were more dangerous, and those shipping companies with the highest rate of delivery quickly dominated.

Some pirates were supported by their governments as a form of economic warfare and when they wanted to retire, all they had to do was exchange their last big booty for a knighthood. This was the case with Sir Francis Drake (knighted in 1580) who had been pre-sponsored by Britain's Queen Elizabeth.

English pirates even doubled as the royal navy during this period. In a lot of cases the pirates had more sway over the royal navy than if they had the Queen's commission in their pocket. Pirates like Sir Francis Drake were able to mix socially with royal naval officers and walk into their meetings with casks of Spanish sherry under their arms. They often had more power than those with gold braid on their shoulders. Drake was renowned for making suggestions and he virtually taught the royal navy the tactics used against the Spanish Armada.

English cannon balls were lighter and their fire was far more accurate than the Spanish. English sailors could lob a cannon ball into the crow's-nest of the mizzenmast at 2000 yards then board the galleons, knife in mouth, cutlass in hand. Drake was a thinking pirate who conjured up all aspects of terror and focussed this on the Spanish. Terror then became the ultimate English tactic and the ports of London produced more pirates than any other.

Drake was adept at reading the tides and the winds and picking on the Spanish out of thin air. The Spanish called him 'el Diablo' ('The Devil') and Drake always seemed to know instinctively when to hit the Spanish when they least expected it.

Drake was adept at forging alliances with natives, whose language he did not speak. He hated the Spanish with all his might and was constantly looking for other races to join in his Holy Crusade. There are lines in the poem 'Drake's Drum' by Sir Henry Newbolt that are really true.

Drake despised most of the gentlemen that he was often called upon to serve with, but he was adept at massaging egos. The royal navy was impressed by his ability to predict and read the Dons (Spanish). He could look at the Dons' sails and rigging and predict when they would tack and when they would strike their colours (surrender). He'd acquired an instinctive feel for his enemy from the many years of preying on them, but was often magnanimous in victory and not in favour of dishing out ill-treatment.

There is a famous line from a conversation between Drake and Sir Walter Ralegh. Ralegh questioned what the crew were doing when they were supposedly mucking around and this occurred nearly 20 years after the battle of the Armada.

Drake said, "There not idle, they're busy manufacturing souvenirs from the Armada.

Whereupon Ralegh said, "But that was twenty years ago".

Drake replied, "Well they will age them and its best not to disturb them while they're doing this." He pointed to a group in the fo'c's'le [crew quarters at bow] firing bullets at various flags. "The last person that disturbed them accidentally was shot dead. Do I rest my case?"

Drake was always on the lookout for hideouts and he acquired an eye for land from having to defend these isolated places. During WWI German commerce raiders put into a lot of these hideouts and often found traces of previous inhabitants – Francis Drake and his pirates. These islands and coves were nearly all off the sea routes and were isolated by geography as much as any other factor. Drake used them to the best of his ability, never defending them for too long and using fallback positions and reassembly points like the seasoned guerrilla he was.

Out of the use of pirates to eliminate competing shipping, the Tonner's Club quickly became a powerful force in merchant shipping.

Kurt Waldheim, Secretary General of the United Nations (1972–81) was part of this, as well as being a Sonder Führer and giving instructions to kill the untermenschem.

Crimes even make organisations completely malleable. In the 1970s, Interpol were completely malleable due to their involvement in a major paedophile scandal in Brussels. Interpol were running a hotel for paedophile victims, but were caught using them in a kiddy-porn film, thus achieving the opposite of what they set out to do.

Spymaster: "Interpol never recovered from its formative years when it was part of the Gestapo. Interpol claimed major changes were made, but the spy who spoke with me said: 'Yes, Hitler's picture was taken down'."

Churchill has since been exposed as being involved in at least three assassinations in England. Britain has been so desperate to cover up Winston Churchill's war crimes and failings that BBC Television ran a one-sided campaign in 2002. In November 2002 Churchill was voted "The Greatest Briton of All Time", with Winston promoted and no one else portrayed as being in the running.

In a country of 60 million people, only 1 million votes were received and Winston Churchill, formerly known as 'the Butcher of Gallipoli' was crowned 'The Greatest Briton of All Time'.

59 million people didn't vote. The BBC did the rest.

Meanwhile what we don't know stagnates history. What is still not clear – Hitler's attempted peace talks, the Hess flights to Britain, the real Hess death, Hitler's escape out of Berlin and where and when he died – lies under Britain's 100-year suppression rule.

Hitler is considered the man who turned Europe into a 'Howling Wilderness', but this was originally an American plan of war for Samar (circa 1900). Plans of war and invasion were sold privately to other countries so that they would go to war with someone else.

America sold its plan to create a "'Howling Wilderness' for the extermination of Samar" to Britain in 1900 without Britain ever knowing they had bought it (1900–39); and Britain sold its plan to attack America's Pearl Harbor, to Japan in 1925. This one took 16 years to eventuate (1925–41). Touché, old chaps.

Hitler was a British agent and double agent who worked with the British Freemasons and monarchy to destroy France. Army Captain Walther Stennes talking to an English guest in Berlin in 1930: "Hitler had a strange sneaking regard, almost an affection for your country. Certainly he never meant to fight you, although it is equally certain that from a very early date in his career, he was determined to have a war."[4]

The German General Staff started planning WWII in November 1918, as soon as WWI had finished.

In support of England, Hitler banned his own Secret Service from spying on the British. To cover for this, he also banned the Freemasons and Catholics in Germany, which only had a small public effect on Thursdays and Sundays, but allowed and encouraged the British Secret Service to live underground in Germany.

Many British spies completely ignored the British–German animosity and continued trading as though it was peacetime, but with bargains to boot. After all, you could buy the plans of the Luftwaffe for the price of finishing a house. Hitler, being part of the plan, turned a blind eye to the free flow of influential information across the globe. As long as he had motors and firepower behind him, he was happy.

Adolf would lose himself in fantasy by watching two feature films each night like the 1938 *The Star is Bright* (*Es Leuchten Die Sterne*), about an isolated male in a suit of armour being courted by a single harem girl. It was a mixture of King Arthur and a Turkish delight; but his favourite film was *The Lives of a Bengal Lancer* (1935) about the British rule of India in exchange for the protection of India's northern borders – a Mafia tactic if ever there was one.

'We'll protect you by occupying you,
and if you don't let us,
we'll activate your enemy,
whom we control.'

---

[4] *The Amiable Prussian*, p. 81.

Herbert Döhring, a member of Hitler's SS Bodyguard (1936–43): "It was his favourite film and he couldn't wait to see it. He'd sit down and rub his hands together, 'It's starting. It's starting'. He'd talk about this huge English Empire and how such a relatively small number of people could establish and manage India and keep it in order."[5]

To Hitler, the British rule of India was perfect proof of the superiority of the Aryan race. "Let's learn from the English, who with 250,000 men in all, including 50,000 soldiers, governed 400 million Indians. What India was for England, the territories of Russia will be for us."[6]

Not all the German generals went along with Hitler's ambitious plans. General Beck was frightened Hitler was leading Germany into another world war and he communicated this to the British through underground means, contacting Sir Frank Roberts of the British Foreign Office (1930–68).

This was fatal because the British were arranging the war and had been working on it for the previous sixty years with a very focused effort since 1907 when Stalin was trained, 1912 when Hitler was trained, and from the last days of WWI (November 1918). Stalin had lived and trained in England for almost four years and spoke perfect English, as indeed did Hitler.

Sir Frank Roberts: "He [General Beck] said, if only you and the French would stand up to Hitler, then we'd do something about him. The British replied, 'Well hadn't you better start doing something about him, then perhaps we can help you.' However, with Hitler's success, this group had less chance of doing anything about him."[7]

General Beck desperately needed the British to stand up to Hitler at Munich. Instead, the British rolled over and watched their protégé Hitler continue.

Britain's Prime Minister, Neville Chamberlain, made three trips to Germany to broker for peace with Hitler (15, 22, 29 September 1938). On the last trip he had a press conference by his plane before he left for Munich and said: "When I was a boy, I used to repeat, 'If at first you don't succeed, try, try, try again'. That's what I'm doing. When I come back I hope I may be able to say, as Hotspur in Henry IV, 'Out of this nettle danger, we plucked this flower safely'."

[5] *The Nazis, A Warning from History.*

[6] Ibid.

[7] Ibid.

Chamberlain was a naïve fop. He was genial with dimples and looked like everyone's favourite uncle. He was not a wartime Prime Minister at all. He was, however, a British puppet filled with hope and misinformation, destined to achieve nothing.

The British government were so embarrassed by this speech, they took out "as Hotspur in Henry IV" and muffled "nettle" so that it could barely be heard, but sounded more like "metal". His speeches were so terrible, Churchill looked brilliant when he replaced him and all the British eagerly followed Churchill, but it was into war, not into peace.

The Munich conference took place inside the brand new Führerbau Nazi building on 29 September 1938 and lasted into the early hours of the following morning. Attended by Hitler, Chamberlain, Mussolini and the French Prime Minister, Edouard Daladier, the Czech representatives were there, but Hitler refused to let them in. Mussolini presented his own demands at the meeting, but these had been supplied to him earlier in the day by the Nazi's and were essentially the same demands Hitler made.

At the meeting Chamberlain said, "You have thousands of young people in uniform?" and Hitler replied, "But so do you. You call them the Salvation Army and the Boy Scouts" – to which Chamberlain had no reply.

Hitler had all the information he needed from the British and he increased his demands to take over Sudetenland (the outer areas of Czechoslovakia) with no British resistance. In exchange for a country, he gave Chamberlain a piece of paper saying "Peace for our Time". The two fascist radicals, Mussolini and Goering, ran roughshod over the very genial and very British, Chamberlain. Hitler's demands were agreed to so long as it was "Hitler's final territorial demand". Hitler was so chuffed, he was skipping like a madman.

Germany demanded Sudetenland because all the Czech fortifications were in that area. General Beck told Hitler that if the Czechs fought, the German Army would have immense problems. General Beck further promised the British that Hitler would be arrested the moment he ordered war.

Just after 1.00 am on 30 September 1938, the four leaders signed the Munich Agreement allowing Germany to occupy Sudetenland, beginning the following day, Saturday 1 October 1938, with the Czechoslovakian takeover to be complete by 10 October 1938.

Upon returning to London, Chamberlain said:

> "The settlement of the Czechoslovakian problem which has now been achieved is in my view the prelude to a larger settlement in which all Europe may find peace."

Virtually every British politician disagreed and Churchill loudly called the Munich Agreement "a total unmitigated defeat".

Just as planned, on Saturday 1 October 1938, the German Army rolled into the Sudetenland and the Czech people fled with only the clothes on their backs. Hitler was welcomed into Sudetenland, but not into inner Czechoslovakia where there was resistance, but to little effect.

Hitler said:

> "I did not think Czechoslovakia would be virtually served up to me on a plate by her friends."

As the representative of the Western Allies, Hitler thought little of Chamberlain: "Our enemies are little worms. I saw them at Munich." Hitler and the Nazis were now drunk on power. All German plans to overthrow Hitler were shelved and the generals resigned themselves to follow Hitler into his future. Chamberlain had ensured that WWII was a certainty.

The takeover came as a big shock to the naïve Chamberlain who wondered why Hitler had not consulted him. Der!

It was all over in ten days and the British Freemasons who backed Hitler told Chamberlain he was a jolly good fellow and promoted him to Lord President of the Council. With the Czechoslovakian takeover complete, WWII had begun in earnest. Chamberlain had run out of uses and excuses and was killed by in-house liquidation, dying on 9 November 1940 of 'cancer'.

Churchill was in on this and did not attend Chamberlain's funeral. He paid non-committal homage by calling him an "English worthy". This set the level of his respect amongst the public and the warmongers. Any kudos Chamberlain was remembered for, he did not deserve.

Chamberlain was used as 'a vehicle for war' without his knowledge and his naïvety led to WWII lasting longer. Germany had prepared for war during his naïve prime ministership and they now had land and weapons from other countries, at least in part, gifted by him.

Chamberlain, Hitler and Mussolini at Munich Accord, 29/30 Sept. 1938 (above and left). Note the paper in Chamberlain's left hand. Below: Chamberlain returns with the two pieces of paper: "Peace for our Time" and Hitler's thank you note to the Lance Corporal of the Green Jacket Regiment.

Molotov-Ribbentrop Non-Aggression Pact on 23 August 1939 . . . with British approval, followed by Doppelgänger Hitler in Paris, in mid-June 1940.

Hitler's Doppelgängers

To top it off, once the occupation was secure, one of Hitler's doppelgängers went to Prague in place of Hitler. He overlooked the city from the third floor of the castle of the Czech kings, 17 metres above the street, and stood there like a bad actor, without waving, as the German military paraded past stunned and silent Czechs. Hitler was in conference with the British at the time, and the actor Andreas Kronstaedt was Hitler's doppelgänger in Prague.

The English brought no enemy against Hitler, and by non-interference encouraged the war to develop, and develop, and develop. Hitler then applied to the Bank of England and had £6 million of Czech gold released to him. The Bank of England did this without hesitation or delay and this money was used to finance Hitler's leap-frogging war effort.

During this time the English and Germans had a 'swinging door policy' in their backrooms for both nationalities. They were still working together, albeit undercover, through spies and diplomats. Military secrets were traded like sports cards, some for personal gain, and others for the pack. Certainly Hitler's "intuitions scored massive triumphs in the first two years . . ."[8]

France was next. It was not supported by Britain or Russia and was crushed from all sides. After June 1940, WWII became a war for profit, selling arms, grabbing land, and setting up the Americans as the new world superpower with Prescott Bush selling American-made arms to the Nazis contravening the Treaty of Versailles and making enough of the green stuff to buy two US presidencies.

Doppelgängers for Everyone

The British Air Force Intelligence Officer Fred Winterbotham was intrigued by the way everyone ran out from their chauffeur-driven cars in Berlin and then turned at a right angle and ran into the building. One of the SS said, "We do this because of the *Swallows*, the communist party assassins".

They got sick of this by the mid-1930s and organised a doppelgänger contest amongst the ranks of the Storm Troopers, for anyone who looked like anyone important. Every region or 'Gau' was judged, and the finalists were sent to the main centre for one of the most bizarre

[8] *The Cambridge Biographical Encyclopedia.*

competitions in history – the "Gau doppelgänger contest" – the Hitler lookalike contest. Some of the doppelgängers were touched up and improved with plastic surgery. None of the contestants here said: "I want world peace".

There were doubles for Goering and doubles for Hitler. The Gestapo then checked their background, giving preference to fathers with large families who really loved their children. Those who didn't love their children enough were dismissed because they weren't able to be bribed. The body doubles would be encouraged to turn a blind eye and a deaf ear to much of what the Nazi party was doing.

After the war a stunning German double of Hitler was located, complete with surgically altered nose, but he was financially well off and remained a bachelor all his life. As such, despite similarities, he was deemed unsuitable for the role as doppelgänger.

All the top brass, the Storm Trooper leaders, and the 'Gaulieters' (Area Commanders) had doppelgängers. The only one who didn't have a body double was Joseph Goebbels, who had a limp from a clubfoot. Because of this, Goebbels and his wife and children were served up to the Russians at the end of the war. They were the only true bodies left in Hitler's bunker at the Chancellery and they lent an air of legitimacy to the so-called bodies of Adolf and Eva. The Russians identified them all and then erroneously jumped to the conclusion that all the bodies were who they were supposed to be. Unfortunately they told Stalin this and then stuck to the story, even after they found it to be a deception.

In the book *I was Hitler's Maid* (1940), the author Pauline Kohler recalls five of Hitler's doppelgängers sitting around the table in her kitchen. They had come from poor working-class backgrounds and were kind men who spoke about their children a lot. She said she always felt an empathy for these guys and could relax around them, something she couldn't do around Hitler. These were fathers who had been commandeered and were as committed to Hitler's service as they were to their families.

Some of these were Gustav Weber (also spelt Weler), the actor Andreas Kronstaedt, Hitler's favourite driver, Julius Schreck (d. 1936) and Heinrich Bergner who was killed when Colonel Claus Schenk Graf von Stauffenberg planted a bomb under Hitler's table on 20 July 1944.

A clear signal of a double agent (rather than a doppelgänger) is that they leave you feeling on edge, like you've been talking to a ghost, or an ideology, that is deathly forceful but not physically present. The same experience can be had talking to a Catholic priest, who simultaneously represents the Holy Ghost and the paedophile movement. This has the effect of suspending reality and leaving one on edge with trust and distrust at loggerheads.

The effect was quite hypnotic, almost as though both the priests and double agents were similarly trained.

Double Agents and Double Agents

By March 1941, Hitler began to realise how he had been set up by the British. As a 'begrudged national' and 'British double agent', he wanted power over Germany, but he didn't want to die in the process. The war was supposed to be over in 18 months and the first part of the war had gone more or less according to plan. British and German counterparts had each other's phone numbers and any deaths were strategic, most of them French and occurring in France.

'C' (General Sir Stewart Graham Menzies): "The fact is that all sophisticated intelligence services maintain contact with their enemies . . . [The German General] Canaris was never a British agent in the accepted sense of that term . . . Canaris never betrayed his country's secrets to me or to anyone else on the British side, although his men did . . . he did contact me and ask me to meet him on neutral territory with a view to putting an end to the war . . . I never saw Canaris. But I did like and admire him. He was damned brave . . ."[9]

When the former Commander-in-Chief of the German Forces in Italy, Field Marshal Albert von Kesselring was on trial in Venice, "a sensation was caused by a British Intelligence Corps officer, Colonel Scotland, who told the court that he had served in the German Army during the war, and knew at one time the disposition of nearly all German armed forces".[10] In Germany Colonel Scotland was known as General von Schotland – a British agent in the German High Command. He'd bought kudos ahead of time by fighting for the Germans in the trenches in WWI.

This is not dissimilar to Hitler's story.

[9] General Sir Stewart Graham Menzies (C) talking to author Anthony Cave Brown at Luckington in the winter of 1964, *Bodyguard of Lies*, p. 816.

[10] *The Illustrated London News*, 8 March 1947, p. 247.

The first part of WWII was considered a 'fake war' as all the battles happened at sea. Hitler had received all the information needed to invade France from Britain's sexually dubious fascist King Edward VIII (head of the Freemasons and the monarchy) and Wallis Simpson (the American-born German bisexual spy and prostitute), thus bypassing all points of resistance and capturing France, like a 'walk in the park' (mid-June 1940).

Hitler's pact with Britain's warring Freemasons was to occupy and destroy France in exchange for Germany. This was completed after just nine months in June 1940. The French could do nothing, so formed a 'resistance' against the fascists – a black beret-wearing communist resistance. It was a brilliant scam to make France a socialist country.

Britain and Russia didn't come to France's rescue and France has remained a dedicated socialist country ever since.

Peter Fleming (1907–71), Ian Fleming's older brother was in hospital during March 1940. While hospitalised he wrote *Flying Visit* in which Hitler dropped in on London via parachute and the following day buildings were silhouetted as fires lit up the daytime sky like the sun. Within 14 months, the fiction the British wrote had become the reality the Germans enacted.

Ian Fleming (1908–64) knew that Hitler had been trained as a British agent in Tavistock (Lord Callaghan was also trained there). He knew that there was an agreement between Hitler and his British trainers that the war would only go on for nine to eighteen months and that the first nine months was to be a phoney war. (As a result Hitler tried to commit suicide on 10 March 1941, 18 months and 1 day after the war started.) Ian Fleming knew that Hitler was gunning for peace and would send his second in command to negotiate – so he played on this.

"Ian Fleming knew that Hitler, Himmler and Hess were all fascinated by the occult, particularly astrology, but also by occultist rituals. Secret Agents such as Frau Nagenast, an astrologer who Hess consulted and paid, were employed to produce charts that pointed to the 10th of May [1941] being a portentous time for Hess to fly to Britain. Fleming carefully made sure that the astrological forecasts that Hess received from his usual astrologers contained very similar information. This was accomplished using intrigue, bribery and forgery."[11] Fleming

[11] *The British Conspiracy, Secret Agents, The Real 007's* website.

used astrology, double agent contacts through the Peace Party, and forged letters from Mrs Mary Violet Roberts.

Fleming used Hess's usual astrologer, occultist Ernst Schulter-Strathaus. In an intelligence file Ian Fleming read about 'The Link', an Anglo-German organisation founded by Admiral Sir Barry Domvile, a diminutive occultist, as so many are.

Admiral Sir Barry Edward Domvile KBE, CB, CMG (1878–13 Aug. 1971) was the son of an Admiral and had been promoted through the ranks at great speed. His naval career spanned from 1892–36. He was the Director of British Naval Intelligence (1927–30) and the Vice-Admiral Commanding War College (1932–34). As such he was a prime target for subversion. He visited the Dachau concentration camp in Germany (1935) and the Nazi government impressed him. On Joachim von Ribbentrop's invitation he attended the Nuremberg Rally in September 1936.

Admiral Sir Barry Domvile then founded 'The Link', which operated as an Anglo-German cultural non-party organisation with a journal that reflected pro-Nazi views to its 4300 members. MI-5 investigated and closed the organisation down in late 1939, soon after WWII began.

Admiral Sir Barry Domvile was considered a serious enough threat to be interned in Brixton Prison (7 July 1940–29 July 1943). Here he developed a view similar to jailed doppelgänger Hess – that there was "a Jewish-Masonic conspiracy". He was released to his home in Hampshire on the understanding that he would be interned as soon as the Nazis invaded.

Admiral Sir Barry Domvile's expressed view was that Hitler "would soon be in this country, but there was no reason to worry about it, because he would bring the Duke of Windsor over [formerly King Edward VIII who was successively exiled in France, Spain and Portugal] as King and conditions would be much improved".

Via agents, Fleming fed the line to Hess that 'The Link' had been driven underground and was in a position to use the Duke of Hamilton to negotiate peace and overthrow the Prime Minister, Winston Churchill. The Duke of Hamilton was less well known as the Duke of Hamilton and Brandon, and a few histories refer to Brandon as being the agent. The Duke of Hamilton was the agent!

Christened Douglas Douglas-Hamilton (1903–73), from 1940 he was the 14th Duke of Hamilton and the 11th Duke of Brandon, the hereditary keeper of Holyroodhouse, hereditary bearer of the Crown of Scotland, and acted as Lord Steward of the Royal Household (1940–64). In the 1920s his father destroyed Hamilton Palace (the family seat in South Lanarkshire), but Douglas Douglas-Hamilton made enough out of WWII to purchase Lennoxlove House (East Lothian) in 1946.

Douglas Douglas-Hamilton, the Duke of Hamilton and Brandon, was the Squadron Commander in the Auxiliary Air Force (1927–36), flew the first flight over Mount Everest in 1932, commanded the Air Training Corps, played a senior role in the Royal Air Force and was responsible for air defence over Scotland. He played a significant role in setting up the aircraft manufacturer, Scottish Aviation Ltd, at Preswick Airport. In 1978 this became part of British Aerospace Plc. Whatever Brandon wanted over Scottish airspace Brandon got over Scottish airspace.

Englishwoman Violet Roberts was the aunt of Walter Roberts, a close relative of the Duke of Hamilton and Brandon and was in the political intelligence and propaganda branch of the Secret Intelligence Service (SO1/PWE). Walter Roberts was also friends with Karl Haushofer, Hess's occult mentor. Walter Roberts wrote a letter to Karl Haushofer[12] and Hess took a great interest in this. Haushofer then replied to Violet Roberts suggesting Walter Roberts's post office box in Portugal for further correspondence. This letter *only* was conveniently intercepted by the British mail censors.

After the war had been going for 20 months, Hitler, a 'British trained and deconstructed Psych-Ops double agent', sent his close friend Rudolf Hess to Britain and Karl Horn to America to instigate one or more of the following:

Plan A: 'Negotiate for the end of WWII'.

Plan B: 'Hitler's anonymous escape to America'.

Plan C: '*Peace for our Time* with Britain and America'.

With Hitler out of the picture, Germany could fold with minimal damage, Berlin would return to its merry ways and Hitler could live out his days in South America as so many other Nazis did. Hitler sent his deputy and pilot Rudolf Hess (47) to negotiate for the end of WWII with Britain. Knights Cross holder and ace Messerschmitt 110 pilot Karl Horn accompanied him.

[12] The Duke of Hamilton was having an affair with his son, Albrecht Haushofer.

This was told to the Spymaster by one who had taken a part in the interrogation of the real Hess. At the time he did not understand the full picture and the interrogation haunted him ever since. He told the Spymaster of the psychotic Austrian G-Man and suggested that Hauptmann Karl Horn (Squadron Commander) was hauled off the Battle of Britain operation and did not enjoy the special flights. Horn didn't look forward to the Hess peace mission, but felt obliged to obey the Führer's commands as he was a Knights Cross holder. There's even some question of whether it was Horn or Hess who flew the aircraft to Scotland.

Hess's tutor at university, Professor Karl Haushofer (1869–1946), played an important role. He was an occultist and one of the conduits between Hess, Hitler and MI-6. Horn took direct action because Hess was rendered incapable of going to America for fear of capture and execution. Instead his capture happened in Britain. Horn went to America because it was virtually their only chance of stating the case for peace.

The British and Germans had each other's phone numbers and it was not unusual to fly to each other's country during the war on 'diplomatic missions' and for these flights to be cleared of attack. The British even had German 87 octane avgas refuelling stations at designated MI-6 airstrips when no Allied aircraft flew on 87 octane. British planes used 100 octane avgas.

In the 1930s, the US Government passed a law prohibiting the sale of fuel additives or their formulae. Despite this, an American company gave Germany the secret to flying on low octane avgas by supplying them with the necessary chemical additive, ethyl lead.[13] (See *Not Without American Help, Appendix 3*)

The Danes purchased a German Condor Bomber in 1937/8 and it was very obviously used as a bomber. Although it had been fitted out as an airliner and was flying for Air Denmark, the stewardesses almost had to crawl up the aisles on their hands and knees to get to the passengers.

When the Nazis invaded Denmark, some Danes managed to load the Condor with fuel and fly it to England in 1940. By 1942 it was reported that the Condor had become so tatty that the British wanted to break it up for spare parts, but they had no other Condors and the parts were not transferable. There was no way a Condor was in good

[13] I. G. Farben and Rockefeller's Standard Oil.

condition in 1940 and bad condition in 1942. The German Condor was used for special work – intelligence speak for intelligence operations.

The German Condor became the ideal aircraft to fly in and out of Europe on special missions and was used safely in German territory. As is typical in wartime, the plane was acquired by an airline in Britain that soon went broke. This left the German Condor plane without an itinerary.

A lot of aircraft from both sides were written off as navigation errors when they had landed intact. Britain now claims MI-6 aircrews were trained to fly Luftwaffe planes and that some Luftwaffe aircrew were MI-6 trained.

This coincided with the British-owned German transport aircraft (ex-South Africa) which allowed German and British meetings to take place in either country, or in any other country. This was done on numerous occasions and entirely in secret.

This is how World War II was progressively agreed upon.

Hess and Hess Fly to Britain
10–11 May 1941

The British summoned the real Hess (the Deputy Führer from 1933) through secret channels to Scotland and had arranged 10 May 1941 as his most portentous day. Switzerland, Portugal (British) or Spain (Fascist), Scandinavia, and Czechoslovakia were other possible destinations for his flight, but these were all optional decoys. At the same time a doppelgänger Hess flew to Scotland from a different location in Germany.

The dates on both the real Hess's and the doppelgänger Hess's three weather maps illustrated these other destinations. The fact that they had three weather maps meant that the real Hess did not know where he was going until after he had refuelled in northern France and received additional directions. The lack of clarity was intended from the beginning so that the myth of the real Hess (1884–1941) being an accidental defector or madman could be maintained and he would never be found.

The real Hess, Hitler's best friend and second in command, left Germany in secret on 10 May 1941 and landed his Messerschmitt Me110C near Abbeville in north-west France in a makeshift airfield. The Germans had secured these airfields all over France for the Battle of Britain (over eight months earlier). These were essentially flat grassed strips with a tower holding gravity-fed fuel and a telephone.

The real Hess refuelled himself and received further instructions by telephone as to his destination and departure time. He camped the night and was due to fly out the following evening, setting himself above the tail end of the Luftwaffe blitz on London. Karl Horn was with him.

The Omega Files say that Hess flew to England on 10 May 1941 to stop the war with Britain and was arrested as a 'war criminal'. However, they do not say that Hess spent a layover-night in France in order to wait for cover from the blitzkrieg. The blitzes went from September 1940 to May 1941 and Hess's cover was the last of the blitzes. Six weeks later Germany was focusing on Russia.

Hess's body double was well trained and this mission had been planned for a long time by both the British and the Germans. Doppelgänger Hess knew all of real Hess's history and had become an expert pilot.

The following day as 5.45 pm on 11 May 1941, doppelgänger Hess took off from Augsburg airfield near Munich in a not unpublicised event. The last person to speak to him was Hitler's radio dentist, Dr Friedrich Kohn, who belonged to the same secret Tibetan Lodge as Hitler, as did his quack doctor, Theodor Morell.

Augsburg is 50 km north-west of Munich and 30 km north of Landsberg Prison. Doppelgänger Hess took off in the next model of Messerschmitt, the Me110D, and flew low and north at 385 kmph (238 mph) to Cologne in northern Germany and refuelled. He took off from Cologne at 7.35 pm, heading across the islands off Holland and into Dutch airspace, where he linked up with the head of SS Intelligence, Reinhard Heydrich, who was an avid pilot. He was flying in Dutch airspace with Allied attention elsewhere on the blitzkrieg. Heydrich had three special SS pilots with him.

The real Hess was given specific instructions when to leave the makeshift airfield near Abbeville on the evening of 11 May 1941 and what flight paths to take. He was instructed to avoid the flak corridors, where they were most likely to get hit, and to fly at different heights and different speeds until he met with the blitzkrieg raid ('lightning war') on London. He was instructed to fly over the top using the Luftwaffe for cover during his most exposed time. Hess then met with the three escort planes by flying parallel on a bearing over Waddenilanden, the chain of islands stretching across northern Holland.

Goering was the commander of the Luftwaffe and a German-born British agent. This meant the British controlled many aspects of the German Air Force and knew what they were doing most of the time, including the London blitzes. Even before a blitzkrieg was predicted by the full moon, or detected by radar, the British knew what the Luftwaffe plans were. They were also prepared to assist them into battle.

Prior to WWII the Germans had been having problems with their aircraft's fuel injection and coughing during turns. In the late 1930s, under MI-6 advice, Rolls Royce invited German officials to visit their factory where MI-6 had got them to turn their engines upside down. According to MI-6, the meeting was designed to lead the Germans up the garden path, but 'engine inversion' solved the German problems, and many others besides. As a result, German fighters were superior to British Spitfires . . . totally by accident of course, old chaps.

As a German-British agent, Goering was opposed to any genuine peace talks and he supported a stitch-up against the gay married-for-cover Hess. Hess was queer for Hitler but had a devoted wife. Goering phoned Leutnant Colonel Adolf Galland, the Gruppe Kommandeur on the French airstrip at Abbeville, the most north-west airstrip in France, and requested that he intercept Hess and shoot him down. Goering had good cover to do so as Hitler had grounded Hess.

"Early in the evening of May 10th Galland got an extraordinary telephone call from Goering, who sounded 'very agitated' and ordered Galland to take off immediately with his entire wing. When Galland pointed out that there were no reports of any enemy aircraft flying in, Goering shouted, 'Flying in? What do you mean flying in? You're supposed to stop an aircraft flying out! The Deputy Führer has gone mad and is flying to England in an Me110. He must be brought down.'"[1]

Leutnant Colonel Galland failed to accomplish the mission. Hess was not shot down over France or Holland and made it to Scotland.

Once the real Hess had established the three escort planes, the four Messerschmitts flew over the English Channel towards Scotland. Hess (with Karl Horn) flew above doppelgänger Hess for the rest of the journey. They turned north-west until the Hesses found the signal from their night navigation radio direction signal. Both Hess planes had been specially fitted with a Kleve Knickbein radio night navigation receiver positioned for the pilot rather than gunner-navigator control. Hess's Me110C and doppelgänger Hess's Me110D were both fitted with two 66 gallon drop tanks for the final leg of the journey.

It was a clear moonlit night with little or no cloud cover and the planes were clearly visible from any ships below. Doppelgänger Hess continued to fly very closely below the real Hess, protecting him from any seaborne assault. Southern England was far better protected by fighters than northern England and there was even less threat during a blitz.

If the Hesses had been intercepted before they were able to enter the Duke of Hamilton's airspace, Heydrich and his decoy were there to lure away interceptors in their Me109E's. According to the British version on 11 May 1941 Hess's plane was spotted by eye and radar just after the blitz in the well-lit full-moon sky as it flew towards Scotland. "But even as the bomber streams made their way toward the burning

[1] *The Murder of Rudolf Hess*, p. 47 and *The First and the Last*, pp. 108-9.

capital, to their north flew a single Messerschmitt 110 fighter flown by the Deputy Führer of the German Reich, Rudolf Hess. The single aircraft was detected by British radar. British nightfighters were sent up to intercept and shoot it down, but they failed to make the intercept."[2]

Heydrich and his special SS-flown Me109E escort protected the Hesses Me110's halfway across the North Sea (north of the English Channel) and then split off. The Me109E's didn't have the necessary navigation equipment or fuel capacity to fly all the way to Scotland. The Hesses then banked, travelling north at about 220 mph (350 kmph) climbing slowly to 15,000 feet (4500 m).

There four planes flown by Heydrich, the SS pilots, Doppelgänger Hess and real Hess were all 350 km away and well out of British airspace. Hess's plane had no ability to fire, as it had been stripped of extra weight for the long journey, and when doppelgänger Hess's plane was investigated after the crash it was discovered that all of the guns had been greased up. Neither Hess nor doppelgänger Hess could shoot at each other if they caught on to what was going on, nor could they retaliate against any fire from the British.

As it turned out, the Hess Me110 planes were allowed to pass with overriding orders given not to shoot them down (shades of 9-11). It was Scotland's highest-ranking Freemason, the Duke of Hamilton and Brandon who called off the Bolton-Paul Defiant Nightfighters sent from London. This allowed the real Hess and the doppelgänger Hess to land safely in Scotland.

The winner of the war always writes the dominant history. "To their north flew a single Messerschmitt 110 fighter flown by the Deputy Führer" was just British propaganda – confusing the truth, as is commonly found in victorious history books. This was another layer to the British part of the Hess cover-up and the British sabotage of peace. The blitz had stopped the real Hess and his escorts from being spotted just hours earlier.

Hess had no idea that the plane flying closely below him was his doppelgänger. Doppelgänger Hess remained close and out of view so as not to be seen by Hess or spotted by radar. At the time, radar was in its infancy and two planes flying close, one over the other, appeared as one plane.

[2] *The Secret Servant*, p. 343.

This can still be done today as long as the planes have the same radar signature. The 'two planes become one' by flying to the edge of the radar screen, aligning their paths and then re-emerging onto the screen. In this way a fighter plane can be introduced to airspace under cover of a passenger plane. When Heydrich and the SS escort parted, the two Me110's flown by the Hesses banked north off the radar screen.

The Hesses proceeded north with the real Hess closely above doppelgänger Hess until they intercepted the Stavanger Knickbein radio direction signal at 9.24 pm. They then banked sharply to the west and headed towards RAF Acklington. They had a tailwind and it was perfect flying weather. The moon was reflecting off the water and they were able to recognise coastal features.

Approaching Scotland the Hesses dived for cover amongst what clouds they could find until they reached about 5000 feet (1500 m). They crossed the coast at 10.25 pm and flew off the Knickbein and circled around the visible Holy Island showing all the world that they were not concerned about the Bolton-Paul Defiant Nightfighters. This is a Secret Operations and doppelgänger signature.

Doppelgänger Saddam Hussein did the same thing when he touched his jaw with the fingers of both hands on the night of his capture, 13 December 2003.

The Hesses then headed for the Duke of Hamilton's Dungavel Castle and overshot it as they headed for the glistening waterways on the west coast of Scotland. Doppelgänger Hess had overshot Dungavel castle by 60 km to purposely escort Hess and Horn to the Liberator flights at Preswick (35 km from Dungavel Castle and 5 km north of Ayr). They were travelling at 238 mph (385 kmph), so this would have taken another 5 minutes there and 7 minutes back.

Karl Horn, the gunner in the real Hess's plane, was an Olympic long-distance runner from the previous Berlin Olympics (1936) where the Duke of Hamilton had attended. Karl Horn parachuted out before they circled West Kilbride, landed and made his way to a rendezvous with an American General and caught a Liberator flight to America in an attempt to plead his case for peace there.

Hess and doppelgänger Hess then flew around West Kilbride below radar. The real Hess slowed down, peeled off, and landed at the

Liberator landing strips at Preswick under cover of a mass of planes leaving for America at exactly the right time. Hess's landing had been precisely coordinated with the Americans.

This confused the radar and no one was alerted by the noise. Hess landed safely and was detained amidst secrecy, then interrogated with as much information as possible extracted from him before he was killed. His execution was kept secret.

Rudolf Hess (26 April 1894–13 May 1941).

"The radar noted that at a certain point over Scotland – near Dungavel, Stratheven, Lanarkshire, seat of the fourteenth Duke of Hamilton, premier peer of Scotland [and very high ranking Freemason] the aircraft began to spiral and then disappeared. It was thought at the time that it had been intercepted by a nightfighter, a Defiant [Bolton-Paul Defiant Nightfighter], and shot down."[3]

The Secret Servant does not note that the plane circled around Holy Island, that there were two planes, that they circled around West Kilbride and that one plane landed at Preswick. The winner of the war always records the war, with history rewriting interference, and always omits the details of its double agent dealings.

Doppelgänger Hess maintained his speed, made a chaotic circuitous route in order to sight Hess' landing, then followed the Scottish landmarks and glistening railway lines over Western Scotland finding his way back to Dungavel Castle (near Glasgow).

King George V's fourth son, the Duke of Kent (39) was waiting with a group of Polish officers at Dungavel Castle. Special Operations 1 (SO1) had all the correct players in place just in case there was a double agent leak. The Duke of Kent then flicked on the runway lights. Doppelgänger Hess realised the runway was too short and he'd crash into the trees at the end, so he overshot it and looked for a field to land in.

Doppelgänger Hess did not have enough avgas to make it back east 160 km to the RAF airstrip at Acklington. Not finding a suitable field and having already accomplished half of his mission, he flew another 20 km north to Eaglesham Moor, where he ran out of avgas, flipped his plane upside down and bailed.

---

[3] *The Secret Servant*, p. 343.

Heydrich and his SS guard flew Messerschmitt Me109E (German Bf109).

The Hesses flew Messerschmitt Me110C & Me110D (above), which the Germans called Bf110. Below, a Liberator B-24.

As doppelgänger Hess bailed out he chipped a bone in his foot on the plane's tail. He landed by parachute on a field not far from Floors Farm in the Eaglesham Moor. His plane crashed and exploded at 11.09 pm, 20 km from Dungavel Castle. It was close enough to walk through the night, but his foot was a problem.

"Hess had abandoned the aircraft by parachute, hoping to land in the grounds of Dungavel where he might have a conversation of a highly secret nature with the duke, a man Hess admired. But Wing Commander the Duke of Hamilton was on duty that night at an RAF base in Scotland [Preswick] and was not at Dungavel. In parachuting, Hess also failed to land on the grounds of Dungavel estate – the only mistake he made in what was otherwise a technically remarkable and flawless flight, especially in regard to navigation. Hess had flown from an airfield near Munich to a pinpoint near Glasgow, a distance of some seven hundred air miles in which he traversed two heavily defended air-spaces and steered his way through major bomber streams proceeding both east-west and west-east."[4] This was hardly a stroke of luck for the second in command of Germany.

Doppelgänger Hess was a test for the real Hess to see if the British really did want peace. With two Hess's one had to go, so they killed the real Hess as the capture of a doppelgänger is always more valuable (Saddam Hussein's doppelgänger is a case in point).

The secret death of the real Hess and the capture of the doppelgänger Hess was a minor victory for the British. Doppelgänger Hess was never sure of the fate of the real Hess and was placed into a deconstruction programme as soon as the original interviews were over. This was designed to make him believe he was the real Hess.

Peter Allen's *The Crown and the Swastika* suggested that Hess was killed in Britain by intention, or in an aircraft accident with the Duke of Kent and a doppelgänger was brainwashed into being Hess.

In Canada the OSS (the CIA from 1946) developed a method of brainwashing using electrical shock and drug treatments capable of changing a personality. This would explain doppelgänger Hess's strange behaviour and different appearance at the Nuremberg Trials (30 September 1946).

---

[4] *The Secret Servant*, pp. 343-4.

Doppelgänger Hess, wearing the name tag Alfred Horn on his brand-new uniform, had been trained to imitate Hess by the Germans and was trained to believe he was Hess by MI-6 who had been sharing data with the OSS. As a coping mechanism, to avoid revealing the true plans of Hitler and what he knew about the war (a Freemasonry stitch-up) he pretended to be mad, lost focus, complained of being poisoned and made fake suicide attempts.

The madness was partly real due to his German doppelgänger training and OSS subconscious personality alteration. The poisons were very likely real and designed to stop doppelgänger Hess thinking clearly. Doppelgänger Hess was eventually murdered in a fake suicide. It really was a horrible life being the fake Hess, the fake gay lover of Germany's ruler – the world's most feared 5'9" bisexual coprophiliac.

The fact that Churchill kept doppelgänger Hess hidden from public view lends weight to the theory that the real Hess was dead and doppelgänger Hess (Alfred Horn) was being altered for limited viewing. That a tailor was ordered to replicate Hess's uniform strengthens this. The 'replicated Hess uniform' was stolen from Spandau Prison in the 1970s.

At the same time as the real Hess and the doppelgänger Hess were flying to Scotland, the Luftwaffe were bombing London at low tide. This meant the British couldn't use the Thames to put out the more than 2000 fires from the incendiary bombs (which explode into fire on impact). Amid the mass of confusion more than 3000 people were killed or injured and the British House of Commons was destroyed for years to come. This was hardly a day for peace, but it was a perfect day to sabotage peace. Peace was sabotaged by both the British and the Germans on 11 May 1941.

All the incendiary bombs dismantled by the London Fire Brigade were made in Illingford, England and carried a manufacture date of 1938.

Spymaster: "The Fire Brigade were in charge of dismantling any-incendiary bombs that failed to explode. MI-5 then monstered the Fire Brigade, silenced all the fire-engineers and swore them to secrecy. It was essential to MI-5 that the manufacturing identity of the exploded and unexploded incendiary bombs remained secret.

"MI-5 then leaked a cover story that Germans recovered the British-made incendiary bombs from an RAF bomb dump in France. This was a lie as all of these incendiary bombs were thoroughly demolished.

"The RAF were fastidious about destroying ordnance and the record of their demolition was well and truly noted. The government story was a cover story. The Fire Brigade were asked not to say anything as it would be considered unhelpful."

A third of the square mile of London was destroyed, but the British monarchy's many palaces were rarely hit, many of them not at all. A British monarchy/German alliance for sure!

"Landing in a field, Hess was captured by a farm-hand. He was still wearing the blue uniform of captain of the Luftwaffe [a set-up]. Hess was handed over to the assistant area controller of the Royal Observer Corps, Major Graham Donald."[5]

Major Graham Donald was complicit to the German subterfuge and German–English Freemasonry agreements. Major Graham Donald looked at the doppelgänger Hess with the name tag Alfred Horn and said, "You look exactly like Hess."

Doppelgänger Hess replied, "That is nothing new to me. It's a fact which has embarrassed me often enough."

From then on Major Graham Donald acted as though this was the real Hess, although he knew otherwise. This was part of the stitch-up, as was confusion over the name Horn, when Horn was on the other flight. Major Graham Donald remained complicit to the German–English Freemasonry agreements and SO1 operations. When he met with the next interrogator, Major Graham Donald once again identified 'Captain Alfred Horn' as "Rudolf Hess" when he knew damned well he was the doppelgänger Hess they had been expecting.

"At the outset, [doppelgänger] Hess told Donald that 'he had a secret and vital message for the Duke of Hamilton, and that he must see the Duke at once'. Donald then asked the German where he expected to find the duke, and [doppelgänger] Hess replied, 'At Dungavel house', producing a map with a red ring drawn around the estate.

"After the brief interrogation, Donald reported to his duty controller and asked him to contact Wing Commander the Duke of Hamilton. 'After this . . . I came to the conclusion that the safety of the realm was now securely in other hands and no longer the sole responsibility of our Group. So I went to bed [as I was told].'"[6]

[5] *The Secret Servant*, p. 344.

[6] Ibid.

When doppelgänger Hess was being interviewed, he requested the British send a telegram to the real Hess's wife, Ilse Prohl (m. 1927) saying that he was okay. He didn't speak to her as voice recognition would reveal him as a fake Hess, and he refused to meet with Hess's family for another 28 years (until 1969).

This message comforted Hess's wife, but when it was passed on to Hitler it meant that doppelgänger Hess had arrived at Dungavel Castle and not the real Hess. It also meant that the real Hess and Karl Horn (in his regular service uniform) had landed safely at Preswick where the Liberator Flights left for America.

Doppelgänger Hess had confirmed the landing during what appeared to be a chaotic circuitous route. He was, in fact, dropping his wing for better sight and ensuring radar picked him up over and above the mass of planes leaving Preswick.

This telegram was the way in which doppelgänger Hess (whom Hitler knew about), contacted Hitler saying that the Reichsführer (Deputy leader and occasional lover) had landed safely. If Hitler knew Hess was dead, he might have become disheartened and not attacked Russia in six weeks' time.

Hitler usually lay in bed until lunchtime. He was a lazy administrator who left much of the administrative work to Hess. However, on the morning of 11 May 1941, after sending both Hess, Karl Horn and Hess's doppelgänger (under the name Alfred Horn) to England to plead for peace (or an unobstructed war) Hitler was up and dressed at 7.30 am and was able to officially receive the letter from Hess' Adjutant Pintsch which read, "And if my Führer, this project . . . ends in failure . . . simply say that I was mad".

Doppelgänger Hess's telegram to Ilse Prohl was a 'successful mission to date' signal but Hitler was never to see the real Hess, Karl Horn, or the doppelgänger Hess (Alfred Horn) again.

Hitler had publicly grounded Hess from flying. This was designed to make Hess's peace mission look like a rebellion against Hitler in case it failed. However, as firstly a British agent and secondly a German agent, Hitler was right behind the mission from its inception. It was in fact his idea, as he was already tired of the war.

Hitler had tried to commit suicide two months earlier on 10 March 1941 and it was Rudolf Hess who had saved him.

London after a blitzkrieg.

The Rudolf Hesses.

The war was only supposed to go on for 18 months (9 September 1939–9 March 1941) after which the secret agreement between Britain and Germany, the British and German Freemasons, and Churchill and Hitler began to fizzle and the real war began. Hitler reacted to this by attempting suicide on 10 March 1941.

Lt.Col. Scotland: "This much, however, is in my view certain. There could be no question of Hess having flown from Germany on his own initiative. It is highly improbable that he could have taken his aircraft without the express knowledge and concurrence of three men: Adolf Hitler, Hermann Goering and Field-Marshal Kesselring or some equally high-ranking air force officer.

"Hitler, in short, would have to grant Goering permission for the trip, and for a machine, with extra tanks, to be made available. This work could only be done with the knowledge of someone like Kesselring (then Air Chief of Staff). And Goering, also, would have to issue precise instructions not only for the aircraft's route and planning, but for the temporary abatement of the German anti-aircraft units while Hess was on his way out."[7]

As it turned out, all three were British Agents. Adolf Hitler, Hermann Goering and Albert Kesselring.

The dates of 10–12 May 1941 are regularly confused by both sides as part of the ongoing cover for the Hess and Hess mission, which was both a peace mission and a mission to sabotage peace. It was a propaganda exercise acted and counteracted by both sides.

Hitler punished Hess's astrologers, whom he knew had been compromised by the British, but he did not punish Willi Messerschmitt (Mr Smith) who had helped doppelgänger Hess obtain and fit a brand new Messerschmitt Bf110D with a Knickbein radio night navigation system positioned for pilot rather than gunner-navigator control. Hitler also failed to punish the ground crew at Augsberg or Cologne. Nor did he punish Heydrich who guided the Hesses over the North Sea.

This is completely at odds with Hitler's standing orders about Hess not being allowed to fly. It shows that the Luftwaffe had official sanction to guide and assist Hess, using the biggest air raid ever as cover – the blitzkriegs over London. It shows Hitler's total complicity in the peace mission, and from his British training, the designated failure of that peace mission.

[7] Lt.Col. A.P. Scotland OBE, *The London Cage*, p. 69.

Hitler knew that in the writing of history, this would make him look good and also allow him to get rid of 'Fraulein Anna', the nickname of his gay lover Rudolf Hess. Hess was beginning to make the Third Reich look like a 'Gay Reich', and the 'mean Hitler' look like a 'gay Hitler'. "Not self-seeking and unswervingly loyal, he [Hess] was promoted by Hitler to posts of increasing importance: Deputy to the Führer in 1933, Minister without Portfolio . . ."[8]

Rudolf Hess saved Hitler's life on 10 March 1941, and two months later Hitler repaid him by sending him on a suicide mission. His British agent status had taken hold. "The war, however, eclipsed his importance, which his meagre talents in any case scarcely justified, and in 1941 he flew on a self-appointed mission to Scotland to negotiate peace."[9]

If Germany knew Hitler was suicidal, Germany would lose its spirit to fight. The British goal was to extend the duration of the war, expand the fronts and get more countries involved. Hitler had no option but to obey his British Tavistock training. In his subconscious, he knew the war was expanding and he was heading north to Russia.

Secret Service: "To further cover this up and add confusion, essentially the name of the game, when the British got to Augsberg in Bavarian Germany they insisted on taking it ahead of any other Allied force. They burnt all the factory werke nummer [work number] records of the Messerschmitt Me110's. To this day, the records of the Me110's are an area of confusion unto themselves. There is no way to work out when they were manufactured or how many there were. The same thing happened in Austria.

"Russian Polikarpovs used to dive on the tails of the Me110's, chew the rudders up, and the Me110s would fall out of the sky. Records were destroyed to thwart any research confirming any double-dealings."

Doppelgänger Hess provided cover for the murder of the real Hess, who actually did want peace, and may have had enough charisma to make others question the war. The apparent capture of Hess appeared like a minor victory for the British. The doppelgänger Hess may have been unaware of the murder of the real Hess and probably believed Karl Horn had made it to America.

---

[8] John Keegan, 'The Men in the Dock', *Purnell's History of the Second World War*, No. 117, p. 3264.

[9] Ibid.

At the time of the blitz, Churchill was at his retreat at Ditchley Park, near Oxford, at the estate of Sir Ronald Tree, a place he went on moonlit nights – blitz nights. Churchill was watching a Marx brothers movie at the time and when he was advised that the Duke of Hamilton wanted to speak to him on the phone regarding the arrival of Hess in Scotland, Churchill said, "Will you kindly instruct the Duke of Hamilton to tell that to the Marx brothers . . . Hess, or no Hess, I'm going to see the Marx Brothers." Churchill knew in advance that Hess and a doppelgänger Hess were arriving and that the real Hess was already being interrogated and would be killed.

The Duke of Hamilton then flew to Oxford that night and met with Churchill who appeared after the movie had finished and began grilling the Duke. Doppelgänger Hess had come fully loaded with proof positive of Hitler's previous attempts to create peace in September 1940. Churchill received the Duke, swore him to secrecy and then dismissed him.

The Duke of Hamilton was actually sworn to secrecy the moment he became Scotland's leading Freemason, and was further sworn to secrecy when he was pre-briefed on how to carry out this scenario. His flight to Oxford to see Churchill was partly for show.

Churchill then selected three people to interrogate the doppelgänger Hess: Roman Battaglia; the Duke of Hamilton; and Lord Simon.

Alfred Horn (doppelgänger Hess) was then taken to Maryhill Barracks in Glasgow where he emptied his pockets for the Duty Officer. One of the items was a letter from Hitler to the Duke of Hamilton. This letter was removed by Major Graham Donald and never reached public records. The war could not continue if there was written record of Hitler trying to create peace.

Major Graham Donald (Observer Corps) was a Freemason and Special Operations insider. First to meet with Alfred Horn, he instructed all the interviewers Alfred Horn was Rudolf Hess.

The first person to interrogate Alfred Horn/doppelgänger Hess was Roman Battaglia, an interrogator and language expert from the Polish Consulate. This following day it was the Duke of Hamilton's turn.

Doppelgänger Hess was then interviewed by Lord Simon who was Chamberlain's protégé. Chamberlain, the naïve fop used to secure war with Germany, had died six months earlier (9 November 1940).

The interview was conducted under the supervision of 'C'. 'C' was General Sir Stewart Graham Menzies who was one of the many illegitimate son of King Edward VII.

Many of King Edward VII's closest relatives believe he arranged WWII, despite the fact that he had died in 1910.

This is very similar to the interview of Saddam Hussein being conducted under the supervision of the CIA on 15 December 2003. It meant that no useful information would be gained, all scenario-information would be colluded, the war would continue to be justified and expanded, and huge profits would continue to be made. It was war and lives were as dispensable as writing them off as 'collateral damage'. It could not have been a bigger set up.

Doppelgänger Hess's offer for peace was completely at odds with real Hess's offer for peace. Doppelgänger Hess's offer for peace was that 'England would return all of Germany's ex-colonies, stay out of the war and allow Germany to take over Europe, including Russia [in 41 days' time]. In return Germany would not touch the British Empire. This 'Peace Talk' was straight out of Hitler's British deconstruction.

England decided Germany needed another enemy to weaken its attacks against England, so they encouraged Germany to attack Russia. Germany kept its part in the bargain. The blitzkriegs of Britain stopped and Germany attacked Russia under Operation BARBAROSSA on 22 June 1941. Britain had an agreement to warn Russia, but they failed to do so. This strained British/Russian relations – but what did it matter, Stalin was also a British agent and had been since his 1907–1911 British training.

Britain did warn Russia but warned them in such a way that they didn't take it seriously, as they knew they wouldn't. The British used letters and diplomatic notes. Stalin was so deluded that he even ignored a warning from the German Ambassador to Moscow. The German Ambassador said he felt he had an admiration for Bismarck, the German Chancellor in the mid-1800s. What was unsaid at the time was that Bismarck was an admirer of Russia and never wanted war with Russia. Bismarck wouldn't even contemplate war with America.

Bismarck was in favour of exhibitions of force close to German borders. He had been a keen intellect and used to call the generals a bunch of dummkopfs, calling Kaiser Wilhelm II the biggest dummkopf of them all.

Bismarck: "All you have to do to understand what German strategy ought to be is to take a glance at a map of Germany and it immediately demonstrates three given truths:

1. Germany is placed geographically to attack in all directions.
2. Germany is also placed geographically to be attacked from all directions.
3. So obviously Germany should only fight with very limited war aims and not get involved in any war protracted beyond a year and a half.

Because dummkopfs could not read a single map, you had to watch them like a hawk."

At the end of the meeting, doppelgänger Hess said that Germany would not negotiate with Churchill. The interviewer's reports were never made public.

After the takeover of France, Hitler moved his headquarters to the Black Forest near Freudenstadt. WWII was designed to bring all the neutral WWI countries into war. The desire for oil crosses all national boundaries and national deaths are of no concern to oil companies. As such, Royal Dutch Shell asked Hitler to launch his armies into Russia for oil. In the Black Forest, in July 1940, Hitler agreed. Almost as soon as Hitler made a decision the British knew about it and acted accordingly. This little pearl was quietly recorded by Hitler's Dr Morell in his diary. The operation was first named 'Fritz', then 'Directive 21', then 'Barbarossa'.

Hitler's intelligence reports were actively compromised by the British. With British assistance Germany concluded in early 1941 that unless Russia was attacked within the year, she would arm and prove to be too strong to defeat. Hitler therefore decided that his July 1940 decision to attack Russia was a good one and he launched Operation BARBAROSSA with 121 German divisions, 19 armoured divisions, three air fleets and summer in mind.

Doppelgänger Hess's offering was hardly a peace talk. It was more of a finger pointing skite and a declaration to create a 'howling wilderness' everywhere but Britain and its colonies. It is hardly likely that Hess would negotiate for peace with Britain in earnest, by blitzing Britain just hours before. Doppelgänger Hess's peace mission was intended to fail and leave no room for success. After all, the British prided themselves as rescuers and there was no way they would let Western Europe fall to the Germans. It just wasn't in their blood.

The real Hess was on a peace mission whereas doppelgänger Hess was pleading with England not to support Russia so that Germany could expand WWII. It was the same peace agreement Hitler tried with Neville Chamberlain prior to the invasion of Eastern Europe – Germany would help protect the British Empire as long as Britain did not oppose Germany in Europe. Britain and Germany would take over Europe without war between the two 'cousins'.

This is why the British Freemasons killed the real Hess and supported the doppelgänger Hess. Germany did attack Russia and the British did not come to a physical rescue. The British only supplied support on paper, which, in war, is as useless as tits on a bull.

In an attempt to limit the PR damage of a captured Hess on the German psyche, Ribbentrop advised the world that "Hess suffered from gallstones and through the pain he had become an 'astrological faddist' and was mad. The German underground movement took this to mean that the man Hitler had been promoting for years was partly or completely insane."

The truth of the matter was that both Hitler and Hess were bisexual and occasional lovers. Hitler had been promoting his lover Hess. They were not the first politicians to invent this strategy.

This encouraged more German High Command to become double agents, which then secured their freedom after the war. Some of them were even decorated by the Allies.

Eight days after Hess's landing Hitler sent two SS officers to parachute into the same location as doppelgänger Hess (19 May 1941) with the same maps, and with the same locations circled. They were interrogated, then executed, with no mission statement ever revealed. The war had only been going 19 months and the British were already furiously sabotaging peace talks and silencing everything around this effort.

The American President Franklin D. Roosevelt remarked, "I wonder what is really behind this story?"

Doppelgänger Hess was then placed in the Tower of London, Aldershot, Mychett Place (Camp Z), the Nuremberg Trials and Spandau Prison for a life sentence and eventual assassination 46 years later. For the last 21 years of his doppelgänger life, Hess was the only prisoner at Spandau Prison.

"He was indeed brought to Nuremberg apparently suffering from amnesia but was judged fit to plead and later recovered his memory. He was indicted on all four counts, convicted on counts 1 and 2, and sentenced to life imprisonment, and refuses all contact with his family."[10]

During his confinement in Britain (1941–45), the RAF guard asked doppelgänger Hess where he had learnt chess. "When I was in hospital in France after Cambrai" came the answer. In 1917 the real Hess was elsewhere on the Eastern Front.

In the 1980s when doppelgänger Hess began mumbling to his guards about being on a peace mission for Hitler, WWII being a British and German Freemasons' war against the French Freemasons, and a war to create 'ORDER OUT OF CHAOS', his execution became imminent. Germany, America and England intervened and doppelgänger Hess was assassinated in the Summerhouse of Spandau Prison by strangulation on 17 August 1987.

There is sufficient evidence to say that this is so. Freemasons dominated all positions of influence right through Britain and Germany. At the beginning of 1930, Germany had 75,000 Masons. Two-thirds of these refused to allow Jews to join and one third, the humanitarian lodges, allowed Jews to join. In 1922 these two lodges separated, with one-third of German lodges supporting Jews and two-thirds not.

> "There is a border which strongly differentiates humanitarian from Old Prussian national Freemasonry. We, the three Old Prussian Grand Lodges refuse to take part in the general humanitarian fraternization movement between people in the world."[11]

This was acknowledged by the Nazis who gave protection to the Old Prussian Grand Lodge Freemasons and treated the Humanitarian Freemasons with contempt.

On 28 March 1933 the unrecognised 'Clandestine' Freemasons resolved to dissolve and become dormant. In their final resolutions they also resolved to support Hitler, as did the National Mother-Lodge, 'The Three Globes'. In late March 1933, the three (Berlin) Grand Lodges sent a congratulatory address to the Reich Chancellor Hitler, and The

[10] John Keegan, 'The Men in the Dock', *Purnell's History of the Second World War*, No. 117, p. 3264. Hess first saw his 'family' in 1969.

[11] Steffens, p. 332; taken from Alain Bernbeim, MPS, *Philaltethes Magazine*, 'German Freemasonry and Its Attitudes Toward The Nazi Regime', February 1997.

Grand Lodge of Saxony (Dresden) sent a telegram expressing its faithful support to Dr Goebbels.[12] By 31 March 1933, all German Freemasons were in support of Hitler.

Hitler was actually worshipped by the P2 Masonic Lodge Grand Master Licio Gelli, as well as a host of other Freemasons including Juan Peron and Thule Society cult founder, Rudolf Blauer (alias Rudolf Freiherr Von Seboottendorf).[13]

> *Omega Files*: "The Freemason's Scottish Rite can be traced back to the Jesuit college of Clermont in France, and at the core it advocates a global government and the destruction of all national boundaries, sovereignties and cultures; the dissolution of all traditional 'family' structures making all children the wards of the world state;[14] and the destruction of the idea that man has a soul, or rather that humans are merely evolved animals having no spiritual nature and therefore no need for God. In other words a homogenized collective society which does not tolerate individual expression but instead enforces absolute conformity to the controlling establishment."

In 1950, Masonic Brother C. William Smith wrote the article 'God's Plan in America' which gives some insight into Freemasonry's goals.[15] There are three plans in action today and they all have different purposes:

1. God's non-sectarian plan.
2. The Roman Catholic denominational sectarian plan.
3. The anti-Capitalist Communistic plan.

God's non-sectarian plan is dedicated to the unification of all races, religions and creeds, to the new order of things, to make all things new – a new nation, a new race, a new civilisation, a new non-sectarian religion, 'The Great Light' (which already exists) and a 'New Age' (Novus Ordo Seclorum).

---

[12] *Nationale Zeitung*, Essen, 30 March 1933.

[13] 'Von Seboottendorf' was sometimes written 'von Sebbetendorf'. Name changes and spelling alterations to those names were a signature of high-ranking Freemasons who considered themselves above the law as they played their role in 'the game'.

[14] This is why so many Family Court judges are Freemasons.

[15] Heavily paraphrased from the archaic writing of Masonic Brother C. William Smith, 'God's Plan in America', *New Age Magazine*, September 1950, the official organ of The Supreme Council 33rd Degree A. & A. Scottish Rite of Freemasonry, S.J.U.S.A., pub. at 1735 Sixteenth Street N.W., Washington, D.C.

Great light non-sectarian Masonic Brotherhood Monarchs include: King George VI of England (1936–52), King Gustav V of Sweden (1907–56), King Haakon VII of Norway (1905–57), and the late King Kristian X of Denmark (1912–47).

The Nordic people are not church worshippers, but avid readers of the Bible. The Nordic-Anglo-Saxons make up 95% of colonists, were the first people to print the Bible in great quantity, were known as the people of the book, and are the great Bible-reading people of the world today. [With six-month long nights and no TV in the Arctic Circle, there was only sex and the Bible.] In Norway there has been no illiteracy for more than a hundred years. The Nordic people [with Greenland's Thule as their centre] are bringing a new order to the world.

At the time, the British thought Hess's history of WWII being a battle between the British and German Freemasons in order to create ORDER OUT OF CHAOS was dead and buried and wanted to keep it that way. Hess's guards at Spandau Prison were rotated every month and the murder occurred under US tenure.

On 17 August 1987 Hess's male nurse Abdallah Melaouhi passed two strangers in the Summer-house. They were British SAS assassins dressed in American Army uniform. According to Wolf Rudiger Hess, his (doppelgänger) father was murdered by British SAS assassins dressed as American soldiers, sent by MI-6 and his death was made to look like a suicide. (See *Doppelgänger Hess's Murder, Appendix 5*)

According to Dr Seidl, doppelgänger Hess could not have committed suicide in this way because the 93-year-old could not lift his arms above his head. The suicide came complete with fake note, expertly forged by a specialist organisation, but not convincing to anyone who knew Hess.

Hess was never allowed to meet anyone from the public. If either the real Hess or the doppelgänger Hess had met with the public either may have told of how:

1. The British organised a fake peace treaty to flush out the German peace activists.
2. Britain could have accepted peace and saved the mass deaths of the Jews.
3. Hitler was encouraged to attack Russia to take the pressure off Britain.

4. If Germany had continued to attack Britain, Britain would have folded and lost the war within two years of its inception.
5. The British sabotaged Hitler's attempts at peace.
6. Hitler, as a British agent, sabotaged his own peace mission and extended the war to Russia. This meant he was fighting on two fronts. Even Hitler said he would 'not repeat this mistake of WWI', but he did.
7. The deaths of the Jews had been a British goal since Nathan Rothschild took over the Bank of England on 21 June 1815 using homing pigeons. (See *The Bank of England Heist, Appendix* 6)
8. Any of this information coming from doppelgänger Hess would have eroded any justified propaganda against Russia and would have delayed the Berlin Wall coming down 27 months later (9 Nov. 1989).

According to the *Cambridge Dictionary*, "In June 1941, on the eve of Germany's attack on Russia, Rudolf Hess flew alone to Scotland to plead the cause of a negotiated Anglo-German peace. He was temporarily imprisoned in the Tower of London, then placed under psychiatric care near Aldershot. At the Nuremberg Trials (1946) he was sentenced to life imprisonment, and remained in Spandau Prison [just west of Berlin] until his death."

The truth of the matter is that both Hess and doppelgänger Hess flew into Scotland on 11 May and landed within 35 km of each other. The real Hess landed his plane safely at Preswick and the doppelgänger Hess crashed his plane at Eaglesham, near Dungavel Castle. The real Hess was then killed, while the doppelgänger was detained, written off as mad, had his personality altered, was placed in prison and then assassinated 46 years later.

Karl Horn, the companion of the real Hess, parachuted out of Hess's plane and went on the very dangerous mission of 'doing the same thing' as Rudolf Hess, but with America. Karl Horn made it to America and pleaded for peace.

Karl Horn was someone the Americans would recognise and who had the highest connections in Germany. He was a Hauptmann or German Captain in the Luftwaffe, Knights Cross holder from the Battle of Britain (August–September 1940) and 1936 Olympic long-distance runner. His uncle was Colonel General Karlheinz von Horn, who later led the German Army in the Ardennes offensive of 1944–5. Karl Horn was a pilot from a famous flying lineage who would be respected by the American military.

It was not uncommon from WWI to WWII for athletes to also be agents and for their names to be suppressed or confused. The agent might get a medal in the event, while another stood on the podium and was photographed. The name, sex and image of agents in the Olympics was regularly obfuscated between the wars. In this way the prize was awarded to the country, with the true identity of the agent remaining secret. There were even men competing in women's events.

It is not untypical for the Polish to look transgender. Stella Walsh, born Stanislawa Walasiewicz, won the 1932 100m Olympic gold medal and came second at the 1936 Olympics at Berlin. It wasn't until she was shot in 1980 that it was discovered she was a man. But these transgender types have a way of using the media to their advantage and she had a Polish reporter accuse the winner, Helen Stephens, of being a man.

In this way, the closest official record of Karl Horn being a 1936 Olympic long-distance runner is Karl Hein who won the gold medal for the hammer with an Olympic record of 185' 4". Erwin Blask (Germany) got the silver for 180' 6.5" and Fred Warngard (Sweden) got the bronze for 179' 10.5". Such is the nature of military-Olympic competitors and the obfuscation that surrounds their public achievements.

Secret Service: "Karl Horn made it to his rendezvous with an American General that had been sent to England and negotiated a flight to America on the 'Liberator Transports of the American Ferry Command' from the Scottish West Coast. These Liberator flights were flying in and out of Scotland all the time, transporting planes to Britain and munitions to both England and Nazi Germany, courtesy of Prescott Bush – grandfather to the current US president.

"Karl Horn made it to America and tried to approach the big-wigs in the United States but instead was hunted down by a joint British MI-6 and FBI firing party which included his British Olympic long-distance competitor. The FBI troop included a sadistic, homosexual, ex-Austrian serviceman who used to beat people to death. The cross-dressing blackmailed director of the FBI, J. Edgar Hoover, used the former Austrian when he didn't care if the subject died."

Karl Horn, a man negotiating for 'world peace', the end of

Germany's advancement in WWII, and Hitler's escape to America, was hunted down as a forerunner to the psycho-thrillers that were to come. Exhausted, Karl Horn eventually committed suicide by swimming out from the New England coast into the Atlantic Ocean and drowning. If only he had made it south to Yaphank, Long Island. There, the 'potato-field fascists' would have covered for him and even given Hitler a bed for a decade or two.

When the fake Hess was on trial at Nuremberg (from 30 September 1946), the Germans High Command smirked and accommodated him as a retard. The real Goering laughed and ridiculed him because he knew he was a doppelgänger and a British agent. After all, Goering had ordered the death of the real Hess at Abbeville and had given approval for both flights to arrive simultaneously in Scotland.

At the Nuremberg trials, the Russian judge dissented and found Hess guilty of 'Crimes Against Humanity' but the British and other judges were extraordinarily lenient and did not. The British judge refused to get into matters of politics and Secret Operations. It would have placed Churchill in a bad light and been an embarrassment to the British monarchy, aristocracy and government. As a result, Hess was not found guilty.

Over 99% of those charged with war crimes were not convicted. Because of double agent dealings, most of the war criminals had fake deaths (Hitler), had doppelgängers at the trial (Hess), were Anglophiles (Schellenberg), had turned up to the trial under British cover complete with plastic surgery to witness their own sentence in absentia (Martin Bormann), or had been compromised during the war and had become British double agents (most of the German High Command).

The Nuremberg trials quickly turned into a farce and the judges were powerless to act with such military/intelligence interference.

In the 1970s the medical officer Hugh Thomas, a Welsh surgeon treating the doppelgänger Hess, noticed that the prisoner did not have the same dunchesse, the chest scar from the through-and-through gunshot wound from the Russian Nagant rifle that almost killed the real Rudolf Hess in Romania on 8 August 1917, after which he was hospitalised for four months.[16]

[16] Leutnant Rudolf Hess's military service record is held in the American Mission (the Berlin Document Centre) which houses several hundred thousand captured German WWII documents. It was formerly the fortified headquarters of Hermann Goering; *The Murder of Rudolf Hess*, pp. 28–29.

When Hugh Thomas pointed this out he got monstered by British Intelligence. Nevertheless, doppelgänger Hess was detained and executed 46 years later in 1987, when he was some 93 years old. He maintained silence for almost all of that time.

When doppelgänger Hess did finally speak out, he was executed: "The war is a war of secrets. I knew you would come for me. I alone won the war. My family are all grown up now." This was delivered to the SAS assassins in fluent English.

The information doppelgänger Hess could reveal would have been bad for the justification of the Cold War against Russia and Britain wanted to look like a top dog with clean paws while it lasted. The death of doppelgänger Hess became the long fuse for the end of the Cold War and made the Russians a little happier about their lot. It also maintained their ignorance.

The 'Progrom' was to maintain the Berlin Wall until 30/31 December 1999, once Helen Clark and her minder Vladimir Putin had got into power. Helen Clark is the KGB operative 'IE', pronounced 'E'. "She trained in St Petersburg"[17] from 1968 and worked with Vladimir Putin from 1978–91 in an attempt to launch a nuclear strike on American property (Canberra, Adelaide, Sydney, Taupo) from a Russian nuclear-armed submarine in the deep New Zealand waters. This was known as the "Trawler Wars".

Vladimir Putin lived in Wellington for two years as a Fisheries Inspector (between 1980–82) and returned for the sinking of the *Lermontov* (16 February 1986). At least some of Putin and Clark's clandestine meetings were held on Wellington's Wharf No. 3 in the early hours of the morning and these were recorded. These records were then read and discussed on a political level, but did not reach the public domain due to ideological similarities.

Through Fred Winterbotham (Air Force Intelligence) the British knew the SS were running doppelgängers. The British knew the second pilot was not the real Rudolf Hess and they knew the real Hess had been tortured to death. To avoid retaliation and looking like 'peace saboteurs' the British sustained the mystery of the real Rudolf Hess for 46 years after his death. Both Britain and Germany and the British and German

[17] The author announced this on televisions on 29 November 2005, replayed on 8 February 2006. There have been no law suits, and worse still, no contact from any media. This includes the Head of Television who has a copy of the first edition.

Freemasons have kept up the pretence that doppelgänger Hess was the real Rudolf Hess to this day.

If the British thought the captured doppelgänger Hess was the real Hess he would have been executed at the Nuremberg trials in 1946. Because various levels of the British and German command were uncertain, or knew otherwise, he was kept alive to live out most of his days.

Rudolf Hess's guards at Spandau Prison all knew that he was a fake Hess, a doppelgänger, because he (Alfred Horn) had spent time in Cambrai in 1917 when the real Hess was in Romania from 1916–18. The real Hess had been nearby in Ypres and Artois in 1915, but in Romania from 1916 where he was shot and then trained as a pilot from March to November 1918.

Secret Service: "All of the Air Force personnel who guarded Hess were swished out to New Zealand on a boat and they didn't know why they had been moved here until I interviewed them. The last Nazi in New Zealand was a wheelchair-ridden invalid nursed to death in 1973. The spy Garbo was also smuggled out to New Zealand."

The truth of the matter is that the British military had trained both Hitler and Stalin. They had both been gifted their countries with ample MI-6 support and the British wanted to watch Russia and Germany fight it out to the bitter end. It gave the British and their secret societies a sense of command to watch two nations battle to the death. By destroying Russia and Germany completely, it made England comparatively stronger.

The British wanted the secrets the Nazis had plundered from the French Freemasons, the direct descendants of the Knights Templar who had invaded King Solomon's tomb in 1127AD. Raiding King Solomon's tomb brought untold riches, wealth, knowledge and style to France. This was followed by envious wars from other countries and retaliatory invasions from the Catholic Church.

The British royalty and Freemasons had this to say to Germany and Russia: "As you depose our royal cousins from the monarchies of your countries, we will introduce new leaders (whom we control) and turn them against you, turning your country into a 'Howling Wilderness'."

The British monarchy's removal of the European monarchies was full of cover ups and arranged events shrouded in the mystery of new ideologies. The deaths of the Czar's family were faked. They didn't die at Yekaterinburg in Russia in 1918 as was popularly believed, but were removed from power and swished out to Southern Ireland (Eire from 1922) by Lieutenant Colonel Meintzerhagen.

Germany's Kaiser wasn't killed either, but removed to Harlem in Holland a week after WWI ended. The British royal family was related to both of these families. They were prepared to depose them, but they were hardly going to have them killed. The ties between Britain and Russia, and Britain and Germany, were so strong at the time that the Russians were referred to as 'uncles' and the Germans as 'cousins'.

Germany and the Soviet Union signed the Molotov-Ribbentrop Non-Aggression Pact on 23 August 1939 (with British approval) but secretly planned to divide up Eastern Europe between them. As soon as the Russo-German Non-Aggression Pact was signed, Germany knew it was going to war with Russia. As Germany overran Poland, Russia overran Finland and the Baltic States. Both countries were expanding under British instruction in order to create an excuse for World War II. Both Stalin and Hitler were British agents and shared Poland by splitting it down the middle.

With the peace plan with Britain thwarted, Hitler broke the Non-Aggression Pact with Russia and invaded the Soviet Union at Lithuania, Belarus and the Ukraine on 22 June 1941. This placed St Petersburg under a siege for a famous 900 days, to February 1944. A bitter four-year Russian-German war was created that Britain sat back and watched. The Russo-German war lasted from the German invasion of Russia, to the Russian invasion of Berlin in April 1945. As a result, more Russian blood was spilt in WWII than by any other nation and both Britain and America fought against a weakened German side[18] . . . and when the Cold War began they fought against a weakened Russian side.

Literally, as kindergarten children playing war on maps with tin soldiers and toy tanks, in libraries containing the great histories of 'propaganda and paedophilic heroism', the British watched as Germany, having been given France, went to war with Russia.

Both Stalin and Hitler had similar backgrounds, were British Psych-Ops trained, and trained using the same methods. Stalin's training in Britain began in 1907 and Hitler's training in Britain began in 1912. Both were used as Britain's retaliators.

[18] *The Wind, June* 2003; 26 million Russians died in WWII.

Prior to WWI, London, St. Petersburg and Berlin were opulent cities of equal wealth. After WWI, WWII and the Cold War, London was by far the wealthier city. The battle between these countries continues in the realm of WAR-IN-PEACETIME. It is now fought around the distribution of drugs and the induction of feminism into each other's societies.

Feminism was invented in Russia as a method of war, and during the Cold War feminists in Russia were deported to the West. Feminists break down the family, reduce breeding and create infighting.

War-in-peacetime is the war of family attrition. Vladimir Putin's agent Helen Clark is a feminist and lesbian. She became Prime Minister only after another female PM lost to her, so there was no choice. Clark has taken the feminist motto, "If it works, break it" to the nth degree and in just six years of her communist/fascist leadership, NZ has become a country without an identity where the citizens fear and distrust the police and paedophiles have been elevated to the highest office.

Like Marilyn Monroe and Jackie Bouvier-Kennedy-Onassis, Hitler and Stalin were each other's admirers and competitors, and all four were after the same thing – enough attention to compensate their earlier years of an absent father.

Hitler came to understand what WWII was about and made three attempts at "Peace for Our Time", sending his top men to get the message across. Most of the upper echelons of the SS had several doppelgängers, as did the Reichsführer and pilot Rudolf Hess. Hess was invited by the British to rendezvous and discuss peace on 11 May 1941. The German attempt to shoot real Hess down came via double agents in the German High Command, namely Goering, who was acting on British orders.

The previous Reichsführer, the gay Captain Roehm, was also murdered. He was a British agent and Hitler's Psych-Ops minder but he was still killed on Hitler's orders during the Night of the Long Knives (30 June 1934).

The German-instigated peace negotiations of September 1940 and May 1941 were sabotaged by both sides under British Freemasonry orders. The Freemasons were out for war. They had created enough of them and lived and died by their motto 'ORDER OUT OF CHAOS'.

This historical event, the Hitler/Hess-instigated peace talks, is fraught with cover-ups on a scale only found in war. The cover-ups included the Luftwaffe air raid resulting in the misconstrued dates for the London blitz, (10 May, 11 May or 21 June 1941), fake Hess plane sightings, the use of doppelgängers, doppelgänger Hess being named the real Hess, doppelgänger Hess being altered to believe he was the real Hess, the deaths of British and German players, and history rewriting interference, employing the best writers, in which two-thirds of all history books ensure 95% of the information is false – after which there has been six decades of complicit silence.

The two Hesses flying to Britain was a cover-up to make Britain look good while sabotaging peace, encouraging their German cousins' war expansion into Russia, thus weakening both Russia and Germany while saving Britain and extending the war.

World War II was an English and German Freemasonry stitch-up against the French and Russians. Britain and America won the war by extending it and ensuring that it took place (predominantly) on others' soil. The British monarchy barely got touched and America suffered little damage at home.

In all its forms, peace had everything to fear in the face of a profitable war and the transfer of power to the West. America was out of the war but selling arms to both sides. It had also remained out of WWI until it was drawn in by the organised sinking of the American passenger ship, the *Lusitania*. This pissed the Americans off no end, but it was the Zimmerman telegram that brought them into war.[19]

British Intelligence Officer: "During the First World War, the British were at desperation point. By 1915, they had virtually sold all their invisibles[20] in America and the Amis now wanted cash up front. The British were absolutely bled white and they came up with the idea of sinking the *Lusitania* to bring America into the war.

"War has a history of inciting its allies into battle by bombing them and blaming the enemy. The ship was loaded with American passengers, arms and munitions, and the hull was lined with gun cotton in the size and shape of bricks. The *Lusitania* had an auxiliary status as a fleet reserve, so she was a naval ship and the Germans were quite within their rights to sink her as it was carrying war cargo.

[19] The Zimmerman telegram was manufactured by the British to infuriate the Americans into WWI.

[20] 'Invisibles' are income generating shareholdings, shares, loans, insurance payments, payments for services, bonds, IOUs, interest and any non-finite goods.

"Churchill knew the gun cotton was stacked around the hull below the water-line and that a glancing blow from a torpedo would blow the gun cotton and then the whole ship. When Nobel was discovering dynamite in the 19th century, gun cotton was one of the variations – an explosive and charge in one.

"The *Lusitania* went on several voyages with this gun cotton stacked up around the hull, and as First Lord of the Admiralty, Churchill was consulted as to its removal. 'Do the British remove it each time, or do they remove it in England or America?' The British were paranoid about it. The potential of the gun cotton lining the hull split British loyalties between America as a trading partner versus bringing America into the war.

"Churchill didn't want the *Lusitania* to sink on the way to America as it would have British cargo and passengers on board and wouldn't bring about the required retaliation. He wanted it to sink on the return journey from America while loaded with Americans, in order to swing tax-free America into war.

"In the Port of New York, the Chief of German Naval Espionage, Von Rintelen (who called himself 'The Dark Invader') boarded the *Lusitania* to see if she was indeed carrying war cargo. It was very important that the facts be verified before she was sunk. Von Rintelen passed the information back to Germany in code that the ship was indeed carrying gun cotton, ammunition and explosives. The *Lusitania* left New York from Qunard's Pier on 1 May 1915 and sailed towards Liverpool.

"In a naval cipher the Germans could understand, Britain broadcast instructions to the Navy in Queenstown in Ireland to withdraw their escort cruiser in the Irish Sea, while at the same time telling the Germans what course the cruiser was taking.

"Eyewitnesses talk about a huge explosion. The German torpedo hit the ship and ripped the bottom out of it. The *Lusitania* was a very fast ship and she was travelling at 15 to 18 knots. As soon as the torpedo hit, the gun cotton blew out the bottom of the ship and she ploughed under. It would normally take 1–2 hours for a ship like this to sink, but because gun cotton lined the hull, she sank in 18 minutes. That's why the death toll was so high. If it had just been ordinary cargo she may have remained afloat and even been towed to an Irish Port.

"This act of enemy-informed Allied sabotage was designed to bring the Americans into the war, which it did for the most part. Six days after the *Lusitania* sailed with 1,959 passengers (including 123 Americans), she was sunk by a German submarine (U-boat) in the Atlantic. It was 7 May 1915."

Secret Service: "When divers started diving on the *Lusitania,* British Intelligence got really jumpy. They decided around 1998 to blow the rest of the ship up, to hide the fact that there was Naval gun cotton lining the hull of the ship and that nearly 1200 had died in an informed enemy attack on an allied ship, in order to bring America into the war. The sinking of the *Lusitania* was enemy informed Allied sabotage (EIAS)."

"The anti-German feeling that this event generated in the US was a factor in bringing that country into the First World War."[21]

The British then used the same tactic against the *Zamzam* in WWII, which was carrying a lot of American passengers. In April 1941 it was intercepted by the *Atlantis,* a well-informed German commerce raider. Commerce raiders often carried English-speaking Intelligence Officers to tune into Allied radio channels which forecast the locations of the ships hunting for them. These Intelligence Officers were often ex-merchant officers who had dealt with English passengers before. The Germans knew about the *Lusitania,* caught on to what was happening, secured the passengers of the *Zamzam* and then scuttled her.

Then in 1941 the British bombed the Dutch submarine that had prior knowledge of the Japanese attack on Pearl Harbor. Ironically, the attack on Pearl Harbor was based on the British Bywater Plan that the British had given the Japanese over a drinking session some 16 years earlier. Pearl Harbor worked and America joined WWII. Rather than supply both sides with arms and munitions, America joined WWII in earnest with full navy, army and air force involvement.

As more profits were made by the munitions factories, and more fathers died, orphaned children were becoming more and more common and available. Paedophilia and the military would be in bed forever.

As it turned out, there was no need for Hitler to send his best deputies and most convincing doppelgängers to negotiate for 'world peace'. It all turned out okay for Hitler. What he hadn't counted on was that once an agent of war you are always protected by those who profit from it most. "Blessed are the war-makers."

The most serious threat to Hitler's power had been the Stennes

[21] *The Oxford English Reference Dictionary.*

Rebellion. After 1945, Walther Stennes said: "Hitler might be dead (he was not even sure of that at the time) but it seemed that his spirit was very much alive . . . his next and highly characteristic step was to investigate the truth of the various stories of Hitler's death . . . He soon succeeded in tracking down an old friend who had served in Hitler's personal bodyguard and this veteran assured him that, although the direct evidence of his death was inconclusive, his physical and mental state when Berlin fell had been so bad as to make it certain that he could not have survived."[22] This was essentially a fob-off to a friend, saying, 'If he ain't dead, he soon will be, and don't bother looking'.

Jimmy Byrnes: "While in Potsdam at the Conference of the Big Four [7 July–2 August 1945], Stalin left his chair, came over and clinked his liquor glass with mine in a very friendly manner. I said to him: 'Marshal Stalin, what is your theory about the death of Hitler?'

"Stalin replied: 'He is not dead. He escaped either to Spain or Argentina.'"[23]

In August 1945, Stalin personally accused the British of "concealing the real Adolf Hitler". "A new feature in this belief was where Hitler was supposed to be hiding. In the summer of 1945 I had been told Hitler was in Spain or South America."[24]

Secret Service referring to the conversations with the IRA undercover 'Cuchullain': "Similarly the British also hid the fascist sympathiser King Edward VIII and Wallis Simpson in Portugal five years earlier in July 1940. Spain and Portugal have for centuries been in the hands of the British Secret Service and their compliance is guaranteed. Portugal is still referred to by the British as 'our oldest allies'."

There is another theory that Hitler died in the mid-1970s but this involved another doppelgänger. It was the same scam the British used with Martin Bormann allowing a reclusive doppelgänger to appear after Bormann's death. The illusion was always to be the denial of truth, with no timescale disregarded, and no expense spared.

As early as September 1944 orders were issued concerning the storage of papers belonging to Special Operations 1 which was linked

---

[22] *The Amiable Prussian*, pp. 180, 185, 186.

[23] Former Secretary of State Jimmy Byrnes in his book *Frankly Speaking*.

[24] Walter Laufenberg, *Hitler's Double*, quoting British Intelligence Officer, Lieutenant Colonel W. Byford-Jones on 20 April 1946.

with Ian Fleming's Naval Intelligence. The four rules, 'A', 'B', 'C' and 'D', lay down specific guidelines pertaining to the destruction of files belonging to SO1. Only category 'A' states anything to do with the files surviving. This resulted in most of the evidence being destroyed. No files containing sensitive material would reach the Public Record Office. As a result, there is little or no chance of any correspondence between key players surviving.

Scores of Nazis fled to South America after WWII. Argentina opened its Nazi files on 30 January 1992 but none of them were of Hitler. Hitler's file is most likely kept under presidential guard in Switzerland.

The British Public Record Office contains files under reference number FO898/257 dealing with Swiss matters. It is on permanent loan to the Foreign Office and is unlikely to be released in the foreseeable future.

Crashing the Duke of Kent
Flying Boat's Holy Ghost

King George VI installed his younger brother, the Duke of Kent as Grand Master Mason in 1939 and he became the Hereditary Grand Master of Anglo-American Freemasonry. The fourth son of King George V[1] married Marina, the Princess of Greece and Denmark (1906–68) and they had two sons.

The Duke of Kent was addicted to cocaine, morphine and sex, both with men and women. He didn't care which. He had a long string of affairs before marriage and continued these during his marriage making his wife one of the most cuckolded women in history, next to the Queen.

His better known female partners included Ethel Margaret Whigham who became the Duchess of Argyll, Indira Raje, the Maharani of Cooch Behar, banking heiress Poppy Baring, musical star Jessie Mathews, black cabaret singer Florence Mills, and American socialite and drug addict Kiki Preston (née Alice Gwynne) with whom he had an illegitimate child. Parenthood didn't slow them down and they had a ménage à trois with the bisexual Jorge Ferrara, son of an Argentine ambassador.

The Duke of Kent also had affairs with his distant cousin, Louis Ferdinand, Prince of Prussia, his half-bother Anthony Blunt (making him an incestuous homosexual) and actor Noel Coward for 19 years, explaining why so many of Coward's plays were inflicted upon us. (Whoever gets to root the most royals for the longest gets the patronage). The Duke of Kent wrote love letters to Noel Coward and these were stolen from Coward's house in 1942. He also wrote love letters to a male prostitute who responded by blackmailing him.

The Duke of Kent's eldest son, Prince Edward, was the son of a cocaine and morphine addict and was born with a face like sin in a silly mirror. Lacking the required looks for royal acceptance, the family moved from London to Buckinghamshire in 1936 to keep all male members out of the public eye.

---

[1] The fifth son of King George V, Prince John (1905–19) was retarded and largely ignored. All were the half-brothers of the treasonous spy Anthony Blunt.

The Murder of Lord Erroll

Josslyn Victor Hay was the 22nd Lord Errol. He was the son of the British High Commissioner in the Rhineland, had a photographic memory, was an excellent public speaker and was part of the Clivedon set.

Lord Erroll came to see both sides of the war – the British side, the German side . . . and the bankers side. He understood Hitler's fascism to be a front for the communism that was to come and he had enough connections to understand the occult links between Churchill and Hitler. Erroll was aware of how the Crown bankers had used Hitler to create a war of profit and social change to their liking and he said as much within earshot of MI-5.

Little did Lord Erroll know,
the privately owned Crown bankers, the Rothschilds,
had also grown and developed Hitler.

MI-5's primary role was protecting the national status quo and any insightful revelation was an unwanted revelation. Churchill was advised and Errol had to go.

Churchill discussed this with the Duke of Hamilton and they colluded to murder the 22nd Lord Errol, Josslyn Victor Hay. On 7 September 1940, the 14th Duke of Hamilton met with others to discuss the murder. Five days later the contract was handed over to the Special Operations Executive from where it went to Cairo under the name Operation HIGHLAND CLEARANCE.

Lady Diana Broughton had a penchant for forcing men to perform cunnilingus on her at gunpoint and she literally came with a bang. Sir Henry and Lady Broughton were two MI-5 assets. In November 1940 they travelled to Happy Valley, north of Nairobi, in Kenya and involved Lord Erroll in a love-triangle.

The following month, in December 1940, an SOE couple entered Kenya and late on the night of 23 January 1941, Lord Erroll dropped Lady Broughton off at her home and then drove past the SOE couple who were pretending to have engine trouble by the side of the road. Lord Erroll gave the female a ride back towards town. With two radio-controlled MI-5 teams following, she pointed the gun at Erroll who stopped the car. She had him kneel in the passenger foot-well of his car. It was close to midnight on 23 January 1941 and she shot him in the back of the head execution style.

Lord Erroll was wearing his army uniform at the time and up to the point of death, the whole experience was not dissimilar to the way Lady Brougthon had treated him.

Diana's husband, Sir Henry 'Jock' Broughton was charged with the murder. MI-6 usually fit people up, but because 'both were MI-5 assets and party to the intelligence hit, and Jock had been knighted, the trial was a distraction so that any real evidence by the real killers was never followed up. Jock was found 'not guilty'.

Even before this information came out, it was widely accepted in intelligence circles that Lord Erroll's murder was an intelligence hit on the orders of Winston Churchill – one of many for Winston. In this case he used the 14th Duke of Hamilton to come up with the plan and have it executed.

The Duke of Hamilton was a homosexual occultist. He was having an affair with Albrecht Haushofer, the son of Rudolf Hess' mentor, Karl Haushofer, who had originated the concept of lebensraum. This gave Churchill leverage over Hamilton who was a higher-ranking Freemason than Winston.[2]

Such cause célèbre (big fuck ups) were common and this one was illustrated in the movie *White Mischief* in 1987. The movie makers brought it to our attention, but they still muffed it.

Flying Boats

Most large cities were on the coast or rivers and in the late 1930s runways didn't exist. Airfields were short, often rough, and before retractable wheels, planes were no faster than flying boats. Nevertheless, Sunderland flying boats were not the best of planes. They were much loved but underpowered, slow to take off, had limited range, were sabotaged by their manufacturers and their service crews, and were involved in every political machination of blind patriotism, royal anarchy and overt sabotage. As a result Sunderlands were in a constant state of ever-changing non-development.

Sunderlands appeared to be capable and threatening, had plenty of small .303 weaponry and were known as "Flying Porcupines".

[2] Kevin Abrams & Scott Lively, *The Pink Swastika*. See the chapter 'Homo-Occultism'. The remainder of this 'White Mischief' section was updated using the 30 April 2006 article posted by Henry Makow PhD, "The 'Ugly' Cause Of World War Two, The Murder Of Lord Erroll".

However they were large and slow, fuel and explosives were stored together, they were prone to self-sabotage, sabotage, forward radar detection and attack.

Sunderlands were "Flying Turtles". They were much loved flying death traps and those who survived even reconnaissance missions were lucky to survive reconnaissance missions.

Arthur Gouge, Sunderlands and Saunders-Roe

Oswald Short and Francis Webber designed the first metal-hulled flying boat, the diminutive Cockle which first flew on 18 September 1924. Arthur Gouge then succeeded Webber as chief designer and designed the Singapore I from which the Sunderland emerged. The Seaplane Works at Rochester built 27 flying boats of eight different designs from the launch of the Singapore I flying boat on 17 August 1926 (a bi-plane flying boat) to the first Sunderland/Empire/C Class flying boat in 1936.

In 1934 the British postmaster general declared that all first-class Royal Mail should go by air.[3] This effectively subsidised air travel and led to a contract for long-range flying boats which went almost immediately to the Short Brothers of Rochester, England. It was an inside job, but their only competition was the Supermarine and they were busy with the Spitfire.

The head of the design team, with a huge influence over research and development, was Arthur Gouge (later Sir Arthur Gouge) and he ensured that underpowered and overtaxed British engines were used for as long as possible. This led to slow and expensive travel, a high turnover of engines, many unnecessary crashes, many failed rescues and many failed escapes.

Saunders-Roe Ltd believed flying boats were going to be the next big thing after the war so they took over Shorts in 1943 in what was as close as you could get to a company takeover during wartime. At the same time Oswald Short resigned as Chairman of Shorts to become Honorary Life President and Arthur Gouge become Vice-Chairman of Saunders-Roe Ltd. This meant that Arthur Gouge had taken over from Oswald Short and was now in charge of design and construction.

[3] Sources: Terry Gwynn-Jones, *The Flying Porcupine Earns Its Name*, Aviation History, March 1999, 30:36; *British Warplanes of World War II*, edited by Daniel J. March, Airtime Publishing, 1998; Robert L. Gandt, *China Clipper*, Naval Institute Press, 1991; William Green, *War Planes of the Second World War*, Vol. 5, 'Flying Boats', Doubleday and Company, 1962; Geoffrey Norris, *The Short Sunderland*, Profile Publications, late 1960s.

The first thing Saunders-Roe did was sell Americans the idea that German flying boats were aiding German communication and escapes. The Americans then shot down German flying boats and this eliminated much of Saunders-Roe's post-war competition. The only competition left was American and mainly the Spruce Goose.

As Vice-Chairman of Saunders-Roe, Arthur Gouge's main responsibility was to direct the design and construction of the Shetland R 14/40 flying boat. It was assembled in October 1944 at the Short's factory at Rochester and weighed 56,700 kg, three times the size of an early Sunderland.

The Brabazon committee met in 1944 to establish the shape of British post-war commercial aircraft and were considering flying boats for the South Atlantic and Pacific routes. Saunders-Roe had detailed proposals for large flying boats up to 150,000 kg, three times the size of the Shetland and nine times the size of the Sunderland. The huge passenger aircraft was designed to steal all passenger travel around the world. The Saunders-Roe SR 45 Princess was launched on 29 August 1952. The second Princess never received any engines. It was launched on water on 13 February 1953 and towed straight to storage. The third Princess never received engines and all were scrapped by 1967.

The Princess (top) and the Spruce Goose flying into oblivion.

The Princess, which turned out to be a flying pig, was smaller than Howard Hughes' Spruce Goose flying boat. The US Government was on Hughes back and denied him the use of aluminium so he built his 180,000 kg plane out of birch wood and flew it a short distance on 2 November 1947. Other than that, it too went into storage, as did much of flying boat history.

Howard Hughes

Howard Hughes had made himself as rich as God during WWII and had multiple world air-speed records. He was a truth talker and had no feelings for anyone else in the American Aviation Industry. Hughes became too much of a problem for the American Military Industrial Complex and the Mafia, so they had the Mafia kidnap him in the late 1950s during post-war manoeuvring. The Mafia then gave Hughes to the Mormon Mafia who guarded him on contract, blacked out the windows of any penthouse he was living in and turned him into a heroin junkie.

Officially "Hughes only had his hair cut and nails trimmed once a year, was addicted to codeine and valium, was surrounded by Mormons because he trusted them, had contracted syphilis as a young man and had obsessive-compulsive disorder." In November 1966 Hughes moved Las Vegas and within two years he bought the Desert Inn and lived on the ninth floor. He then bought Castaways, New Frontier, The Landmark Hotel and Casino, Sands and the Silver Slipper. All of these hotels were purchased off the Mafia, essentially for the Mormon Mafia. This suited the FBI down to the ground as it severed Mafia ties to Las Vegas. The Mormon Mafia committee mainly consisted of Latter-day Saints.

> The FBI, via Hughes and the Mormon Mafia, were buying up Las Vegas.

Howard Hughes' kidnap was covered by a marriage to Jean Peters on 12 January 1957, although the whole relationship was carried out by phone. He spent the last twenty years of his life as a prisoner and was then killed on "5 April 1976".

In 1970 the Mormon Mafia sold Clifford Irving a copy of the computer-generated biography of Howard Hughes before it was published. Clifford published it as the co-author and made a fortune out of *Autobiography of Howard Hughes*. The biography was denied by Howard Hughes on television on 9 January 1972. Hughes denied it by telephone conference by talking to seven journalists he'd known prior to his kidnapping. Hughes did not appear on the TV. Irving claimed "the voice was probably fake". The Mormon that sold Irving the computer-generated manuscript was hunted down and killed and Irving had to go to prison for 17 months (from 16 June 1972) which really pissed him off.

Autobiography of Howard Hughes appeared on the net in 1999 and it is the most truthful account of Howard Hughes' life. Lies and cover ups are not limited to any media or any time frame and filming for *The Hoax* began in July 2005. *The Hoax* is based on Clifford Irving writing *Autobiography of Howard Hughes* as a hoax. It wasn't. Meryl Streep's daughter Jane Gray stars in the movie. That should give *The Hoax* all the kudos it doesn't deserve.

When Hughes died in 1976 he only weighed 41 kg (90 pounds). He was such a changed man that the FBI had to resort to fingerprint identification. His real death occurred much later in the 1980s. I spoke with someone who was contracted to kill him, but he was removed from the job due to benevolence on a previous contract.

Sunderlands/C Class/Empire Flying Boats

Sunderlands were collectively known as 'Empire flying boats' from a Short Brothers self-promotional letter dated 25 May 1935, a year before the first was launched. Use of the word "Empire" helped to sell them as a luxury and justify the expense of the flights. Sunderlands were way behind the Boeing Clippers and Sikorsky transatlantic flights and this was a huge embarrassment to the puffed-up British. American Clippers were flying from San Francisco to Hawaii in 1939 whereas the Sunderlands needed refuelling every 800–965 km. The British compensated for this by loving their flying boats, all 42 of them.

"All the 42 Empire 'boats were built in the main assembly shop – No. 3 Shop – of the Seaplane Works at Rochester, beside the River Medway in Kent. The first s.23, Construction number S. 795 G-ADHL CANOPUS, went down the famous, and still existing, slipway outside the Shop in July 1936 and the last S.1026 G-AFRA CLEOPATRA, in May 1940 . . . 12,000 drawings were needed to construct the first Short Empire flying boat. It seems that all the originals were later destroyed . . . All the original tracing masters and stress calculations have been destroyed. The fact that nearly every single print has completely disappeared is difficult to believe but seems to be true . . . none of the aircraft themselves have survived."[4]

[4] Brian Cassidy, *Flying Empires, Short 'C' class Empire flying boats*, Queen's Parade Press, 2004.

The first Sunderland model, the s.23 flew on 4 July 1936 and was named CANOPUS. It weighed 16,846 kg and took 17 seconds to leave the water. They were commonly known as Empire flying boats. Imperial Airways Limited (IAL) that flew them called them the 'C class'. The names were always in full capitals and all began with the letter 'C'. They were also prefixed with who they were flying for, like RMA (Royal Mail Service, 1936–40), TEAL for New Zealand, and QEA for Qantas.[5]

As with the development of all war planes, the pressing into military service of civilian planes, the names of the planes and even the drawings of those planes were an area of confusion, sabotage and self-sabotage. The CANOPUS was the name of the first Sunderland, but it was also the common generic name of the shorter flying boats made before the Sunderland, both of which were made by a company called "Short". Hence a short Short Sunderland was a Canopus and the first Sunderland was a long CANOPUS made by Short.

In order the Sunderlands were named CANOPUS, CALEDONIA, CENTAURUS,CAVALIER,CAMBRIA,CASTOR,CASSIOPEIA,CAPELLA, CYGNUS, CAPRICORNUS, CORSAIR, COURTIER, CHALLENGER, CENTURION, CORIOLANUS, CALPURNIA, CERES, CLIO, CIRCE, CALPYSO, CAMILLA, CORINNA, CORDELIA, CAMERONIAN, CORINTHIAN, CHEVIOT/COOGEE/VH-ABC, CORIO, COORONG, CARPENTARIA/G-AFBJ, COOLANGATTA, COOEE/G-AFBL, CHAMPION, CABOT, CARIBOU, CONNEMARA, CLYDE, CAPTAIN COOK /AO-TEA-ROA/AWARUA, CANTERBURY/AUSTRALIA/CLARE, CUMBERLAND/AWARUA/AOTEAROA, CATHAY, CLIFTON, CLEOPATRA and another never named, but referred to as G-AFRB.

The last three planes (CLIFTON, CLEOPATRA and G-AFRB) were ordered on 7 June 1939 by which time at least 7 Sunderlands had crashed.

This last Sunderland was registered on 27 January 1939, the hull was stored on 12 April 1940 and it was scrapped in 1943. It was never flown.

[5] Names beginning with 'C' was repeated by TEAL and BOAC when the Boeing 377 Stratocruisers were delivered in 1949 and they even used the same names: Caledonia, Caribou, Cambria, Canopus, Cabot, Castor, Cathay, Champion, Cleopatra, Coriolanus, Cordelia, Cameronian, Champion, Clio and Clyde. This was repeated again in 1963 when the US named their de Havilland Comet 4C XS 235, Canopus. This helped to maintain confusion over the names of pre-WWII planes, WWII planes, post-WWII planes, British planes, American Planes and Australian planes. When it comes to planes, confusion is the name of the game before, during and after war and identifies long-term allies.

With a shortage of aeroplanes during WWII this was pure sabotage, but there was purpose to this sabotage. Almost all salvaged parts were attributed to this last stored unflown plane.

Name Changes

Eight flying boats had their original names changed. Three of these were delivered to New Zealand and another three to Australia. The other two name changes are not listed.

Sunderland produced three boats (Construction No.s S.884, S.885 and S.886) and named them CAPTAIN COOK, CANTERBURY and CUMBERLAND. All of these names were changed and they were changed in the most confusing fashion. New Zealand and Australian flying boats had a second use covering for anything and everything Britain wanted covered up. Flying boats were also paid for by New Zealand, were not delivered, and were retained, flown and destroyed by the British.

S.884 CAPTAIN COOK was registered as G-AFCY CAPTAIN COOK and delivered on 21 April 1939. Strangely its much celebrated entrance onto Auckland's Waitemate Harbour was four months later on 28 August 1939, just 12 days before WWII officially started. It had flown 20,000 km from Southampton and done the Horseshoe route, but this would only take four days. CAPTAIN COOK was sold to New Zealand as AO-TEA-ROA with the New Zealand registration ZK-AMC, but the New Zealand government protested over the hyphenated name and it was renamed AWARUA. It was broken up in Auckland after 1953.

S.885 CANTERBURY became G-AFCZ AUSTRALIA, but never reached Australia or New Zealand who had paid for it. It was 'delivered' on 24 April 1939, retained by IAL and BOAC, ran aground at Basra on 10 August 1939 after 4 months service and was renamed CLARE. CANTERBURY/AUSTRALIA/CLARE was destroyed by fire on 14/15 September 1942 off Bathurst, West Africa.

S.886 CUMBERLAND was launched as G-AFDA AWARUA and delivered on 25 May 1939, arriving four months later. It had the New Zealand registration ZK-AMC (the same registration as S.884). It was then renamed AOTEAROA (the same name, but without the hyphenation) and re-registered as ZK-AMA (a new registration). "This became the first of the TEAL flying boats" and "was broken up in Auckland after October 1947".

CAPTAIN COOK changed its name to AO-TEA-ROA and then AWARUA.

CANTERBURY changed its name to AUSTRALIA then CLARE.

CUMBERLAND changed its name to AWARUA and then AOTEAROA.

Both CAPTAIN COOK and CUMBERLAND had the same New Zealand registration, ZK-AMC and both were called AOTEAROA and AWARUA, but in a different order.

ZK-AMC AWARUA and ZK-AMA AOTEAROA criss-crossed the Tasman countless of times and were used countless of times to search for enemy vessels. Both were fitted with bright Leigh searchlights.

CANTERBURY/G-AFCZ AUSTRALIA/CLARE never made one flight over the Tasman Sea and never landed in New Zealand waters. Britain owes New Zealand £36,200 for this Sunderland they never delivered – NZ$ 2.5 million in todays money. I'll take a 5% finders fee.

Strange Goings On in Australia

The CARPENTARIA was delivered to Australia on 3 December 1937. It was broken up in Hythe in January 1947.

The COOEE was delivered to Australia on 30 March 1938 and was broken up in Hythe in February 1947.

The COOGEE was officially delivered on 3 January 1938 and was named CHEVIOT by the British, with construction number S849. It officially crashed in Townsville on 1 March 1942 after 4 years service. In reality (not the faked record books and press releases), it was delivered to Australia in February 1942 (4 years after it was officially delivered) and underwent a 50 hour inspection.

COOGEE was parked on the water outside the Queens Hotel in Cleveland Bay, Townsville and the Australian pilots were about to take it on its maiden test flight, late on the Friday summer afternoon.

The British were there and they wanted the plane back after having not delivered it for four years, so the British did a Scottish marriage number on the Aussies.

A Scottish marriage is when the bride's father gets the groom-to-be drunk before the wedding and marries him to the wrong daughter. The son-in-law then elopes with his intended bride and the married daughter keeps his land and titles, with the Scottish father effectively in control.

Drinking before a flight during wartime warrants a court marshal. Townsville is tropical and February is peak summer, so the British invited the pilots and crew for a celebratory drink on the Friday afternoon. The COOGEE Sunderland crashed during takeoff at 6.02 pm on Friday 27 February 1942 and of the 11 pilot-and-crew, six of the crew were officially written off as "missing believed killed".

The crewmembers were picked up, advised of the impending court marshal, and hidden under canvas. Half of the crew (those that were not injured) were given fake funerals and commissioned to work Sunderlands for secret wartime missions. In return the injured crew were not charged (the pilot was seriously injured) and their places of burial are given, but the dates are not.

COOGEE was only partially submerged. The British salvaged it from the water and returned it to Britain. It was repaired and returned to British service under an unlisted name, probably with the same name as another plane.

The COORONG was delivered on 26 February 1938 and stranded at Darwin 10 months later on 12 December 1938. It was rebuilt at Rochester (UK) and reverted to British registry in 1939 as G-AEUI. It was broken up on 10 February 1947.

The COOGEE VH-ABC being loaded.

The COORONG is not present in Brian Cassidy's *Flying Empire* list of crashed or stranded Sunderlands. The book published by the Queen's Parade Press, lists downed Sunderlands. This included planes holed while taxing to shore, but does not include planes stranded during take off.

After the repair, the COORONG was effectively unnamed (except as G-AEUI) and became involved in special work under British tenure. A plane with letters not read as a name was all the more difficult to follow.

The CORIOLANUS was 'delivered' on 17 June 1937, although it officially reached Australia in 1942. It was broken up in Sydney at the end of 1947.

The CAMILLA was 'delivered' on 13 September 1937 and crashed 5 miles west of at Port Moresby on 22 April 1943, although it officially reached Australia in 1942.

The CLIFTON was 'delivered' on 17 March 1940 and crashed in Sydney on 18 November 1944, although it officially reached Australia in 1942.

The CORIOLANUS, CAMILLA and CLIFTON had three to five years of British service before they officially reached Australia in 1942. When they officially reached Australia in 1942, the CARPENTARIA and the COOEE were re-registered in Britain as G-AFBJ and G-AFBL. Before and after 1942, the CARPENTARIA and COOEE appeared on both British and Australian registries.

COORONG changed its name to G-AEUI.

CARPENTARIA changed its name to G-AFBJ.

COOEE changed its name to G-AFBL.

These Sunderlands were not given any further names and were moved to British registry for use in special work. Due to Short's self-sabotage, this was no work at all followed by crashes in place of more memorably named planes.

Changing plane names to a previous plane's name, registering planes with the same number, registering planes with the same name but not hyphenated, registering planes with the same name but in a different order, changing plane names after repairs, changing plane names to letters only, changing plane registries, having planes registered in two countries, exchanging planes between countries and naming a plane after a country for another country again and then retaining it under British command, official delivery years after actual delivery, using salvaged parts and attributing them fixed to an unflown plane . . . all helped to confuse the Sunderland registry. This was common practise amongst the British both before, during and after WWII and the British continued this with the Messerschmitt manufacturing records when they took over Germany and Austria in April 1945.

Short Self-Sabotage

Shorts also modified Sunderlands to client requirements and gave them ordered names like Mark I, II, III, IV when little of that order existed. The second flying boat off the Short Shop line, CALEDONIA, is cited as both a Mark I and Mark III.

Constantly "upgrading planes" in non–effective ways, and disregarding all beneficial requests for effective upgrades (often at the last minute) meant that it was diabolically difficult to follow the progress of the Sunderland – if indeed there was any. Even the Australians request for 20 mm cannons was sabotaged at the last minute.

It appears that any 'effective progress' made by Shorts on the Sunderland was immediately withdrawn. Any progress on the Sunderland, or any progress by Shorts was either stopped, sabotaged, or shipped to Germany for Germany to have as 'their invention', to be used to 'their advantage' during WWII.

Short, Saunders-Roe, the Sunderland and the Mistral were heavily sabotaged against the British for the benefit of the Germans and the British royal family. The Mistral, for instance, was invented by Shorts and then shipped to Rechlin, a small remote village in Mecklenburg-Vorpommern, Germany, from where many of the British royal family originated, including Princess Luise, Prince Albert's mother.

Sunderland Crashes

The Sunderland flying boats were an icon. Every country wanted one as it pegged them in the 'modern' age just as sky towers and EFTPOS did in the 80s. Sunderlands were a symbol of pride and they were bought by countries. Shorts made a lot of money out of their sabotaged Sunderlands and when they crashed, countries simply bought another one . . . at £37,000 . . . and these crashes were frequent, sometimes occurring within days of service.

1. CAPRICORNUS crashed at Ouroux in France on 24 March 1937 after 8 days service.
2. COURTIER crashed in Athens on 1 October 1937 after 5 mth serv.
3. CYGNUS crashed at Brindisi on 5 December 1937, 9 months serv.
4. CALPURNIA crashed at Lake Habbaniyah, 27 Nov. 1938, 17 mth serv.
5. **COORONG** stranded at Darwin on 12 December 1938 after 10 mths service but is not listed as a "down plane" in *Flying Empires.*
6. CAVALIER crashed in the North Atlantic on 21 January 1939, 3 yrs serv.
7. CAPELLA was holed in Batavia harbour on 12 March 1939, 26 mth serv.
8. CENTURION crashed in Calcutta on the Hoogly river at Calcutta on 1 May 1939 after 2 years service.
9. CHALLENGER crashed at Mosambique on 12 May 1939, 2 yrs serv.
10. CONNEMARA was destroyed by fire in Southampton water on 19 June 1939 after 3 months service.
11. **CANTERBURY** ran aground at Basra on 10 August 1939 after 4 months service.
12. **CARIBOU** was lost between Bodo, Norway and an undisclosed location on 4 May 1940. Because nothing was found, it was not listed as downed. Its crash is debateable and is not counted as "downed" in *Flying Empires.* CARIBOU was swished for special work including the back up plane for 'Crashing the Duke of Kent'.
13. **CABOT** was destroyed off Mauren Island near Bodo, Norway on 5 May 1940 (14 months service). It is debateable whether it was the CABOT or the COORONG/G-AEUI that was destroyed.
14. CLYDE was wrecked by a hurricane while at anchor on the Tagus river in Lisbon on 14 February 1941 after 23 months service. CLYDE was not counted as "downed" in *Flying Empires.*
15. CLIO was modified September 1940–March 1941. It did one patrol and then crashed on its test flight at Loch Indal, Islay Island, Argyllshire on 22 August 1941. Test flights could last up to 400 hours. CLIO's effective service was 3 years.
16. CASSIOPEIA crashed at Sabang on 29 December 1941, 4 yrs serv.
17. CORIO was shot down near Koepang on 30 January 1942, 4 yrs serv.
18. COOLOANGATTA crashed at Sydney on 2 February 1942, 7 yrs serv.
19. CIRCE was lost without trace between Broome and Tijlatjap (seaport on Java's southern coast) on 28 Feb. 1942, 6½ yrs serv.

20. **COOGEE** (not the COOEE) crashed in Townsville on 1 March 1942 after 4 years service.
21. CENTAURUS was destroyed on its moorings at Broome on 3 March 1942 after 3 years service.
22. CORINNA was also destroyed on its moorings at Broome on 3 March 1942 after 3 years service. *Flying Empires* did not list this plane.
23. CORINTHIAN crashed at Darwin on 22 March 1942, 4½ yrs serv.
24. CALYPSO crashed at Daru, Papua New Guinea, 8 Aug. 1942, 3 yrs serv.
25. The **Duke of Kent's Sunderland** crash on 26 August 1942. This was not listed in *Flying Empires* probably because it was published by Queen's Parade Press. The plane was either the **CABOT, CARIBOU, COORONG or COOGEE.**
26. **CANTERBURY/AUSTRALIA/CLARE** destroyed by fire off Bathurst, West Africa on its way to Lisbon on 14/15 September 1942 after 2 years service. Four crew were never recovered. It was owned by New Zealand, but never delivered.
27. CERES was destroyed by fire at Durban on 1 Dec. 1942, 5½ yrs serv.
28. CAMILLA crashed 5 miles west of Port Moresby on 22 April 1943 (1–5½ years service). Although it crashed in shallow water, the wreck has never been recovered, not even by recent divers.
29. CLIFTON crashed in Sydney on 18 November 1944, after 2–4½ years service.

In the authoritative *Flying Empires, Short 'C' class Empire flying boats,* Brian Cassidy does not list the crash of the Duke of Kent's Sunderland on 26 August 1942, nor whether it was a Mark I, Mark II, Mark III or Mark IV; what s. number it had, what Construction No. it had, its registration number, modifications, the name of the plane, the time or date of the crash, nor where it crashed. To all intents and purposes, the Queen's Parade Press does not acknowledge that the Duke of Kent died in a Sunderland flying boat. Ipso facto, nor does the Queen.

Swishing the Duke of Kent's Plane

The Duke of Kent's Sunderland may have been the Mark II listed as "special". That is, with modifications that were not specified, like a starboard door or an escape hatch through the floor of the cabin. All doors and hatches could be opened from the outside.

The 'special' plane is identified as CABOT from its production schedule and was ordered ten months into King George VI reign. George VI was the Duke of Kent's brother.

Both the CABOT and the CARIBOU had two passenger doors and both were capable of refueling in flight. Both were s.30s.

The CARIBOU was built to replace the COURTIER that crashed in Athens on 1 October 1937 after only 5 months service. CARIBOU was a Mark III, construction No. S.881. CABOT was construction No. S.880 and also a Mark III. "It is thought the unspecified Mark II (S.880) boat ended up in New Zealand"[6]

Although flying boats that ended up in New Zealand and Australia were an area of confusion unto themselves and Australasia was the blaming ground for flying boats, S.880 CABOT did not end up in New Zealand, nor did S.881 CARIBOU. The two New Zealand boats were both Mark IV. Brian Cassidy's remarks are a lost leader that comes straight from the Queen's Parade Press/the Queen.

Further on Queen's Parade Press has another crack at confusion.

"The standard s.23 'boats were known at Rochester as Mark I aircraft, the two 'Bermuda' 'boats as Mark IIs and the two first generation 'Atlantic' 'boats, as Mark IIIs. The first s.30 – a replacement for G-ADVC COURTIER with Construction Number S.879 – was known as Mark I. [It was a Mark III.] The Mark II s.30 is listed as 'unspecified' [It had a starboard door.] The four second generation 'Atlantic' 'boats – Construction Numbers S.880 to S.883 – were known as Mark IIIs [correct] and two 'New Zealand' 'boats as Mark IVs [correct]. It seems that the 'unspecified' Mark II became the third 'New Zealand' 'boat – on the British register as G-AFCZ AUSTRALIA."[7]

Big ruse – the third New Zealand boat was the S.886 CUMBERLAND which changed its name to AWARUA and then AOTEAROA and had the British registration G-AFDA and the New Zealand registration ZK-AMC followed by ZK-AMA.

This may seem as dull as dishwater, but war was full of lies and it is important to expose the lies from every angle to ascertain which side your royal family was gunning for.

[6] Brian Cassidy, *Flying Empires*, p. 7, slightly paraphrased.
[7] Ibid, p. 7.

There was no great sequence to the order of Sunderlands. "The first order was for one Mark I 'boat – the 'prototype' (Construction No. S.759) and one Mark III 'Atlantic' 'boat (S.804). The first production batch comprised one Mark II 'variation on the Bermuda' 'boat (S.811), the original 'Bermuda 'boat (S.812), the second 'Atlantic' 'boat (S.813) and nine standard Mark Is (S.814–822) . . . The second production batch of fourteen Mark I s.23 'boats (S.838–851) was covered by the third order, placed on 2 September 1935. This batch brought the total fleet to twenty-eight aircraft.[8]

Equally, either one of the returned Australian planes could have been used to 'kill' the Duke of Kent including the COORONG/G-AEUI, CARPENTARIA/G-AFBJ, COOEE/G-AFBL, or COOGEE/VH-ABC. If asked to do so, the Australians would have supplied a Sunderland to kill the Duke of Kent, just because he was queer. That he didn't die in the crash didn't bother the Aussies, as long as they didn't know about it.

Sabotaging the Duke of Kent's Flying Boat

The s.30 is touted as being a heavyweight long-range Mark III. The CABOT, CARIBOU, CONNEMARA and CLYDE were the long-range Sunderlands. They had a Short and Medium wave receiver, a D/F receiver, a telephone control unit and a Type 240A On-off switch. Some of the s.30 were fitted with voice-pipes between the Captain's seat and the Navigator's position, but not all of them.

The Persus engines of the CABOT and CARIBOU were fitted with Graviner fire suppression equipment which operated automatically at 60 degrees Celsius and sprayed the engine surface, especially the manifold pipes and inside the cowling. Initially oil from the Sperry oil supply leaked on the discharge heads rendering them useless. This sabotage was noticed and these were replaced.

Nevertheless CABOT was still sabotaged and had a reconditioned starboard propeller off the salvaged CAPELLA (12 March 1939) or CHALLENGER (12 May 1939). Records attributed these to an s.33 when the CABOT was an s.30 – this is more sabotage, this time, records sabotage.

CARIBOU was originally fitted with Bristol Perseus engines (Serial No. 20505–20508) and de Havilland 5000 series constant-speed propellers (Serial No. 55997, 55998, 50008 and 55996). The port inner airscrew 50008 out of sequence and probably off the COORONG/AEUI.

[8] Brian Cassidy, *Flying Empires*, p. 54.

Three of the s.33 boats were equipped, partially or completely with reconditioned airscrews. This included the CABOT. In some records the CABOT is a Mark II special. In other records it is a Mark III s.30 and in other records it is a s.33. This is even more record sabotage.

De-icing equipment was fitted to the planes after production in 1938. CARIBOU was fitted with the latest de Havilland equipment and CABOT was fitted with the oldest equipment, the old Dunlop slinger rings.

Late in April 1940 V3137 CABOT and V3138 CARIBOU (RAF numbers) were stripped of their ASV radar and converted as transport aircraft for special missions to Norway. CABOT and CARIBOU were armed with seven Vickers .303 K guns with 4500 rounds and a fake gun made of a broomstick painted matt black installed in the tail's refueling cup – as shonky as shit. It was well-known at the time and reeks of self-sabotage. A working gun would have sufficed and a cannon would have been much better.

Many of the flying boats originally fitted in 1937 were re-equipped in 1939. Even this was sabotaged. On 10 September 1941 Modification 10141 referred to "the fixed fittings of complete Lorenz equipment, but actually received the 1124A only". Even some of these modifications didn't happen as the boats were sold back to BOAC on 19 September 1941 without the changes being made.

Defective parts within the first year or first 1000 hours of travel were to be replaced by Shorts. Disagreements were subject to arbitration by the Air Ministry. At Safety for Flight certificate inspections, the boat was swung and compass corrections were made.

Just before the summer trans-Atlantic season was to begin CABOT and CARIBOU were involved in a dispute over ownership (April 1940). BOAC assumed they were to be handed back for trans-Atlantic mail service and the RAF assumed they could do what they wanted with them. CABOT and CARIBOU were then sent to Hythe for their first 200-hour check. The War Cabinet then wrote a memo: "The two planes were to stay in military service and the mail service was cancelled". The trans-Atlantic mail service was only resumed after both planes were 'lost'.

> It was obvious the RAF and War Cabinet had special plans for these two planes and needed to 'protect' them.

Swishing a Plane for the Duke of Kent

CABOT left Hythe on 3 May 1940 heading for Invergordon. At midnight they left Invergordon to Harstad in the Lofoten Islands. With the long northern twighlight they could search for landing strips while darkness gave them some cover and they landed at Lofoten at 8.21 am. They slept through the day and searched for more fuel.

At 8 am on 4 May 1940 CABOT departed Harstad for Bodo, 248 km to the south and arrived in the middle of an *air raid alert* so the plane changed its flag to a Norwegian national flag and landed, or rather alighted on the water and moored up next to some Norwegian float planes and fishing boats and began to unload.

On 4 May 1940 CARIBOU left Hythe for the quick flight to Invergordon arriving at 8.05 pm adding three RAF gunners to their crew and a Norwegian translator. CARIBOU then left Invergordon and arrived at Harstad at 8.30 am on 4 May 1940. The 3 RAF gunners and the Norwegian translator then disembarked.

At 9.30 am CARIBOU departed [it doesn't say where to] and became a total loss at 9.45 am on 4 May 1940. CARIBOU was the 12th Empire boat and second s.30 to be written off.

CABOT was then moved out of Bodo harbour by two motorboats (including M.V. Sissy) during the long twilight. CABOT was moved 6.5 km north up the coast and moored off Mauren Island with the help of anchors borrowed from boats. The roundels were covered with blankets and the plane was covered with brush. The electrical system was to be repaired onboard the CABOT and the Vickers K guns were to be given ground mountings to ward off any Luftwaffe planes, but none of this happened.

All the RAF crew returned to Bodo with the Norwegian seamen who had helped them.

A Luftwaffe Junkers Ju 88 'discovered' CABOT the next day and destroyed it with incendiary bombs. The plane caught fire and sunk in the steeply shelving seabed. It was the 13th Sunderland and third s.30 to be written off.

The reports say there were no crew on board and also that the crew on board were injured and lay up in hospital listening to the radio salvaged off the CABOT.

Sabotaged Post-Swish History

CLIO and CORDELLA were then purchased by the Air Ministry from BOAC to replace the CARIBOU and CABOT lost at Bodo in Norway. CLIO and CORDELLA were then flown to Queen's Island in Belfast in September 1940 for much more extensive conversions. They were equipped with two Bolton-Paul four-gun power-operated turrets and internally stowed depth charges stored inboard as well as ASV radar (Anti-Surface Vessel) making them look like an Asian apartment.

CLIO and CORDELLA were ready in March 1941 (which kept them useless for 10 months) and delivered to 119 Squadron on Islay off the west coast of Scotland. CLIO flew one convoy protection patrol on 27 April 1941 and then crashed on its test flight near Bowmore on 22 August 1941. It was the 15th Sunderland to be written off and was the only plane that showed the ladder connection between the control deck and the lower deck.

119 Squadron was then disbanded and CORDELLA was given to 413 Squadron and then sold back to BOAC to be converted back to a standard s.23.

This effectively tied up four planes as useless from May 1940 to August 1941.

CARIBOU was lost, 'CABOT' was bombed, CLIO crashed in a test flight and CORDELLA went back to BOAC and was broken up at Hythe in 1947.

> After this string of loses, no one wanted to look at these planes, nor the history of these planes. That was the plan.

How the Swish was Done

Here's what really happened.

At midnight on 3/4 May 1940, CABOT was swished for a lesser Sunderland – the G-AEUI, previously Australia's COORONG. It was not uncommon for the CT & MGT (Colonial Trash and Machine Gun Thieves) to swap planes at midnight. This being the pattern, they were used as such. They also doubled for each other, stole and traded weaponry and mucked about with whatever was loose on any plane.

> Colonial Trash recognised the stupidity of the British and broke any and all rules to survive, which they did a whole lot better than the British. The British utilised this to their advantage on important missions.

At 8 am on 4 May 1940 'CABOT' (COORONG/G-AEUI) left Harstad and landed on nearby water at Bodo, Norway in the middle of an air raid *alert*, so they changed their display flag to a Norwegian flag. Due to the air raid *alert*, people were running for cover and no one had a good look at the plane. The air raid alert was arranged by the British.

On 4 May 1940 CARIBOU left Harstad (close to Bodo) at 8.30 am (half an hour after CABOTat 8 am) and was never seen again. There was still post air-raid alert panic about which took the attention off other plane details – like where CARIBOU was heading.

On the night of 4 May 1940 'CABOT'/COORONG/G-AEUI was towed 6.5 km north to Mauren Island and sunk, officially by Luftwaffe incendiary bombs. The fire destroyed any identifying aspects of the plane, including markings and modifications and the Sunderland sunk on a steeply shelving seabed. The Germans had been alerted to the location of the CABOT and sunk it. 'CABOT' was easy enough to spot. It was covered in brush, the roundels were covered in canvas, it had too many anchors, it was moored in a remote hideaway location . . . and German spies at Bodo harbour would have seen it towed out of the harbour at twilight.

The British had intended to move their guns off 'CABOT' and install them on a cliff top and had intended to repair their radio equipment, but none of this happened.

A result both the CABOT and the CARIBOU were swished.

CABOT was swished at Invergordon at midnight on 3/4 May 1940 and replaced with the COORONG, renamed G-AEUI. For its final trip the name on the side was painted "CABOT". COORONG had been returned to Britain in December 1939 and underwent repair work over 11 months. It was renamed G-AEUI and officially broken up in 1947 along with about fifty other Sunderlands at the same time. Even the breaking up of these planes had muffed records.

CARIBOU flew into secret work oblivion at 9.45 am on 5 May 1940.

CABOT was swished at midnight on 3/4 May 1940 and hidden under the control of the Duke of Hamilton. It was probably towed ashore in Argyllshire where Simon Fraser was still unpopular. CABOT was hidden until service on 23 August 1942 at Oban.

The service included final maintenance and checks which officially included "compass correction" and "refueling". In reality they included remote control devices, sabotage of the magnetos and maintenance on the starboard door (referred to as the "second hatch") that the CABOT and the CARIBOU both had. CABOT was then flown to Invergordon on 25 August 1942 for the Duke of Kent's flight on 26 August 1942.

CABOT and CARIBOU then became the plane and the seconder for the Duke of Kent's crash on 26 August 1942. They were modified to engineer the Duke of Kent's escape and crash afterwards.

CLIO and CORDELLA were then purchased as replacements and both were sabotaged. After that, no one wanted to look at the saga in any meritous detail.

So why go to such enormous trouble to hide two planes. The CABOT and the CARIBOU both had two passenger doors either side of the fuselage and were the only recorded Sunderlands to do so . . . so they needed to be lost. Manufacturing and fitting the second door was too risky. Someone would mention it in their memoirs.

When the Duke of Kent walked into the portside door of the Sunderland into the promenade cabin he gave instructions to the Flight Steward and then walked out the starboard door, complete with his entourage of homosexual cross-dressing royal party, all of whom would become his sexual partners in the after life. The Master Mason was about to become the Golden Dawn coven's new Holy Ghost.

> The Holy Ghost mission was so important no resources were spared. The CABOT s.30s Mark II "unspecified" was the 33rd Sunderland made and it had modifications that were not made known. This was ordered on 21 October 1937, five months into King George VI's official reign[9] and it was ordered to engineer his brothers disappearance. After all his brother was second in line to the throne and even the thought of a drug addict transvestite King of England made the retarded King of England blush and run for cover.

Eventually modifications to the CABOT and CARIBOU included radio control ability, complete with override. Radio control had been used since 1918 by Jewish British and was redeveloped by Shorts as the Mistral and gifted to the Germans as the Mistel. This was done publicly on the suggestion of a German pilot and then successfully used by the Luftwaffe from 1943. The Americans also went public with it in January 1947.

[9] King George VI's coronation took place on 12 May 1937.

The date of the Duke of Kent's crash is given as both 25 August 1942 and 26 August 1942. The earlier date could have been for the official photographs. On 26 August the Duke of Kent and his royal party simply walked out the starboard door onto the tender or the refuelling vessel. This done under cover of running the plane through its tests. These tests were noisy and everyone moved off.

Sabotage at Refueling

Sunderlands were the first British planes to use 87 Octane gas. This was mainly used by the Germans and showed extreme German leanings on the part of Arthur Gouge. The 87 octane aviation spirit, derived from crude oil in Mexico, required tetra-ethyl-lead additive, aromatics or both.[10]

In hot weather at over 1500 metres (5000 ft) the fuel system suffered from vapour locks as the 87 octane gas was highly flammable with a boiling point anywhere between 50–180 degrees Celsius. If two engines died the speed dropped below 240 kmph the loss of height was over 100 metres per minute, a straight course was difficult to maintain due to rudder flutter, and flap adjustments caused the plane to stall from 142 kmph. When flying over deserts a static discharge built up around the fuel tanks and this was also of great concern during refueling as the plane could explode.

In 1937 Shell ordered 27 self-propelled steel refueling barges for the Empire/Sunderland routes. These refueling barges were all named MEXSHELL, followed by a number. MEXSHELLs were 15.25 metres long (50 foot) and 3 metres wide (10 foot) and sat 1.45 metres (4 foot 9 inches) above the water. They were 15.5 tonnes empty and 27.6 tonnes[11] full and had a speed of 7 knots.

Each Sunderland took 11,250 litres in four tanks and the MEXSHELL pumped 9 litres per second through a Kent indicating meter (30 minutes to fill). Oil was also delivered through a flexible hose-line. Multiple pump lines could be used, but this proved dangerous as it required more than the usual three hands plus British Officer.

[10] Brian Cassidy, *Flying Empires, Short 'C' class Empire flying boats*, p. 175.

[11] The metric ton equal to 1000 kg or 2204.6 lbs is the only form of legal trade. The metric spelling is 'ton' and the European spelling is 'tonne'. The Imperial ton or long ton is 1016 kg or 2240 lbs and is used to measure aviation fuel and the capacity of ships. This was not used in the conversion of weights for the flying boats. With flying boats a ton/tonne is 1000 kg or 2204.6 lbs.

The test bucket was knocked over on the CONNEMARA on 19 June 1939 and it caught fire and sank resulting in one death and one serious burn victim. The plane had only been in service for three months.

On the MEXSHELL was the Coxswain, Pumpman and Deckhand. The Coxswain was in charge of the barge and seamanship. The Pumpman was responsible for refueling and the Deckhand was responsible for mooring the barge, casting off and assisting with refueling.

In important and remote locations a British Officer was also on board. In some instances he used his First Officer to replace him. Occasionally this First Officer was replaced with an ingénue, especially when 'accidents' occurred, either because of him, or to be blamed on him.

Refueling was done through the side or over the top. In sheltered harbours like Hythe or Invergordon it was done through the side via the refueling cock on the starboard side of the aircraft. In fast flowing harbours it was done over the top directly into each fuel tank. In rough weather it was done by cans directly into the tanks on top of the wing.

At each refueling the tanks were dipped to check the levels. At this point it was easy enough for the Pumpman to place a petrol pill in two of the tanks on one wing. These are usually wrapped in some form of plastic broken down by petrol. Today glad wrap is used.

This was not the method used on the Duke of Kent's Sunderland as refueling would have occurred through the starboard side and not over the top. A petrol pill could have been placed through the starboard side refueling cock, but this would not have provided enough control for the accident as it panned out. That is, the Duke of Kent's Sunderland crashed in a specific remote location, with a specific fall rate and not during the flyover farewell salute at Invergordon which would have caused the plane to lose altitude over water, thus enabling landing. The fall rate had to be swift and over land, preferably over recently traversed high ground.

It was the Coxswain, Pumpman and Deckhand's job to take the Royal party on board the MEXSHELL (hidden under canvas), or to cause distraction and cover while the tender did it. It was not the MEXSHELL's job to sabotage the plane.

Passengers were not allowed on board the Sunderland or the MEXSHELL during refueling. Refueling took place before passengers boarded and if refueling was to occur once passengers were on board, they were taken off on the designated tender. In tourist flights these were IAL tenders that brought passengers onto the flying boat when they were anchored rather than docked. So if the MEXHSELL was around for a fuel top up, there was an excuse for the tender to be around as well. The two worked hand in hand.

Heavily laden refueling barges were cumbersome vessels. Away from the main bases, seamanship was not the best and MEXSHELLs were known to hole Sunderland floats. At Hythe and Invergordon, seamanship was the best and both were sheltered harbours. The refueling of barges was left to the professionals and only the Coxswain, Pumpman and Deckhand were on the barges, although a British Officer was likely on board during important refueling as with the Duke of Kent.

When refueling through the side [normal] the supervisor opened up the mail loading hatch on the starboard side of the control deck. A bucket was placed inside the plane with a chamois over the top. Two litres of fuel was then pumped into the bucket to check for water. Fuel passed through and the water stayed on top of the chamois. This was a perfect time for various forms of sabotage and "the aircraft's main electrical switchboard, the fuel gauges and tank cocks were all within his easy reach."[12]

Refueling was a perfect place for last minute sabotage, like replacing switches with faulty switches or adding remote control devices. There was 30 minutes for the Pumpman, Coxswain, Station Officer or First Officer to act, but all up, refueling took around an hour and was prone to sabotage, explosion, escape and swish.

> As long as the MEXSHELL crew and British officer were in on it, any passenger on any refueling Sunderland could be swished on or off. A starboard passenger door just made it easier. For tenders and MEXSHELL's this was not uncommon practise. The author even did it as late as 1990, lying on top of airmail bags, avoiding the one's marked FRAGILE. All that was required was a phone call to the right person.

In the Duke of Kent's case, the MEXSHELL refueled, stayed alongside, the royal party boarded the flying boat, the pilots boarded and the royal party disembarked with the help of the tender and MEXSHELL, which motored off as the Sunderland underwent its rather noisy pre-flight checks.

[12] Brian Cassidy, *Flying Empires*, p. 176.

> Official records show the Sunderland refueled at Oban, but all offical records relating to the Duke of Kent's flight were faked. Due to the swish in progress anything went.

This was a military operation with military precision and had support from on shore (the Duke of Hamilton), on board the Sunderland (via instructions to the Flight Steward and base instructions to the pilot) and on board the tender and MEXSHELL – from the Duke of Hamilton, premier peer of Scotland, uncrowned king of England, leading Freemason, Wing Commander, and the Duke of Kent's lover.

> The Sunderland flew off without the royal party. If the royal party were caught, it would have been laughed off as a joke. There were no repercussions for getting it wrong.

The Duke of Kent becomes the Holy Ghost

Sunderlands had a history of self-sabotage. The British loved the planes but they rarely returned home. With this in mind, on 26 August 1942, Air Commodore HRH the Duke of Kent was reported to have taken off in a Sunderland and crashed 40 miles from take off.

Prince 'George' Edward Alexander Edmund of Great Britain and Ireland (20 December 1902–26 August 1942), 1st Duke of Kent (1934–42) and Grand Master Mason in (1939–42) was the fourth son of King George V, half-brother of lover Anthony Blunt, and a transvestite.

As Air Commodore HRH Duke of Kent, he was reported to have died in the crash of the Short Sunderland W4026 flying boat of 228 Squadron on 26 August 1942. His capacity was as the Inspector-General of RAF Welfare and he had intended to meet senior members of the US Military in Iceland as well as isolated RAF stations where bottles of whiskey would have been welcomed . . . other's say he was fulfilling his intelligence role and heading to Sweden for secret peace talks with Germans.

The Sunderland took off from Invergordon at 1.10 pm on 26 August 1942 bound for Iceland carrying a royal party of four plus a crew of 11. (Three of the four have never been named). It was heavily laden with fuel, ammunition, depth charges, whiskey, supplies, four royal party passengers and their kit (which was bulky and heavy), as well as the 11 crew.

The takeoff was lengthy with a slow climb due to the weight of the royal kit. When it reached its required altitude of 2000 feet it returned to Invergordon for a flyover farewell salute.

On the day of the crash the weather conditions were mild. It was summer. For the first part of the journey there was cloud at 1000 feet, clouds at 300 feet at Wick and bright skies North of the north coast of Scotland, but the Sunderland never got to Wick.

Flying north-east the Sunderland turned North 27 miles before it should have and crashed 18 miles south of Wick and only 40 miles from take off.

The flight crews instructions were to remain East of the east coasts of Scotland and one of the ways this 'mistake' could have occurred was by remote control. Remote controlled aircraft had been used since late 1918 when David Ben-Gurion used a Farman biplane against German artillery positions on top of Mount Kilimanjaro. It was the first flying bomb.

The crew did their pre-flight checks and duties in base HQ while the royal party boarded. They were the only passengers. The crew boarded and the Sunderland took off just a few minutes later. There was no chance of passing the pre-flight checks drunk and no time to start drinking before taking off.

The four final systems checks were the airscrew pitch controls, the engine fuel pumps, the magnetos and the engine boost. These were either done while the plane was stationary or while the flying boat taxied for take-off. In this case, they were done while the plane was stationary. The noise moved everyone away and made for an easier escape.

When the First Officer moved each of the four pitch levers from fine to coarse, it would cause a drop in engine speed. If any of the pitch-levers got stuck on coarse, it would cause one wing to drop on take-off. If this happened, take-off was abandoned.

The magnetos (On/off button for the engine) were also tested. The magnetos controlled the park plugs and there was one magneto for each spark plug with two magnetos and two spark plugs per engine.

In flight magnetos could be switched off by remote control and this would stop the engine. If two magnetos were switched off a Sunderland flying at 142 kmph with ¼ flap open at 380 feet over the new high ground would fall for 1 minute 16 seconds and crash 3 km from descent. If the Sunderland went into a dive, this would increase the height from descent and decrease the horizontal distance travelled.

With control over the two engines and flaps a Sunderland flying at 1000 feet could be crashed within 3 km in under 45 seconds. The Flight Steward would have been thrown about and possibly killed before the plane crashed. The noise in the cabin would have exceeded 60 decibels and the crew would have had difficulty hearing each other even when shouting.

The favourite method of communication from the Sunderland to base was by morse code. This was not possible when the plane was diving.

Drinking alcohol in the hours before flying warrants a court martial, so drunkenness can be dismissed as the cause of the crash, as can incompetence.

In the No 1 seat was commanding officer Wg Cdr Moseley and in No 2 seat was Flt Lt Frank Goyen, a highly experienced and competent pilot. The Duke of Kent was the commanding officer on the plane and "Everybody on board came under his orders, as the entire crew and the royal party must have known full well."[13]

Spymaster: "Before take off the Duke of Kent was standing between the two pilots which meant he was in a position to pressure them. The usefulness of this tactic varied in proportion to the colonial origin of the aircrew. New Zealand pilots would politely tell any interfering passenger to 'go boil your head'. Australian pilots, on the other hand, were quite rude."

> The plane was flying fine and "The crash must have occurred as the result of a navigational error, as almost everyone who is competent to comment on such matters agrees."[14]

As is common with 'destiny' air crashes, like Erebus in 1979, the plane had just been serviced. A few days prior the Sunderland had been serviced, checked and refuelled at 228 Squadron's base in Oban from where it was flown directly to Invergordon. Its navigational equipment had been reset. The bearing of the flight was correct, it's just that the turn north was made at 40 miles instead of 67 miles. How much the plane was refuelled was not stated, nor whether there was a top up at Invergordon.

Immediately after takeoff it was the role of Flt Sgt Andrew Simpson William Jack (the only survivor) to go the rear turret, close the steel doors behind him, face backward and turn the turret from side to

[13] Rob Nesbit, 'A Travesty of the Truth', *Aeroplane monthly*, p. 28–29.
[14] Ibid.

side only communicating if there was something vital to be said, like, "enemy air traffic".

The navigator and pilots could talk directly to each other, but the rear gunner was only connected via intercom and he had no view of the interior of the plane. There was also no communication with the passengers on the lower deck.

British planes were also peculiar in that the gunners could not look down. The Germans knew this and always did their best to attack from below. The rear gunner could not see below him, or what was happening in the plane on the upper deck, the lower deck, or if someone had parachuted out over the sea just before the plane crossed high ground.

These were all possibilities and due to the Freemasons draconian rule over Scotland, especially during WWII, many witness accounts have proved contradictory and many 'respectable' accounts, 'official' accounts and 'authoritative' accounts have been the work of down right liars working towards an agenda. Even the servicing records of the Sunderlands differed from what actually occurred.

Part of that agenda was avoiding the British royal family's shame at having the King's brother being a number carrying Abwehr agent, rampant homosexual, cross-dresser and drug user. The Duke of Hamilton assisted in this cover up using his role as Commander of the Air Training corps responsible for the defence of Scotland, Head Freemasons, premier peer and uncrowned King of Scotland . . . because he was one of the Duke of Kent's homosexual lovers and he wanted him all to himself.

The big flying boat had two decks – an upper deck for the flight crew and a lower deck with luxury passenger accommodation. When the Sunderlands were converted to delivering mail (stored on the upper deck), it is not clear how many passenger seats were left, but most importantly for this story, the Flight Clerk's office was moved down to the lower passenger deck, with no clear indication of either a direct ladder to the pilots or the normal circuitous route with stairs.

Extensive photos showed a ladder between the Flight Clerk on the lower deck and the pilot mail area on the upper deck, but no one who worked the flying boats has any record of the ladder. Thus there is a dispute over whether the Flight Clerk could access the pilots quickly and easily. The Flight Clerk/Steward did have intercom but it was 60 decibels inside the lower cabin, so shouting was common and even intercom conversations with the pilots were difficult, although it was quieter in the pilot's cabin.

CLIO crashed on 22 August 1941 and it was the only plane that showed the ladder connection between the control deck and the lower deck.

The s.23 could seat 7 in the Forward Cabin, 3 in the Centre Cabin, 8 in the Promenade Cabin and 6 in the Aft Cabin – a total of 24. Each cabin was on a different level and each rose two steps (0.5m) towards the rear. The pilot sat above and forward of the forward cabin in a completely enclosed area. The mail sat behind them.

Despite the pilots vast experience, and with no prior warning, the 'newly serviced' Sunderland banked 27 miles too early. It crashed 32 minutes after takeoff at 1.42 pm on Eagle's Rock, the highest rock in the area. Three miles inland from Dunbeath in Caithness, Eagle's Rock also had the advantage of being very remote.

This was exactly 15 months, 15 days, 15 hours an 15 minutes after Hess and doppelgänger Hess had cirlced Holy Island. Who says the occult wasn't involved? In Golden Dawn coven language '15.15.15.1.5' means "occult master (of themself) cheating death four times".

Arranging the Crash

Plane crashes are usually arranged via first hand knowledge of the plane. Sunderland crashes are no different, except that the technology of the planes were quite simple and methods of sabotage were also quite simple, frequent and not widely recognised. It appears that there were a dozen or more Sunderland 'practice' crashes prior to the Duke of Kent's crash.

Sunderlands were usually flown by automatic pilot in fine weather. When the weather got rough the passengers in the Aft Cabin were thrown about with the planes continual pitch, bank and yaw and this upset even the most hardened travelers. In rough weather the automatic pilot was disengaged and both pilots flew the aircraft together using combined maximum force. The normal arrangement when flying manually was for each pilot to fly for 20–30 minutes before handing over.

In the Duke of Kent's flight it was fine weather so they were flying on automatic pilot.

Stall Speeds

The lowest possible speed for take off (alighting speed) was 109 kmph.[15]

The minimum flying speed was 112 kmph.

Stalling speed with the flaps unextended was 116 kmph.

With FULL flap, the stalling speed was at 120 kmph.

With ¾ flap, the stall occurred at 129 kmph.

With ½ flap, the stall was at 131 kmph.

With ¼ flap, the stalling speed was 142 kmph.

The flaps were not fully extended over 184 kmph.

The maximum range cruising speed in still air was 211 kmph.

Against the standard 35 knot head wind, the optimum speed was 223 kmph.

The Sunderland's natural cruising speed was 236 kmph.

At 10,000 feet the economic cruising speed was 237 kmph.

Over 21 772 kg the maximum permitted speed was 304 kmph.

The maximum speed in level flight at 5 500 feet was 316 kmph.

The maximum speed with an automatic pilot engaged was 313 kmph.

The maximum speed of the Sunderland was 320 kmph.

Sunderlands could dive without vibration or instability up 320 kmph. With the throttles $^2/_3$ open they would pull out easily and quickly. However with a full fuel and cargo load it was difficult. With one engine down, low fuel levels and no cargo the Sunderland could not pull out of a dive. If one of the flaps were stuck it just got worse and if two engines were down, the plane simply fell out of the sky.

A Sunderland loaded to 21 772 kg could not maintain height on three engines and could not pull out of a dive. The Duke of Kent's Sunderland had a full load of fuel, was heavily laden and noted as "slow to take off". There was not enough time to throw the cargo and the ability to jettison fuel did not come about until the Mark IV TEAL s.30 'A' 'boats were fitted with fuel jettison pipes. The New Zealand boats had them but the Duke of Kent's Sunderland did not.

Climbing

The maximum rate of climb for a laden s.23 Sunderland from 1000 to 10,000 feet was 920 feet per minute taking 12½ minutes. When the weight was increased by 9 500 kg of cargo the climbed was reduced by 40% to 575 feet per minute.

15 All these speeds from Brian Cassidy, *Flying Empires*, pp. 160–61.

Sunderlands had a quirk. If the throttles were opened to increase speed during the climb, the flying boat would simple level off until the increased speed was reached, and then resume its climb. This made life difficult for pilots who needed to climb fast, especially if they had just flow over high ground and had just lost altitude.

At a height of 400 feet and climbing, the override was taken OUT and the mixture control levers moved forward through the gate to the NORMAL position and the flaps brought IN. As the engines changed from the FULL throttle (FULL boost condition to NORMAL boost) the engine note dropped to more normal sound levels. The variable blade propellers were then changed from FINE to COARSE pitch. It was at this point that the Sunderlands had a second quirk – they dropped 50 feet before climbing again.

If one magneto went out at this point the plane would crash.

As the plane flew over high ground towards Eagle's Rock, the override taken OUT and the airscrews were changed from FINE to COARSE, if the two magnetos went out of action on one engine, a fully laden plane would crash. Lack of flap control would only add to the disaster.

Flaps

Flaps control the drag of the plane. The more flaps are opened, the more drag the plane has and the more control the pilot has over take off, landing and turning, even creating level turns.

The three most commonly used flap settings are 8 degrees (${}^{1}/_{3}$ OUT), 12 degrees (${}^{1}/_{2}$ OUT) and 25 degrees (Full OUT). The extended flap at any setting did not interfere with the efficiency of the elevators and the drag was low. At a take-off the flap setting was ${}^{1}/_{3}$ OUT. Just before leaving the water it was ${}^{1}/_{2}$ OUT.

However in certain situations, if the flaps are stuck in the wrong position, there was less control over the plane and disaster could strike, especially at take off, when the override was taken OUT, when the propellers changed from FINE to COARSE, or while trying to pull out of a dive.

On the first official flight the flaps got stuck on CANOPUS while approaching the Seaplane Works at Rochester and the plane landed without the use of flaps. This resulted in recommendations which included a ladder to the flap motor. This ladder also gave access to the elevators, magneto/starter motors and the engine speed indicator generators.

The flaps on standard s.23 flying boats were moved by a single small electric motor, which took a full minute to wind to full flap and a minute and a half to retract the flap. This 90 seconds provided plenty of time to crash the plane without the extra stability flaps provided.

The flap operating motor is not mentioned in the Production Chart which is very curious. However "the standard equipment was a Rotax split-field series-wound 0.373 kW electric motor, mounted in the storage space over the forward end of the promenade cabin. [These were underpowered at only 0.5 Hp/0.373 kW.] The flaps could be operated manually by disengaging the clutch on the port side and winding the flap in or out by means of a winding handle inserted in the starboard side of the gearbox. The torque tubes that drove the flaps extended from the gearbox to the wing roots."[16] In the Duke of Kent's case, having recently flown over high ground, there was not enough time to do so.

Rotax were not the best flap motors and some s.30 were fitted with Delco-Remy flap motors. These weren't that great either and in January 1940 1 kW motors with an extra battery were considered . . . but not installed. As a result flap operating motors were a third the desired size.

A 4 amp fuse was used for the flap indicator, a 15 amp fuse for flap motor changeover switch and a 50 amp fuse for the flap motor. It was simple enough to swap the 50 amp fuse for a 30 amp fuse to cause a delayed blow out. Alternatively highly acidic acid could be dripped on the fuses and/or cables causing a delayed blow out. Passengers with know-how could access the flap motors, elevators, magneto/starter motors and engine speed indicator generators if the Flight Steward had been sent to the upper level.

When the nose of the plane went up or down, the pilots had a manual control on the underside of the coup, which could be worked by either pilot. A handle was turned 6.38 turns to trim the elevators through its full movement.

The flap, elevator, magneto/starter motor, engine speed indicator generators wiring and batteries were all in the same area, in the terminal block in the wing-root. These were accessed through the compartment over the centre cabin, between the wings (spar booms).

The manual override operator (Flight Steward) had to clamber into the compartment, de-clutch the motor and insert the winding handle into the gearbox, to move the flaps IN or OUT.

[16] Brian Cassidy, *Flying Empires*, pp P. 77.

The saboteur only had to climb in and drop acid on the Telefex cables or fuses to the flaps/elevators/magneto/engine speed indicator generators or replace their fuses with faulty fuses or smaller fuses.

> "The engine starter solenoid circuit wiring and the starter circuits, were connected through the junction boxes in the wing-roots in 35/012 copper core cable to the Rotax N5CP solenoid switches, which energised the starter motors."

The control wiring was only single core copper cable and the limit switch gearbox drove both the flap-angle indicator and extension indicator, but these applied to the port flap only. This meant that the starboard flap could be faulty without causing alarm.

The flaps, elevators, magneto/starter motor and engine speed indicator generators could all have been sabotaged by access to the wing-roots and this could have been done by any of the unnamed three in the royal party by distracting the Flight Steward (which he was) and opening the cover plates. With practice this sabotage can be done very quickly. Equally the sabotage could have occurred while in service during the previous few days.

The sabotage could have been done during servicing, on the plane or as a back up to remote control. The possibilities were not limited.

> The magneto/starter motor was sabotaged on two of the four engines and there was a remote control override to the magnetos, rudder and communications just in case they were needed.

A Sunderland Crashing

A simple method of crashing a Sunderland was to turn off the magnetos on two engines, reduce the speed to 142 kmph and open ¼ flap. This would cause the flying boat to stall and fall 300 feet per minute. Having just flown over high ground, it wouldn't take long to hit the ground, certainly less than 90 seconds. This could have been done as soon as the propellers had moved to COARSE and the plane had just dropped 50 feet.

Once the plane had stalled and begun to fall the magnetos could be turned on again. The pilots would have the engines on full throttle as they tried to pull out of the dive. If this occurred under 116 kmph the plane would continue to stall and continue to dive, at best levelling out. If the pilots judged they were too close to ground to pull out of a dive they would have gone to throttle off and waited for their demise.

The Usual Method of Sabotage

Sabotage was also taught by taking apart and reassembling the fuel-monitoring unit. This would have been looked for, however, since MI-5 and MI-6 were well in on the act, it was simple enough for them to destroy this small piece of evidence.

Remote control was not widely known and was not looked for. Those MI-6 agents on the inside would have looked for any evidence of sabotage and removed them as soon as they arrived at the crash site.

The Unusual Method of Sabotage

In Burma, India and Assam planes were downing in 1943–45 like there was no tomorrow. This included passenger air craft. The British checked this out and found the Japanese were lacing chewing gum with hashish and giving it to the native ground crews to put in the pilot's cabin. The pilots were chewing the gum, getting stoned and crashing.

The hashish was discovered when some erk (Ground Crew) pinched the chewing gum and dived off the 50 foot control tower injuring himself.

This was how the plane crashes got solved in reality, but it only became public knowledge when the Royal Flying Corps veteran and editor of *Popular Flying* magazine, Captain William Earl Johns attributed it to Captain James Bigglesworth in the Biggles novels. Biggles was so big he influenced wallpaper.

Remote Control and Instructions from Inside

To steer the plane from inside, all that was needed was control over the rudder. This was done by command from inside the plane, from the cockpit, from outside the plane, or by remote control over the rudder. The steward could easily have been given instructions from the Duke of Hamilton prior to boarding:

> "If the Duke of Kent gives you any instructions, follow them. He is the commanding officer on the plane."
>
> Once on board the Duke of Kent's instructions may have been: "We are going to the Aft Cabin. Do not disturb us until we have passed Wick. Have the pilots fly over Eagle's Rock. I hear the scenery is spectacular."

After this the Duke of Kent and his party made their way to the Promenade Cabin and climbed out the starboard door of the Sunderland Special, directly onto the waiting craft, no steps required.

The North Sea is largely fed by the Baltic which has no tide at all. It is also partly fed by the Atlantic which does have tides. Rochester had small tides. No ramp or stairs were required from the Sunderland to either the dock, tender or MEXSHELL refuelling craft.

MI-6 to the Rescue

Eagle's Rock was 18 miles from the small town of Wick which meant MI-6's rescue team were assured to be the largest number of people first on the scene.

There were 15 officially on board. MI-6 had done a 'coffee run' and visited the morgues in Britain in search of bodies. It was preferable they had died as the result of car crashes, plane crashes, or by fire. They needed a body for the Duke of Kent, the other three in the unnamed royal party and a spare. It's always good to have a spare body when you're MI-6.

MI-6 arrived in their Army lorries converted into ambulances with their best canned meat ready to place. The bodies were often preserved with ice. This idea was first put forward by Squadron Leader O'Reilly – MI-6's serial murderer until the Russians got him.

The five bodies were all dressed in appropriate uniforms and pre-stressed in a manner commesurate with a plane crash. MI-6 failed to adequately stress the Duke of Kent's uniform and his body was found thrown well clear of the plane and not too far from the Army lorry loaded with the canned meat. This meant that MI-6 found little reason to carry the Duke of Kent's body double very far. The smashed face must have been something horrible. His briefcase was found near the body and it was 'his' uniform and briefcase that identified the body. The face did not.

> The body was not that of the Duke of Kent. It was a canned meat body brought in by MI-6.

When Flt Sgt Andrew Simpson William Jack turned up alive, "The reported additional and unexplained body at the scene was [erroneously] attributed to Rudolf Hess." It was not Rudolf Hess, but was a canned meat spare attributed to rear gunner Flight Sergeant Andrew Jack. Andrew Jack was not meant to survive and MI-6 had planned on there being no survivors. Andrew Jack was discovered after the bodies had been counted and placed and was lucky not to have been executed on the spot as part of MI-5's tidy up.

Given something of a silent mythical status as 'surviving hero', it was unwise to kill Andrew Jack, but it was necessary to silence him. Part of this has involved discrediting him, even after his death. Officially known as 'boiler-plating', this is often employed against low-ranking survivors of incidents.

There were meant to be no survivors. Either the pilots had managed to slow the plane down, or the Oban saboteurs had not taken into consideration that under 240 kmph (150 mph) there was a chance of survival, especially for the rear gunner. The tails of Liberators and Sunderlands were known to snap off and if the tail gunner said the bolts were coming loose, the pilots headed the plane for home . . . so whenever the tail gunner wanted to go home, he would tell the pilots via intercom that the bolts were coming loose.

The tail of the Sunderland snapped off and rear gunner Andrew Jack was badly burnt, but survived. Having an understanding of the British from his family background, he escaped the scene as quickly as possible and staggered to a crofter's (farmer's) cottage.

Jack did not alert anyone and was discovered the next morning exhausted and burnt. The rescue party did not know he had survived until the following day. As a result an extra body found.

Spymaster: "Stinks of MI-6."

The 16th body, explained as Rudolf Hess, was a car crash/burn victim who had died days earlier and was picked up during the MI-6 coffee run and packed in ice.

Once Flt Sgt Andrew Simpson William Jack had identified the Duke of Kent's back as he stood between the two pilots, the Duke of Kent walked down to the passenger level to see his unnamed royal party of three. The Flight Steward had been instructed not to go to the Aft Cabin until after passing Wick (after the crash). Curtains between cabins and the royal party luggage blocked his view. At 60 decibels (as loud as shouting) the Flight Steward could not distinguish whether or not there was any conversation coming from the Aft Cabin. Just prior to flight, the Duke of Kent opened the seaward starboard door in the Promenade Cabin and simply walked onto the tender.

This was a Holy Ghost operation.

MI-5, Air 3 and Jack

The Duke of Kent was MI-5 as of right. Another in the royal party was most likely an MI-5 officer proficient in sabotage and intelligence operations and from Air 3.

Since three of the 'four' passengers in the royal party remain unnamed and were at a level below the crew, there was no communication between the crew and royal party during flight and no way of ascertaining who the royal party were.

Having survived, Andrew Jack went to the East Grinstead hospital for burns, retired as a flight lieutenant on 6 June 1964 and worked as a telephone engineer. He had vast scarring, and officially "suffered from depression and was a changed man".

Documents were released by the Public Records Office under the 30-year rule around 1972. (His brother King Edward VIII/Duke of Windsor had died on 28 May 1972.) The PRO records shed no light on the matter, such that they contradicted Andrew Jack's reports – the only eye witness.

Flt Sgt Andrew Simpson William Jack (8 May 1921–22 March 1978) died at Brighton General Hospital, officially of bronchopneumonia, pancreatitis and cirrhosis of the liver.

Considering MI-6 had probably been threatening to kill Jack for 36 years, with veiled threats and hints, it was no wonder Jack was depressed. The MI-6 rescue team were very concerned that there was a survivor and would have preferred there were none so they spent the next four decades ensuring that rear gunner Andrew Jack did not have a voice.

Spymaster: "The liver diagnosis is typical of MI-5/MI-6 boiler-plating and is completely in line with how MI-6 treats people even after death. Citing alcoholism at death provides another avenue for deniability."

Britain – a Liar's Paradise

The substance of the Court of Enquiry is encapsulated on the Aircraft Accident Card held by the Ministry of Defence. Based on this, the Secretary of State of Air, Sir Archibald Sinclair made a statement six weeks after the crash in the House of Commons on 7 October 1942, yet a diligent search at the Public Records Office (also by its director) has confirmed in writing that the original Court of Enquiry cannot be

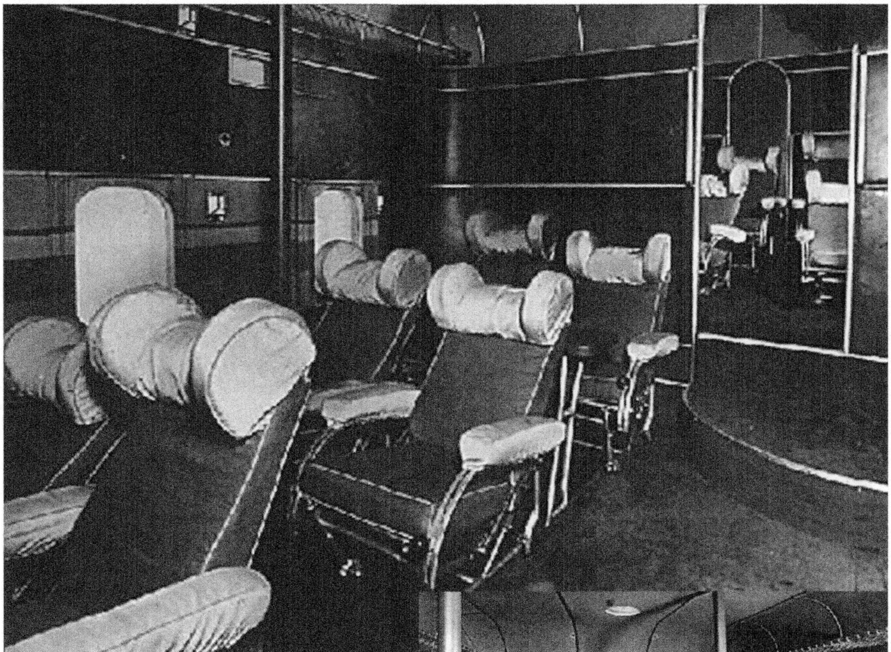

Sunderland Empire Flying boat lower level interiors.

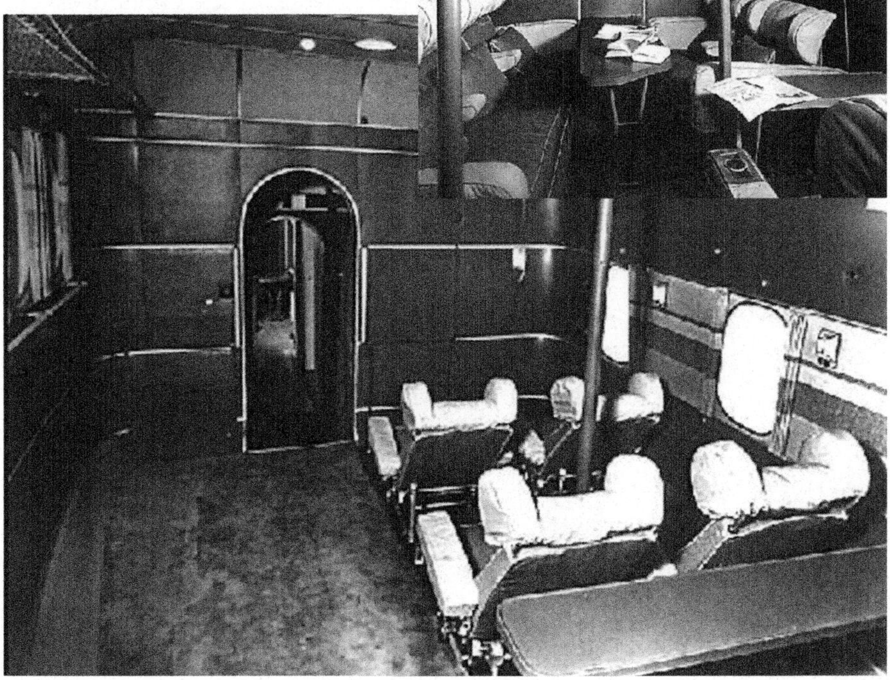

found in either the "open" or "closed" files and the Royal Archivist has also confirmed that these have never been sent to the Public Records Office.[17]

> This indicates that, regarding the circumstances of the death of the Duke of Kent, the Secretary of State of Air made his statement in the House of Commons based on information that did not exist.
>
> This also indicates that all enquiries into the Sunderland crash were stopped by the British Royal Family, in particular, by the Duke of Kent's brother, King George VI.

Spymaster: "King George VI happily cooperated in all these cover ups because he was virtually retarded, and was guided by more worldly military figures who pretended to advise him beneficially. His only genuine friend was the New Zealand VC Charlie Upham who treated the King like one of his own men and never called him George."

The King of England, the British Royal Family, the House of Commons, the Ministry of Defence, the Court of Enquiry, the Secretary of State of Air, Commander of the Air Training corps, the Duke of Hamilton, the Freemasons of Scotland, MI-6 and all embedded historians were complicit in the cover up of the death of Air Commodore, Inspector-General of RAF Welfare and Grand Master Mason, the cross-dressing Duke of Kent . . . and his new role as the Holy Ghost.

> King George VI was not very bright and Princess Elizabeth had been attending war meetings since she was 13 (1939). If the Duke of Kent were to have survived, Elizabeth may not have been queen until after his death. The Duke of Kent had been cited for King, but was considered too similar to King Edward VIII.

Based on the Duke of Kent's homosexual and occult practises, his cross-dressing, his cuckolding and his snobbish Nazi wife demanding she was "the most blue-blooded royal of them all", the Duke of Kent was removed from the public picture and his death was framed.

This is backed up by the hushed and rushed funeral and the royal family's near complete lack of mourning for their brother and uncle.

---

[17] In Golden Dawn coven/Thule Society language, 'six weeks' is "all 6s and 7s – all madness", with the '6' referring to death and the '7' referring to heaven, meaning it was "a heavenly death surrounded by madness". This too was part of the Holy Ghost operation.

The 'Duke of Kent' was originally buried at St. George's Chapel, Windsor, but once the real Duke of Kent had died (morphine and cocaine overdose post-1968, the same as his father, King George V), the canned meat Duke of Kent was removed and the real Duke of Kent was buried at the royal burial ground at Frogmore. It was here that the real ceremony took place.

Homosexual Lovers raise Prince Edward

The Duke of Hamilton was born Douglas Douglas-Hamilton (3 February 1903–30 March 1973) and became the 14th Duke of Hamilton and the 11th Duke of Brandon upon his father's death on 16 March 1940.

Previously the Duke of Hamilton had worked in coalmines as 'Mr Hamilton', although the coal was on their property. He served in the Auxiliary Air Force as Squadron Commander (1927–36) and was the first to fly over Mt. Everest (1933). He was a prominent Conservative MP (1930–40) and made friends with several prominent Nazis during the 1936 Olympics in Berlin. He was also Lord Steward of the Royal Holyroodhouse (1940–64) and during WWII, Commander of the Air Training Corps responsible for the defence of Scotland.

The Duke of Hamilton and Brandon was also a German agent with an Abwehr V-Mann number and was referred to in both British and German occult circles as Brandon – yet after WWII he was styled GCVO (1946) and KT (1951) for services to Britain.

After the 'death' of his lover the Duke of Kent (39), the position of Duke of Kent was filled by the Duke of Kent's six-year-old son, Prince Edward George Nicholas Paul Patrick, born 9 October 1935.

As a six-year-old, Prince Edward could not fulfil the role of his future titles so these were carried out by his father's close friend and lover, the Duke of Hamilton . . . with his lover, the surviving Duke of Kent, living at Dungavel Castle with him, often in a dress. The Duke of Hamilton wore the pants.

The Duke of Hamilton acted as mentor to Prince Edward for the quarter of a century from 1942–67 when he handed over his Freemasonry titles. Whenever Prince Edward and the Duke of Hamilton met there was an opportunity for Prince Edward to met with his father who often dressed as a woman for sexual preference as much as for disguise.

The Duke of Kent in Air Force and Naval uniform and as pretty boy (top); with fiancée Princess Marina of Greece (middle); and with lovers Albrecht Haushofer (bottom left) and the 14th Duke of Hamilton (bottom rights).

The 2nd Duke of Kent Field Marshal Prince Edward George Nicholas Patrick Windsor (1935–) KG, GCMC, GCVO, ADC. The Grand Master of the United Grand Lodge of England and Hereditary Grand Master of Anglo-American Freemasonry.

The first and second Duchess of Kent.
Stalwart wives look upon their sons and wonder – what have I done?

> Just imagine it:
> A transsexual cocaine and morphine addict as of King of Great Britain.
>
> Just imagine it:
> The current Duke of Kent looks nothing like his father and was probably conceived during a Golden Dawn coven ritual – a gang bang with the males acting as the Father, the Son and the Holy Ghost. Conception took place 33 days after their marriage at 1.30 am on Christmas Day 1934 at exactly half-waned moon. Feeble and illegitimate royals are often conceived in the first half of the waning moon. It was the same for King George VI's illegitimate son conceived near the bottom of New Zealand's South Island and born on Christmas Day 1927. Let's call him Harry.

The most likely fathers were the Duke of Kent, his lover the Duke of Hamilton, and his lover Albrecht Haushofer. Albrecht Haushofer was the son of Rudolf Hess' mentor Karl Haushofer. Karl had originated the concept of lebensraum, something the British royals absolutely needed.

The current Duke of Kent has Albrecht Haushofer's hairline, eyes, nose, ears and jaw. Albrecht Haushofer could well be the Duke of Kent's biological father . . . although his unfortunate looks can also be explained by his father's cocaine and morphine addiction. The Duke of Hamilton, who specialised in magnanimous vanity, looks nothing like Prince Edward/Duke of Kent.

Royal Titles

As Queen Elizabeth II's cousin, Prince Edward eventually became Field Marshal, KG, GCMC, GCVO, ADC. Upon joining the Masons he immediately became a 33 degree Mason and The Grand Master of the United Grand Lodge of England and Hereditary Grand Master of Anglo-American Freemasonry – all in 1967.

Indicators of the real Duke of Kent's death are his son's elevation to Grand Master Mason in 1967 with the deceased father in the galleries role playing the Holy Ghost; his wife's death on 27 August 1968; and his reburial at Frogmore, the date of which seems to be protected.

Royals have got away with giving each other titles and post-nominal letters for a long time, so let's look at what the post-nominal letters mean.

The Knight of the Garter (KG) is given to the Sovereign (themself), his eldest son and 24 nobles, which included his third son. Its motto 'Honi soit qui mal y pense' – 'Shamed be the person who thinks evil of it' – brought about the Age of Chivalry. Of all the orders it includes the most degraded knights. These include King Charles I (appointed in 1611 and beheaded in 1649); James Butler, Duke of Ormonde, Viceroy of Ireland (appointed 1689 and executed for treason 1716) and over thirty other Garter Knights executed from 1388, after which the government took over their appointments from the late 1700s to 1946 when the royal family reclaimed the right.

The Order of the Garter is also given to foreign monarchs "as a means of marking and securing alliances" including Emperor Nicholas II of Russia in 1893 (we're going to swish you and end your monarchy); King Alfonso XII of Spain in 1902 (we won't help you against the Germans); the Shah of Persia in 1903 (we want your oil); the Emperor of Japan in 1929 (we don't want you to fight alongside Germany);[18] the King of Sweden in 1954 (thanks for rejecting Hitler's Non-Aggression Pact) and King Olav V of Norway in 1959 (thanks for rejecting Hitler's Non-Aggression Pact while allowing him to take over your country and really getting the war in Northern Europe under way).

The Order of the Garter has become an order for complicit cover utilising those from lower down the ranks such as Lord Kitchener (KG). "You deny for me and I'll deny for you." The Order of the Garter has come to symbolise closeted homosexuality, wife cheating, paedophilia amongst royals and peers, and trading in countries' fortunes.[19]

The Knight of St Michael and St George (GCMC) is the 'Spies and Traders' knighthood and is given to those who have dealt with delicate British foreign matters. Anyone with the letters GCMG, KCMG or CMG after their name should be treated as a British spy, whether retired or not. Part and parcel of being a British royal is dealing with delicate British matters overseas. As such, many honorary members are royals. Its motto 'Auspicium melioris aevi' (We are doing this for a better Age) may as well refer to the Masonic New Age – Novus Ordo Seclorum.

---

[18] Hirohito, Emperor of Japan was appointed Knight Garter on 3 May 1929. This was removed in 1941 and reinstated by warrant on 22 May 1971. That he was allowed to survive after WWII amazed all historians and points to complicity in war.

[19] King George VI qualified in all these areas.

The Royal Victorian Order (GCVO) is given to family members and servants of the royal household among others. There is no limit to the number given and its really just the home-help award.

The Aide de Camp to Her Majesty (ADC) is just that. It signifies that the ADC carries out the will of the monarch without question.

The Duke of Hamilton and Brandon/Douglas Douglas-Hamilton was a pro-Nazi conservative MP who travelled through Germany returning to nobble the British Government into *not* supporting France over the re-militarisation of the Rhineland (1936). He also encouraged the British Empire to "come to an understanding" with the New World Order of Nordic-Anglo-Saxon colonising and advised King George VI on the advantages of Naziism.

The British monarchy took this on board and Queen consort Elizabeth (King George VI's Scottish wife) said: "I don't care who wins the war, as long as we retain the monarchy".

> As "the uncrowned King of England" this was the Duke of Hamilton's gift to the Nordic-Anglo-Saxon coloniser Adolf Hitler. He had the British monarchy on board with Hitler and they tasselled between supporting Hitler and retaining the monarchy. As it turned out, they did both.

The 14th Duke of Hamilton (GCVO, KT) was doing the work of the KG, GCMC, GCVO, ADC – the work of 'shameful delicate British foreign matters that directly serve and aid the British monarch and trade in countries fortunes'. As the uncrowned King of England, the uncrowned head of Freemasonry, Scotland's premier peer and a German V-Mann agent, the 14th Duke of Hamilton ensured the Freemasons did everything they could to ensure German Freemasons had every assistance in taking over England.

> Of many knights, you could comfortably say, they were "creating mass crime behind a veil of dignity".

Each Knight provides a reference for the other and justice is never done. Delaying the charge of treason and making those look stupid who would lay the charge is common to 80% of knighthoods. It also puts the knights completely in the pockets of those in power to do their bidding, both up and down the elevation scale, developing and sustaining the British monarchy's New World Order goals.

The 14th Duke of Hamilton, Douglas Douglas-Hamilton was a homosexual and a lover of the transvestite, cocaine and morphine addict, the Duke of Kent. He was also the occultist 'Brandon' and used the surviving Duke of Kent as the Holy Ghost in all Golden Dawn coven occult rituals.

> Whenever you have a high-ranking homosexual fronting as a married heterosexual, you have a malleable spy who will go to any treasonous lengths and use all their resources just to maintain one or all of their positions.

Many homosexual Freemasons use Freemasonry and marriage as a form of cover. Freemasons have a high rate of child-sex abuse, paedophilia and incest, with accounts suggesting that Freemasons sexually abuse a third of their daughters and granddaughters.

> Paedophiles control Freemasons, because Freemasons consider paedophiles to be close to royals. Royals use their illegitimate children for supply and control for paedophiles. Police are a Freemasonry organisation and serve the British Crown. Thus Police cover for paedophiles and expect promotions when they do so. Freemasons admire paedophiles and a Freemason will do anything a paedophile asks them to do. This does not exclude dropping the Berlin Wall.

Because the Freemasons control the police and judiciary, Freemasons are rarely charged for their incest, child-sex abuse and paedophilia. When they are discovered, the first step is to cover up. When it becomes too obvious they are often murdered. Sometimes these murders are real and other times they are fake with new identities established elsewhere. In the case of really important secret society members, they are retained, hidden and used for ceremonial purposes. One of those purposes was to act as the 'Holy Ghost' in Golden Dawn coven occult rituals. In Germany these were called Thule Society rituals.

Secrets give power
and rituals with a manifest secret have more power.

On 11 September 2004 the Freemasons opened their doors to the public for membership in order to spread the blame of an increasingly exposed history. (See *Spreading the Blame, Appendix 4*)

Frogmore

Frogmore is named after the preponderance of frogs in this low-lying ground in Berkshire. The British royals are usually buried at Frogmore, St. George's Chapel in Windsor, or Westminster Abbey.

Frogmore refers to Frogmore's burial grounds and includes the Royal Mausoleum containing the graves of Prince Albert and Queen Victoria (only), the Duchess of Kent's Mausoleum (Queen Victoria's mother only, slightly smaller but close by), and the royal burial ground.

Frogmore is 33 acres of private gardens which adjoins Home Park grounds of Windsor Castle, Berkshire. It was purchased by King George III for his African Queen Charlotte, for use as "a country retreat". They had 15 children, and in real terms, it was a place to get rid of the kids. Frogmore House is therefore a former royal residence. Lord Louis was born in this large white mansion.

Queen Victoria set Frogmore House aside as the royal burial ground a few days after Prince Albert died in 1861. This was on the advice that the usual and more public Westminster Abbey would, at some point in the future, make it easier to ascertain whether a royal was of illegitimate parentage. The other royal burial ground is St. George's Chapel at neighbouring Windsor.

The mausoleum at Frogmore was designed, not by a Britisher, but by the German architect, Ludwig Gruner, in the form of a Greek Cross. Work began in 1862 and the mausoleum was finished in 1871.

There was grave robbing at Frogmore. This removed all non-royal graves from the site and some royal ones too. King George III's body would have been swished by the Freemasons so his poisoning could not be analysed and Queen Victoria would have organised the site with the words "prepare the site". Some grave robbing was organised by the victims to cover for more disingenuous activities, especially when pride was a part of history.

The royal burial ground, behind Victoria and Albert's Mausoleum contains the bodies of "most" members of the royal family (1861–1928), although it only includes three of Victoria's nine children: Princess Helena (d. 1923); Princess Louise (d. 1939); and Prince Arthur (d. 1942). Prince consort Albert was the father of Arthur, but the parentage of the two daughters is suspect. King Edward VIII (d. 1972) and Wallis Simpson (d. 1986) were also buried at the royal burial ground.

1861 to 1928 was a period when a lot of illegitimate high-ranking British royals were dying and buried at Frogmore. Consequently the royal burial ground at Frogmore is only "open six days a year". This includes 17–19 May (Mausoleum and garden), 25 May (Mausoleum only, closest Wednesday to Queen's Birthday) and 27–29 August (Bank Holiday, House, Gardens and Mausoleum).[20] This means the royal burial ground can be viewed over a fence only 5 days a year from 10 am–6 pm. This excludes casual DNA testing.

Consider Frogmore the Pharoh King's sealed crypt. The Duke of Kent was buried there because his death was delayed for over a quarter of a century. The DNA in Frogmore hides the secrets of the British royal family, their illegitimate origins, their murders including MAD (medically assisted death) and their delayed deaths.[21]

Before Marina, Duchess of Kent married she was a princess of Denmark and Greece (the Greek bit was by invitation and was quickly followed by exile). When Marina married on 29 November 1934 she became the Duchess of Kent, Countess of St. Andrews and Baroness Downpatrick. Just before her son married, she changed her title to HRH Princess Marina, Duchess of Kent as she was entitled to do. Her son, the new Duke of Kent then married the violinist Katherine Lucy Mary Worsley on 8 June 1961 and Katherine became the new HRH Duchess of Kent.

The new Duchess of Kent suffers from depression and chronic fatigue syndrome. (No wonder, look at what she married.) "I do love guidelines . . . I have wanted that all my life. I like to know what's expected of me. I like being told: 'You shall . . ." In 1994 she converted to Roman Catholicism, the first senior royal to publicly do so since the 1700 Act of Settlement (touted as 1701) and in 2002 she voluntarily gave up the style HRH (Her Royal Highness) to become publicly known as Katharine, Duchess of Kent and privately as Katharine Kent.

The 1700 Act of Settlement has been interpreted with every form of excuse and the Duke of Kent did not lose his place in the line of succession to the British throne because his wife converted to Catholicism after they were married. Similarly a King could marry an Anglican and she could become a Catholic Queen and no one would do anything effective

[20] These are the 2005 dates.

[21] King George V was killed by MAD as was the Duke of Kent.

about it. Sure there would be the usual discussion in the papers, but what has that ever achieved. The Duchess of Kent became a Catholic and gave up her succession to the British throne, although her children are still in line to the throne by way of their Anglican HRH father.

Her predecessor, HRH Princess Marina, Duchess of Kent died from a brain tumor at Kensington Palace on 27 August 1968. She was a 61-year-old Nazi and Colonel-in-chief of the Essex and Kent Scottish Regiment. She was originally buried at St. George's Chapel at Windsor, but was later reburied at the royal burial ground at Frogmore to be next to her husband, fellow Nazi-in-a-dress, the Duke of Kent.

The date of his reburial is not given, but is post 1968 and probably within a week of his actual death.

Catch 22

Fleet Air Arm: "I was in the desert arming and maintaining Beaufighters, but ended up receiving everything – South African Kittyhawks, Hurricanes, Mark V Spitfires, Free-French Baltimores, Free-Greek Baltimores and every other thing that could fly. The joke amongst ourselves was 'If anything came in and it was flown by a complete and utter Kraut and it had some variation of RAF markings that looked like the Krauts had painted it; and if they had a uniform that looked like it had been put together by a shoplifter working at Madam Tussaud's wax works; and if he couldn't speak English and all they could tell you was "Ya flieger, schnel schnel" ("I am a flyer, hurry, hurry")' – they were probably all right.

"All these foreigners were usually dripping in guns, nearly all German, and Luftwaffe flieger watches. A sure case of suspicion was a foreigner with a Mark V Webley in its correct holster and a Pommy watch."

The Webley was British. The German guns were better, so any one dripping in British guns was either a German spy or a dumb British and if a dumb British returned twice, he was a German spy . . . No one carried a British watch because they didn't work in the desert.

Fleet Air Arm: "They called on me one day saying, 'We are bringing you these Commandos and we need to teach them how to sabotage aircraft.' I tried to teach them how to attack the fuel-monitoring unit by taking it apart and reassembling it. The Commandos, the Marines, Popski's Army, NZLRDG (NZ Long Range Desert Group) – they could all understand, but the SAS couldn't and even the SAS Officers couldn't.[22]

"You could try to teach them how to stuff a rag under the sump and set fire to it and that was too complicated. SAS never understood anything that wasn't accompanied by a big bang. Anything else was an anathema to them. They really were the dumbest bastards in the whole of the Western Desert.

"There was this 10-year-old Bedouin kid [desert-dweller] everyone called 'Farouk.' He was thin and skinny and used to coat himself in a mixture of grease and tyre black and he' go around German aircraft and drill a hole with a corkscrew stolen from Shepherds and given to him by a New Zealand Army officer. Farouk probably got more Germans in the Western Desert by drilling holes halfway through the landing wheel than the rest of us.

"When the Me109G came out Farouk transferred his attentions to drilling a hole halfway through the supercharge inlet. He's believed to have downed Joachim Marseilles – the famous German pilot Ace. Marseilles certainly fell victim to an engine fire.

"We asked Farouk why he did it and he told us, 'I'm just here for the money.' He was Tunisian. He was paid in British pounds into an account in Switzerland and he'd been promised resettlement into his own restaurant in a British colony in South America.

"If he survived it would have been a miracle. The kid lived for the day he would be able to sit in his restaurant in a clean white shirt and be able to handle a white menu and not leave black marks everywhere. He'd been recruited by one of Popski's men working on Italian aircraft in his native Tunisia with a thorn from a bush called the Jerusalem Thorn. 'The vital thing was not to go to far with the thorn so the tail-wheel only gave out when the plane landed.'

"The trickiest thing in the Western Desert was sorting out the Allied aircraft from the German aircraft and Farouk told me that the markings had nothing to do with it. You actually had to go and listen to the pilots in order to tell which aircraft were targets. Farouk said, 'A lot of the high up pilots in the Luftwaffe actually spoke English together and were German aristocrats. I'd been told by British Intelligence to give them a wide birth. It was only the low class that spoke German together.'

[22] All Czechs during WWII wore Polish uniforms and Polish titles but spoke Czech. All wearing Czech uniforms during WWII were Poles. All of Popski's Army were Czechs who spoke Czech, but didn't wear the uniform or carry the title of a Czech or a Pole. The desert was full of Catch 22s.

"We took Farouk into town once, into Cairo and dressed him up. When we were passing Gray Pillars we were challenged by an MP. I was asked 'What are you doing with this boy?' I became nonplussed and didn't know what to say and then Farouk said, 'He makes me wash his socks and bums me every night' and the MP turned to me and said, 'You'd better hire another to wash your socks. You have to treat these Wogs right, after all Egypt is there country.' I wandered off admonished and Farouk led the way from behind."[23]

Spymaster: "I was told this story by another army officer who had been in intelligence and the only spies that were any good and wouldn't rob you blind were whores and they were Jewish whores that worked for MI-6, the Mossad and God knows who else.

"They befriended me and looked after me all the time I was in the UK. They told me some amazing things. They told me that the whole place was run by Prince Philip but they were right because they knew what he liked.

"The only ones you had to watch out for were the KGB and Jews and some of them could be quite nasty. They told me that New Zealand was regarded by all British and American military personnel as 'The Dump' and anything that was no longer of any use went there, and in Britain's case, at a huge expense to the New Zealand taxpayer.

"One night two of these ladies came up to me and told me to watch out for this British Admiral. He was particularly nasty and was getting backhanders from all directions including Vickers and was intent on getting rid of some Leander Class frigates.

"The particularly nasty Admiral was told by the First Sea Lord at the party, 'Any luck getting rid of those Frigates Old Bean?' and the Admiral said, 'No, even the Indians don't want them. They know they're clapped out.' Whereupon the First Sea Lord said, 'Have you tried the Kiwis?' and the Admiral replied, 'No, I haven't. Never thought of them,' and the First Sea Lord replied, 'Do try them. Their money is just as good as anyone else's and they're still as thick as the bulkheads on the Bismarck.'

[23] Gray Pillars was a distinctive building owned by Omar Sirry. It was the British Headquarters located at 10 Tolombat, Garden City, Cairo and was headed by Ministers' Oliver Lyttelton (July 1941), Richard Cassey, then Lord Moyne. The locals called it 'Assicurazioni' and believed the British, war or no war, had overstayed their welcome. The British set up a football field and a cricket pitch around Gray Pillars and the locals used this to stage quick Sieg heils (gun shots) before they dived for cover in the undergrowth.

"Of course I reported my knowledge back through the chain of command to Wellington [NZ]. Not long after I received a rocket [telling off]. On the day I received the rocket for sending half-arsed information through service channels, I noted two things in the British papers the next day. My ladies of the evening had disappeared to Israel and New Zealand had purchased a number of Leander Class frigates."[24]

Of course Kiwi Keith had been dipping his 'keel' in a bowl of 'rice' and the only people using their real names in London in the 70s were the guys stealing cars for London TV.

Spymaster: "Sunderlands couldn't land on choppy water. They used to land in Wellington (NZ) at Evans Bay, to the side of Shelley Bay on an RNZAF Base. It was still in use after WWII until at least 1969. They used to fly up and down the Bay two or three times before they'd come in and the water used to plane off the hull beautifully and the pilot used to make it look comparatively easy to set down. The reason it was so easy landing was the sheltered bay. This big bow wave would come off the hull and pour salt water all over the tail of the aircraft. Being RNZAF aircraft the engines used to perform like Swiss watches – they were maintained up in Hobsonville. The other RNZAF base was Lualatha Bay in Fiji. New Zealand Sunderlands were all white, whereas WWII aircraft had all white hulls with grey and green across the tops.

"The RNZAF would add Molybdenum Sulphate to the engine oils and get 10–20% more power. The Americans developed this for use in Flying Fortresses flying at extreme heights for the attack on Germany. It was shipped out to New Zealand in May 1945 for the attack on Japan. The RNZAF had big drums of it at Hobsonville and would share it with the civilian flown demilitarized Sunderland s.45, known as the Solent.

"A Warrant Officer/mechanic at Hobsonvillle knew all the interchangeability of Sunderland parts. Officially he was meant to be retired, but was retained and worked on operating Sunderlands until 1970. He managed to blackmail the RNZAF so ended up with a commission rank as Wing Commander which is not bad for a mechanic.

"The first to fly a small fighter attached to a long-range bomber were Shorts of Sunderland fame. It worked so they stopped doing it. The next to do it were the Luftwaffe. The Germans called these 'Mistel' [Mistletoe – probably a reference to kissing cousins]. This was always treated like a top secret aviation programme of the Third Reich, but in actual event the idea came from England and was first developed and trialled by Shorts.

[24] Leander Class frigates arrived into New Zealand 1968-73.

"I have had high-ranking Luftwaffe personnel tell me 'this is a fact' and could not understand why the British didn't continue with it. It was in common use in Germany and was considered to be the ideal end for a number of worn-out aircraft. Germans filled them with explosives and sent them into attack in heavily defended locations – most of which happened to be on the Eastern Front."

> "The original concept was proposed to the RLM in 1941 by Siegfried Holzbauer, a Junkers test pilot. His idea was to make use of 'tired' Junkers Ju 88 airframes by packing them with explosives, fly them near a target and crash them into the target after the fighter had released itself. The fighter pilot would control the missile after release by *remote control.* The first conversion flew in July 1943 . . . a further 15 conversions, with the code name Beethoven . . . an eventual thickness of 60 feet of reinforced concrete was breached . . . over 250 Mistels of various combinations were built . . ."[25]

Spymaster: "I know the KG200, the elite bomber Geschwader [organisation] of the Luftwaffe used these aircraft and that at the end of the war, they were used in an attack on Russian bridges on the Western Rhine which was captured in tact by the US Army.

"At the end of the war, the British held a famous air show at Farnborough where they exhibited a number of new inventions from Germany. Nearly all these aircraft had hastily applied British roundels and hastily applied Air Ministry numbers on the tails blocking out the Swastika.

"No one noticed apart from MI-6 entourage that the upside down engines in all German aircraft were courtesy of MI-6 and that the revolutionary Mistral design had been stolen from Shorts. [The Mistel was gifted by Arthur Gouge to the Freemasons who then gave it to Nazi Germany].

"The latest German-fighter ejection seats were not exhibited because they were busy being stolen by the executives of Martin-Baker who were touring the Luftwaffe base at Rechlin[26] [and Lärz] with an

[25] Warbirds Resource group, Mistel – Composite Aircraft; also called Mistral.

[26] Rechlin is a small remote village in Mecklenburg-Vorpommern, Germany – an area closely related to, and heavily influenced by the British royal family. Rechlin was a testing ground for aircraft from 1916 and was the main testing ground for new Luftwaffe aircraft during the Third Reich, up to 1944/45 when Lärz was included. Plane construction was carried out by forced labour from the nearby Ravensbrück concentration camp.

assortment of tools, stealing many things and intent on bringing them back to be discovered anew in the United Kingdom.

"No doubt there was similar activity from Rolls Royce and the Russians who stole early Rolls Royce designs of jet engines, among them the Rolls Royce Nene which turned up on a MIG-17 bearing a striking resemblance to a Messerschmitt fighter. In the 1980s the Russians ended up paying manufacturing rights to Rolls Royce for the use of these stolen designs.

"Similar things were happening down at Vickers with the Vampire. This is all just post-WWII and the gun ports had just gone cold."

British Intelligence Officer: "Confusion in wartime is the result of the British being as bent as a dingo's hind-leg whereas confusion in peacetime is the result of the British government's arms and drug dealing – euphemistically called 'Black Velvet" – organised by MI-6 and covered by the Air Police.

"One could delve into the history of any type of British aircraft and find a mass of confusion. Whenever a plane is pressed into or out of military service there's an opportunity for confusion.

"MI-6 and MI-5 got very excited in the early days of WWI when they suddenly realised that mastery of the air provided them with a whole new environment in which to stage accidents. No longer would they have to rely on people falling down gang-planks, poisoned by a Chief Steward, crushed by a cistern falling off a ship's toilet wall, or eaten by a shark. Now there was a whole new environment brimming with possibilities, completely at their beck-and-call.

"The RAF used to have huge rows about how someone had supposedly died in the air, but they found Winterbotham hugely accommodating and never looked back. A special section of the RAF was formed to master this new environment – Air 3 – and F. W. Winterbotham became Wing Commander responsible for the distribution of Ultra intelligence.

"All the museum historians are picked solely for their ability to swallow the bullshit from the officially embedded historians as they die off. In Short/Sunderland's case, none of their buildings remain at Rochester – there is no plaque and no museum, only a ramp going into the sea and a new motorway. In extreme cases museum historians are left uninstructed and in highly secretive cases they are left without a museum."

Sabotaged Sunderland Development

The Sunderland model s.23 had a maximum speed of 320 kmph with a cruise speed of 265 kmph, a laughably small range, an empty weight of 10,900 kg and a loaded weight of 18,400 kg meaning it could carry 7500 kg. It had four 686 kW engines, a length of 27 metres and a wingspan of 35 metres.

The Sunderland model s.23 (4 July 1936–38) was a very slow and heavy plane with a laughable payload and range. This made it next to useless, which made it all the more loved by the British and utilised by the British monarchy. It was a flying turtle.

In 1937 the second and third C-Class flying boats were stripped down and given additional fuel tanks to make the transatlantic flights, but its payload was minimal, maintaining its overriding characteristic – Sunderlands could fly, but little else.

In 1938 the Sunderland model s.30 was delivered with Pegasus 22 engines providing 753 kW each. This was a 10% improvement in engine output, but only eight were built.

In September 1939 three bigger-and-better Sunderland s.26 G-Class flying boats were built powered by four Bristol Hercules engines providing 1030 kW – 50% up on the first model. This increased the range to 4800 km and could carry a combined weight of 34,000 kg – 85% up on the first model. The plane was starting to become useful so it underwent a name change.

When WWII started in September 1939 these flying boats were pressed into military service for ocean patrol with four 7.7 mm guns (.303).

When the slow and cumbersome s.23 Empire boats were pressed into military service, the RAF called it the s.25. With much love and little quality they became "one of the most famous flying boats ever built" and the first Sunderland Mark I flew on 16 October 1937 (15 months after the first s.23).

The new Pegasus XXII engines with 753 kW were not ready and the planes were fitted with Bristol Pegasus X engines 709 kW making them 10% less powerful. This required a new wing design. The new Pegasus XXII engines were ready on 7 March 1938 with 21 production models on order dating back two years.

The modified military version, the A.33 was delayed for 5 months to October 1938. The new flap system shortened the length of takeoff. It was fitted with three .303 guns which meant it could kill in all directions but do little damage to other aircraft. Due to the heavy .303 machine gun tail turret, the wings were swept back 4.25° which meant the engines and floats had to be canted slightly. This was tinkering without forethought. The A.33 suffered structural failure during taxi trials and was scrapped – never to fly.

The new thicker wings carried four Pegasus XXII engines, six drum fuel tanks with a total capacity of 9200 litres. Four more fuel tanks were later added behind the rear wing spar giving 11,602 litres. This could then carry 900 kg of bombs, mines and later depth charges. Ordnance was carried inside the fuselage (the body of the plane) and winched out under the wings through wide hatches on each side of the fuselage.

Originally the number of crew was 7, but this increased to 11 and later to 13. The Sunderland Mark I had six bunks and a galley with a stove for cook-ups. The first Sunderland Mark I was delivered in June 1938. By September 1939 at the outbreak of WWII the RAF were operating 40 Sunderlands. The Sunderland had no ability to land on land and could only take off from water. If it landed on land, it was a crash.

The Sunderland quickly proved themselves to be inadequate against German submarines and U-boats. They were adapted with depth charges which would bounce off the water back up into the air and hit the tail of the Sunderland and explode. With sufficient embarrassment the depth charges were designed to sink before they exploded (Torpex depth charges from early 1943), but this was countered by a new form of self-sabotage, early warning-to-the-enemy radar.

In October 1941 Sunderlands were fitted with Anti-Surface Vessel radar (ASV Mark II) meaning it could only detect vessels on the surface. This was a primitive form of low-frequency radar with a wavelength of 1.5 metres and featured 22 stickleback aerials dotted all over the plane making it look like an Asian apartment.

The ASV Mark II radar (and not the plane) were picked up by the German radar warning system, Metox. This reversed the kills from German to British for the 18 months from October 1941 to early 1943. The British fitted ASV Mark II radar downed a lot of British planes.

German U-boats and submarines with longer range and more powerful weapons could detect the Sunderland crawling along the sky and would fire while the flying turtle was still out of its range. The Sunderlands had become completely useless against German submarines and U-boats and any British who went out in Sunderlands from October 1941 to early 1943 went out as cannon fodder. This was a crucial turning point in the war.

> The Sunderlands would have been more effective without the radar as it was their ASV Mark II radar that made them detectable and not the plane. For this their British CEO of design and development, Arthur Gouge, was cited for a knighthood.

A total of 75 Sunderland Mark Is were built – around 30 by Short's factories in Rochester, England, 15 by Blackburn at Dumbarton, and around 30 by factories in Belfast in Northern Ireland. The Irish did not like the British and equally supported the Germans. This meant that up to 40% of the Sunderland Mark I were up for sabotage and it only takes one sabotage to make history.

Short knew this and vetted all the Irish workers ensuring they were all Protestant, British loyalists and loyal members of the Lodge. It was a well-known Protestant boast that "It was harder for a Cattle Dog [Catholic] to get a job at Shorts than it was for a camel to squeeze its way through the eye of a needle."

After 18 months of pro-German/anti-British kills and with the loss of many Sunderlands, the new barely-improved Mark III was fitted with ASV Mark III centimetric band antennas.

Production had moved to the Sunderland Mark II for a short period (August–December 1941). The Mark II featured Pegasus XVIII engines with two-speed superchargers providing 794 kW each and a high turnover of engines. This was an improvement on the Pegasus XXII engines of 5% and a reduction in power on the September 1939 Bristol Hercules engines of 30% – providing a new version that was underpowered from 2 years prior. The near useless .303 rounds were maintained, but with twice the ammunition capacity – 4000 rounds. 43 Sunderland Mark IIs were built (5 by Blackburn at Dumbarton, 15 miles downstream from Glasgow in Scotland).

In December 1941 production moved to the Sunderland Mark III with improved seaworthiness – less water inside and a new hull step that allowed the plane to come unstuck from the water in a smoother curve as opposed to an abrupt separation. Happy with this, a total of 461 were built; 170 by Blackburn (Scotland) and the remaining 291 by the Short Brothers in Rochester (England), Belfast (Northern Ireland) and a new plant at Lake Windemere in the Lake District (north of Manchester).

A Mark I Sunderland in war colours belonging to No. 210 Squadron. The Pegasus engines were massively underpowered and the engines would fail on a regular basis, sometimes three on one trip. Ocassionally the crew had to run up and down inside the cabin space to try and break the suction from the water. The Mark I could take off on one engine but it took up to 10 miles to leave the water. This Mark I Sunderland had side blister guns prior to the dorsal turrret.

The Sunderland Mark III had a maximum speed of 340 kmph, a range of 4800 km, an empty weight of 14,970 kg and a maximum load weight of 26,130 kg meaning it could carry 11,160 kg. It was 26 metres long, 9.8 metres high, had a wingspan of 34.4 metres and a service ceiling of 4575 metres (15,000 feet).

This was supposed to be an improvement on the Sunderland s.23 which first flew five years earlier. It wasn't. It was still a flying turtle.

After more than five years of British improvements the maximum speed had increased by 10 mph, the length had decreased by 1 metre, the wingspan had decreased by 0.3 metres, the empty weight had increased by 4070 kg and the range was the same as the G-Class built in September 1939. The only improvement after five years was that it could carry 3600 kg more, but it still had a laughably small range.

The Sunderlands stemmed from a competition for long-range aircraft and they struggled to make the distance, only doing so with additional fuel tanks. With these designs and self-sabotage in mind, designer Arthur Gouge (1890–1962) was knighted and promoted to President of the Royal Aeronautical Society. Neither now exist.

Some of the Sunderland's were only used for search rescue and on 21 September 1939 two Sunderlands rescued 34 crew off the torpedoed merchantman Kensington Court in the North Sea. All Sunderlands were available to be fitted with a bright Leigh searchlight to make night rescue possible. These Leigh searchlights were fitted to very few Sunderlands thus ensuring any British shot down in the afternoon had a maximum chance of drowning. The Leigh searchlights were not rare as both New Zealand Sunderands had them. It was just that they weren't fitted to the British flying boats.

Propaganda was high and all records of kills were well kept. A Royal Australian Air Force Sunderland (RAAF) managed its first kill, a U-boat on 17 July 1940, after which the new early warning-to-the-enemy ASV Mark II radar was installed. This sabotaged every Sunderland opportunity from October 1941 to early 1943.

On 3 April 1940, a Sunderland operating off Norway was attacked by six German Ju88 fighters (exactly a month after the CABOT and CARIBOU incidents). The Sunderland shot one Junkers down, damaged another and drove off the rest. The British then said the Germans named their Sunderland the "Fliegende Stachelsweine" (Flying Porcupine) referring to its abundance of small short range fire and lack of big fire-power (cannons). The Sunderlands were well built and could take many hits, but it was better named the 'Flying Turtle', or 'Show Pony'. It was only luck if a Sunderland downed a plane and only luck if it returned home – 93 % of them didn't.

On 2 June 1943 an RAAF Sunderland Mark III did battle with eight Ju88 long-range fighters. There were nine Australians on board and only two British. They were under the command of Australian Lieutenant Colin Walker, so they had a better chance.

The Sunderland was searching for the remains of the actor Leslie Howard whom they were told had crashed in the Bay of Biscay the day before (1 June 1943), but Leslie Howard was covering for his homosexuality by doubling for Winston Churchill and was shot down over the English Channel after his 'location, departure time and direction' were leaked to the Germans through known double agents.

Eight Ju88s were spotted so the Sunderland immediately dropped all its depth charges (making it useless against German submarines and U-boats) went to full revs (which all the earlier models had to fly at normally) and did corkscrew evasive manoeuvres. One engine got knocked out. On the fighters' third pass, the top turret gunner managed to shoot one Ju88 down and on the fourth pass a second was shot down.

On the fifth pass most of the crew were hit and one was mortally wounded. Only two Ju88s made it back to base. The others were nicked and faltered. The Sunderland Mark III crew threw everything overboard and nursed the flying boat back to the Cornish coast, beached it in the surf, waded to shore, then watched the waves break it up.

Lieutenant Colin Walker got a DSO and a ground job, sick of the Flying Turtle. The surviving nine crew went up in another Sunderland and were shot down by six Ju88 two months later. There were no survivors.

What makes this tale all the more interesting is that there were no Sunderlands listed as downed in August 1943. The closest was the CAMILLA which crashed at Port Moresby on 22 April 1943, followed by the CLIFTON at Sydney on 18 November 1944.

Throughout the entire six year war 749 Sunderlands[27] managed to

[27] Some say approximately 600 Sunderlands.

destroy 28 U-boats and assist in sinking 7 more. To say that they were a reconnaissance aircraft and not a defensive or attack aircraft is a cop out. This was the worst ratio of any aircraft in the history of WWII.[28] By the end of the war less than 50 Sunderlands in service had survived.

The circumstances of the demise of most Sunderlands were not listed as flying boats were a matter of public pride. Sunderlands were lost leaders.

In early 1943 the new centimetric radar completely baffled the German's Metox radar at first, which meant the British Sunderlands could see German surface vessels before the Germans could shoot them down.

The Germans reacted by increasing the size and range of their firepower to two 37 mm and eight 20 mm flak guns. This was far bigger than the British 7.7 mm guns and Sunderlands that were hit then tried to crash into the German submarines, but only one Sunderland managed it. With no improvements coming from the government, the crew adapted their own Sunderlands with 12.7 mm (0.5 calibre) machine guns.

This was officially frowned upon and was usually resorted to only by Colonial Trash and Machine Gun Thieves (the CT & MGT). Quite often they doubled for each other and swapped places at midnight. It was quite common in the early part of the war to see Italian 20 mm Breda Machine Guns fitted to British aircraft under Colonial control. The Greeks and the French preferred German weaponry.

A Maori Warrant Officer received over thirty warnings that his mounting German machine guns on a Bren Gun carrier was illegal and action would soon be taken against him. As a good Maori he wrote back saying, "As I'm planning to be killed soon, I won't be taking this seriously". He was eventually sent home. This was simpler and less painful than shooting himself in the leg.

The Sunderland Mark IV was then developed with more powerful Hercules XVII 1253 kW engines (a 66% improvement), seven 12.7 mm machine guns and a twin 20 mm cannon. Two prototypes were made and 30 production models were ordered with Hercules 1720 Hp XIX engines (1283 kW, a 70% improvement). These Sunderlands were so different and so vastly improved they were redesignated the s.45 Seaford.

---

[28] There were minor exceptions, mainly British.

The s.45 Seaford was finally an effective and far superior flying weapon, equal to the improved German Junkers Ju52/3m g10e. Intended for the Pacific, it did not see any combat and was sabotaged by production too late to see any action, creating yet another period of self-sabotaged British development. Even the prototypes were not used in action. The first Sunderland Mark IV/s.45 Seaford's flew in April 1945, just weeks before WWII ended, so it was too little too late.

The s.23 Sunderland/s.25 Sandringham engines suffered from overheating. This caused them and their successors' engines to be replaced more than any other plane's engine, and this was on a very regular basis. The Sunderland V developed out of crew concerns for the engines which had to be run on full combat power at all times.

Australian crews were not self-saboteurs and refused to love things that didn't work to capacity, so they demanded the Pegasus engines be replaced with Pratt & Whitney R-1830-90B Twin Wasp engines. These 14-cylinder engines provided 895 kW each, were an improvement on the high-maintenance Pegasus XVIII supercharged 794 kW engines by 12% and the 753 kW Pegasus XXII engines by 18%. The main advantage of the American engines was vastly reduced maintenance and the ability to fly when two engines were down on the same wing.

If two Pegasus engines on a Sunderland got hit, it steadily lost altitude and crashed dead in the water, or very dead on land.

To produce the Sunderland Mark V, two Sunderland Mark IIIs were taken off the production line in early 1944 and fitted with four American Pratt & Whitney engines. The plane could now maintain altitude with two engines down on one wing and could cruise without the engines running in combat mode, and the range was the same. This was the first development of the Sunderland that was not self-sabotage, but it was also too little too late.

The first non-sabotaged Sunderland made it to operation in February 1945, two months before the end of the war, but were still fitted with near useless .303 machine guns and the new centimetric AV Mark VIC radar which had been used on the Mark IIIs for some time. The 12.7 mm guns and 20 mm cannon on the Mark IV were dropped for no apparent reason other than the British sabotage of Australian crews.

155 Sunderland Mark Vs were built and 33 Mark IIIs were converted (which meant changing the British engines to American). The last Mark V was delivered in June 1946 with a total production of 749 Sunderlands since their inception.

In 1940 the British Air Ministry requested another four-engined flying boat, this time for long-range reconnaissance with heavy defensive armament and an offensive war load of 1815 kg. The first prototype was flown on 14 December 1944 with dummy nose and tail turrets and no guns. The Shetland was substantially bigger, had a greenhouse cockpit for better vision and twice the takeoff payload. It was powered by four Bristol Centaurus XI 18-cylinder radial 1865 kW engines and 4-bladed propellers. Its range 7100 km, speed 423 kmph and service ceiling 5180 metres (17,000 ft) made it far superior to the Sunderland, but it never made it into production and caught fire on its moorings on 28 January 1946.

A second passenger carrying prototype was made and flown on 17 September 1947, flown several more times and then scrapped, never to fly a commercial flight.

> All the Sunderlands, Shetlands and Princesses were sabotaged, either by using under-powered high-maintenance engines that if two failed the plane crashed, early warning-to-the-enemy ASV Mark II radar, using .303 machine guns, not using or removing 20 mm cannon, by the timing of the improved models, and by delayed production.

To increase the sabotage, six Sunderland Mark IIIs were stripped down and used as mail carriers by the BOAC (British Overseas Airways Corporation) and another 29 were refitted as mail carriers and passenger liners carrying (wait for it) 24 passengers. Another form of sabotage, this removed 35 Sunderland Mark IIIs from wartime service.

> This was such a shameful period in British aviation history that it was covered up by the most impractical of last resorts – 'love'. In war, love is as useless as tits on a bull. It is the equivalent of expecting a sexually bent Air Commodore, Inspector-General of RAF Welfare, or Commander of the Air Defence of Scotland to act in the best interests of their country.

CUMBERLAND/AWARUA/AOTEAROA (G-AFDA/ZK-AMC/ZK-AMA).

According to Shorts this Sunderland was delivered on 25 May 1939. Other official records show it arrived in August 1939. The newspapers note its first flight was Auckland to Sydney on 1 May 1940. Pictured is the return maiden voyage over Auckland on 2 May 1940.

ZK-AMA AOTEAROA was replaced in 1947 and then broken up. The replacement was a complete failure and was replaced again in 1950 with the Mark IV variant specifically built for TEAL (Tasman Empire Airways Limited) with a steeper inset hull. The Mark IV/Solent final service was on 14 September 1960. It was then stored at Hobsonville, officially until May 1966 and then onto the Auckland Museum of Transport and Technology.

KIWIs recognise there was a flying boat, but not that there were three different types. They also note Sunderlands still skimming Wellington waters in 1969.

Post War Refitting

After WWII, a number of Mark IIIs were refitted as Sandringham Mark I and a number of Mark V were refitted as Sandringham Mark II.

In 1946 the second production of Sunderland Mark V/Seafords were loaned to BOAC for evaluation as a civil airliner and 12 were converted into Solent Mark 2. Most of the early RAF Mark V were rebuilt as Solent Mark 3s. These were then sold to the civilian public as Solents and not Sunderlands. A Solent is a demilitarised Sunderland with the front and rear gun turrets removed and the nose and tail reshaped.

Sunderlands continued to be used by the RAF after the war in 1948, landing on Hitler's ill-famed Lake Havel. They then resupplied the British Greenland expedition (1951–54) and were then phased out.

In 1951, 19 Sunderlands were recondition in Belfast for Aeronavale (French naval air arm) and 16 were reconditioned in England for the RNZAF (Royal New Zealand Air Force). France used theirs until 1960 and New Zealand until the early 60s.

The New Zealand flying boat was actually launched in Belfast (not England) by Queen Elzabeth II in 1949 (not 1950) which helped to sell it to New Zealand as a new Solent with no mention, ever, that it was a converted Sunderland with altered nose and tail.

> The Sunderland was used until 1970, not the early 60s and always drew a crowd of Kiwis – Keen Interest Without Intelligence.

But what's worse is that this was done three times and each series of flying boat sold to New Zealand was sabotaged. The first two Sunderlands had the same two successive names but in reverse order (AO-TEA-ROA/AWARUA/AOTEAROA). These were both replaced twice and the new planes retained the same name and serial number so when the civilian and military talk about a Canpous, Sunderland, Solent, Empire class or C class and how to differentiate between the planes, it was all wrong. One flying boat could be all of these things. This ruse was backed up by the RNZAF who still teach-to-confuse onto all matters Sunderland and Solent. The RNZAF do not even complain that one of their planes never arrived.

> Getting ripped off by the British was akin to getting sodomised by the British, so for the RNZAF, Mum's the word.

More Colonial Confusion

In 1938 Union Airways placed an order for the three Empire class flying boats to be delivered to New Zealand. "Certificates for work carried out were presented by Short Bros. to Imperial Airways Limited, to be honoured within seven days. The final certificate, when the aircraft was handed over at delivery, was due for payment within 14 days."[29] Often this delivery took place months later, or not at all.

Twelve days prior to WWII Britain delivered two of the three planes to New Zealand which arrived four months after the official April delivery date on 28 August 1939. These were s.30 Sunderlands romantically referred to as Empire class and operated until 1947. The third boat never arrived, but New Zealand still made all the progress payments. Three years after the official delivery date this third Sunderland was destroyed at Bathurst off West Africa on 14/15 September 1942 while still under British command.

"Four larger 30-seat Short s.25 Sandringham class flying boats replaced the two smaller Empire Class craft in 1946, but these proved unreliable through overheating engines and were replaced by s.45 Solent flying boats."[30]

> The s.25 Sandringham suffered from overheating engines, but New Zealand stuck with them from 1947–50. The s.23 Sunderland/Empire boat was the same was the s.25 but with military applications. When these were removed the s.23 and s.25 were the same. The Sunderland Mark IV, s.45 Seaford and Solent were also the same plane. Their difference was in the romantic attachment placed on them.

Solent Mark IV flying boat ZK-RMA ARANUI was built by Short Brothers and Harland Ltd in Belfast and delivered to TEAL on 30 November 1949. It was the last of four Solents to be built. Its inaugural flight was from Wellington to Sydney 5/6 October 1950, 11 months after it was officially delivered. The last officially recorded flight was Cook Islands – Samoa – Fiji – Auckland on 15 September 1960, but it was still flying in 1969 between RNZAF bases in New Zealand and Fiji.

When Queen Elizabeth II and Prince Philip boarded the Sunderland Mark IV/s.45 Seaford/Solent Mark IV flying boat in New

[29] Brian Cassidy, *Flying Empires*, p. 53.
[30] *Otago Daily Times*, 30 April 1990.

Zealand in 1953, they walked 7 metres apart with another standing between them. (Wing Commander George Gudsell in full fruit salad.) Their sexual relationship was already over. They entered into a portside door 0.6 metres above the tide, the same level as the dock. One could step straight from the dock into the cabin door and down to the lower level. Any ramp was just for tidal convenience. The portside door sill was at the same level as the lower level window sills.

> Eleven years earlier her uncle had walked in the portside door and out the starboard side door. This is how history is made for the oligarchy and confused for the masses.

Sabotage by Salvage

The British have a way of writing history that puts them in gentlemanly stead and none of the crashed Sunderlands were attributed to have any salvaged parts. The G-AFRB was retained as unfinished and never flown because almost all of the salvaged parts were attributed to it, yet it always remained 75% complete. Salvage was expensive. Little of the salvaged planes was ever put to use and crashes were never blamed on salvaged parts.

Parts of the crashed CYGNUS (December 1937) were used in the G-ARFB that never flew. The mainplanes were stored in the open and when High Duty Alloys came to test spar boom extrusions, they were under strength and had to be scrapped. The tail unit, engine nacelles and rear section of the hull were most likely reused, but this plane never flew.[31]

The CAPELLA was salvaged almost entirely and shipped back to Rochester. The wing floats, some of the control surfaces and the anchor were re-used. Salvage and recovery cost £2100, 20% of the price of new Sunderland, so salvaging was "scrapped", but in reality continued. The date of the CAPELLA crash is given as both 12 March 1938 and 12 March 1939.

When the CHALLENGER was salvaged after only three days immersion in the sea, a knife could be pushed through the magnesium alloy reduction gear casing of the engines. The alloys were that bad. Regardless, the airscrews, with their bent blades, mainplanes, tail unit and engines were salvaged in May 1939.

---

[31] Brian Cassidy, *Flying Empires*, p. 57.

The CENTURION crashed on the Hoogly river at Calcutta on 1 May 1939 (or 12 June 1939). The aft end of the hull, the tail planes, the fin and rudder, three engines and airscrews and the fuel and oil tanks were salvaged.

The CLYDE flipped over in a hurricane and four engines and airscrews, oil tanks, the two elevators, one aileron, the port wing float and the radio equipment were salvaged. The Relunit fuel tank valves were reconditioned and officially used in the tanks of the G-AFRB that never flew.

The engines of CONNEMARA were brought up from the bottom of Southampton Water and stripped down.

Many of the flying boats were ordered as replacements for the ones that had crashed. Many crashed, so there were many orders. Obviously there was collusion with the insurance companies, so Lloyds was probably involved and salvage was probably demanded. The last order on 7 June 1939 was for three s.33 hybrid aircraft, the CLIFTON, CLEOPATRA and G-AFRB (Construction No. S1025–S1027). Work on the 43rd boat was stopped when it was about 75% complete and it became the blaming ground for all salvaged parts. The G-AFRB was never flown and never attempted to fly.

Sabotage of Sunderlands was prolific as the Queen's world expert Brian Cassidy states in *Flying Empires*:

> "Why was CAPRICORNUS descending in a snow storm with the engines throttled back, just before it struck the ground? How many of the Horseshoe route 'boats were re-engined with Pegasus XXII engines? Some of the Horseshoe route 'boats had their fuel tankage increased from 650 gals. to 1010 gals. What effect did this have on the mainplane spars? Indeed, how many spar designs were there? There is reference in the Type Record of a Mark II. Why was the hull of the forty-third 'boat kept in its crate in the Barge Yard until as late as 1943? How did CORSAIR get so far off course before setting down on the River Dangu? And what really happened to CIRCE and CLARE, both of whom disappeared over the water with their passengers and crews? Traces of CLARE were found but nothing was heard or seen of CIRCE."[32]

Nothing was heard of the CARIBOU either.

[32] Brian Cassidy, *Flying Empires, Short 'C' class Empire flying boats*, Preface.

The CAMERONIAN over Windsor Castle in 1938.

The rare starboard side passenger door as shown in *Raiders of the Lost Ark* (1981). The real *China Clipper* crashed in 1945 and none of the American Pan Am Flying boats survived past 1946.

This *Raiders* flying boat was British built and found in a museum in San Francisco with one engine still working. The Pan American logo was added and the plane was superimposed at Treasure Island Naval Base by Industrial Light and Magic.

The *Raiders* flying boat is the surviving CARIBOU – the back up for the CABOT. Some things are best hidden in plain sight and the homosexual occult is full of such jokes.

Filming for *Raiders of the Lost Ark* began in the summer of 1980. This points to the Duke of Kent dying before this date, otherwise the CARIBOU would not have been used.

The Duke of Kent's lover, the Duke of Hamilton flew to the west coast of America in 1946 for no formal or declared reason. Perhaps it was to offload the CARIBOU. His landing was noteable in that one landing wheel failed to open and he walked away unharmed.

Dunkirk
Operation DYNAMO

19 May–4 June 1940

Early on in the war, it was evident that Goering and Hitler were both British agents, although they may not have known each other were. Doentiz, Raeder, Milch, Canaris and Oster were also British agents, as was Rosenbaud who was codenamed 'The Griffen'. Most of them were accessed after WWI when they were POWs in British hands. Canaris had many heart-to-hearts with British Interrogating Officers as did Doenitz, who was under psychiatric care in Manchester (October 1918–July 1919).

Rosenbaud was an Austrian Army Officer captured by the British. He was turned around by a lowly British Regimental I.O. in Italy at the end of WWI. Rosenbaud went on to report to British Control Officers right through the 20s, 30s and 40s and was ultimately taken over by the Americans. At the end of WWII Rosenbaud was awarded the American Medal of Freedom, while his ex-wife became the chief of the Stasi. Whoever said spying wasn't in the family.

A huge number of other German officers would rewrite reports, fudge documents and not work in Germany's interests. Defeatism was rampant right through the entire German Armed Forces and played a part in nearly all battlefield loses, including Dunkirk. The loss of the four German battleships is a case in point.

Every loss was accompanied by a massive breach of standing orders and procedures. In virtually none of these cases was the offending officer prosecuted and someone else always became the scapegoat. This was controlled warfare on an enormous scale that breached both sides to the point of musical chairs.

British Captain Liddel Hart (Ret.) was renowned as a newspaper columnist and military strategist for the press. He had written several books on armoured tactics which the German General Guderian praised as giving him all his ideas. Liddel Hart ran around with a suitcase containing groceries and pad paper and was well-known by German officers in every Allied holding camp as a virtual shop steward for German Generals. He was on very friendly terms with most of them and practised the time-honoured ritual of feeding them from his picnic basket disguised as a suitcase. Then he got down to the details. Hart had no secretary and was not worried by keeping notes as the conversations were taped.

At all times Hart denied anything other than academic interest. He wrote letters for German Generals complaining about their treatment, their wife's treatment and even the schoolwork of their children. He got American camps to hand over their German Generals and accomplished tasks with such ease, that he was very obviously connected to the higher rungs of SIS and Army Intelligence.

When denied favours, he would say, "Do you mind if we just ring George or Trevor [his handlers back in Britain] and I'm sure everything will be all right" . . . and it always was. Moments later all obstructions were cleared and Captain Liddel Hart (Ret.) could do whatever pleased him or the German General he was either feeding, supporting, interviewing, or influencing.

Spymaster: "British Intelligence was a monumental fuck up. There were so many different outfits doing exactly the same thing that nobody could figure out what they did, what was going on, or what the outcome was supposed to be. Working with them were the Czechs, the Poles, the Greeks and the Free-French, the Danes, Norwegians and even the Free-Finns, so it was an orgy of malconstructed misnomers and faux pas of intelligence gathering. As such, British Intelligence was the Keystone Cops of misconstruction and indeed the Keystone Cops were films based around intelligence gathering.

From 15 to 22 May 1940 the Germans made their famous sickle-stroke move (Sichelschitt) sweeping southwards into France and then northwards towards Dunkirk and Calais. The French and British who had advanced into Belgium found themselves separated by the German Panzer tank corridor.

On 19 May 1940 British Commander Viscount Gort considered withdrawing the British Expeditionary Force (BEF) to the coast for escape by sea, but the British government refused. The same day Admiral Bertram Ramsay was ordered to prepare for an evacuation. The person who gave this order is left out of the history books. "On 19 May, had ordered Admiral Bertram Ramsay to prepare for an evacuation [sic]."[1]

[1] *WWII*, p. 15.

Mistakes and omissions in history are the strongest indication of where the real history lies.

By 22 May 1940 the French and British were threatened with encirclement. All the Channel ports were taken by the Germans except for Dunkirk and all the Allied hands withdrew to Dunkirk in hope of a sea rescue. British Commander Viscount Gort realised he was running short of supplies and ammunition and ordered the British to fall back towards the coast. The Allies set up their final line of defence at Canal d'Aire outside Dunkirk.

On 24 May 1940 the Germans broke through this final line of defence and 340,000 British and Allies were trapped. Two-thirds of them were British and their most experienced troops. Another 220,000 Allied troops were trapped at Cherbourg, Saint-Malo, Brest and Saint-Nazaire. In three weeks the German army had taken more than one million Allied prisoners and trapped 560,000 British and Allied troops, while sustaining only 60,000 German casualties.

Goering promised Hitler he could finish off the British and Allies at Dunkirk with the Luftwaffe alone. But Hitler ordered the German troops to stop advancing and to stop attacking.

Germany could have been 1.5 million men ahead in the first ten months of the war but they decided to let 560,000 British and Allied men escape to fight again.

History notes that Hitler's reasons for this are unclear.

Under Operation DYNAMO the British and Allies escaped by sea from 26 May to 4 June 1940 on 848 British, French and Belgium craft. Destroyers, private motor cruisers and everything in between picked up 560,000 men off Dunkirk's ten-mile stretch of beach during eight days of disorganised and panicked evacuation. Even British Naval crews mutinied because it was too dangerous to go.

The Germans had every chance to kill the British and Allies and they did strafe the beaches, but not as much as they could have. All the Germans had to do to increase the body count was to use their usual air-dropped contact-fused or pressure-switched airburst munitions which were absolutely lethal to unprotected men on the ground, but the Germans even failed to do this in great numbers.

The only excuse that this was not done in abundance was that the Germans had run out of the correct munitions and resorted to using delayed action devices that went 3–4 metres into the sand. Many of the German warheads were purposefully changed from contact and airburst explosives to delayed-action devices before the attack. This resulted in spectacular vertical explosions. They were good for the cameras but caused minimal damage.

The history books say that the Luftwaffe held back because of the RAF. At this point in time the operating RAF had very small numbers, but it was their first use of Spitfires and the Germans were expecting a cakewalk.

The Spitfires were flown aggressively, mainly by Colonials, each carrying eight machine guns. German air-gunners weren't expecting Spitfires to pop up out of nowhere and shred them. The German Me109 and Me110 crews were all huddled together in the front cockpit and they had to decide between self-defence or strafing and bombing the beach. As a result, the few Colonial-flown Spitfires managed to draw the larger number of Messerschmitts away from the escaping Allies, but even this was still not enough to engineer the relatively peaceful outcome.

Hitler and Goering's Luftwaffe had the opportunity for eight days of near unobstructed bombing and total annihilation but they let the opportunity go. Of the 41 destroyers only 6 were sunk. Of the 807 other craft, only 19 were damaged.

The British press had instructions that discouraged them from photographing dead bodies at Dunkirk, soldiers with torn and missing clothing, and soldiers who had stripped their own clothing to swim out to the Allied rescue craft.

The British authorities are renown for making out they did everything to a plan after the war was over. Their numbers of dead men, rescued men, rescue craft and aircraft should be considered (at least in part) one of the casualties of war. When German spies inspected the British hospitals afterwards, many of those on the stretchers were already dead and many of these were nearly dead by the time they arrived at Dunkirk. It is presumed the British counted these as injured.

As soon as Viscount Gort was gone Hitler resumed his attack on the remaining Belgian Army (27 May 1940). The British did not evacuate the Belgians with them and they were left to face the German army and Luftwaffe alone. The Belgians were left for slaughter, surrender and annihilation. King Leopold of Belgium saw this and surrendered unconditionally the same day (27 May 1940).

This left eight days of attack opportunity on Operation DYNAMO with no land resistance, little or no sea resistance, and a small contingent of RAF aircraft 'having a go'.

As an extra present to the Germans, the British and Allies left all their equipment behind, which aided the German occupation of the low countries throughout the war.

Hitler and Goering had given the British a 24-hour window, which was extended to an eight-day window and 560,000 Allied troops were set free with only minor harassment.

By this time the French had lost 45% of their divisions and to all intents and purposes the Battle of France was lost 12 days later on 9 June 1940.

The Italians finally decided to side with the Germans in 'The Pact of Steel' on 22 May 1940, the same day the Germans encircled the French and British. Bu that time the Germans had taken all the Channel ports except Dunkirk.

The Italians weren't out to win the war, but they wanted to be on the winning side. Many Italians couldn't give a rat's arse about the war, hence the sensible *Italian Book of War Heroes* being the shortest book in the world – 'sensible' because the heroes died and the cowards survived.

When the Italians finally got around to attacking the French frontier on 20 June 1940, they made little progress and Hitler soon realised they would be of no strategic importance. The French and Italians swapped recipes at their WWII frontier and cooked their way through the war, boasting as to who were the greater lovers.

The French and Italians differ from the English and Germans in that they are romantic and enjoy living. The English and Germans, on the other hand, seem to enjoy dying. To them, death justifies the hero. To the French and Italians, making love justifies the hero.

WWII could not have been set up better. Germany had Belgium, France and much of Eastern and Northern Europe. The British had been stung and were now willing to fight, but they lacked the military might.

"Controversy still rages about why Hitler stayed his hand and allowed the British Army to get away. It may have been one of the several key mistakes he made during the Second World War, though some believe that Hitler still wanted to make peace with Britain and thought that this might be more easily achieved if the British Army was not forced into a humiliating surrender.

"Although the action at Dunkirk was a retreat, it was hailed as a victory by the British. In the long run, it proved decisive. The bulk of Britain's most experienced troops had been saved."[2]

The war could now continue in force. Without this British-influenced move by Hitler, England would be speaking German today, America would have never got into the war and WWII would have been between Germany and Russia with Britain watching handcuffed, rather than with a ruling pen.

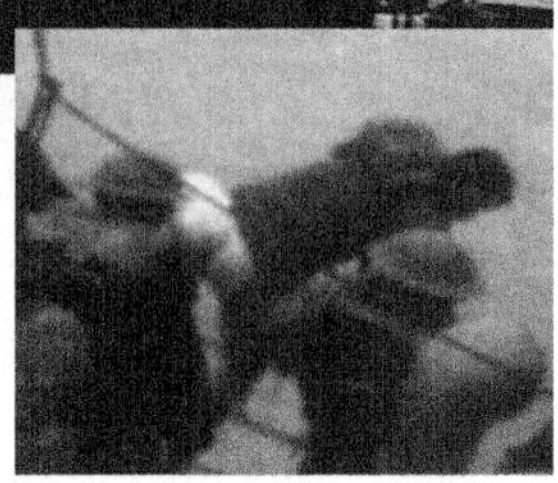

Dunkirk's Operation DYNAMO is the most blatant example of organised war extension and double agent activity the world has ever seen. It screams so loud, it gives historians a headache and makes the Freemasons blush and run for cover.

[2] *WWII*, p. 16.

James Bond

Enter the cult figure – James Bond (18), morphic resonances' main man of the twentieth century. All hail Bond, for through him, we shall bond. His name is laced with British and European history: James, Jesus' brother, second born in AD1 (or AD0 for the pedantic), conceived in the first week of December 1BC, and born to set the clocks on the 15 September AD0, having the highest qualities of integrity and investigative intuition, the Joseph of Aramathea, the Prince of Aramathea, deposed King David and leader of the exiled Davidic teachings, head Druid, tin trader, the original creator of Westminster Law and deposer of Roman Law, Jesus Justice, magic-mushroom eater who sought health and life extension through mineral-rich cunnilingus with virgins of royal lineage, the ladies' man, the holder of secrets, the true spiritual teacher, the second son of Joseph and Mary, the former prince and priestess of the Davidic and Zadoc lines; James, the original acknowledged parent of the monarchies of Europe, the man who brought culture to babarian Britain – yeah that guy, James, for through him we shall all bond; either that or Ian Fleming actually did pick up the classic ornithological book on his first trip to the Caribbean in November 1944, *Field Guide to Birds of the West Indies*, written by one James Bond.

On 14 October 1963, Ian Fleming, author of the James Bond books and inspiration of the James Bond movies, wrote to John Ainsworth-Davis: "Without any doubt, you and your operation were my secret inspiration for all that followed; a secret that I have never revealed to anyone else."[1]

John Ainsworth-Davis was also known as Lieutenant-Commander C. J. J. Creighton RN, Christopher John James Creighton, Chris Creighton, Christopher Ainsworth-Davis, Christopher Robin, C.R., with a nom de guerre of 'Leading Seaman John Davis'.

He was born on 13 March 1924, is 6' 2½", did his first mission at the age of 15½ in 1940 and became Lieutenant-Commander at just 21 years of age. He was the second leader of Operation JAMES BOND in April/May of 1945 into Berlin. He wrote this up in his 1996 book,

[1] *OPJB*, p. 229.

OPJB under his given name – Chris Creighton. He was undoubtedly the inspiration for the James Bond series.

His father, John Ainsworth-Davis, went to school at Christ's College with Lord Louis Mountbatten, Prince Henry and Bertie, the future King George VI. John Ainsworth-Davis was a gold-medal winner at the 1920 Antwerp Olympics for the 4 x 400 relay[2] and later became a doctor specialising as a genito-urinary surgeon. He raised Chris Creighton at 69 Harley Street, London until he was eight years old. Harley Street was a spies paradise.

One of his 'uncles' was Joachim (von) Ribbentrop, the German 'Champagne General', a close friend of his father. He took the young James Bond (5) to rugby matches including the All Blacks/Lions game at Twickenham in January 1930. By 1936, this same man was the Nazi Ambassador to London who had sex with Wallis Simpson once a week and passed the British and French secrets on to Hitler.

Ribbentrop was later condemned at Nuremberg to die by hanging. His sentence and execution confirmed he had too many MI-6 connections. If his story got out the entire view of WWII would have been more like this one sixty years earlier.

When he was eight, Chris Creighton's parents separated and he moved in with his mother onto Winston Churchill's estate. There, Winston Churchill (1874–1965), Lord Louis Mountbatten (1900–79) and Major Desmond Morton (1891–1971) took the young Christopher Creighton under their wing – as one of their own.[3]

With their paternal guidance, he entered the Royal Navy College at Dartmouth (close to Tavistock) in September 1939, aged 15½. During his training the young Chris Creighton was given German POWs whose records had been fabricated with atrocities and was encouraged to kill them. He was given a licence to kill but there wasn't a tuxedo in sight. Almost immediately he went on his first mission and was issued with a silent single-shot Wellrod pistol. His cover was often as a boy pushing a bicycle and most German officers didn't give him a second look.

[2] He ran with Cecil Griffiths, Robert Lindsay and Guy Butler in a time of 3:22.2. This is an av. 400m of 50.55 sec. with the world record set in 1912 (av. of 49.15 sec). Speed was something John Ainsworth-Davis II/Chris Creighton inherited.

[3] During his wilderness years (1929–39) Winston Churchill also took on the Paladin, who was then 12–13 years old.

Ian Fleming (1908–64) had been the *victor ludorum* (champion athlete) at Eton for two years, went to the Royal Military College at Sandhurst, became an agent, worked with Reuters in Moscow (1929–33), learnt German in Austria and further studied languages at Munich and Geneva Universities (1933–39) and was a banker and stockbroker as cover.

Ian Fleming had the luck of the Irish. Part of his brief was intelligence gathering from POW camps and one of these was at Grizedale Hall in the Lake District which he used to visit from London in his open-tourer Bentley. Early in 1941, using leather laundry hamper straps, the German POW, Dieter von Hassel, strapped himself underneath the Bentley. Fleming drove off, got lost on a country road (most road signs were taken down during the war) and got stuck in a wide stream.

As Fleming went for help the stream flooded, and the German officer, one of the Luftwaffe's greatest escape artists, drowned. Fleming knew nothing about it until he was towed out of the stream and back to Grizedale Hall by a woman on a horse.

Fleming was quite upset and said, "It's absolutely tragic to have killed a chap in such circumstances." The Guard Sergeant replied, "I wouldn't worry about that Sir. He's still dead."

The horsewoman had been hiding German prisoners of war (Leutnant Herbult Shultz and Leutnant Victor Molde) using them as concubines and farm help. The last escaper surrendered to police in 1949 not knowing that the war had ended or that Hitler had reportedly suicided. He was being used as a sex-slave long after everyone else had gone home. He was reportedly gutted by his own discovery that he had stayed on four years after the war. He wanted the horsewoman arrested but the police declined amid great mirth.

Mrs William Heelis was the tea lady at Grizedale Hall and she got more out of a German serviceman with a cup of tea than interrogators could with pincers (tongs used in torture). She illustrated and published books under the name Beatrix Potter.

The German officer in charge of the POW camp, Commander Otto Kruger, was in contact with Germany and ran the camp as an intelligence-gathering exercise and was very annoyed that the Luftwaffe officer had even tried to escape. Grizedale Hall was a *Hogan's Heroes* in reverse.[4]

[4] *A Cage of Eagles.*

Kruger's spectacular coup was offering to repair the roof of the Hall. This was undertaken by German labour and closely supervised by British Guards. A year after it was completed a young RAF pilot, who had got lost earlier that day, contacted the British Commanding Officer and thanked him for the directions painted on the roof of the RAF base. The roof was painted (**RAF →**) for the benefit of the Germans.

By 1943, Ian Fleming had distinguished himself in at least five top-secret operations and became Lieutenant-Commander Ian Fleming of the Royal Navy Intelligence Division. He was also the personal assistant to the Director of Naval Intelligence, Rear-Admiral John Godfrey.

Fleming was always ahead of the game and operated with such style and ease that he was referred to as 'the Chocolate Soldier'. He was a master spy with great connections. His father was Valentine Fleming who was an MP and close friend of Winston Churchill. Ian Fleming was the first 'James Bond', if only for a day, and he too took Christopher Creighton under his wing.

Major Desmond Morton created 'M' in 1932 as 'Special Secret intelligence operations' and was financed and protected by successive monarchs: King George V, King Edward VIII, and King George VI etc. M was directed from Morton's home in Crockham Hill, near Westerham in Kent, with the enthusiastic support of Winston Churchill, who lived below Desmond Morton's house in Kent, two miles south of Westerham, in the Vale of Chartwell.

Churchill took all the credit for M and it was written up that Churchill, in his 'lost years' set up a private intelligence network in his home in 1929. However, Churchill was substantially Morton's public cover and confidant. M meant 'mother', and as art imitates life, 'M' is still the name of the governing agency both in the British Government and in the James Bond movies, as in "REPORT IMMEDIATELY HQ M".[5]

Major Desmond Morton, or Morton as he was known, was the Supreme Chief of the Special Secret intelligence operations (M) and his role was pitched above the Prime Minister and his secret circle. It was above MI-5 (Internal), MI-6 (External) and the military. It was the monarchy's special force.

M had free reign, not being controlled by any outside body other

[5] *The Spy Who Loved Me*, 1977.

than the reigning monarch – and when it reigns, it pours. Rather than patriotism, 'M's role was to ensure that the larger events of WWII went according to plan. Such larger events were:

1. Conflict was to be prolonged until the profits were made and the power structures were in place for the next sixty years of social policy.
2. All peace negotiations were to be sabotaged.
3. America was to be drawn very publicly into WWII with America's full knowledge.
4. Britain was to control all the assets of Nazi pillage.
5. All double agents were to be returned to safety with their deaths faked.
6. Doppelgängers to be released as dead, living in other countries, or alive posthumously.
7. Any incriminating evidence against Britain or America was to be destroyed.

Three such incidents were *Pearl Harbor* in Hawaii, *Dieppe* in France, and *Operation James Bond* in Berlin. A study of these OPs gives us a clear understanding of 'Special Secret intelligence operations', the transfer of power, the pointlessness of battle, and the games secret societies play.

Churchill and Roosevelt
in Days of Infamy.

Pearl Harbor
1921–7 December 1941

Pearl Harbor took 16 years to plan and it was either a masterstroke or a complete cock-up. Either way, all sides knew about it at the time. One method of drawing an ally into war is to give the mutual enemy (Japan) enough information to attack the ally (America) without retribution, thus giving the country attacked (America) a clear mandate to join the war. Pearl Harbor was just such a mission and it occurred with full British and American Chief of Staff knowledge.

Britain started planning its next war in 1919 in order to utilise its existing military and to prevent them from getting restless and turning in on themselves and the nation. Britain planned a war with America and it was due to start in 1927. The conflict was based around 'naval tonnage', but was eventually settled with diplomacy and the *Washington Treaty.*

However, a plan to attack Pearl Harbor was commissioned by the British Admiralty and awarded to the consultant Hector C. Bywater, who came up with the *Bywater Plan* which involved dropping torpedoes from planes into Pearl Harbor. It was believed at the time that the harbour was too shallow at 12 metres, but Bywater correctly forecast that adapted torpedoes could be dropped safely and efficiently into the shallow harbour.

Hector C. Bywater (21 October 1884–17 August 1940) was an English and American journalist, author and spy who could hold a packed pub room in rapt attention when he told anecdotes. He wrote *Sea Power in the Pacific* (1921) and *The Great Pacific War* (1925) and knew more about the navies of the world than a roomful of admirals. He published numerous articles on Pacific strategy as the European naval correspondent for the *New York Herald*, the *Baltimore Sun* and the *New York Times.*

When Bywater wrote *Sea Power in the Pacific: A Study of the American-Japanese Naval Problem* (1921), it was an immediate sell-out among Japanese and American Navy General Staff who studied it line by line. The US Naval Institute's *Proceedings* magazine called it "the most important recent estimate of the situation . . . in the Pacific".

It was so 'considered' that it set a special 5:5:3 tonnage ratio between America, Britain and Japan on 15 December 1921 at the Washington Disarmament Treaty.

"What Bywater wrote powerfully influenced Admiral Isoroku Yamamoto, the architect of the Pearl Harbor attack . . . who served as a naval attaché in Washington in the late 1920s. At least once Bywater and Yamamoto met face to face and wiled away an evening discussing the prospects for peace and war over a bottle of Scotch."[1]

Hector C. Bywater was killed 16 months before Pearl Harbor at the age of 55. He was supposedly found in bed alone at his home in London, some time between 16 and 17 August 1940, and was declared the victim of acute alcoholism. The physicians didn't check for any other cause and he was immediately cremated. Modern investigation techniques and circumstantial evidence suggest he was murdered by poison.[2] The order came from the Japanese High Command and was administered with British complicity.

Churchill had already been involved in many assassinations and Hector C. Bywater had a very good chance of sabotaging Churchill's efforts to bring America into the war, all the more so if he were alive. The one man who knew all of Japan's plans for Pearl Harbor, and America's dedication to ignoring it, was killed in the build-up to Pearl Harbor.

With Bywater dead, Yamamoto adapted the *Bywater Plan,* increasing the attack on the Philippines and British possessions and grafting them onto the original attack plan against Hawaii. The adapted British *Bywater Plan* became the plan for Japan's December 1941 attack on Pearl Harbor that brought America into WWII.

The *Lusitania,* Pearl Harbor and 9-11 all get protection under the umbrella of American self-sabotage – DENY, OBSCURE, COVER UP – 1915, 1941 and 2001 are all very questionable years for US patriotism.

Hardly had WWII started when President Roosevelt (Freemason) wrote to Britain's First Lord of the Admiralty, Winston Churchill (Freemason), suggesting they work together via a secret system of communication.

---

[1] William H. Honan, *Visions of Infamy*, p. xiii–p. 8.

[2] William H. Honan, chief cultural correspondent for the *New York Times*, sourced from Raymond L. Puffer, Air Force History Program, Los Angeles, Reed Business Information Inc.

President Roosevelt, 11 September 1939: "What I want you and the Prime Minister to know is that I shall at all times welcome it, if you will keep me in touch personally with anything you want me to know about. You can always send sealed letters through your pouch or my pouch."

Churchill responded enthusiastically: "I am half American and the natural person to work with you. It is evident that we see eye to eye. Were I to become Prime Minister of Britain we could control the world."[3] This happened eight months later.

In January 1941, the Japanese sent an amazingly generous offer to the Americans to retire from the Rome-Berlin-Tokyo Axis (Italian, German, Japanese alliance) in return for peace with the United States. President Roosevelt and Secretary of State Cordell Hull rejected it.[4] British and American joint-staff conferences were then held in Washington DC (January–March 1941) to arrange a plan for military collaboration called the ABC-1.

It was thought that Pearl Harbor was too shallow to launch torpedoes. The anchorage was only 12 metres deep and torpedoes dropped from planes sunk to 20 metres before beginning their run. But the Japanese tested torpedos with wooden fins at Kagoshima Bay and this gave them extra buoyancy. The strike rate reached 70% and the British knew of these successful torpedo tests.

The key to Pearl Harbor became the long-lance torpedo 21" warhead. It was quiet, fast, straight running, could out-distance everyone else's torpedoes by 2–3 times and the warhead always blew. It was far better than American or German torpedoes which were prone to misfire. American torpedoes failed as much as 90%, partly because crews were constantly on a hunt for alcohol and would drink the torpedo juice after they'd filtered it through bread.

On 27 March 1941, the Japanese spy Takeo Yoshikawa arrived in Honolulu and began studying the American fleet at Pearl Harbor.

Prior to Pearl Harbor, American ships were immune to attack, despite their cargo, or who they were delivering it to. During the spring and summer of 1941, in Europe and the Atlantic, Roosevelt did

[3] Harry Elmer Barnes, *Pearl Harbor After a Quarter of a Century.*

[4] Cordell Hull (1871–1955) received a one-year law degree in 1891 and was made a judge in 1903 (aged 31). After this, he was nicknamed 'Judge' by all and sundry. He served as Secretary of State from 1933–44 and then retired due to ill health.

everything he could to provoke Germany and Italy into producing some "act of war" against an American ship. He even convoyed supplies and munitions to Britain and Russia illegally and with full advertisement, but neither Germany nor Italy would take the bait. They remembered the *Lusitania* well and weren't about to repeat that mistake.

"One of the [British] XX-Committee's first and most important double agents was a thirty-year-old Yugoslav businessman named Dusko Popov. [Ian Fleming described Dusko Popov as the perfect British Intelligence recruit]. A member of a well-to-do royalist family, Popov had been approached by the Abwehr at the outbreak of the war [he regularly had lunch with the chief of Paris Gestapo] with the suggestion that his family's political ambitions might be enhanced if he worked for Germany as a spy against the British. Popov agreed – and promptly informed the MI-6 representative in Belgrade of his Abwehr connections.

"He arrived in England on December 20, 1940, and made a 'most favourable impression' when closely questioned by the British secret intelligence services. [He was suave and sophisticated, enjoyed wine, women and song and could talk his way in and out of anything]. He was then passed on to the XX-Committee and rechristened 'Tricycle' [his German codename was 'Disco'], and he opened up secret communications with the Abwehr in Lisbon.

"He established himself as a highly placed agent in England; and in the next several months he supplied the Abwehr with a great deal of information fabricated by the XX-Committee that beclouded all German estimates about British strength for the remainder of the war.

"Then in June 1941, the Abwehr, pleased with Disco's [Tricycle's] performance in Britain, instructed him to go to America on an espionage mission to investigate in detail, among other targets, the air, military and naval installations at Pearl Harbor, which the Japanese had asked the Abwehr to reconnoitre because of the difficulties that ethnic Japanese agents in Hawaii were encountering.

"Popov informed the XX-Committee of his assignment and, through the American Embassy, the XX-Committee informed the FBI . . . But [when] Popov arrived in the United States . . . on August 24, 1941, he encountered the full wrath of the director of the FBI, J. Edgar Hoover.

"Hoover did not want agents of any foreign power working in America. At their only meeting, he treated Popov with disgust, and declared . . . 'I can catch spies without your or anybody else's help.' He accused Popov of being 'Like all double agents. You're begging for information to sell to your German friends so that you can make a lot of money and be a playboy.'

"Popov, who had taken a woman friend to Florida for a holiday, would find himself threatened with prosecution under the Mann Act [the illegal transportation of women across a state line for the purposes of sexual intercourse], and agents of the Internal Revenue Service were also set on him.

"The British extricated him . . . with the IRS hot on his heels . . . and the Japanese attacked Pearl Harbor. Although the American government had some foreknowledge from other intelligence sources of the impending attack, notably from its naval cryptanalytical bureau in Room 1649 of the Navy Department on Constitution Avenue in Washington . . . The United States declared war upon the Axis powers, and for Churchill, America's entry into the conflict was the answer to a constant prayer."[5]

Although both British and American Chiefs of Staff knew about the planned attack on Pearl Harbor years beforehand, both wanted America to join the war and were waiting for an excuse. All they needed was a swing in public opinion. Before Pearl Harbor, 60% of Americans did not want to get into the war. After Pearl Harbor, 99% of Americans wanted to get into the war.

Spymaster: "When the US started advertising for pilots with multi-engine experience to fly Lockheed Hudsons, the Japanese became alarmed and started to cast around America to see what was on order in the American defence works. They uncovered a large contract to manufacture incendiary bombs, paid for by the British.

"The Japanese then checked the runways in North China and concluded that the Chinese were going to launch an attack against Japan from these new runways, with British and American backing. The Japanese concluded that the date of the attack was to be January 1942. From this they knew they had to attack Pearl Harbor beforehand, so they attacked in early December 1941."

America had advertised for pilots and built runways knowing that it would force the Japanese hand to attack before January 1942.

The wisdom from all sides was that making a surprise attack against Pearl Harbor some 6500 km away was virtually impossible. The only

[5] *Bodyguard of Lies*, pp. 60–61.

way this could be done was with complicity from all sides – so Japan was given complicity from all sides.

What is even more shameful is that President Franklin D. Roosevelt could decipher the Japanese diplomatic code faster than the Japanese Embassy in Washington. Pearl Harbor was deliberate self-sabotage to draw America into the war.

On 17 November 1941 Joseph Grew, the US Ambassador to Japan, cabled the State Department stating that Japan had plans to attack Pearl Harbor, but his cable was ignored. This gave the US twenty days' warning.

On 26 November 1941, a fleet of six aircraft carriers commanded by the Japanese Vice-Admiral Chuichi Nagumo left Hitokapu Bay for Pearl Harbor under strict radio silence. Twelve days later the Japanese Navy were to launch their surprise attack on Pearl Harbor on 7 December 1941 (6 December Japanese time). The only surprise was to those patriots who had not been warned.

To achieve this end, M was used. The British contribution to the cover-up of events leading to the Pearl Harbor attack was called Operation SUBEND. Ian Fleming (33) was the naval control officer and Chris Creighton (17), with the nom de guerre 'Leading Seaman John Davis', was the sole boarding operative.

Since Germany's invasion of Holland, the Dutch submarines in the Pacific were acting as a proxy for the British Royal Navy. They were doing tasks for the British and were under British control. The Dutch submarines were essentially a picket line watching for the Japanese battle fleet.

One of these Dutch submarines saw the Japanese battle fleet head towards Pearl Harbor and wired a storm warning to the British. The 17-year-old Chris Creighton was immediately flown to the Far East, plonked into a naval uniform and made a Brevet junior officer.[6] He boarded the Dutch submarine delivering explosives disguised as gifts and delaying devices for torpedo warheads. These blew up the Dutch submarine with all its crew. This prevented the Dutch from warning the Americans that the Japanese fleet was about to attack Pearl Harbor.

[6] 'Brevet' signifies that it is an elevated title in use only for the duration of the Special Op. Chris Creighton's first job was to destroy French and Belgian supply dumps (specifically fuel) in the path of the German army, but he failed to act as he was overwhelmed by the speed of the German attack. The Germans were dependent on stolen fuel for their advance.

Ian Fleming: "Five minutes after midday on 28 November 1941, Dutch submarine *K-XVII,* commanded by Lieutenant-Commander Besançon, approaches a position in the Pacific, latitude 43° 30' north, longitude 155° 20' east, approximately 280 miles off north-east of Japan's Tankan Bay. There she sights a fleet of Japanese warships. They've been making a three-leg zig-zag course. Commander Besançon correctly calculates this to be a course-made-good – a direct track – of 88° (true). This will bring them to Hawaii and Pearl Harbor eight hundred miles ahead."[7]

Chris Creighton: "In November 1941 I alone had wiped out the entire ship's company with two tiny cylinders of cyanide inserted into their oxygen supply, and a box of high explosives, disguised as whiskey, both timed to release their venomous contents when I was safely away. Those Dutch submariners' only sin was that they had seen, and reported, the Japanese fleet sailing toward Pearl Harbor: news of it had to be suppressed, to ensure the attack went home and America came into the war, and it was deemed essential that the Dutchmen and their secret must die.[8]

"I related how I had witnessed the destruction of *K-XVII* and all her crew, whom I had come to know well over the previous few days. I related how fused canisters of cyanide gas and high explosive had been taken aboard at my direction, disguised as Christmas gifts of food and drink from Queen Wilhelmina and our Admiral, Submarines, Sir Max Horton. From the safety of a Berwick flying boat I had watched as the aircraft suddenly shuddered, and an enormous explosion vomited out great spouts of water, together with broken-up crates of stores, bits of men, oil and oddments of equipment. It was as if a colossal underwater creature had swallowed a submarine, chewed up its human and mechanical contents, and then been violently sick.

"Above all, I wondered what they would say or do if they knew that their valiant submariners had been sacrificed simply because the highest authorities in Britain and America did not trust them to keep their mouths shut."[9]

James Bond (Chris Creighton) then flew back to Britain in a clean-up operation to supervise and assist in the murders of the Royal Navy

---

[7] Chris Creighton, *OPJB*, p. 112.

[8] Ibid, p. 81.

[9] Ibid, pp. 112–3.

signals staff who had sighted the Dutch submarine's *K-XVII* signals. One of the woman was attacked by a sex-criminal specifically paroled from His Majesty's prison for this purpose. Under police control and supervision the criminal was allowed to have his way with her before she was murdered.

Spymaster: "Hilda Murrell met with a similar fate in the 1980s during the hunt for the missing pages of the log of the HMS *Conqueror* which sunk the Argentine heavy cruiser, the *Belgrano*, as it attempted to surrender during the Falklands War."

This is called an 'intelligence-involved coup' – not dissimilar to 9-11. Complicit enemy-attacks are the *usual* method of bringing a third party ally into war. Operation SUBEND was a British 'war-escalating exercise' as was the sabotage of Hitler's peace initiatives of May, June, and July 1941. Conflict was to be prolonged and up-scaled and America was to be drawn into the war. This was a British secret intelligence operation run by M.

In order to further hide these 'Cover-Up Operations', the true identity of James Bond is being misconstrued and applied to lesser entities who could not have been involved in the Cover-Up Ops. As such, Buckingham Palace is dishing out press releases that apply the James Bond identity to others with such squeaky-clean records that they appear to be under-achievers, such as "Commander X" and the "Bond Inspiration Dies".

"A British war hero *said to have been* the inspiration behind secret agent James Bond has died age 90. Former Royal Navy Lieutenant Commander Patrick Dalzel-Job [1913–2003] carried out a series of daring exploits behind enemy lines during WWII including some while serving under Bond author Ian Fleming. Fleming *had told him* he was the model for the spy. In 1940, Dalzel-Job *disobeyed orders* in order to rescue all the women, children and elderly residents from a Norwegian town just before it was destroyed in a German bombing raid."[10]

"Commander X , a real-life Bond . . . Ernest Bond was . . . a tough founder member of the Special Air Service, he was known to the press in the 1970s as 'Commander X' (for security reasons Scotland Yard did not release his name) . . . and on the outbreak of WWII . . . he joined 'L Detachment' of the embryonic SAS."[11]

[10] *New Zealand Herald*, 16 October 2003, B1.

[11] Ibid. 29–30 November 2003, A27. Author's emphasis.

"No top military or civilian authority in Washington on December 7, 1941, should have been surprised at either the place or time of the Japanese attack on the Pacific fleet at Pearl Harbor. The only element of surprise, if any, should have been over the damage that the Japanese planes delivered to the fleet."[12]

What happened to British Prime Minister Chamberlain in the beginning of the war happened to American President Roosevelt at the end of the war. Both were killed with the complicity of their own sides. Chamberlain was killed after he was successfully used to start WWII and Roosevelt was killed three weeks before the end of WWII to ensure he did not write his memoirs about his part in bringing America into the war . . . or face questioning about how American Intelligence failed so badly at Pearl Harbor.[13]

> "The government of Britain was forced to aid the international bankers' plan for the Bolshevik revolution in Russia in 1917 in order to obtain their promise that they would bring America into the war on the side of the Allies. It can be assumed that SS *Lusitania* was sunk to provide the necessary incident to justify the change of American policy, just as Pearl Harbor was used as an excuse for America to enter World War II."[14]

Similarly, 9-11 was used to start WWIII. This too was, according to the writings of Adam Weishaupt, the agenda of the Illuminati, and the military industrialists who make their money selling FEAR AND SECURITY.

The entire Pearl Harbor scenario was repeated in 9-11 and the 2003–06 Iraq war. But this too won't become public knowledge for another hundred years, unless America's Vice-President Dick Cheney admits to meeting with Saddam Hussein on 20–22 April 2003 during Saddam's three-week sojourn out of Iraq – Kuneitre, I presume.[15]

---

[12] *Pearl Harbor After a Quarter of a Century*, pp. 21–22.
[13] Medicine withdrawn, altered or diluted is 'medically-assisted death'. 'MAD' is a current favourite for political assassinations and limits query to doctors.
[14] Commander William Guy Carr, R. D., *Pawns in the Game*, p. 108.
[15] Dick Cheney actually met with Saddam Hussein many times prior to his capture just in time for Christmas 2003.

The absent Pearl Harbor Fleet, 500 nautical miles southeast of Honolulu on exercise. The fleet regularly left Pearl Harbor, Tuesday–Friday (4 days) and Friday–Saturday week (8 days).

The USS West Virginia bombed, burning and sinking.

Dieppe
19 August 1942

Dieppe was another devious distraction designed to establish 'Leading Seaman John Davis' (Chris Creighton) as a British traitor in the eyes of Germany's military elite. Creighton could then pass false data to the Germans with credibility.

In order to achieve this, sacrifices needed to be made. These were not to be British, or American, but a third party, the Canadians – second-rate allies whose only crime was excessive belligerence.

In Ireland, Chris Creighton, under cover as 'Leading Seaman John Davis', revealed to General Canaris that Canadian Divisions and some minor Allied forces were going to attack at Dieppe on 19 August 1942.

Both Canaris and his 2IC, General Hans Oster, were German double agents and had supplied Dutch, Belgian and French forces with the dates of their German attacks. Creighton appeared to be doing a favour in return. Canaris took the information at face value and alerted his troops.

Chris Creighton (18) was then detained and tied to a gun emplacement above Dieppe from where he was made to watch the slaughter of 4000 Canadians and tertiary allies.

Chris Creighton's 'uncle', Lord Louis Mountbatten was a paedophile,[1] adulterer and homosexual incestuous lover for 10 years with his pro-Nazi cousin, the former King Edward VIII.[2] Born in Windsor Castle as 'His Serene Highness Prince Louis of Battenburg', he was a British Admiral, First Sea Lord, uncle and mentor to Prince Philip. When the German styles were dropped in 1917, he became Louis Mountbatten in exchange for further elevations, making him instantly Lord Louis Mountbatten, later elevated to viscount and Earl.

---

[1] This was confirmed in November 2003 when Mick P tracked down a sailor off the HMS *Kelly* whose job it was to second children for Louis Mountbatten. MICK P is a 'Member of the Intelligence Community Knowledge Pool'.

[2] This semi-incestuous homosexual relationship continued during the Royal Tours of India and New Zealand.

'Dickie' Mountbatten was the driving force behind the Dieppe raid. It was an ill conceived raid and even his fellow paedophile Montgomery told him it was ill conceived from the start. Despite this, Mountbatten did not act entirely independently of Creighton and even confirmed his 'nephews' message to the Germans.

As such, Dickie remained a favourite of Churchill (they were related) and Churchill promoted him to Supreme Allied Commander of South East Asia in October 1943, where he was largely self-publicised "as gifted as Eisenhower, Montgomery and Churchill". Dickie was further elevated to Knight of Justice of St John (KJStJ, 1943) and Viceroy of British India.

As the Viceroy of British India, Mountbatten couldn't keep it together. His wife Edwina Ashley was shagging his best friend, Jawaharlal Nehru, as Mountbatten watched India collapse into a Partitioned Independence, assisted by British sabotage resulting in appalling carnage (1 million dead) and the largest migration in history – 12 million were relocated across new borders. Both Louis and Edwina were frequent adulterers[3] with Mountbatten preferring sex with those too young for sex.

After his failure at Dieppe and India, Louis Mountbatten was further promoted to Chief of Defense Staff (1959–65) and in 1967, he was invited to stage a coup and take over Britain's government. When it was pointed out that this was treason, Mountbatten stuck to his knitting, failing in the style to which he had become accustomed.

Lord Louis Mountbatten (Chris Creighton's 'uncle') was truly troubled by the revelations that he too had betrayed the Canadians to the German Army (the Abwehr), resulting in the open slaughter of those 4000 men. The Royal Canadian Legion went to great lengths to distance themselves from him and the rest of Canada soon followed suit, even distancing themselves from Britain, which lead to Canadian Independence and Canadian citizenship in 1949.

Mountbatten was troubled by what other's knew and showed signs of coming unglued and seemed about to blunder and confess.

After a lifetime of personal/professional failings and public promotions 'Dickie' became isolated spending his days fishing in Donegal Bay, near

[3] This was confirmed quite openly by their daughters.

his summer home in Mullaghmore, Ireland. He managed to publicly deny his role in Dieppe until Brian Garfield raised it, leaking his response prior to release of *The Paladin* (1980), a book about Chris Creighton's exploits leading up to Operation JAMES BOND.

Almost immediately the British monarchy arranged MI-5 (Internal Intelligence) to blow up his boat (1979), happily covering their trail by fitting up four IRA men who were jailed for 10 years before being released due to lack of evidence. They kept staunch because they thought some other IRA men had done it.

The tactic of blowing up one of your own leaders to cover up any incriminating evidence on Britain or America was a face-saving device to distract from even more damaging intelligence about the British monarchy working for the Germans, against peace, and for a prolonged war. This covers point '7' of 'M' in which: "Any incriminating evidence against Britain or America was to be destroyed."

When the adulterous paedophile Earl/Viscount/First Sea Lord/Lord Louis 'Dickie' Mountbatten was killed (aged 79), he had six knighthoods and was the last of Morton's fellows, the last of the M senior staff.

In exchange for these titles Prince Philip selected his uncle 'Dickie' as the authority to rebut Anastasia's claim to 'her' father the Tsar of Russia and all that was hers and not theirs.

Lord Louis Mountbatten, KG, GCB, KJStJ, GCSI, GCIE, GCVO
(25 June 1900–27 August 1979)
'Dickie' is remembered for inventing 'Mountbatten Pink',
a naval camouflage that allowed homosexuals and paedophiles
to blend in with ships and remain unnoticed.

Nehru seduces Lady Edwina Mountbatten and cuckolds Lord Louis. An agreement is reached. In exchange for having an affair with his wife, Nehru will turn a blind eye to Mountbatten's penchant for young Indian boys. Meanwhile one million die.

Anthony Blunt

Anthony Blunt's mother was Hilda Master. She was the daughter of a magistrate in the Indian Colonial Service. She married beneath herself to a poor Anglican Priest named Stanley Blunt, who achieved his role through zealous preaching and his ability to blind and deceive others – a talent much valued by spying, double-handed, sly-rooting monarchies.

Three-and-a-half years before his coronation, the future King George V had an ongoing 'sex-for-dress' exchange programme with Hilda Master. The sponsor was his wife Mary of Teck, (daughter of 'Fat Mary') and future Queen of England (m. 6 July 1893).[1]

Mary of Teck would have dresses made for A-List occasions. She couldn't be seen wearing them twice so she gave them away. King George V would do the giving away in exchange for sex. One of the recipients of the future Queen-consort Mary's dresses and King George V's armours was Hilda Masters and, after many A-List occasions and many dresses, they conceived a child together.

He was 41 at the time and his wife didn't particularly mind. Sex for them was a matter of facing ugliness and dim-wittedness, only since found in the realm of Boy Scout masters.

During one of these sex-for-dress exchange programmes, the Prince of Wales from 9 November 1901, the Vice Admiral of the Royal Navy from 1903, the sailor prince and future King George V showed Hilda Master his large blue and red dragon tattooed on his right arm. They then conceived an illegitimate son a fortnight before the Christmas of 1906. The illegitimate child's name was Anthony Blunt (26 September 1907–26 March 1983) and he was to become a royal spy.

Anthony was gay, as is so common with those who grow up without their biological father. His housefather was penniless, a religious replacement in denial, and none too bright. It was virtually impossible for them to bond.

---

[1] Mary of Teck (Victoria Mary Augusta Louise Olga Pauline Claudine Agnes) was previously engage to her husband's brother, the Duke of Clarence, but "he died six weeks after the engagement from a mysterious illness" . . . "pneumonia".

As a ranting proselytising priest Stanley Blunt was well capable of self-deceit and believing his far-less sporting and far-more intelligent son was actually the product of the Holy Ghost – Abracadabra.[2] As is common with priests, anything too hard to confront is left to the realm of mystery.

If the Blunts were not married, the children would have carried the pre-name Fitz, meaning the illegitimate child of royalty. This would have made Anthony a 'FitzBlunt'. Fitzes were usually given a small parcel of land in Ireland, called a 'cunt', an Anglo-Norman word meaning 'a small parcel of land too small to farm', hence the saying 'It's a cunt' meaning 'there is no way to work it'. If they were of German farming stock, their chosen trade would have made them 'Fuckers', making them the FitzBlunt-FuckerCunts, an entirely appropriate surname for Anthony.

Instead the family were given a religious posting to France.

In 1912, two years after the coronation of his biological father-in-denial, when Anthony Blunt was 5 years old and becoming recognisable (the resemblance was remarkable), the family were changed from poor to rich and given a posting in Paris, Stanley becoming the Anglican vicar at the British Embassy. This posting-in-exile stopped the English public from 'noting, pointing and laughing' at Anthony Blunt's astonishing resemblance to King George V, more so than his acknowledged sons, the future King Edward VIII (18, David to his peers) and the future King George VI (17, Bertie to his peers).

Anthony and Edward in particular, were from the same physical, social and moral gene pool – that of languid, non-ideological homosexual – easily manipulated by both sides. These two were Freemasonry in the making.

In the 1920s and '30s Anthony Blunt proudly wore a red tie, continuing the long association between gays and Marxism. He maintained contact with Moscow until the 1930s, and despite obvious qualities and ideologies of 'everything England did not stand for', he was recruited into Britain's Internal Secret Service – MI-5.

MI-5 was more of a 'Freemason's protectorate' than it was an organisation that gathered intelligence and disseminated it for the benefit of the country. When Anthony Blunt became a member of MI-5, he was reapproached by Moscow to hand over security documents. He

[2] Abracadabra is supposedly Arabic for 'Father, Son and Holy Ghost'.

did this is in such abundance and in such gay abandon that even the KGB described him as "ideological shit".

King George V's full son, the future King Edward VIII, as Duke of Windsor was willingly used by the Nazis prior to WWII. After the war, this became a hangable offence. He was attending a diplomatic party when the Abwehr alerted him to the derailment of a freight train in Switzerland. The Germans were trying to make out that they were abiding by the Treaty of Versailles, yet a German railway carriage derailed and illegally acquired 15-inch Italian naval shells fell out. The Duke of Windsor was then asked to keep the British ambassador at the party and to entertain and distract any and all ambassadors who might react to this. The next day they played golf. There were no mobile phones.

Just before Churchill declared the end of WWII on 7 May 1945 (for 0.01 am on 8 May) Anthony Blunt was sent to Germany as a British spy. He was entrusted by the monarchy with the delicate task of destroying all trace of the treasonous activities of Edward VIII and the other British traitors. To do this, he had to go into the ruins of Nazi Germany and recover all communications between Edward VIII (his half-brother, 13-years-his-senior) and the Nazis at Schloss Kronberg, a castle near Frankfurt.

Blunt was part of the British monarchy backing the Nazis and was a German Army Intelligence agent. He had been assigned a 'V-Mann number' meaning he was a registered card-carrying member of the German forces and was actively passing information on to them. While he did this he also stole the Kaiser's crown jewels which Queen Elizabeth II returned only recently.

As is so common with traitors, Britain's most notorious spy was knighted for services to the British Empire (1956), and then spent his Christmases in the 1960s with Dick White, Head of Britain's internal/external Secret Services (MI-5, MI-6) and Victor Rothschild.

Nathaniel Meyer 'Victor' Rothschild was a secret society leader who profited enormously from WWII. He was the principle shareholder of the Central Banking System, 'the Fifth Man' of the Cambridge Five spy ring and the primary supplier of British secrets to Russia from 1935 to 1963.

Anthony Blunt was also very, very good friends with his Queen consort sister-in-law (1936–52), whom the current generation knows as the Queen Mother (4 August 1900–30 March 2002) and her daughter, Queen Elizabeth II.

The Queen consort and Anthony Blunt were both privy to the previous king. One's illegitimate father was the other's father-in-law. It was a case of one non-ideological spy talking rings around Queen 'Liz-nice-but-dim', who was the wife of one 'George Dunce', to those who worked under him. The intelligence community and much of the public considered King George VI to be one IQ point above retarded (66 + 1 = ?).

Anthony and the Queen could talk frankly of their lineages' sexual secrets, and the state secrets poured out as easily as the tea. As is so common with straight, gay and paedophile traitors, Blunt was knighted in 1956 for services to Queen and country. The knighthood stood between him and a charge of treason (1973). This worked for 24 years until he was stripped of his knighthood by Margaret Thatcher in 1979. He died four years later on 26 March 1983. Three weeks later the fake *Hitler Diaries* became public.

Despite being gifted everything required in life, Anthony Blunt spent his entire existence in psychological torture. He was never allowed to say who he was or what he wanted. He was a highly valued, yet unwanted pawn, despised by all authority and used by all authority. Like most of the royal family, all Blunt wanted was to be a little more intelligent and a little less ugly – the curse of the Windsors.

Anthony Blunt was a major trader in a 'homosexual, non-ideological, secrets-trading, spyring' and his greatest value was to Freemasonry and the Illuminati who so desperately wanted to continue the managed wars for continued profit – wars that would make them wealthier than all of England and all of Europe.

WWI and WWII financed America
to become the superpower it is today
and placed it ahead of all other nations.
It also did wonders for the Rothschilds.

King George V and Anthony Blunt,
father and son.

Opposite: Anthony Blunt as young man
and as the surveyor of the Queen's pictures, 1945–72,
seen here with his neice, Queen Elizabeth II.

The Duke of Windsor and Wallis Simpson.

Dear MI-6,

A DNA match here would not go amiss.

PS. To cement any epiphany a press release wouldn't be a bad idea. Remember to get authorisation and keep in mind the Einsatz Kommando camp's motto, "The truth shall set you free". British camps were also familiar with this phrase.

The Champagne General, Joachim von Ribbentrop,
German Ambassador to London and another of Wallis Simpson's lovers.

King Edward VIII abdicates, then marries a treasonous spy
and meets with Hitler ASAP.

The Duke and Duchess of Windsor.
A couple of life's tragedies.

Wallis Simpson and King Edward VIII

Sex and German Spies in the British Monarchy

The *Oxford Dictionary*, which takes final editorial input from the monarchy, describes "Wallis Simpson (1896–1986) as the American wife of King Edward VIII [26 June 1894–28 May 1972], who reigned for 11 months in 1936 after King George V. Her relationship with the king caused a national scandal, and her second divorce forced the king's abdication. They moved to France. He died and she remained a recluse until her death."

In late 2003 the author was interviewing the Spymaster who said: "I spoke with a British Intelligence officer who told me this story . . ."

> "Wallis was the subject of a round robin in 1930. A round robin is where all intelligence are circulated with a request. They were asked if they could provide a woman that might revive the future king's jaded sexual appetite. This was Edward VIII, later famous for his 11-month reign, gay fashions, the Windsor knot and abdication.
>
> "King George V had visited the front lines at the beginning of WWI and his horse rolled on top of him breaking his pelvis. Thereafter he suffered ill health, mainly bronchitis and was in continual pain. His eldest son John was retarded, ignored by his mother and left to randomly garden on one of their estates. David was a little less retarded, but not much. He was to become Edward VIII. As King, it was essential to all who had designs on England, that David become their pawn. This was as easily done as said.
>
> "Somebody remembered having sex with an American naval officer's wife in a Chinese brothel in the Forbidden City in Peking, China. She was learning the secrets of 'Chinese amour' while working for free, and it was this 'free' aspect that drew British Intelligence attention. They knew they were dealing with a lifetime actress who survived on attention rather than food.
>
> "The agent replied back to London and London said, 'That's just what we need; we'll be coming straight out to get her'. The woman was Wallis Simpson, the future partner of King

> Edward VIII, and the gym instructor to his jaded, disinterested sexual appetite. She was brought back to England and the King liked her. She had sexual relations with David, the future King, but she also had sex with Ribbentrop, the Nazi German Ambassador to London, an American car salesman, and pretty much anybody else who could come up with the required attention. Flowers, a keen interest, and some form of status were generally enough.
>
> "Just as Prince Charles was another Edward VIII (his grand-uncle), Diana also survived on attention more than food. Both Diana and Wallis Simpson were 'sexual-bulimics' in a pattern of desiring and denying; and both Charles and Edward were social misfits, incapable of being employed in the ordinary world. Both women were primarily concubines to disinterested, incompatible, and incompetent sexual partners.
>
> "She [Wallis Simpson] introduced him [King Edward VIII] to homosexuality and photographed him in the process."

The First market 'Petite Camera with matching lipstick holder and compact', from Kodak, was available to the elite from 1930, some four years earlier. Photographs of royalty and politicians in compromising sexual positions immediately became the most valuable piece of intelligence any secret service or hostile country could obtain. Cameras became big business, the smaller and the more hidden, the bigger the business.

Wallis' role, as far as the Germans were concerned, was to enmesh the weak future King Edward VIII into a sexually perverse world and then threaten to reveal reports of his sexual habits to 'high society' and the British public at large, via American newspapers if necessary.

The conscious and unconscious illusion he adhered to was that he was successful in bed for the first time and this made him want to marry the woman. Wallis encouraged the future King to vent every pro-German/anti-English sentiment he could. The future King of England was being bribed by his mistress. These bribes were so successful he became completely dependent on the illusion she provided, despite all outward appearances to the contrary.

The truth was that Wallis was cheating on him left, right and centre and the future King was completely useless in bed and preferred prostitutes, the greater the actress the better. Having a sexually-based ego for the first time in his life, the future King was foolish enough to buy Wallis' husband out of bankruptcy and the three of them were living in the same house for several years.

Wallis was half-American, half-German and actively spied for the Nazis. The sessions photographed included the future King of England having a ménage-à-trois with another man. Wallis would get up from the bed, put on her lipstick, and at the same time take a photo from her 'Kodak compact' make-up case. This petite camera became a main agent for WWII and the invasion of France, which astounded even its inventors.

As many British secrets as possible were passed from the British Monarchy to Germany, obeying the Prince of Wales crest 'Ich Dien' ('I serve, Germany'), honouring the family name, Saxe-Coburg-Gotha, their origins, and David's uncle, the Kaiser of Germany. To King Edward VIII, revealing the British secrets to Germany was akin to sending a letter to his relatives.

Wallis Simpson's German contact was the German Ambassador to London, Joachim von Ribbentrop, the Champagne General. He would read the state secrets, then check the homosexual photographs of the future King as proof of the information's authenticity.

Ribbentrop would send Wallis roses every day, 17 being a reference to the number of times they had exchanged information and had sex – about once a week for four months, from August 1936 until the King abdicated four months later on 10 December. Wallis was having sexual relations with the King six days a week (for secrets) and rooting the Nazi ambassador one day a week while passing them on – that's a lot of secrets and one of history's most successful sexual-information highways.

Wallis and Ribbentrop were two hysterically horny international spies, laughing at the British monarchy as they made way for the invasion of France with the joining of their libidos. This was pure knife-edge fun. They had the monarchy by the balls, and the fact that they both got away with their reputations intact during their lifetime showed total complicity from the British press, MI-5, MI-6, Freemasonry and the gay community – all to the country's detriment, but for the expansion of war.

Spymaster: "The British Monarchy should have fallen. Almost every other European monarchy fell in the 1920s, but the British monarchy survived because it had become such a non-nationalistic spy network that it virtually condoned the bleeding of sensitive military information to countries like Germany and Russia. This ensured the monarchy survived, Britain was severely damaged and the war lasted longer."

The British monarchy's spy network took rule only from the British Freemasons, the highest-ranking Freemasons being the King and currently the man with the world's lowest EQ (emotional quotient), HRH Prince Phillip (33° Mason) who is married to his second cousin, the current Queen. Both are the great-great-grandchildren of Queen Victoria.

The British monarchy was not serving its people, it was serving its secret societies, its Freemasons, its Illuminati, its Mercer's, the Livery Companies, the Anglican Church, the Boy Scouts, the paedophiles, and the creation of orphaned children as playthings for all of the above. The proof of this is in the near complete preservation of royal buildings during the war, while a third of the square mile of the City of London was completely destroyed.

The bribed King of England collected British secrets and passed them to his concubine, Wallis Simpson, who passed them to the Nazi Ambassador, in another sexual encounter, who then passed them to Hitler, who sniffed cocaine, snorted speed and masturbated over them. It was an orgy of information and one giant blowjob of secrets and it served to keep the Freemason's war going. France was invaded at all its weak points (including its Prime Minister) and virtually without resistance. It fell within two weeks while Britain stood back and watched, fiddling over paperwork.

Prince Edward (later King Edward VIII) "regarded WWI as futile and stupid and a result of unnecessary conflicts between his grandfather King Edward VII and his father's cousin Kaiser Wilhelm of Germany."[1] Reasons for WWII were equally vain. More than one secret service agent has mentioned that WWI and WWII were managed wars and WWII was a battle between the French and English Freemasons, or British royalty and French royalty.

Edward VIII, King of England, was surprisingly stupid and Wallis Simpson was surprisingly clever. She had spent most of her life entertaining two or more lovers at the same time and 17 yellow roses received daily from the Nazi Ambassador, was a lot to ignore – still, the constantly inebriated King Edward accomplished this with even more alcohol.

Abdication was a solution that saved the monarchy from certain extinction and prevented the King of England from being executed. Can you imagine a treasonous, bribed, homosexual king – surely that

[1] *Wallis*, p. 96.

is a dead thing, except he was a Freemason which meant there would be no fall from grace in his lifetime and his true history would be covered up for generations to come.

Britain's King Edward VIII was so entrenched in the German Nazi movement that the German Military Intelligence's Abwehr even issued him with a 'V-Mann number' giving him special German military status. After 11 months as King, Edward VIII abdicated, retaining his title as Duke of Windsor (10 December 1936). As is so common with those on the sexual fringe, Wallis and Edward were actively destabilising their own family-based societies.

During WWII, the abdicated King Edward VIII and Wallis Simpson were both placed as far away as possible from Europe, its allies and from America. Consequently, a position was invented for them and they were made 'Governors of the Bahamas Islands' from 1940–45. Here they were both under strict surveillance.

Spymaster: "Wallis Simpson was investigated by the FBI in 1941 for passing information to Ribbentrop, the Nazi Foreign Minister in London, for being his lover, and for their involvement in the murder of the Canadian millionaire, Sir Harry Oakes, who inspired the private purchase of Spitfires for the RAF in 1940. When the Duke and Duchess of Windsor (Edward and Wallis) were accused of manipulating currency in France after WWII, the Labour Government had to step in and save them both from prosecution."

No action was taken against Wallis Simpson; however, Ribbentrop, her German lover, was hanged on 16 October 1946, primarily for his knowledge of the Duke of Windsor's sexual proclivities. At the end of WWII they were both asked to leave the Bahamas. This was a slap in the face with a wet bus ticket, but a shameful one nevertheless.

Wallis Warfield-Spencer-Simpson-Windsor was a woman primarily interested in her own sexuality. She was born in 1896 and died in 1986. Her father died when she was five months old. She (20) married a navy Lieutenant pilot, Earl Winfield Spencer Jr in 1916. He was an American-born Briton who was 'Earl' by Christian name only. They divorced in 1927. During this time she had an affair with Ernest Aldrich Simpson and they married in 1928, changing her name to Wallis Simpson (32). They divorced in May 1937.

Between 1922 and 1928 Wallis and her first husband Spencer were separated. In 1928 he suggested reconciliation and she sailed to China to join him. He then suggested she accompany him to a few Chinese brothels. They soon separated but she remained in China for a year, "haunting brothels by herself, enjoying close male friendships and a heady social life, refining her already considerable social/sexual skills". Of this time she wrote: "without doubt the most delightful, the most carefree, the most lyrical interval of my youth – the nearest thing to a lotus-eater's dream any young woman could expect to know".[2]

She still wore fashion influenced by the Chinese brothel to the end of her days. British Intelligence later claimed she had learnt techniques in Chinese brothels that helped her snare a king. They should know, they arranged it. "The [famous China dossier] file contained interviews with brothel madams confirming that Wallis had entered into perverse practices in the singsong houses."[3]

Wallis met the future King Edward for the first time in January 1931 and again in May. By January 1932, Edward, Prince of Wales was staying at Wallis and her second husband's house in London. By 1934, Edward was a frequent visitor to Wallis' home and she slept with both Edward, the future king, and her second husband, who didn't move out for another two years. Prince Edward (David) and Wallis were a couple of swinging bisexuals. It was four years later, and six months into Edward's reign (July 1936), that Ernest Simpson finally moved out of the marital home.

By January 1936, Edward, although King, was obsessed with Wallis. Despite Edward's several more available mistresses, Edward was characterised as Mrs Simpson's lapdog and their relationship, "sadomasochistic", he, "relishing contempt and bullying", and she finding him "dependent, burdensome and claustrophobic".

Edward's relationship with Wallis Simpson was now being reported in the foreign press; however, the British government had instructed the British press not to refer to the relationship. The British monarchy controlled the British press to the country's detriment.

Wallis Simpson was described by the Queen Mother as "the lowest of the low", presumably because she was conceived out of wedlock, from a solo-parent family that begged for survival, developed flirting as a survival skill, was a drug-dealer and gambler, trained as a sex-concubine

[2] "Lotus-eater" refers to lesbian acts.

[3] *Wallis*, p. 163.

in Peking's Forbidden City at no charge, was twice divorced, falsified her own divorce papers, had affairs in each marriage, one of which began as a cuckolding affair, was involved with a high-powered group of society lesbians, had communist connections, spied for the Russians, was a Nazi sympathiser, and was having an affair with Ribbentrop, the Nazi foreign minister to London, and a married American car salesman (Guy Marcus Trundle[4]), while dating the King, whom she got to abdicate, married him in Nazi Germany and then cheated on him with a homosexual.

Wallis Simpson was no beauty, but she was seductive. All of her relationships revolved around her being in control of the new man, while destroying the masculinity of the live-in partner. She was as successful at attracting men as she was at fleecing them and rebutting them. (See *Was Wallis Simpson A Man, Appendix 13*)

When she got sick of men, she had affairs with bisexual women like the German Marlene Dietrich (1904–92) who acted in *The Blue Angel* (1930), *The Devil is a Woman* (1935) and, rather ironically, *Judgement at Nuremberg* (1961). In his autobiography, Laurence Olivier writes of the two of them dancing tit-to-tit with their hands up each other's pants. Marlene Dietrich was a Nazi spy.

From 1949–53, while still married, she (53–57) began another affair with the gay playboy grandson of Woolworths. Twenty years her junior, it lasted four years, and Edward the Duke of Windsor (55–59), fully aware, trailed along behind. Edward, once King, had been usurped by a gay man. As the Duchess of Windsor once rebutted: "You can't abdicate and eat it."

You'd think by now that her given surname 'Warfield' meant something. She still wore fashion influenced by the Chinese brothel, her most cherished moments, till the end of her days. She remained, until her death in 1986, the Step-Aunt to the current Queen of England.[5]

"He was not skilled in doing anything physical."[6] Despite the fact that Prince Edward was a failure at everything – education, sports, relationships, sex (including erections), reproduction (no children), sleep (he was an insomniac), sobriety (he was a lush), family (they shunned him), public relations, the press, politics, service at war, kingship, and

[4] Trundle lived at 18 Bruton Street, Mayfair, London. Ref., *BBC News*, 3 Feb. 2003.
[5] Chris Jones, BBC News Profiles Unit, 29 January 2003 and several other related websites; also Charles Higham, Wallis, Secret Lives of the Duchess of Windsor, 1988.
[6] *Wallis*, p. 145.

was vain to boot, the press still managed to maintain a level of popularity between Edward and the public.

Edward was a poor student and after two years of failed study it was decided he should be given a commission in the British Army. On the insistence of King George V (3 June 1865–20 January 1936) and Lord Kitchener (24 June 1850–5 June 1916), Edward was excluded from any discussion on political issues and restricted to serving as a courier (staff appointment) during WWI.

As Prince 'David' Edward, he had a gay liaison with his Oxford tutor Henry Peter Hansell. In 1918 he had an affair with the wife of the Liberal Whip, Freda Dudley Ward, then a homosexual liaison with Louis Mountbatten during the Empire Tour (1927). By 1930 Prince 'David' Edward was lingering in the Tate Gallery picking up boys and men. Six years later he was king. "He was an unsatisfactory lover with homosexual leanings."[7]

His father King George V encouraged him to find a wife and start a family. "In January 1923 it was announced in the press that the future King Edward VIII would marry Lady Elizabeth Bowes-Lyon."[8] On discovering his penis was so small as to be impractical, that he was bisexual, liked to be dominated, could not maintain an erection and was an insomniac, Elizabeth went with his brother Bertie instead, despite his bad stammer and shyness. "A week later her engagement to his brother Albert was announced; today she is the queen mother."[9]

The future Queen of England and Queen Mother became engaged to his brother Prince 'Bertie' Albert even though Bertie (the future King George VI and the current Queen's father) had already an affair with a black actress and a homosexual affair with a young Parisian boy who later blackmailed him.

King George VI followed this up during his marriage to the Queen with an illegitimate son named Michael Canfield (1926–69). He was brought up by Cass Canfield of Harper & Row Publishing and was the half-brother to the current Queen. Michael 'Fitz' Canfield later married the Duchess of Marlborough and 'died' soon after the wedding. There was no way he was going to be allowed to have children.[10]

[7] *Wallis*, p. 94.
[8] Ibid, p. 92.
[9] Ibid.
[10] King Edward VIII tried to pass this off as the Duke of Kent's illegitimate son.

But even this was pre-empted in the colonies and became known as New Zealand's worst kept secret. Recently married and on Royal Tour with his wife (Elizabeth), newborn child (Elizabeth II) and homosexual incestuous partner (Louis Mountbatten), the future King George VI conceived a child with a Maori woman in March 1927.

As an adult, he was in charge of DoRAs (Defence of the Realm Acts) for British paedophiles on holiday in New Zealand, especially in Rotorua. He would cover for those who were caught or who had complaints against them, ensuring that there was no police record and that "the British tourists" got out of the country safely. His job was to cover up for British paedophiles, but it was also to ensure there was a ready supply of young Maori boys available for paedophilia who were encouraged to swim naked in the Priest and Radium pools.

Secret Service (NZ): "King George VI's illegitimate son was an effeminate housebound homosexual who looked like a British royal who had been nuggetted. He was the Queen's half-brother and 18 months her junior. She spent five days with him at Moosewood Lodge in Rotorua during the Royal Tour from 23 December 1953 to 30 January 1954. The previous Royal Tour in 1927 had sired the child."[11]

The author has a bakelite cigar case stamped "·ROYAL VISIT··N·Z· 1949·", but this was made in anticipation. The Royal Tour was delayed as King George VI became ill with a strange form of lung cancer called syphilis. He died of lung cancer/syphilis on 6 February 1952 and the newly crowned Queen Elizabeth II and her husband/second cousin Prince Philip went on the Royal Tour instead.

The former King's doctor then came out to New Zealand, made child introductions to King George VI's illegitimate son and was then promoted and elevated to Governor-General. Elevations and paedophilia go hand in hand, especially when the little hand meets the big hand.

After the future King Edward VIII's week-long engagement to the current Queen Mother, the monarchy did a 'round robin' amongst the secret service, chocolate soldiers and diplomats. They searched high and low for a woman to revive the sagging libido of the inheritor of the British Empire. They tried the American Thelma Furness, but David rejected her. (She was normal, he was not.) The best they could find for 'the most eligible bachelor in the world' was a divorced American

[11] The author mentioned the existence of Queen Elizabeth II's half-brother as born and having lived his life in New Zealand on television on 29 November 2005.

woman working at no charge, in a Peking brothel, in the Forbidden City of China – Wallis Simpson.

The King's challenged sexuality was confirmed by Wallis Simpson who told guests at a Paris party: "The duke is impotent and although he had tried sexual intercourse with numerous women they had been unsuccessful in satisfying his passions." "The duchess in her own inimitable and unique manner has been the only woman who had been able to satisfactorily gratify the duke's sexual desires."[12]

The 5' 5" (1.65 m) King Edward VIII had a small penis, could not maintain an erection and preferred to wear nappies and be dominated by Wallis Simpson.

Countess of Romanones: "The techniques Wallis discovered in China did not entirely overcome the Prince's extreme lack of virility. It is doubtful whether he and Wallis ever actually had sexual intercourse in the normal sense of the word."[13] It was a sadomasochistic relationship in which she had total control. She despised him and he adored her.

Wallis was considered unsuitable for the monarchy by the public and this caused Edward's abdication. After abdicating in December 1936, they both confirmed their Nazi sympathiser status by visiting Germany in October 1937 and being entertained by Hitler and other senior Nazis. Edward VIII: "Dictators are very popular these days."[14]

Edward VIII had supreme influence over the Freemasons and the Masonic Lodge. It becomes increasingly obvious to all who read history that control of the press is the key to allowing secret societies like the Freemasons to carry out their own agenda for war (British/German versus French Freemasons), while the monarchy's reputation is left untarnished.[15]

Control of the press always leads to some form of civil unrest. It may maintain stability at the time, but 'essential delayed knowledge' is always detrimental to history. It is an expression of an 'affective power vanity' which always results in an 'effective power vacuum'. It is the stuff of double agents.

On colonial visits Edward drew large crowds and his obvious

[12] *Wallis*, p. 115. The second quote refers to the author.

[13] Ibid.

[14] *Wallis*, p. 116.

[15] The Metropolitan Police had a huge file on Wallis Simpson. The file was instigated by her partner Prince Edward, but was not released until February 2003.

popularity made him increasingly vain. As one observer noted, he had "difficulty in understanding the symbolic nature of his position and tended to assume that the attention focused on him was a direct consequence of his own particular gifts".

Edward had no children, thank God, but his father, George V, had given him a few half-brothers and sisters, the most famous of which was Anthony Blunt. His younger brother Bertie became King George VI, whose daughter became the present Queen (QEII).

A sexually bent King and a prostitute/sexual compulsive for a prospective Queen made Britain an invaders' paradise. War was planned and happened within three years.

It was essential for invading countries to find weaknesses in the key figures of opposing countries and then exploit those weaknesses. Embarrassment was something that was delayed as long as possible and, not surprisingly, the cover for such a plot always came from the country's own media under government instruction. Edward VIII had weaknesses to be exploited in abundance and his shortcomings made England a spy's paradise.

It was Edward's weaknesses as a king, his naïvety around politics, his lack of sexuality, his liking for prostitutes, and his continual intoxication, making him 'non compos mentis' most of the time, that almost brought down the British monarchy and perhaps should have.

With the British media's continual suppression and virtual blackout of anything 'Edward and Wallis', Edward VIII maintained his cover and provided an easy source of information for WWII's most competent and ingrained spy, Wallis Simpson, the Duchess of Windsor, and the King of England's partner. "Edward VIII turned to Wallis for advice in doing everything."[16]

By August 1935, Wallis was surrounded by French and British special agents and a detective from Scotland Yard. In order to pass secrets she employed a lawyer (Gregoire) who was also the lawyer for Ribbentrop (Nazi Ambassador to London) and Otto Abertz who soon became the German Ambassador to Paris. When she couldn't get through to them, she sent crucial secrets to Berlin via Italy.

Anna Wolkoff, the daughter of Admiral Wolkoff, was a Nazi spy sending crucial secrets to Berlin via Italy and was considered a leading

[16] *Wallis*, p. 144.

figure in British fascism. She was the dressmaker to Wallis Simpson and Princess Marina of Greece (the widow of the Duke of Kent). Five associates of Anna Wolkoff were listed by MI-5 as being Nazi sympathisers. This list led right into the household of the British royal family.

For Pro-Nazi suspects, MI-5 had divided the country into regions, and when they were released 60 years later (October 2004) all but the central region of London involving British establishment figures were released, though the more obvious ones, the Duke of Bedford, the Duke of Windsor, Sir Oswald Mosley, Sir Barry Domvile (the former head of Naval Intelligence) and Lord Rothermere (owner of the *Daily Mail*) were included. These leading British fascists were quoted as saying "A victorious Nazi invasion would place the Duke back on the throne".[17]

None of their spying or sexual secrets made it to the British press as there was a media blackout on anything to do with Wallis and King Edward. Only overseas papers dared show the stories. Viscount Lord Rothermere,[18] fascist sympathiser and owner of the *Daily Mail*, often published pro-Hitler messages:

"In England, many people imagine Hitler as a cannibal; but I would like to say . . . he conveys good comradeship. He is unpretentious, naturally and apparently sincere . . . There is no human being living whose promise on important matters I would trust more readily. He believes that Germany has a Divine calling and that the German people are destined to save Europe . . . No words can describe his politeness . . . He is a man of rare culture."[19]

"Hitler's political aim and policy is directed toward attaining his goal without loss of blood. He succeeded in ascending to the highest power position in Germany with very little spilling of blood or loss of human life in a land of 68 million inhabitants. Austria was annexed without one shot being fired."[20]

King Edward and Wallis Simpson were a couple of swinging

[17] Ben Fenton, *The Daily Telegraph*, Nobles and Admirals on War 'Suspect List', 12 October 2004.

[18] Lord Rothermere was born Harold Sydney Harmsworth. He was elevated to baronet in 1910, baron in 1914, made Britain's Air Minister (1917–18) and then further elevated to viscount in 1919.

[19] Viscount Lord Rothermere, *Warnings and Predictions*, pp. 180-3.

[20] *Daily Mail*, 20 May 1938.

bisexuals. She divorced in May 1937 and they married on 3 June 1937. Their official wedding photo in France showed Herman Rogers and Major Edward 'Fruity' Metcalfe. Wallis had had a ménage-à-trois with Herman Rogers and his wife and 'Fruity' was a bisexual in a front marriage. These were sexually incompetent bisexuals and gays in show marriages attending dinners sponsored by German and Italian Fascists.

As his father King George V put it: "My son has not a single friend who is a gentleman and does not see any decent society." Wallis was also sexually involved with "Thelma and Gloria Vanderbilt in a high-powered group of society lesbians".[21]

Snubbed by the royal family and the British establishment, the Duke of Windsor was forced into exile in France, Spain, Portugal and the Bahamas. He was considered a drunk and she obnoxious. Despite their exile, Wallis Simpson continued to provide Ribbentrop (the Nazi Ambassador in London) with the information required for the invasion of France in 1940.

The former King Edward VIII, abdicated and reduced to the Duke of Windsor, was posted to France to liaise between the British and French armies; however, "the Duchess of Windsor was in constant contact and communication with Ribbentrop . . . Because of their high official position, the duchess obtained a variety of information concerning the British and French official activities and passed this on to the Germans."[22]

With this information, the Germans invaded northern France in May 1940 with virtually no opposition. The couple then fled to Biarritz in the south of France. Wallis Simpson had informed Ribbentrop where they were going, and arrival to their secret hideaway was simultaneously announced on German Radio, along with their room number. This lifted German war spirits to new levels of hilarity not enjoyed since.

Within a month they travelled to Spain and communication with Ribbentrop was facilitated through Spanish Fascists. A month later they travelled to Portugal where the Duke made indiscreet remarks that Britain stood little chance of resisting a German invasion and may as well try to settle for peace with the Germans.

---

[21] *Wallis*, p. 107.
[22] Wallis website.

Edward VIII was allowed to leave Spain under the direct intervention of Walter Schellenberg, the Nazi Intelligence Officer. For this favour, Schellenberg was not prosecuted for War Crimes in 1946, but 1949. He was placed in British custody and made to sleep on a mattress with radioactive material inserted. He died soon after from stomach cancer (1952).[23]

Schellenberg had managed the Venlo Incident for Germany but was never forgiven by the British for 'acquiring possession' of the Prince of Wales' homosexual secrets. For this, in the end, he was ultimately condemned to die. The Intelligence Officer's comment that often appears on British files and believed to be penned by 'M' read:

"Well done, true and faithful servant".

The Duke and Duchess of Windsor spent the month of July 1940 in Portugal, during which time Winston Churchill arranged for the Duke to become the 'Governor of the Bahamas' from August 1940. The Bahamas were selected to prevent the Duchess from coming into contact with any British officials and from "establishing any channel of communication with Ribbentrop".

FBI memo: "It was considered absolutely essential that the Windsors be removed to a point where they would do absolutely no harm."

> *London Guardian*, 2002: "When the Duke and Duchess of Windsor sailed into Palm Beach, Florida, on the SS *Berkshire* from Nassau on April 18 1941, they were looking forward to enjoying three days of relaxation at the Everglades Club, playing golf and drinking and gossiping with American high society. Little did they know that the previous night instructions had gone out from President Roosevelt to FBI chief J. Edgar Hoover to launch what was to be an extraordinary covert intelligence exercise that had to fool both the exiled royals and the US secret service agent who was guarding them.
>
> "The exercise was launched after the FBI had been passed intelligence that the Duke and Duchess were being used by the Nazis to obtain secrets which could wreck the Allies' war effort. The US investigation became even more lurid when FBI agents interviewed a Benedictine monk in a Franciscan monastery in the United States; Father Odo had once been the Duke of Wurttemberg, a minor German royal with connections to Queen Mary, the duke's mother, and her brother, the Duke of Athlone, then governor-general of Canada.

[23] The same method was used on New Zealand's Prime Minister Norman Kirk (1972–74) dying on 31 August 1974.

"He told them that a prime suspect in the investigation – Joachim von Ribbentrop, then the Nazis' foreign minister – had been the Duchess's lover when he was ambassador to Britain in 1936. The minister was already thought to have been supplied with information by the Duchess during the German invasion of France in 1940. Now it was suggested that there was a far closer arrangement.

"A year after war broke out, the FBI sent a memo to President Roosevelt outlining the agency's worries about the couple. It stated: 'It has been ascertained that for some time, the British government has known that the Duchess of Windsor was exceedingly pro-German in her sympathies and connections and there is strong reason to believe that this is the reason why she was considered so obnoxious to the British government that they refused to permit Edward to marry her and maintain the throne.

"Both she and the Duke of Windsor have been repeatedly warned by representatives of the British government that in the interest of the morale of the British people, they should be exceedingly circumspect in their dealings with the representatives of the German government."[24]

From their base in the Bahamas, the couple made frequent visits to the United States during WWII. After tailing the Windsors, on 2 May 1941 an FBI agent wrote to Hoover: "The Duchess of Windsor had an intense hate for the English since they had kicked them out of England . . . and he [FBI agent] had definite proof that the Duke of Windsor, former King of England, had reached an agreement with Hitler's deputy, Herman Goering. After Germany won the war, Goering, through control of the army, would overthrow Hitler and reinstate the duke as King of England."[25]

This pipedream of Goering's was sympathetically treated in the higher echelons of MI-6, but was only for the consumption of Goering and the Prince of Wales.

This saga was not only circumstance, but also hereditary. Edward's father, King George V, was described by his biographer Robert Lacey:

[24] Chris Jones, BBC News Profiles Unit, 29 January 2003; Rob Evans and David Hencke, *Wallis Simpson, the Nazi minister, the telltale monk and an FBI plot, London Guardian*, 29 June 2002.

[25] Ibid.

"As his official biographer I felt compelled to admit, King George V was distinguished by no exercise of social gifts, by no personal magnetism, by no intellectual powers. He was neither a wit nor a brilliant raconteur, neither well-read, nor well-educated, and he made no great contribution to enlightened social converse. He lacked intellectual curiosity . . ." and it was these qualities that King Edward VIII inherited, as did his brother King George VI, the father of the current Queen Elizabeth II.

King George V had the perfect parenting style for creating sexual repressives and moody ne're-do-wells. He was a remote and stern figure who treated his sons like cadets on a battleship – they were always on parade when in his presence. He reprimanded them with savage anger and employed a succession of nannies, at least two of which were sadistically cruel. The children were raised by an unavailable, angry father, for whom they had to perform. Both Edward (David) and George (Bertie) grew up to be effeminate, non-performing, easily bribed bisexuals whose sperm had no morals.

King George V was killed by his doctor, Lord Dawson, who injected him with a mixture of morphine and cocaine so his death announcement could make the morning papers. He died within 15 minutes at 11.55 pm on 20 January 1936 at Sandringham, Norfolk, England. Hitler sent a message of sympathy and his entire cabinet attended a synchronous memorial in Berlin on 28 January 1936.

Hitler was infatuated with Wallis Simpson and assigned a German agent to film Wallis at the funeral procession. Both Hitler and Eva Braun were mesmerised by Wallis's hair, make-up and severe, classic, timeless clothes. Hitler deeply admired Wallis and giggled uncontrollably in ecstatic pleasure when he viewed her on film in Obersalzburg.

Something drastically changed between 1936 and 1939. The continued use of hard drugs began to tax high society. Hitler was a speed and cocaine addict and the elite of Britain and Berlin were in a white powder epidemic. Cocaine (snow) was widely used in the 1920s and from 1933 the Nazis campaigned against their use.

Despite this, from April to December 1939 German soldiers were supplied with 29 million pills of Amphetamine Pervitine (Benzedrine, or speed) designed to keep the paratroopers awake. From 1942, Adolf Hitler's personal physician (King George VI's agent, Dr Theodor Morell) injected him daily with methamphetamine or 'speed', very similar to 'P' which caused Hitler's premature ageing and charismatic dementia.[26]

[26] Wolf Kemper, *Nazis on Speed*, 2003.

Many Nazi servicemen of all kinds took emergency packets of supplied drugs. A paratrooper who jumped on Crete in 1941 said: "It was as if someone had boiled my blood. I suddenly had superhuman strength and could not sleep. I was capable of superhuman feats."

Allied Officer: "I was assigned to guard a German 'naval commander' – a ship saboteur. He had dangerous knowledge but was not physically capable. He showed me shots of his children and I pretended to relax. He talked to me in English and one night when I came on duty, his eyes had changed. His pupils had got a little bigger and he moved a little more quickly. He suddenly tried to grasp my throat and it took a full magazine from a Lanchester SMG4 in .45 calibre to bring him down. He was dead on the deck before he fell. If I had engaged the safety he would have killed me. I have no doubt the previous guard had missed him taking something."

The use of drugs and alcohol was a major feature of the life of Wallis Warfield-Spencer-Simpson-Windsor and her greatest supporter was the drug addict Lady Emerald Cunard. Wallis suffered from recurring bleeding ulcers from her ever-increasing alcoholism which resulted in delusions, and in the last 10 years of her life she would pick up objects and talk on them as though they were a telephone.

The ambition of the British monarchy from 1837–1910 had been to exert political influence (Queen Victoria, 1837–1901; King Edward VII, 1902–1910) in the tradition of Queen Elizabeth I (1558–1603). However, King George V (1910–1936) did not have the sufficient IQ required to manipulate the destiny of nations. As such, his royal perspective was considerably more humble, understandable in that he could comprehend little. Instead, George V chose, or rather, it was chosen for him, that he would do whatever he was capable of. This was limited to embodying qualities which the nation was to see as its greatest strength – "diligence, dignity and duty". This involved being seen parading in a glorified uniform and little else.

These new traditional values were to march men into war as proud cannon fodder. It was a well-dressed borderline retard leading the impoverished into deaths of glory and risking their lives for medals made of brass and silk.

Despite the lack of intellectual status assigned to King George V, even less was assigned to his son King George VI.[27] Queen Elizabeth II

[27] King Edward VIII was assigned a little intellectual kudos, but this was mitigated by his inability to grasp 'cause and effect' and his sexually libertarian antics.

is no bright spark either. Her lack of intelligence and inability to spell her own name correctly during signing is often confused with her not being amused. She is not amused because she does not get the joke. "She is a child in a woman's body, does not understand murder and has little concept of Emotional Quotient."[28] In that regard, she is well matched to her husband/second cousin, Prince Philip.

As a result, Buckingham Palace is described as a sterile emotional void, and yet another generation morbidly waits on her passing the crown and the couple dying their way out of the history books. For such honoured people, at the end of their lives, we have to ask ourselves: "What have they done?"

More importantly, historians have to ask: "What have the royals done that the public generally don't know about?" This usually takes 50 years or so to uncover, but in the case of Prince Philip's tour of South America it is passed the the 50-year rule and still not released.

Going back to the late 1800s, the British royal family is a collection of German bisexual cuckolders and wife-cheaters. The bisexuals include King George V, King Edward VIII, King George VI, Lord Louis Mountbatten, Prince Philip, Prince Charles and Prince Edward. The cuckolders and wife-cheaters include King Edward VII, King George V, King Edward VIII, King George VI, Prince Philip, Queen Elizabeth II, Prince Charles and Princess Diana.

Prince Charles' servant, George Smith, claimed he was anally raped in 1989 by a royal servant and had seen Prince Charles in a compromising position with the same servant. Diana recorded Smith's affidavit and died within the year. Smith went public in 2003 dying two years later, apparently of post-traumatic stress disorder following military service in the Falklands War, 23 years earlier (1982). His illness was acquired soon after accusing Prince Charles. George Smith died 'ex-military fit' aged 44 on 24 August 2005. Unfortunately his late-detected long-time illness proved fatal.[29]

By no means is this history a good look. It looks more like a low grade American soap, a kind of super-rich *Days of our Lives* without the daily toil. The public at large can be justified in saying: "We are not amused".

[28] Spymaster.

[29] *The London Free Press News*, 'Palace rape claimant dies after long illness', 27 August 2005. His death was announced by his father.

Operation JAMES BOND 1–10 May 1945

From the very beginning of the war, the British ran German Army Intelligence and had insight into what the General Staff were doing. This made the war a very planned war which Britain continually expanded and prolonged. Essentially Britain trained Hitler and Stalin, gave Hitler Germany, and Stalin Russia, and then ordered Fascist Germany to attack Communist Russia, watching as they destroyed each other.

In the last days of WWII, America halted outside Berlin allowing Russia to destroy the Germans and many voluntary Scandinavian fascist units. At the same time, Britain pulled out its double agents from the inside.

America and Britain had this inside/outside thing going on the whole time. The British and American High Command were making decisions that troops on the ground could not understand. America could have taken Berlin two weeks earlier, but the British had not yet extracted their agents Martin Bormann and Adolf Hitler.

All the characters from Operation JAMES BOND took their names from *Winnie the Pooh.* Winston Churchill had been known as 'Winnie' since WWI. Ian Fleming was 'Pooh'. Adolf Hitler was 'Rabbit' and Eva Braun was 'Ms Rabbit'. Admiral Canaris, a British agent in the German High Command, was 'Eeyore'.

Hitler had Admiral Canaris killed on 9 April 1945 and by the time OPJB came into action he had been dead three weeks. "If Canaris was not actually working for the British, it is clear that he was working against Hitler."[1]

Operation JAMES BOND was designed by 'M' and consisted of:
Director of Special Secret intelligence operations, Major Desmond Morton;
Prime Minister and 2IC of 'M', Winston Churchill;
Director of Naval Intelligence, Rear-Admiral John Godfrey; and
Lieutenant-Commander of the Royal Navy Intelligence Division, Ian Fleming (Godfrey's personal assistant).

[1] *Bodyguard of Lies*, p. 816.

The operation was sabotaged by King George VI using his half-brother, Anthony Blunt, who was also a KGB operative.

In *OPJB* Chris Creighton claimed his mission was, according to its subtitle, *The Last Great Secret of the Second World War.* Churchill referred to the mission as 'The Operation that never was'. What was not acknowledged about OPJB was that there was another mission tacked onto it. The Lieutenant of OPJB, Ian Fleming, only knew about it when he was switched to the second, and even more secret, mission on 1 May 1945.

Germany was losing the war and Britain needed to control all the assets of Nazi pillage (M's, point 4), get its double agents out (M's point 5), and remove any incriminating evidence on Britain or America (M's point 7). To achieve this they had to pluck Martin Bormann, Hitler's secretary and head of the Nazi Party Chancellery (the money) to England in exchange for the Nazis' Swiss Bank account numbers. Britain would thereby become the hero of WWII's surviving victims, especially the Jews.

This had been pre-negotiated with Martin Bormann. Training had started four months earlier in January for a mission date in May 1945. Those in Operation JAMES BOND were trained at Birdham Military Camp near Portsmouth in a large country house in Hampshire for four months.

Christopher Creighton (21) led Operation JAMES BOND out of Berlin on 1–10 May 1945. He was the real inspiration for Ian Fleming's James Bond books (1953–64) and the cult movies that followed (1963–2006). In Chris Creighton (alias James Bond) we have one of the luckiest men alive. Luck was his nursery rhyme, his star, his life's work, and like the Fraud Squad, he was simply never suspected.

Operation JAMES BOND was of such a nature as to be considered unpatriotic. Therefore every measure of cover was put in place for the British agents.

"Extended cover was therefore put in place to show that for the duration of OPJB, from early January to early May 1945, he [Ian Fleming] had been either in the Far East, liaising with intelligence divisions of the Commonwealth navies, or else in Jamaica, where he had visited Sir William Stephenson (head of British Intelligence in the Americas and referred to as the 'quiet Canadian') at the end of February. So thoroughly was the deception planned" . . . he flew between England and Jamaica between training just to keep his alibi intact.[2]

[2] *OPJB*, p. 224.

Christopher Creighton's record was also continually altered and the record of his alias 'John Davis' was continually blackened making him appear as a convincing traitor.

Christopher Creighton was called to the underground war-room in London. King George VI "confided that he was worried about correspondence lodged in Schloss Kronberg, a castle near Frankfurt belonging to the Hesse family, of which Mountbatten was a scion[3] ... Worse, he feared other letters might contain embarrassing evidence that his brother, the Duke of Windsor, formerly King Edward VIII, had shown pro-Nazi leanings. Unfortunately, he said, there were valid reasons for believing this to be true, and he was extremely anxious that the correspondence should not fall into the wrong hands. Anthony Blunt [KGB spy] had been assigned the job of finding the letters and bringing them out."

Christopher Creighton: "I could see he did not want to believe what he had just admitted."[4] Other officers who were contemporaries of George VI were amazed that he even enunciated such a difficult and complex sentence. They suspected that a double was used.

The Duke of Windsor, the abdicated King Edward VIII, was a V-Mann with an Abwehr number. This meant that he was an active German agent passing vital information to the Germans.

King George VI acknowledged this but failed to reveal his half-brother Anthony Blunt as a communist sympathiser and numbered Soviet operative. Anthony Blunt joined Operation JAMES BOND.[5]

While training at Birdham Military Camp over the next few days, Anthony Blunt copied the plans for Operation JAMES BOND and gave them to the Russians who were desperate to stop all top Nazi brass leaving Berlin, as they too wanted everything the Nazis had looted – money, gold, paintings, artefacts, Freemasonry war plans and occult secrets. Anthony Blunt was removed from the mission for being lazy, insolent, refusing to train, and stealing documents. If less connected, he would have been shot on the spot.

---

[3] Hesse was an area of Germany formerly under British control. As such, the Hesse family never closed their doors to the British. A 'scion' is a descendant.

[4] *OPJB*, pp. 136–37.

[5] Prior to Stalin's death in 1953, the KGB was called the NKVD.

Martin Bormann was Hitler's secretary and head of the Chancellery. A doppelgänger was found for him and was only ever referred to as 'Günther'. Doppelgänger Bormann was given plastic surgery and matching dentalwork in England. German dentalwork was completely different from that practised in Britain and MI-6 had long used Continental dentists in specially equipped British clinics.

Doppelgänger Bormann was then taken back to Berlin where he accidentally protected the real Martin Bormann from a bomb blast during their escape on 1 May 1945. As he lay dying, the real Martin Bormann put his mouth close to his, virtually kissing him as he thanked his doppelgänger for saving his life. This allowed him to finish him off with a phial of potassium cyanide poison stored in one of his teeth.

Operation JAMES BOND then kayaked down the River Spree and Hitler's chief deputy Martin Bormann was taken back to Britain, given plastic surgery, and taught how to speak and walk differently. He was given a life in London, and when that got hot, life in a country town as Herr Martin Schuler. Becoming depressed, he was given a fake death in 1956 and on 29 April 1956 flown to Paraguay in central South America where he died in February 1959.

At the time of the real Martin Bormann's death, Peter Broderick-Hartley, a doppelgänger in training for the previous eight years, surfaced in the south of England and took Martin Bormann's place in 1960, dying in 20 June 1989. He specialised in overacting in public and giving German/Jewish relations a bad name.

Even after the real Bormann's death (1896–1959) British Intelligence still faked his life with doppelgängers in England, Italy and Germany. 'The Martin Bormann illusion' became a competition for the longest-running doppelgänger (44 years) and the longest-running unnecessary doppelgänger (30 years) and was recognised as a secret intelligence coup over the media and the masses.

In 1946 rumours were put out that SS men were guarding Martin Bormann in the Alps near Hitler's old retreat at the Berchtesgaden on the Austrian/German border. Later in 1946 the hideout was bombed by the Americans in a rather public display and they captured one of the SS 'actors' who confirmed they had been protecting Martin Bormann.

Then a motorcade, apparently carrying Bormann, drove through Austria and Italy followed by a British war-crimes investigator

The Bormanns.

(forerunner to the pitifully useless UN). He was to follow at a distance and was repeatedly denied permission to arrest the fake Bormann.

> "When they reached the Italian port of Bari, the dummy Bormann and his vehicle were hoisted in cargo nets aboard an unmarked ship which sailed away to an undisclosed location, 'rumoured' to be South America."[6]

This was the Rat Line – many rats used it. It was jointly funded by the US Army and the Vatican and when they arrived in South America they were protected by Vatican documents. This is why there were reports of Bormann in Argentina ten years before he actually arrived . . . and by then the search was over.

The Argentine documents released in the 1990s state that Bormann got through Italy by moving from monastery to monastery by way of Lake Garda and left Genoa on an Italian ship, landing at Buenos Aires. However, this is the fake story of his doppelgänger and made it all the way to Argentina as the official story. It even duped the spy ace, Ladislas Farago, author of *Aftermath* (p. 333) and at least 15 other books.

The lengths the Secret Service will go to, even in a foreign country, to hide the identity of a doppelgänger are endless. But their real mission was to hide, for as long as possible, the story that follows.

Just as Operation JAMES BOND had got Martin Bormann to the edge of the River Spree in central Berlin, on the evening of 1 May 1945, and were scaling down the river walls into their kayaks, Susan Kemp (who later became Director of 'M') gave Ian Fleming, the Commander of OPJB, "*an urgent but totally unexpected order.* He had been *recalled to London immediately. No reason had been given,* but he was to *return upstream to Müggelsee* [south-east of Berlin] as soon *as the escape party was safely away.* At 0200 a Lysander would come in to land on the disused road along the south-west shore of the lake, and pick him up . . . *an order had been given. Fleming was recalled*: that was it. Caroline Saunders had come downstream in one of the motorboats: in a matter of moments, Fleming [37] had gone down over the wall on a rope and was aboard it. As they pulled away, I [Chris Creighton, 21] called out, 'Good luck!' Fleming's reply was typical: 'Don't go and ponce up all our good work now, Christopher."[7]

---

[6] *OPJB*, pp. 221–22.

[7] *OPJB*, p. 178. Author's emphasis.

Chris Creighton then became commanding officer of Operation JAMES BOND. Soon after, they received a signal directly from General Donovan of American Intelligence saying that "Anthony Blunt belonged to a *homosexual Marxist* secret society called *The Apostles* at Trinity College in Cambridge, and that he had been a member of the *Communist Party* for the last nine years."

These facts were all covered up by MI-5, generally run by the Anglicans (British Catholics) and Freemasons. The head of all three was King George VI – Anthony Blunt's half-brother. King George VI was sabotaging M's mission and the James Bond operatives.[8]

Spymaster: "George VI would not have understood what he was presiding over and would have been used merely as a rubber stamp."

As a favour to Morton and Churchill, MI-5 did a back-room deal and pulled Ian Fleming out, but not James Bond (Chris Creighton) whose mission was paddling straight into alerted Russian fire. The only thing that saved them was a Russian-speaking beauty on board, who was one of their agents.

Ian Fleming didn't go straight back to London. He was being shifted to another mission that had been tacked on to Operation JAMES BOND. After the Führer had faked his death the day before, he made contact with his British opposite (Winston Churchill) and confirmed as much. He also reminded Churchill, in perfect English, that he was a British double agent, trained in Tavistock[9] from February to November 1912, gave his British military number, and confirmed that he had completed all missions (and then some), and requested to be evacuated to the "pre-negotiated safe haven".

Winston Churchill complied. It gave him the excuse to save one of his best friend's sons, the personal assistant to the Director of Naval Intelligence, Lieutenant-Commander of the Royal Navy Intelligence Division, and commander of Operation JAMES BOND, Ian Fleming.

What Ian Fleming experienced in the next 24 hours was an even bigger mind-bender and one that drove him to drink and bank debt for the next eight years.

---

[8] From 1940 the 14th Duke of Hamilton (Nazi) had huge control over the Freemasons. MI-6 is currently run hands on by QEII and MI-5 is controlled by Prince Charles.

[9] The Psych-Ops school was called Tavistock from 1920/21 after the school in Ireland was closed down due to civil war and new land was gifted by the Rothschilds.

If OPJB was 'the mission that never was', then the secret mission tacked on to it would be the most secret, shredded, and disavowed mission ever, and bound to remain secret until all parties were dead and even after that. Ian Fleming had already got all he needed from Martin Bormann and the JAMES BOND mission was about to paddle for 10 days into a Russian trap instigated by the communist sympathisers, Anthony Blunt and King George VI.

OPJB paddled during the night and camped under cover during the day in the Wannsee near Pfaueninsel Island where Goebbels gave his phenomenal party during the 1936 Olympics for two thousand guests, with huge fireworks many thought predictive of war. The next day, on the afternoon of 2 May 1945, under no German fire, but under heavy Russian fire, something really interesting happened.

> James Bond (Chris Creighton):
> "Now the Pfaueninsel [an island in Lake Havel, south-west of Berlin] was again under intermittent bombardment, this time from Soviet armour, which had advanced into the suburbs of Kladow, on the western shore of the Havel. During the afternoon a *Junkers sea-plane* came in to land on the Wannsee, close to the big island [Pfaueninsel]. *We speculated that this might represent a last-minute attempt to lift high-ranking Nazi to safety,* and sure enough, *two small boats, one a motor yacht, the other a gaff-rigged yawl,* came out, apparently to make contact with the pilot. No sooner had they appeared than the Soviet gunners took up target practice on both. The motorboat headed away at full speed and made good its escape. *The Junkers took off, also unscathed.* But the slow-moving yawl was less lucky: a direct hit blew it to pieces, and it went down, so far as we could see, with all hands. For us professional sailors, at action stations and highly trained in search-and-rescue techniques, it was terrible to have to stand by and watch helplessly as people drowned in front of our eyes. The incident shocked us, and made us all too well aware of what would happen if one of our kayaks were hit by a Soviet shell.[10]

---

[10] *OPJB*, pp. 185–86. Author's emphasis.

Plane Sailing

This is a point of history that's worth looking at in detail. If Hitler was to escape out of Berlin by plane, he would have put a great deal of effort into selecting the right plane, or planes, to escape in.

Hitler would have debated between three categories of plane. The first choice would have been the most capable VTOL evacuation seaplane (the German version of Short Take Off and Landing) and that would be the Heinkel 115. The second choice would have been an easily recognised unarmed passenger plane, unlikely to be seen as a threat, the least likely plane to be shot down and with as big floats as possible. The third choice would have been whatever was available.

Any of these three choices should have been able to fly the 1500 km from Berlin to Barcelona in one stretch at a minium speed of 190 mph/ 300 kmph to match the Lysander he was eventually to fly with.

Although the point of view of the James Bond team was very distant and obscured, they were all trained in plane spotting and reported a Junkers landing on Lake Havel. According to *The Last Days of Hitler* it was a JU52. I don't disagree, but there were scores of Junkers planes of which many could be mistaken for other aircraft and there were at least 28 different models of JU52s.

WWII aircraft expert: "The first choice of plane for the VTOL on water would have been a seaplane that was: (a) available with spares so as to be readily employed by the RAF version of KG200, which operated captured British and American aircraft; (b) fast; (c) capable of diving; (d) able to stop and start in a short distance; (e) relatively quiet; (f) able to carry heavy loads like gold; and (g) proven as the best aircraft in the fleet.

"Seaplanes are weighted differently from land planes and land horizontally with their weight over the wings. Land planes tend to land with the tail wheel first and have their weight behind the wings.

"Seaplanes have a higher torque for take-off and a lower cruising speed, so they tend to have three or four propeller blades. The JU52 had two propeller blades and its single engine was underpowered which made water take-offs unreliable to say the least.

"For the JU52 to be adapted as a seaplane, it would need greater torque for take-off. It would have to have been the 3-engined version, the JU52/3m, and most likely with the propeller blades increased from 2 to 3. This still left the problem of the weighting of the plane and this was compensated for with very large floats.

"No one with half a brain would try and land a twin-blade propeller single-engine JU52 on a lake (especially in rough weather) and if they did, no one with experience would expect to take off again. The JU52 was too risky to use on such an important mission. The later three-engined JU52/3m was a better bet and had the advantage of being recognised as a non-fighter transport aircraft.

"Junkers never made Catalina-type planes that landed on their bellies, planes with roof-mounted wings, or bi-planes. Junkers did make the twin-engined glass-nosed JU88 from December 1936 and these matched with the Dornier Do17 and the Heinkel 111 quite closely.

"They were all similar length (14.2–16.6 m), similar wingspan (18–22.6 m), similar height (4.2–4.7 m), similar speed (440–510 kmph) and all had enough range (2108–2150 km).

"The problem with all of them was they were known to be combat aircraft carrying 1–2 tonnes of bombs and machine guns. This made them a target and ruled out the more modern JU88 as a possible EVAC seaplane."

The Heinkel He115 (August 1937–44) was also similar in that it had a glass nose, twin engines, was 17.3 m long, had a 22.2 m wingspan, a height of 5 m, a slower speed of 349 kmph and a range of 2100 km. The Heinkel had 9-cylinder BMW radial engines while the Junkers had 18-cylinder BMW radial engines. The wingspan, dimensions and height, as well as the engines and look of the plane, were very similar.

The Heinkel He115 had an aluminium and rope ladder and the Heinkel He115B had a torpedo belly that could be modified with a retractable harness falling out to lift two people with ease. This would have been very difficult to see from a hidden low-level position.

The Heinkel also had six struts per float which would have further obstructed the view and these may well have been modified with bulletproof side walls. It would have been simple enough to drive right under the Heinkel and for the passengers to be transferred without getting wet.

The Heinkel He115 was described as "a wholly outstanding machine in all respects. It was tough, beautiful to fly at speeds down to 75 knots and carried a substantial load at relatively high speeds. In 1938 the prototype was specially streamlined as the A-1 to set class records.

"By 1939 the long-range B models were in production which could carry 1420 kg at 240 km/hr for up to 3300 km. They were also used by the British RAF for secret agent dropping between Scotland, Malta and North Africa.

"The 141 E-models were built in 1944 to bring the total past 400. They were used for armed reconnaissance, shallow dive bombing and casevac [casualty evacuation]."[11]

WWII aircraft expert: "The Heinkel He115 was a reliable seaplane with plenty of spare parts. The KG-200 squadron used special Allied aircraft and also German aircraft, which they dressed up to look like foreign aircraft. JU88 'fighters' were also painted to look like JU88 'bombers' with the bomber's glass noses painted on. This was done to lure the RAF into attacking from the front, the most lethal part of the JU88 'fighter'."

The Heinkel He115 would have been the perfect choice for Hitler as an escape plane because it was more than capable of flying the return trip from Berlin to Barcelona (3000 km) without refuelling and was considered one of Germany's most solid fighting aircraft.

The problem with the He115 was that it was too good an aircraft and was known to carry one tonne of bombs, plus machine guns. The He115 was the best plane for the job, but it was too much of a target.

The second choice, the easily recognised unarmed passenger plane, unlikely to be seen as a threat, was best satisfied by the Junkers JU52/3m.

Single engine Junkers JU52 were built from 1930 with two propeller blades and a top speed of 250 kmph (155 mph). They were poorly armed and slow so many were shot down. As such they always needed an escort and weren't considered a threat without one.

From April 1931 these were upgraded and fitted with three engines (BMW 132T Radial Piston Hornet engines, 725 hp each) giving the JU52/3m a maximum speed of 316 kmph (195 mph) and a range of 1300 km (808 miles). These were built as seaplanes from 1932–45 with the later models having three-bladed propellers.

The JU52/3m had a length of 18.9 m, a wingspan of 29 m and a height of 4.5–6.0 m, depending on wheels, skis or floats. But most importantly they had very large floats, 12 m long by 1 m high. This was enough to hide the top of a conning tower from a rising submarine.

[11] *Hitler's Luftwaffe*, p. 186.

The JU52/3m were reliable and had plenty of spare parts, but had little else going for them. They were not fast, great divers, VTOL, or quiet, and could only carry moderate loads off the water. They were considered an unthreatening transport aircraft and people had affection for them. This was their main advantage.

The JU52s were variously nicknamed the 'Iron Annie', 'Auntie Ju' and 'The Corrugated Coffin' because of the corrugated iron fuselage that protected a very solid airframe.

During the Spanish Civil War[12] the Junkers JU52/3m ferried more than 10,000 Moorish troops from Morocco to Spain as well as dropping 6000 tonnes of bombs. They generally carried 2 x 7.92 machine guns and could be fitted with a variety of bomb brackets. They were commonly used by the Condor Legion in Spain (German troops) and would not attract any special attention there.

The JU52/3m entered into service as troop transport and bombers. They were used by Lufthansa and served Madrid as airliners, which was slightly embarrassing when the same German planes were used to drop bombs less than a mile from the airport during the Spanish Civil War essentially a practice war for WWII.

From 1937 the JU52/3m were purportedly withdrawn from their bomber role and used for transport and bomber training only. By 1939 over 1000 JU52 were in service and eventually 5415 were built. As a Lufthansa airliner they could carry (only) 17 passengers and travel from Berlin to Rome in 8 hours, which at the time was considered fantastic. They also served as airliners in Finland, Spain and Sweden, as mail carriers in China, and hauling lumber in Canada.

In delivering mail, carrying lumber, passengers, troops and doing bomber training, the JU52s developed a friendly and unthreatening reputation. After 1939, JU52s were recognised more and more as a civil transport plane.

During WWII the JU52s dropped paratroopers into the Netherlands, Ardennes, Crete, the Mediterranean, North Africa and the Baltic States. The 'Iron Annies' were popular, reliable, generally recognised as an unarmed plane and became the most famous German transport of WWII.

---

[12] Spanish Civil War, 16 July 1936–1 April 1939.

Top: Heinkel 115.
Middle: Condor Focke-Wulf 200C-1 Condor, SG+KS.
Bottom: Junkers JU88.

The JU52/3ms were continually improved upon and not all of these improvements were made public. Later models were powered by 3 Pratt & Whitney Hornet radial engines with a maximum take-off weight of 10 tonnes.

The JU52/3m g5e had interchangeable ski gear with an exhaust that de-iced, and even later JU52/3ms had three cells capable of carrying 1.5 tonnes of bombs in the fuselage and 3 x 7.92 mm MG15 rearward-facing guns with a total of 1800 rounds. Improved versions had more modern radio equipment, upgraded bomb-release mechanisms and a take-off weight of 10.5 tonnes with an economical cruising speed of 210 kmph.

The JU52/3m g10e was an improvement on this again with wheels, skis or floats and was powered by 3 BMW 132Z radial engines, a glider tow coupling and strengthened landing gear for a maximum take-off weight of 11.5 tonnes.

The final production version of this was the JU52/3m g14e with additional armoured protection for the pilot, 13-mm MG131 guns to the rear, 7.92-mm MG 15 guns in each beam position and another over the cockpit in the low drag cupola position.

By manipulating public perception Hitler had transformed a successful bomber plane into a much-loved transport aircraft. The appearance of the plane was not improved upon from 1930 and their latest improvements were largely kept out of the public eye so that by the end of the war the JU52/3ms were the aeronautical version of a hotrod – highly powered, strong on take-offs, able to carry huge loads, well protected and defended, but still an 'Iron Annie' – all affection and no threat. The plane was also in common use in Spain so landing there was not of any particular note. This was the perfect plane for Hitler's RAPWI (Recovery of Allied Prisoners of War and Internees).

In addition to these general improvements, the belly of the JU52/3m g14e seaplane could be modified into two long trapdoors as was common to many planes. The 12-m-long floats on the JU52/3m seaplane tapered from 1 metre to 0.6 metres and sat about 0.5 metres above the water. The distance from the top of the float to the belly of the plane was another 1.5 metres. With two trapdoors 1 metre wide, this only left a gap of 0.5 metres from the top of the float to the bottom of the doors and this gap was further obstructed by eight struts each side.

If the conning tower of a submarine rose to 0.5 metres above the surface there was no way to sight it and if it rose to within 1 metre of the belly of the plane there was no way to sight who travelled between. This was near perfect protection that only the bombing of the plane could have destroyed, and Hitler had organised German bombing on the Russians just for this occasion.

The Junkers JU52 was selected for the very reason of all its failures. It was recognised as a slow passenger aircraft, had not carried bombs in many years, was known to have the minimum of machine guns, was a relatively old and easily recognised design and was not considered a threat by anyone[13] . . . but the vastly improved JU52/3m g14e was capable of travelling at over 316 kmph (195 mph), had a range of 1300 km (808 miles), and additional mileage could be supported using fuel bladders inside the aircraft. Most importantly the JU52/3m g14e could keep up with a Lysander on a trip to Spain.

The Junkers that landed on Lake Havel was a JU52/3m g14e, with 3 BMW 132Z radial engines, a maximum take-off weight of 11.5 tonnes, 13-mm MG131 guns to the rear, two 7.92-mm MG 15 beam guns, a 7.92-mm MG 15 cockpit gun, armourplated cockpit, 12 metre x 1 metre floats, an opening belly with 1-metre wide doors, oxygen, and a typewriter. There were no reported shots hitting the plane and it left Lake Havel "unscathed" at 4.24 pm on 2 May 1945.

It appears that Hitler had planned the history of the Junkers JU52/3m with this escape in mind. 'Iron Annies' had drawn on the affection of almost everyone. They were not considered a threat and their 'hotrod' improvements were not noted. As such they became the best escape aircraft from Lake Havel on 2 May 1945.

Hitler's destination to Barcelona was pre-empted 11 days earlier on 21 April 1945, the day after his birthday celebrations. In the process, many of his Berlin staff were killed and many of Hitler's secrets died with them. This terminated links with his new destination and meant that Hitler arrived in Barcelona as a disempowered individual rather than a world dictator.

---

[13] Most JU52s were destroyed at war's end, but a small number were still manufactured in Spain (170 by CASA in Getafe) and France (400) after 1945 and most of these were fitted with 3-blade propellers. Some JU52/3m g4e were used by the Swiss air force as transport until 1981.

> "The last flight made by a Fw 200 *Condor* (and also the last flight of any great distance by the pre-war *Lufthansa*) was on the evening of 21st April, 1945. The plane, hastily loaded with the luggage of the Berlin head office staff, was to fly the staff to Munich, and then on to Barcelona. The plane was to be flown by Flug-kapitan Kunstle. It is known that the plane duly took off for Munich, overloaded in the confident knowledge that no enemy plane would appear in such bad weather. The *Condor* was never seen again, although enquiries were made and continued for years, in Germany, Switzerland and Spain. But it was not until ten years after the war had ended that any explanation was forthcoming. Then traces of a four-engined aircraft were discovered near Munich, just outside a place called Müldorf. The plane had burnt out, but investigation showed that the surviving wreckage was of the last German *Condor*."[14]

Pommie Spies: "The Fw 200 *Condor* was carrying the Führerbefehl [the Führer command], the colonels, majors, captains and leutnants – all of Hitler's high staff that did not want to stay in the bunker with Hitler. Hitler treated this act as somewhat treasonous.

"The Fw 200 *Condor* had 'D-ASHH' over-painted on its side indicating that it was a C-3 *Condor* manufactured before 1939. Still fitted with its seats, it had been used for VIP transport throughout the war and was now being used to transport the Führerbefehl to Barcelona.

"It was important that this plane exploded. It had the escaping Führer command, all their documents, and contained evidence of many high-level meetings during the war, including those with British, American and Russian high command. This terminated any leaks they may have provided after the war and was a vital connecting piece that needed to be destroyed for official history to remain unchallenged.

"When the Fw 200 *Condor* D-ASHH landed in Munich for refuelling, a time bomb was put on the plane. It exploded in the air soon after, with its remains scattered over a Bavarian pine forest, just as planned.

"If the aircraft had crashed intact then it would have gouged a landing strip through the pine trees, the fuel would have incinerated everything on the plane and the forest would have caught fire. This would have been a crash without mystery.

"It was essential that the plane blew up in the air so that everything was scattered far and wide with no tell-tale gouge through the pine trees

[14] *Design for Flight*, p. 92.

or the forest catching fire. It was essential to delay discovery until as much of the evidence as possible was destroyed and for the event to remain a mystery. This worked and the plane was not discovered for another nine years, in 1954."

Spymaster: "If one walks in that Bavarian forest today, it is a place of deadly quiet. There are the odd bird sounds, but no major animal noises. The pieces of *Condor* are scattered widely. Most are small pieces from around the rear spar [aircraft part]. The rear spar was always a problem and those with extra fuel tanks for Atlantic flight had their spars extensively strengthened. This was one of the early Condors whose rear spar may not have been extensively strengthened.

"It would not have taken a huge charge to destroy the aircraft and would have been quite easily accomplished with a British barometric bomb, with an incendiary included for good measure. One of the pieces I picked up from the forest floor was fuselage, schwarze grün on one side [black green is a Luftwaffe camouflage colour] and charred on the other side. Charring is the sign that the fuel load had been ignited, probably in the air. Whoever said the British weren't thorough?

"I could find no human remains, but I had no doubt they were there all around me. There would never be a memorial here for these people. In serving their Führer faithfully, they had come to know too much and paid the ultimate price."

Another top secret KG200 transport was downed in March 1945. The B17 'Flying Fortress' crashed shortly after takeoff from Echterdingen, near Stuggart. It was fully crewed with an American pilot (Oberseld Webel Knappenschneider) and carried ten members of the French 'Vichy' Government. All died except for the tail gunner.

When Luftwaffe HQ investigated the crash, one Luftwaffe officer quickly declared the cause as 'sabotage and probably a British barometric bomb detonated prematurely'.

There was much speculation amongst Detachment Olga (the sub-Squadron of KG200) and the officer was asked for further comment. He declined on the basis that stopping to comment would probably guarantee his death and instead concentrated on perfecting his disappearance.

The lower ranks of the Luftwaffe had run out of rations and the Quartermaster used the luxuries that survived the fire as food to the end of the war. "It was just dumb luck that we never lost all that lovely grub."[15]

[15] Story partly sourced from P. W. Stahl, *KG 200*, pp. 147–48.

Real Doppelgänger Deaths and Faked Real Deaths

Spymaster: "When Stalin expelled the ethnic Germans out of Russia, some were trained in the GRU Spy Factories in the Baltic Republics. One of these was then infused into the German Army as a driver. He initially drove for the Abwehr, but was eventually transferred into the SS and rose to the equivalent rank of sturmbannführer.

"On 22 April 1945, the first Soviet armies reached the outskirts of the still fiercely defended Berlin. Stalin had organised special teams in his WWII military counter-intelligence service, Smersh, to locate Hitler dead or alive. [*See Smersh, Appendix 7*]

"Late in the afternoon of 1 May, the Russian SS sturmbannführer walked through the smoke and ruins of Berlin towards the Russian lines where he began whistling a Russian folk song. This was whistled back to confirm their shared origins. The sturmbahnführer then told the Russian troops that Eva had acquired a new blue dress and Hitler had pinned his Gold Party badge on Frau Goebbels dress. He left as the Goebbels children's deaths were being prepared and walked through the Russian lines with the troops in awe."[16]

When the Russians invaded Hitler's bunker they were tired, fearful and on edge, just as the Germans knew they would be. If Hitler was dead, his body must be somewhere. The first bodies they identified were of the Goebbels' family. Magda Goebbels was wearing the Führer's Gold Party badge just as the Russian SS spy had told them. The bodies of the Goebbels children were also there as was their father with his easily recognisable clubfoot.

A body was found with a small moustache and a bullet hole through the centre of his forehead. The corpse looked barely 40, whereas Hitler was 56 and looked 70. One of the men from headquarters of the first Byelorussio Army said, "No, this is not Hitler."[17] The Soviets then called in some captured Nazis and they all said, "No, no, not Hitler", but they still photographed the body with a correspondingly aged photo of Hitler placed on his chest. They just happened to have a 17-year-old photo of Hitler aged 39 (1928), which corresponded to the age of the dead doppelgänger and did not use a recent photo of Hitler (56) for

[16] The spy was deliberately kept alive by the order of an SS General, probably Fegelein.

[17] Byelorussio is a big part of Russia above the Ukraine. They consider themselves 'White Russians'.

identification. The Russians were exhausted, dead keen on capture and susceptible to fooling even themselves in order to please Stalin.

The Fritzes (Germans) were not being difficult as they easily could have been and they led the Soviets to a second proposed Hitler body buried on top of a shell hole near the entrance of the bunker. The crater was filled with loose earth, and when stood on, it sank.

A body of a man and a woman were dug up. Both were scorched beyond recognition but the remains of a blue dress was unearthed with them. The dress helped convince the Russians that the female body was Eva Braun and that the male body next to her must be Adolf Hitler. Being Russians they began celebrating as soon as the Commissar (Soviet Party official) had informed Stalin of the find. The autopsy would be performed the following day.

The next morning, in the cold light of day, things were not looking so good. Fifteen bodies were found in the Chancellery garden including Joseph and Magda Goebbels, their six children, Adolf and Eva Hitler's doppelgängers and five other Hitler doppelgängers. The Goebbels family deaths on 1 May 1945 were designed to lend credibility to a scene of forensic fraud.

The Soviets placed the bodies in wooden crates and took them to Buch, an old lunatic asylum outside Berlin. The Freemasons love creating wordplay jokes in history and here "It's madness by the book."

Blood testing had indicated that neither 'Hitler' nor 'Eva Braun' had died from the poison inserted in their mouths after death. 'Eva' had died from shrapnel wounds and had dental cavities in her teeth. They realised that the cunning Fritzes had tricked them after all.

Spymaster: "They had a vote: 'Ring Stalin and tell him the truth, or carry on lying.' They voted unanimously to carry on lying."

Hugh Thomas's *Doppelgänger* (1995) showed that all stories contradicted each other in some way. With the bodies found outside the bunker, Eva Braun's teeth did not match Eva Braun's dental records; and the woman had died from shrapnel wounds, not cyanide as the SS had claimed.

With the supposed body of Hitler, all the teeth were loose as if they had been plucked from other bodies. The left leg had been burnt away, "as if to conceal some defect Hitler did not have, while the rest of the body was only lightly torched", but enough to remove all fingerprints. This concurs with the actions of Otto Günsche, Hitler's SS Adjutant, who soaked the fake Hitler and Eva Braun bodies with gasoline in the courtyard and threw an ignited rag on them at 4 pm on 30 April 1945.

The Soviets refused to tell the Americans or British what they were up to, let alone ask for help. The autopsy was not a perfect autopsy. It was crude and carried out under less than ideal conditions between 3–8 May 1945. The teeth were the only clue as to Hitler's identity so the Soviets scoured Berlin looking for Hitler's dentist.

Miraculously they found two people who said they were part of Hitler's dental team. They drew pictures from memory of what Hitler's teeth looked like, and according to the ever-so-keen Russians, the dentists' hand-drawn pictures matched the body on the slab. Hitler's last dental work was seven months earlier, in September 1944.[18]

The chances of Hitler's dental assistants being alive, available and remembering his dental records is absolutely astounding and all too convenient. It was part of a hoax to identify the fake unrecognisably burnt body as that of Hitler's. This worked for a while and fooled a few, but was completely dismissed with the work of Hugh Thomas in *Doppelgängers* (1995).

> "A medical report dated May 8, 1945, of an autopsy of a severely charred body came to the conclusion that this was 'presumably Hitler's corpse'. Other statements shortly afterwards cast doubt on this assertion. Then again Soviet sources maintained that Hitler had after all been identified on the basis of dental studies; but this statement, too, was questioned, and rumours arose that the British authorities were hiding Hitler in their zone of occupation."[19]

No X-rays were available at the time and Stalin held back the findings on the autopsy, turning Hitler's fake captured body into a State secret.

Hitler had now either shot himself, poisoned himself, been burnt beyond recognition, died at the head of his troops, or escaped. Stalin didn't believe it was Hitler's body and he placed a 7–15-year prison sentence on anyone who revealed the erroneous capture of Hitler.

[18] Dental assistant Kathy Frankerman was then immediately removed to a Soviet prison for the next 12 years.
[19] *Hitler*, p. 750.

Bormann Dies Again and Again

As for Bormann, there were two bodies found. The doppelgänger 'Günther' Bormann with plastic surgery was found on the night of 1 May 1945, then in 1965 a tip-off was received that Bormann's body could be found at the Ulap Fairground in Berlin, but no body was found at the time. It was not until 1972 that Bormann's real body was found there, 14 years older. That is, Martin Bormann had lived for another 14 years after 1 May 1945. The British knew this as they had arranged his escape, plastic surgery and supply of doppelgängers even after his death.

In the real Bormann (found dead in 1972) the teeth were close but had extra fillings indicating that he had lived beyond 1945 and had visited a dentist. Paraguay clay was also found in the cranium. The body had been brought back to Berlin after being buried in Paraguay for six years from 1959 to 1965.

Spymaster: "Apart from the Russians, the British also went to enormous trouble compromising the Germans. Many of the German nobles, who were related to their royal cousins in England, began to 'turn' during the war. They were convinced by an 'attached' British agent that they were serving a bohemian corporal and should become double agents. This resulted in the British running German officers in intelligence schemes. The proof of this is the number of German officers who were awarded British decorations and resettled in Commonwealth countries after the war. The Americans tended to award German military personnel who served them with a US decoration known as the 'Medal of Freedom', some of which were awarded posthumously."

The Germans issued a coloured book every month and the colour changed from month to month. In it were listed deserters and military personnel gone AWOL; German military personnel involved in the officers' revolt against Hitler (20 July 1944); and those who had been turned by the Allies and reinserted into the German military. The Americans called these people 'Joes' and most of them were recruited from POW cages.

One such death occurred while Hitler was visiting Kiev in Russia, just before the German offensive into Russia in 1943. The anti-Hitler group of Wehrmacht (army) officers that resisted Hitler were supposed to have smuggled a mercury bomb onto Hitler's plane, which would explode at a certain height.

Secret Service: "It was a Courvoisier brandy bottle with a mercury barometer bomb inside. This was wrapped around three brandy bottles and placed in the Focke-Wulf 200 in Kiev that the Hitler doppelgänger unit was flying in. It had a solid nose and no gun turrets. Leutnant von Schlabendorf delivered the bomb to von Treskow who didn't have the stomach to put it on board, so he asked an SS Officer to do it for him.

"The SS Officer was very touchy and refused to load it, but when von Schlabendorf threatened him personally, he relented.

"One theory says that it did explode and the real Hitler was killed. Martin Bormann then brought a doppelgänger in to double for Hitler and duplicated the bomb, returning it to Leutnant von Schlabendorf saying nothing. The new Hitler even changed his routine to make it convincing."

The Russian intelligence viewpoint at the time was that the real Hitler died at Kiev in 1943 and that a doppelgänger replaced him thereafter. This eventually became known as "the theory that was never enunciated".

'The theory that was never enunciated' was considered too hot, too secret, and too confusing for historians, who tend to write to the edges of a pre-defined cube, as opposed to juggling the cubes and letting them fall on the floor.

Spymaster: "The Russians have a completely different view of the history of WWII. They believe Hitler was killed in 1943 in Kiev, Russia, and that a doppelgänger took over Hitler's role and started rooting Eva Braun for real."

Hitler had complete doppelgänger units who were so convincing that their true status would only show up under extensive interrogation. (This is not unlike 'made-for-viewing' Saddam Hussein doppelgänger units.)

The German Intelligence understanding of the Russian belief that Hitler had died meant that the Germans were surprised at the intensity of the Russian defence at Kursk. The Germans had always hit the Russians where they least expected trouble, but the Russians were given ample time to prepare defences at Kursk.

Many of the weapons delivered to the German army arrived full of undisclosed faults and design errors. Self-propelled guns had problems with engines, Panther tanks suffered engine overheating and turret traverse problems. Tiger tanks also had problems with engines. This combination of events, coupled with a Soviet artillery strike on the

German attack as they organised, was enough to bring eventual disaster to the whole German operation.

Such a combination had never occurred before on any front involving German arms. This smacks of war sabotage and intelligence sabotage on both sides in order for the bigger picture to remain confused. The Russians believe that it was the real Hitler who died in Kiev in 1943 and a doppelgänger Hitler took over. The Germans believe the Hitler death was a doppelgänger, but thought it convincing enough for the Russians to relax their defences. At Kursk the Germans were expecting a disorganised Russian army and the Russians were expecting a disorganised German army. The result was pandemonium.

Evidence of the death of 'the Hitler' was obscured in battles and war damage. When Hitler was later found to be alive again and again, it gave him immortal status. The same year Churchill used exactly the same tactic with Leslie Howard who, as Churchill's doppelgänger, was killed over the English Channel.

This in turn leads to the question of whether or not this was an elaborate hoax so that Hitler and Churchill could meet in Cyprus. Cyprus remained a backwater during the war, whereas Crete, only a few miles away, was a hotbed of conflict. All of these islands including Kos are in the eastern Aegean, near Turkey.

Secret Service: "Cyprus, under British administration since 1878, is a place where something should have happened, but it is a Freemason stronghold and many of those who arranged the war were on Cyprus at the time. Nothing happened here during WWII. Cyprus doesn't appear in any of the war histories. It falls into the zone of Italian occupation, which is suspicious as it's a place where something should have happened."

Greek Intelligence Officer: "After WWII, Greece was the last country fought over. Britain wanted it the right side of socialist and Stalin wanted it farther left. Since Churchill and Stalin had worked together for over four decades, a compromise was reached. In 1947, 25,000 children, all under 12, were taken to Russia and trained as communists, with the intention that they would be repatriated back into Greece as adults and drive Greece left of socialist.

"Most of the 25,000 stolen children were between 7 and 9 years. At this age, children are most easily reconstructed, or to the Western way of thinking, deconstructed – that is, their subconscious thought patterns were shifted to conform with the Russian State.

"The programme was delayed, and it was 2005 before the former Greek children applied for Greek citizenship. Greece refused. There is no way they wanted communists in their country. In 2005, those Greek children were 63–70 years old, with Russian and Greek wives, children and grandchildren. They weren't 25,000 Greek children any more. They were 80,000 Greek Russians."

After WWII, Cyprus went to arms and virtual civil war, first between the British and the communist-backed Cypriots, then between the Greeks and the Turks. This lasted until 1975. Georgeios 'Costas' Grivas (1898–1974) became head of the underground campaign (EOKA) against British rule in Cyprus (1955–59). In 1971 he secretly returned to Cyprus and directed the terrorist campaign against the Turks (EOKA-B) for the unification of Cyprus with Greece. He died just before victory in 1975 – just as planned.

Archbishop Makarios III, the primate of the Orthodox Church of Cyprus (Mikhail Khristodoulou Mouskos, 1913–99) took over the administration as president of Cyprus (1959–77), and after his death the archbisopric and head of state were separated. It was no longer possible to gift 25,000 Greek children to Russian paedophiles.

Spymaster: "When the Cyprus Civil War finished, the Illuminati (those who organise war for profit and social engineering) moved to Kos between 1976–78. Kos has been a British base for over two centuries with British memorials and graves going back two hundred years. During WWII, Kos was protected by guerrillas prepared to fight to the death for their cause – partisans and the British together. Today it is used for important Freemasonry and paedophile meetings.

"This area is renowned for its war preparations. In the caves about Croatia, Tito stored arsenals, casing gear and military machines capable of manufacturing Mauser 98s, which meant they didn't have to import their arsenal. Tito (Winston Churchill's cousin) built this military manufacturing plant into the hills, expecting the Russians to invade after WWII.

"Bob Hawke, former Prime Minister of Australia, lost his brother in tragic circumstances when Group Captain Hawke, while on leave from the RAF, was accidentally blown up by a bomb flying an unauthorised flight of British ammunition into Croatia for the last round of British-inspired hostilities in the Balkans. When his plane was shot down, the CIA operative, Australian Prime Minister Bob Hawke, kept very quiet about it."[20]

Similarly, one of Martin Bormann's doppelgängers was Stalin's fabled spy 'Der Specht' (The Woodpecker). He faithfully supplied Stalin with information direct from the top for years, to the extent that Stalin believed he was the real Bormann and Kiev flight bomb had killed the real Hitler.

Stalin was a British Agent and had been gifted Russia in order to destroy it and create war with Germany – essentially doing Britain's job for them. The job of the British-run German doppelgängers was to supply people like Stalin with enough correct information to keep them involved, confident and advancing. In this way, the doppelgänger Bormann did a brilliant job, everything the British and German double agents wanted.

This particular Bormann doppelgänger died in Moscow soon after Germany's collapse on 1 May 1945. After the war, virtually all of the doppelgängers were killed. They had become useless curios and enormous security risks capable of inciting the world's most disillusioned people into mass riot. Until now, history has supported their demise and kept quiet about their role.

Ironically, Britain preserved its last doppelgänger until 1987, when he too was murdered for saying wildly true things about WWII . . . "everything was arranged . . . everyone had doubles". When the British SAS death squad, uniformed as American servicemen, came to kill doppelgänger Hess, he was hardly surprised. He probably welcomed death after 46 years in custody under a false identity.

Following page: Nuremberg Rally; destruction in Germany; the former Europen Union flags at Kos; the island off Kos; Kos ruins; and the famous Kos hotel.

[20] Officially Bob Hawke had one brother who died aged 19.

Operation WINNIE THE POOH
26 April–4 May 1945

With the use of doppelgängers, Hitler's entourage were specialists in deception, deceiving each other, themselves, the staff and any witnesses. Any witnesses they failed to control were either killed, ordered to suicide, suicided or swore the dreaded Holy oath of silence on penalty of death to themselves and their entire family. Such was the depth of their oath, secrecy and in-house revenge.

The Germans have Teutonic brains and always planned everything three years ahead and right down to the last detail. On 22 April 1945 Hitler announced to General Alfred Jodl (adviser on strategy and operations) and General Karl Koller (Chief of Luftwaffe Staff), among others, that he was intending to suicide.

Field Marshal Wilhelm Keitel (chief of Armed Forces High Command), General Alfred Jodl (adviser on strategy and operations) and Albert Speer (Minister of Armaments) then left the Bunker, with some impetus, and spread the news to the wider world. Once the 'secret from no greater source' got out, everyone was expecting Hitler to suicide and it was a big relief when he evidently did.

Hitler and his entourage had been in the Bunker from 16 January 1945, and from 21 April 1945 there were many permanent escapes out of the Bunker. These occurred on 21, 22, 23, 29, 30 April and on 1 May 1945. The Allies knew about them and did little to stop them, except when there was agreement with the Germans to stop them.

Operation WINNIE THE POOH deals with Adolf Hitler and Eva Braun's escape from the Bunker on 30 April 1945 and their flight out of Berlin between 4 and 5 pm on 2 May 1945.

On 30th April 1945, there were ample opportunities for Adolf and Eva Hitler to escape from the Bunker. As cover for this, no less than six Hitler doppelgängers were terminated around the Chancellery Bunker. These were later found by the Red Army's mopping-up squads.

As the Intelligence version of history is studied more and more, Hitler's death reveals itself as a 'canned meat' operation. Stalin would have recognised this immediately as he had enacted the same thing on 2 January 1911, some 44 years earlier, during his escape out of the Sidney Street siege.

Both 'canned meat' operations came with Churchill's active complicity.

Many histories have exposed the burnt Hitler and Eva bodies as fake. Anomalies in the bodies prove this well enough. The dead Hitler had no gunshot wound to the skull, although it was first reported that he had shot himself through the mouth. Eva was supposed to have died from poisoning, although the autopsy showed the female body in the blue dress died of shrapnel wounds, was bleeding from the breasts and had abundant dental cavities. If this had been allowed to happen to the Führer's mistress there would have been courts martial and trips to the wall for everyone involved.

According to the Spymaster: "The use of the blue dress was a case of 'sheep dipping'. It was a key part of the cover story that Eva Braun was to be wearing a blue dress during the escape, just as the Soviet undercover told the Red Army . . . There were also two skulls of Hitler, one found in the crater/grave attached to the body and another presented prior to autopsy."

If anything, this points to a higher level of cover-up and the possibility and probability of complicity from all sides.

No war is ever finished
and each portion of unsolved war
leads to the next war.

From the point of Hitler and Eva's bodies being brought out of their rooms there was no positive identification. Hitler was identified from his trousers and boots and Eva from her blue dress. In preparation for the exhausted Russians this was a classic case of 'Keep It Simple Stupid' – in this case, the KISS of death.

Once Hitler and Eva Braun had faked their deaths in their quarters, Goebbels went in followed by Reich Youth leader Artur Axmann. Axmann had ascended to the heights of the Hitler Youth on the basis of the loss of an arm in combat at the exact time that the previous director's wife Baldur von Schirach had embarrassed Hitler. The one armed Director of the Hitler Youth was hardly a man to be trusted and more a man to comply with any and every deception.

With Goebbels having himself killed 29 hours after Hitler, Axmann became the most unreliable witness testament could provide.

The German name for Hitler's escape plan was "Testament" named after Hitler's will and those sections of the Bible the Nazis were enacting to make the Bible prophesies come true. For the British it was "Winnie the Pooh". Neither carried the prefix 'Operation' and little of these combined operations ever appeared in writing. As such, both plans could be spoken about openly without raising suspicion.

Sometime after Hitler and Eva's doppelgänger deaths, the three doors to the Bunker-Chancellery bulkhead passage were locked. (See page 311.) These bulkhead doors separated the Bunker and the bulkhead passage, the bulkhead passage and the Chancellery, and the bulkhead passage and the Foreign Office. This provided ample space for Adolf Hitler, Eva Hitler née Braun and their escorts, SS Chancellery commandant Wilhelm Mohnke and five Hitler doppelgängers to hide while the mourners attended their Viking funeral pyre. **This was Plan A**.

There was also a 10-minute window for the same group of eight to climb up the round concrete watchtower, out the 0.6 x 0.6 metre (2 foot x 2 foot) opening, onto the reinforcing bars 1.4 metre (4½ foot) below, dropping the same distance to the ground and then making their way east, while all the focus was on their funeral on the southwest side of the building. **This was Plan B**.

Thus two clear exits were provided after the faked Hitler and Eva suicides. To assist in this, the guards had been ordered out of the Bunker and out of the Chancellery. The telephone exchange workers and the secretaries (Gerda Christian, Gertrude Junge, Elizabeth Schroeder, Johanna Wolf and Else Krueger) were relieved of their duties and took fresh air whenever it was offered. The Goebbels' were locked in their room, spending their time with their children and mourning their impending murder-suicides. The ordered exit of all the guards, police guards and mourners attending the funeral provided a clear exit through all the Bunker passages.

This was the basic scenario, now let's look at it in detail.

On 26 April 1945 Hanna Reitsch and her partner Field Marshal Ritter von Greim flew into Berlin and landed at Gatow Airport in West Berlin amongst heavy Russian small arms fire. The Russians were deliberately taught to fire at anything that flew over that wasn't theirs, as opposed to the Americans that fired at anything that flew. While landing in Berlin, von Greim's ankle was injured quite seriously and he was unable to fly any great distance, but they managed to change to a small plane and flew into central Berlin landing on the main East-West Axis the same night.

At their meeting that night Hitler 'officially' repeated his suicide plans to them, but this was cover talk. To add weight to this, Goebbels strode about the bunker ranting, "We are teaching the world how men die for their honour" and Hitler talked incessantly about General Wenck freeing Berlin and saving him. This was a message through his radio teeth to the ever-listening British. Meanwhile Bormann documented Hitler's every word creating a false history of his impending doom.

Hitler then stripped Goering of his post and made Field Marshal Ritter von Greim 'General of the Luftwaffe' and Hanna Reitsch 'Commander-in-Chief of the German Air Force'. Hitler then spent much of the next three days consulting with them in infinite detail over his escape flight out of Berlin.

Later that night, 26/27 April 1945, the first heavy barrage of Russian artillery hit the Chancellery and the details for Hitler's flight plan out became more and more pressing. On the night of 29/30 April, less than 15 hours before Hitler's show suicide, Reitsch and Greim flew out of Berlin in the tiny two-seater plane they had hidden near the Brandenburg Gate. Hanna Reitsch was a daredevil pilot and one of the few woman to win the Iron Cross during WWII. Von Greim was injured and she did the flying.

WWII was coming to an end and thousands of Berliners were injured, exhausted, desperate and hungry. Along with their nursing staff they took shelter in their cellars, in tunnels and in the underground railway, which was clearly marked under the Red Cross as a hospital. When the Russians broke into the subway tunnels Hitler ordered (27 April) the locks of the River Spree to be opened (28 April) and the tunnels flooded. Thousands of wounded drowned along with their nursing staff and Russian soldiers.

This was not the first time the wounded had been deliberately killed in the name of the Führer. A military hospital full of wounded soldiers on the Eastern Front had been blown up earlier in 1945. As it was, the River Spree was ready to become a floating mortuary stained red with blood.

Around 6 pm on 29 April the locks to the Upper River Spree were closed and the waters were allowed to recede enough for kayak travel. At midnight on 29 April, Major Bernd Freytag von Loringhoven (aide to army chiefs) and his aide-de-camp Rittmeister Gerhard Boldt[1] (Boldt was also General Krebs' aide-de-camp) and Leutnant-Colonel Weiss left the bunker, got a number of kayaks out of storage, placed them in preparation for the escape teams, then paddled through the tunnels and dead bodies, killing any and all survivors. They then secured the exit and waited for the next escape team. Two groups of three bodies were then tied together and retained near the exit.

The Last Days of Hitler (repeated in *Hitler, The Survival Myth*) reports that Boldt's escape was down the East-West Axis towards the Kantstrasse under Russian fire and then to the Reich Sports Field where he met up with the adjutants Loringhoven and Weiss and continued south along Kaiserdamm (under more Russian fire), where at Pichelsdorf bridge they jumped in sailing boats (under heavy Russian fire) and sailed down Lake Havel (where the Russians would have seen their sails). But this was another lie for cover. It was a ruse and a nearly impossible ruse at that.

Leutnant-Colonel Nicolaus von Below (Hitler's Luftwaffe adjutant) and his batman Heinz Matthiesing (a resourceful barman) were the next to escape (just short of midnight 29 April). They each used a group of tied bodies as cover and floated down the River Spree using snorkels between the bodies to breathe. They made it to the west bank of Lake Havel by the morning of 30 April. Officially von Below was carrying Hitler's will and was supposed to deliver it to General Keitel, but he left before the official will was finished and only carried Hitler's 'cover will'.

They sent word back confirming their survival, equipment in place, and the best route to take. As such, von Below and Matthiesing were the scouts for Hitler's entourage the following night.

With confirmation of safe passage, at 2.30 am on 30 April Hitler said goodbye to about 20 people in the conference passage, but hardly moved. He mumbled to each individual and then said goodbye en masse, once again announcing that he was going to commit suicide. He mentioned this so many times to so many people that this has to be viewed with suspicion. When someone talks about suicide, they rarely do it, and it is usually a show suicide.

[1] Rittmeister is a cavalry rank.

Hitler honours the Hitler Youth outside the Chancellery
on his 56th birthday, 20 April 1945.

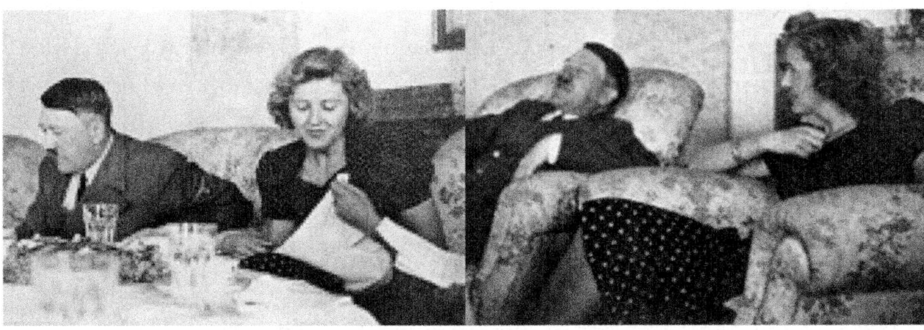

Hitler and Eva in the last photos taken in the bunker.

The Bunker watchtower (Plan B escape),
with the reinforcing bars noticeably removed.

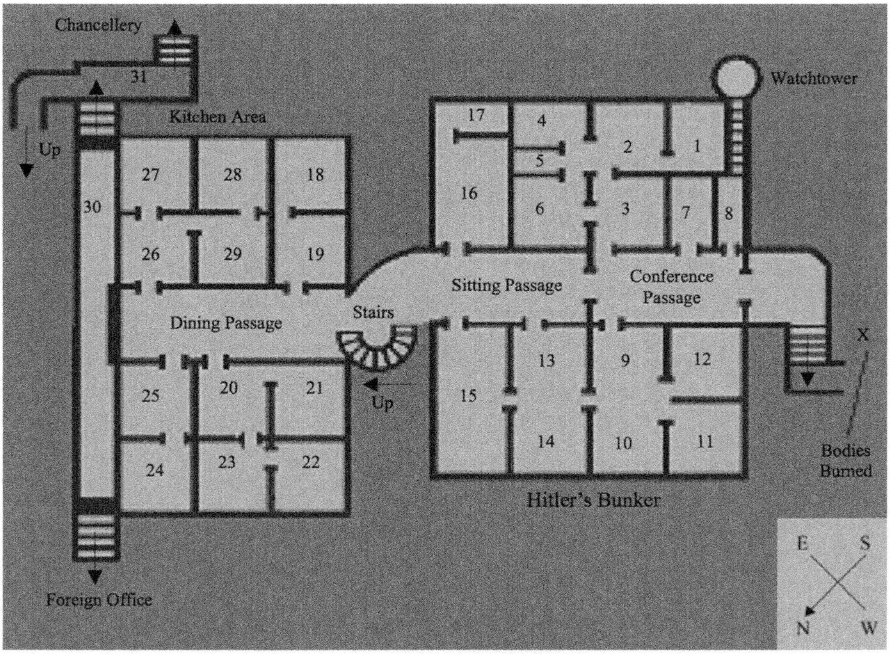

Chancellery Bunker

1	Hitler's Bedroom	13 Telephone/Secretary/Guard Room
2	Hitler's Study	14 Emergency Telephone Exchange
3	Hitler's Anteroom	15 Diesel Generator
4	Hitler and Eva's Bathroom	16 Toilets
5	Eva's Bedsitting Room	17 Switchboard for Electric Lights
6	Eva's Bedsitting Room	18-19 Lumber Rooms (Timber)
7	Map Room	20-23 Magda Goebbels' and Children
8	Guards' Rest Room/Dog-Bunker	24-25 Servant's Quarters
9	Drawing Room	26-29 Kitchen Area
10-11	Dr. Ludwig Stumpfegger's Rooms	30 Bunker-Chancellery Bulkhead Passage
12	Dr. Joseph Goebbel's Bedroom	31 Butler's Pantry

Goebbels squeezed and SS Chancellery commandant Wilhelm Mohnke.

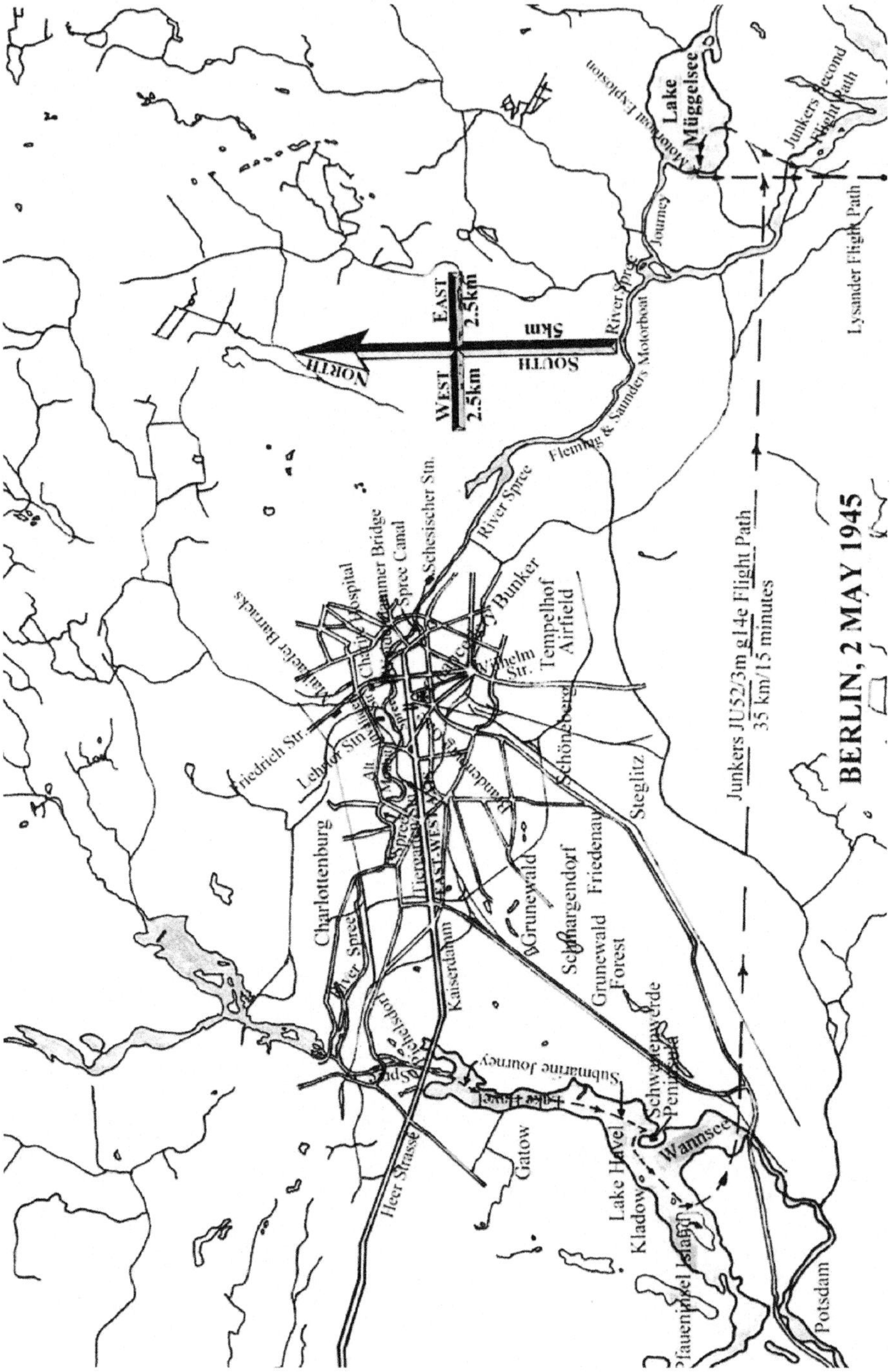
BERLIN, 2 MAY 1945
Junkers JU52/3m g14e Flight Path
35 km/15 minutes
Lysander Flight Path
Junkers Second Flight Path
Lake Müggelsee
Motorboat Explosion
Journey
River Spree
Fleming & Saunders Motorboat
NORTH
SOUTH
EAST
WEST
2.5km
5km
Schesischer Stn.
Spree Canal
Tempelhof Airfield
Schöneberg
Steglitz
Friedenau
Schmargendorf
Grunewald
Grunewald Forest
Charlottenburg
Friedrich Str.
Kaiserdamm
Heer Strasse
Gatow
Submarine Journey
Lake Havel
Schwanenwerde Peninsula
Wannsee
Kladow
Potsdam

Between 2.30–3.15 am 30 April 1945, Hitler and Bormann conspired in Hitler's rooms. Bormann had already arranged his rescue via the British some four months earlier and Hitler had been a British agent since his training at Tavistock from February to November 1912, some 33 years earlier. They were discussing their codes to alert the British to assist their exit and who could be trusted to support their British rescuers in their escape. Goebbels did not know of this plan, so his telegrams were not in full code.

The pressure of three months in a bunker brings out a lot of cabin fever and cabin fever expresses all sorts of suspicions. Since Bormann had sold out to the British (1 January 1945) and since the Bunker had been occupied (16 January 1945), Bormann had been particularly unpopular. In three months he had made no friends and spent his time documenting Hitler's every word – creating a false history of Hitler's impending doom as final cover.

Bormann's official records of what Hitler said were largely a fabrication so people would believe Hitler was desperate, sick and suicidal and would die even if he had survived the Bunker.

As further cover for this, all the bunker staff were allowed to get regularly drunk. This stopped them noticing anything strange, like an escape plan that excluded them and Bormann's notes being a literary version of Dr Morell.

At 3.20 am 30 April 1945, Bormann sent a telegram to Admiral Doenitz at Ploen near Hamburg in North Germany, but sent it through the Gauleiter of Mecklenburg rather than through ordinary communications. This was picked up by the signals officers on both the German and British sides and alerted the British. The double send meant that the British were especially alerted.

The telegram read:

> "Doenitz! – Our impression grows daily stronger that the divisions in the Berlin theatre have been standing idle for several days. All the reports we receive are controlled, suppressed, or distorted by Keitel. In general we can only communicate through Keitel. The Führer orders you to proceed at once, and mercilessly, against all traitors. – Bormann.
>
> PS. The Führer is alive, and is conducting the defence of Berlin."

This was in Open Code, Reverse Code and Aesopian language combined. Open Code meant that it could be understood by knowing the events that were to unravel and with a few key words, like "Testament" meaning Hitler's escape plan. The British version of "Testament" was "Winnie the Pooh", and "Rabbit" for Hitler and "Ms Rabbit" for Eva Hitler née Braun. (They had married at midnight on 29 April 1945.)

Reverse Code meant that one could say, "conducting the defence of Berlin" and it meant, "escaping to save one's arse". "Against all traitors" meant, "pro-war traitorous Allies would assist their escape" and "Lead the way" meant, "the leader was on his way, play your part."

Aesopian Code was a background and refers to family structure and common literary works like *Winnie the Pooh, Peter Rabbit* or Wagner's writings. "Our cousins are all too quick" would mean "the Russians are advancing on the Bunker. Advance on them and they will fire over the top."

So "Testament against all traitors defending Berlin" would mean "Hitler is escaping with the Swiss Bank accounts and the secrets the Nazis had gathered from 1933–45 with the assistance of Ian Fleming, Chris Creighton, Anthony Blunt, Hanna Reitsch and his primary concern is his own welfare. All positions covered and all equipment functioning. Hitler in position for evacuation."

It is interesting that the Soviets have never released this information before. Stalin, having been through British deconstruction, was the Soviet expert in unravelling Aesopian messages, but ensured the rest of this department was full of babushkas so only he got the message.

To the Gauleiter of Mecklenburg, Doenitz at Ploen and the British linked with Operation JAMES BOND, Bormann's 3.20 am telegram translated as:

> "The British are ready and waiting to complete the rescue and are set up in all their locations. German protection has been in place for several days with no shots fired. The escape route has been tested successfully and is secure. Anthony Blunt has the protection of Keitel and the Russians for Hitler's escape. Keitel is our man on the inside who will obfuscate till the end. Provide flak as cover and flares to light the way. Berlin has been sufficiently compromised for the escape. All doppelgängers and traitors are in place.

[Anthony Blunt, Ian Fleming, Chris Creighton – Bormann's evacuation team and Hitler's evacuation team]. The Führer has announced his death and all suspicions have been covered. He is ready to escape into the open from midnight. The criminal Goebbels and his family will *really* die._
PS. Despite reports of death, Hitler is alive and ready to kayak through the tunnels, which have been cleared of all survivors. Destination Fireworks Island [Pfaueninsel Island] and flight out."

On 30 April 1945, Hitler took lunch at 2.30 pm. Eva was not present. It is hard to get briefed for such a mission in the wee hours and take it on board for action. Eva was being briefed for her escape and waited for the arrival of her new signature blue dress. After lunch, around 3.10 pm, the secretaries were relieved of their duties.

"In the morning [of 30 April] the guards had been ordered [by an SS Escort officer] to collect all their rations for the day, since they would not be allowed to pass through the corridor of the Bunker again."[2] They were also given arms. This stopped the guards from checking anything going on in the Bunker or from using the Bunker-Chancellery passage. Their focus was to be on external protection and not on the internal workings of the Bunker.

Since their quarters, the "dog-bunker" or "guards' rest room", linked the conference passage with the stairs to the concrete watchtower (Plan B escape), it was essential that this passage be kept free of any witnesses. The watchtower had never been finished and the external protruding reinforcing bars allowed people to climb out of the tower window and onto the Chancellery garden, as was commonly done.

Hitler's personal SS adjutant Sturmbannführer Otto Günsche never let Hitler out of his sight. At 2.40 pm Otto Günsche telephoned Hitler's personal chauffeur Sturmbannführer Erich Kempka to send 200 litres of gasoline to the Chancellery garden. This gasoline had been carefully hoarded and guarded for months just for this purpose. Kempka went to the Chancellery and managed to locate 160–180 litres.[3]

On his return, he passed through the Chancellery-Bunker passage doors, which were still open at 3.38 pm. At Hitler's door he was greeted

[2] *The Last Days of Hitler*, p. 219.

[3] This would require at least 8 jerricans, but the photos only show 6 jerricans, amounting to 130 litres. This would have significantly reduced the bodies combustion.

by Kempka who said "The Chief is dead" and then made a gun with his right fingers and pointed them into his mouth. It was 3.40 pm.

Kempka carried the jerricans to the emergency exit of the Bunker. All of the remaining guards in the Chancellery were then ordered to leave the Chancellery and stay away from the Bunker. This removed any witnesses capable of defending themselves and opened up the Bunker-Chancellery passage as an escape route (Plan A), as well as the escape route from the watchtower over the Chancellery garden and into the Chancellery (Plan B).

After lunch, Hitler went back to his room, spoke with the newly briefed Eva and emerged for another farewell ceremony (3.10 pm) to his inner circle Martin Bormann (Hitler's secretary and head of the Nazi Party Chancellery), Joseph Goebbels (Propaganda Minister), Werner Naumann (Goebbels assistant and State Secretary in the Propaganda Ministry), General Hans Krebs (the last German Chief of Staff), Vice Admiral Erich Voss, General Wilhelm Burgdorf (Army adjutant) . . . and to Ambassador Walter Hewel (Foreign Office liaison officer and old-time Nazi), Brigadeführer Johann Rattenhuber (RSD head and chief bodyguard for Hitler's private police SS guards), Chief Inspector Peter Hoegl, Sturmbannführer Otto Günsche (Hitler's personal SS adjutant), Heinz Linge (Hitler's SS Orderly and personal valet), Konstanze Manzialy (Hitler's Austrian cook) and Hitler's secretaries Gerda Christian, Gertrude 'Traudl' Junge, Elizabeth Schroeder, Johanna Wolf and Else Krueger (Bormann's secretary). Magda Goebbels remained in her rooms with her children the whole day.

Everyone was then dismissed to their rooms with the doors closed as they mourned the imminent death of their leader. This provided ample opportunity for Hitler and Eva to simply walk through the bulkhead door into the Bunker-Chancellery passage with the door closed behind them, but they returned to their room at 3.20 pm.

At their door stood Bormann and Goebbels. Bormann was a British agent and Goebbels had agreed to kill his family, himself and his wife the following day. Goebbels was in an emotive state, something approaching complete denial and there was no way he was a threat as a witness. Nor was Goebbels in a state to tell the difference between a real Hitler and a doppelgänger Hitler with a bullet through the back of the skull.

Hitler is said to have shot himself through the mouth with a 7.65 mm Walther pistol and Eva is said to have taken poison. Neither were true. The red carpet in Hitler's room hid the blood and the blood found was of a different type from Hitler and Eva's. Of the two Hitler skulls found, one had no bullet wound and the other had a 10.5 mm hole signifying a SS-controlled state-sanctioned killing. Eva had apparently taken poison, but the autopsy showed that she had died of shrapnel wounds. The Eva corpse had been removed from the streets and bled from the breasts. This made it a 'canned meat' operation.

As if on cue, straight after the complicitly timed shooting, the one-armed Hitler Youth director Artur Axmann arrived at the Bunker and was admitted straight into Hitler's rooms where Goebbels sat with the two bodies, no doubt torn over the apparent Hitler and Eva deaths, his own impending death and that of his family. It was the Goebbels family deaths that would make the whole scenario appear real. Without them, Hitler and Eva's deaths would have been exposed as fake in the weeks that followed. This would have led to a results-oriented hunt for Hitler, rather than the wild-goose chase that followed.

The wild-goose hunt for Hitler was the beginning of the Cold War. It allowed all sorts of British and American spy agencies to set themselves up in whatever country they chose to suspect. These were countries where there had been Nazi influence and the locations Hitler had chosen as options to escape to. These included South America, Norway, Greenland, south-west Africa, New Zealand, Antarctica and Spain. Spain was where Hitler went to, so the search teams stayed well away from there and the press always treated Spain as a joke location and diverted attention elsewhere.

If you had a Nazi problem you automatically received the cure whether you wanted it or not. Many of the repatriated Nazi spies went to South America followed by G-Men and to New Zealand followed by MI-6 retirees who posed as Rolls-Royce salesmen and wore cashmere coats and bowler hats up and down Queen Street at to-the-minute lunch hours. We used to watch them as kids, kick their umbrellas and stand on their heels so their shoes came off. "Frightfully . . ."

Antarctica was the place where the most advanced Nazi experiments were held, including their medical experiments, a eugenics society (dead at 45), Foo-Fighters and the attempt to create a new master race

– more or less Homo sapien 1.52, that is, a race of technocrats – so Nazi and American military scientists went there . . . say it isn't so.[4]

The communist Russians planned to take over a third of the world and did the same thing with Eastern Europe, although with a different excuse. As communists, they fought fascists and became fascists.

Politics is like a big ship and big ships have big rudders. The ship's gearing is never strong enough to move the big rudder so they have a smaller rudder behind which moves in the opposite direction and this moves the big rudder, which moves the ship of nations. Politics is first guided under the direction of the small impetus and against the direction of the big impetus.

Germany, under fascist leadership, became a socialist country, as was planned. Russia, a totalitarian communist country, became a fascist country (that taught the world the value of freedom) and directed Russia to socialism for the masses and fascism for the oligarchy. This is now the model of America – a fascist oligarchy controlling socialist masses. This too was planned.

Goebbels left and Axmann remained alone with the bodies for a short while, giving the latest briefing to the still alive Hitler and Eva who were hiding in cupboards in the room. He told of von Below and Matthiesing's successful escape down the River Spree, the tunnels loaded with bodies for cover, the kayaks and submarine in position, and Boldt, Loringhoven and Weiss ready to assist the kayak journey to the submarine.

Hitler had been exchanging his life with his doppelgängers ever since the mid-1930s "Gau doppelgänger contest" and was used to hiding – Eva less so.

Hitler's SS Orderly Heinz Linge then entered the room and wrapped doppelgänger Hitler's body in a blanket, completely covering the head, but showing his familiar trousers, the same ones every doppelgänger wore. Two other SS officers then carried the body up the stairs. The exchange occurred at the intersection of the conference passage and the guards' rest room so that it could be seen by the guard in the concrete watchtower.

Bormann (Hitler's secretary) then entered the room and picked up the Eva doppelgänger body and carried it to the passage where he

[4] This can be taken as Homo sapien 2.51, depending on whether you understand the human race to be evolving, devolving, or just mucked around with.

handed it to Kempka (Hitler's personal chauffeur) who took it to the foot of the stairs and handed it to Günsche (Hitler's personal SS adjutant who never let Hitler out of his sight) who then gave it to another SS officer who carried it up the stairs to the garden.

Hitler's orderly, personal chauffeur and personal adjutant were chosen because they were physically closest to Hitler and their ID testimonies were the most likely to be believed. This commotion was seen from the watchtower by police guard Erich Mansfeld who became very intrigued.

The only people to enter Hitler's room after the gunshot were Goebbels, Axmann, Linge and Bormann – none of whom could be trusted to reveal anything of Hitler's Operation TESTAMENT.

Goebbels was dead within 29 hours. Axmann gave the latest briefing to the very much alive Hitler and Eva. Hitler's SS Orderly Linge was familiar with the doppelgänger scenario and had long sworn the Holy oath to secrecy. Still, he was sorry to see one of them go. Bormann was a British agent who planned his escape parallel with that of Hitler and Eva and had been a British agent for the last four months. As such, the immediate witnesses to Hitler and Eva's deaths were all completely unreliable.

As the bodies were taken upstairs, Hitler and Eva had two escape options. Plan A was into the Bunker-Chancellery bulkhead passage to wait for clearance into the Chancellery. This had a four-hour window. Plan B was up the watchtower and down the outside assisted by the reinforcing bars midway, and then into the Chancellery. This had a 10-minute window.

For Bunker security, only the bulkhead door between the Bunker and the Chancellery passage needed to be locked, but the bulkhead door between the bulkhead passage and the Chancellery (southeast), and the bulkhead passage to the Foreign Office Garden (northwest) were also locked. This kept people out, but it also kept the people inside hidden as long as the air lasted. The bulkhead passage was easily capable of holding eight people for four hours, from 3.50 pm to 8 pm.

The moment after Police Guard Erich Mansfeld left the watchtower (3.50 pm) Hitler and Eva left their room with SS Chancellery commandant Wilhelm Mohnke and five doppelgänger Hitlers providing cover.

They made their way through the Bunker passages, through the bulkhead doors, into the bulkhead passage, locked themselves in and waited for the wake, which never came. It turned very quickly into a party. The bunker occupants smoked, drank and danced and the whole atmosphere was very happy.

Once security was lax and there was some promise of darkness Hitler's entourage made their move.

What joy Hitler could detect shamed him somewhat. It is always British practice to humble their agents on their war exit. It reduces the need to make phone calls and write letters to friends and relatives while under exiled house arrest.

In some ways Hitler's escape was reminiscent of the capture of Napoleon in 1815 and the escape of the Kaiser to Holland after WWI. These were also managed by the British, but the biggest British signature was the James Bond movies that were to come – always leaving with the girl, massive destruction behind them. That's Hitler and Eva and it kind of makes Hitler the original James Bond character. Hitler was the best double agent the British ever had.

Hitler's entourage of eight then left the Chancellery, escaped through vaults and tunnels, to the underground station at Wilhelmsplatz and walked along the underground tracks to the Friedrichstrasse and then into the semi-flooded tunnels.

Around 10.30 pm the tunnel's exit floodgates were opened. This let many of the bodies out into the River Spree and would provide advanced cover further down stream.

Hitler's entourage then met up with Boldt, Loringhoven and Weiss (11 pm) who assisted Adolf and Eva Hitler into tandem kayaks. As the tunnels continued to drain, they travelled swiftly with the current.

With the bodies surrounding the kayaks, providing cover and distraction, Boldt, Loringhoven and Weiss then assisted Adolf and Eva Hitler up the conning tower and into the half-sized submarine (11.30 pm), less than 0.5 metres of the which was above the waterline.

With four crew on board, as well as Adolf and Eva Hitler, Major Bernd Freytag von Loringhoven (aide to army chiefs), his aide-de-camp Rittmeister Gerhard Boldt and Leutnant-Colonel Weiss, the submarine submerged (11.40 pm), motored out into the current (11.55 pm) with minimal engine power and then cruised down the River Spree under cover of the recently drowned hospital bodies. Flares lit their pathway from just before midnight.

At the beginning of the kayak journey, SS Chancellery commandant Wilhelm Mohnke waited for the signal that the passage had been successful then marched the five doppelgänger Hitlers back to the Chancellery and executed them around the Chancellery using a variety of guns including the 10.5 mm SS state-sanctioned signature gun on a doppelgänger Hitler whose dental work best matched Hitler's.

SS Chancellery commandant Mohnke then returned to the Bunker at 1 pm to take word back to Hitler's secretary and former head of the Nazi Party Chancellery, Martin Bormann, that the Testament was in force – the fully laden submarine escape was under way.

With no lights and without using sonar, which at the time, went 'beep' rather loudly, they waited until the flares lit the way from 11.55 pm. At midnight, using the engines to start and then principally for direction, they coasted down the River Spree as quietly as possible, using their three-tone grey paintwork and the mass of floating hospital dead as cover. They coasted down to Lake Havel at the same speed as the bodies and directed themselves into the middle of the lake, using their engines when the lake was wide and slow-flowing to catch up to more bodies in front.

By 4.30 am they had positioned themselves off the Schwanenwerde Peninsula and stationed themselves in the shadow of the morning light. From here Boldt, Loringhoven and Weiss were offloaded under cover of darkness and no flares, to be used as the eyes and ears of the submerged submarine. They were also used as decoys and sitting ducks on the water.

By morning the submarine with Adolf and Eva Hitler and four crew lay between the east of Schwanewerde Peninsula and the east bank of Lake Havel. In the afternoon they followed the shadows and moved several hundred metres to the northwest of the peninsula towards the middle of Lake Havel.

Private German boat builders began constructing submarines in 1891 and Germany established a submarine service in 1906 with the U-1. In 1942, the English built the X-craft, a two man mini-sub, part of the X5-X10 series. Even the British WWII magician Jasper Maskelyne built a mini-sub which sunk a German cargo ship carrying heavy water to their A-bomb laboratories. The same year the Germans built a mini-sub called the WK202 and by 1944 they were using Hydrogen Peroxide as an additional fuel source, providing more oxygen for greater combustion (as in the U-791). At the time many people did not believe mini-subs existed, including much of the British Navy.

"During the advance through Southern Holland a German one-man submarine was found washed up on the beach at Walcheren [Westkapelle, after the RAF bombing had turned the dykes into a lagoon]. Ralph Izzard inspected it and then excitedly telephoned Admiral Bertram Ramsay, Naval Commander-in-Chief of the Allied Expeditionary Force. 'Nonsense,' said Ramsay, 'there is no such thing as a one-man submarine.'

"'Very well, sir,' said Izzard. 'I'll have it sent round to your headquarters immediately [early November 1944].' And he had the submarine loaded onto a tank transporter and shipped off like a tiny tin whale. It arrived as the Admiral was finishing breakfast. He was still unimpressed. 'The thing's a toy,' he said.

"'I suggest, sir,' said Izzard, 'that you have a look down the periscope.'

"The Admiral did so, and staring at him from the other end was the still open eye of the dead German submariner who had been killed when his vessel foundered."[5]

Germany's 1942 WK202 mini-sub was 36.5 metres long, 6 metres deep, 3.6 metres wide and painted various shades of grey, doing its best to look like a shadow. The conning tower added another 2.6 metres and the breather pipes another 2.3 metres, which could be made retractable. The main chamber was 24 metres long and 3.6 metres high with the cabin 10 metres long. The torpedoes were retained just in case they were required to terminate Operation JAMES BOND as they carried Martin Bormann further down the River Spree.

The WK202 looked like it was straight off the Beatles album and when the yellow, red and green flares and parachute flares exploded over the River Spree from 11.55 pm on 30 April 1945, the grey submarine shone yellow in the murky and bloody waters . . . but then the Beatles were a Tavistock-trained MI-6 cover band and the Intelligence community are not immune to making historical jokes, especially since

[5] David Fisher, *The War Magician.*

their lives and work are sworn to secrecy. "Yellow submarine" was also a play on Hitler's submerged Testament scout, Colonel von Below.

Spymaster: "I was told the 'Beatles' name was acquired from MI-6 and the name came from the Pharaohs who considered beetles significant."

Oxford Reference English Dictionary: "Beetle – an insect of the order of Coleoptera [Cleopatra, the last Ptolemaic ruler]; a type of compact rounded Volkswagen [created under Hitler]; *British useage*, a dice game in which a beetle is drawn or assembled" . . . war has its jokes.

Spymaster: "MI-6 asked me if I was an accountant because they always need accountants.

"I said, 'No, but if I said yes, you'd kill me when you'd finished with me.'

"They said, 'That's true.'

"MI-6 need accountants for transferring all the money away from the successful bands. They make 'em – they break 'em."

Pfaueninsel Island was the perfect regrouping and evacuation point and many of the high-ranking Nazis headed there for RAPWI (Recovery of Allied Prisoners of War and Internees). It lay in Lake Havel and was surrounded by water wide enough to land a seaplane in any direction. It was also downstream from the Bunker. If the submarine had to go upstream against the current its turbulence and extra noise could have become a factor in detection and therefore survival. The submarine went in the opposite direction to Lake Müggelsee and the flares lit its way.

The last German Chief of Staff, General Hans Krebs, had presented a ceasefire plea to the Russians but it had been unsuccessful. ETA on Pfaueninsel Island was just prior to dawn on 1 May 1945 and the first RAPWI plane was expected that night (1 May 1945) but was to be delayed. The flying part of the escapes would now have to wait until the Russians had taken Berlin and were celebrating.

Hitler had ordered SS General Felix Steiner to launch an all-out counterattack in the southern suburbs of Berlin in which "important prisoners were being moved".[6] Adolf and Eva Hitler were those important prisoners and General Steiner's counterattack gave Hitler enough protection for his submarine not to be attacked, not to be detected, but to light its way down the winding River Spree. It was truly a Teutonic plan.

[6] *Captured official Nazi documents.*

At 3.50 pm on 30 April 1945, Police Guard Erich Mansfeld was in the watchtower. Noticing the commotion and aware that no one was allowed in the dog-bunker (guards' rest room), he climbed out of the tower window (southeast), onto the external reinforcing bars of the unfinished structure and walked to the southwest side of the building to the Bunker emergency exit. The scurrying of men, the shutting of apartment doors and the shutting of the bulkhead doors had raised suspicion, just as it was supposed to do for Plan B to be a possibility.

At the Bunker emergency exit, Mansfeld met the SS officers carrying the bodies up the stairs and saw the unmistakable trousers of Hitler and the unmistakable blue dress of Eva Braun. Behind the SS officers were Bormann (Hitler's former secretary), Goebbels (the new head of the German government, also replacing Bormann as Reich Chancellor), General Burgdorf (Army adjutant), Günsche (Hitler's personal SS adjutant), Linge (Hitler's SS Orderly and personal valet) and Kempka (Hitler's personal chauffeur) but not the SS Chancellery Commandant Mohnke who was noticeable by his absence.

SS ex-adjutant Sturmbannführer Otto Günsche shouted at the Police Guard Erich Mansfeld to get out of the way. He stood back, waited till everyone passed, took in what was about to happen and went inside the Bunker, down the two storeys of stairs (7.3 metres/24 feet), into the conference passage, through the guards' rest room, then up three flights of stairs back to the watchtower (9 metres/30 feet). On the way up the stairs, through a loophole, he noticed black smoke rising from the burning bodies (4.02 pm). Mansfeld was out of the tower for at least 12 minutes.

This gave Hitler's entourage ample opportunity to escape into the bulkhead passage and seal it off (Plan A), or up the watchtower from where everyone had been excluded and down the reinforcing bars, then to the Chancellery from where everyone had been excluded (Plan B).

Russian shelling ensured that the bodies were placed close to the Bunker emergency exit and that the mourners took shelter in its exit. This stopped them from seeing any activity to the east and there was no one in the watchtower. Günsche lit a rag and threw it on the corpses (4 pm). The mourners gave the Hitler salute and then withdrew back into the Bunker as did the High Command who carried on with practical business as though they had just been to a service they knew was fake.

The Bunker-Chancellery bulkhead passage door was now locked and had been since 3.51 pm.

SS men were all reserve police by virtue of their SS rank, but not all police were SS. Historians sometimes refer to the Police Guard when they mean the SS. Such confusion was designed to thwart further investigation.

SS Hermann Karnau, a policeman from the Detective Guard, had been in the Chancellery canteen. Disobeying orders, he decided to go back to the Bunker. He tried to get through the bulkhead door into the Bunker-Chancellery passage, but it was locked. Against orders, he came past the watchtower, ducking the Russian shelling and walked around the corner (4 pm) just as SS adjutant Otto Günsche had thrown the flaming rag on the bodies which combusted right in front of his eyes. "Possibly someone threw a match from the doorway."

This reduces the timing available for Hitler and Eva's Plan B escape out of the watchtower from 3.50–3.58 pm. This was still plausible. Karnau didn't know at the time that Hitler was dead and if he had seen the entourage he could have been variously invited along for further protection, shot, or any scenario in between.

SS Detective Guard Hermann Karnau got to within a metre of the bodies and judged that the bodies were Hitler and Eva because he could recognise Hitler's moustache, trousers and Eva's blue dress. He also noted that Hitler's head was "smashed" and "repulsive in the extreme" which stopped closer investigation, as did the flames.

Karnau then went into the Bunker by the emergency exit and down one flight of stairs where he found Franz Schedle, the commanding officer of the SS Escort distracted with grief: "The Führer is dead. He is burning outside" – but who would believe the word of an SS Escort commanding officer. These were crocodile tears with another successful doppelgänger mission accomplished – three final ones – the death of one of the last doppelgängers; the first part of Adolf and Eva Hitler's escape; and the impending deaths of a further five doppelgängers, whom he had come to know quite well.

This was also the fulfilment of Schedle's mission and his own impending death. An injured foot prevented survivable escape and Schedle committed suicide in the Chancellery the following night (1 May 1945), along with many other officers.

Hermann Karnau then helped Schedle down the emergency stairs.

In the watchtower Police Guard Erich Mansfeld, looking west, watched the bodies burning and noted SS men pouring petrol on them from time to time. SS Detective Police Guard Hermann Karnau joined him, helped Police Guard Mansfeld climb out of the watchtower and then followed him down the tower to view the bodies at close range. By now the shin bones of the bodies were visible (5.30 pm). Mansfeld returned an hour later and was joined by another police guard, Hans Hofbeck, who came up the emergency stairs but quickly returned due to the stench (6.30 pm).

Later that night (30 April), Brigadeführer Rattenhuber, the head of the Police Guard, went to the now packed guards' rest room and requested the sergeant of the SS Escort to report to Schedle. When he returned, the SS Escort sergeant picked three men to bury the bodies who were sworn to Holy secret over the events of the day. Anyone talking about them would be shot.

The bodies were buried around 11 pm.

Brigadeführer Johann Rattenhuber (Chief of Hitler's private police SS Bodyguards) and Heinz Linge (Hitler's SS Orderly and personal valet) claim to have buried the remains with the help of several policemen.

When Police Guard Erich Mansfeld returned to the watchtower just before midnight (30 April), he saw the graves had been dug on top of a bomb crater, that Russian shells were falling and the sky was lit with flares. This would be dangerous for surface travel, but essential for nocturnal submarine travel down a winding river.

In *The Last Days of Hitler*, Trevor-Roper reports many options for the demise of Hitler including that the bones of Hitler and Eva were never found and were most likely mixed with the bodies of soldiers killed in the defence of the Chancellery, and reports that Günsche said the ashes were collected in a box and taken out through the Chancellery.

The latter was impossible and shows Günsche as a complicit liar because the bodies were never reduced to ashes. Tests show that even 180 litres of gasoline would only melt the fat and drain the bodies of moisture and would not turn them into ashes. None of these stories were true, but they are important to history as they represent an ever-present cover-up.

Trevor-Roper states that the Russians never searched the Bunker properly, pilfered it for souvenirs and then neglected it. He also reports that Hitler's engagement diary was left unobserved on his chair for five months. It is more likely, however, that a fake engagement diary was placed there to assist Trevor-Roper in a misdirected history.

Colonel W. F. Heimlich, an American military intelligence officer in their intelligence service enquiry admitted that it was unlikely Hitler had died in the bunker.

We should keep in mind that the combined British, German, American and Russian Intelligence forces were in on this scam and have supported it ever since.

Hugh Trevor-Roper was promoted and elevated to Baron Dacre of Glanton for writing *The Last Days of Hitler.* If he had got closer to the truth, his book would never have been published and he would have been shot for heresy. As it was, he survived, wrote eloquently and provided fantastic research material, some of which was a record of hoaxes. As such, he picked the nose, but couldn't pick the face. Trevor-Roper failed to identify the scenarios as he had no magic training, little intelligence experience and he still trusted people on their word.

> To write the grand war tale of our times, you have to trust the worst that training can bring out in people. WWII was an occult hit and one of its goals was to take the Western focus off Jesus and place it onto Hitler. It did that.

The secretary's office and telephone exchange was right next to the diesel generator. Diesel fumes dulled the senses of everyone in the Bunker, but especially the sense of difference. Whenever the telephone and secretarial staff got a chance to get some air, they took it – although with cigarettes.

The secretaries had been dismissed from service at their last meeting with Hitler (3.10 pm) just prior to his death and had surfaced to witness petrol being thrown on the bodies and set alight (4 pm). When they returned from the emergency exit, the atmosphere of the entire Bunker changed, like a magic theatre before and after a trick.

With the deconstructed Hitler now removed, the Bunker moved into party mode. Despite the constant diesel fumes, all and sundry lit up cigarettes, started drinking and began dancing. Banning cigarette smoke is something that deconstructed double agents do.

It was most important that the secretaries were relieved of their duties and absent from their offices as their door looked out onto the conference passage (escape Plan A), diagonally to Hitler and Eva's doorway and the guards' rest room (the entrance to the watchtower), escape Plan B.

If the secretaries were in their office, they would have seen the doppelgänger bodies of Hitler and Eva carried out and then the real Hitler and Eva scurrying out after them. Unlike the other doors, the secretarys' doors could not be closed as they were adjacent to the diesel generator and the fumes would quickly make them ill.

Bormann, Hitler's brown-noser for so long, now had no ministerial post, which removed some of the guilt from the British who rescued him. Around 8 pm on 30 April Bormann sent a final telegram to Doenitz:

> "Grand Admiral Doenitz, – In place of the former Reichmarshal Goering the Führer appoints you, Herr Grand Admiral, as his successor. Written authority is on its way. You will immediately take all such measures as the situation requires. – Bormann."

Bormann did not mention that Hitler was dead, because he knew he wasn't. He had colluded with Hitler over their escape earlier (2.30–3.15 am 30 April) and knew that Adolf and Eva Hitler were hiding in the room when he went in to view the bodies.

Bormann's telegram translates as:

> "The Führer's death has been faked. Hitler has left the Bunker and is currently en route with the Testament. Assist where possible. I'm leaving in 24 hours. – Bormann."

Officially Doenitz replied not knowing that Hitler was dead. In real terms, he knew that Hitler was en route and sent a reply to cover for this:

> "I shall do everything possible to relieve you in Berlin. If fate nevertheless compels me to rule the Reich as your appointed successor, I shall continue this war to an end worthy of the unique, heroic struggle of the German people. – Grand Admiral Doenitz."

This roughly translates as:

> "Everything possible is being done to ensure Hitler's safe passage. There is still some luck in it, but all countries are assisting. America is holding back. V-Mann Blunt has the

> Russians and a small German unit on his side. The Hitler escape takes priority before the Bormann escape and one may succeed the other at the last minute, but delivery of the Testament to the British is paramount. Hitler's rule is over, but British rule isn't. The excuses of this war will create the next British war so the British will assist.– Grand Admiral Doenitz."

Through Hitler's Tibetan occult practices and connections, he had utilised the Buddhist tradition and predicted the time and place of his reincarnation.[7] His last actions in Berlin were an indication of the time and place and this was something the British occultists were interested in for their next cycle of war. So were the Russians, and even the Americans were prepared to counteract it with scholarships. As such it became imperative that Hitler's escape out of Berlin remain secret.[8]

By virtue of Hitler's will and testament, Bormann and Goering were now members of the new government, although Bormann was considered to have no official posting. They *could* walk as a privileged envoy through the Russian lines and from there travel to the new German headquarters in Ploen, North Germany, but the war had challenged the Russians' manners. They were unpredictable and unlikely to bother with such niceties.

On the evening of 30 April 1945 the remaining Nazi command worked on a treaty with the Russians, but had nothing to bargain with. Bormann, Goebbels, Krebs, General Burgdorf and Axmann were present. Mohnke hadn't yet returned from Hitler's escape and the murder of the five Hitler doppelgängers.

They made radio contact with the Russian headquarters and sent a messenger to enquire whether Marshal Zhukov would receive a representative of the new German government. Krebs, the last chief of the German High Command, had been a military attaché in pre-war Moscow, spoke Russian, had once been publicly embraced by Stalin and was probably a graduate of the secret Reichswehr training camps.

[7] After WWI, 1000 Asian bodies were found buried under Berlin, all well-preserved (poisoned), wearing Nazi SS uniforms and green gloves. Presumably these were Tibetan Monks whose leader was known as 'The Man with the Green Glove'.

[8] These numbers, corresponding dates, place, person and name change of country can be made available – courtesy of a former esoteric Nazi officer, a Tibetan doctor and an intelligence head. "Look for the big and the small" . . . on . . . "the 14th Family Tree".

General Hans Krebs left with a letter from Bormann and Goebbels at midnight. In the letter Bormann mentioned Hitler's death, because he wanted to be sure the Russians would look for a dead Hitler. It also encouraged something of a ceasefire during Hitler's escape down the River Spree and was supposed to provide a long enough ceasefire for Hitler to escape by plane that evening (1 May), but this didn't eventuate and the flight out had to be delayed until Berlin was taken (2 May). This was the primary purpose of sending Krebs as a diplomatic envoy – to create a ceasefire for a few hours (the submarine journey) or permanently (the flight out).

> General Krebs reached Chuikov's headquarters around 4 am: "I am authorised to inform the Soviet Command, and through them, the Soviet Government that yesterday on 30th April, the German Führer, Adolf Hitler, voluntarily left this world. In his will the Führer appointed Grand Admiral Doenitz his successor, and Dr Goebbels is appointed head of the new German government. I have the honour to represent this new government, and am reporting to you with a personal message from Goebbels. The German government considers further resistance in Berlin useless and asks that the Soviet Union agree to a one-day ceasefire in order to prepare the conditions of our capitulation."[9]

At the time, all but a few square miles of Berlin was in Russian hands. General Krebs had a second meeting with Chuikov around 6.30 am and asked that the Doenitz-Goebbels government be officially recognised. It was also important to the British that they were not assisting in the escape of the Führer, but the previous Führer and a dead one at that. Chuikov smelled a rat, rejected the ceasefire proposal, and resumed attacks on Berlin around 7.15 am.

Nevertheless, Krebs had achieved a partial success. The Russian ceasefire from 4 am–7.15 am on 1 May was perfect for Hitler's escape. His path had been lit by flares followed by a short ceasefire. This allowed Major von Loringhoven, his aide-de-camp Rittmeister Boldt and Leutnant-Colonel Weiss to scurry out of the submarine, across Schwanenwerde Peninsula and onto Pfaueninsel Island.

Hitler's escape from submarine into a plane was arranged for 1 May because this is the most significant day in the political, occult and social

[9] Cited in *Hitler, The Survival Myth*, p. 56.

engineering calendar. But it had to be delayed from the 1st to the 2nd May and this really pissed off the occultists. It made them suspicious that this was not the perfect scam and Hitler was not their perfect agent, but merely the best they had developed so far.

By 11 am 1 May 1945 there was no reply back to the Bunker and Bormann agreed to telegram Doenitz that Doenitz was now running things. Once again, Bormann refused to mention Hitler's death. Another coded message, it read:

> "Grand Admiral Doenitz, – The Testament is in force. I will join you as soon as possible. Till then I recommend that publication be held up. – Bormann."
>
> Translated this reads:
> 'Everything according to plan. Hitler made it to the submarine and the skies were sufficiently lit up with German flares for him to make it to Schwanenwerde Peninsula. The eyes and ears have made it to Fireworks Island. I am leaving at 8.40 pm and surfacing at 9.30 pm. I have told the Russians Hitler is dead so they will be looking for a body. We have killed the doppelgängers around the Chancellery. Don't tell the Germans yet, I still need their firepower for cover as my journey doesn't have a submarine or the Russian protection that Hitler's does. I'll be paddling down the River Spree in open kayaks.'

An hour later, at noon, Krebs returned from Chuikov's headquarters with the Soviet message demanding unconditional surrender. Another meeting was held in the Bunker and they decided on a massive exodus with smaller escape parties when in the open and to relay a message to Zhukov that negotiations were over. This would bring unprecedented Russian firepower towards their Bunker and hopefully bypass Pfaueninsel Island and the British and American zones where they were all headed.

At 3.15 pm on 1 May 1945, Goebbels (with Bormann's coded assistance) sent the last telegram from the Bunker:

> "Grand Admiral Doenitz - Most secret - urgent - officer only. The Führer died yesterday at 15.30 hours. Testament of 29 April [the cover will] appoints you as Reich President, Reich Minister Dr Goebbels as Reich Chancellor . . . By order of the Führer, the Testament has been sent out of Berlin to you, to Field-Marshal Schoerner, and for preservation and

> publication. Reichsleiter Bormann intends to go to you today and to inform you of the situation. Time and form of announcement to the Press and to the troops is left to you. Confirm receipt. – Goebbels."

Although Goebbels was not in on everything and was kept ignorant to maintain his status as 'sacrificial lamb', this roughly translates as:

> "Hitler's death was faked at 3.30 pm yesterday and we haven't heard a disbelieving word from anyone who slept on it [the alcohol and hangovers helped]. The illusion was convincing so you can announce Hitler's death as cover for our escape at the time arranged. Hitler is out of Berlin. Bormann has been officially downgraded to a non-existent position and I am now in charge of the money and the government, but will be dead in five hours, an hour before British contact with Bormann, thus ensuring that at the time of the transfer of the Nazi money to the British, there is no Reich Chancellor and no head of the new German government. I take Bormann's place in name only. Hitler is in position to be taken out of Berlin. Use the announcement of Hitler's death to distract, create relief, grief and celebration to provide cover for all survivors."

Goebbels had made no secret of his planned suicide since 4 March 1945 and had published this intention as an appendix to Hitler's 'cover will' and retired with his family to his apartment opposite the guards' rest room. Erich Kempka (Hitler's personal chauffeur) and the one-armed Artur Axmann (Hitler Youth leader) visited, more or less to ensure the Goebbels family *were* preparing for their murder-suicide. This was essential for Hitler's suicide to look authentic.

Frau Goebbels poisoned all six of her children then, at 8.30 pm 1 May, Frau and Herr Goebbels walked through the Bunker, up the emergency exit stairs and outside where they were immediately shot and burned without ceremony. The Russians found them charred and on the surface of the ground the next day, but still recognisable right down to Hitler's Gold Party badge still pinned to Frau Goebbels' dress – history's greatest sheep dipping.

Spymaster: "Sheep dipping is when you attach something to encourage the other side to positively identify a person, something akin to a bull's-eye drawn on the body. The Party badge on Frau Goebbels was history's ultimate sheep dipping exercise."

SS Chancellery commandant Wilhelm Mohnke, who had been in Hitler's escape party the night before, hastily ordered the conference passage set alight. Everyone then left the Bunker at 8.40 pm on 1 May and walked through the bulkhead door, through the bulkhead passage and into the Chancellery under the nominal command of Hitler's former secretary Martin Bormann, taking the same route as Hitler the night before.

General Hans Krebs (the last German Chief of Staff), General Wilhelm Burgdorf (Army adjutant) and Franz Schedle (Commanding SS Escort officer with injured foot) stayed behind at the Chancellery and shot themselves when the Russians made demands at the door. This also helped to limit suspicion and knowledge of Hitler and Bormann's post-war survival.

The rest made their way through vaults and tunnels, drained of the bulk of their water, to the underground station at Wilhelmsplatz. From here they walked along the tracks of the underground railway station to Friedrichstrasse Station and to the surface around 9.20 pm.

Doenitz drew his radio announcement out for maximum distraction, effect, and escape timing. At 9.30 pm, 1 May 1945, Hamburg radio said "a grave and important announcement would be made". At 10.20 pm Doenitz himself announced that Hitler was dead and that he was his successor. This brought 50 minutes of silence when people withdrew to listen to their radios, rather than fire bullets. They also listened afterwards for more news which was slow coming.

In Munich, Seymour Carmen got it right when he announced on radio: "There is some caution about accepting the German announcement as fact. It might be a trick. It might be a desperate effort by Hitler to disguise himself and escape."[10]

If Doenitz had announced that Hitler had committed suicide then every German soldier would have been relieved of their posts and the Russians would have advanced on the Bunker without resistance and all too quickly.

With Hitler announced dead at 10.20 pm on 1 May, there was still enough last-ditch German resistance to slow the Russians down and provide something of an escape corridor. Doenitz' radio announcement also indicated that Hitler was in place ready to be evacuated by plane at the predesignated location.

[10] *Hitler of the Andes*, 1 May 1945.

The first radio announcement came 50 minutes into the Bunker escape (9.30 pm) and the second 100 minutes into the escape (10.20 pm). The Bunker party surfaced around 9.25 pm.

SS Chancellery commandant Wilhelm Mohnke headed the first party with Günsche (Hitler's personal SS adjutant), Ambassador Hewel (Foreign Office liaison officer), Vice Admiral Voss and Guppenführer Hansl Baur (Hitler's pilot), three secretaries and Konstanze Manzialy (Hitler's Austrian cook). The entire German Wehrmacht was engaged in a mad scramble to the West to surrender to the Amis (Americans).

The flaming ruins of Berlin made surface travel a real danger for the lead group, so they went back underground and made their way through the recently drained tunnels that Mohnke was familiar with, to the River Spree, crossed it on a footbridge parallel to the Weidendammer bridge and reached Charité hospital. Mohnke, Günsche, Hewel, Voss and the seriously injured Baur (Hitler's pilot) were the only group to make it across the River Spree. They made their way to the Maikaefer Barracks and then underground. Vice Admiral Voss went missing but Brigadeführer Rattenhuber (head of Hitler's private police SS guards) was unexpectedly carried in wounded. The next day (2 May) the Russians demanded surrender of the bunker and the men offered suicide. The four women were set free and made their way to much preferable American surrender.

Former Reich Chancellor Bormann wanted as many people as possible around him to be picked off instead of him, the more the better. He was dead keen on living and was secure in the expectation of British assistance. The rest followed in groups of four or five, with Bormann placing himself in the middle. He carried the last copy of the much-valued Hitler Testament as protection, his part in the British RAPWI bargain. Bormann was an integral part of the Testament. He was its deliverance and back-up along with the Nazi Swiss Bank account numbers.

A second miscellaneous group containing Bormann (former Reich Chancellor), Axmann (Hitler Youth leader), Kempka (Hitler's personal chauffeur), Standartenführer Beetz (Hitler's second pilot), Günther Schwaegermann (Goebbels' adjutant) and SS Colonel Alfred Rach surfaced from the Friedrichstrasse station at 9.30 pm, just as the first "important announcement" was made. It was here that Chris Creighton and Bormann's doppelgänger 'Günther' joined them. Trevor-Roper refers to them as "and one other".

Martin Bormann said to Chris Creighton: "The Führer is dead." Chris Creighton was not convinced. His kayaks were parked very close to where the submarine had disembarked 21½ hours earlier. Suspicions were further aroused 20 minutes later when Ian Fleming took a look at Martin Bormann, put Chris Creighton in charge of Operation JAMES BOND, then left the team.

Chris Creighton, Martin Bormann, doppelgänger 'Günther' Bormann and the others made their way along the blazing Friedrichstrasse to the anti-tank barrier at the Weidendammer bridge where they took refuge from heavy Russian fire. Chief Inspector Peter Hoegl, in another group, was killed here.

When German tanks came to the rescue they ran behind them reaching the Ziegelstrasse about 300 metres ahead. *The Last Days of Hitler*: "A Panzerfaust then hit one of the tanks, which exploded." If this wasn't Russian ordnance misreported, then this was German war sabotage and may have been prearranged.

Kempka was temporarily blinded. The one-armed Axmann was wounded as was Hitler's pilot Beetz who was never seen again. (Standartenführer Beetz may have been extracted for work in Spain.) Ludwig Stumpfegger, the Chancellery doctor who had poisoned Blondi, was thrown to the ground but not injured. Doppelgänger 'Günther' Bormann was severely injured as he protected the real Bormann from the blast. The real Bormann thanked his body double and virtually kissed him as he transferred the phial of potassium cyanide from his mouth into Günther's. Dr Stumpfegger was similarly poisoned.

Axmann later found doppelgänger Bormann's body lying face up with no apparent injuries and Dr Stumpfegger's body close by. Russian fire prevented closer examination as to whether or not it was the real Bormann, but there were no obvious wounds. Both were cyanide assisted deaths.

Artur Axmann escaped to join the Hitler Youth in the Bavarian Alps for the next six months. Axmann's exit was protected because he had brought the final Testament escape plans to Hitler and Bormann immediately after the death of Hitler's doppelgänger.

Axmann (Hitler Youth), Naumannn (Goebbels' former assistant and Propaganda State Secretary), Schwaegermann (Goebbels' former adjutant) and SS Colonel Rach followed the railway tracks, or what was left of them, to the Lehrter station and went west towards Alt Moabit. Schwaegermann and Rach managed to avoid the Russians and made it into American captivity.

Kempka (Hitler's personal chauffeur) crossed the river by footbridge and hid under a railway arch for all of 2nd May while the Russians celebrated the capture of Berlin. He then swam by night straight into American captivity. This was pretty much the difference between a short prison sentence with food, followed by employment opportunities, versus a long prison sentence without food, followed by endless interrogations.

The James Bond rescue package split up from the rest of the group taking the real Bormann to the banks of the River Spree where they met the rest of Op JAMES BOND and scaled down ropes on the flood banks and jumped into kayaks. As soon as Ian Fleming sighted Bormann and recognised him as the original, he left for Lake Müggelsee and was briefed along the way. Martin Bormann also recognised Ian Fleming, knew something of Hitler's escape plan and their separation ensured no familiar chit-chat.

By the morning of 2 May 1945, Pfaueninsel Island was crowded with escaping Nazis, British rescue teams and no Russians. Leutnant-Colonel von Below and his batman Matthiesing had arrived first, early in the morning of 30 April 1945.

Corporal Hummerich, SS officer Standartenführer Wilhelm Zander (who had Hitler's cover will designed for capture), Heinz Lorenz (Hitler's Bunker news/inner circle) and Major Willi Johannmeier (who claimed to be their bodyguard) had arrived just before daybreak on the morning of 1 May 1945 on kayaks and by floating downstream under bodies. Boldt, Loringhoven and Weiss had stepped off the submarine at Schwanenwerde Peninsula and arrived around the same time. They met and briefed each other, but only claim to have been suspicious of each other's presence. By evening, Operation JAMES BOND were close by on the Wannsee. Martin Bormann would have been aware of the planned positioning of the other seven German players.

Adolf and Eva Hitler and four crew remained on board the WK202 submarine waiting for protection and RAPWI. Boldt, Loringhoven and Weiss were their eyes and ears on the surface as well as their cork duck decoys.

They waited all the next day for a plane. Russian artillery positions were the main factor, hence the Nazi challenge for them to advance on the Bunker as quickly as possible. On the night of 1 May the Russians bombarded the island so Corporal Hummerich, Lorenz and Zander hopped into some kayaks (specially left there for escape groups), paddled out into the lake and boarded a moored yacht where they hid.

The Junkers JU52/3m g14e rescue plane arrived a day late on 2 May. To break continuity, Boldt, Loringhoven and Weiss who had come off the submarine, remained on shore and Hummerich, Lorenz and Zander approached the rescue plane. Major Johannmeier remained on the moored yacht and acted as the signals officer for the plane to position itself over the submarine's conning tower.

Of Hitler's three pilots, Hanna Reitsch was the only one available. She was a test pilot and such a good one that she was the first person to fly a helicopter indoors. She made her famous name infamous by flying a Focke-Wulf Fw 61 helicopter inside the Deutschland Hall in Berlin in February 1938 with only three hours' training. It took another 50 years for this to even make it to the movies.

At 4.15 pm on 2 May a Junkers JU52/3m g14e landed on the water, just as requested from Doenitz. Zander motored out in a yacht and Lorenz and Hummerich went out in a slow-moving gaff-rigged yawl. Johannmeier remained on the moored yacht they had slept on and signalled the plane to position itself over the conning tower of the WK202 submarine – forward stop.

Zander, Lorenz and Hummerich drew their two boats up alongside the plane and attempted a last-minute bargain to take them also, or they might be dead in the water. Any vision of the three-tone grey submarine as it rose up (4.20 pm) was blocked by the Junkers' 12-metre-long floats 0.5 metres above the water, the Junkers 1 metre trapdoors, the eight struts each side and the two boats. To complete the distraction away from the rising 6-metre-long conning tower, Zander upset his boat and Lorenz and Hummerich jumped into the water and onto the motor yacht. Hitler and Eva stepped out of the submarine's conning tower at 4.21 pm and clambered up the clearance distance into the belly of the plane.

For a German soldier reporting this, it would be attributed to the methamphetamine that most soldiers took. For a Russian soldier, it would be attributed to his drunkenness as he celebrated the conquest of Berlin all day – the Russians had been stealing and hoarding alcohol on their way to Berlin.

Such 'hilarity' is an old escape trick of the British. It harks back to MI-6 agents like Bunny Aldon, most likely Jasper Maskelyne. Rather ironically, Jasper Maskelyne had designed and built a working submarine that had downed a cargo ship and could easily have been consulted to make this part of the plan work, not knowing that it was going to be used for Adolf Hitler, the British war machine's most valuable agent. Through his illusions Jasper Maskelyne had been invaluable in winning the desert war for the British. He could make entire divisions disappear and painted materials look like a tank division.

Those Intelligence Officers who did see this realised it was above their station and the next part of their operation, so they were never going to say anything. It would have ended their careers with a bullet. Still it took Chris Creighton 51 years to publish his *OPJB* story, an essential lead to this.

What sun there was blurred the lines of definition for those on the west bank of Lake Havel. It was the last day of fighting, the war had exhausted everyone, and any soldiers who did see would rub their eyes in disbelief and then it would all be over. The witnesses did not believe what they had seen, let alone report it. No one did and no one survived who did. WWII was the most complete history of doppelgängers, double agents, cover-ups and ridiculous scenarios the world had ever seen.

Standartenführer Zander, Lorenz and Corporal Hummerich all ended up on the motor yacht. The Russians were too far away to see any of this and had their view from the west bank of Lake Havel obscured by the plane's struts, two boats, the boating incident and whatever sun refracted any outlines. As if on Anthony Blunt's cue the Russians began shelling around the plane but never hit the plane, submarine or motor yacht. The Junkers JU52/3m g14e flew off with Adolf and Eva Hitler on board and the submarine submerged and headed for the shadows. The vacated gaff-rigged yawl was blown to pieces giving the Russians, many of whom were drunk, a sense of win.

The RAPWI pilot was almost certainly Hanna Reitsch who had been Commander-in-Chief of the German Air Force for six days (26 April–7 May 1945). She then flew Hitler and Eva the 33 km to Lake Müggelsee and landed on the water near the southwest shore (4.36 pm).

Adolf and Eva Hitler then climbed down the aluminium ladder onto the waiting British-held motor launch (4.41 pm) where they were greeted by two Britishers dressed as Russian Army Lieutenant Majors – 2IC of British Naval Intelligence, Ian Fleming and Caroline Saunders, later the first female head of MI-6.

Ian Fleming was fluent in German and the natural choice to accompany Adolf and Eva Hitler to the British safe haven in British Intelligence-controlled Fascist Spain. After all Hitler, with the help of Mussolini and MI-6, had installed Franco as Spain's leader.

With Caroline Saunders as witness and piloting the boat towards shore, Ian Fleming greeted and briefed their passengers in perfect German without ever acknowledging who they were.

> "Mr and Mrs Rabbit, congratulations on your marriage. I can confirm that Adolf Hitler's successor, Joseph Goebbels killed himself yesterday and Admiral Doenitz is leading Germany into surrender.[11] Doenitz announced yesterday that the Führer was dead.
>
> [*By the time the announcement was made at 10.20 pm Goebbels had been dead for 110 minutes and six doppelgänger Hitlers had been killed.*]
>
> "The Reich Chancellor is also dead.
>
> [*This meant Goebbels again and also referred to doppelgänger Bormann's death.*]
>
> "Germany has no Führer and no Reich Chancellor. In the last two days there have been two changes of command in Germany and there is now no trace back to the Führer of WWII. The airfare for the journey out of Berlin is the Testament of Adolf Hitler."

Adolf Hitler, acknowledged only as Mr Rabbit, signalled to Hanna Reitsch who lowered the Testament down the undercarriage of the plane (4.45 pm). Ian Fleming and Caroline Saunders examined it noting some Swiss Bank accounts, some more with a few numbers missing and the promise of more to come. Like all wars it started and finished with a bank robbery.

---

[11] Just before the end of WWI, Karl Doenitz was captured by the British (4 October 1918) and placed in a mental hospital in Manchester where he was 'turned' into a British Agent, to be activated when required. Once his training was complete (9½ months) he was released (July 1919), seven months after WWI had ended.

After a few minutes (4.49 pm), Fleming confirmed that it would be good for two airfares out of German airspace to British Intelligence-controlled neutral territory and exiled permanent homestay until natural death. No status, nor acknowledgement of whether they were alive or dead, would ever be given to their two passengers. The two rabbits were never to have alive status as humans again. They were to live out their days in Intelligence-controlled purgatory.

Sure enough this did happen. After Adolf Hitler died in 1950 the West German Courts began meeting in 1952 after a request for Hitler's official death certificate was issued. In January 1954 West Berlin's Central Registrar Office reminded the world that:

Hitler was "not officially dead yet".

In 1955 this task was passed on to the Berchtesgaden court and the decision was finally made in 1956:

"Adolf Hitler was dead".

The whole process was drawn out long enough to lose all public interest, but it is interesting that the process started in 1952, two safe years after Hitler had died. Eva Hitler's death was never an issue and no tribunals were set for her.

Ian Fleming and Caroline Saunders had been waiting at Lake Müggelsee since 10 pm 1 May (the night before) and at 2 am on 2 May a British Westland Lysander IIIA had landed on a disused road near the southwest shore of Lake Müggelsee.

These both served to confirm Operations WINNIE THE POOH/ TESTAMENT and saved Hitler flying out of Germany on a German plane with German markings or continuing his journey down the River Spree in the WK202 half-sized submarine and risking the narrow gap between Pfaueninsel Island and the shores of Lake Havel so fiercely dominated by the Russians.

After the pick-up on Lake Havel they could have flown directly to Spain, but for surety, witness confusion and the need for British cover they flew for 15 minutes in the torpedo hold from Lake Havel (southwest of Berlin), to their second pick-up point at Lake Müggelsee (southeast of Berlin) where they were met by two British officers in Russian uniform.

Once they were safely loaded onto the motor launch, had been briefed as to the conditions of their journey and fulfilled their part of the

British bargain (4.49 pm) they were driven to the shore and the motor launch was beached (4.52 pm). Ian Fleming then set explosive devices on the boat for 10 minutes and they scurried to the waiting Lysander which, to all intents and purposes was on a RAPWI (Recovery of Allied Prisoners of War). Their Allied prisoners were Rabbit and Ms Rabbit – Adolf and Eva Hitler – the former Führer of Germany (retired for 48 hours, six times dead and replaced twice) and his new wife of 41 hours (who had also died).

When the Special Secret Intelligence Service sent a plane on a top-secret mission they would wax over the plane's serial number and paint over it with another plane's number. When the mission was complete, they would heat up the wax and the paint would drip off revealing the original serial number. Confusion over the identification of a plane, the whereabouts of that plane, and a plane with different markings before and after a mission, were all part of the cover.

The single-engined, high-winged Lysanders were British Intelligence 'Moon Squadron' aircraft with excellent low-speed handling and capable of short-takeoff-and-landings (STOL). The MkI were built from 1936 and the MkIII built from July 1940. Their British markings gave them some protection from Russian and American fire. They had been used by the RAF's Special Duties squadrons delivering and collecting Allied agents in occupied territory, usually in the dead of night, during full moon periods, when the mist rising over the lakes and boggy ground gave cover. These landings were minimally guided by three battery-powered hand torches in a 140m L-shaped pattern.

"These Lysanders differed from the norm in several respects. Their undercarriage spats no longer carried winglets for light bombs, all the machine-guns had been removed, and a streamlined 700 ltr fuel tank was carried under the fuselage which gave the plane a range of 1,780 km; however, it took 40 km/hr off the speed [reducing it from 370 kmph/230 mph to 300 kmph/190 mph with the time to reach 5000 ft a little over 4 minutes. Post 1940 some were produced with rear cockpit winches].

"German military opposition to the flights was negligible. The Luftwaffe had other overwhelming priorities, and the location and interception of low-level flights by single, slow, highly manoeuvrable aeroplanes did not figure large in their thinking . . . By the end of the European war, Lysander special operations had made 323 sorties, 1,074 passengers successfully transported to France or England.

"The main problems were betrayal (10%), pilots killed (6), being shot down (4) and landing in bog (2). In the last year of the war, operations were widely mounted to Germany for RAPWI, the Recovery of Allied Prisoners of War and Internees."[12]

The RAF's Special Duties Lysander squadron was located about 100 km north of London at Tempsford in Bedfordshire (east of Milton Keynes) with a forward base for refuelling 130 km south, in Tangmere (15 km east of Portsmouth) on the south coast of Britain as it joins the English Channel. They were flown successively by No. 419 Flight, No. 1419 Flight, No. 138 Flight and No. 161 Squadrons in the UK, by No. 149 Squadron in North Africa and by No. 357 Squadron in the Far East. In September 1943, eight Westland Lysander MkIIIs went to Portugal.

The Special Secret Intelligence Service Operation, JAMES BOND, operated out of a large country house near Birdham Military Camp, 10 minutes' drive from Tangmere. The SOE (Special Operations Executive) agents were sent to Tangmere cottage for debriefing and SIS (Secret Intelligence Service) agents went 20 minutes northeast to Bignor Manor, the site of an old Roman villa, before being transferred 90 km to London for debriefing.

The pilot of the Lysander would have been an experienced pilot and one of the best. He would have spoken Spanish for landing in Spain, and probably French from previous multiple bail-outs in France. It was preferable that he did not speak German, to avoid any verbal contact with the German passengers during the last days of the war. He would have had a distinguished record and been above the rank of Squadron Leader and would have been retained in the RAF service after the war, most probably at a consultancy level.

Before the mission he would have been blackmailed, most likely for homosexual activities in a highly distinguished institution like Oxford University, as opposed to Cambridge University, which had already been compromised with the likes of Anthony Blunt and *The Apostles.* "At Cambridge it was estimated that a quarter of the students and a third of the staff were homosexual."[13]

Hugh Beresford Verity (b. 6 April 1921, Jamaica) was highly competent at mathematics and studied at Queen's College at Oxford

[12] John Maynard, *Aeroplane* magazine, December 2001, p. 46.

[13] *Cambridge Spies.*

University from September 1937 – "having read French and Spanish at Oxford, he had proven language skills".[14]

Two months before the Battle of Britain (August–October 1940) in June 1940, Hugh Verity underplayed what was to come. When Lord Trenchard (nicknamed Boom) approached him and asked whether he would like a plane with cannons or machine guns, he replied "both"; however, it was not a question normally asked of the RAF's version of a car washer.

Within four years, he was heavily decorated with the Distinguished Service Order (DSO) and the Distinguished Flying Cross (DFC) with Bar, meaning he was awarded the medal again for an additional mission. There were very few medals awarded at that time, except for the North Africa Star. The DSO was second only to the Victoria Cross (VC). His medals record acts of courage, service and gallantry that had placed him in a very elite club.

He rescued 97 people from France flying Lysanders by moonlight. When he was captured in early 1944, he was sent to the world's cushiest POW camp in the neutral territory of Eire, in Southern Ireland. This was made popular by the movie *The Brylcream Boys*. The POWs from both sides went to dances on Tuesdays and the horse races on Thursdays. Both sides were paid their military wages and were encouraged to bet on the race horses, buy drinks and lead a near-normal civilian life, dropping their hard-earned money in Ireland. (That'll be the Irish for yer.) The only rule was that they had to be civil to each other. Fighting at the races or anywhere in public meant a loss of civil liberties.

There had been British POWs in Eire for five years, but when Hugh Verity arrived in early 1944, Britain's *Escape and Evasion Team* (MI-9) mounted a rescue.

His medals and history show that the British took special care of him and even more care to downplay his role. He continued with the RAF until he was 47 (1968) when he retired with the rank of Wing-Commander, one rank above squadron leader. For his interview with *Aeroplane* magazine (2001) he wore a tie with parachutes revealing membership to the elite Special Forces Club which he frequently represented in retirement. He also kept in touch with former French Resistance members.

[14] Ibid.

If an RAF pilot of lower rank than 'squadron leader' piloted for OP WINNIE THE POOH they would have been swished to the colonies after the war; however, Hugh Verity remained in Britain.

When the V9673 Lysander was modified in the 1990s, it was repainted in satin-black (formerly matt-black with charcoal cloud-patterns) and the serial number was changed from **V9673** to **V9367**, while still claiming 161 Squadron allegiance. Serial numbers do not usually change from the time the aircraft is made to the time it is scrapped as the serial number is keyed to all the maintenance records. It is usually only the squadron markings on the side of the plane's fuselage that are changed.

All RAF aircraft have two letters and three digits. So this lysander was an anomally in 1945, just as it is today. The extra digit continues to mark this plane as "the one".

At 4.50 pm on 2 May 1945, the camouflage net on top of the waiting Westland Lysander IIIA was removed and the plane was readied for takeoff. Hugh Verity, who spoke no German, but very good French and Spanish, recognised Ian Fleming and Caroline Saunders from the Birdham Military base 10 minutes from Tangmere, but not the other two passengers, Adolf and Eva Hitler. Rather than a leader of fifty-six, Hitler looked like a harmless dependent old man of seventy. His appearance had degenerated from nine years of excessive drug use and not even his German public could recognise him.

Under cover of some really crap weather the four of them scurried towards the Lysander, engines running, and climbed up the white-painted rungs into the rear cockpit (4.56 pm).

The German Junkers JU52/3m g14e took off first in an effort to draw fire. Soon after the Lysander's wheels left the ground (5.00 pm) the motor launch exploded (5.02 pm) and all evidence was destroyed. All decoys were important decoys. At 190 mph direct flight took 8 hours plus lift-off and landing. ETA in Barcelona was 1.30–3.10 am 3 May 1945 depending on wind and flight corridors.

Hanna Reitsch, the Commander-in-Chief of the German Air Force, then flew the Junkers (with armourplated cockpit) below the Lysander in a predetermined pattern to alert all commands that this was a RAPWI not to be messed with. Neither planes were considered a threat. By 2nd May there was a ceasefire and all British planes were allowed to leave without being shot at. There was only sporadic street fighting, Berlin was taken and the Nazis were scarpering without weapons trying to find any capture other than Russian.

Hanna Reitsch then reported in code to her injured partner Field Marshal Ritter von Greim, General of the Luftwaffe – "Located warren but failed the rescue". Von Greim reported the same code to Doenitz via a third party. The message meant the successful extraction of the two primaries and completion of the German part of Operation WINNIE THE POOH/TESTAMENT.

The submarine that transported Adolf and Eva Hitler then followed Martin Bormann and Operation JAMES BOND down the River Spree waiting for instructions to terminate them using their two torpedoes. The order never came because Ian Fleming refused to acknowledge "Rabbit" as anyone with any status, not even human status and he refused to take orders from a rabbit. In doing so he saved the life of his friend Chris Creighton and the rest of the James Bond team, a scenario repeated throughout Ian Fleming's James Bond movies.

In *OPJB* Chris Creighton wrote that he sensed he was being followed down the River Spree from 2–10 May 1945.

After Adolf and Eva Hitler left, and knowing what Rittmeister Gerhard Boldt knew, he tried to commit suicide, but Major Loringhoven and Leutnant-Colonel Weiss forced him to vomit up his morphine. Boldt was the aide-de-camp to Loringhoven who was the adjutant to General Hans Krebs and Krebs had committed suicide the night before (1 May) just as he was programmed to do. Major Bernd Freytag von Loringhoven was the aide to army chiefs and he knew what was going on, so much so that he later became the German representative to NATO.

The group then moved westward dodging Russian patrols and were captured by Allies, non Russian allies though, and that was the minimum goal for all of them.

Major Johannmeier, Standartenführer Zander, Heinz Lorenz (Hitler's bunker news/inner circle) and Corporal Hummerich, now without Adolf and Eva Hitler, spent the next day on Pfaueninsel Island (3 May), then made their way to Potsdam, eventually found workers clothing, waited for the German surrender (7 May 1945) and for Churchill to declare the end of hostilities (8 May 1945) and then walked into the Western Allied area as foreign workers. Zander made it to Bavaria, told a few friends he was dead and began a new life as Wilhelm Paustin, having rather obviously buried Hitler's 'cover will'.

Leutnant-Colonel Nicolaus von Below (Hitler's Luftwaffe adjutant) and his batman barman Heinz Matthiesing had scouted the path for Johannmeier, Zander, Lorenz, Hummerich, Weiss, Loringhoven, Boldt, the former Führer Adolf Hitler and his new wife . . . and left the west bank of Lake Havel on the night of 1 May, sick of waiting and being bombed by the Russians. Below and Matthiesing travelled by night and hid in remote forests by day. Eventually they met up with Sergeant Major Pardau who had escaped the Russian capture on 2 May when Mohnke, Günsche, Hewel and Baur (Hitler's pilot) were captured. Foreign Office liaison officer Ambassador Hewel died there.

Leutnant-Colonel von Below made his way to Bonn University and studied law. Heinz Matthiesing returned to his hometown. Both were eventually captured by the British, von Below with Hitler's cover will.

Hitler's inner circle newsman, SS Orderly and personal valet Heinz Linge fared worse and was captured by the Russians. His potential information was the most dangerous of all the captives (except for Himmler who was killed by the British in captivity) but he was sworn to the Holy oath and only ever gave out the believable cover scenario.

When the Lysander landed in Spain (1.30–3.10 am 3 May 1945) they were greeted by Rámon Serrano Súñer, General Franco's former 2IC. The pilot responded in perfect Spanish. The Lysander was then taken into a hangar and the markings were heated up so that the wax paint melted off. The Lysander was now where it was supposed to be, in Spain. The Junkers did not stand out amongst the Condor Legion's Junkers and the Lysander did not stand out amongst the eight Westland Lysander MkIIIs in Portugal from September 1943.

Spain had declared itself a 'safe haven' for war criminals in April 1945. This was immediately covered up by the Allies' 'Operation Safe Haven' to recover gold and other assets stolen by the Nazis.

The operation to remove Hitler (OPWTP) was tacked onto the operation to remove Bormann (OPJB). If any M operatives knew about the planned removal of Hitler beforehand, they would never have accepted the mission.

Hitler carried with him all the Chancellery documents that Martin Bormann had. The James Bond mission was intended to fail as soon as Ian Fleming, Caroline Saunders and Adolf and Eva Hitler had reached Spain. The mission to pluck Adolf and Eva Hitler out of Berlin was tacked onto another mission so that no one could string it all together. Everyone in Operation JAMES BOND was supposed to die and all knowledge of the mission was supposed to die with them.

After Adolf and Eva Hitler were safely in Barcelona they had to cover all their tracks. The same day that Rabbit and Ms Rabbit escaped out of Berlin (5 pm, 2 May 1945), Admiral Doenitz, the new leader of Germany (1 May–7 May 1945) moved his head-quarters from Ploen to Flensburg (closer to the Danish border) and took Minister of Armaments Albert Speer with him. Himmler followed with his entourage of vanity.

> Hanna Reitsch (Commander-in-Chief of the German Air Force) flew Adolf and Eva Hitler into British Intelligence-controlled Fascist Spain, to General Franco's MI-6 handler, Rámon Serrano Súñer. As soon as she had secured Adolf and Eva's acceptance into British Intelligence safe haven, Hanna Reitsch left Spain late on 3 May 1945 and returned to Germany in the early hours of 4 May. (See *Hitler's Host for Hitler's Ghost, Appendix 11*)

Hanna Reitsch then met up with her injured partner, General of the Luftwaffe, Field Marshal Ritter von Greim and briefed him with Hitler's latest wishes, just in time for a meeting with Himmler at Schleswig-Holstein the same day (4 May 1945). The two dressed him down as though they were the voice of Hitler from beyond the grave.

Himmler, long compromised by the British, failed to receive his promotion, was rejected by the others and relieved of all duties and postings. He was on his way to give himself up at an American outpost when he was intercepted by the British on Churchill's orders and killed by 'Mr Thomas'.

It is commonly thought that Himmler bit on his cyanide capsule during a doctor's examination and committed suicide, but when he died his nose was broken and his cyanide capsule was still in tact. Churchill did not want Himmler interviewed by the Americans and refused to allow him to reveal what he knew at trial. This removed one of the most troublesome witnesses to Hitler's survival and Churchill's part in it.

The Yellow Submarine, WK202.

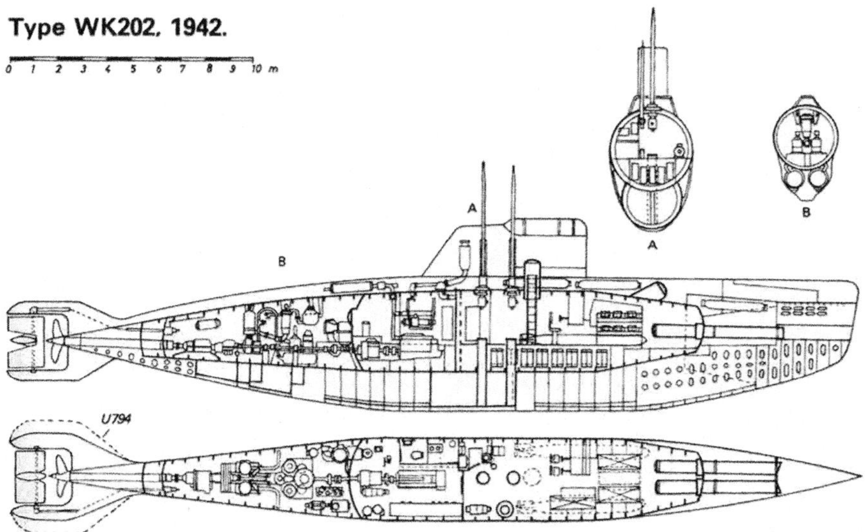

The Junkers JU 52/3m g14e.
This was the final WWII production version of the Junkers.
Only a very small and unknown number were built.

Westland Lysander IIIA, Serial No. V9673,
modified in the 1990s with the serial number changed to V9367,
while still claiming 161 Squadron allegiance. Note the drop tank.

Hanna Reitsch (29 March 1912–24 August 1979)
Commander-in-Chief of the German Air Force (26 April–7 May 1945).

Ian Fleming in Room 10 of Royal Navy Headquarters and smoking rights.

After five days of independent negotiations with Hitler and Bormann regarding their new identities, plastic surgery, places of residence and where the loot was, Germany surrendered (7 May 1945). The same day Winston Churchill announced WWII would end at 0.01 am 8 May 1945, with the death of Hitler officially noted as 30 April 1945, and Martin Bormann's as 1 May 1945.

This was a signature MI-6 act – one of their greatest ever. They are constantly into double-dealings that appear on the surface, and at depth, to be treasonous.

MI-6's primary role is as an agent of war.

The same day (8 May 1945) Luftwaffe General Karl Koller visited General of the Luftwaffe Ritter von Greim and Commander-in-Chief of Luftwaffe Hanna Reitsch (both 26 April–7 May 1945) and they all said:

"No one would find Hitler's corpse."

They should know. They organised his flight out and covered all bases.

For all the month that Ritter von Greim was General of the Luftwaffe he was injured. He "committed suicide" on 24 May 1945 and his 'suicide' removed any chance of him being a witness.

Hanna Reitsch was captured in the summer of 1945. The death of her partner was enough to keep her quiet and her true confessions were either never ascertained or never made public.

Hanna Reitsch returned to Spain to live after the war. In Spain there was another attempt on her life as her plane caught fire, but she was a survivor.

Fieseler Storch

Léon Degrelle also headed to Barcelona flying a Fieseler Storch, a German VTOL (short takeoff and landing). This was the same plane the Germans used to fly Benito Mussolini (1883–1945) out of Italian captivity at Grand Sasso in northern Italy in 1943, and the same type of short single-engine aircraft Rommel used to fly around the African desert. The Fieseler Storch was a well-trusted plane, enough for German High Command intelligence work.

In Spain, Léon Degrelle, a Jesuit from father to son, Belgian Fascist, former Chief of the Belgian SS and father of seven daughters, was known as Dr Sanchez. Here, he and Hanna Reitsch crashed in his Fieseler Storch on a beach in 1945 with Degrelle suffering disfiguring burns to his face and body. They were both supposed to die after the testament mission was successfully accomplished.[15]

Hanna Reitsch had many world gliding records including the longest distance (305 km, 1936) and another for being the first to glide over the Alps. In 1952 she attained third place in the world gliding championships in Spain. Hanna Reitsch eventually died from a massive heart attack at the age of 67 (29 March 1912–24 August 1979).

In the early 1990s, Léon Degrelle (15 June 1906–1 April 1994) was commissioned by the US to write a revisionist history of WWII. He completed this, including his plane crash in Spain with Hanna Reitsch which left his face and body badly burned and scarred. Days after the book came out, he was killed (87) in Malaga (Spain) and the book was withdrawn. (Sometimes MI-6 go around and buy them all).

> It was Ian Fleming, the future author of the James Bond series, and Caroline Saunders who flew out of Berlin with Adolf and Eva Hitler to their final destination in British Intelligence-controlled Spain.

M Section's 'shred, doctor and forge' unit went into overdrive expunging every trace of Operation JAMES BOND to remove Bormann, thus removing any trace of the parasite Operation WINNIE THE POOH to remove Hitler.

---

[15] 'Dr Sanchez' was Léon Degrelle. This was the testimony of the Spaniard Don Angel Alcazar de Velasco in 1962, formerly a German V-Mann (V.312), known by the German secret service as 'Guillermo'. In the found 'lost archives' of the Abwehr he was a press attaché to the Spanish Embassy in London in 1940 where he managed a dozen other Spaniards involved in espionage for the German secret service. *Aftermath*, pp. 332–333.

Ian Fleming then became an alcoholic. His financial state was so bad by 1952 his bank manager insisted he write books in order to recover his debts. His first book *Casino Royale* appeared in 1953 and was based on actual events – the money followed and was shared with all of his James Bond team.

In the British elections immediately after WWII, Churchill was ousted and replaced at the Potsdam Conference (17 July–2 August 1945) by Prime Minister Attlee (July 1945–51). In this way, Churchill didn't have to answer any of Stalin's questions about Hitler's whereabouts. At Potsdam the Soviets and the Allies quarrelled about everything. The only thing they agreed on was that:

Hitler should be left off the list of war criminals
and not tried at Nuremberg or elsewhere.

A few weeks later General Eisenhower told Dutch radio that there was reason to believe Hitler had slipped away to freedom.

Russian and American officers who had been to the Chancellery Bunker agreed that Hitler had slipped out of the Bunker and that his body was not found. Berlin newsmen confidently announced that Hitler was still alive. In the United States, Gallup Poll I:527 showed that 70% of Americans believed Hitler was still alive.

Stalin developed an obsessive suspicion that Hitler had escaped and was still alive. One Soviet report suggested that Bormann and Hitler left the bunker together, and this simple summation was reasonably close to the truth.

Hitler left the Bunker at 8 pm on 30 April 1945
and Martin Bormann left at 8.40 pm on 1 May 1945.

Stalin correctly implied that Hitler had backed General Franco's forces and accused Franco of harbouring the fugitive Hitler. Frustrated by increasing distrust and paranoia, Stalin had every contact with Hitler jailed. With them he jailed Russian, East German and Polish undercover personnel and plugged everybody for years about what they knew. The Russians did learn a lot but seemed to be baffled by an overabundance of bullshit which is the natural German reaction to major catastrophes.

In desperation Stalin ordered the infiltration of the Vatican, which produced even more bullshit. In 1953, not much closer to the truth, he had a stroke and died. "Now a new Hitler Youth Director, I mean Pope, presides over all."[16]

[16] British Intelligence Officer.

> Retired Intelligence Officer on guarantee of anonymity:
> "The difference between the CIA, the KGB and the Catholic Church is the KGB may shoot you, the CIA may shoot you full of drugs and the Catholic Church will guarantee to fuck you up the arse. This is why it has always been difficult to find couriers to the Catholic Church except for a certain breed of agent who doesn't mind. The Russians have always treated the Catholic Church as another spy agency, and an odious one at that."

MI-6 Officer: "Hitler's death was a shonky load of shit. Doppelgängers may have died in the bunker for Adolf and Eva, but the real Eva Braun and Adolf Hitler were swished out of Germany by the British to Spain in the same manner the British swished the Kaiser out of Germany in 1918.

"Hitler returned to Spain where the Germans had been practising for WWII from 1936 to 1939 and was referred to as 'the German Gardener' for his own protection.

"He lived out his days in the Montserrat Monastery just outside Barcelona and in the Citadel overlooking Barcelona. He worked [in the Parc de la Ciutadella opposite the Natural History Museum] as a gardener, dying in early 1950 of stomach cancer. He died from radiation plates fitted into his mattress [six weeks to die], a favourite British method of getting rid of 'sensitive alien allies from former warring countries'."

The Montserrat Monastery is incredibly isolated and currently requires a funicular (cabled railway) to get to it. But it is a very beautiful building in a stunning isolated location. When you get there you are completely dependent on the monks. Above the monastery are two outbuildings where Adolf and Eva Hitler spent their time when things got really hot. Montserrat was built in 1592 and rebuilt in 1858 after being destroyed. Now 10,000 people visit there every day.

Spymaster: "Hitler was definitely in Spain. Circa 1949/50, a group of IRA were in Spain (about 15 years before they were needed) being billeted just outside the Citadel in Barcelona. One IRA billet went for a walk in the Parc de la Ciutadella on New Year's Eve and met the 'German Gardener', Adolf Hitler, and spoke with him about his roses, in English.

"When Spanish Intelligence heard about this they went berserk. They interviewed the billet and said, 'How did you speak to the German Gardener? He doesn't speak English'

"The young IRA man replied, 'We spoke about the roses and he spoke English.' He was pistol-whipped for his troubles.

"The same IRA soldier didn't surface again until 1987 when he was around 60 years old, appearing on TV walking beside Ypres Road, one of the long straight roads below the Poelcappelle (Poplar trees) in Belgium. The British were accusing him of being a Quartermaster General in the IRA (head of the army department in charge of stores). He replied: 'I am only a poor parish priest going about my business.' He was referred to as Father Ryan. A week later the British attempted to deport him to England, for trial, but failed, because he [too] could show that the British had removed Hitler to safety and Spain, and that the potential embarrassment of this was enormous, riotous and very unpatriotic for England.

"When I met Father Ryan, he showed me a vellum Vatican bull. It was written in English, French, German, Spanish, Italian and one other language I didn't recognise. It read:

'This Priest is on urgent mission work
and whomever impedes or obstructs him
will be instantly excommunicated from the Church.'"

Such a statement is quite comparable to that of Pope Gregory XIII (1958–63), formerly Angelo Giuseppe Roncalli, who in 1962 issued a confidential document to all Bishops, stating that they should:

"not move any claims of paedophilia to discussion"
on penalty of being excommunicated.

Spymaster: "Father Ryan also said he had high blood pressure and if you live long enough, you'll come down with exactly what I've got."

Sure enough, every capable Intelligence Officer I've spoken to has had high blood pressure. Not surprisingly, it lowered when they found someone who would record their stories and lowered again when they read this. Recording these stories takes a certain IQ – bright enough to understand and dumb enough to write it down.

Hitler started learning English when he trained in the British Psych-Ops Schools in Tavistock and Ireland, when he lived in Liverpool for six months, and during his frequent visits to London. Not speaking English was part of his cover as a British double agent and speaking English (and not German) while living in Spain was also part of his cover. It gave him the edge, and helped to make the Austrian, 'a trusted German'.

That the young Irishman was close to the same age as Hitler was when he was in Liverpool and Ireland (23) raised enough affinity, rapport, and longing for family, for Hitler to break cover. From this point on, "the curio that Hitler had become was not worth the risk that he posed", and a decision was made to terminate him (3 January 1950).

Radioactive plates were slipped into his mattress (5 January 1950), as per the British, and he died of stomach cancer some six weeks later (19 February 1950).

Due to Dr Morell's toxic thrice-daily medication during the war, Hitler looked 80 rather than 60 years, 10 months and 19 days old. Adolf's *Will* of 1938 was discovered three years later in 1953 and it left 60,000 marks to his half-brother Alois who was Hitler's seconder. This disregarded the last will and testament Hitler and Bormann brought out of Berlin on 2 May 1945 which would have exposed operations JAMES BOND and WINNIE THE POOH as something akin to complicity to mass war crimes.

Alois Hitler was also Psych-Ops-trained and was encouraged to pick up the pieces immediately after Adolf's actual death. He didn't have a hope in hell. He had gambled in Monte Carlo and was bankrupted in 1914. He continued setting up businesses and gambling in Monte Carlo and changed his name from Alois Hitler to Alois Eberle and then to Alois Hiller. He took up politics and became leader of an extreme right wing nationalistic movement in the early 1950s. This also bombed.

By 1953 he was selling portraits of Hitler signed by Alois, as though they were signed by Adolf. The seconder agent had become a spoof. To finish it off, all these records have been confused and it is only input from 'living libraries' and 'talking dictionaries' that cut the wheat from the chaff.

Like Martin Bormann, there was another story floating around that Adolf Hitler had died in 1958. Folklore ideas with serious consequences are usually introduced under the guise of non-reality, usually through part-fantasy, part-reality films. Sometimes the entire film is a front for a single statement.

This was repeated in 2004 when Professor Trevor Broom (sweep it under the carpet) as Head of America's Bureau of Paranormal Defence and Research makes this statement in the action/fantasy flick, *Hellboy*: "1958 – the occult wars finally come to an end with the death of Adolf Hitler."

Agent John T. Myers: "1945 . . . you mean Hitler died in 1945."

Professor Trevor *Broom*: "Did he now? Oh, ah, *Myers*, this is Agent *Clay*. Take his lead. He'll make the introductions."[17]

There was another more alive action/fantasy story floating around that Adolf Hitler was running a menswear store in Levin, a small drive-through town an hour north of Wellington, New Zealand's capital. Through my research I met one of the two assassins who were assigned to kill this 'Hitler' in February 1964 (the same year Ian Fleming died). They were paid £1000 up front with another £2000 due on completion. One of the two assigned to kill this Hitler was good friends with the New Zealander Dan Davin, head of Britain's M at the time – the same organisation that had brought Martin Bormann and Hitler out of Germany 19 years earlier.

Dan Davin (1913–1990) came from humble beginnings. He grew up in the small town of Oamaru where his father was a fencer and scrub cutter. He played rugby and cricket for the South Island and became a Rhodes Scholar, which is a diplomatic spy network using sporting intelligentsia as founded at All Souls College, Oxford University, England. He wrote *The Gorse Blooms Pale* (1947) and *For the Rest of our Lives* (also 1947), a strange book about New Zealanders in Greece and the Desert of Cyrenaica and Libya during WWII. He was the inspiration for Graeme Greene's character 'Smiley', was an Oxford Don as a Classical Scholar, and held the Oxford Chair in Rare Classics, which meant he had no students. He became head of Britain's MI-5 – the British Intelligence Council (some say he became 'M' after Major Desmond Morton) – and he did all of this without the New Zealand Government ever acknowledging him.

Two charismatic ruffians, John and Tom were having an innocent drink in the Regent Hotel lobby on Manners St in Wellington, New Zealand early in February 1964 when a respectable Jewish man approached them and said:

"I know you boys do bad things. I have found Hitler.
He works in a menswear store in Levin.
Heading north, it's the one on the left.
I want you to kill him for me."

---

17 *Hellboy* was a movie about a boy born out of the occult with a military arm (Columbia Pictures, 2004). In the occult Golden Dawn coven language, '8' means '∞'. This was as close to '0' as they were allowed to publicly state.

The Jews were quite obsessed about Hitler and John and Tom were prepared to take advantage of this.

This Jew was the largest furrier (fur coat dealer) in the country and a very successful businessman. John and Tom considered him successful enough to be someone who should not be deluded, but as things have turned out, there were more Slavs gassed in the ovens than Jews.

Double checking this story in April 2005, John said to me: "More of mine got killed" and finished off with a joke:

> "After all the kindness from the Germans paying for Israel, the Huns got sick of it and sent the Jews a gas bill."

As soon as John and Tom got the £1000 down payment they jumped in a taxi and got as far away from the hotel as quickly as possible. They didn't want the "obsessed Jew" to change his mind. Tom then suggested they'd better check this guy out, so the two assigned assassins went to see the supposed Hitler.

> "He did indeed look like Hitler, right down to the height and the small moustache, but he was the wrong age . . . By then Hitler should have been 74, but this guy barely looked 60 . . . So we went back to our employer and told him we had done the job and collected the other £2000."

No Hitler and no Hitler lookalikes were killed, but it was a notable distraction that perpetrated the theory that Hitler was still alive, and it only cost £3000. The people chosen to do the job were white, believable and likeable charismatics. Their rumours would be believed, spread and misinterpreted throughout the pubs of New Zealand and abroad. The fee, the price of a house and section in those days, was never requested back. This was part of a deliberate and ongoing hoax. It was myth building.

The 'Tom' in this microcosm of history was Tom Stanford, also known as 'Tom Ward' and 'Big Tom'. He had been the cook and bodyguard for Noel Coward in England and through an actor friend of Noel's got work in the movies. He was 6'7" (2.1 m) and built well enough to be the loin-clad man who bashed the gong in the signature opening act for the J. Arthur Rank movies (later Pinewood Studios).[18]

---

[18] Other's who banged the gong were "Bombardier" Billy Wells, Ken Richmond, Carl Dane and Phil Nieman. Noel Coward had been the lover of King George VI's brother for 19 years.

In New Zealand Tom was a croupier for church and bingo halls ensuring that the promoter got their cut. When Tom Stanford died in the late 1960s he was cremated at Karori in Wellington. Four years later Jockey John went looking for him and found an undertaker who was a drinking buddy of Big Tom's. The undertaker had held on to Big Tom's ashes for a couple of years waiting for someone to claim them. When Jockey John arrived he pointed out where, two years earlier, he had "released Tom Stanford's ashes under these rose bushes here." Jockey John assures me it was quite a nice spot.

Rather ironically, three years before the Hitler contract, Hitler's assassin was cast in the leading role in the first James Bond movie *Dr No* (1962), but was replaced, due to a drinking problem, by the Scottish milkman and truck driver Sean Connery. He was, however, an advisor on the 1969 James Bond *On Her Majesty's Secret Service* where he gave George Lazenby acting lessons. (See *James Bond – Sir Sean Connery, Appendix 10*)

Conspiracy theories amass in cover-ups and there were plenty around Hitler's multiple deaths during his career, his many faceted escapes out of Germany and the many sightings of him after the war. At each level there is another theory and these are developed to occupy the minds of varying intellects and belief systems with varying amounts of research. To decipher these you have to understand that the groups behind Hitler were the most powerful and resourceful organisations in the world. For them, Hitler was an agent of war and as long as the focus was on him, it was not on them.

> Operations JAMES BOND and WINNIE THE POOH were designed so that nobody would believe they ever existed and nobody could prove them. They left no evidence other than a Junkers JU52/3m g14e that witnesses described as a Junkers/Junkers 52, a camouflaged submarine too small to be a submarine, a bombed-out motorboat and a Lysander with dummy wax-painted serial numbers proved to be elsewhere. This was enough to discredit any witnesses. The mission was designed so that nobody would believe it and nobody could prove it, making Ian Fleming the star attraction to the end of the century.

It was essential for the British to suppress details and confuse the outcome of WWII for as long as possible. If those who fought, and those who lost parents and children during the war, discovered that Britain had taken many of the leading Nazis out of Berlin and given them safe haven in Britain, Spain, South America and New Zealand, then patriotic people would have rioted.

> The British went to enormous trouble removing Martin Bormann and Adolf and Eva Hitler out of Germany, creating doubles for all of them in life and death, as well as doubles for their transport planes.

"It was rumoured that Hitler had perished, but nobody really believed this."[19] Hitler survived for another five years and Martin Bormann for another 14 years with doppelgängers operating for both.

> Operations JAMES BOND was a success and a secret for the next half-century. Operations WINNIE THE POOH and TESTAMENT were a secret for the next 60 years.

There are jokes in Intelligence work and one of them is the number on the dates on which pertinent events occur. When the West bombed Tavistock Square as an add on to the London Tube bombing, under the guise of being oil-rich Syrians, they did so on 07.07.2005 – 007.007^7.

The joke here is that the original James Bond characters pulled Adolf Hitler out of Berlin at 5 pm, 2 May 1945 or 1700 hrs on 02.05.1945, with the numbers being $007^{\infty}.007^{\infty}$ or $(007^{\infty})^2$ – the 'squared' being another allusion to Freemasonry.

Ian Fleming left a lot of leads, just as in-house sabotage does today.

> The old boys who laugh at history – the old Freemasons with nothing to make them radical and enough protection to make them feel like life's a day's fishing amongst friends – they laugh and say the Spanish government were still making remarks about Hitler in 1965:
>
> "Our soil is tilled by the smartest people of Europe" and
> "Our soil is tilled by the finest minds of Europe".

From this they believe Hitler died in 1965 or 1975. That may be so for one of his doppelgängers, but there was cover upon cover and the real boy died on 19 February 1950.

[19] *Agent Extraordinary*, later known as *The Man Who Saved London*, p. 187.

Lost Leaders

If you want to study history, you need to follow the murders.
The history of war – for instance – is the study of mass murder.
It is mass murder that makes history and culture that makes home.

War is the destruction of cultures and homes.
The primary target for the destruction of the home
is the man with integrity.

We call this man husband and hero.
Traditionally he takes care of the animals and protects the region.
Without him culture is as malleable as clay.

It shouldn't be so surprising that Hitler was a British agent. Not only was he completely supported by Churchill and Stalin (they sabotaged attempts to kill him), but the same pattern is repeated over and over again in war today.

Two of the groups that tried to kill Hitler were the Black Orchestra (Schwarze Kapelle – German intelligence) and the Red Orchestra (Rote Kapelle – communist intelligence). Both, the Black and the Red Orchestra were prepared to risk their lives to kill Hitler. As such, both groups should have had the support of Churchill and Stalin. Instead both groups were sabotaged by Churchill and Stalin.

The Black Orchestra constituted the only anti-Nazi resistance movement in Germany and had the best access to Hitler as they worked within Hitler's ranks. They were in constant contact with Churchill, but Churchill refused to return their calls.

Churchill, on the other hand, took the less effective Red Orchestra more seriously and assisted them occasionally. The Red Orchestra were communist intelligence who wanted to kill Hitler on behalf of Stalin, but would always be less effective than the Black Orchestra.

As part of the *Russo-German Non-Aggression Pact* (23 August 1939), Hitler asked Stalin to surrender the Red Orchestra. These were all highly trained and motivated German, French, Belgian and Dutch spies. In a fit of ambivalence Stalin ordered the Red Orchestra to Moscow by rail to receive medals. When they passed through Germany the Gestapo sealed off an entire train station and had them all shot. So perished the best Intelligence service the Russians ever had in the West.

In this way, Churchill and Stalin had Hitler's most motivated and resourceful enemies killed with little reference in the history books. Churchill and Stalin were conspiring together in support of Hitler. Whatever Hitler wanted, Hitler got. All three were working together for the continuation of war with Churchill pulling the strings.

"By their [Churchill and Stalin's] actions towards the anti-Hitler conspiracy they sealed the fate of Europe and the world in a pact of blood on D-Day."[1] Now Churchill's war could continue in earnest.

There were a few hard-core spies who weren't on the train, were sick or chasing poontang (sex) so a few survived, but very few. Leopold Trepper, one of the brightest, said, "Who ever heard of spies getting medals?" and never showed up.

Hitler also had enemies within Germany, many within his own ranks. "Hitler entered the war with grave misgivings of the German High Command."[2] The Black Orchestra were similarly done away with.

In 1942 a second Black Orchestra resistance (the defacto Schwarze Kapelle) was founded within the German Army and by June 1944 Colonel Claus Count Schenk von Stauffenberg had appointed himself its head. This was well known to the British. On 20 June 1944 Count von Stauffenberg was appointed as chief of staff to General Friedrich Fromm, commander of the army reserve, the home army. This gave him admission to military conferences with Hitler in his headquarters.

On his first day Count von Stauffenberg openly told his boss General Fromm that he was planning a coup d'état. General Fromm listened silently and then asked Stauffenberg to assume his duties. On 6 July 1944 Count von Stauffenberg, carrying explosives, attended a military conference with Hitler at the Berghof. Stauffenberg did not activate the timer on the explosive because he also wanted to kill Goering and Himmler simultaneously. The same thing happened on 11 and 15 July 1944.

MI-6 supplied the bomb and detonator. Both were faulty.

Rommel, who was to support Count von Stauffenberg after a successful coup, was then severely wounded, as if on British cue. By mid-1944, British fighter bombers had the Cab rank system which

[1] Eminent German-American military historian, Charles V. P. von Luttichau, *Bodyguard of Lies*, p. 820.

[2] *The Cambridge Biographical Encyclopedia*.

was capable of targeting any German vehicle. They had also sent in ground troops to assassinate Rommel. The Führer's headquarters were then transferred from his residence in the Berghof in Obersalzberg in Berchtesgaden in the Bavarian Alps to Rastenburg in north Germany.

Rastenburg, known as the Wolf's Lair, is just south of the Russian border. It is near Gierloz, 8 km east of Ketrzyn, 100 km (64 miles) southeast of Konigsberg and near Karlsof with its seven bridges. In the old language it is East Prussia. It lies on the flat sandy plain of the Guber and had 2.5 km of bunkers with walls six metres thick. It was built by the dreaded Todt Organisation (notorious for their ill-treatment of prisoners) and served as Hitler's headquarters from September 1941 to September 1944. Hitler spent most of his days here except for short trips to Berlin and Berchtesgaden in Bavaria.

The Wolf's Lair had been built on cheap swampland surrounded by deciduous forest and marshy pools which were perfect breeding grounds for fungi, mosquitos, worm eggs and dysentery. As a result, the bunkers were damp and cold as were all the Nazis' underwear and uniforms. In combination with Dr Morell's toxic treatment, Hitler suffered from diarrhoea, stomach cramps, nausea, aching limbs, shivers and fever.

The British knew this. Koch had overseen the building of the Wolf's Lair and had told British agent Winterbotham. It would have been easy enough to bomb the various German headquarters during the war, but this would have ended the war. The Berghof was the only German headquarters to be bombed, but this only happened at the end of the war and only after it had been emptied. It was more or less a symbolic gesture.

As everyone was sitting in their cars ready to leave the Berghof, Hitler returned for one last look, and commented to a bystander that he would probably never return. His apparent psychic ability was a reflection of his Intelligence reports, much of which came via British sources and via his teeth.

Von Stauffenberg then received an appointment to see Hitler on 20 July 1944 at Rastenburg, with the compromised British agent Goering attending. The British were quite happy killing Goering towards the end of the war. He was outliving his usefulness and his death would secure their shared secret – Carinhall was financed and bugged by the British.

At the last minute the conference was shifted to the barracks, with its thin timber-panelled walls. Stauffenberg was interrupted in another building while setting the timer on the bomb with pliers. As if with complete complicity, he then managed to place the bomb under the heavy map table in Hitler's meeting room. This was reported to Hitler minutes later. Under threat of assassination Hitler used one of his ever-ready doppelgängers to represent him.

The bomb was powerful enough to blow much of the wall and ceiling panels off and seriously injure or kill ten of the 25 people, but it was not as powerful as it should or could have been. As soon he recovered from the shock, General Wilhelm Keitel ran towards the doppelgänger Hitler saying "Where is the Führer?" He then immediately helped the severely injured doppelgänger Hitler out of the room.

Doppelgänger Hitler's reported medical condition afterwards is the least one could expect in that situation. It was reported that he had splinters in his legs, slight bleeding to his right elbow, trival bruises on the back of his left hand, both of his eardrums had been ruptured, and he had head traumas for weeks afterwards.

With the use of doppelgängers, all the expected signs of damage seemed to disappear. "After the bomb blast his left leg stopped trembling and even his hand tremor almost completely vanished. To outward appearances, the bomb left Hitler unscathed."[3]

Soon after, the real Hitler entered the room with singed hair and a blackened face. He carried tattered trousers and a jacket with a square of cloth removed from it. It is difficult to rip a jacket in any pattern that is not a square, whereas an explosion does not rip a square hole, but leaves the jacket, like the trousers, in tatters.

> Hitler's experience of the explosion became a collusion.
> "Like everyone else in the room Hitler had experienced the explosion as an 'infernally bright darting flame' and a deafening crash. When he got up out of the burning, smoking debris with blackened face and the back of his head singed, [General Wilhelm] Keitel came running towards him, shouting, 'Where is the Führer?' and helped him [doppelgänger Hitler] get out of the room."[4]

---

[3] *The Secret Diaries of Hitler's Doctor*, p. 60. Historian Hugh Trevor-Roper goes as far as to say that Hitler wasn't even hurt in the 20 July explosion.

[4] *Hitler*, p. 708.

Hitler was leaning over the desk at the time of the explosion and his legs would have been broken and smashed with splinters of wood. He would have been knocked unconscious from the table rising to hit his upper body and head. Hitler was very close to the bomb and two people around him were killed, yet he was not counted amongst the seriously injured. His injuries "seemed to miraculously disappear within hours".

Six people were seriously injured and four died including stenographer Heinrich Berger who sometimes acted as Hitler's doppelgänger. General Heusinger who stood next to Hitler was seriously injured. Colonel Brandt, General Korten and General Schundt were all very close to Hitler and all very dead after the explosion.

In all, 226 Germans were involved in the plot to kill Hitler, so many in fact that Hitler was forced to continue working with the people who had planned to kill him.

Dr Erwin Geising treated Hitler's 'bomb plot' doppelgängers for head trauma for weeks after. "But he had suffered considerable damage"[5] and was killed by Dr Morell who treated him with his fake [toxic] 'penicillin powder'. Typically Morell used a sulphonamide of which U_1 iron was the most toxic and would have caused a violent allergic skin reaction with extreme anger as a side effect. Both of these were reason enough to die.

Once the real Hitler entered the room (after blackening his face, singing his hair and carrying the torn clothes of his doppelgänger) he told the shocked meeting that he had long known of a conspiracy to kill him and he would now unmask his conspirators. He then displayed the tattered trousers and jacket that had come off the doppelgänger Hitler moments earlier. This comes from a long practice of role playing. Role playing various scenarios is still practised by the Freemasons today (7.30 pm Tuesdays and Thursdays at a lodge near you).

That same afternoon, on 20 July 1944, Benito Mussolini arrived at Rastenburg and Hitler greeted him with his left hand (his only visible anomaly) and calmly used the bomb blast to his advantage while carrying on a conversation with full hearing. Mussolini, who believed in heroes and posing like a Greek God, said "This was a sign from heaven". More likely it was a sign from the British.

---

[5] Ibid.

Around 5 pm back at the Führer's bunker, Hitler and Mussolini met with Marshal of the Reich Hermann Goering, Foreign Minister Joachim von Ribbentrop, Commander-in-Chief of the German Navy Admiral Karl Doenitz, Supreme Commander of the Armed Forces General Wilhelm Keitel, General of Artillery Alfred Jodl, and Hitler's Chief Advisor and Chancellor Martin Bormann.

Bormann had already begun negotiations with the British. He had been forewarned and was not in the barracks during the explosion. He was in the official photographs but Bormann was not mentioned in any of the *Hitler* text as being present.

Hitler was advised that Germany was losing the war, yet he refused to capitulate. Part of Hitler's British deconstruction was the all-or-nothing approach and the all-or-nothing annihilation of Germany.

The conversation then centred around getting Hitler out of Germany alive after the war was lost. Hitler seemed lost in thought, drugged from a lozenge provided by British agent Dr Morell. These drugs exacerbated Hitler's short fuse and allowed it to be lit with key words. One of those words was 'Roehm' and it referred to Hitler's homosexual past and the control the British had over him.

When the Freemason agent, Commander of the Armed Forces General Wilhelm Keitel brought up 'Captain Ernst Roehm and the Night of the Long Knives', Hitler's subconscious hatred was activated and he rose to his feet declaring he would kill all those involved in the coup, including their wives, families and relatives.

The bomb was not powerful enough and historians blamed this on Hitler transferring from a concrete-walled bunker (which would have enclosed the blast) to a timber-lined barracks which allowed much of the explosive forces to escape. Regardless, the lack of power of the bomb had the opposite effect to which Colonel Count von Stauffenberg desired.

Over the next nine months, to April 1945, there was a wave of executions of the conspirators, the de facto Schwarze Kapelle and the German High Command with links to England. Count von Stauffenberg, his wife and sister were killed, but the children were swished. They were put in custody under false names and repeatedly moved. Many other von Stauffenbergs were hunted down and killed. Effectively all of the high-ranking intellectual Germans – the von Intellectuals – were killed.

Mussolini celebrates his chin (above).

Mussolini and Hitler parade.

This Nine Months of Long Knives did not occur without British support.

> "In fact both Nazi and Allied propaganda, in one of those dreadful harmonies they exhibited more and more frequently at this stage of the war, denounced the conspirators."[6]

The British, by providing Count von Stauffenberg with an ineffective explosive with forewarning and a doppelgänger replacement, had drawn the final curtain over the German aristocracy with any influence or military connections. Those who survived the Nine Months of Long Knives were put through the Nuremberg trials and killed afterwards.

> The only thing left for the British was to kill as many Germans as possible in the last nine months of the war and to destroy whatever vestige of infrastructure Germany had left. This too happened in a killing spree so great that more Germans died in the last nine months of the war than during the rest of the war put together. The last nine months of WWII became a massive depopulation exercise.

The killing of the Jews pales in comparison to the Allied killing of the Germans (July 1944–May 1945), which pales in comparison to the killing of the 26 million Russians, which pales in comparison to the 50 million that died from the British 1918–19 Spanish Flu epidemic.

War, it seems, is an organised killing epidemic.

Hitler went into hiding and forgot about defending Germany. His military decisions became irrational and were no longer based on the strength of his forces, but what he dreamed them to be. He spent the remainder of his time in bunkers developing jaundice, dental problems and a heart attack, all in September 1944. He also required the extremely suspicious second vocal chord operation in the same month. The first was in the Autumn of 1933.

This is a lot of sickness and operations for one man and one suspects that this sickness was spread over all of his surviving doppelgängers. The doppelgängers were bribed with the promise that their families would be safe as long as they acted for Hitler. As the security of that promise waned, so did their health. With the death of one of their comrades, they chose 'operations' as a means for time out and time off.

---

[6] *Hitler*, p. 716.

Because Mussolini was present at the meeting for the planned escapes of Hitler out of Germany, the British ensured that he too was killed before the end of the war, before he could speak out. Of the others present at the 20 July 1944 meeting, Goering was tried at Nuremberg and committed suicide (11 pm 15 October 1946) with American assistance just before he was due to be executed. Ribbentrop was tried and hanged at Nuremberg two hours later at 1 am 16 October 1946.

Keitel (1882–1946) and Jodl (1890–1946) were totally fluent and complicit with the doppelgänger Hitlers and it was essential that all of their secrets died with them. They were both tried and executed.

"A major-general in 1934, he [Wilhelm Keitel] was serving as chief-of-staff to the Minister of War in 1938, and, on Hitler's abolition of that office after the Blomberg/Fritzsche crisis, became head of the unified defence staff which was set up to replace it (OKW). He held the post throughout the war. It involved constant attendance on Hitler and he was therefore privy to all his major strategic decisions, besides being responsible for their transmission to the operational commands . . . In practice, his age [63] made his advice of little use (he was known in the army as Lakaitel – 'Lackey') and Hitler depended more on Jodl."[7]

"Colonel-General Alfred Jodl was chief of the Operations Section, High Command of the Armed Forces, and Hitler's personal operations officer. He was born in 1890 in Bavaria [the cradle of Naziism], into a traditionally military family. Commissioned into the artillery in 1910 he served throughout WWI. He was appointed Chief of the National Defence Section of the General Staff (war plans) in 1935 and Chief of the Operations Section in the new OKW in 1938 and held that post throughout the war. His chief tasks were to inform Hitler of military situations as they developed and to transmit his orders to the operational commands. OKW was not itself a command staff, but it was the one with which Hitler was in most frequent and intimate touch and Jodl came eventually to act as Hitler's principal military adviser, since Keitel lacked the courage to disagree with him."[8]

"Admiral Karl Dönitz [Doenitz] was Grand Admiral, Commander-in-Chief of the German Navy and Hitler's successor. He arranged the

[7] John Keegan, 'The Men in the Dock', *Purnell's History of the Second World War*, No. 117, p. 3269.
[8] Ibid. p. 3268.

surrender of Germany to the Allies and insisted throughout the trial that his career had been solely that of a professional naval officer, a submission to which the tribunal went some way towards accepting. He was convicted on two out of three counts and sentenced to ten years."[9]

> Admiral Doenitz had been a submarine commander and knew all the secrets of German Antarctica and was far too useful for the Americans to kill. He had also been a British agent from early 1919. As a result, Doenitz survived until 1980 – longer than anyone else.
>
> Martin Bormann escaped the Nuremberg trial by providing the British with the Nazis' Swiss Bank account numbers. He did attend the Nuremberg trials, but only after plastic surgery, attending in the spectators gallery with M, the head of British Special Secret Intelligence Operations. M had got Bormann out of Berlin in OP JAMES BOND and Hitler out of Berlin in the piggyback mission impossible, OP WINNIE THE POOH.

The 20th of July 1944 was an important day in history. From a failed British sabotaged coup, all the de facto Schwarze Kapelle and their families were killed. The 'von Intellectuals' were wiped out, as were their families. The Germany military tradition was wiped clean and the fate of the entire German command was sealed.

"Thus Hitler not only destroyed Germany, he also put an end to old Europe . . . ultimately it must be granted that he could not have destroyed Europe without the help of Europe."[10]

> The killing of Germans began in earnest at six times the rate of the rest of the war – and all for what? So that Adolf Hitler, an Austrian-born British agent running Germany into the ground, could be brought out to safety, and hidden, until the propaganda of war had taken over the post-war recovering world, the Cold War begun and the mystery man would take all the blame for the social engineering and military profits of the war-makers.

The Wolf's Lair headquarters in East Prussia (Poland) was built under British supervision. Group Captain Fred Winterbotham visited the site in 1935 and knew it was built for the attack on Russia which

[9] Ibid. p. 3268. Slightly paraphrased.
[10] *Hitler*, p. 750.

had been planned from 1919. The attack on Russia was self-sabotage for the German war effort – hence it was supported by the British. The Germans also lost WWI by fighting on two fronts.

> Spymaster: "Nothing succeeds like making the same mistake twice."
>
> From this point on, Hitler prepared many options for his escape. He also kept well hidden, and virtually gave up on defending Germany. This was also part of the British plan. Why should Hitler defend Germany when his own men were trying to kill him? Hitler gave up and waited for the destruction of Germany as per his British training. He knew he was to be guaranteed complete assistance in his escape.

Hitler sowed confusion as to his whereabouts using surviving doppelgängers for his public appearances. One, in a hospital, was shown on Movietone News in 1945 with the title *German Newsreels on Hitler's Escape*. Newsreel narrator: "Looking rather more round-shouldered than usual, he goes from bed to bed commiserating with the casualties. Maybe this is Hitler's double or perhaps his double was killed by the bomb. Though there are scores of theories, the facts are not yet known."[11]

The fact that Movietone News had the newsreel showed that it was leaked for PR purposes.

The Movietone News doppelgänger was an entirely bigger person, with round shoulders, a chin, jowls, different-shaped ears, hairline and neck thickness. He was 1–2 inches taller (25–50 mm), had muscular arms, a thick chest and large farmer's hands. He was a bigger man altogether but wore the trademark moustache which drew attention away from all other features. He had also had plastic surgery to imitate Hitler's nose.

Hitler, at this stage, was square-shouldered and thin, with a hollow chest.

Narrator: "In the final months of the war, even the Germans couldn't be certain. Since the 1944 bomb plot, Hitler kept well out of sight hidden away in bunkers. The last ordinary Germans who saw him in the open were a handful of the Hitler Youth."[12]

---

[11] *Hitler of the Andes.*

[12] Ibid.

There were seven plans to get Hitler out of Germany. These are separate from the faking of his death. Some of the plans for his escape became active false trails and these were pursued relentlessly by complicit intelligence agencies. These seven plans included South America, south-west Africa, Switzerland, Norway, Antarctica, Spain and New Zealand where a hit against a Hitler was ordered in February 1964, well after his actual death.

The main East-West avenue was used by the Nazis as a runway right up to the last moments when Berlin fell with Hanna Reitsch flying out on 29 April 1945. The Nazis had captured British planes at hand to try and make their escape without being shot down, one of which was an Auster with RAF markings.

Flight out of Berlin was certainly possible. Hitler's switchboard operator: "There were two planes waiting to the North of Berlin. One of them was the [large] JU390 and a Blohm and Voss that could fly the same distance. It could fly 18,000 km without refuelling, so Hitler could have escaped if he wanted to."[13]

Professor Hugh R. Trevor-Roper, a wartime MI-6 officer and British Army Major and more recently the Regius Professor of Modern History at Oxford University: "Up to 22 April [1945] when the net closed, they could get out by air. Big airplanes could take off on the 22nd and a whole convoy of them went off from Berlin to Berchtesgarden on the 22nd carrying quite a large number of people who wanted to get out – all those who opted to get out. The Russians couldn't be everywhere."[14]

Despite Trevor-Roper's confidence, a packed Condor, including Dr Morell, flew out on 23 April to Munich.[15]

Stalin's deputy, Marshal Zhukov had announced Hitler was dead on 1 May 1945, but had changed his mind. *Hitler could easily have escaped.* The runway was open and he was probably in Spain or Argentina, both of which were fascist. So the newspapers published articles with the headings, "Hitler's Argentine Connection". This was another cover-up. Spain was a fascist country under British Intelligence control and Hitler was a British agent.

Hitler was in Spain.

[13] *Hitler of the Andes.*

[14] Ibid.

[15] This was additional to the Condor that flew out and crashed two days earlier.

Hitler's destination to Barcelona was pre-empted with the Condor that crashed on 21 April 1945 in Müldorf as it left Berlin headed for Barcelona. Despite the strong indication that Hitler had escaped to Barcelona, all search efforts were directed elsewhere.

To counter this, the British sent out a young army major and MI-6 agent, Hugh Trevor-Roper who was someone with no authority, but breeding. He was 31 years old but looked 23. This is called 'send a monkey, get peanuts'. Hugh became Baron Dacre of Glanton for his efforts.

In *The Last Days of Hitler,* British Army Major Hugh Trevor-Roper gives an illuminating account of his vain efforts to obtain information or co-operation from the Russians:

> "The Russians accused the British of harbouring Hitler and Eva Braun in their zone for some nefarious and unstated purpose in the future. And at this point my superior officer, Dick White [who later spent his Christmases in the 1950s and '60s with the treasonous homosexual spy Anthony Blunt attending] said, 'Enough is enough. It's perfectly ridiculous that the facts have not been established' and he charged me with this mission."

Starting a month after the report of Hitler's death (approx. 30 May 1945), Hugh Trevor-Roper's mission was fraught with difficulties. The bunker had been ransacked by the Russians and was 0.3 metre (1 foot) deep in water with no electricity. Neither the Soviets, British or Americans shared information or evidence. Hansl Baur, Hitler's pilot and Hans Rattenhuber, the head of Hitler's guard, people who were in the bunker at the time of Hitler's escape, were in Soviet imprisonment and unavailable for interrogation.

All the important conclusions of Hugh Trevor-Roper on Hitler's death were based on the evidence of one man, Sturmbannführer Erich Kempka, Hitler's personal chauffeur who was also present at the Night of the Long Knives. According to Kempka, Hitler was shot. This became the official version, but the British found no bloodstains that matched Hitler's blood type, no bullets, and no bullet holes in the room where he was supposed to have shot himself.

To continue his 'milk and cookies' version of history as the official British history of 'maximum depth and endeavour', Hugh Trevor-Roper was made Regius Professor of Modern History at Oxford University in 1957. (See *Hugh Trevor-Roper, Appendix 8*)

A month prior to sending Hugh Trevor-Roper, the British had sent Anthony Blunt (37, King George V's illegitimate son) to Schloss Kronberg (a castle near Frankfurt) to retrieve any evidence of the former King Edward VIII's Nazi involvement. British half-royal Anthony FitzBlunt was German Army Intelligence with a 'V-Mann number' and a numbered Soviet operative.

These connections gave Blunt a free pass anywhere in wartime Europe. He had spent the war actively passing information to both the Germans and the Russians and was known by the Russians as "ideological shit". This made him one of the best non-ideological spies the world had ever seen.

> Anthony Blunt represented one thing – the British monarchy: a non-ideological spy-unit 'loyal only to itself' – perhaps the best definition of 'royal' ever.

Spymaster: "On his mission, Anthony Blunt took liberty and stole the Kaiser's crown jewels from the Czech castle Karlstejn, which had been purposely built to safeguard the inheritance."

Russia Looks for Hitler

By late July 1945 at the Potsdam conference, Stalin knew the bodies of Hitler they'd discovered were fake and the British were hiding Hitler either in Spain or Argentina. Stalin said as much to President Truman (Freemason) and to Secretary of State Jimmy Byrnes as recorded in *Frankly Speaking* and *Hitler.*

> "At the Potsdam conference in July, 1945, Stalin assured his Western colleagues that the Russians had not found the corpse and that Hitler was hiding in Spain or South America."[16]

> Hugh Trevor-Roper:
> "In Spain there was General Franco [general & dictator from 1936–75] and in Argentina there was Colonel Perón [soldier and president from 1946–55, 1973–74]. From Stalin's point of view, these were both semi-Nazi reactionary dictatorships who supported the Germans."[17]

To support the Argentina theory, before, during, and after the end of WWII, the large German population in Argentina would give each

[16] *Hitler*, p. 750.
[17] *Hitler of the Andes.*

other the Nazi salute . . . even on the beach, where they could be seen from submarines, and in places where they were openly filmed on land.

Smersh and the KGB did their best to prove that Hitler hadn't killed himself, but had somehow vanished. This marked the start of Operation MAPTA (MYTH), N° 655-A/OP. Operation MYTH was the cornerstone of Stalin's claim that Hitler had escaped and was being looked after by Western fascists. It was made public in the 1990s. Of detailed note is that the typewritten 'P' in 'OP' had been changed by ballpoint pen into a 'B'. The 'B' stood for 'observation' rather than 'operation'.

The Soviets never looked at the bodies found in Berlin after the first autopsy of 3–8 May 1945. They knew they were doppelgängers of Adolf and Eva Hitler. The Russian commission autopsy report (Document 12) showed no bullet wounds to the skull, nor any detectable fragments from the claimed shooting, but the remains of a crushed ampoule in the mouth of the corpse. There was no smell of bitter almonds given off by cyanide compounds observed in the other bodies, but those bodies weren't burnt.

The bodies were treated with exemplary neglect by the Russians and buried secretly in a shallow grave, in a little wood, so that even dogs could dig them up. Then the Russians placed a guard at the site – until the earth settled.

The KGB then claimed to have "flushed Hitler's corpse" into a Magdeburg river in April 1970. These were the skeletal remains of a doppelgänger Hitler or Hitler's killed 29 April–1 May 1945.

> "In a memorandum to the U.S. Joint Chiefs of Staff, dated August 5, 1945, they [the British] requested that all those concerned with compiling the official histories of the war not 'be given access to any original special intelligence material'.
> "They [the British] further proposed that the British Chiefs of Staff 'write up important battles, using personnel already indoctrinated', and it was this information that would be given to official historians for incorporation in their volumes . . . The U.S. Joint Chiefs of Staff . . . agreed in a memorandum to the British Chiefs of Staff, dated September 7, 1945."[18]

To continue this, Stalin was blamed for covering up true information and putting out false information about Hitler.

[18] *Bodyguard of Lies*, p. 825.

> "In the end the Russians managed to swathe the whole question in such obscurity that the wildest versions concerning the end of Hitler circulated . . . *fleeing in a submarine to a remote island, living in a Spanish monastery* or on a South American hacienda."[19]

Amongst those most taken with the news that Hitler was alive was General Eisenhower. Months after Berlin was taken, he said publicly:

> "*We have been unable to find one tangible piece of evidence of Hitler's death.* Even though I initially believed Hitler was dead, there are now *reasons to assume that he is alive.*"[20]

A radio bulletin stated "*The United States Army does not know whether Hitler is alive or dead.*" An Associated Press heading read "Zhukov Says Hitler Wed Actress In Berlin, May Be Alive in Europe . . . Berlin, June 9 [1945] – *Adolf Hitler not yet found.*"

On 19 December 1945 a newspaper article read: "*Soviets not convinced Hitler Dead*". Other articles read, "Far from being brought to justice, Hitler had melted away" and "*Court Ruling sought on Hitler's Death*".[21]

> After all of these headings the Soviets then claimed the British were holding Hitler alive. Stalin should know. He was a British agent and had been a criminal in London's East End underground. He still had contacts in Britain and knew as much as most as to what was going on.

After the Potsdam conference the false trail was developed to Argentina and was continued through into the mid-1970s. This involved a U-boat leaving Norway for Argentina in great secrecy and was followed by a well-publicised landing and surrender on the coast of Argentina on 17 August 1945.

The FBI then became involved and searched for Hitler from the subways of the Bronx to the jungles of Latin America. This was only ever going to be a wild-goose chase. The FBI were already discredited by their director J. Edgar Hoover (1924–1972) who looked like a Russian with a crooked jaw and mouth. "He was a paranoid and suspicious neurotic man who had built his career on finding the enemy within."[22]

[19] *Hitler*, p. 750.

[20] *Hitler of the Andes.*

[21] Ibid.

[22] Ibid.

Soon after Hoover (1895–1972) died the hunt for Hitler ceased. A discredited person is always required to pursue a fruitless mission and J. Edgar Hoover was a cross-dressing, bisexual, inside-crime boss, who was given the Hitler-hunt for 27 fruitless years. Hoover was regularly sodomised by the Mafia while dressed as a woman.

J. Edgar Hoover was useless for integrity and could be guaranteed to support crime at whatever level, whenever it was required. He was as much an agent for chaos as anyone and it was only through having intelligence files on everyone else that he was able to take his intelligence role to the top and to keep his weird sexual behaviour under wraps. The Mafia didn't care about reputations and used his secret to screw him every which way. While the FBI were hunting Hitler, the Mafia were creating crime.

The FBI (America's CID) began to investigate if Hitler had made it across the Atlantic, and recently released FBI documents point to worry and hysteria surrounding the possibility that Hitler was alive and in their neighbourhood. The FBI documents presented had all traceable detail blacked out, so little or no follow-up was possible. Some of these documents were letters sent in by players to create false leads and other leads were treated as hoaxes, like "If you want to know where Hitler is call xxx-xxx". The name and address was also blacked out.

Polls at the time showed that over 50% of people believed Hitler was still alive and this led to a lot of Hitler sightings. Every FBI bureau in the US received sightings of Hitler somewhere in America. There were a thousand FBI agents working on these reports at any one time. This produced over 1200 documents on Hitler's escape – all of which were decoys.

The maths on this is fascinating. If 1000 FBI agents hunted for Hitler over 30 years from late 1945 to the mid-1970s and produced 1200 reports, then each FBI agent spent 25 years completing one report. The hunt for Hitler was cover for every other FBI operation under the sun.

A hoax is always built upon a previous hoax
and never the truth of history.

This is how history is hidden and how history is formed. It is also why 95% of all history books contain information that is two-thirds false. The longest hoaxes are always reason for the next war.

The most enthusiastic Hitler hunter was *The National Police Gazette – Sports, True Adventure, People* (America's first pictorial, established 1845). In the December 1945 issue, the front cover showed two American actors looking like suburban versions of Hitler and Eva at 40 and 30 years of age. The cover read "Hitler is Alive! His Marriage to Eva Braun – Their Fake Suicide and Escape from Berlin".

One story goes that a double had died for Hitler at the bunker and Adolf Hitler and Eva Braun had escaped to Norway (north Germany, through Denmark, to Norway) and from there were taken by the U-boat submarine U-977 to Latin America.

U-977 crew member: "We left Norway on 6 or 7 May [1945] and then practically became a phantom boat, all the way around the North of Scotland, past Ireland, past France and the Bay of Biscay. They were looking for us and searching for us and all we could do was listen for anyone above us."[23]

This was a voyage many thought physically impossible but the U-977 made it to the coast of Argentina on 17 August 1945. On the same day the newspaper headline read "102 Days Late, German Sub Surrenders to Argentina". The crew were immediately taken prisoner and accused of hiding Hitler on board. During their interrogation many Nazi U-boat officers were castrated.

John Walsh, an American FBI G-Man (a spy working for the American Embassy in Buenos Aires on the fruitless Hitler-hunt in Argentina): "The U-boats came and surrendered to Argentina. The press reports there indicated that someone in Montevideo [Uruguay] or Argentina suggested that Hitler had been on these boats and that caused a number of people to say, 'Well, we have to look into that possibility'."[24]

More reports of U-Boat landings came into the FBI over the next couple of weeks. "Reports of Hitler Hideout – Los Angeles, [muffled] Bureau, 21 September 1945 – The first sub came close to shore after it had been signalled safe to land and a doctor and several men disembarked and Hitler and two women. Another doctor and seven more men said Hitler had suffered from asthma and ulcers and had shaved off his moustache and had a long 'but' on his upper lip."[25]

[23] *Hitler of the Andes.*

[24] Ibid.

[25] Ibid.

Hitler was supposed to be hiding in the foothills of the Southern Andes but reports remained unconfirmed. Argentina's navy tried to capture the U-boats but the huge coastline made it easy for the Nazis to evade capture and get ashore on German-owned coastal farms in Patagonia.

The FBI then set up an operation behind the walls of the American Embassy in Buenos Aires but the FBI's power of interrogation was restricted and their agents had to operate covertly. They had difficulty establishing the crucial network of informants on the ground and were limited by their conspicuousness. They were also under constant surveillance from local police and Nazis who hid behind newspapers.

This was a game of **Spy versus Spy** for the Nazis, with the Nazi spies looking exactly like the FBI's G-Men except that they all had moustaches. This pre-empted the movies that took them seriously and the comic strips that lampooned them later.

Messages from outside Argentina were relayed to the FBI Hitler-hunters by the FBI Radiogram system. These instructions kept the team of G-Men busy chasing the ever-elusive, never-present Hitler for over four decades.

The FBI G-Men would even report on footprints found in mudflats near San Gelling (25 June 1948), leading to a car and would then follow up in Veronica. There were thousands of lost leaders. Another U-boat was spotted on 18 July 1948 at Mar del Plata, then Hitler was seen heading across the Argentine pampas towards the southern Andes towards the German-owned Eden Hotel in La Falda, a remote region of Cordova nestled in the foothills of the Andes. This was a crop circle investigation, defined by the *Oxford Reference Dictionary* as caused by "whirlwinds, fungi, alien spaceships and/or hoaxers".

In November 1945, the FBI had linked Hitler to the Eden Hotel, a centrepiece of a long-established wealthy German community. This was an international hotel where aristocrats from Cordova and Buenos Aires danced to the orchestra into the early hours.

Since the 1930s, the Eden had been a paradise for its predominantly German clientele. It was run by Eda Eyckhorn whose connections reached the highest echelons of the German Reich. She was definitely dykey-looking and went to Europe each year to attract guests.

One suspects that the principal guests she attracted were those Germans with an unnatural interest in children. Kiddy porn is still not illegal in Germany and fascist Germans are renown paedophiles, including the Stasi.

According to the FBI, who established a dossier on Eyckhorn after the war, she had close links with the German Reich. Before the Nazis had come to power she placed her entire bank account of 30,000 marks at Goebbels' disposal. Over the years she became one of Hitler's closest friends and confidants although there is no mention of her in Joachim C. Fest's authoritative *Hitler*.

This was a fabrication and showed the FBI's collusion in taking the world's attention off the scent, onto Argentina and away from Spain.

Spain was where Hitler was and, quite purposely, no post-war-controlled media published anything of him being there.

It was difficult for the FBI G-Men to get to La Falda in person, because they stuck out like sore thumbs. The FBI *never* went to the Eden Hotel. They used locals and got all of their information second-hand. A lot of photos of Hitler had been placed around the hotel and the hotel was in a constant state of readiness for his arrival. It was considered to be the natural place for him to be in Argentina.

Catalina de Mero, a seventeen-year-old maid at the Eden Hotel, said Hitler came to the hotel in 1948. "He arrived one night and was put up on the third floor [of the two-storey hotel]. I took breakfast up to him, placed it at his door, knocked and then left. It was German food including cheese soufflés [beaten egg] and he ate everything."

According to Catalina de Mero, the Hitler of the Andes was clearly recognisable as the Hitler of so many people's imagination, even though he'd lost his moustache and most if not all of his hair. He wore a wig. For the three days he was there, the third floor was private, but everything carried on below as normal.

The hotel proprietor, Eda Eyckhorn, told the 17-year-old maid: "Whatever you saw, pretend you didn't." Two weeks later Eda and Catalina drove up to a wooden house in Pandazucar in the mountains and delivered a picnic basket of German food to the supposed Hitler. From here he went to La Rioja after which they lost trace of him. Pandazucar means 'sugar bread' and is still a lodging place today.

The Angel of Death, Josef Mengele (1911–79) chief doctor at Auschwitz, and Adolf Eichmann (1906–62) an SS organiser of anti-Semitic activities, arrived in South America the following year (1949). Mengele befriended the Nazi Wolfgang Gerhardt in Brazil in 1961 and assumed his identity when Gerhardt died. Eichmann reached Argentina in 1948 and was traced by Israeli agents. He was taken to Israel in 1960 where he was tried and executed. (See *Was Wallis Simpson A Man, Appendix 13*)

The FBI didn't close the files on Adolf Hitler until the mid-1970s, after the useful hoaxer J. Edgar Hoover had died in 1972. After this the Americans started to liberalise their attitude towards the secret matters of WWII and a flood of documents were declassified in the spring of 1975 containing secret papers on cover and deception.

> John Walsh, FBI G-Man in Buenos Aires:
> "Much of the information was not credible . . . others where there was a possibility of some credibility . . . we made enquiries . . . but [in] none of them we found any true indications that Hitler was in Argentina or the United States, or in any place where we had any responsibility. All the investigations we made came to a dead end because nothing really specific had been found."[26]

The narrator of *Hitler of the Andes* states that these revealed Stalin had deliberately confused and misinformed the West about Hitler's fate in Spain or Argentina. This is an interesting end to the documentary as it never investigated Spain. It is designed to confuse, introduce an erroneous story, affirm lost leaders and discredit truthful leads.

Stalin tried to find the truth about Hitler's escape. It is what fellow agents and mortal enemies do. They look out for each other, whether they like them, admire them, or fear them. After all, Stalin and Hitler were both fellow foreign British agents in a plan to make the Great War (WWI) even greater (WWII).

Eisenhower then became America's 34th President on 20 January 1953 and Stalin was killed by MAD 44 days later.

Spymaster: "With his interest in Hitler, Stalin's protection from being poisoned was suddenly removed. In his diet kitchen there was an amalgam of secret services who all tasted his food. These included Smersh and the GRU, the forerunner to the KGB. They watched each other and tasted everything. It was quite the tense kitchen.

[26] *Hitler of the Andes.*

"Stalin was treated in much the same way as Hitler and the Queen, receiving all these homeopathic medicines, but Stalin never received any medicine, homeopathic or other, for high blood pressure, nor was he treated for high blood pressure. High blood pressure is a common condition amongst top secret agents, especially deconstructed agents at the head of the programme.

"When Stalin suffered his stroke, his sentries enforced his privacy. He was most likely guarded by White Finns (Finnish) who worked for the British government on contract. White Finns were also used to guard Lenin in his last days. There is a long history of foreign troops guarding key assets in Russia. The Czech legion guarded the trans-Siberian railway in the last days of WWI because it was a foreign asset."

Modern Equivalents

The Hitler-Hunt was the FBI's most incredible manhunt, but the whole scenario reeks of Saddam Hussein and Osama bin Laden – they too are more useful as 'enemies to incite ongoing hatred' and therefore defence spending, as opposed to 'succumbed and conquered' enemies. The myth of Hitler was kept alive for the same reason – the development of fear and arms.

British SAS: "Saddam Hussein is an American agent, but may have been taken over by the Israelis at one point. Osama bin Laden has been an American agent for the last 30 years and his CIA codename is Tim Osman. He was educated in Britain and is described by a former school buddy as 'Harry bin Laden' (his British name) and as 'a family man, full of integrity, with a nice nature'."

High ranking ASIO officer: "I have seen Bin Laden in a safe house in London. Perhaps that's why he doesn't appear to age as he walks down the rocky slopes of yesteryear."

James Bond III: "Bin Laden is in on the oil scam. The 007, 7 July 2005 London Tube bombing was arranged by the Americans and Israelis with everything attributed to the Syrians as Syrian oil is the next American mark. They won't attack Iran because they have nuclear weapons, but you watch, Syria is the next country America will attack making Syria the 74th country since 1945. It's the same scenario as my namesake pulled."

Spymaster: "Arafat was an Egyptian brought in to run Palestine as an Israeli-American agent of war, which in turn profits the Americans who supply Israel with arms, hence Yasser Arafat's inability to conclude peace."

"But many Palestinians now believe he [Arafat, 75] could not have served Israel's cause better had he been a card-carrying member of Sharon's Likud party."[27]

Spymaster: "Palestinian President Arafat [4 Aug. 1929–11 Nov. 2004] was poisoned during the build-up to the American elections when his protection from poisoning was suddenly removed. The first poisoning on 20 October 2004 gave him stomach pains making him really sick by 29 October. He was vomiting and unable to eat or drink. This was made to look like 'leukaemia or some other blood disorder' with an 'abnormally low count of blood platelets'. This took him out of the country to a Clamart military hospital in Paris where his wife Suha has lived for the last two and a half years with their daughter Zara Arafat (8).

"The second poisoning was powerful enough to put him into a 'reversible coma' (5 November 2004), the day after the American election result. The first poisoning hospitalised him and the second was to keep him in a coma on life support. Because he had never named a successor, Palestinian leadership was placed in hiatus, making the Palestine Liberation Organisation vulnerable to takeover, by yet another American/Israeli agent."

On 9 November, on Al Jazeera TV, Suha Arafat accused Palestinian officials of conspiring to kill her husband. "They're trying to bury him alive."

High-ranking ASIO officer: "To discredit her the International Monetary Fund [part of the UN and an American patsy] found US$1 billion in one of Arafat's offshore accounts. The money was missing from the Palestinian Treasury. The technology for this search was provided by America who monitor all the world's money transfers. Eventually closer to US$6 billion was found in Arafat's purse.

"Arafat took this money on American instructions and with American assistance. It is a common tactic of those offering bribes to give money in exchange for a favour, in this case more conflict, and then discredit that person and retrieve the money."

MICK P: "In this version, Arafat took someone else's money, not America's but the Palestinian Treasury's. Consequently the Israelis never took Arafat seriously and buried him alive, playing cat and mouse with him for his last three years, keeping him alive only as a toy

[27] *New Zealand Herald*, 12 November 2004, A22.

incapable of negotiating peace. Arafat was then discredited and killed, creating a power vacuum, while morally empowering Israel. This is called 'demonising the opponent' and was also used against Hitler and Stalin. They all deserve it, but they were all double agents."[28]

British SAS: "America wants to install puppet governments in every area of conflict. Because up to a third of America's gross national product is based in and around the military industrial complex, and because America is so dependent on oil, America is setting up puppet governments in all areas of conflict, and in all areas where there is oil, which, surprise surprise is the same thing. Afghanistan (drugs), Iraq (oil) and Syria (oil) are cases in point. These countries always 'attack' the West before America goes in and takes over their resources."

Arafat lived simply but was reported to pay his wife a monthly allowance of US$100,000. The fight for his power and fortune now begins with Suha Arafat. Her deceased husband has been sufficiently discredited, and his wife is now unable to return to her own country, having lost all influence. It's a tidy little stitch-up not dissimilar to those of WWII.

Arafat was poisoned (20 October and 5 November 2004) at the same time as the American election (28 October–3 November 2004) with the self-confessed war-maker George W. Bush re-elected (4 November 2004) and Arafat dying on 11 November 2004 (11.11.2004). Whenever such symmetrical dates are attached you know it was a planned event.

Spymaster: "Britain's prime minister Tony Blair is also not immune to bribes. The war-maker George W. Bush called again for Britain to support the war in Iraq in early October 2004 as a part of the 'Coalition of the Willing'. This was a month before the American election and Bush needed Britain's support in order to get re-elected. Many other countries, including Spain and Japan, had pulled out."

On 8 November 2004 a radio bulletin said that Blair was beginning to look like "The greatest British prime minister since Winston Churchill". Churchill himself was a war-maker and both were heavily compromised. Both were occultists and both were rock spiders (paedophile minders).

British Intelligence Officer, 12 November 2004: "On 10 November 2004, it was revealed that Tony Blair had bought a £3.5 million apartment on the Thames – the ferrets are all over this.

[28] 'MICK P' is a Member of the Intelligence Community Knowledge Pool.

"In order to get countries to support America in the Iraq war, Bush had the FBI pull out all the smut files on every political leader. Tony Blair, it was found, was covering for and promoting those involved in a paedophile ring involving knights and at least one prominent royal, a second cousin to the queen.[29]

"Britain's Tony Blair is now a fully-fledged puppet for the American military industrial complex, which is why he has been in power for so long. The media is the propaganda machine for the war machine. It's just as Winston Churchill said:

'The first casualty of war is the truth'.
All the war media are embedded
and the media is *bound* to tell the lies
the military industrial complex want told."

In the Iraq war, America's death toll was minimised to 1500 and the civilian death toll as officially 17,000, but in the real world it was over 100,000 as of April 2005.

By June 2006 the official American death toll had risen to 2,500 and the official Iraqi civilian death toll had dropped to 50,000. This meant that in the 14 months of American-Iraq war from April 2005 to June 2006 at least 50,000 Iraqis have miraculously not died. This would make the truth very dead in Iraq and Allied media capable of raising the dead.

Even the Iraqi Health Ministry has acknowledged the 50,000 death toll as an undercount.[30] The problem is that the violence has been so extreme in the north and the west with the used of plutonium-tipped missiles and rolling thunder (a rolling wall of fire 100 metres high and 800 metres wide) that often there are no bodies left to count and no one left to say how many died. The 'body count war lie' has been purposefully exacerbated by cut telephone and power lines, but we all know the real reason for America's atrocious acts in Iraq.

> The worse Iraq gets, the more justification there is for oil price increases and those oil prices are set worldwide. It is not diplomacy that controls the world, but oil. Diplomacy is just something sodomists fake under the guise of being employed by governments whose employees are elevated depending on their level of involvement in shame

[29] This was the Dunblane massacre in 1996 in which 16 school children were murdered by Thomas Hamilton.

[30] *Los Angles Times*, 25 June 2006.

. . . and the measuring stick of shame is paedophilia . . .
hence rock spider Prime Ministers.

James Bond III: "Iraq is being depopulated by 'Rolling Thunder', 800 metres of ground-level rolling flame . . ."

Spymaster: "And the Israelis have developed plutonium-tipped rockets. The bodies are simply vaporising and vaporised bodies can't be counted."

All this for American access to oil upon which its superior survival depends, with the doubling of oil prices to fund the war. It's just as the American comedian Craig Kilborn said:

"How did our oil get under their sand?"

A week after the election, America went into Fallujah with its "biggest military assault since WWII". They decimated Fallujah killing several hundred rebels (breeding males) each day and untold civilians (these are not reported).

MICK P: "They were due to attack oil rich Iran anytime from October 2004, using Israeli aircraft off American aircraft carriers, with the intent to drop low-radiation nuclear bombs, decimate the population, and take over the oil fields . . . but on 9 October 2004, through an Israeli-Iranian treff in a chip factory in the colonies, Iran confirmed that they had a large number of nuclear weapons hidden under the likes of school buildings.

"These were purchased from India, via Sweden (India's nuclear weapons agent). Sweden has a nice name, so no one suspects. So instead, tens of thousands of Indians and 3000 Swedes were killed and another oil field was taken over on 26 December 2004 in what became known as the Boxing Day Tsunami."

Spymaster: "Much of the technology used in the tsunami was trialled by the New Zealand Army off Whangaparoa Peninsula during WWII. In those days it was destined for use against low-lying ground in Japan."

MICK P: "HAARP[31] was used to create the main earthquake. The six minor earthquakes around Diego Garcia, the US military base in

[31] 'HAARP' stands for 'High-frequency Active Auroral Research Program' based in Tok Road, Gakona, 300 km southeast of Fairbanks in Alaska. It is run by the Phillips Laboratory of Hanscom AFB in Massachusetts and is sponsored by the Office of Naval Research and the US Air Force. It has the ability to control the weather, volcanoes, earthquakes and tectonic plates, and is part of the 'Global Warming' scam.

the upper-middle of the Indian Ocean ere caused by NZ-styled bombs placed well before the Tsunami hit. Consequently, Diego Garcia suffered no damage, despite the base being 0.6 m (2 ft) above sea level. US ships were also given two-weeks notice to leave the Indian Ocean.

"There is also a move to disappear islands off maps for use as military bases. Diego Garcia is disappearing, just as Kodak Island has already disappeared."

If Burma's high casualty rate made it to the media, it would have brought unwanted attention to Diego Garcia, a nuclear missile base. Burma colluded and denied the bulk of their casualties.

Control of the media is essential to acts of war.
Truth is still the first casualty of war.
Lies are told before and after strikes.

It seems that nuclear arms are a strange form of peace that protect oil fields. Ironically, no-radiation nuclear bombs are also the symbol of the anti-patriotic movement.

Vet: "The war in Iraq is now having a demographic effect on the Iraqi population for the simple reason that there are so many car-bombings and shootings, all entirely concentrated on the young. This is a sure indication that the Mossad and the CIA are at work. Whenever they run an insurrection, they engineer demographic change and one of the largest groups hit in Iraq have been the 'breeding cows' (females anywhere from 2- to 20-years-old).

"Concentrating war on a very finite section of population is a known Israeli and CIA tactic. The CIA used it in South America where they ran genocidal conflicts in conjunction with the Mossad. When school came out there were no breeding cows (schoolgirls). This was even noticeable after the CIA coup against Allendé in 1973.

"The CIA trained the local Argentine Army Special Forces in the College of the Americas where they did the short graduate course, 'How to be a paedophile'. As a result, the Argentine Army Special Forces couldn't drive their international 6 x 6 trucks passed school bus stops without arresting nearly every schoolgirl in sight."

The CIA have never been an intelligence organisation.
The CIA's motto is TO PROTECT AMERICAN BUSINESS INTERESTS.
The CIA cherry picks its intelligence to suit its business goals.

This becomes obvious in the light of George Herbert Bush who was born oil rich, ran Saddam Hussein in oil rich Iraq, became the head of the CIA, and then became President of the United States. When George installed his son George into the same position, a large amount of American self-sabotage occurred with 9-11 being called "another Pearl Harbor".

The George Bushes used the Georg Ludwig trick and blamed 9-11 on any country they wanted to go to war with, especially ones with their dictators running them. This had long been back-engineered and Iraq was an oil rich country with a different religion.

These new Christian-Islamic wars (YOU HAVE – WE WANT) were created with increasing the price of oil in mind. Because the oil price is fixed internationally, regardless of who attacks who, any war by anybody, as long as it hits the media, profits all the oil owners.

The bigger the media hit,
the bigger the oil hike.

To humans at war, war is everything.
To the oil companies,
war is an itch that makes them rich.

Wars have been back-engineered. That is, treaties, agreements and contracts (cause and effect) have been placed on paper beforehand to ensure maximum profit and minimal interference. The United Nations is a case in point. Since the UN receives 50% of its funding from the US, it has come under the thumb of the CIA.

The UN has no opposition
when conflicts serve American interest.
No American can be charged by the UN
for international war crimes.

The UN is now a white paper on war, drugs and paedophilia and only those with secret CV's of corruption, murder, bribe taking, drug use, paedophilia and front-marriages (intell. files held by the CIA, the FBI, the Mossad and the KGB) are considered for any position of influence.

Secretary general of NATO Lord George Robertson: "Jaap [de Hoop Scheffer] has a distinguished record as both diplomat and politician that make him superbly qualified to be secretary general of NATO . . . I am delighted that we have found the right man to ensure NATO remains the world's most successful defense alliance." Lord Robertson went on to become deputy chairman of the British-based Telecoms group Cable and Wireless – the ultimate position for spying on drug and paedophile markets . . . and supplying them.

NATO's new secretary general is Amsterdam born Jaap de Hoop Scheffer. Jaap was a reserve officer in Dutch Air Force, senior diplomat before entering Parliament in 1986 and is described as "as extremely talented professional". Jaap: "the enemy is international terrorism . . .. that is why NATO is in Afghanistan."[32]

After near bankruptcy post-WWII, Monaco's bank was taken over by Aristole Onassis. Monaco then became a meeting point for drug shipments, washing drug money . . . and a tax haven.

The Pope John Paul II (Karol Jozef Wojtyla) and Prince Rainier were both terminally ill and NATO went in search of new drug markets for their newly acquired role of drug trafficking Afghan heroin. The paedophile Lord Robertson (Dunblane massacre) knew of the New Zealand government's paedophilia through the US Customs naming of Jonathan Hunt (Speaker of the House) as a paedophile in September 2004 and the ongoing intelligence documented homosexual child-sex abuse of Peter Davis (husband of Prime Minister Helen Clark) from pre-1979 to his arrest at San Francisco's Airport on 7 June 2006 where he propositioned an underaged Mexican boy by grabbing his crutch and saying "How about it?" The underaged boy turned out to be a policeman and Davis was arrested. First Laddy Davis claimed diplomatic immunity and was rescued by the RNZAF and three diplomatic officers (Sodomy Olympics).

Jaap de Hoop Scheffer went to Australia and New Zealand and gave a speech at Wellington's Victoria University on 31 March 2005: "We have come closer together over the last three years . . . Australia and New Zealand were the top candidates for NATO partnerships . . . NATO is everywhere." He arrived into New Zealand with 10 kg of Afghan heroin via diplomatic pouch. Once this new market was accepted the two previous drug lords were knocked off.

The next day (1 April 2005) the homosexual paedophile Jonathan Hunt became New Zealand's High Commissioner to Britain. The following day the Pope died (2 April 2005) and Prince Rainier (codenamed 'Tax') died four days later (6 April 2005). Both were involved in drugs and money laundering. Tavistock's MI-6 drug activator Peter Frampton

[32] *BBC News*, 23 September 2003.

then appeared in New Zealand on television (11 May 2005) using words and coded phrases to activate the baby boomer's drug habit. Tavistock's Frampton was the popular culture hook into the heroin market.

Minister of Health Annette King was responsible for the cover up of police paedophilia at Banks Ave in Christchurch. She moved the focus to a Christchurch kindergarten and this was written up by Internal Affairs agent Linley Hood in *A City Possessed*. The excessively weak Minister of Police George Hawkins was then replaced by the 'sustainable-corruption Minister' of Health Annette King on 19 October 2005.

In order to become the Minister of Police, Annette King delivered the Afghan/NATO heroin to the police for distribution prior to the 17 September 2005 rigged election. As a reward, Annette King became Associate Minister of Defence, Trade, and Race Relations (all 19 October 2005–3 May 2006). The police distributed the Afghan heroin to the gangs on 30 November/1 December 2005 and planted drugs on any gang member who did not comply.

On 3 May 2006, once the Afghan heroin had taken hold, all of Annette King's positions were upgraded to Minister of Police, State Services, and Transport. This provided Annette King with full cover. Annette King has a Bachelor of Arts, a Post Graduate in Dental Nursing and was a practicing dental nurse from 1967–81. Her daughter was involved in drug dealing and was struck off as a teacher.

New Zealand's Minister of Police is a heroin enabler.

Intelligence officers: "The Afghan heroin definitely came into New Zealand by diplomatic pouch." It arrived in March 2005 with street word that it had arrived in February 2005, thus diverting the focus of the search. All of this came as a backdrop to Helen Clark's status as the highest-ranking KGB operative in New Zealand, former St Petersburg prostitute and Tavistock St Petersburg graduate.

Helen Clark is the prime contender for the position of Secretary General of the United Nations. She was filmed having sex with another woman at Anderson's Cottage (better known as Lincoln Cottage), near the White House on the night of 3/4 January 2003. This gave the crooked American President George W. Bush full control over her, hence his backing for the KGB operative Clark as the Secretary General of the pitifully useless and massively corrupt United Nations.

During WWII, MI-6 and the OSS were never intelligence organisations. They were BIG BUSINESS MAFIA with leanings towards the occult and homosexuality, just as they are today.

The Americans have dismembered Iraq so thoroughly they are now ready to hollow out their old enemy Iran for the simple reasons that:

1. Iran has oil.
2. Iran has a different religion.
3. Iran is not part of the Rothschild central banking system.
4. Politics is a sodomite's holiday; DIPLOMACY IS THE SODOMY OLYMPICS; peace accords merely set the boundaries for the next conflict; the media are compromised talking hairdos and any conflict the media releases, staged or otherwise, increases the price of oil.
5. The only politics that counts is oil.
6. America is powerless without oil.
7. America is all-powerful with oil.
8. If Iraq had no oil, there would be no war there. Similarly if Iran had no oil, there would be no war there. Without oil Middle East wars would be considered humanist conflicts and the UN would step in, no doubt taking bribes of paedophilia before handing out food rations.
9. Tony Blair won't speak out against war in the Middle East because the FBI files link him to the Dunblane massacre paedophile ring.
10. Oil is not the product of 10 trillion dinosaurs dying in one place. Dead dinosaurs produce soap, not oil.
11. Oil is the natural product of the Sun's energy and Earth's Outer and Inner Cores. Oil greases the friction between the Outer Core rotating at 8.3 revolutions per day in one direction and the Mantle and Crust rotating at 1 revolution per day in the other direction. This creates the mythical interface speed of 1000 miles per hour.
12. Superman got it right. Watch your cartoons. They have more news than a talking hairdo, especially during times of war. For rational thought watch *The Simpsons* and *South Park* cartoons. For irrational propagandist talking hairdos spouting war, watch *Fox* televison.

Lost Leaders

Common to all of these men is that they succumbed to the positions given them and took on the beliefs of their own subjects. They all began to believe in their own greatness. By and large their place in history is by way of emptiness, fault, and double agent training, rather than working patriotically for their people.

Hitler, Stalin, Churchill, Roosevelt, Truman, Hussein, bin Laden, Arafat, Blair and Bush have all been, or still are, puppets of war. They were not the prime makers of war, for if they were to make peace, they would have been liquidated with the rest of the peace-makers – Neville Chamberlain (1940), Rudolf Hess (1941), Karl Horn (1941), Colonel Claus Count Schenk von Stauffenberg (1944), Wilheim Canaris (1945), Mahatma Gandhi (1948), John F. Kennnedy (1963), Martin Luther King (1968) . . .

> It was the West who deliberately confused and misinformed their citizens to avoid linking the dots that WWII was an organised war, a massive depopulation exercise – with the British sabotaging peace talks at every turn, the Americans getting into the war with complicit self-sabotage (Pearl Harbor), and the British developing a hatred for their German cousins with Dieppe and D-Day.

Pseudo documentaries such as *Hitler of the Andes* by David Howards and Madoc Roberts are yet another propaganda exercise for the British. It promotes the myth and avoids the evidence at every turn right down to the detail, making important names inaudible, interviewing fifty percent of the people without naming them and showing documents with any information that could be followed up, blurred out.

The 2002 *Hitler of the Andes* mystery/doco concludes that few now believe Hitler was ever in Argentina, but that fantasists still follow Hitler from the foothills of the Andes to Antarctica. It concludes that they solved the mystery of Hitler by giving evidence that Hitler was not in Argentina or North America, but was buried outside Berlin and flushed down the River Elbe. But this story, although true of one of Hitler's doppelgängers, is not followed up. It contains within it all the hallmarks of another lost leader –

A mystery wrapped in a riddle inside an enigma.

Adolf Hitler lived with Eva Braun in Spain, in Barcelona, in the Parc de la Ciutadella opposite the Natural History Musem and in the Montserrat Monastery. Hitler wanted to continue his most far-reaching missions, and these did involve Antarctica, particularly the secret German submarine base at South 69° 10' and West 4° 15'.[33]

"The Germans had frequented Antarctica since the 1920s. Here they discovered an undersea entrance to a cavern south of South America in Queen Maud Land on the Princess Astrid Coast and named the mountains of their chosen area after German bureaucrats of the time like the Mühlig-Hofmann Mountains and the Wohlthat Mountains. These names remain today.

"Richard E. Byrd was the most famous American Antarctic researcher and was the first person to fly over the South Pole in 1929. In mid-November 1938 (10 months before WWII) he showed a movie of his Antarctic flight in Hamburg, Germany. Very soon after Byrd was promoted from civilian to high-ranking US Navy Admiral.

"The Germans went to Antarctica two months later based on what Richard E. Byrd had shown them. Under polar-experienced Captain Alfred Ritscher, the Germans made 15 flights over some 600,000 square kilometres (4%) of Antarctica from 19 January 1939 and took 11,000 pictures of the area. They discovered ice-free areas with lakes and small signs of vegetation. These aerial photographs showed that the 1931 Norwegian maps of the interior were fake.

"Immediately after this, Nazis began building an underground city on the Princess Astrid Coast, and in 1940 Nazi engineers began construction of buildings to withstand 60°C below zero. During the war, underground bases were the de rigueur for protection and secrecy (Harz and Thuumlringen) and the Germans have maintained underground construction activity at Antarctica since 1941.

"The Nazis referred to this impregnable city as New Berlin (Neuberlin) in an area called New Schwabenland, Neuschwabenland, Neu Schwabia or Base 211. It is built to withstand an atomic attack and a nuclear winter. Schwabenland refers to a place 'where the population is as thick as pig-shit and reluctant to take orders.'

"Neuschwabenland refers to a place "where the population are intelligent innovative technocrats and take to orders impulsively". It also refers to "New Cockroach Land", a place where atomic survival is possible.

[33] With receding ice, this entrance has now moved.

"In 1943, four years after they began in earnest, the Commander-in-Chief of the German Navy, Admiral Karl Doenitz (1891–1980) stated, 'The German submarine fleet has even now established an earthly paradise, an impregnable fortress, for the Führer, in whatever part of the world.'

"In 1947 the American Naval Task Force 68 led by Admiral Byrd under Operation HIGHJUMP tried to roll the remaining Germans out of New Schwabenland, but they failed. American Operation HIGHJUMP maps say that the Americans left the German side of Antarctica 'unexplored'. Instead an agreement was reached between the Americans and Nazis. This usually occurs when the riches or technology are more than the both of them could share."[34]

> WWII was an agreement between all parties. It was planned in 1919 with players tagged as early as 1836 (Maria Anna Schicklgruber). The major players were trained at Britain's Tavistock from 1907 – Stalin (Koba, Losif Vissarionovich Dzhugashvili) and Adolf Hitler (Edmund Hitler, 1912).
>
> "All his life Hitler owed his success largely to one or the other of his enemies. Now, once more, his ill-wishers – as if in a last display of all the mistakes of the era – made it possible for him to live a mythical posthumous life . . . only a mind that has learned nothing from the misfortunes of these times will call him the man of a single nation and refuse to recognise that a powerful tendency of the age culminated in him, a tendency that dominated the entire first half of this century."[35]
>
> Official history still covers for him.

Adolf Hitler died of stomach cancer on 19 February 1950 – a death entirely in keeping with British Intelligence traditions dating back to Napoleon.

As a neurotic empty man, Hitler was made evil and great by virtue of others playing puppeteer on his emptiness.

---

[34] *Flying the Planet*, Volume II, CLASSIFIED.

[35] *Hitler*, p. 750.

"Conspiracy, fact and fiction rushed to fill the vacuum
left by Hitler's absence . . ."[36]
and what we got was every government in the world
immitating Hitler.

Hitler has become the new standard.

Roosevelt outsmarted at Yalta (4–11 February 1945) while Stalin and Churchill share a memory.

[36] *Hitler of the Andes.*

Churchill, Hitler and Stalin Work Together

Chaplin Plays the Muse

When the British soldiers returned from war on the Continent and compared notes with British Intelligence in Britain, they suddenly felt very sick. The British Intelligence chiefs woke up in 1945 and realised they had been had, that the war was an arrangement, a fallacy, a pre-organised hoax with goals well defined before WWII ever broke out. This led to personal disillusionment amongst many high-ranking soldiers who then refused to talk about the war – the tight-lipped, big-eared generation, as indicative of determined survivors (large noticeable ears), who were bitter about their responsibilities (tight-lipped).

British Agents – Adolf Hitler and Dr Theodor Morell

Hitler's doctor, Dr Theodor Morell, was a British agent, Freemason, secret Tibetan Lodge member and 'Vril' practitioner, placed there by King George V and VI. These were all qualities he shared with Adolf Hitler, although Hitler denies the Freemasonry connection.

'Vril' was the life force as taught in Tibet to Gurdjeiff, who taught Hitler's dentist, Dr Friedrich Krohn and Professor Karl Haushofer, both of them Hitler's primary spiritual mentors in the occult. Vril was so popular as a concept in the early 1900s, it led to the brand name 'Bovril' – 'Bovine and Vril'. Karl Haushofer's son Albrecht was the Duke of Hamitlon's lover, who was the Duke of Kent's lover, who was King George VI's brother.

Dr Morell was offered a position as doctor to the Shah of Persia. This is a tell-tale sign that he was a British agent, as the Shah of Persia was a British hostage, allowed to function, but completely under British rule.

Dr Morell had been a doctor on board elegant trans-Atlantic liners between Hamburg and Buenos Aires and was a fashionable dermatologist at the Berlin Tennis Club, making him something of a VIP. Although he was recognised and well received by high society (he was a short fat curio), the opinions of his colleagues and historians were that he was a complete charlatan. I don't disagree, but he was a purposeful charlatan. The fact that Hitler's own staff didn't stop his over-medication defies logic and points to a phoney war with disaffected double agents.

Hitler's photographer, Heinrich 'Heini' Hoffmann was an alcoholic and latent homosexual with gonorrhoea whose wife had just died. Dr Morell switched to specialising in venereal disease from 1936 and was invited to treat 'Heini' who just happened to be employing Eva Braun. Only those with British intelligence connections had access for the drugs required to treat venereal disease and this gave Morell access to Hitler in the weeks afterwards.[1]

From January 1937 Dr Morell was Hitler's preferred doctor and like Winston Churchill with Lord Moran, Hitler preferred doctors of dubious repute.

Dr Morell didn't drink or smoke, but he ate like a horse, belched like a mule, stunk like a pig and had chronic flatulence as did Hitler under Morell's treatment. The 5' 6", 105 kg (16½ stone) Dr Morell was not popular in Hitler's circle, was refused an SS uniform, was a social outcast and chuckled at anything Hitler said, just in case it was funny.

Hitler didn't eat meat, poultry, fish or eggs. He ate fruit, vegetables and pastries. By October 1937, Hitler's consumption of pills overtook his consumption of food and his health declined rapidly. Morell gave Hitler morphine, hypnotics, dextrose, hormones and vitamins and endless anti-gas pills compounded with strychnine and belladonna, up to 16 per day.

Dr Morell systematically ruined Hitler's health, feeding him banned drugs, toxins and narcotics which aged him prematurely. Dr Brandt even alleged that Morell had systematically poisoned Hitler with strychnine disguised as anti-gas pills. Morell more or less admitted to this in their shared prison cell in 1945: "Hitler was never ill".[2]

"Morell converted the largely healthy man that Hitler had been earlier into one constantly plied with injections and tablets which made Hitler more or less dependent on him; he played on Hitler's neuropathic nature by spouting utter rubbish about how Hitler's heavy workload meant that he was burning energy at the same rate

[1] The Scottish Freemason Sir Alexander Fleming had pioneered the use of Salvarsan for syphilis.

[2] *The Secret Diaries of Hitler's Doctor*, p. 67.

as people in the tropics, and that the lost energy had to be replaced by all manner of injections like iodine, vitamins, calcium, heart-and-liver extract and hormones."[3]

Dr Morell kept Hitler heavily medicated with an antagonistic cocktail of uppers and downers – an action which suggested he was deliberately medicating Hitler into insanity. He gave Hitler 28 different pills and injections each day, some of them more than once. These were a combination of stimulants, digestive aids, anti-influenza drugs, vitamins, hormones, and glucose including Prostacrinum (an extract of sperm and prostatic tissue), and Bromnervalit against depression, Indelan to stimulate appetite, Eupaverin to alleviate colitis, Eufrasin against colibacillary infection, ecalyptus lozenges and even Dr Körster's quack pills.

After Hitler's second attempt at peace, which the British sabotaged, as well as his planned escape to America in June 1941, the doses were increased with injections of strophanthus and nicotinic acid. By August 1941 Hitler was nauseous and had uncontrollable shivering. His legs became oedematous (they held water), he became weak and deteriorated rapidly.

Dr Morell ignored the side-effects and increased his doses adding Cardizol, Coramine, and Sympatol and even more anti-depressants. When that didn't work, he gave Hitler caffeine, Pervitin (speed) and Vitamultina (amphetamines with even more caffeine). The bulk of the Nazi military were also on speed and they had containers to be accessed in an emergency.

Hitler had a heart attack, arterial hypertension, icteric hepatitis, his eye haemorrhaged, his right eye closed up, he had long and frequent lapses of memory, constantly burped and aged five years to every one. His staff reacted to him in much the same way that most people react to heavily medicated old people – they sold off his assets. By 1942, Dr Morell's drug-induced condition of Hitler had become such a success that even the Allied Headquarters kept an eye on Hitler's 'psychiatric situation'.

Hitler's own generals were completely baffled by his ever-changing battle plans. This gave them further impetus to 'run away from that crazy old person' and defect. As a result of Hitler's drug-induced

[3] Dr Erwin Geising, 'Report on My Treatment of Hitler', June 1945, cited, ibid. p. 19.

madness there was a plan to kill Hitler using Martin Bormann's gun (a universal agent) and there was another attempt by the German High Command/British agent Hermann Goering, who attempted a Palace Revolution in early 1945. Hitler's madness was deliberately induced and he was meant to die many times, but the assassination attempts kept failing or the doppelgängers were killed instead.

This was a direct result of having MI-6 arm and finance Hitler's would-be killers, when MI-6 were also in charge of looking after Hitler's life . . . so only the doppelgängers died.

There is no doubt that Dr Morell was a quack and an expert quack. His treatment history showed that he wanted Hitler to 'govern in a mad rage of irrational forgotten decisions' which he achieved on behalf of King George VI. It was quite brilliant really. Hitler spent most of his time burping and leaning to the right, rather than carrying out war strategies. His movements, moustache and hairstyle certainly usurped those of Charlie Chaplin and this gave great mirth to the Freemasons.[4]

Between 1939 and 1941 Hitler started WWII with the masterful intuition of a double agent. Between 1941 and 1945 he spent four years in a heavily medicated stupor. This was followed by five years (1945–50) of recuperation, after which he was assassinated by the very people who trained him, drugged him, and gave him the information he needed to achieve his international status. It was a 40-year wind-up and wind-down that created a platform for experimentation, which gave rise to a plethora of inventions, and killed 50 million people in the process.

World War II was a 'how can we most easily rule' experiment. Regrettably the answer was:

1. The deconstruction of disgruntled foreign nationals as double agents, activated at will and deactivated by debriefing.
2. The medication of the masses with a daily cocktail of uppers and downers and mild poisons like beer, coffee, cigarettes, medication, drugs, fluoride and radioactive water.
   (See *The Fluoride Con, Appendix 2*)
3. Government department and police-enforced socialism, or communism, of which today's brand is *sex-communism* or *gender-feminism* where children are removed from their fathers at 45 times the rate of war.

---

[4] *Very Illustrious Patients*, pp. 91–107.

War has been a huge success.

What happens rapidly in war, happens slowly in peacetime. War has always been the acid-test blueprint for what the next society will become.

According to the medical records on Dr Morell, he suffered from partial paralysis and lost his ability to speak on 17 June 1945. He was formally arrested a month later on 17 July and remanded in the prison at Reichenhall where he shared a cell with Hitler's competent doctor, Karl Brandt. Morell's last words to him were:

"I wish I were somebody else."

With British complicity, Dr Morell was judged too sick to attend the war trials of the 23 other Nazi doctors which began on 15 November 1946. Only the competent doctors were accused. Ironically, it was the competent Dr Brandt who was hanged in 1947 and Morell was allowed to live out his days, although with Hitler's curse.

Dr Morell was "cleared of war crimes" and discharged on 20 June 1947 (Prisoner No. 52,160) and went straight to the local clinic in Munich, where he was treated for arteriosclerosis in the same way that Hitler was – by injection. Within eleven months he was dead.

"There is some evidence that Himmler, the Gestapo chief, Martin Bormann, Hitler's executive officers and the ill-famed Dr Morell conspired in a plot to slowly poison the Führer."[5]

Dr Morell was a self-convinced suspiscionist who did more to destroy Hitler in the last three years of the war than anyone else, or anything else. (See *Unlikely Heroes, Appendix 9*)

The fat man is an unsung hero. In war, even the delusional have their uses. British agent, Dr Theodor Morell (22 July 1886–26 May 1948):

"Well done, true and faithful servant."

James Bond Revisited

While working as the intelligence officer at Grizedale Hall in 1941 Ian Fleming met a woman raising Herdwick sheep in the Lake District. Her name was Mrs William Heelis who wrote and illustrated *The Tale of Peter Rabbit* (1900) under her maiden name Beatrix Potter (1866–1943). Fleming promised her he would become a thriller writer and that his books would appeal to children.

[5] *Collier's* weekly, 4 May 1946.

Ian Fleming was a wartime-only sailor and after the war he became 'the foreign manager of the *Sunday Times*' (1945–59). However, this was more or less a cover for other operations including his heavy drinking and womanising. He would go through women like there was no tomorow.

In 1952, at the age of 41, Fleming was approached by his bank manager who insisted he write books as his only possible method of paying back his increasing debts. His first book, *Casino Royale*, appeared in 1953 to good reviews. On 21 October 1954, CBS screened a television version of *Casino Royale*. The show was quickly forgotten but a James Bond comic strip appeared. In 1960 film producer Harry Saltzman paid Ian Fleming US$50,000 for six months' rights to the Fleming novels.

Sean Connery (32), in the British Royal Navy from 1946–48 (aged 16–18), was cast for the lead role. On 16 January 1962 the filming of *Dr. No* began. Ian Fleming recommended his author/singer/actor/composer/playwright and witty friend Noel Coward (1899–1973) for the part of *Dr. No*. Noel Coward was Fleming's homosexual neighbour on the North Shore of Jamaica and had been the lover of the Duke of Kent for 19 years. The written reply came back, "No, no, no".

Rather ironically, two years later, in an act that linked reality, fake reality and illusion, Noel Coward's cook and bodyguard Big Tom Stanford was commissioned to kill one of M's doppelgänger Hitler's (February 1964). This theme was followed up in the trademark James Bond opening shot, using a pinhole camera photographing the inside of a pistol barrel, the person who appears as James Bond is not Sean Connery, but doppelgänger stuntman Bob Simmons.

Looking down the barrel of a gun, it was a stunt man.

Dr. No premiered nine months later on 6 October 1962 in the Pavilion Cinema at London's Picadilly Circus. It was an instant hit. In the spring of 1963 *Dr. No* also became a smash in America. The initial gross takings of US$20 million was 20 times the US$1 million budget.[6]

In 1963, Ian Fleming sent Chris Creighton, the real James Bond, £20,000 in £5 notes to be shared amongst the survivors of OP James Bond. In those days £20,000 would buy each OP James Bond survivor a house.

---

[6] John Cork, *Inside Dr. No*.

"Many of James Bond's experiences have some basis in fact. Facts that Fleming came across while serving as assistant to Britain's Director of Naval Intelligence [Rear-Admiral John Godfrey] during WWII, which he has used to embroider the exciting adventures of secret agent 007, James Bond."[7]

Ian Fleming was a big drinker and James Bond's drink was a medium dry vodka martini with a twist of peeled lemon, shaken, not stirred. The James Bond movies were satires of Fleming's personal and operational experiences in government Black Ops. As in the movies, the British Secret Service was indeed on the eighth floor of a building in Regent's Park, London. In the movie the intelligence company was known as 'Universal Exports'. In real life they have very similar names.

After the war, Major Desmond Morton (M) sent Christopher Creighton to become an actor, training at the Royal Academy of Dramatic Art (formerly the Old Vic) where he met Roger Moore who later played James Bond, and made contacts for Creighton to become a movie director with Warner Brothers in Hollywood.

In Hollywood Creighton wrote and produced *Murder at 3 am* (1952), acted with Noel Coward and Eva Gabor in *Nude with Violin*, acted in *Present Laughter* on Broadway (1957) and directed *Judgement in Prague* (1967) while under cover for NATO. He also acted and directed for television.

Of all the James Bonds, Roger Moore was Creighton's closest lookalike starring in seven films from 1973's *Live and Let Die* to *A View to Kill* in 1985. The real James Bond, Christopher Creighton, remained active in secret intelligence work until the early 1980s.

After the war, M continued to give Chris Creighton a bad name, adding "supposed villainy, psychopathic tendencies, gambling, bad debts and bankruptcy to his list of failings". M also encouraged this reputation amongst his father and his stepmother, which saved Creighton's life many times. He was, for undercover reasons, in the RAF as the disaffected pilot, John Davis, turncoat, arch-hater of Britain, and not in the Royal Navy. His name appeared in the Nazi list as an ardent disciple of the Fascist leader Oswald Mosley, which caused him to be disowned by his father and stepmother, who passionately abused the name Chris

[7] *Dr. No* trailer, 1962, *Inside Dr. No.*

Creighton whenever they were questioned. It was full cover.[8]

Laurence Olivier and Ralph Richardson (both ex-Fleet Air Arm Lieutenant-Commanders) and Somerset Maugham (gay) were all active in counter-espionage, some triple agents, and all becoming famous actors. They were rewarded with a life of luxury for their efforts, and good on them.

Spies were often retrained as Shakespearian actors. They are trained into people others want to be and will therefore talk to, spilling the beans. It used to be Shakespearian actors, but now it is televison and movie actors, musicians and DJs.

The British Mitford sisters took their lead from the heads of the British Conservative Party and via them it was the done thing to be pro-Hitler. As a result, Diana Mitford (1910–2003), the most outstanding beauty of her time, met Sir Oswald Mosley in 1931 and married him in Berlin in 1936 at the home of Hitler's propaganda minister, Josef Goebbels, with Hitler attending.

Her sister Unity Walkrie Mitford (1914–48) went to live in Germany and soon met Hitler and slept with him. She attempted suicide in the British Garden outside the Bavarian Interior Ministry on the day Britain declared war on Germany. She was shot in the right temple with a small automatic pistol but survived another eight years as a brain-damaged invalid. Her father was Lord Baron Redesdale (David Mitford, 1878–1958) who had seven daughters, all notable beauties and brought up in isolation on the Cotswald Estates, almost as an experiment.

When Diana Mitford was interviewed recently she was rational and knew what the Nazis were involved in: "Hitler made the trains run on time and it was only afterwards we discovered the cost." She was, however, as shallow as a puddle, but these people too have their place.

The world celebrates simple-mindedness wrapped in beauty
and makes them famously so.

---

[8] *OPJB*, p. 230.

Churchill and Stalin

Stalin spoke perfect English and had spent almost four years training in England as a British agent. He could understand innuendo which showed that he had more than one English-speaking trainer.

Stalin later worked very closely with Churchill, using 'C' (Colonel Stewart Graham Menzies, 30 January 1890–29 May 1968) as his intermediary and they had over 1500 meetings. Stalin executed those whom he thought closer to C than him and eventually killed over 20 million people. C was trained at the Sandhurst Military Academy and in the Grenadier Guards.

The chiefs of the British Secret Service were always known as 'C'. "C's job was to direct espionage, sabotage, counter-espionage and much of the political warfare outside the British Empire . . . and to report to the Prime Minister."[9] Despite Winston Churchill and Colonel Stewart Graham Menzies being half-brothers, they did not get on and neither publicly declared who their shared father was. "Despite Churchill's animus for Menzies at this time, Menzies subsequently became Churchill's most important advisor."[10]

Spymaster: "Stalin had a similar relationship with his spook director, Sudopolotov, but treated him more harshly. Due to Stalin's paranoia, Sudopolotov was in and out of prison like a yo-yo. Eventually the prison staff allowed him to wear his uniform in prison and referred to him as 'Comrade, Major General' because they never knew how long he was going to stay."

Churchill warned Stalin of the imminent attack by Germany on the Soviet Air Force on the first day of Germany's invasion of Russia on 22 June 1940, as did Germany's Soviet Ambassador. Strangely Stalin chose to ignore both warnings and Germany wiped out most of Russia's air fleet on the first day.

All three, Churchill, Stalin and Hitler were operating under higher powers, powers that were controlling the war. These were the Freemasons, the Illuminati and the Rothschilds who were funding both sides of the war. They wanted the war to go on for as long as possible and to be as all-encompassing as possible. Profit and depopulation were the goal – even of their own people, the Jews.

[9] *The Secret Servant*, p. 14.

[10] Ibid.

Stalin's Intelligence was a mess, a reflection of the bloody chaos within the military. Every spy dreaded any communication from Moscow. No news was good news. Britain's greatest intelligence coup occurred when a spy in Germany was summoned to Moscow over travel expenses. Instead of turning up to Moscow, he walked into a British Embassy and spilled the beans.

Communism had a real appeal in Europe in the 1930s. It was a Utopian dream placed before the masses with the vision of unified wealth. To most, the Industrial Revolution had brought a poverty of work conditions and a loss of quality of life and Communism was to do the same over a third of the planet.

Nothing succeeds like making the same mistake twice.

Churchill made a special visit to see Charlie Chaplin in America in 1929 and then went underground for 10 years from 1929–39 while he planned the war that would serve all sides but cost the populations dearly. Both Churchill and Hitler were Psych-Ops trained. It would be silly to train Hitler without training Churchill. If Churchill wasn't trained, Hitler would have run rings around him. Churchill, Hitler and Stalin were all trained at the British Military Psych-Ops War Schools.

Chaplin Plays the Muse

Four days before Hitler's birth, Charlie Chaplin was born in Lambeth, London, on the 16 April 1889. Hitler (20 April 1889–19 February 1950) and Chaplin (16 April 1889–25 December 1977) had a similiarity to their lives and Chaplin mirrored and mocked Hitler, as any good mime artist should do. Both had questionable grandfathers and were fatherless at young ages (3 for Chaplin and 13 for Hitler). Chaplin was raised in an orphanage from 9 and Hitler lived in dosshouses from 19. Both were trained by comedians and knew that success depended on appealing to the sympathies of their audience. Both had their first loves die on them. Both were romantics, a soft touch, loved women, but couldn't live with them. Both were sexual deviants and raged against monogamy (Chaplin was into young girls and Hitler was a bisexual coprophiliac). Both were immigrants and had mental illness in their families. Both had confusion over their names of origin – Chaplin (née Tbonstein, Bodges and Harley) and Hitler (née Hiedler, Hutter, Schicklgruber). Both were accused of being Jewish.

The Jews often claim successful British-trained agents as having Jewish lineage, and rightly so. Often the agents are created two generations ahead. Hitler lived in Germany for 18 years before he got citizenship and Chaplin lived in America for 42 years and never got citizenship. Both were trained by British Intelligence and used to change the social landscape towards a One World Order.

Like Hitler, who studied under the Munich comedian Weiss Ferdl, Chaplin studied under the British comedian Fred Karno. Fred and Charlie went to Hollywood in September 1910. Hitler used his training for public speaking and Charlie went all the way in acting.

Charlie Chaplin's first play role was as 'Billy' in *Sherlock Holmes*. In the West he was set up to mock Hitler so the American public wouldn't treat Hitler as a threat. This worked very well with Chaplin adopting his out-turned feet, walking cane, British bowler hat and comical short moustache for his second silent movie *The Kid* on 6 January 1921, after which Hitler adopted his short moustache, first photographed on 8 November 1923.

Chaplin also made *The Gold Rush* (June 1925), *City Lights* (1931), wrote, directed and produced his first political film *Modern Times* (1936), wrote, directed and produced *The Great Dictator* (October 1940) based on Hitler, and Churchill's favourite movie, *Monsieur Verdoux* (1947) in which he takes on the persona of the nearest person or machine, and *Limelight* (October 1952).

As a result of the visual similarity between Charlie Chaplin and Adolf Hitler, Hitler was constantly in the funny pages, and Chaplin was used to play down the Hitler threat in America. In 1933 "If they had heard of Hitler at all, they probably thought he was just a comical fellow with a loud voice and ridiculous moustache".[11]

Chaplin admired Hitler and Hitler put up with Chaplin, knowing that he smoothed the way for him.

Chaplin had a front as a communist sympathiser, which he accomplished with actor's credit (FBI File No. 100-127090, p. 45/2063). This gave him access to communist connections in America and overseas. Chaplin spied on France, Africa, Germany, Italy, Switzerland and Japan (September 1931–June 1932) and on his return wrote the script for *Modern Times* based on Hitler. He then visited China and the South Pacific (April–June 1936) before WWII broke out.

[11] *The Amiable Prussian*, p. 86.

Many British agents were in the entertainment field and Charlie Chaplin was a huge success, his acting career far outshining his British Intelligence role. By 1916, at the beginning of his career, he was the highest-paid person in the world at US$10,000 per week, now the equivalent of US$2 million per week.

Hitler was first filmed silently giving speeches and looked ridiculous. He looked very Chaplinesque. The first talking picture (1921) was *The Jazz Singer*, a movie by Jews about Jews. By 1923 sound made Hitler a powerful film presence and Chaplin considered Hitler one of the greatest actors he had ever seen.

Hitler saw every American film he could. *The Lives of a Bengal Lancer* with Gary Cooper and Franchot Tone was his favourite and he loved Greta Garbo movies. Like many world leaders, Hitler couldn't tell the difference between a lesbian and a breeder.

The Nazis were convinced Chaplin was a Jew and Chaplin never denied it. Chaplin had the balls to visit Berlin in 1931 and the Nazis loathed his rapturous welcome. Chaplin then visited Venice expecting to meet with Mussolini, but Mussolini took his line from Hitler, banned his films and refused to meet him.

Against a background of aggression and appeasement where Jews were cleaning the pavement with toothbrushes, Chaplin announced (18 October 1938) he was going to make *The Great Dictator*. Many thought Chaplin was a comic David against a German Goliath. Three weeks later Kristallnacht brought a wave of violence against the Jews (9 November 1938) and on 20 April 1939 Hitler celebrated his 50th birthday with one of the biggest military parades in history.

Chaplin financed *The Great Dictator* entirely himself and filming began on 9 September 1939 under conditions of strict secrecy. This was six days after WWII broke out in Europe with America not officially joining for another two years.

No sooner had the filming finished than Hitler began his blitzkrieg. France fell in months and Denmark in a matter of hours. Chaplin was so appalled he spent another 111 days filming, changing the final speech, which became a parody of Hitler's latest actions. The same day this speech was filmed, Hitler drove into Paris to view his conquest. When Hitler returned to Berlin, he drove through a carpet of flowers, but it was a doppelgänger Hitler in the parading Mercedes (more portly with a smaller nose) as Hitler was in constant fear of being assassinated.

Chaplin gave his final speech in front of a flag with a double cross, wearing a hat with a double cross, alluding to Hitler and the war being a double cross. Chaplin wanted to premier *The Great Dictator* in Berlin but the British war-makers said they would ban the movie. After all, Chaplin's dictator was a caricature of their own 'double agent of war'.

Despite what the war-makers wanted *The Great Dictator* opened on 15 October 1940 in London at the height of the blitzes – almost as an attempt to destroy the movie theatres. It received standing ovations and calls for Chaplin, yet it was banned in Ireland, across Europe and in parts of South America. Roosevelt, who was Jewish but could not admit it, guaranteed its release in America. *The Great Dictator* was to become Chaplin's biggest moneymaker.

Hitler watched *The Great Dictator* and then watched it again two days later. Even the German Army saw the film.

In Belgrade, Yugoslavia, the 17-year-old Nikola Radosevic (now a filmmaker) working in film despatch, discovered a print of *The Great Dictator* and showed it to the Blue Ribbon, a group which never fired a shot. Their modus operandi was to make fun of the Germans. "We wanted Hitler to hear what Chaplin thought of him."

Nikola Radosevic substituted the German feature the Nazi soldiers were to see for *The Great Dictator*. "At the start of the show, the people didn't immediately realise what was going on, but after 40 minutes an SS man pulled out his gun and opened fire at the screen. All the others rushed out of the hall. They didn't want to stay any longer because something was against Hitler."

Chaplin was officially written off as a lefty of the far left, when he was, in fact, a non-political British agent who maintained his cover throughout his life. As with Christopher Creighton (James Bond) the cover went deep. On 13 March 1944, the communist newspaper *People's World* stated: "Charlie Chaplin had been a friend of the Soviet Union since 1917" (FBI File, 47/2063). He was a generous man who helped a lot of people out and said "I am for the little people". He was 1.65 m and 65 kgs, some 5' 5" and 145 lbs.

Charlie Chaplin's brief was to spy on communism in America, feed it back to Britain and to mollify Americans regarding Hitler and communism. He was playing the communists in America. As part of his British Intelligence briefing, Charlie Chaplin spent a week's camping holiday with Clare Sherridan, Winston Churchill's free love cousin.

". . . in September 1946, Chaplin will be subpoenaed before the United States House Committee on UnAmerican Activities where he will be questioned regarding his communist affiliations amid concern of his alleged partnership with a third political party" (FBI file p. 49/2003). That third party was Britain's MI-6 – essentially Winston Churchill, via Clare Sherridan (who had sculptured Lenin and Trotsky) and whatever other contacts Chuchill provided from 1929. After 42 years producing a 2063-page file, the FBI still didn't get it.

Chaplin wouldn't take American citizenship and the FBI were so desperate to get him, they considered charging him with purchasing too much cheese – more than the war rations would allow for one household. How cheesy is that? "Mr Charles Spencer Chaplin, you will receive the maximum penalty for the excessive consumption of war-rationed cheese. You are hereby sentenced to sit next to people who talk in talkies."

Chaplin had a weakness for young girls. His first two wives were 16 and his last was 18. Others look for such traits as it makes the agent controllable on threat of reputation alone. Both sides of this coin were a common trait in British agents and Chaplin was available for blackmail right throughout his career. Those blackmailed will usually even cover their own expenses in exchange for return cover. In exchange, Chaplin gave a respectable face to child-sex in Hollywood, was a British agent and was never charged.

At 59 Charlie Chaplin had an 18-year-old wife and a 21-year-old girlfriend, and went some way in inspiring Hugh Hefner's *Playboy* enterprise. As is typical of British agents into underaged girls, he was knighted as Sir Charles Spencer Chaplin in 1975, aged 86. This would have placed his last act of child-sex 18 years earlier in 1957, aged 68, while living in Switzerland with his most troublesome daughter Geraldine (b. 31 July 1944), just 13 years old at the time. It is typical of a child who sees or senses her father with another young girl to have attention tantrums, for which Geraldine was renowned.

Chaplin died on Christmas Day 1977, aged 88, having married three times (a fourth marriage was a Mexican farce to keep her relatives happy), with 10 surviving children from two marriages between May 1925 and July 1962. Charlie sired his last child, Christopher Chaplin (b. 6 July 1962) at the much-celebrated age of 72. His wives were Mildred Harris, 16 (15 when they met), Lita Grey, 16 (whom he married on his boat, the *Panacea* within two weeks of meeting her), and Oona O'Neill, 18.

Politically, Sir Charles Spencer Chaplin was very well informed, enough to take politics lightly.

> "I have no political views. I'm a comedian, not a politician...
> I don't want radical change, I want evolutionary change . . .
> I don't want spy censorship . . . I'm against dictatorship . . .
> I'm against everything . . . I believe the purpose of language
> is to conceal ideas rather than convey ideas."

He never revealed to anyone he was a British agent and he never told anyone when Hitler died, except through his artform.

As soon as Chaplin got word of Hitler's death at the end of February 1950, he wrote *Limelight,* started shooting in 1951, editing in spring 1952, with the first screening in London on 23 October 1952. It is the story of a fading clown who helps a paralysed dancer regain the use of their legs and achieve great fame. After the screening, Chaplin moved to Switzerland. Chaplin was connected to Hitler via British Intelligence and *Limelight* was his last movie. He was 63 at the time, and like Hitler, the most famous actor the world has ever known.

In the 1990s Charlie Chaplin was voted the greatest actor in movie history. Chaplin remains the second most famous person in the world. The first is Hitler. In the end, comedy is the most powerful tool for war.

> Chaplin: "Courage doesn't do it, Laughs do. Please parody
> me wherever you can" – It's *The Fool* who owns history.

For Hitler to be referred to later as 'the German Gardener', his death in 1945 had to have been faked. This was drawn on by Peter Sellers (born Richard Henry Sellers, 8 September 1925–24 July 1980). Sellers was a stand-up comic, impressionsist, one of the original *Goons* from 1951 and a humorous chocolate soldier of the Secret Service with all the correct contacts, career, and support. He was also a Freemason and Freemasons placed a lot of value in having the wars they've created put in a humorous context.

Peter Sellers played the role of Chancey Gardener (also known as 'Mr Chance', 'Chance the Gardener', and 'Chance') in the movie *Being There* (1979), as in 'YOU HAD TO BE THERE'. The gardener portrayed by Peter Sellers was a simpleton who became famous for repeating lines others attach esoteric meanings to. This parodied Hitler's early years, *Mein Kampf*, the repetition in his speeches, and the conversation the IRA billet (Father Ryan) had with Adolf Hitler over the roses.

Being There has many parodies of Hitler from 1945 to his death in 1950. His love interest is named Eve (Eva Braun) and even the voice-overs from the TV are pertinent. One of the most profound parodies is that the most malleable people, with the most hidden history, become the rulers of their countries.

At that time photocopiers were a rare thing and copies were cyclostyled with the print quality particularly bad. It may have been that Peter Sellers mistook the 80-year rule for a 30-year rule and this oversight killed him.

The movie was first screened on 19 December 1979 and Peter Sellers received an Oscar nomination for best actor in 1980. Spymaster: "His other reward was a pre-emptive death by heart attack brought about by an overdose of digitalis disguised in a dish containing apples – a favourite method used by British Intelligence."

Peter (Richard Henry) Sellers (54) died on 24 July 1980, seven months after *Being There* was first screened. His life was then misportrayed in *The Life and Death of Peter Sellers* (2005) which showed him to be a miserable son of a bitch. Using misery to show a comedian's life is cheap pop-psychology designed to write off any importance Seller's had. To a degree it worked.

Being There was written in 1971 by Jerzy Kosinski (1933–91), a political scientist. He grew up in Lodz, Poland and studied political science at Lodz University where he taught from 1955–57, after which he emigrated to America and pursued an academic career, writing four books. *The Painted Bird* (1965) is a classic of holocaust literature. Although the numbers are up for debate, the ongoing emotionalism around Jewish deaths, rather than the more prolific Russian deaths, continues – 6 million Jews versus 26 million Russians.

A common theme to Kosinski's books are characters who machinate to make the most of their situation, similar to Chaplin's *Modern Times*.

This is the vacuum we live in today.
That vacuum can at least, in part, be filled
with an anotomically accurate historical correction.

Peace kills and immortalises a few.
War kills millions and they are remembered,
for the most part, as unknown soldiers
of inaccurate statistics.

War traps surviving generations into a refusal to accept
that their war was tried and executed
with a predetermined plan of chaos,
followed by order (peace) and then chaos (war) again,
so that each generation always experiences a war (chaos),
and boundaries are forever shifted,
until finally,
all that we have that is human,
is lost.

Perhaps war is the fifth element:
Earth, Air, Fire, Water & War.
Perhaps humans are dependent on war as one of their elements.

World wars do have a habit of not occurring
in places of active volcanoes and earthquakes,
but in places of storms and harvests,
where traditions and cultures
create freedom worth dying for.

Perhaps humanity
is just another clay on the world stage,
and the world stage,
for all its players,
is there to be moulded.

Blessed are the war-makers,
for the heroes are all dead.

Greg Hallett

Afterword
Counter Intelligence

I knew that from 11 May, in the six months leading up to 1–11 November 2005, I would be able to talk and allowed to communicate. Suffering from media shyness dating several years back, I never knew how this was going to happen. The date is partly due to the 60th anniversary of the end of WWII, partly because the Black-Ops peace agreement was developed 12 years earlier and had an 11½-year silence, and partly due to the media having come some way to catching up.

On 11 May 2005, it was also released that investors were claiming back US$8 billion for dishonoured bonds (off Germany) for their financing of Hitler. The British banks had funded Hitler and hadn't asked for the money back.[1] They probably thought it was money well spent. Things regarding Hitler's history were hotting up.

I had been renovating my house down the line and had tools in the truck (4WD, 5 m long), along with a pair of $400 sunglasses, a $5 note, and a disk containing all ten books to date. I intended to lodge the disk in the painting shed but ran out of steam at the end of the day, so the disk remained in the glovebox.

The Spymaster came around at 1 pm on Wednesday 11 May 2005 and he had lost the paper 'Gifting the United Nations to Stalin' from Volume III. We searched through his car but couldn't find it. It was then that I noticed that my truck had been entered. After completing the search we went back to the house. At 1.11 pm (11.05.2005) it was confirmed that the disk containing a copy of all books had been taken and nothing else (apart from the sunglasses).

The driver's seat had been slid and tilted forward, something that only a large person would need to do. The glovebox was left open, as was the central console. The spare set of keys for the car was not taken and $1000 worth of tooling was also left in place. It looked like a professional job and there was no sign of forced entry. It looked like a fast job by a large person, with the sunglasses taken for cover.

---

[1] *New Zealand Herald*, International section, 'A bond is a bond', 11 May 2005, C7.

The sunglasses or DNA off them could easily be used for planting at a crime scene using DNA replication lice, the same lice that changed the DNA structure of migratory Polynesians to Maoris during their migrations from the Pacific Islands to New Zealand. This is nature's way of adapting to the new environment. It was discovered by a brother-and-sister team at Massey University in Palmerston North. One hopes that publication is still protection.

On the Monday prior, a friend had come around and we chatted for four hours. He gave me the lead for the 'Missing History' story (Volume III). When we went out onto the footpath we saw a new black Audi 4WD a spotter's distance away.

The driver was at the bonnet and as soon as he saw us, he got back into the driver's seat. He was huge, about 6'4", 18 stone of muscle, dark brown hair, slightly balding (35). His partner was a similar description. The front bumper and indicator of the black Audi were removed. Most importantly, it had easily borrowed temporary yellow dealer plates.

They had been there for a while. When we got to the pavement, they took off, not noticing us, even though we looked at them quite intently, but in a way that anyone else would acknowledge us. It was after all, a domestic street and a reasonably friendly neighbourhood. They were really trying not to see us.

Without prompting, my very experienced friend said, "That's weird."

I replied, "That'll be the SAS. They're interested in all of my visitors, all of my movements, anything I say or write and whoever I contact. Part of it is to isolate me from anyone I ever knew. It's all part of boiler plating [harassment]."

My house is thoroughly bugged. My car has a military tracking device on it and the SIS paid for the re-piling of the house next door in exchange for using it as a bugging station, reading off my computer screen, logging keystrokes, that sort of thing. Thus, everything that is said in my house goes straight to Intelligence and I use it as such. Because of this, Army Intelligence refuses to visit and I always have to meet them at 'the place'.

On 28 March 2005 the Spymaster had come around with the Knowledge Carrier, a black woman in her early twenties who did not know her country of origin or her birth parents, yet the information she provided was beyond both of us and the detail and breadth of her knowledge was such that we were both gobsmacked, continually. That takes a lot of doing.

She provided a different perspective. It was a history from the black person's point of view. I told her I was a mulatto short of a quadroon and she said it didn't matter. I wasn't black.[2]

I had managed to gather some psychological training in my travels, and after our third meeting I told the Spymaster, KC was working for MI-6, had been downloaded with information and was gathering a hit list to keep history suppressed and this would be released through scopolamine.

On the Monday (9 May 2005), I was travelling down the line to fit some hardware to my front door (knocker and lock). It took me five hours and I qualify as the world's slowest builder. My shingle should read, 'Sloth Builders, $6/hour'. On the way down, the Knowledge Carrier rang and left a message for the Spymaster who was also down the line. Previously I was in a naturally ecstatic mood, but became grumpy immediately after her call. Not only is the KC demanding, but it occurred to me that I was about to get robbed as both the Spymaster and myself were away. When I got back Monday night, I was surprised to find that nothing was stolen. That's not to say it wasn't copied.

The following day I went to both of my cars on the street. I noticed that a white van with red markings was at the house next door. The guy had a look in my direction. I was his 'mark'. He was SIS tech support. In exchange for tapping my place, the house next door had its garage foundations re-piled four months after I moved in. Again I thought things were hotting up.

The next day, after the Spymaster came round and we had established that one of my papers from Volume III was missing from his car and the 10-volume history had been stolen from my truck, I asked him who he thought had done it.

"Well it could have been thieves because they're lazy and don't steal tools. Those guys in the black Audi 4WD were SAS. It was most

[2] A mulatto is a tawny-coloured mixed race person, named after a mule. A quadroon is their offspring. A 'mulatto short of a quadroon' is the next generation after this. You can trace your black race, but you don't look the part. No handouts for me.

likely school kids. They'd steal sunglasses and a CD. They'll probably write over the CD. Don't worry about it."

This is a common attitude amongst Intelligence – 'Don't worry about things you can't change.'

I said, "It's not rewriteable. They may try it as a new history with their teachers and we'll see what happens to them. What happens to them would happen to us if we published under our own name. I knew the leaking would start on 11 May 2005. Still, it's a good buffer for us. Someone else gets the initial blame . . . I rang JBIII today."

Spymaster: "An Intelligence Officer is all over him at the moment. He's trying to get any and all information he can out of him, including his contacts."

"Is he from Australia?"

Spymaster: "Yes."

"So is the Knowledge Carrier. I want all reading done here now. Try and lose her for two weeks. I don't trust her, the other girl, or the drunk. He'd give away any and all information for a peck on the cheek from either of those two."

Spymaster: "That's true."

"Don't bring any of them around. It's almost finished and we're changing history. I want all the reading done here . . . It's important now. We can't afford to fuck it up at this stage."

A week prior KC was around here claiming that her surrogate father was the James Bond of the Pacific. She certainly carries the knowledge of someone whose sat around briefing tables from a very young age. She had complained to the Spymaster of symptoms that matched scopolamine and freely rings American Intelligence, Echelon and detective constables, calling them by their surnames and in a demanding tone. What's most surprising is that she has all their phone numbers.

In private, I suggested to the Spymaster that she had been drugged, briefed with all the New Zealand cons ASIS knew of, and told to spread them around in order to draw out those able to acknowledge and correct them. She would then be put under scopolamine again to draw out the information she'd gathered in New Zealand.

"Spymaster: "She certainly told the police who killed who in infinite detail. They were completely taken aback."

Some of the ASIS stories on New Zealand were wrong and some of them were deliberately wrong to fish for those with the information . . . but my biggest worry was with the Mossad who now control Australasian Intelligence. Tasmania is targeted as the new Israel and New Zealand as their holiday home, slave colony, information mine and gateway to Antarctica with all its shenanigans.

But then New Zealand is a listening post with the highest rate of retired and swished spies. If you listen in New Zealand, you find out more than anywhere else.

"I won't ring JBIII."

Spymaster: "See ya."

4.45 pm, 11 May 2005: I get into my car and drive it three metres and then repark it. I get out and walk to the shops with my mobile phone in my pocket. My mobile has been tracked and tapped for the past three years, part of the discredited Operation *Leaf* – discredited by the Prime Minister/Minister of Security and Intelligence who was doing the bugging. Through my phones they listen to everything I say.

Shopkeeper: "How are you?"

"I'm fine, but I've just been robbed. My car's just been robbed. Nothing was taken except a disk with 10 volumes of books on it – three years' work."

Shopkeeper: "What are you going to do?"

"I dunno. Probably lodge an affidavit with the High Court, registering the thefts and what the titles were."

Shopkeeper: "Can't you go to the police?"

"The police were behind it. They operate thieves in 90% of all crimes, all thefts."

Shopkeeper: "Nooo."

"Yes."

Shopkeeper: "What are you going to do now?"

"I'll probably lodge all the information with the High Court and let them deal with it."[3]

I returned at 5.15 pm, open the truck driver's door, removed the drink bottle, threw a box in the back and looked in the pouch behind the driver's seat. The disk was there, returned.

---

[3] The shopkeeper and his family emigrated to England soon after this was published.

It was the big SAS guy driving the black 4WD Audi import. That would explain the seat slid and tilted forward, no tools taken, the disk missing and then returned once my Merc had moved, my mobile phone was on walkabout and my conversation with the shopkeeper.

The SIS bugged and sabotaged my car from 26 March 2002 and changed this to a military device on the night of 13/14 August 2003. As soon as I moved the car, they knew they had a window of opportunity to return the disk to the truck. There was a spare key in the car and they took a soap impression and then had a copy made.

This was actually done 18 months prior. I changed my house keys but that was pointless. There was a period where break-ins to my house occurred two and three times a week. The front door was either left ajar, or with the keys in the outside of the door. This was boiler plating, designed to intimidate, saying 'my life was theirs' and they could terminate it whenever they felt like it. The reason I survived was that they really wanted to read the finished product . . . combinations of people who can write such books are few and far between.

It was just a normal day. It was a good day's fishing for them and I've had three good years fishing for information they stole off me. There's probably some mutual respect thing happening. It could act for or against me, but . . . 'I can't do anything about the things I can't change'. Tomorrow, if I'm still amongst the living, I'll have forgotten what yesterday began. The times they are a-changing . . . I wish someone would come and push back the clock for me . . . But I'm already there in my mind and it's good enough for now.[4]

Friday 13 May 2005: My immediate neighbour on the other side has his power connection to the house repaired. Connections here are a classic surveillance technique. I spoke to the electrician, but he failed to give me any information and refused to look at me.

Saturday 14 May 2005: The Spymaster had come around at 9.30 pm to baby-sit for me. This was the first and only time he did it, but it gives me a great sense of kudos to say the Spymaster was my babysitter. My child should be able to dine out on that for a few years, but still, it's service that brings results and results bring status.

That night, the Spymaster told me of a conversation he had with the Knowledge Carrier the night before.

[4] Apologies to Robert Zimmerman.

Spymaster: "You're working for MI-6. If you're going to kill me, kill me. Get it over and done with. I've lived my life and I've done everything I wanted to do."

Knowledge Carrier: "I promise to take care of your kids."

Now this may not seem like an actual conversation, but it is the gist of the conversation without all the ums and ahs. She had an accent that came from everywhere. It was Irish, Trinidadian, Australian and Fijian. She came with no confirmed history, could not identify her biological family and was the Spymaster's honey-trap, designed perfectly for him. She was the only person I've ever met who could keep up with his knowledge of history and intricate detail of events suppressed.

I had already established she had spent time in a mental hospital in Melbourne, Australia on the way here (Callan Park). This is standard practise to be referred to later for writing off the person as of no consequence and as cover if any charges were laid.

> New Zealand is the spies' holiday and retirement home. In New Zealand it is not illegal for a woman to kill her male partner, as long as she is dark brown, lesbian, lesbians are attracted to her, or she has a history of mental illness. The KC has 3 out of 4 of these attributes. New Zealand's legalising of 'female murders male' came under the KGB operative Prime Minister Helen Clark, a renowned feminist and lesbian herself.[5]

Sunday 15 May 2005: At 6.45 pm (dark), a 1.8 m (5'11") tall black man walks over to my stairs, then turns back, opens the gate to the house above and tries a key in the front door. The woman inside looks out and then calls me. The key he had was for my house and made from soap impressions taken when my truck was broken into (mailbox key included). It didn't fit her lock. He left, waving at the women behind the door – a typically relaxed protected non-traceable operative (NTO).

I thought about what to do if the NTO (black guy) came to my door. I'd leave the curtains drawn and take a leaf from James Bond III's hit on

[5] This law was tested in Whangarei in 2002 when a female Maori rugby player stabbed her husband and father of her two children to death in front of her mother in her own kitchen during a party. She didn't lose custody of her children for a minute and wasn't even convicted of manslaughter. This set in concrete the New Zealand judiciary as an 'occult mafia'.

Adolf Hitler in February 1964: "Are you the shooter? . . . The job's done. Tell them you did it and take the money." The black NTO was later revealed to be a Rhodesian NTO known to New Zealand Intelligence.

I wanted to change my door lock barrel first thing, but was going fishing the next day so I decided to leave the front door deadlocked so the key wouldn't work. I went out the back door and took the large key with me, of which there are only 12 variations. I also left my phone behind, turned off, so if they rang, it would go straight to message . . . and I left the radio on. Such was my security.

The Spymaster has been around every day reading and adding last-minute stories. Various intelligence communities from various suppressive governments want the finished product. My fear was they would add a virus to my non-net-connected computer. I copied this 'Afterword' and left it on the dining table, at the front of the manuscript, and on the keyboard, I copied all of the work to date and gave it to my fishing buddy's friend to stick in his mattress, delivered another copy to the Godfather, then put this sign on the front door, emulating James Bond III:

Job done.

Tell them you did it.

Take the money . . .

I got back after fishing, the sign was still on the inside of my door and there had been no break-in. It's no wonder, the large back door key was incredibly hard to fit, something to do with rusty locks. The Spymaster came around the next day at 11 am and told me what happened to him the previous night.

The Knowledge Carrier told him she wanted to start seeing a South African guy (white) and the Spymaster said, "Fine, Go."

KC: "You're not jealous or angry?"

Spymaster: "No, just go. Do what you want to do."

It's curious that the key had been stolen (SAS), a black Rhodesian NTO had tried to get into the house above using my key and the Knowledge Carrier had started seeing a white South African – all within the same week.

The Spymaster came around to my place the next day (17 May 2005) and did some editorial work and confirmed the KC was MI-6. The KC then came around uninvited. I remained in my office and changed from being a nice guy to saying: "Get rid of her. Don't let her in." She hears this, sees the sign "Job done. Tell them you did it. Take the money . . ." – but doesn't see me.

The next day two ex-British MI-6 officers (white, in their 30s) phone up requesting false names: 2.19 pm, "Is Gary there"; 2.31 pm, "Is Ben there". I haven't added question marks, because they weren't asked as questions. They were actually recording and comparing voice recognition (Echelon) to see if I had been replaced by a doppelgänger. I mentioned this to the Spymaster and gave a description of the people from their voices. He was worried very worried and said, "They are MI-6". He suggests I take the book to the editor early.

James Bond III was equally worried.

Thursday (19 May 2005), the Spymaster came around and confirmed my worst fears. The KC is not even the stepdaughter of the man she claims to be her father – the James Bond of the Pacific. "He is her controller and we already know him to be an evil S.O.B. having caused many coups, even ensuring that some fail." I tell the Spymaster that she's here to clear out any intelligence rings. It's her job to confirm the 'Marks' for the killers.

Just as I was finishing (20 May 2005) my printer broke down two-thirds of the way through the final print job. The paper tray had jammed half in. I took it to the dealer and it was like nothing they had ever seen before. I got a brand-new printer, straight out of the box and that failed on a technical matter, twice, which meant that my CPU had been fiddled with and I lost hours. They never asked for the loan printer back.

While I was out I got a call from my sub-landlord that builders would be around tomorrow doing an unspecified job. Now that both neighbours were bugged, they were moving in for the kill. I took my computer in and insisted repeatedly that they not put it online to download any printing programs. Three unknowns turned up, but double jeopardy, my computer had been at the dealers or was in the car. One of the builders knew the entire family of my closest relatives. This helped with their rapport-building.

The Spymaster came around (28 May 2005) and told me he had taken the KC to ONI (Office of Naval Intelligence) for an IQ test and confirmed everything I had said. She had an IQ of 95 – low enough to know you're not getting it, but bright enough to keep asking questions (annoying). The fantastic amount and detail of historical information she had, had been dumped into her subconscious via MK-Ultra.

The Spymaster suggested, "She was the illegitimate daughter of someone famous". Yeah, with a maid.

A friend popped by to make it a proper treff and slipped something out that solved a case the Spymaster had been working on for three years . . . something about a judge wearing nappies during filmed S&M.

On 2 June 2005, the Spymaster confirmed more information, that her father (illegitimate) was a seriously high-ranking British MI-6 officer. All these events just confirm my suspicions aired two months earlier. It was a severe case of botulism all round.

After I had given the book to the editor and had mentioned, in my very bugged home, that it was at the editor's, the driver's licence and credit card stolen six months earlier were returned (9 June). Then, on 11 June, my other credit cards were stolen.

On 13 June it was known that I was going charter fishing. When I got into my car, the minor electrics had failed – radio, CD, rear window. This is all part of boiler plating. The message was: "Are you sure you even know how to tie your own shoelaces?"

When I got home early, the Spymaster rang just as I was putting two and two together. The Spymaster had been grievously assaulted in the previous three weeks. Eleven days later the assailant killed for the second time – this time his father (40), but because he was a minor, he would be let off to kill again. He's tough, the old Spymaster. When he rang me after the assault, he didn't even mention it, but you wouldn't believe how much I laughed when I saw the nasal strapping. He mentioned that the 18 year-old double murderer was being groomed as a government hit man. As it turned out he killed again (for a third time) six weeks later.

I've been working on ten books and took one book to my editor on 2 June 2005. The day before, mail was sent and I was being sued by a school buddy of the Prime Minister, a person who owed me money.

It was obvious from their search that they received a lot of inside help, even discounting that their timing was perfect. The hearing for their case ended up at the same time and day as another hearing of mine. Each time I raised the sexuality of the Prime Minister (lesbian married to a homosexual child-sex abuser), the case was interfered with, postponed and I was charged. Rather than receive the amount due I was ordered to pay the amount due.

Interference or coincidence? What are the chances of that? It's corruption and sexual collusion in the Courts.

So far three Courts have failed to sight my evidence and keep delaying me into higher Courts. There are changes being made in the Courts, but they are all to do with cosmetics, like delays.

> The real question Western world citizens need to ask is:
> 'To what degree are our Courts an occult mafia?'

While writing these books, including the constant thefts out of my home, car, bank account and insurance, I've experienced at least 50 incidents, over half of which were criminal attacks by the police or courts, including three lawyers through my architecture practise.

> The legal system is primarily an occult mafia, but it is also a history mafia when challenged. The legal system is based on the current version of social history. As such, the Courts believe it is their right for others not to know right, and their version of false history is the only version that should be known. The truth hurts and it seems that I have taken many of the hits.

Mother rang me shortly after the London Underground bombings (7 July 2005, with '777' signature as the Bible definition of evil) and invited me to lunch. Mother talks away and then slips something in. "You know, no one believes in your conspiracy theories." I hadn't given him any information. He had obviously read off the disk the SAS stole on 11 May. At the end of the day, Mother's allegiances are towards the status quo. Information is not there to rock the boat, but to keep it on edge, levelled by the next report.

On Wednesday 13 July 2005 I rang the Godfather to make an appointment to see how his reading was going and arranged an appointment for Saturday morning 16 July. On Friday 15 July I lodged a High Court appeal against the Prime Minister's school buddy who had employed me with fraudulent documents on 24 May 2004. This was two days after I had ended eight days of Mossad reconnaissance (16–22 May 2004) with a debriefing on their previous murder of the government historian, Michael King, on 29 March 2004 by ipecac and impact explosive on the petrol tank.

The Mossad were quite annoyed to have been discovered, but quite pleased to find someone to talk to. It was 4 February 2006 before they invited me to a meeting and even the Spymaster rang prompting me to be on time.[6] They queried me on space. I found what they had to offer, dull, and the report came back, "He's highly intelligent". I would have been happy with "He's quite bright" . . . M had told me my work on space was shit.

On Saturday 16 July 2005 I drove the truck to the Godfather and on my return the Mercedes rear right quarterglass had been smashed. I spoke to the neighbour and established that it had occurred between midnight and 8.30 am on 16 July 2005. Inside nothing had been stolen, not the money or the CD player, but the rear interior light (video & sound) had been pulled apart, the front overhead seatbelt light had been pushed in (video & sound), as had the passenger's electronic seat adjuster (receiver) and the passenger lock cover on the door as it meets the frame had been removed (receiving signals, tracking & sending). All the parts were there as were the tools for the job – a 14 cm black slot-head screwdriver and its 12 cm Phillips adaptor. The Phillips adaptor was used to pinch the quarter light and break the glass. The slot-head was used to pinch off the light and seat control covers and it was this one that was in the black handle when they scarpered.

I later found out they had left the tools behind to illustrate their confidence in the system not to catch them and a slow leak in my rear left tyre as a little indicator that this was also boiler plating, just for the hassle of it all. The fingerprint department isn't open until Monday and fingerprints only last three days, or so I thought. Given low priority, there was no chance, or so I thought.

The SAS had obviously read at least some of the ten books on disk they had stolen two months prior (including much of this one), saw the mention of the SIS planting tracking devices in my Merc (26 March 2002, 13/14 August 2004, 16 July 2005), and had them removed.

[6] This was two years to the day that I had returned with this info. What are the chances.

It also confirmed my suspicions about Mother, that they did believe what I had written and gave it enough credibility to try and remove evidence of their part in it, first by saying no one believed what I was saying and second by removing the tracking devices. Ironically Mother had popped in for a social call 18 hours before the car was broken into and spoke directly to the SIS, framed as a question, "I don't understand why the police employed Graeme Capill as crown prosecutor when they knew he was a paedophile 21 months before he was charged?"

At 5 pm I drove the Merc to my regular takeaways/restaurant where I always purchase on credit card and by chance, inside was an SAS man. They stand out like dog's balls – well built, late twenties, black receding hair, wearing a black polo neck and having to concentrate on having a civilian dinner with another couple as opposed to eating out of a tin can. As I walked in I noticed him checking out the rear light dangling inside the Merc and then checking me out. Initially I thought his stare was a bit camp but it seemed to have a certain admiration attached to it.

About three hours later the Spymaster popped in and I mentioned the break-in. He asked to see the tools the SAS had left behind. Looking at them he said, "It was a semi-professional job . . . at least we now know you're not paranoid, but others will still need some convincing."

We got to talking and he explained how few people still active had his experience. We established that the SAS and the SIS did have this information and then so did the Prime Minister. Then I mentioned that this SAS guy in the restaurant was actually looking at me with some admiration, kind of looking up to me like a student to a teacher. The Spymaster didn't say anything, but word will get to him soon enough. If he starts being treated with more respect then we know we've hit the believability button at the coalface.

A month later the SAS approached him and said, "You know we didn't used to believe you, but now everything you've been saying has come true, well most of it."

On Sunday I met the Spymaster again and he confirmed that international investigations had confirmed everything we had said in this and the other nine books and a summarised version was about to be published in magazine form prior to the election. These people are the old boys of an organisation so powerful they have access to all information currently available, unavailable, suppressed and stolen.

I queried whether they had accessed information stolen by the SIS and whether it had muddied the waters, but there were still things we had solved that they weren't aware of – bigger than God and clearer than the wide blue sea – it came out soon after.

On Monday 18 July 2005 I drove to the police station and filled in the 'Offence Report'. Senior fingerprinting officer Struan Ferguson was serving someone next to me and took an interest in my case. He took fingerprints off the screwdriver and came down to the car. He saw the rear interior rear light dangling, the safety belt light pushed in and the electronic seat adjustor with its covers off.

Struan Ferguson: "I've never seen anything like it." He also said fingerprints lasted longer than three days.

I told him I thought the SIS had done the job and he replied, "SIS fingerprints would not be on our database."

Welcome to the world of NTOs – Non-Traceable Operatives.

I had long suspected the Prime Minister's school buddies of being NTOs. When I first tried to get money out of them through the District Court, my Merc was scratched the same night, the hood ornament was wrenched out and the driver's window was pushed down, but nothing was stolen. The same thing happened this time when I lodged in the High Court and again before the night was out.

I showed the car to Mother. He said, "The Prime Minister's people have done it. They're on to you . . . You're too friendly. Too many people know you linked the Prime Minister to Vladimir Putin." But I never told him that.

Mother's read it and Mum's the word. So what am I, just an interested recorder of events, an active historian caught up in the politics of the Cold War as the New World Order emerges? A week later the "Police Complaint Acknowlegement Form" came through the post, "File Ref: No. 050722/5468".

I lost a High Court Appeal of the same case to a feminist judge on 28 July 2005, got into my truck and parked outside the bank in Mt Eden village. There was a driveway in front of the parking space, so parking was easy and a few cars passed me before I'd finished parking. A $150,000 Black CL500 Mercedes coup (CAW834) then stopped the traffic for 45 seconds and parked in the middle lane of the main road right next to me. A large fit 58-year-old male in dark sunglasses got out of this car and started yelling and gestating in high anger, "Fuck you, fuck you . . . I fucked your wife."

It looked like he was coming for me so I locked my doors, wound up my windows, closed my sunroof and then wound down my driver's window a few inches to, "I fucked your wife".

I said, "I don't have a wife".

He appeared to be on methamphetamine. With three witness names gathered, I filed a complaint "File Ref: No. 050728/2968" and later asked the police for his address so I could send him a get well card.

They said they wouldn't have a case officer for two months. Sometimes people do contract boiler plating for the government (police and intelligence) in exchange for not being charged for other crimes ranging from drug use and drug dealing to murder.

At 5.25 pm on 11 August 2005, police officer Graeme Bruges phoned and said he was working on the case, that the other witnesses had agreed with my statement and they had been to the listed address of the driver, but he had moved, and according to his record, he probably was on P.

No kidding.

Officer Bruges then said, "I'm going on holiday for two weeks, and when I come back I'll try and locate him."

Straight after the High Court appeal against government NTO's, driving a flash car with a history of road rage, on P, moving house, no forwarding address and the policeman on holiday . . . this was perfect NTO material. It'll be at least four weeks before they locate him. I wouldn't be surprised if he's overseas already, or if pressured, catches the trans-Tasman Seatow to freedom.

On 30 August Constable Graeme Bruges invited me to give a statement. I went into the station and it was all very cordial. He noted that it was strange that a person driving a $150,000 car should be living in a rental state house in a bad area. He said he would arrest him and the hearing would be in a year or so.

The next morning the Spymaster asked me which station I had been to and then told me that the driver of CAW834 was protected.

Authors work for years without pay and I had been after a loan on my rental house. After six weeks of haranguing it finally came through the same day.

Three hours later I got a fax from the High Court requesting payment for the defendants lawyers fees stating that my case had been abandoned . . . 18 days before the election. The case was not due to be abandoned until 1 October, 14 days after the election.

Both the Disputes Tribunal judge and the High Court judge were lesbians and the District Court judge had been very cordial to me on one case and had jumped so far down my throat on this case I was still pulling his shoe-laces out of my throat a month later.

I had two separate cases scheduled for exactly the same time and day to be heard by the same judge who acted completely differently on the two cases. What are the chances of that? Judges are influenced by politicians, especially when that politican has had their hit thwarted.

Within minutes the Spymaster contacted me and said: "You'll never believe this. Westfield property bought the Twin Towers two months before 9-11. Westfield is a front for the Mossad who bought it for Silverstein Properties – the Mossad. There was a clause in the purchase that they didn't have to do any maintenance in case of terrorism . . . The building was insured."

The Mossad purchased the Twin Towers in July 2001 when they required extensive maintenance and were near the end of their life. The buildings were attacked in an act of terrorism, the government cleaned up the mess, the insurance companies paid out, everyone else's premiums went up worldwide, and Silverstein Properties ended up with a freehold empty section and enough money to build again from scratch. Nice little stitch-up. Problem is, it changed the face of the world.

Things were hotting up. The KGB operative Prime Minister was under attack and erroneously thinks I'm involved. Who, me? I'm just a struggling architect who was the first to expose her. On 25 March 2002 I mentioned she was a KGB operative on radio. There was an attempt on my life on 2 April 2002, I put my comments to print on 11 April and the early election was leaked on 15 April 2002.

> "Hitler continues to pose a dreadful problem . . . If we don't get Hitler right, the critics insist, we might not recognise the next Hitler."[7]

[7] *Sunday Star-Times*, 15 May 2005, C2.

Hitler is everywhere now. There are parts of him in every leader in the world. Governments are occult organisations dedicated to the destruction of their citizens' lives by whatever means is most profitable. We live in a Mafia State. You do in your country too.

New Zealand is ruled by a mafia of paedophiles.

What we are witnessing is the transfer of control from national governments to the Shadow World Government and from there to the One World Order where heterosexual male individuality is treated with the utmost suspicion – as virtual treason.

Patriotism is now treasonous.
All that defined yesterday's heroes is now under attack.

Regarding the 11 May 2005 truck break-in, when I filled in the complaint form the Spymaster advised me to say that it was the SIS and Israeli's who did it. In the computer disk stolen and returned the same day, I had mentioned that Hitler was a British agent and was trained at Tavistock, but reference to this was the least concrete part of the book.

The Israeli's answered all my prayers. They confirmed Hitler's Tavistock training eight weeks later on 7 July 2005 with their signature hit on Tavistock Square. In Golden Dawn coven/Freemason language 07.07.2005 is 007^7 or '007 on the square', in direct reference to James Bond and Ian Fleming's escort of Hitler out of Germany at 1700 hours on 007.1945 – '007 squared'.

Tavistock Square is part of an estate owned by the Dukes of Bedford and takes its name from the courtesy title given to the eldest male in the line of the Duke of Bedford – 'Lord Tavistock' – with the younger males styled 'Marquess of Tavistock'.

The Lord Tavistock's had not been having a good run of it lately. The 13th Duke of Bedford had organised an open-air concert headed by Neil Diamond in 1977 attended by 56,000 people (56 people died in the London bombings). This Lord Tavistock died on 25.10.2002.[8] Two years later in October 2004 MI-5 labelled WWII's Duke of Bedford "a Nazi sympathiser".

His son, the 14th Duke of Bedford died eight months later, aged 63, on 13.06.2003. The 15th Duke of Bedford was born on 30.03.1962 and

[8] The 13th Duke of Bedford's estate included a safari park. The author had dinner at his Woburn Abbey in 1989 and it was here that he found out just how unpopular thinking was with the British.

had just had a son, the 16th Duke of Bedford, born on 07.06.2005, exactly 30 days prior to the bombings. He is the Marquees of Tavistock and when his father dies, he will be the new Lord Tavistock.

Bus No. 30 was driven off its route into Tavistock Square and blown up. It was an add on to the London Tube hits. The front of the building at Tavistock Square was all covered in blood – blood on its hands – and with this allegory still in tact, those in the front of the bus were left unscathed.

The Marquees of Tavistock was born on the same day as Adolf Hitler's father, exactly 168 years later (Alois Hitler, b. 7 June 1837). In the Golden Dawn coven language, '168' translates as "infinite one dead".

Hitler was trained in the Tavistock military Psych-Opps war school from February to November 1912, 103 years prior – 7 July occurs right in the middle of that training.

Initially 13 died, plus the bomber (18) and then another died, an architect, the namesake of an author who had written about such matters, one Lee Harris.

Developed in the 1820s, Tavistock Square contains a memorial to conscientious objectors. This was unveiled in 1995, 56 years after the beginning of WWII and 56 people died.

The bombing occurred in the 56th year of Hitler's death – 55 years and 136 days after he died. In Golden Dawn coven/Freemason language '55' represents "the master of occult history" and '136' is "dead bad luck".

The bombers were all from England and from low-paying jobs. There is a theory that they undertook the bombings on the understanding that they were time-delay bombs and that they were organised to take the emphasis off Sir Bob Geldof's focus on the depopulation of Africa – for its resources.

Of the people who died, all were British except for 12 foreigners. No American's died and the only Israeli to die was a charity worker who was scared of suicide bombs on Israeli buses, so she moved to London – dead bad luck, '136'.

During the London bombings, the surveillance cameras were all monitored by an Israeli so there was little fear of pertinent evidence catching up with them. The London policeman who said the bombings were done with military explosives was sacked prior to 6 August 2005 (when this information came to author) and the official release said that the bombs had been made out of common household products, but no one believes this.

It was an American and Israeli hit with Tony Blair's complicity. In covering up the Prince's Greek attraction to youth (Thomas Hamilton's Dunblane massacre), Tony Blair had signed a document prior to 7 March 2003 allowing the US government to kill up to 60 Britisher's or people on British soil in order to create the next oil grab (Syria) and sure enough, it was the Syrian's who were blamed by the press the next day, with no evidence to back it up.

Between 60 and 160 dead would mean a proportionate reduction in oil prices for Britain and over 160 meant that the British government could kill American's on American soil in agreed retaliation (another Israeli employment scheme), which would also suit the Americans who would also blame this on the Syrians.

> This is the value in shame over a British aristocratic paedophile ring and it was what America used to bring Tony Blair's Britain into the 20.03.2003 Iraq war.

This was followed by the promotion of back bench MP George Robertson to Cabinet Minister (1997), Lord George Robertson (24 August 1999) and then Secretary General of NATO (11 August 1999–5 January 2004) for his part in supplying the Freemasonry letter of reference for the purchase of the gun for Thomas Hamilton's massacre of 16 school children (16 March 1996). Robertson was accused of this on 11 March 2003, nine days before the Iraq war started, using FBI files as a reference.

Lord George Robertson, Secretary General of NATO, repaid the favour by protecting Afghanistan and ensuring that 98% of the heroin in Britain comes from Afghanistan. How regular are those NATO flights? Have they got their air-to-air refuelling yet? History is built on shame. Those with the most shame are promoted. Politicians regularly fail their way to the top.

The same month as the London bombings, Israel's Prime Minister Ariel Sharon was exposed by the *Haaretz* newspaper as having an affair with his wife's sister, killing his first wife Margalith on 6 May 1962 (car accident), marrying his wife's sister Liala (Lily) in 1964 (date unavailable) and then killing his first son Gur on 5 October 1967 (shooting accident), with their new son Omri (b. 8 August 1968) conceived the same month.

This shows a heavy influence of the occult.

Ariel Sharon had became Israel's Prime Minister by special election on 6 February 2001 with much shenanigans. His son's, Omri and Gilad were both involved in corruption over the 1999 election campaign, with Omri convicted of corruption and dishonesty on 26 July 2005 and Gilad refusing to give self-incrimination evidence.

Given Ariel Sharon's history this is not beyond belief. He has been in the military since the age of 14, became an intelligence officer at 22 and then a major, reading Animal Farm (1945) and leading 'Unit 101' as a 25 year-old.

When his brutal disregard for human life was noted after the Six-Day War in 1967, he resigned and moved straight into politics. As Israel's Defence Minister (1981–83) he was responsible for two refugee massacres in September 1982 and was forced to resign again. He has been successively known as the Butcher of Qibya/Lebanon/Sabra/Chatila and Beirut and has failed and murdered his way up the ladder to become Israel's Prime Minister.

With the assassination of Israel's Prime Minister Yitzah Rabin on 4 November 1995 and no killer found, the warring Ariel Sharon is not off the list of suspects. He bores us with news of Middle East conflict every night, stories of his own making, which force out less violent and more relevant news.

> Israel's Foreign Minister Silvan Shalom, mid-July 2005:
> "Suicide attacks around the world are driven by a common hatred for freedom. Ultimately terrorism can strike any country in the world that has an ideology of freedom, of democracy, that has an ideology of openness."

Shortly after this Ariel Sharon ordered his minister's not to comment on the London bombings and within a month passed into law:

> 'Any expression critical of Israel or any anti-Semitic remark warrants extradition and interrogation, without limit to any country. That it is true, is no excuse.'

This was done with the London bombings in the forefront of his mind and these texts in the background – two months after they were stolen, three months prior to completion and four months prior to publication it's already influencing history.

When Israel attacks foreigners they make it as significant as possible in order to give it mystical qualities. Tavistock is a very significant place and '007 on the square' or '777' was a very significant hit.

According to Hebrew interpretations '777' represents God and '777' is an offence against Jesus Christ. When written in the original Hebrew '777' looks remarkably like '666' which looks remarkably like a track of paw prints of a large animal, hence 'the beast'. Later numerology got hold of '666' and was supposed to represent someone's name, either the Roman emperor Nero (Neron) or Hitler, but these are all just riddles that leave their mark.

With British complicity and under American orders those who organised the London bombings were intelligent enough to leave us clues. They were also intelligent enough to pick up on mine. Thank's for the confirmation of Hitler's British training . . . my condolences to the victims throughout history.

Israel is a wolf in sheep's clothing barking that it is a sheep.

In an unpublished article to *TIME* magazine (9 March 2005) I had predicted New Zealand's election would be at the end of September 2005. (A minium of three weeks notice is required.)

On 28 June 2005 I had written another unpublished article, "The Rainbow Warrior Bombing, An update on the *Sunday* programme on 26 June 2005" and vetted it with Mother and the Spymaster. The following day I phoned Donna Chisholm at the *Sunday Star Times* and met with her predicting former Labour Prime Minister David Lange would publish an autobiography just before his death and his death would be just before the election.

> "When the nuclear issue came up for New Zealand . . . David has written about this in his book, which is timed to come out immediately upon his death, as is another biography on Lange's life by Dr. Michael Basset."

I spoke with Mother on Sunday 24 July 2005 and he told me the election would be announced on Wednesday. Being highly bugged, it was announced the following day, on Monday 25 July for 17 September 2005.

David Lange's book came out on Tuesday 9 August 2005. On the afternoon of Friday 12 August 2005, Mother contacted me and said: "David Lange's life support was switched off at 11am. I just thought you'd like to know. He has a matter of hours or days to live. Keep it secret."

I couldn't help myself. The Spymaster was standing right next to me and after the call I asked him if he could keep a secret. I asked him three times and each time he said "No", so I told him anyway. We then sat outside and he told me the KC was back. I said "Don't let her in. Where is she?"

Spymaster: "Up the top . . . They've read your books. They've gone to the highest levels. They were going to kill you and everyone involved and then someone else read the books and said, *'No, they serve our purpose. It's about time the truth came out'*, so they're going to write you off as a Nutter."

I just sat back and laughed and the Spymaster watched me for a while and said, "The books have gone to the highest levels."

"Have they got the latest information or just the information they stole on 11 May?"

Spymaster: "I don't know how they've got it, but they've got all the information. The third nuclear bomb really threw them."

"They must have been reading keystrokes . . . who, the Brits and the Jews?" There was no answer. The Spymaster always protects his sources with no response and a completely unreadable face whenever he wants to protect his sources. "I can imagine you and me as the North Going Zac and the South Going Zac with the British and Israelis firing bombs at each other overhead."

Spymaster: "This is the dinkum oil."

I laughed again . . . couldn't help myself and the Spymaster said, "I thought you'd react this way . . . I reckon they'll delay Lange's death so it won't be announced on the late news, but in the Sunday papers."

David Lange died at 10 pm Saturday 13 August 2005. His death was announced in the Sunday papers the following morning as having occurred at the start of the Bledisloe Cup rugby test match, which New Zealand won. If the government wants to stay in, test matches are bought and the All Blacks have been winning hands down. This was followed by full Sunday television coverage of David Lange.

9 March 2005: predicted election in late September 2005 to *Time* magazine; 28 June 2005: predicted David Lange would publish an autobiography and die soon after, but before the election; 24 July 2005: knew election was to be announced, as it was the following day; 9 August 2005: Lange's book came out and he died four days later on the suspicious date of 13 August 2005. The election was due five weeks later and Lange's death caused a lot of sympathy to the incumbent government.

It's easy enough to rig a rugby test match with the awarding of penalties. The winning team has penalties awarded in their opposition half and the losing team has theirs awarded in their own half. If the bribe is big enough, the loosing team's kicker, kicks for touch, rather than for goal. This is how the Lions lost all three test matches to the All Blacks in June/July 2005. It came with the complicity of Tony Blair's paedophile minder, Alistair Campbell (ex-military) who fronted as the Lions maître d'.

The Prime Minister had a consultation lunch with Alistair Campbell on 26 June 2005 regarding rigging the next election. First there was to be no KGB or lesbian information on Helen Clark, no homosexual child-sex abuse information on her husband, Peter Davis, no paedophile information on Jonathan Hunt, the High Commissioner to Britain; no coverage of Sir Peter Elworthy's 'death', or Michael King's 'death'; butch lesbians were to hide from the public, no lesbians were to drive convertibles and lesbians were to disappear from public view in general; all Labour women were to get new bright pastel clothes and were to dress like heterosexuals; Helen was to lose weight and have her 55-year-old lesbian XY-self made to look like a 28-year-old heterosexual complete with manufactured teeth. This image was to be placed on an election pledge card. David Lange was to die just before the election – engineering sympathy, and the leader of the opposition Don Brash was to be accused of being CIA backed. The latter was to prevent last minute accusations that Helen Clark was the KGB operative IE and had worked with Vladimir Putin in Wellington to launch a nuclear strike on American property during the Cold War – namely Canberra, Adelaide or Sydney in a rotating fashion.

After the chicken salad had arrived, the NATO delivered Afghan heroin was not to reach the market until after the election, regardless of who won. In exchange for no information on Tony Blair's rock spider activity, Campbell would throw the Lions Tour of New Zealand which would make Helen Clark popular in the eyes of rugby fans. He would also ensure the world's media remained silent on Helen Clark's filmed sex with Heather Simpson at Lincoln Cottage. He could only guarantee W. remained quiet on it as long as she continued to not criticise the Iraq war. This was the deal. This was how it was engineered and this was how it was done, complete with carbonated water.

Another interesting aspect of election rigging is the engineering of fine weather during the winter leading up to the election providing that feel good factor.

Under Operation CLOVERLEAF (1997–) aerosol and electro-magnetic operations, high frequency microwaves are used to manipulate the charged atmosphere for weather modification. Along with this are 4 beats per second extremely low electro-magnetic frequencies breaking down human biological and mental functioning . . . and aerosol poisons dissipated by planes.

These particles (10% the width of a human hair) are made up of barium salts, aluminium and radioactive thorium, viruses, bacteria, fungi, desiccated bovine (cow) blood cells and mutated spores which secrete a powerful microtoxin, Ethylene Dibromide (a carcinogen and toxin banned in 1983) and Mycoplasma Fermetens Incognitus, the same Mycoplasma that created the Gulf War syndrome.

Weather modification is bought via bribes to the CIA who fly unregistered planes stolen off the American military and America companies as well as pre-modified commericial planes like the KC-10A, KC135 (707) and C-130s. These have been adapted with 500 litres of poisons stored amongst the sewerage bowels and are dissipated through the modified static discharge wicks at the rear of the plane's wings.

Spymaster: "The CIA just waltz in with their bogus and forged documentation and commandeer the planes. They are not all commercial flights and some of the planes are unregistered."

The poisons are so fine they are breathed in and enter the blood cells. Their toxic metals suppress the immune system, weakening muscles and cause cancers, Alzheimer's, blood clots, strokes, heart attacks, changes to the endocrine and nervous system, respiratory problems, coughing fits, shortness of breath, sinus headaches, respiratory failure, severe infections to the throats and sinuses, swelling of the lymph glands and liver damage . . . and it only costs US$0.73¢ per kilo to disseminate.

The cover for this is that the aerosols contain fine metalic particles which reduce the sun's electromagnetic radiation to stop global warming, but GLOBAL WARMING IS A HOAX.

> DuPont's CFC patent was due to run out in 1985 and they wanted to stop Asian companies producing CFCs cheaply, so they banned them and introduced HCFC's having the sole patent for this. HCFC's are more expensive and less effective, but DuPont has the patent.
>
> Mt Erebus releases more CFCs than all the rest of the world's volcanoes put together and these are sucked up into the atmosphere during the spring and autumn equinox. To prevent this being measured, a plane crash was engineered.
>
> When the 28 November 1979 Air New Zealand crash was arranged to hit Mt Erebus, DuPont and the CIA were present at all meetings. The CIA's motto is to PROTECT AND ADVANCE AMERICAN BUSINESS. The Erebus crash now prevents anyone climbing Mt Erebus to test its CFC emissions.
>
> The hole in the ozone layer was caused by a nuclear explosion in Antarctica in 1958. It was measured for 60 years and when the ozone hole began to contract in 2002, it was no longer news. Erroneously the GLOBAL WARMING HOAX is still with us.

Instead of spraying fine reflective particles to stop global warming, poisons are being sprayed to assist the new Avian Flu (H5N1) which has been designed to be as strong as the 1918–19 Spanish Flu that killed 50 million. The Bush administration has been having discussions as to the optimum number of people to 'work the planet' and their current estimates are around one billion (May 2005). This has resulted in experiments to kill 5 out of 6 people.

"United States health officials said this week they have started human tests of a vaccine against Avian Flu, which experts believe could kill tens of millions of people if it becomes easily passed from person to person . . . Usually, people catch the virus directly from birds such as chickens or ducks. Geese and wild birds and mammals such as cats can also carry the virus . . . To date, there has been a small number of cases where human-to-human transmission of the virus may have occurred

. . . public health experts fear that the virus may evolve into one that is more easily transmitted between people . . . If this were to happen, a worldwide pandemic could follow . . . the public health community is concerned that the virus will develop the capability of efficiently spreading from human to human and thus create a risk for a worldwide pandemic . . . the vaccine [is] made by Sanofi Pasteur [with] Chiron Corp. of Emeryville, California."[9]

Prime Minister Helen Clark stuffed up the importation of the vaccine ensuring that a less effective vaccine was purchased . . . just as previous Prime Minister William Ferguson Massey (1912–25) carried the Spanish Flu into New Zealand personally, refusing to be quarantined. In Freemasonry he was 'M. W. Bro. W. F. Massey' and for his efforts in eugenics (mass murder) a Freemasonry lodge was named after him – the 'William Fergusson Massey Royal Arch Chapter No. 60'.[10]

Deaths in New Zealand are due to happen with a cold snap in late October after the election and after a warm winter. The Avian Flu is due to arrive into New Zealand (the world's test population) via planes carrying Chinese 'Chicken-Sleepers' from Manchuria on 10 October with the virus taking hold on 14 October,[11] followed by an extreme cold snap in late October.

Almost all natural disasters are man-made and governments arrange emergencies to keep them in power. For the Bush government it was 9-11 and the Iraq War. For Blair it was the Iraq War and the London tube bombings. For Helen Clark it is 250,000 deaths from the Avian Flu.

The rules of Nordic-Anglo-Saxon colonising are that you have to limit the killing of 'people with integrity'. These are noted as white heterosexuals. The plan from 1500 years ago is for those from Thule (Greenland) to sweep down to Antarctica over 1500 years and then to sweep back up again with a different species – modified humans – for the next 1500 years.

---

[9] This Reuters article 'Human tests of avian flu vaccine underway' made public on 25 March 2005 was published in the *New Zealand Herald* five months later on 1 September 2005.

[10] Freemasons often misspell a persons name by one letter. It is a sign they believe they are above the law. Sure enough, Massey belonged to the British-Israel-World Federation with an office next to Buckingham Palace (1924–90). Federated on 3 July 1919, its roots can be traced back to the 1800s.

[11] As it panned out, H5N1 struck in Romania and Turkey on exactly these dates and New Zealand was saved by the Mossad accused.

From 1945 this new species of humans – homo sapien 1.52 – has been developed with their 'human' aspects breed and trained out of them. They are now a race of technocrats – capable servants – 21st Century serfs rasied amongst the world's largest geothermal lakes between Neuschwabenland and the South Pole, first accessed by U-boat under the ice.

Israel has taken over Tasmania on condition that the Australian population be disarmed (2003). At the same time the Avian Flu was successfully tested as a human killer in Korea, but its contagiousness needed to be improved. The Israeli government then enforced the withdrawl of its people out of the Westbank (15 August 2005) and gave each family US$800,000 and placed them in rental accomodation. They will soon be emigrating to Tasmania en masse, followed by the depopulation of New Zealand resulting in extremely cheap housing and an influx of very wealthy Israeli's without the grief of the incubent population. At the same time the Antarcticans (Homo sapien 1.52) will merge into New Zealand, purchase houses with counterfeit money of a foreign country, but accepted by New Zealand banks (most likely the Euro). Their move from Antarctica to New Zealand will go unnoticed amongst the confusion. This is the way migrations happen.

History rarely notes the intricate details of a migration
and rarely if ever survives to record another species.

That's the plan, but gang aft agley – things fuck up.

Normal peace agreements say 'this is peace now',
with no definition of what peace is,
and 'if you cross this line, it is war'.
War is defined, but peace is not.

Peace was always some static thing on a spring
summers day when nothing went wrong.

In between wars there is
PEACE, FREEDOM AND CULTURE
which is maintained with 'AAA' –
Acceptance, Acknowledgement, Attention
– and it is this simple formula that was used
to send the above plan astray.

Yet another example of migration engineering and population control. It is how the face of the planet is altered.

J' Accuse . . .

J'Accuse Helen Clark of training with the soviets in Tavistock St Petersburg from 1968 and being the KGB operative IE.

J'Accuse Helen Clark of using the nuclear free treaties as cover for launching a nuclear strike on American property between 1980 and 1989.

J'Accuse Helen Clark of complicity in the murders of Diplomat Chris Beeby, sailor and greeny Sir Peter Blake, Sir Peter Elworthy, historian Michael King and Green politician Rod Donald.

J'Accuse Helen Clark of letting out a contract in October 2003 for the murders of Sir Peter Elworthy, Michael King, Sharon Crosby and Alison Holst.

J'Accuse no one of picking up the contracts so they went to Chief Justice Sian Elias who organised and funded the Mossad to murder.

J'Accuse Sian Elias of stealing over half a billion dollars and transferring the money to the Cayman Islands in 1989.

J'Accuse the Mossad of spotting this transfer and bribing Sian Elias. The Mossad would take over New Zealand and in exchange they would carry out any murders for Sian Elias.

J'Accuse Sian Elias of ordering the murder of her accountant brother-in-law in 1993.

> Most of the money stolen was due to the Chinese and China threatened war on New Zealand. The Mossad intervened and an agreement was reached resulting in the Asian immigration of 1995. China would take over New Zealand by immigration, just as it has.

J'Accuse Helen Clark of three attempted murders on the author.
The first on 2 April 2002 using the SIS and the KGB.
The second on 23 August 2002 using the SIS and the Police.
The third on 14–22 May 2004 using the Mossad. The later was ordered with complicity of the Labour Party and initiated and funded by the Chief Justice Sian Elias.

J'Accuse Helen Clark of contract killing.
J'Accuse Dame Sian Elias of contract killing.
J'Accuse Helen Clark and Dame Sian Elias of competing to be the Mafia bosses of New Zealand and the South Pacific.

J'Accuse Helen Clark of promoting Jonathan Hunt to New Zealand's High Commissioner to Britain after he was exposed as a paedophile by US Customs.

J'Accuse Helen Clark of being in an arranged marriage to a homosexual child-sex abuser.

J'Accuse moi of running a program to drop the Berlin Wall 10 years early.

Appendix 1
Information and Inventions

Still Camera

The first permanent photographic image using a Camera Obscura occurred in 1825. The first production camera was made in 1839 and weighed in at a whopping 55 kg. By 1850, the photographer's kit required a horse-drawn wagon. The first pocket camera became available in 1899, the first folding camera in 1890 and the first market camera from 1917 (Kodak 1A, US$21). The first market petite camera with matching lipstick holder and compact hit the espionage scene in 1930. Cameras became digital in 1990 and this posed a problem with the veracity of the finished image.

Photos can now be taken from paint (camera paint) and this technology is now available in make-up, which means that your honey-trap can be filming you from your first date. "I can't believe it's you. Are you really .... [fill in name]?" ... then you're dead with no wake-up call.

Fax

The facsimile (fax) was invented in France in 1843. The first commercial fax service was up and running 22 years later in 1865. Forty-one years later, newspaper photographs could be faxed (1906). The fax was originally called a 'Mojo' and by 1973 it was capable of sending one page of text every 18 minutes. For its first 130 years, the fax was the dinosaur of communication.

Calculator

The calculating engine was invented in 1855. IBM formed in 1924 and the first pocket calculator was available in 1972 for 15% of the price of a new car (US$400).

Telephone and Dictaphones

Italian American, Antonio Santi Giuseppe Meucci (1808–1889), was considered a revolutionary and incarcerated (aged 25–26). He discovered the principle of the telephone in 1849 and developed a working model by 1859. He also registered at least 11 patents for such things as the stearic candle process, paraffin candles and electroplating.[1]

Officially Bell patented the telephone in 1876 and the first

[1] *Antonio Meucci: The Inventor and his Times*, Basilio Catania. (Vol. 1), Seat – Divisione, Editoria per la Comunicazione, Rome, 1994. 107th CONGRESS 1st session H. RES. 269.

exchange opened two years later in 1878, making Bell incredibly rich. Trans-Atlantic telephones were in operation from 1927 (51 years later). Telephone answering machines were invented in 1930, dictaphones in 1935 (available from 1939) and cell/mobile phones from 1982. The invention of the telephone was attributed to the Scotsman, Alexander Graham Bell (1847–1922), and it was only attributed to the much older, actual inventor, Antonio Meucci, on 15 June 2002 by the US Congress.

Alexander Graham Bell still has the memorable phrase attibuted to him: "Give us a bell." If the similar "Give us a Meucci" were in use, the Germans and Japanese would be very confused.

The Freemasons claimed Antonio Meucci, as they used to claim Alexander Graham Bell, and they do it by the following rider from the website of the Grand Lodge of British Columbia and Yukon, entitled 'A Few Famous Freemasons'.

> "The following list has been compiled from primary references or creditable authors. It is neither comprehensive nor definitive, but merely attempts to demonstrate the interest in Freemasonry found in all facets of society. Although the authors noted at the end of the list write with some authority, they do not always provide citations. Membership therefore cannot be considered confirmed unless a lodge name is supplied. Biographies for some of those listed can be found in our Biographies section. Although these men were Freemasons, they neither represent nor speak for Freemasonry."
>
> No lodge citation was provided for Antonio Meucci.

The Freemasons have an invested interest in the Patent Office and many inventors falsify their patents so that they do not work and cannot be copied. Regardless, Bell was still an interesting cat. He built the biplane which flew the first public flight in America (1908), designed a hydrofoil capturing the world water speed record (1918) and designed the 'photophone' based on transmitting speech by light which anticipated optical-fibre communications, although it did not work.

Lie Detectors

The hilarious Alphonse Bertillon system was in operation from 1887 to July 1901, when it was phased out by fingerprinting, which fingered its first criminal in June 1902 (the Fingerprint Bureau at

New Scotland Yard). There are no advertised convictions from the Alphonse Bertillon system which worked off ear prints and racial prejudice. In America, it was 1924 before an Act of Congress established the Identification Division of the FBI. This was the first thing the cross-dresser J. Edgar Hoover did.

In 1921, an instrument capable of continuously recording blood pressure, respiration and pulse rate was devised by John Larson.

In 1926 the polygraph was invented by Leonarde Keeler, but it was found that people could lie and neurotics on pentathol would go on and on and on, giving endless false leads that would take forever to investigate into oblivion. The best way of getting people to tell the truth was to interview them naked and this is still standard military practice to this day.

In 1936 the psychogalvanometer which measured electrical changes on the skin was invented by Walter Summers.

Radio

Radio waves were discovered in 1887 and transmissions in 1895. The valve was patented in 1907 and regular public radio broadcasts occurred from 1921. Transistor radios were invented in 1947 and became available seven years later in 1954.

Electricity

The first alternating current motor (AC) was built in 1888, with alternating current produced for public supply in 1895, courtesy of the Croatian, Nikola Tesla (1856–1943), a man who privately blamed his inventions on aliens. The definition of 'Guru' is 'bringer of light', and since Nikola Tesla brought light to the masses, he is more influential than God, with similar billing rates and line charges.

Moving Camera and Movies

Silent movies were invented in 1895 and movies with sound (talkies) came out in 1929. Many thought it would kill the industry. The first portable movie camera, the Bolex H-16, was in use from 1933 and has been used for intelligence and counter-intelligence ever since. The criminals were also spying on the police and saboteurs were also spying on the military.

Television

The cathode ray tube was invented in 1897 with television demonstrated 29 years later in 1926 by John Logie Baird (not a Freemason) and taken up by the BBC in 1929. This was improved from a 30-line mechanical system (shocking picture quality) to a 240-line mechanical system in 1936, just in time for the first B&W television broadcasts of the Nuremberg Rallies and Hitler's Berlin Olympics.

Hitler, as a Nordic-Anglo-Saxon coloniser, refused to shake hands with a black man (Jesse Owens, 10.3 sec) while a Polish man (Stanislawa Walasiewicz) slipped by the Wolf and won the silver medal for the Women's 100 m sprint.

A rival 405-line system was adopted by the BBC in 1937.

John Logie Baird went further and developed radar and infra-red television called 'Noctovision', which meant that you could also cook on your TV, and cook your family, which is partly why early television was only on for a few hours a day.

As well as screen projection and stereophonic sound, Baird produced 3-D images as early as 1944. Colour television was available from 1953 and in the Colonies some 20 years later in 1973. As far as home entertainment and public brainwashing goes, John Logie Baird (1888–1946) was Mr Big.

Video recorders were invented in 1951 and sold in 1956 for US$50,000 (B&W). At the same time, blank tapes cost US$307. Domestic videos and tapes became available in 1971.

The Freemasons have long been stealing inventions and the previous two centuries were ripe for it. Primarily as warring Nordic-Anglo-Saxon colonisers, they believe that everything great is created by a white colonist, and the Freemasons push this onto the public. So when the brown-blooded homosexual, Leonardo da Vinci (1415–1519), invented the helicopter etc., it was important that he was portrayed as a white heterosexual. This false history was successfully projected for over 480 years.

Other long-standing bluffs are yet to be exposed, but Samuel Colt (Freemason) stole the revolver and Winchester stole the repeating rifle. Winchester improved on Volcanic's repeating rifle, bought out the Volcanic Repeating Arms Company (1857) and created the Winchester Repeating Arms Company 10 years later (1867).

Jewish spies named Singer stole the sewing machine invention (patented 1852) and Richard Gatling, a doctor who never practised, assisted his father in the manufacture of sewing machines. During the American Civil War, Gatling (Freemason) stole a gun (1861–62) and is credited with having invented the crank-operated revolving multi-barrel rapid-fire machine gun, since called the Gatling gun. It was still in use in 1991. Perhaps he learnt something off his father and the Singer spies.

Because much of the Freemason history is assumed, they believe they are from an organisation of greatness and therefore assume it is their right to produce anything great. The Freemasons steal inventions by:

1. Inviting the inventor to become a Freemason.
2. Using a Freemason to reinvent the invention soon after; and
3. Then prove a false history that a Freemason did it first.
4. Assume without citation that the inventor was a Freemason.
5. Purchase backyard inventions off starving inventors never mentioning their name.
6. Kill the inventor on the way to the patent office, or
7. Copy the invention from the patent.

The record of the Mill Valley Lodge is a good example of the gullibility of boring white men who want to be part of something great.

> Mill Valley Record, 19 December 1925: "The New Masonic Temple: All meetings of the Masonic Lodges and of the Mill Valley Chapter of the Order of the Eastern Star are now being held in the remodeled Masonic Temple on Corte Madera Avenue.
>
> "The rooms have been enlarged and equipped with modern accessories. The spacious entrance hall opens off an attractive, small garden spot, next the street. On one side is the dining hall and entertainment room, on the other a thoroughly equipped kitchen. The dining hall has been enlarged and a double floor laid.
>
> "A wide stairway leads to commodious corridors and dressing rooms above and to the temple room. Elegance and simplicity combine to make the lodge room an ideal one for its functions. The floor is carpeted in an emblematic pattern of soft blue and gray. The proportions of the room are impressive and the new system of lighting lends to the atmosphere of the place.

"Before every stated meeting Mill Valley lodge holds a get-together dutch treat dinner. At the last dinner there was 80 in attendance and a large crowd is expected at the April affair which is expected to be an Italian dinner. This is quite a novel idea and should be tried out by some of the rest of our Masonic organizations. (Marin Sciots Monthly **BolOgnA**, Vol. 1, No. 1, April 1928).

"On September 10, 1928, at the age of 20, Inventor Philo T. Farnsworth, produced the first electronic television at San Francisco, CA, for Crocker Research Laboratories, which was later reorganized as Television Laboratories, Inc., and in May 1929 was renamed Farnsworth Television Inc., of California. Philo Taylor Farnsworth's electronic inventions took all of the moving parts out of televisions and made possible today's TV industry, the TV shots from the moon, and satellite pictures."[2] [all sic]

Philo T. Farnsworth claimed the invention of the television and the US government even issued a stamp with his image on it. But television was invented 19½ months earlier by John Logie Baird and shown to the Royal Institution on 26 January 1926. John Logie Baird even made a trans-Atlantic TV broadcast on 9 February 1928, but still, the US government (run by Freemasons) issued stamps with Philo T. Farnsworth's image crediting him with the invention seven months later.

John Logie Baird also patented the world's first record and play-back system (the Phonovisor), the world's first fibre-optics, and developed an all-electric 1800-line 3-D television (patented 1944) called Telechrome-colour. This is more advanced than anything we have today.

Realising they had lost the post-WWI movie race, the British government's Hankey Committee (1941) gave the go-ahead to Baird's 3-D television as the British post-war television standard, but two months after the report came out, John Logie Baird died suddenly and his Telechrome mysteriously disappeared.

Immediately after WWII a number of American companies (including RCA) mysteriously patented similar devices. This was enough to scare off most Brits.

Baird was so good, his Field Sequential Colour System was used for the Moon landings. His 3-D Telechrome television wasn't used because

[2] Mill Valley Lodge website.

it would have revealed the hoax and Russia would have won the moral high ground in the Cold War.

John Logie Baird's 1944 1800-line 3-D Telechrome-colour television would show up all digital hoaxes, so it was not issued to the public.

All those who filmed the 'Moon landings' died within four days of filming – thirteen by car accidents and two by heart attacks. Coincidences are amazing things and history is full of it.

It is common practice in the big stitch-ups to kill those involved and then to kill those who did the killing, with the surviving Freemasons already sworn to secrecy, like the astronauts, Neil Armstrong, John Herschel Glenn Jr., Edwin 'Buzz' Aldrin Jr., Virgil 'Gus' Grissom, Edgar D. Mitchell, Leroy Gordon Cooper, Donn F. Eisele, Fred Wallace Haise Jr., Walter 'Wally' Schirra Jr. and Thomas P. Stafford.

This is what our real history is made of – Freemason stitch-ups followed by Freemason cover-ups.

Sound Recording

Magnetic sound was invented in 1898. Discs for recording sound were invented in 1891, with sound recordings introduced in 1928. Wax discs weren't popular with the public, probably because they could only record once and be listened to once, after which the sound quality diminished exponentially. Wax discs were used to record the sound portion of the sexual practices of political figures of all nationalities in Berlin's Salon Kitty. These were then stored in Russia and the US, and are now worthy of study for historical influence.

The term 'Wax' became slang for its successor, the gramophone record, and 'Wax' is still slang for the raw material used to manufacture vinyl records today.

The first professional tape recorder was available in 1947. Small tape recorders made it to market in 1962, cassette tapes in 1963, 8-Track in 1965 and small chrome tapes from 1969. Digital recorders were available from 1978 and compact discs from 1982. Tapes exceeded vinyl sales in 1984, but you can't 'scratch' a tape.

The First Programmable Computer

Apart from Pascal developing the mechanical computer in the 1600s, the world's first programmable computer, the *Colossus*, was built in 1943 by the post office engineer Tommy Flowers. It contained 1500 valves and was used to decipher German war codes. Ten were built and they broke the German Enigma codes against a probability of 1 in 150 million million million in a matter of hours, sometimes revealing information to the British before the Germans had deciphered it themselves.

The British were aided by the capture of an Enigma transmitting machine and coding documents from the U-110 (U-boat) on 9 May 1941 by the HMS *Bulldog* and the HMS *Aubretia*. The 1500-valve *Colossus* was so successful that when the British Forces invaded France on D-Day, they already knew the location of 60 of the 62 German divisions.

At the end of the war Tommy Flowers was ordered to destroy the machine, smash it up, bury it, and burn all the plans, which he did in 1945. The secret of the machine was kept for another 30 years (1973), thus giving America credit for creating the first computer. The British made the first computer in 1943 from valves and the Americans reinvented programming language in 1954, taking all the credit for the creation of the computer – typical Yanks.

The first silicon chip was created in 1958. The Internet was invented in the 1960s for US military communications and the mouse was invented to aid this in 1969. Both became available to the public in 1988.

This was just preceded by computer-aided financial charging like EFTPOS (Electronic Funds Transfer at Point of Sale). New Zealand was the test country and New Zealanders were told they were following the rest of the world, then the rest of the world followed New Zealand with Interac Direct Payment, debit cards, Redcompra, Maestro and pinnen.

The first word processor was invented in 1964, the first mini-computer in 1965 and fibre-optic cables from 1966 (first used in computer cables in 1985). The first portable computer was available in 1975 and desktop computers were marketed six years later in 1981 with the mouse, Windows interface and magnetic disks from 1984. The first laptop was flown in the Shuttle in 1983 and available to the public in 1991.

The World Wide Web (www) was invented in 1990 and took off immediately to become the greatest information revolution the world has ever seen – more than the oral history of St Francis of Assisi and the 15th-century language race across Europe.

The www was voted most likely to topple *The Forces of Order* ('ordered disorder') and opened up a Pandora's box of otherwise secret information that would never have been published.

This was counter-actioned with equally compelling misinformation, computer crime, and too much information, most of which was government propaganda from *The Forces of Order*.

The www also made it possible to track the thinking and discovery patterns of the world's most belligerent individuals – and dedicated porn addicts – colonial British High Commissioners among them . . . rhymes with Anthony Blunt, he was named by US Customs as Jonathan Hunt.

Ghosts and GHOST

Ghosts were an incredibly popular form of fear, but lost their footing when mobile phones started to block the airwaves in 1982 – then aliens took over as the primary source of fear. But now we have a new form of ghost that runs hand in hand with 'World Anti-Independence Day'. This began on 4 July 2003 with any government department now allowed to hack into anyone's computer and share that information with any other government department – via 'The Privacy Act'!

There are two computer programs called "GHOST/Ghost". One was developed by a member of the test population at the bottom of the Pacific (New Zealand) and called "GHOST". The other was developed as a cover called "Ghost". GHOST can draw down all information on a computer without the computer realising it has been tapped and can work whether you are offline or online.

As soon as GHOST was developed, one of the New Zealand employees was seconded by the US Government to assist in tapping computers in America. GHOST was bought out by Semantec, the same company which delivers Norton Anti-Virus. If you have a Norton Anti-Virus program, you have GHOST, and all of your computer data can be downloaded and read.

There are some 120,000 people in America working for the US Government solely reading the information on your computer, faxes, emails and listening to your phone calls – so send them something funny. Can you imagine how dull their job might be?

GHOST makes thinking and research a dangerous profession. Part of the *One World Order* is One World Thinking (OWT), and ensuring that no one thinks outside the square.

One of the functions of governments now is placing paedophile images on the computers of thinkers, but this is not an excuse when such images are found on the computers of the police, as they were with the New Zealand Police in November 2004. These were placed on the police computers in order to stop the police charging paedophiles who were in the process of being promoted to the highest governmental positions in New Zealand. To further cover this up the Minister of Police was required to deal 10 kg of Afghan heroin to the police who dealt it to the gangs as part of the deal for promotion. Those gang leaders who refused to deal in the heroin were then attacked by the police.

I saw the results of these attacks first hand and they were very expensive for any gang member who stopped dealing. The police and gangs work hand in glove. The police are the hand and the gangs are the glove. The public perception is the opposite. The police are made up of Freemasons whose motto is ORDER OUT OF CHAOS.

Facial Recognition: Mandrake and Biometrics

The facial recognition programme *Mandrake* was publicly dropped in October 2003, with the announcement that it did not work. It was withdrawn to be forgotten about, probably because it worked so well and was considered a military device. It was continually developed and upgraded in secret and then marketed again after the secret testing process and withdrawal from the market had increased its value. It was capable of distinguishing between a real person and a body double and this proved problematic for higher-end politicians who use body doubles as a cover and as a form of political afterlife.

Sure enough, facial recognition was re-released to the public as *Biometrics* in May 2005. It never went away. Whereas fingerprints are not immediate and check 60–90 points, *Biometrics* instantly records and database-compares 50 points on the face and 240 points on the iris. This occurs from further away than one would think possible – like across the street and two storeys up. It also checks the movements of groups of people as to whether a crime is about to take place. When biometrics was reintroduced, the final shot was of Hitler with the statement "Someone is watching you".[3]

As soon as the Web became a common tool, it also became a common tool for crime. From 2003, computer crime has escalated at a greater rate than any other form of crime. Fishing attacks on computers masquerade as official bank websites and invite the target to log in passwords. Keystroke logers also place the Trojan virus silently at the back of the

[3] *Inside New Zealand*, 28 May 2005.

target computer. This activates during telephone banking and passes the logged information back to the Fisher, allowing them to use the passwords to withdraw funds via the target's Internet banking. This gives new meaning to the term 'Fisher King'.

Radio Frequency Identification Device Tags (RFIDT) are now on many purchased products. This is a low-powered tracking device and can be scanned from up to 10 metres away. RFIDT allows the new Tech-Burglars to identify new items in a home without even entering. This gives new meaning to the term 'stealing to order'.

Submarines and Torpedoes

Originally called the 'Intelligent Whale', one of the first submarines ever built was condemned by the US Navy in 1872.[4] The Holland A-1 (1901, USA) was the first real submarine. Powered by diesel electric it carried torpedoes. "By 1904, the 'Automobile' or self-propelled torpedo was erratic and unseaworthy, often proving as great a danger to the ship that launched it as to its intended victim."[5]

By 1904 the world had *intelligent whales* launching *automobiles* – how Jules Verne – but if it was moving, it was good enough for war. The first torpedo war began on 7 February 1904 when Japan attacked Russia without warning in the Manchurian Harbour of Port Arthur. This was the first engine-powered Asian attack against Europeans. Torpedos are now called *tin fish.*

Cars

The internal combustion engine was invented in 1885. Cars were first mass-produced from 1901 and became the first remedy for incest, especially for the slow walkers.

Ernest R. Godward (1869–1936) invented mechanical hedge cutters (from bicycle parts), the posthole borer, burglar-proof windows, a padded draught protector for doors, the hand-rotated egg beater (1900), some power tools, a hair curler and the spiral hairpin. His home was a veritable *Chitty Chitty Bang Bang* of inventive clutter.

His most lucrative invention, the spiral hairpin, came about by accident. His wife's hairpins used to fall out in bed and irriate him. Being a bit of an arrogant shit,[6] he would screw them up and throw them

[4] *Visions of Infamy*, p. 6.

[5] Ibid, p. 2.

[6] These were the author's great-grandparents.

against the wall. Mrs Godward would then straighten them out. Noticing that they sat in her hair better, he (32) took out a patent (1901), went to America, set up his Koy-Lo Hairpin Companies at 280 Broadway, New York, and made a fortune.

For the decade from 1901, Ernest Godward employed the near destitute and penniless 65-year-old Freemason Samuel L. Clemens (Mark Twain) as his vice president until Clemens (75) died. 280 Broadway, New York was no doubt the address from which *Tom Sawyer* and *Huckleberry Finn* were read time and again. Authors write their own life and Mark Twain never had to do another hard day's work.

Samuel Clemens had lost his money by acting on his own words, "Invest in land. They aren't making any more of it." When Samuel Clemens died in 1910, Ernest Godward sold the 'American only' rights to the spiral hairpin for £20,000 (now around $20 million).

During his time in America (1901–10) Godward invented the Petrol Economiser, the forerunner to the carburettor. This vaporised fuel and meant that engines could run on petrol, diesel, meths, turps or bootleg liquor using a third of standard fuel consumption . . . and they were more powerful.

He tried to sell the Petrol Economiser to British public transport, but they weren't interested so Godward got an engineering degree and sold it to the American military (1929) who fitted it to all of their military vehicles. This increased the length of their supply lines while keeping the military sober.

Not long after, the Petrol Economiser was fitted by most car and bus manufacturers and Ernest formed Godward Gas Generator Inc. in New York to fulfil demand. British public transport then followed . . . "If it's good enough for them, it's good enough for us."

By 1931 Ernest Godward was the foremost authority on the combustion engine. He was one of the lucky ones. He proved himself again and again. He (66) eventually died in a skipping competition on an ocean liner. He had ten children, but where is the money? That's the problem with independence. Ernest Godward gave the slow walkers a cheaper option to incest, but incest is highly protected by the *Forces of Order*.

Show me the money. No one in the family can find it.

Penicillin

Dr Morell produced quack pills like 'vitamin chocolate', 'Russian lice powder' and 'Ultraseptyl' for sore throats. When Dr Karl Brandt, Hitler's real German doctor, told Dr Morell about penicillin, Morell thought he meant 'phenacetin'. Morell then got 100,000 marks from Hitler to make penicillin and Hitler got sterile cane sugar for his money. When questioned by the Americans after WWII, Dr Morell said that he had invented penicillin and the British secret service had stolen it off him. This may seem ludicrous, but it is worth looking at.

Up to 1950 inventions were regularly stolen, with the true inventor discredited, gone missing, or terminated, and the credit going to a 'deserving' person, usually a Britisher and usually a Freemason. It was common practice in Britain to disregard backyard inventors and backyard discoveries, steal their inventions and give them no credit.

Penicillin comes from mould, something a quack could discover. It was officially discovered in 1928 by Alexander Fleming. For this, Alexander Fleming received the Nobel Prize in 1945, the same time Dr Morell was captured and claiming to have discovered it.

Sir Alexander Fleming (1881–1955) was the opposite character to Dr Theodor Morell, and was someone Morell could have wished he was – "I wish I were someone else". Alexander Fleming was a bacteriologist from southwest Scotland. He served in WWI and then as a professor at St Mary's Hospital in London from 1919. Fleming was the first to use antityphoid vaccines on humans, pioneered the use of Salvarsan for syphilis (something Morell had access to from 1936) and discovered the antiseptic powers of lysozyme. In 1928 he discovered penicillin, was elected to the Royal Society in 1943, knighted in 1944 and received the Nobel Prize in 1945.

Although penicillin was discovered in 1928 and characterised in 1934, it was not used in the war until 1944. The war was about killing, not about saving lives.

Alexander Fleming was the kind of doctor the British wanted to keep away from Hitler. Morell was the kind of doctor the British wanted for Hitler. Morell was an actor in a play who believed his own superstitions. As such, he was the perfect companion for Hitler. Both kept each other from approaching reality and both were borderline personalities.

Alexander Fleming served in WWI and invented many things particularly useful for war – typhoid vaccine, syphilis treatment, antiseptic and penicillin. Penicillin was first characterised by Howard Florey (Australian) and Ernst Chain (German) in 1934. Alexander Fleming and Howard Florey were knighted in 1944. All three received the Nobel Prize (1945). It took another 26 years for things to cool down and the German Ernst Chain was knighted in 1970.

I have seen inventions and the authorship of books taken off people and it has done much to destroy them. They do tend to become a shadow of their former selves, and under alcohol, legends in their own lunchtimes . . . but it is more common for borderline personalities to claim the news as their own, thus substantiating their own delusions.

But then again, inventors are accidental creatures, prone to accidents.

Helicopters

Helicopters were first mooted by the brown-blooded homosexual Leonardo da Vinci in the 15th century, who was portrayed as a white heterosexual for the next five centuries. Half a millennium later, the Spaniard Juan de la Cierva (1985–1936) developed the autogiro, first flown on 9 January 1923. This has a propeller in the front like a single-engine plane and a helicopter-like propeller on the roof. It flew like a plane, could not take off vertically, but could land like a helicopter. These were still flying in the 1940s.

Helicopters were first flown in Germany in January 1938 by the inventor Igor Sikorsky. The pitch-adjustable blades could be adjusted to provide lift and/or forward motion.

Hanna Reitsch was the first to fly a helicopter indoors. She flew a Focke-Wulf Fw 61 in the Deutschland Hall in Berlin in February 1938. This was one of the few cases where reality preceded the movies by 50 years.

Microwaves

Spymaster: "The earliest people I know in possession of microwaves were the Russians. This was discovered in 1939 and 1940 when the Germans got access to Russian Embassies in Poland and the low countries. The Germans were desperate to get into the Russian Embassies as they were looking for coding equipment and any information to go with it. What they found were small rooms containing bits and pieces of body parts.

"These were believed to have been special vaporising rooms. The entire rooms were microwave ovens and used to obliterate corpses. Smersh and the GRU's standard method was to neck-shot their subject first.

"An ancient Czech agent told me that we would see the Smersh men going out with little paper bags and dump the contents off bridges. We assumed at first that it was sandwiches made by the local Intelligence Officer's wife and nobody wanted to tell her that her culinary skills weren't up to scratch. It was only after the Germans gained access to the Russian Embassies that they realised it was all about 'heavenly transport'."

"When the Americans stole the microwave and found different uses for it, the Russians were quite indignant.

"The typical money-hungry American swine have stolen our idea. Just because they spotted a commercial use for it and didn't categorise it as being solely a method for state termination, they generalised its use and then obtained a patent for it.'"

Microwaves are a form of electromagnetic radiation that occurs when electric current flows through a conductor. The microwave was officially invented by Dr Percy Spencer, a self-taught engineer with the Raytheon Corporation who was working on a radar-related project. Dr Spencer noticed that food cooked around the new vacuum tube he was testing. Yeah Right!

Patented in 1946, the first microwaves, the 'Radarange', were 1.5 m (5'6") tall, weighed 340 kg (750 lbs) and cost US$2,500. Nevertheless they were immediately accepted in certain industrial applications, like drying potato chips, defrosting, precooking, and tempering meat. Dr Percy Spencer was titled Dr Percy LaBaron Spencer and inducted into the Inventors Hall of Fame on 18 September 1999.[7]

Space

The first multi-staged rocket was launched in the United States in 1949 and then leaked to Russians via the United Nations. The first Russian satellite shot its bolt in 1957. The first US satellite went into orbit in 1958 and thereafter space was militarised. Satellite phone calls started in 1960, with the first TV satellite coverage from 1962 and the first satellite broadcasts from 1980.

The first Russian travelled in space in 1961 and walked in the thinnest of air in 1965. In the great Russo-American propaganda war, the first Russian unmanned space craft was claimed to have landed

[7] Invention Dimension at the Lemelson-MIT Awards Program.

on the Moon in 1966. The Russians were never so foolish as to claim to have landed a man on the Moon, citing too much radiation and no atmosphere to block it. The first American space traveller claimed to have docked in 1966 and they went on to claim six highly controversial Moon landings from 1969–72.

Regardless of the truth of the matter, this was the height of the Cold War and Cold War propaganda. The claim served America well, but has never been repeated, not in 34 years.

The Space Shuttle first travelled in space in 1977. The Space Shuttle *Challenger* exploded in 1986 and the Space Shuttle *Columbia,* launched in 1981, exploded in 2003. The most successful space mission was the Hubble Space Telescope which was launched into orbit in 1990. It brought back the best *real* information, but was decommissioned in 2004 after it had rewritten the formation of planets.

Birth Control

The contraceptive pill came onto the market in 1960. The first test-tube baby was born in 1978 and "Dolly" the sheep was cloned in 1997 (d. 2003). The first *official* cloning of a human cell occurred in February 2004.

Hitler's Moustache

I feel compelled here to mention the invention of one of the 20th century's most visible foibles – Hitler's ever-diminishing moustache.

Bridget Hitler: "When Adolf [23] had come to visit us in Liverpool [November 1912] his moustache had been of the handlebar type, rather full and soft. Long before that I had persuaded Alois [30] to cut off the waxed points of his 'à la Kaiser'. When Adolf came, I set to work on him too and succeeded in getting him to trim it. Now [1923] I see that it had decreased still more, almost to a ridiculous degree. Alois's moustache had grown narrower too when I saw him in Monte Carlo. I had started them in the right direction, but Adolf had gone too far."[8]

When Adolf arrived in Liverpool in November 1912, he had a waxed handlebar moustache in the style of the Kaiser. When he left six months later in April 1913, it was a standard-length moustache, but by 8 November 1923 (34), it had been reduced to a ridiculous state and served as a symbolic reaction against the Kaiser's waxed handlebar moustache.

The short moustache also served to cover Hitler's unfeasibly large

[8] *The Memoirs of Bridget Hitler*, p. 44.

nostrils, something not all of his five doppelgängers shared. It also linked him with Charlie Chaplin in the West. This constantly put him in the funny pages and served to play down his threat to America.

Adolf Hitler: "My moustache is political." It was more likely the best doppelgänger tool never to be repeated.

Both Hitler and Chaplin studied under comedians, but only one took themself seriously. The English-American Sir Charles Spencer Chaplin mocked Hitler ruthlessly.

As Hitler became more confident, and more outrageously gay with his faggotty hand-flop wave, the Third Reich was nicknamed "The Gay Reich" and with good reason. Hitler's moustache became narrower, rounder and thicker, until it looked like a lower orifice. Hitler's moustache became so distinctive it allowed his less convincing doppelgängers to be completely accepted. Common thinking went, 'There's the moustache with dark flop fringe on a 5'9" body. It must be Hitler.'

Some of Hitler's doppelgängers were not that convincing and it was the moustache that carried them through. Three-quarters of all Hitler photos are of doppelgängers. The more doppelgängers Hitler used, the more difficult it became to ascertain which was the real Hitler. To date, no historian has risen to the challenge.

From Invention to Mass Use

The Camera had a 14-year delay from invention to production. It took another 60 years to become hand-held, another 18 years to get on the market, another 13 years to be miniaturised, and another 60 years to go digital. The Camera is the most influential invention in world history.

The Fax had a 20-year delay before going commercial, a 41-year delay before transmitting photographs, and a 140-year delay before it became quick enough for human patience.

The Telephone took 51 years to go trans-Atlantic.

Transistor Radios and Calculators had a 7-year delay before they reached the market.

Electricity (AC) took 11 years to reach the market.

Movie Cameras took 4 years to reach the market.

Television had a 10-year delay before it reached the market; 62 years later, we still haven't got 1800-line 3-D Telechrome-colour television.

Videos took 20 years to reach mainstream.

Magnetic Tapes took 64 years to become popular.

Computers took 21 years to reach the market.

Cars took 16 years from the invention of the internal combustion engine to mass production.

Penicillin took 16 years from discovery (1928) to mass use (1944). Many died in extreme agony during the 16 years between.

It took 11 years to move from multi-staged rockets to landing on the Moon. In the light of Cold War propaganda and the Apollo's computers being less powerful than a home PC, men landing on the Moon is still debateable, with less than half the population believing it.[9]

The Internet took 19 years to reach the public and in between was used by the military.

The www took no time at all and grew organically out of a desire for knowledge and synapsis.

---

[9] *The Oxford English Reference Dictionary*, 1996, pp. 1720–21 and the Web under Camera, Car and Electrical History.

Appendix 2
The Fluoride Con

One of the by-products of the manufacture of aluminium WWII planes was fluoride, which is difficult to dispose of. The addition of fluoride to the water was first proposed on 29 September 1939 by Gerald J. Cox Ph.D. of the Mellon Institute. His job was to find uses for industrial by-products. In a PR speech built on something that didn't exist, he said, "The present trend towards complete removal of fluorine from water and food may need some reversal . . . it may help with tooth decay."

There was never a trend towards the removal of fluorine out of food or water at the time. It was not even an issue. Fluoride does nothing for tooth decay; however, it does increase infant mortalities by 36% after five years.

The fluoridation of water was a complete fabrication from start to finish. However, the Germans were building huge numbers of planes and openly tested the fluoride by-product on Jews and found it made them more manageable, reducing their powers of lateral thinking. This made it more difficult for the Jews to link events with larger-scale ideas.

This is why fluoride is still used today – for population compliance. Fluoride, like religion and TV, is an opiate of the masses.

Germany, France, Holland and Japan are some of the few countries without fluoridated water. In Germany it is illegal to put any product in the water. Germans refused fluoridated water for its post-war population, arguing that Adolf Hitler used it mixed it with the water to dumb down populations, thus making it easier to conquer nations.

The Japanese culled out all their lateral thinkers 2000 years ago and the Chinese 50 years ago. Germany, on the other hand, culled out its nutters under Hitler.

New Zealand is a country where the practice of lateral thinking is seriously frowned upon, has restricted media time, if any, and is outlawed wherever possible and by whatever means available. As such, New Zealand was one of the first countries to supply fluoridated water (1950), well before the tests were complete.

Rather than culling out its nutters, foreign powers have been filming Kiwi nutters having 'sex they shouldn't be having' and then elevating them to the highest political positions, up to, and including, Prime Minister.

This scenario has been so successful few Prime Ministers have escaped this sure thing. First they are given fluoride, then they are malleable, then they are filmed having sex and then they are malleable in politics. Once malleable in politics, they are elevated into positions of influence.

Hitler had metal teeth surrounded with porcelain, was a noted and filmed coprophiliac and was then placed in roles where the position accelerated his status. Hitler was the perfect role model for this scenario.

The fluoride in toothpaste is sodium fluoride – a byproduct of aluminum production. It is not a good thing.

Fluoride can be good for your teeth, but it has to be naturally occurring calcium fluoride. There is a region in Denmark where this occurs naturally and the locals have good strong teeth.

Appendix 3

Not Without American Help

The Germans were able to fight WWII through the use of synthetic fuels that were created by the hydrogenation process (turning coal into gasoline). This process was discovered by I.G. Farben. Hydrogenation technology would not have been fully developed by WWII, but I.G. Farben made a deal with Rockefeller's Standard Oil, who were able to complete the research, thus facilitating the war. I.G. Farben plants were not targeted by the Allied bombing raids on Germany and by the end of the war their refineries had experienced only 15% damage. They were not strategically removed.

William Dodd, the American ambassador to Germany prior to WWII, wrote to President Roosevelt: "At the present moment, more than a hundred American corporations have subsidiaries here or cooperative understandings. The DuPonts have their allies in Germany that are aiding in the armament business. Their chief ally is the I.G. Farben Company . . . Standard Oil Company . . . sent $2,000,000 here in December, 1933 and has made $500,000 a year helping Germans improve hydrogenation technology . . . The International Harvester Company president told me their business here rose 33% per year, but they could take nothing out. [No earnings, just goods]. Even our airplanes people have secret arrangements with Krupps. General Motors Company [which was controlled by the J.P. Morgan Group] and Ford do enormous business here through their subsidiaries and take no profits out."

Germany needed the capital of these, and many more, American companies in order to wage a war. I.G. Farben had a holding company in the United States called American I.G. Farben. Paul Warburg, his brother Max (head of Germany's secret police during WWI) and Warburg agent Herman Metz were some of the members of the board of directors of the American I.G. Farben. Other directors included Rockefeller/International banking men like Edsel Ford, Charles Mitchell and Walter Teagle.

After the war three Germans from the I.G. Farben board of governors were convicted as war criminals, but the aforementioned Americans were not, even though they participated in the same criminal decisions as those who were punished.

According to author Eustice Mullins, Hitler met with Allen and John Foster Dulles in 1933. The Dulles brothers were acting as legal representatives of Schiff and Warburg's Kuhn, Loeb & Co, which was an Integral part of the Rothschilds network. Mullins claims Kuhn & Loeb had extended large short-term credits to Germany, and needed to ensure the repayment of these loans. The Dulles supposedly assured Hitler he would receive the funds necessary to be installed as Chancellor of Germany if he promised to repay the debts. One of the largest tank manufacturers for Germany was Opel, which was controlled by the J.P. Morgan Group. Another company connected to the J.P. Morgan Group was Bendix Aviation, "which supplied data [to Germany] on automatic pilots, aircraft instruments and aircraft and diesel engine starters". The examples go on and on . . .

The manufactured Pearl Harbor attack allowed Roosevelt to enter America into the war. A second world war had been created by the Illuminati, with the help of the Rothschild/Morgan/Warburg/Schiff syndicate. According to historian Antony C. Sutton, after the end of the war, the tribunals that investigated Nazi war criminals censored "any materials recording Western assistance to Hitler".

The source of this Appendix (slightly paraphrased) is 'Financial Wizards & Wealthy Cults: The Rothschild Bloodline' website. For this section of their website they refer to: Frederic Morton, *The Rothschilds: A Family Portrait*, Collier Books, New York, 1991; William Still, *New World Order*, Huntington House Publishers, Lafayette, Louisiana, 1990; Antony C. Sutton, *America's Secret Establishment: An Introduction to the Order of Skull and Bones*, Liberty House Press, 1986; Eustace Mullins, *The World Order*, CPA Book Publisher, 1985; A. Ralph Epperson, *The Unseen Hand*, Publius Press, Tucson, Arizona, 1985; Anthony Sampson, *The Money Lenders*, Penguin Books, New York, 1983; Virginia Cowles, *The Rothschilds: A Family Fortune*, Alfred A Knopf Inc, New York, 1973; and Joseph Wechsberg, *The Merchant Bankers*, Pocket Books, New York, 1968.

Appendix 4
Spreading the Blame

New Zealand is a listening post so it is interesting that what happens in the eroding Western society at the bottom of the South Pacific is, more often than not, the test case for the rest of the world. New Zealanders are a population that is constantly being experimented on, first. Hence they are internationally compared to sheep and by the marketeers as 'sheoples'.

New Zealand is the test case for resistance to dehumanisation. It is also the test case to see if covers are to be blown – that is, the believability of conspiracies are tested on New Zealanders via the media, which is why reference to first-screened New Zealand media is so important. Occasionally the programme (whether print media or television) gets it glaringly wrong and the media programme is swiftly changed for the rest of the world.

On 5 December 2003 in a High Court hearing, I asked the High Court judge and the lawyer for the discredited New Zealand police if they were Freemasons. Both said "No" which is what they are trained to do. Regardless, it did have some impact and the Freemasons began opening their doors on 11 September 2004.

Word leaked out that Hitler was a British agent and the Freemasons were about to be exposed for having created WWI and WWII. In response to this, they flung their doors open even wider and began targeting lonely non-thinking groups unable to fight back. The Freemasons are opening their doors to share the blame with geriatrics as this paid advertisement in *The New Zealand Herald* illustrates (Friday 12 November 2004).

Freemasons, New Zealand
Working for the good of all

'The understanding of ageing and the health of older people has been substantially advanced through the support of the Freemasons.'

Over the last 15 years the Freemasons have been instrumental in advancing research, education, training and health policy aimed at improving the health and well being of older people. Their vision, generous support and financial assistance has made a huge difference to New Zealanders, but the work is of relevance to ageing populations all around the world."

(Professor Craig Anderson, Professor of Gerontology, University of Auckland)

In 1990, to mark the centennial of the Grand Lodge of New Zealand, the Professorial Chair of Geriatric Medicine (now Gerontology) was endowed to the University of Auckland through a $2 million capital fund [he was placed there with a $2 million backing bribe]. An enormous amount of new scientific knowledge has since been gained through the array of world-leading research undertaken by Professor Anderson, his staff and students and their predecessors.

Areas of study have included the causes and treatments of stroke, heart disease, dementia and disability, as well as new methods of rehabilitation, health service provision, and ways of improving lifestyle.

In an age of increasing numbers of older people in the community, research into ageing (gerontology) and health care provision for older people (geriatric medicine) are key components of academic institutions and the health care system.

This week representatives of 12,500 New Zealand Freemasons gather in Auckland for their biennial conference and to install their new Grand Master, Mr David Mace, well-known Auckland businessman and community leader. They will celebrate their traditions and plan for the future, upholding their strong values and supporting the whole community, the young as well as the older.

Interested in Freemasonry? 'Freemasons' are in your phone book or visit www.freemasons.co.nz.

This is the first time the Freemasons have opened their doors to the inauguration of a Grand Pooh-Bah. No doubt the police and legal fraternity will be there in abundance.

Appendix 5

Doppelgänger Hess's Murder

The Affidavit of Hess's Nurse Abdallah Melaouhi

TO: The Service Registering Officer for North West Europe

In the Matter of the Births, Deaths and Marriages (Special Provisions) Act 1957 AND in the Matter of the Entry in the Register of Deaths of RUDOLF WALTHER RICHARD HESS

I, ABDALLAH MELAOUHI . . . do solemnly and sincerely declare as follows:

1. I worked as a male nurse caring for Rudolf Hess from 1 August 1982 until his death on 17 August 1987 at the Allied Military Prison in Spandau. From 1967 to 1970 I trained as a technical medical assistant in tropical diseases at the Institute of Tropical Medicine in Hamburg. From 1970, I continued my training as a qualified male nurse until 1973 when I received a Diploma Certificate in Nursing. In 1974 I moved to Berlin and worked at Hohengatow Hospital in the intensive care unit until 1976. I then attended the specialist medical school, Gauschule, Wedding, at the recommendation of the Department of Health at the Berlin Senate until 1977 and upon completing that training I received a Diploma in anaesthesia and the intensive care of sick people.

I was then promoted to Superior Male Nurse and went to work at Spandau Hospital (Krankenhaus, Spandau) in the intensive care unit until 1st August 1982 when I went to work in the Allied Military Prison in Spandau as Male Nurse for Rudolf Hess.

2. On the day of Mr Hess' death, 17 August 1987, I commenced my duties, which involved caring for Mr Hess, as usual at 6.45 a.m. I assisted him, as was usual, with showering and dressing, and was present when he ate a meal at 10.30 a.m. At no time did he give any indication that his state of mind was disturbed or that he was unduly depressed. Shortly after the meal, he asked me to go to the nearby town of Spandau to purchase a ceramic pot to replace one which was defective. Mr Hess would not have made such a request merely to ensure my absence, since I was always absent in any event from midday, during my noon pause.

3. At 2 p.m. I was called to the prison from my flat which was located outside, but in the immediate vicinity of, the prison (to which I had gone on my return from the town of Spandau). After some delay I reached the summerhouse in the prison garden where I was told that there had been an incident. The small door at the front of the summerhouse was closed.

4. When I entered the summerhouse, the scene was like a wrestling match had taken place; the entire place was in confusion. The straw tiled mat which covered the floor was in disarray, although only the day before I had cleaned the floor and had left the straw tiled mat carefully arranged in its usual place. A tall lamp had fallen over, but I clearly remember that the cable attached to the lamp was still connected to the main socket. It was this lamp cable which the authorities later said that Mr Hess had used to hang himself. A round table and Mr Hess's armchair had also been overturned. In summary, none of the furniture or equipment was in its usual place, and there is no question in my mind but that a struggle had taken place in the summerhouse.

5. The body of Mr Hess was lying on the floor of the summerhouse, apparently lifeless. Near to his body stood two soldiers dressed in US Army uniforms. I had never seen either soldier before. I also saw an American guard, whom I knew as a Mr Tony Jordan. There was no cable anywhere near the body of Mr Hess; as I have said, the only cable was attached to the fallen lamp which was still plugged into the wall.

6. I immediately proceeded to examine Mr Hess. I could not detect any respiration, pulse or heartbeat. I estimated that death had occurred 30 to 40 minutes earlier.

7. The guard whom I knew as Jordan stood near Mr Hess's feet and appeared overwrought. He was sweating heavily, his shirt was saturated with sweat and he was not wearing a tie. I said to Jordan: "what have you done with him?" He replied: "The pig is finished, you won't have to work a night shift any longer". I told him to bring the emergency case (which contained a first aid kit) and the oxygen appliance, while I commenced artificial respiration. When Jordan returned with the equipment, I noticed that he had first taken the opportunity to change his clothes. The equipment which he brought had clearly been interfered with. The seal on the emergency case had been broken open and its contents were in a state of disorder. The intubation instrument set had no battery and the tube was perforated. Further, the oxygen appliance had no oxygen in it. Yet when I had checked the emergency case and the oxygen appliance that same morning, as part of my normal duties, I am certain that both had been in full working order.

8. Since I did not have any of the necessary equipment I did the best I could which was to perform mouth to mouth resuscitation on Mr Hess and I asked one of the soldiers in American uniform to conduct a heart massage on him. This was at approximately 3.20 pm. These efforts had no discernable effect.

9. A doctor and a medical orderly whom I did not recognise arrived from the English Military Hospital in an ambulance. They brought a heart-lung machine into the summerhouse. I tried to operate the machine but it did not appear to function. Mr Hess was taken to hospital. I accompanied him and made further unsuccessful attempts to resuscitate him in the ambulance. There were final unsuccessful attempts to resuscitate him by the doctors at the hospital. He was pronounced dead at the hospital at 16.10 hours.

10. During the five years in which I daily cared for Mr Hess, I was able to obtain a clear and accurate impression of his physical capabilities. I do not consider, given his physical condition, that it would have been possible for Mr Hess to have committed suicide in the manner later published by the Allied powers. He had neither the strength nor the mobility to place an electric flex around his neck, knot it and either hang or strangle himself. Mr Hess was so weak that he needed a special chair to help him stand up. He walked bent over with a cane and was almost blind. If ever he fell to the ground he could not get up again. Most significantly, his hands were crippled with arthritis; he was not able, for example, to tie his shoelaces. I consider that he was incapable of the degree of manual dexterity necessary to manipulate the electric flex as suggested. Further, he was not capable of lifting his arms above his shoulders; it is therefore in my view not possible that he was able to attach the electric flex to the window catch from which he is alleged to have suspended himself.

11. Having regard to first Mr Hess' physical condition; second, the scene which I discovered in the summerhouse, in particular the location of the electric flex; and third, the surrounding circumstances as I have described them, I am firmly of the view that Mr Hess could not possibly have committed suicide as has been claimed. In my view, it is clear that he met his death by strangulation [1:30 pm], at the hands of a third party.

Declared before me at: [handwritten "Berlin"]
Signature of Declarant: [signature of Abdallah Melaouhi]

on: [handwritten] 17.2.1994

Qualification of person or officer taking the declaration:

Reinhard Gizinski, Notary Public, Berlin.

Appendix 6
The Bank of England Heist

During the Battle of Waterloo fought in Belgium, Napoleon appeared to be winning. The first military report to London communicated this on 18 June 1815. However, when the Prussians sent reinforcements, the tide turned in favour of Britain's Wellington. On 20 June 1815 Nathan Mayer Rothschild (1777–1836) received news in London, first by carrier pigeons and then by a fast boat trip, that Napoleon was being beaten. He informed the Government, (perhaps in a give or take manner) and they refused to believe him.

Nathan Mayer Rothschild took advantage of this and sold his stock. Everyone followed suit and this caused a crash on the English stock market. As it bottomed out, Nathan bought all the stock back at rock-bottom prices. The next day, at 11 pm, Britain's War Office 'discovered' Napoleon had lost a third of his men and had indeed been crushed. On 20–21 June 1815, the Rothschild family gained complete control of the British economy and forced England to set up a new Bank of England, which Nathan controlled outright. By 1815 Nathan Mayer Rothschild became the Bank of England, becoming Nathan Mayer, Baron de Rothschild.

Two years later in 1817 France secured loans through government bonds from two opposing banks, a French banking house in Ouvrard and Baring Brothers in London. In October 1818, the Rothschild agents (some of them illegitimate Rothschilds) began buying huge amounts of French government bonds. This increased their value. On 5 November 1818 these were dumped on the open market creating a financial panic as their value declined. This meant the opposing banks, and France itself, no longer had security for their loans and Rothschilds gained complete control of France's finances.

Nathan Mayer Rothschild then became Britain's first Jewish MP. During his 15 years as MP until he died in office, he accomplished absolutely nothing in Parliament. He maintained the position merely for the power, insight and influence. He was a Freemason, Illuminati, and hard man. During his life he profited hugely from war.

After his father's death (in 1836 or 1850) his son, Lionel Nathan,

Baron de Rothschild (1808–79) monopolised the family. In 1838, emulating his father, he said, "Permit me to issue and control the money of a nation, and I care not who makes its laws". He monopolised large international loans creating the Irish famine (1845–50) followed by the Crimean War (1853–56) which set up the Rothschild's financially. Lionel Nathan was elected to the House of Commons in 1847, but did not assume the position for another 11 years taking the parliamentary oath in a strictly Jewish manner on the auspicious Golden Dawn coven date of 26 July 1858 – interpreted as "one infinite hidden occult forever, from birth to the promise of heaven and death for the populace".

American and British Intelligence have documented evidence that the House of Rothschild (and other International Bankers) have financed both sides of every war since the American War of Independence (1775–83). One Rothschild agent, Haym Salomon, supported the British patriots during the War of Independence and later made loans to the American presidents from 1801–25 (Thomas Jefferson, James Madison and James Monroe). During the Napoleonic Wars (1800–15) one branch of the family funded France while another financed Great Britain and Germany.

In order to feed their habit of profit from war, the Rothschilds had illegitimate children which they used as agents for either war or money-lending. This was so for Abe Lincoln (A. A. Springs' son); Adolf Hitler (Lionel Nathan Rothschild's grandson); and Bill 'Slick Willie/Bubba/Elvis/Eagle/The Big Dog/Rockefeller Clinton (Winthrop 'Win' Rockefeller's son/Winthrop Paul Rockefeller's brother).

As a family working the banks around Europe, the Rothschild's developed a scam of trusted rescuer and kept this going so that investors had to be rescued, repeatedly. This gave them financial control over Europe, much of America and complete financial control over Israel, now their primary agent of war.

By 1913, the Rothschild's controlled a fortune well over US$300 million. By the time of railroads, coal, ironworks, the Suez Canal, oil exploration, diamonds, the French African empire, the Hapsburg monarchs and the Vatican bankruptcy (1823) their family fortune was over US$2,000 million. This was a family that could buy countries, the Courts, history and silence. The Vatican has remained financially and morally bankrupt ever since – similarly the British monarchy.

Appendix 7
Smersh

Smersh was a contraction of 'Smyert Shpionam' and roughly meant "Death to Spies". It was so powerful and feared that no sane man dared mention its name. With headquarters at 13 Sretenka Ulitsa, Moscow, its earliest operation was the assassination of the Mafia/Russian leader Leon Trotsky (Lev Davidovich Bronstein, b. 1879) on 22 August 1940.

After this successful operation, Smersh specialised in killing cowards (treachery) and double agents during the Soviet retreat from Hitler (from 1941) and was used as an execution squad for the NKVD, the forerunner of the KGB.

Smersh were also supposed to have killed the Russian agent/ Martin Bormann doppelgänger in April 1945. The firing squad were all then shot by someone else. Within days a group of British officers were car bombed outside Palestine's Lod airfield. One of these was Wing Commander Lindsay who had recently been behind German lines and was privy to sensitive information on the leadership challenges within the Third Reich. Smersh and the Betar worked hand in glove on this and it was organised by Joseph Stalin.

Khruschev disbanded Smersh in 1958. It then became Department V (Sabotage and Assassinations). Many KGB *Department V* officers made their way into Canada via the 1967 Montreal Expo and thereafter made their way into the United Nations . . . who turned a blind eye to it.

Nikolai Semenovich Skvortsov (Smersh) was expelled from Canada for espionage in 1949 and was immediately employed by the United Nations in New York.

In 1971, the United Nations Secretariat in New York employed 207 Soviet nationals of which at least 120 were KGB.

On 24 September 1971, 105 Soviet intelligence officers were expelled from the UN for subverting public officials and stealing technological data. Breshnev then ordered all other *Department V* personnel to leave their stations in Europe, Asia, Africa and the West, thus exposing them.

In October 1971, Vladimir Pavlichenko, the Director of External

Relations for the United Nations Public Information Office, was exposed as a senior KGB officer by the *New York Times*. Two days later the United Nations renewed Vladimir's contract for another two years.[1]

Mikhail Mikhailovich Antipov (*Department V*) was the first secretary of the Soviet mission to the United Nations. He had been involved in sabotage and assassinations since 1952 and operated out of the United Nations under diplomatic immunity for 12 years until 1972.

When you hear the words "The United Nations said . . ." hear "Communism and the NKVD/KGB/FSB said . . ."

The difference between the KGB vehicle and the United Nations vehicle is that the United Nations is the new model – it just has better suspension, but like the East German car, the Trabant, everything is backwards and designed to slow progress and disrupt forward-thinking, any forward-thinking ideologies, any foreign industry and any foreign family model that works.

Through intelligence eyes, the UN and the Red Cross are:
". . . the biggest bunch of intelligence sluts the world has ever seen".

---

[1] *KGB*, pp. 18–19.

Appendix 8
Hugh Trevor-Roper
Baron Dacre of Glanton

Hugh Redwald Trevor-Roper (15 January 1914–26 January 2003) graduated from Christ College, Oxford in 1936 (22) and in 1939 qualified for the master's degree as a research fellow at Merton College. At the age of 26, he wrote *Archbishop Laud* (1940). As a religious author with soft hands and no field experience, Hugh Trevor-Roper (31) was then sent to Berlin to investigate the authenticity of Hitler's death.

Trevor-Roper then wrote *The Last Days of Hitler* (1947), *The Gentry,* 1540–1640 (1953), *The Rise of Christian Europe* (1966), *The European Witch-Craze of the 16th and 17th Centuries* (1969), *Final Entries, 1945: The Diaries of Joseph Goebbels* (1978), *Catholics, Anglicans and Puritans* (1987) and *From Counter Reformation to Glorious Revolution* (1992).

Hugh Trevor-Roper was made the Regius Professor of modern history (1957–80) and Master of Peterhouse College, Cambridge (1980–87), during which time he authenticated some 60 volumes of the *Hitler Diaries* which covered Hitler's innermost thoughts from June 1932 to April 1945.

These were fake, fraudulent and another very well funded attempt to disguise the true events of WWII. The *Hitler Diaries* were discovered in

1980 by journalist Gerd Heidemann of the German Stern newsmagazine who paid £2,460,000 for the 60 bogus volumes, around £50 per word. Stern published them on 25 April 1983 and they were simultaneously published by *The Sunday Times* in Britain and sold to *Newsweek* (US).

Konrad Kujau (46, also known as Konrad Fischer) had told Stern journalist Gerd Heidemann that he was receiving the volumes from an East German general who had retrieved them from a German aircraft that had crashed in the village of Börnersdorf near Dresden in 1945, after it had left Berlin.

On Adolf Hitler's posthumous behalf, Konrad Kujau had previously written poems, a sequel to *Mein Kampf* and the beginnings of the opera Wieland the Blacksmith (Wieland der Schmied). Gerd Heidemann (54), a Third Reich aficionado, used his money from the deal to buy Hermann Goering's yacht.

Historian David Irving obtained copies of the *Hitler Diaries* in December 1982, and concluded a few days later that they were fake.

Regius Professor of modern history, Hugh Redwald Trevor-Roper, then Lord Dacre of Glanton, had been hoodwinked. He claims to have expressed serious doubts the day before it was to be published and phoned *The Times* editor Charles Douglas-Home on Saturday 24 April 1983 (not *The Sunday Times*) and his message did not get through to the correct newspaper. His endorsement and his failure to communicate effectively when it really counted darkened his reputation and brought much of his previous historical work into question. The West German Federal Archives then declared the diaries to be "grotesque and superficial forgeries", something which historian David Irving knew all along.

Kujau, a balding, portly, jocular man, who revelled in publicity, was captured by West German police on the Austrian border three weeks later on 14 May 1983. With journalist Gerd Heidemann he went through an 11-month trial and was given a four-year prison sentence for forgery.

When Kujau was released in 1988 suffering from cancer he declared to the press that he was going to write a memoir called "I Was Hitler". Ten years later *The Originality of Forgery* (*Die Originalität der Fälschung*) was published under his name, but he did not write it.[1]

[1] *The Times*, London, 14 September 2000.

Konrad Kujau then became a celebrated forger and made a fantastic living selling genuine forgeries of Hitler, Monet, Rembrandt and van Gogh paintings. With his new-found notoriety he signed the paintings with the original artist's name and his own name. By the 1990s he was so popular his paintings were fetching up to £42,000 each and a counterfeit sub-market appeared in fakes of his fakes.

Such is history – fakes upon fakes.

Kujau (27 June 1938–21 September 2000) then ran for mayor in his hometown of Löbau in 1994 and in Stuttgart in 1996, failing both times.

Despite lecturing propaganda history for 26 years and making the biggest historical booboo of the twentieth century, Hugh Trevor-Roper was retained as the great WWII historian and made honorary fellow and life peer in 1987 – cover upon cover.

Baron Hugh Redwald Trevor-Roper believed in his own intellectual rigour and could make up history with the eloquent language of his breeding. His elevation was enough to give him a following in England.

Hugh R. Trevor-Roper was a naïve intellectual who was easily bluffed by his own employers. His employers, the upper crust of British society and intelligence, gave him kudos, position and status for recording their eloquent status quo of investigative lies. As a result he was made Baron Dacre of Glanton.

Baron Hugh Redwald Trevor-Roper died aged 89 from cancer in a hospice in Oxford and was survived by three stepchildren. He was British aristocracy and wrote their history with a handcuffed pen.

History is the recording of lies
from which to build an uncertain peace
and justify the next war.
As long as that works,
it is the history that is selected.

British Army Major Hugh Trevor-Roper (left) used the testimony of Sturmbannführer Erich Kempka, Hitler's personal chauffeur (right) as the basis for *The Last Days of Hitler* and Britain's history of WWII.

Trevor-Roper was assigned to the task by Dick White (MI-6) later director-general of MI-5 (1953–56) and Head of British Secret Intelligence Service (1956–68).

Richard 'Dick' White was a close friend of the treasonous spy, Anthony Blunt, and MI-5 Security Inspector, Baron Victor Rothschild, 'the Fifth Man' in 'the Cambridge Five'. From 1935–63 the Cambridge Five managed to leak all Britain's military secrets and intelligence operations to Russia.

Appendix 9

Unlikely Heroes

Because Hitler had been a house painter, they were held in high regard in Nazi Germany. If anyone didn't pay a painter in the Third Reich they were in serious trouble. Insulting the Führer or not paying a painter were (equally) reason enough to be thrown into a concentration camp. Those who didn't pay their painter could also have their houses confiscated. As a result painters were treated with kid gloves and generally not questioned. This preferential treatment gave painters enough leeway to be very effective spies.

René Duchez, a French painting and decorating subcontractor took advantage of this. He took a job at the Caen offices of the dreaded Organisation Todt. He was not a spy, but on impulse stole the plans of Hitler's massive Atlantic Wall from the German engineers. These were the plans of the German defences around Cherbourg and Le Havre. The plans showed the position of the gun emplacements, batteries, pillboxes, machine-gun posts, trench systems, supply and ammunition dumps, fields of fire, gun range, communication systems, command systems and the technical specifications.

René's plans of the Atlantic Wall were taken to England via ship. They were tossed on the deck and generally disregarded during the sailing, then tossed onto an office desk at MI-6 with little or no notice given. MI-6 studied the plans lightly and then recognised their importance.

MI-6 feared the plans would be useless believing the Germans would change everything when they realised the plans had been stolen, but the German design engineers were even more fearful of the consequences, so they produced a duplicate copy and never mentioned it to anyone. British aerial reconnaissance then confirmed German construction was continuing according to the plans René Duchez had stolen.

As well as stealing the plans of the Atlantic Wall, René Duchez would hang around the cafés the German engineers used and pose as the village idiot. He'd initate arguments about their engineering practices and volunteer old-fashioned advice. The Germans would then draw him pictures of what was actually going on.

During the air raids René Duchez would crawl all over the Atlantic Wall with the French agent Henri Marigny and during weekends he would cycle with children along the coast and draw maps. On his return journey these were hidden in the handlebars of the children's bikes.

René was eventually betrayed to the Gestapo. When they came around to his house they found his wife arguing with a dissatisfied customer of her husband. The Gestapo escorted him out of the house, only to discover much later, that it was René Duchez they had removed. In this way, René Duchez, the French painter and paperhanger was one of the great spies of WWII.

René Duchez with Mothballs.

Appendix 10
James Bond – Sir Sean Connery

Sir Sean Connery was born Thomas Connery in Edinburgh, Scotland in 1930. He left school at 13 to work on a milk round (1943) before joining the Royal Navy at 16 (1946). He was invalided out of the forces at the very young age of 18 (1948) due to an ulcer and began body-building and truck driving.

His first big break was in the London stage production of South Pacific (1951), a television production called *Requiem for a Heavyweight* (1956), followed by a string of B-grade movies: *Time Lock* (2-minute cameo, 1957), *Another Time, Another Place* (1958), *Darby O'Gill & the Little People* (1959), *On the Fiddle ('Never have so few FIDDLED so many!'*, 1961), *The Frightened City* (1961) and *The Longest Day* (1962).

He was then picked for the role of James Bond (killing with style) by Cubbi Broccolli in 1962, doing *Dr. No* (1962) with Ian Fleming as consultant, *From Russia with Love* (1963), *Goldfinger* (1964), *Thunderball* (1965), *You Only Live Twice* (1967) and *Diamonds Are Forever* (1971).

During this time he also made *Marnie* (1964), *A Fine Madness* (1966), *Shalako* (1968), *Red Tent* (1969) and *Molly Maguires* (1970).

He has since done *The Anderson Tapes* (1971), *Zardoz* (1973), *The Offence* (1973), *The Terrorists* (1974), *Murder on the Orient Express* (1974), *The Wind and the Lion* (1975), *The Man Who Would Be King* (1975), *Robin and Marian* (1976), *The Arab Conspiracy* (1976), *A Bridge Too Far* (1977), *Meteor* (1979), *The Great Train Robbery* (1979), *Cuba* (1979), *Time Bandits* (1981), *Outland* (1981), *Wrong Is Right* (1982), *Five Days One Summer* (1983), *Sword of the Valiant* (1983), *Never Say Never Again* (1983), *The Name of the Rose* (1986), *Highlander* (1986), *The Untouchables* (1987 and Oscar), *The Presidio* (1988), *Memories of Me* (1988), *Indiana Jones and the Last Crusade* (1989), *Family Business* (1989), *The Russia House* (1990), *The Hunt for Red October* (1990), *Robin Hood, Prince of Thieves* (1991), *Highlander 2: The Quickening* (1991), *Medicine Man* (1992), *Rising Sun* (1993), *Just Cause* (1994), *A Good Man in Africa* (1994), *First Knight* (1995), *The Rock* (1996), *Dragonheart* (voice-over, 1996), *Playing by Heart* (1998),

The Avengers (1998), *Entrapment* (1999), *Finding Forrester* (2000) and *The League of Extraordinary Gentlemen* (2003).

Sir Sean Connery has been in over 57 movies and lives in the Bahamas from where he donates money to the Scottish National Party. At 59 years of age he was voted the world's sexiest man.

Ironically, in the 1970s the biggest gang of murderers in Northern Ireland were 'The Milkmen' and most of them *were* milkmen made up of New Zealand Maoris. It appeals to the sense of humour of military spy chiefs to send out operatives disguised as milkmen on the basis that no one would ever expect any harm to come from them. Their link with Sean Connery's first job is purely coincidental and has been included for clarification and, to dispel any rumours to the contrary . . . Sean Connery is no Maori!

England had its nuclear arsenal stored in Ireland and in 1978 Russia attacked Ireland to get at these. While neither confirming nor denying their existence, England hired New Zealand mercenaries to go into Northern Ireland and create strife. The Kiwi's became 'Milkmen' for cover and reconnaissance.

The Kiwi milkmen would dress as IRA, identify their targets from photos taped to the butts of their M16 or Armalite rifles, kill, load the bodies in a Triumph 2.5TC with a Leyland P76 V8 motor, drive to a prearranged location and hand over the bodies to the Garbage Men.

The Garbage Men would then put the bodies in a Land Rover and drive out into the countryside. A posthole borer originally mounted on the left-hand side of the front bumper was later moved to the right rear and these were used to dig a ten-foot hole. The skull, shoulder blades, spine, humerus and femurs were smashed with an engineer's ballpein hammer and the body was dropped in head first with half a sack of quicklime poured over the top. This broke down the remains quicker.

The hole was then sealed with the original grassed plug. Six to ten inch posthole borer-sized plug subsidence is still visible around Ireland and England today although most are now disguised under bushes.

The IRA would get the blame again and again for murders and explosions and the British Army would go in and protect their nuclear arsenal under the guise of cleaning things up – again and again – as long as 'nuclear' was the hot issue.

This is why no one from the British side has come forward to name IRA gravesites. It is something only Kiwi's can do.

For this reason, the New Zealand officer who ran the Garbage Men was 'accidentally' killed in a parachuting accident in a Tasmanian mangrove swamp in the 1980s, from which there was no escape. The tragedy is that he was as loyal to the Queen as any Maori.

New Zealand mercenaries would also go into Asian villages wherever the next war was going to be, kill everyone in the village so there were no witnesses, lay out the bodies, open up their postal bags, pull out Chinese and Russian weapons, place them alongside the bodies, photograph them and report that they had killed communists.

This sheep dipping made the New Zealand mercenaries look like heroes and the communists and Russians a threat. Those who survived the set up of war eventually had to chose a side and take up arms. If they didn't choose a side, they were merely killed and the pattern repeated – the weapons of their assassin's opposition placed next to them and the new dead photographed again and again.

Military Intelligence used these Suitcase Men who seemed comfortable with any and all degrees of the stitch-up. They'd even redress civilian child casualties in military style clothing and supply half-sized weapons to photograph next them, ensuring the child looked like a soldier of some merit. What do the Suitcase Men do now? They take photographs of the All Blacks of course – oh true and faithful servant. (Since publication in Sept. 2005, the photographer has been promoted.)

These photos did have the desired affect. *TIME* and *National Geographic* published them and helped to create the public indignity that put the heart behind the West's funding of these wars, until their own got killed. It was years and sometimes decades later before Western citizens woke up and realised it was just another Military Industrial

Complex fundraiser and a depopulation exercise to keep the population planners in the upper echelons of the United Nations happy.

When the United Nations says, "We estimate that by 2005 one in four people on the planet will be Chinese", you can bet there will be a plan to kill off this population. Sure enough, there are repeated attempts to perfect the killing of Chinese, first with Chairman Mao and his 70 million, then with H5N1 (the Avian Flu, the new Spanish Flu), the virus which is having its fatality and contagiousness continually perfected and tested on "the Chicken Sleepers" in Manchuria. In this case, the Chinese people are the victims at home and the weapons in the West.

Despite this, the paedophile Chairman Mao did his best with the killing of 70 million Chinese from 1936–76, with no books available other than 'The Little Red Book' (*Mao Zedong on People's War*, 1967) and absolutely no advantage to China whatsoever.

Mao Zedong (1893–1976) was Stalin's agent and Stalin had been gifted the United Nations for an eight day war from 8–15 August 1945. Like Hitler and Stalin, Mao Zedong had been deconstructed and was a man of no ideology, who stood for nothing and achieved nothing, other than spending his life in bed having sex on call with under-aged concubines, reading, but not absorbing the information, and 70 million deaths, which was more than Hitler and Stalin.

Chairman Mao's motto was "Political power grows through the barrel of a gun." His 'Great Leap Forward' and 'Cultural Revolution' achieved absolutely nothing for China. When he died, his third wife tried to seize power, but was arrested as part of the 'Gang of Four'.

This is war and this is the pattern of war from Hitler, Stalin and Chairman Mao to the Milkmen, the Garbage Men, the Suitcase Men and now.

So what is that – 130 million down and another 5.87 billion to go? Watch the news. It will tell you everything you don't need to know and everything that will stop you from knowing.

Research is under-funded and continually compromised.
"Truth is the first casualty of war"
and those who tell the truth about war
are continually threatened by The Forces of Order.
By the time a true historian publishes, he is already one-third cat.

Appendix 11
Hitler's Host for Hitler's Ghost

Rámon Serrano Súñer (12 September 1901–1 September 2003) was born in Cartagena, a seaport in the southeast of Spain. His father was José Serrano Lloberes, a distinguished civil engineer who worked on the Valencian port of Castellón. His birthplace was Spain's premier naval port and the largest naval base in the Mediterranean. It was a political town renowned for its Poms and MI-6 presence.

Rámon Serrano Súñer was an excellent student and, despite his father's sane protests, studied law at Madrid's Universidad Central. One of his closest friends was José Antonio Primo de Rivera who also studied law. He was the son of Miguel Primo de Rivera y Orbaneja (8 January 1870–16 March 1930), born in Paris to a family of soldiers. With his contacts in the British Military's General Staff, Primo de Rivera became dictator by coup from September 1923–January 1930, becoming General Pilar Primo de Rivera. He stepped down in January 1930 and died two months later. Officially, "He died in Paris apparently from diabetes, although the exact cause of death has not been determined."[1]

Spymaster: "He was killed in an air accident, a favourite MI-6 method of silencing political leaders, creating an instantly randomised and anonymous death. This is the curse of the 20th century and MI-6." Within three years Franco had overall command of the Spanish Army (1933) and eventually replaced General Rivera.

---

[1] Web, Wikipedia.

Rámon 'Serrano' Súñer graduated from Madrid Central University with the highest honours, then passed the combative legal examinations to join the elite corps of public prosecutors, the 'Abogados del Estado'. He spent a year at Bologna (the equivalent of Bavaria) where he developed a taste for fascism and was then posted to Zaragoza in 1929, where he became friends with General Francisco Franco.

In October 1923, Franco (4 December 1892–20 November 1975) married the strict Roman Catholic, Carmen Polo y Martinez-Valdès (9 July 1900–6 February 1988). Three years later he was made the youngest General of any European Army at the age of 34 (1926). Franco passed the favour on and made Serrano (28) the director of the Zaragoza Military Academy. Zaragoza is the capital of the autonomous region of the former Kingdom of Aragón at the crossroads between Madrid and Barcelona, and Bilbao and Valencia.

Serrano would rock up for dinner and it was here that he met his future wife Zita Polo y Martinez-Valdès, the beautiful younger sister of Carmen Franco. Rámon Serrano Súñer then became the brother-in-law of Franco in what was undoubtedly one of the great MI-6 honey-traps of all time, something approaching Mark Antony and Cleopatra. They had six children together. Zita was the better Catholic.

When they got married (1931), his best friend José Antonio Primo de Rivera (son of the recently deceased dictator) was his best man. José Antonio (24 April 1903–20 November 1936) became one of the founders of the Falange (1933) and editor of *El Fascio*. Five years later while José Antonio Primo de Rivera was awaiting execution at the beginning of the Spanish Civil War (1936), he named Serrano as one of the two executors of his will.

José Antonio was executed without trial at Alicante and became a national martyr at 34. Such was his popularity that Franco had his life artificially extended in order to die on the same day as José, 39 years later, and was buried next to him. This meant that Latino fascists could celebrate on the one day.

The Spanish are such impossible romantics.

José Antonio's brother Fernando was also killed without trial in the Madrid Jail at the beginning of the Spanish Civil War (July 1936), while their surviving brother was the Spanish Ambassador to Britain, abundant with MI-6 connections. Their sister founded the female branch of the Falange, and in the February 1936 election Falange managed to gain 0.7% of the nation's vote.

Rámon Serrano Súñer was one of the outstanding legal minds of his generation. Daily access to Franco and his association with the former dictator's son completed his credentials. At the elections in 1933, Serrano was the successful Zaratoga Ceda candidate (Catholic Authoritarian Conferación Española de Derechas Autónomas) and became the Conservative member for the Cortes Party (1933–36). He was also a prominent figure in the Catholic youth movement and carried much of its rank-and-file over to fascist Falange on the eve of Civil War – something approaching masterful deception.

The Canary Islands are way out in the Atlantic off southern Morocco and the British virtually patrol them. They were run by MI-6 then and they are run by MI-6 now. It remains a retirement home for many Pommy spooks.

Franco, a graduate of the Toledo military academy, was suspected of plotting against the leftist government (1933–36), so he was sent to the MI-6-dominated Canary Islands where he became the military commander. It was from here that he plotted in secrecy and isolation (in conjunction with MI-6) the Spanish Civil War (16 July 1936–1 April 1939), the testing ground for fascism, the training ground for WWII, Hitler's post-war destination and the beginning of the Cold War.

With overall command of the Spanish Army since 1933, Franco flew to Spanish Morocco and led the Spanish troops in North Africa against the leftist Republic government in Spain.

Sanjuro was the official leader of the rebellion (Civil War) but was conveniently killed in a plane crash four days into the war (20 July 1936). Fascist Germany and Italy sent troops and weapons in support on 26 July 1936 and Franco proclaimed himself Head of State (el Caudillo) on 29 September 1936. The government then left the combat zone, moving from Madrid to Valencia, with the inauguration taking place on 1 October 1936.

Fascist Germany and Italy officially recognised the Franco régime on 18 November 1936. They followed up with Heinkel He51 biplanes, the German Condor Legion on 7 May 1937, and later with Junkers JU52 and Messerschmitt Me109s.

Franco's 2IC was then killed on 3 June 1937. This left Franco and Serrano as the outstanding leaders.

Britain and France recognised the regime on 27 February 1939. Officially it was "reluctantly" but their recognition pre-empted the conquest of Madrid (28 March 1939) and the official end of the Spanish Civil War (1 April 1939) by a month.

Franco failed to warn Serrano that the Civil War was about to start (16 July 1936) and Serrano was caught in Madrid with his family. José and Fernando Primo de Rivera appealed for sanctuary at the British and French embassies, but were refused. They were then caught in the crossfire, captured and held in a Republican prison. Many of Serrano's friends were marched out of jail and murdered, Fernando Primo de Rivera among them. José Primo de Rivera was held for four months before being executed.

This experience imbued a hatred of democracy in Serrano, just as it was supposed to do. This is a common theme to fascist heroes (the same thing happened to Hitler) and the Republican marksmen would have been advised by MI-6: "Don't shoot the public prosecutor, the 36-year-old slightly built handsome distinct figure with aristocratic bearing."

As the war turned in October 1936, Serrano utilised an old MI-6 trick dating back to the 1600s and dressed as a woman to escape. Officially Serrano made his way to fascist Argentina where he joined the navy, sailed to France and made his way to Salamanca (20 February 1937) where he joined Franco's office working on the Falangist side of the Spanish Civil War . . . but it is more likely that he spent four months in MI-6 training in exchange for his assisted escape.

Salamanca, in central Spain, is part of the autonomous Kingdom of León and is one of the most spectacular renaissance cities in Europe. Salamanca is nicknamed 'the Golden City' for its aged sandstone, one of the finest squares in Europe, Castle-León, and the Romanesque cathedral that imitates the Hagia Sophia. In 2002 it was voted the European capital of culture, a title it shared with Bruges.

Following the 1936–39 Spanish Civil War, Rámon Serrano Súñer became the Chairman of the Falange Executive Committee, President of the Political Council of the Falange that governed Spain (full effective control), Minister of the Interior (Whom do we kill?

30 January 1938–40), Minister of Press and Propaganda (1939–40) where he developed the Whom do we malign? State News Agency, EFE (1939), and became the Foreign Affairs Minister from 16 October 1940–September 1942.

Rámon Serrano Súñer was in charge of the government, the press, suppression of the truth, the projection of lies, accusations, trials, convictions, the police, judiciary, the military, murder and Spain's international position.

Serrano was also a Nordic-Anglo-Saxon coloniser. He objected to the increasing role of the Roman Catholic Church in the Falange Party. There may have been no increase in Catholic influence, but at least he had made his official statement. One of the goals of WWII was to separate the Church from the State and that theme was common to all political parties right across the globe.

Serrano was Spain's answer to Goebbels, Goering, Himmler, Hess and Ribbentrop all rolled into one with a bit of Churchill and Moshe Dayan thrown in on the side. He was often called "the Spanish Goebbels" or "the Spanish Himmler". Serrano was Franco's aid and handler and his role often transcended that of el Caudillo himself. Quicksilver Rámon Serrano Súñer was effectively the head of the fascist Falange from 1937–42, with Franco taking the blame for Serrano's fascism. The Falangista was Spain's sole political party.

Franco was nicknamed Generalísimo (Cuñadísimo) meaning "a commissioned officer of the highest rank", "General of the highest degree" or "Commander in chief of the entire armed forces". Rámon Serrano Súñer was nicknamed "the brother-in-law issimo" (el Cuñadísimo).

The Spanish had a cool and casual sense of humour considering the number of dead.

As the much-accomplished brother-in-law of Franco, Serrano (the secret fascist) had a skill for building up the relationship with Mussolini and he modelled Spain after Benito Mussolini's fascist Italy. He also brought Franco and Mussolini together which indicates he had MI-6 connections. Serrano still publicly admired Mussolini in the mid-1990s. He was the only one.

Pedro Lain Entralgo worked for Serrano as a press official in the Spanish Interior Ministry (Whom do we kill?). Whenever a foreigner has a Pommy name in their midst, you can bet they are working for the British, and usually MI-6. 'Lain' is a British name and Pedro Lain Entralgo travelled to Nazi Germany three times during 1939 and 1940.

While in Germany, he was supported by Wilhelm Faupel, the Spanish Ambassador to Germany who directed the Spanish-German Cultural Institute (1934–45). This may seem innocent enough, but Wilhelm Faupel was Army General Wilhelm Faupel who received the esteemed military awards, the Pour le Mérite (8 June 1918) and the Oakleaves (4 August 1918), joined the Freikorps as a commander as soon as it started two months after the end of WWI (January 1919) and became Oberstleutnant (Leutnant-Colonel) Wilhelm Faupel.

Wilhelm Faupel, director of the Spanish-German Cultural Institute, was Army General Freikorps Commander Leutnant-Colonel Wilhelm Faupel who ran a Spanish spy agency in Germany with links to the Spanish spy agency in England.

Spain was such a divided nation that when their war ships were in port they would shoot each other across ships and even on the same ship. Heavy ordnance was not ruled out. Spain was the frontier where Britain and Germany met. As cousins, each had their claim and Spain was continually factionalised by Intelligence from both countries. As such, Spain became the trial run for WWII.

While in Germany, Pedro Lain Entralgo called for "Spanish colonial expansion in North Africa". Franco then publicly demanded Gibraltar and French North Africa. They knew that Hitler would refuse immediately and this charade gave Franco enough reason to turn down Germany's request that Spain become one of Germany's serf colonies, just as the Low Countries had.

In this way, Spain maintained its non-belligerent neutrality during WWII. Franco and Serrano had MI-6's military brilliance at their beck and call.

Hitler had been planning his escape to Spain since the war began, and to this end, Serrano had been conversing with the Germans from 1939. This continued with Ribbentrop (the Nazi Ambassador to England) on 17 September 1940 and with Ribbentrop and Canaris prior to the meeting with Hitler. Admiral Canaris had privately advised Spain not to join the Axis powers of Germany, Italy and Japan as England would win the war.

With meetings regarding Hitler's post-WWII escape going on in England, Germany and France, Rámon Serrano Súñer was officially made Spain's Foreign Affairs Minister on 16 October 1940, exactly a week before he accompanied Franco to the meeting with Hitler, Ribbentrop and aides at Hendaye on 23 October 1940.

Hendaye is the last French coastal resort town before entering Spain and is on the border with Spain's San Sebastian, near Bilbao in the Bay of Biscay. Canaris liked Bilbao so much he had properties there.

Officially this meeting was to discuss Spain's part in WWII, and to this end, no official progress was ever made, to the extent that Serrano failed to record anything of the meeting. The meetings were primarily about a safe haven for Hitler's exile.

The next day (24 October 1940) Serrano sent his junior official, Pedro Lain Entralgo, back in his place, to talk more with Ribbentrop over a secret protocol between Germany, Italy and Spain of which only Hitler, Mussolini and Serrano were to have knowledge.

Serrano would only avoid such a meeting if he felt the need to maintain plausible deniability. Spending two days at a meeting for which there were no records is not plausibly deniable.

The meetings contained vague territorial offers, but they were really about Hitler's escape to Spain at the end of WWII. Hitler had a history in architecture and liked Hendaye and the whole romantic feel of the place. Officially Hitler and Franco had "failed" negotiations on 23 October 1940 and nothing was recorded of their meeting. In real terms the whole thing was a smashing success and Serrano made further visits to Germany a month later in November 1940, and again in November 1941, to tidy up the details.

Once this was complete, the cover had to be instigated and all three disowned each other. Franco adopted a cooler attitude towards Germany and Italy and dismissed his 'Hess', Rámon Serrano Súñer, in September 1942, blaming him for the very German alliance he had just torpedoed. Hitler publicly called Rámon Serrano Súñer "the gravedigger of the new Spain" and Serrano was forced to officially resign his posts.

After WWII Serrano wrote a persuasive public letter to Franco, "calling for a transitional government that would have room for intellectuals in exile". Franco replied by scribbling "Ho-ho" in the margin and Hitler now had a safe haven.[2]

---

[2] Web: Facts, Info, and Encyclopedia article, Rámon Serrano Súñer.

Serrano remained a proud Catholic, which placed him at odds with the Nazis who officially regarded him as an enemy – perfect cover for receiving the new Holy Ghost, the six times dead and resurrected Catholic British agent, Adolf Hitler.

In the 1940s Serrano was considered a hypochondriac and in poor health. He officially retired from public life in 1947 and lived quietly thereafter – but at 94 he was still giving authoritative history lectures (minus the history) for 3½ hours before he was asked to stop (1995).

In 1947 Serrano published his first volume of memoirs, *Between Hendaye and Gibraltar* (*Entre Hendaya y Gibraltar*) which also completely excluded Franco and Serrano's meeting with Hitler and Ribbentrop at Hendaye (23 October 1940), his aides meeting the day after (24 October 1940), his meeting with Hitler in the witching hours of 3 May 1945 at Barcelona, and his subsequent meetings with Hitler in his post-life as 'the German Gardener'.

After Franco's death and the end of his reign (1939–75) Serrano published *Between Silence and Propaganda, History As It Really Was* (1977) and severely dented Franco's reputation, but still left out these same historical meetings.

More accurate examples of the Spanish Civil War may be found in Ernest Hemmingway's *For Whom the Bell Tolls* and George Orwell's MI-6 account, *Homage to Catalonia.*

The tragedies of Serrano's life inclined him towards fanaticism, but his legal mind and ministerial responsibilities made him a pragmatist. He was a lawyer, politician, author, MI-6 agent, fascist and prolific liar with a sparsity of morals. Like Hitler, he was also working for the Catholic cause and like most competent diminutive prosecuting lawyers, he believed his own lies unto death. Rámon Serrano Súñer gave himself plausible deniability in the part he played in history by charismatically thrusting his own sectionalised mind onto other's.

Franco and Serrano were the men who set up Spain to hide Hitler. With the help of MI-6, they gave Spain interim status so that no one, and no governorship, could ever take the blame.

As the uncrowned King of Spain, Franco supported this further in 1969 by designating the former King's grandson, Juan Carlos de Borbón, as his successor. This effectively meant that Spain was on loan to the fascists for the duration of WWII and its stitch ups – the 45 years from 1930 to 1975.

Hitler and Franco at Hendaye,
23 October 1940.

The Hitler scenario was very similar to the Jesus scenario and may have been used as a model.

Jesus was crucified on 1 March AD33 when he was 40, with two others to make it look convincing, one of whom was a doppelgänger for Simon ("Simon says, 'Hold out your arms'") and only the guerrilla warfare assassin, Judas Sicarii died (similar to Goebbels).

Simon was the head of East Manasseh and also known as Simon Magus (Simon the Magician), Zadoc Simon, Simon the Cannonite (Simon the Fanatic) and Simon the Leper. He was one of the most powerful people in the land, just as Martin Bormann was.

Similar to Hitler, all public and private records of Jesus' family were burnt by the Roman governors. Those who kept their family records were called the Desponsyni which became the root word for 'desperate'. They were hunted like outlaws and pursued to death by the Roman Empire and its Church. The none-too-bright spies, Peter and Paul, were killed off in AD64 by the same people that later elevated them to sainthood. The sacking of Jerusalem was completed in AD70.

Jesus was resuscitated and physically resurrected three days after the crucifixion to be acknowledged by the Marys. Hitler was transported to Spain three days later to be acknowledged by Eve.

Jesus travelled as far as possible from the clutches of the Roman Empire and went to Srinagar, in northwest India (40 km south of the border with Pakistan) to the highest peak in the area. There is a shrine to him here at Yusamarg – 'Jesus Meadow'. He was acknowledged by both the Christian and Islamic worlds and is mentioned in both teachings.

Similarly, Hitler is acknowledged by both the fascist and communist ideologies and is mentioned in both political teachings. Both achieved mass destruction and the opposite of what they set out to do. Jesus left a destroyed Jerusalem and Hitler left a destroyed Germany.

From Yusamarg, Jesus escaped some 250 km away to the Ladhak region of Tibet (now part of India) where he studied at the Hemis monastery, down the famous Indus River from Leh. Although this area is currently under Indian governorship, the people speak a very ancient form of Tibetan called 'Ladhak'. They are Tibetan traditionalists in language and culture. The Hemis monastery was shown in the movie *Samsara*, but the Tibetan language was modernised for the movie.

Similarly, Hitler escaped from the Parc de la Ciutadella to the Montserrat monastery just outside Barcelona and belonged to a secret Tibetan Lodge and practised Tibetan occultism.

There are four monasteries in the Ladhak region of India (former Tibet). The first is Spituk on the east side of the Indus river. The second is Mato some two hours from Leh on the west side of the river. The third is Stagma, a further hour's walk, and the fourth is Hemis, which is the big monastery. These are at 11,000 ft so there isn't much oxygen.[3] Jesus lived in the Hemis monastery in the Ladhak region of Tibet where he studied Buddhism.

At the council meeting in Ephesus in AD70 Jesus was referred to as "the lamb" and "St John" as in the St John's Ambulance Association.

Hitler was referred to as "Rabbit" and "the German Gardener" and is immortalised through the Volkswagen.

Jesus lived to physically die again around AD73 (aged 80) and his followers hoped he would be reborn again and again. When this didn't happen, a vacuum was created.

Hitler died six times within a day in Berlin (30 April/1 May 1945), was swished to Spain (3 May 1945), physically died in February 1950 (aged 60), but then his doppelgängers kept popping up all over the place for the next 22 years (until late 1972), as do his undressed imitators and dressed followers.

Jesus is preserved on a sadomasochistic cross, continually dying as he takes away the sins of those in denial.

Hitler was a sadomasochist and is preserved above a reverse harmony swastika (representing chaos) and is reborn daily in the sins and denial of every second politician – It's "Church on Sundays, hell six days a week, and at least I'm not as bad as Hitler."

How could anything possibly go wrong?

[3] *Samsara* incorrectly states that the Ladhak region is at 15,000 ft (January 2003).

Hemis Monastery top,
Parc de la Ciutadella (above), or
Montserrat Monastery (right and below).
Two out of three ain't bad.

Appendix 12
The Origins of *Animal Farm*

George Orwell (25 June 1903–21 January 1950) was born Eric Arthur Blair in Bengal, India, the second child of Richard Walmesley Blair and Ida Mabel Limonzin. His father worked for the Opium Department of the Imperial Civil Service (British monarchy/government drug trafficking) and his mother was the daughter of a tea-merchant in Burma (Burma was a harvest zone for drugs later hidden in tea). He then moved to England with his mother in 1904 and saw his father again for three months in 1907. He described his family as "lower-upper-middle class".

When he was six he won a scholarship to St Cyprian's Preparatory School in Eastbourne, Sussex. From here he went to Wellington for a term and then to Eton College where he was a King's Scholar from 1917–21, essentially a spy training network for MI-6 so it comes naturally and they don't have to pay them later. Here he made lifetime friendships with a number of future British intellectuals and spies. At Eton, Aldous Huxley was his French teacher for a term.

Orwell failed to win a university scholarship and it was here that his career diverged from his peers. He left England in 1922 and went to his mother's hometown in Burma and served as an assistant superintendent in the Indian Imperial Police (1922–27). Like his colleagues, he took on a native mistress and then quickly grew to dislike British imperialism. This was the role of Burmese beauties.

With this experience he tried becoming a total immersion author. Between 1928–33 he lived as a tramp, beggar, homeless person and itinerant in England and in France (near his aunt's pantry) and then stayed with his sister, aunt or parents to bring himself back from the depths of society he had immersed himself in. He even managed to get himself arrested for drunkenness, spending 48 hours in prison just to get the feel of it.

In 1933 he wrote for the *New Adelphi* and lived in Hayes in Middlesex, where he taught at a private school. Officially, the beginnings of tuberculosis during this time forced him into part-time work, and he became an assistant at a second-hand bookshop – notorious spy networks and the equivalent of the literary underground. He wrote *Down and Out in Paris and London* (1933) and needed a pseudonym to maintain a cover and save his parents' embarrassment. He considered 'Kenneth Miles' and 'H. Lewis Allways', but settled on 'George Orwell', a name that reflected the '**S**pies and **T**raders' knighthood of the order of St Michael and St George, the reigning monarch (King George V) and the River Orwell that ran through Suffolk. 'George Orwell' was a code name that reeked of MI-6 influence.

Orwell then worked as a shopkeeper in Wallington, Hertfordshire (1936–40) and published *Burmese Days* (1934) and *A Clergyman's Daughter* (1935). Meanwhile, his wife-to-be, Eileen O'Shaugnessy, was becoming very accomplished in her own right.

Eileen Maud O'Shaughnessy (25 September 1905–29 March 1945) was born in northeast England, the only daughter of a customs collector. She attended Sunderland Church High School (founded 1884), where she was once a student of J.R.R. Tolkien's. She studied at Oxford University in the late 1920s and graduated with a degree in psychology. To celebrate the Sunderland Church High School's 50th anniversary (1934) she looked ahead 50 years to the school's centenary in 1984 and wrote a collection of poems of what life would be like then. She included mind control and personal freedom eradicated by a police state. She called these "End of the Century, 1984" and was also a big influence on her future husband's vision in *Animal Farm.*

In 1935 she met George Orwell and they married in 1936. George was working on a commissioned documentary account of unemployment in Nordy country (North England), which resulted in *The Road to Wigan Pier*.

The Spanish Civil War broke out in British Intelligence controlled Spain on 16 July 1936, and as an MI-6 agent George was assigned as a war correspondent (like many other writers). Orwell was an uncompromising individualist and political idealist and argued that writers have an obligation to fight social injustice, oppression and the power of totalitarian regimes. The newly married couple arrived in Spain in December 1936. George soon took up arms and joined the struggle against Franco's fascists becoming a member of the Lenin Division in Barcelona. His wife Eileen was his support and civilian intelligence. She effectively kept him alive and informed.

Orwell looked like a robber chief, being inclined to rough-looking clothing, leather jerkins and high leather boots. He carried a long ex-German Mauser 98 Gewher and topped the outfit off with a large knife. When you think of all the other Poms in Spain dressed up like Christmas trees, it was a practical-looking outfit.

In early January 1937 he was given the rank of corporal, sent from Barcelona to join the offensive at Aragón and from there to the front line of Huesca in February. In early May, he took a week's leave to be with his new wife in Barcelona and exchange information. He returned on 12 May to be promoted to 2nd lieutenant in command of 30 men, one of which was a Scotsman named Jimmy.

While talking to an American sentry near Huesca at 5 am on 20 May 1937, Orwell was hit in the neck by a Franco sniper bullet leaving him temporarily dumb and his left side paralysed. This enabled him to go to hospital where he heard that his unit had been declared illegal and were in danger of being murdered by the communist comrades within their unit. With this foreknowledge (his wife included) he managed to escape what was the utter chaos of the Spanish Civil War. Much of his unit was either thrown in prison or murdered, depending on food rations.

This was described in *Homage to Catalonia* which, after British government interference, was published in 1938. With further government interference it sold less than 100 copies over the next 12 years Orwell was alive.

"I had come to Spain with some notion of writing newspaper articles, but I had joined the militia almost immediately, because at that time and in that atmosphere it seemed the only conceivable thing to do . . . It was the first time that I had ever been in a town where the working class was in the saddle. Practically every building of any size had been seized by the workers and was draped with red flags or with the red and black flag of the Anarchists; every wall was scrawled with the hammer and sickle and with the initials of the revolutionary parties; almost every church had been gutted and its images burnt . . . systematically demolished by gangs of workmen. Every shop and cafe had an inscription saying that it had been collectivized . . . Tipping was forbidden by law . . . There were no private motor cars, they had all been commandeered, and all the trams and taxis and much of the other transport were painted red and black . . . the loud-speakers were bellowing revolutionary songs all day and far into the night . . .

In outward appearance it was a town in which the wealthy classes had practically ceased to exist. Except for a small number of women and foreigners there were no 'well-dressed' people at all. Practically everyone wore rough working-class clothes, or blue overalls or some variant of the militia uniform. All this was queer and moving. There was much in it that I did not understand . . . I did not realize that great numbers of well-to-do bourgeois were simply lying low and disguising themselves as proletarians for the time being."[1]

The 30-strong Lenin Division that George Orwell led in Barcelona was a particular breed of ragtag rebels that wore a unique uniform with scarves. They had Mauser rifles, more ammunition than most other crowds, and a vacancy . . . so the 19-year-old Kiwi joined them, principally because he liked Mauser rifles.

The Kiwi was influenced by a Scottish fella named Jimmy, and Jimmy the Scot clung to a Pom he referred to as 'George the Spook' and he accorded absolute authenticity to any pronouncement that came out of George's mouth. Whatever George said, the Scotsman took as Gospel.

On a Wednesday in June 1937, George jumped up and announced to the Scotsman that he was going back to England and leaving, right then and there. Jimmy the Scott asked him why and George said their unit was going to be slaughtered by the British on the Saturday and they had to leave right away, get to the port and catch a boat back to England.

Jimmy the Scot said, "Right, I'm off then." The Kiwi was inclined to go with Jimmy and said, "Why are you going off?" and Jimmy said, "Where George the Spook goes, I go. If it's good enough for me to go, it's good enough for you to go too." The Kiwi said, "Well, he is George the Spook, so if it's good enough for him, it's good enough for me."

So the Kiwi agreed to go and the three of them made their way

[1] George Orwell, *Homage to Catalonia*, 1938.

to the port in Barcelona. They arrived on Friday and wandered around waiting for their travel documents to come through. George the Spook was paranoid that in the time they were wandering around they might come to some grief. He was certain that they should keep a low profile, that they should dress in civilian clothes and not parade their identities before any number of the varying militias that might put them up against the wall and shoot them. All they had to do to stay alive was to stay out of trouble and not stand out.

George wanted to negotiate with the others everywhere they went, and the Kiwi, being young, wanted to go out and wander around and look at things. The Scotsman, although a little bit more cautious, wanted to go out and have a butcher at things as well, so they decided to go for a short walk late on the Saturday afternoon. They walked along the seafront for about 15 or 20 minutes and came upon an auction held down at the beach. The auctioneers were selling all the travelling effects of a circus and the thing that was put on the lot to go next was a large-breasted female orangutan.

The Kiwi was all fired up in righteousness and said, "We should do something noble in our time in Spain and buy this poor fucking gorilla and we should free it." They were looking hard at the cost of it. In the meantime this English aristocrat came up with a large sum of guineas and made the highest bid on the orangutan.

George the Pommy spook said to the Kiwi, "Now you can't do anything, it's been bought fair and square."

The Kiwi was appalled and said, "That mongrel Pom is going to root that gorilla." At that stage the Kiwi couldn't understand the difference between an orangutan and a gorilla.

George the Spook said, "That's quite likely, but all we can do is go around and pick up the pieces afterwards."

All they had to do was keep a low profile until their ship set sail, but the Kiwi wanted to have a go at the Englishman and started to scrap with the others. Jimmy the Scot kept knocking the Kiwi to the ground and the Kiwi asked the Scot why he kept beating him, and Jimmy replied: "Any fight is better than no fight."

So George the MI-6 Spook and Jimmy the Scot carted the Kiwi back to the hotel and tied him up for the rest of the day, all night and into the next day. On the Sunday afternoon, they finally agreed to release him, and when they did the Kiwi was still adamant he should get back to where this Pom had taken the 'gorilla'.

Very, very reluctantly, George, because he was paranoid about their diplomatic presence in Spain, agreed to go back, but they had nowhere to store their rifles. They were bloody great Mauser 98 Gewhers and stood out like dog's balls, so they stuffed them in their bags and wrapped both in a carpet. To the Spaniards they were known as "the rug pedlars".

They went around to this flash hotel, the best hotel in the whole town. The Pom was right up on the top floor. On the way up, George the Spook was going on and on to the Kiwi about how he must not create a fuss, couldn't damage anything, must say please and thank you, and that they were dealing with a young member of the aristocracy and couldn't afford to annoy or enrage him.

They found his room and George knocked on the door, but there was no answer, so George went back downstairs to the maître d'hôtel to get the key.

While George was away the Kiwi said, "I'll fucking 'enrage' him, I'll fucking kill him" and the Scotsman was going, "I'd like to bash his head in too." Kiwi asked the Scot, "What is this cunt? Is he a Pom or is he a Scotsman?" and Jimmy replied, "He's a Pom" and the Kiwi said, "Well help me smash the door down."

So they busted through the door together and the stench that greeted them inside was absolutely horrendous and the room was in a total shambles. There was shit all over the bedding and at the end of the bed the orangutan was sitting all balled up in sheets, deeply distressed and crying into its arms. Jimmy started looking for the Pom to bash and the Kiwi started to clean up the orangutan and run a bath.

Jimmy said, "Oh, I found the fucking Pom," and the Kiwi said, "Don't bash him. Leave him for me. I'll come out and get him in a second." The Scotsman yelled out, "He's beyond it." The Kiwi rushed out and the aristocratic Pom was lying on the floor, dead as a door nail, all covered in shit with his neck broken. The Kiwi was furious.

George the Spook then came back with the hotel staff, and the maître d'hôtel stood up to his full height and read in his best accented

English telegrams that the aristocratic Pom had sent to England on the Thursday night before the circus auction. There were three of them and he had requested the hand-in-marriage of the three wealthiest single women in England. Each offer came back accepted.

After the maître d'hôtel had left the Kiwi said, "This story should be written up and told" and Jimmy agreed, "Aye, it should be written up and told."

After a long and considered pause George said, "No, there is far too much pathos in the story. It cannot be told" and Jimmy reiterated, "Aye, it cannot be told."

The Kiwi then went back into the bathroom and continued bathing the orangutan. George the Spook and Jimmy the Scot were wondering what to do with the A-list marriage proposals and the dead aristocrat, and when it came to moving the body, the Kiwi shouted out, "Monkey in the bath".

With the help of the British Consul in Barcelona, George Orwell, Eileen O'Shaughnessy 'Orwell' Blair, Jimmy the Scot and the 19-year-old Kiwi were able to escape to France. They narrowly missed being denounced and arrested as 'Trotskyites' when the communists moved in to suppress all the militias of their political unit later in June 1937 . . . like the next day.

George Orwell returned to England a staunch anti-Stalinist and anti-Communist, with the plight of animals firmly imprinted on his mind. He remained a democratic socialist, all of which defines him as MI-6 trained through and through.

When the Kiwi related this story to his son in the late 1960s, he said that George the Pom was a famous author from northern England, was quite a capable man and knew a lot. He was a working man and you would never suspect he was from the middle class.

The son asked his father why he had thousands of zoo animals in his photo album, everywhere from Cairo, Alexandria and right up into Italy. The 50-year-old Kiwi replied, "In 1936, as an 18-year-old in Wellington, my aunt told me, 'If you get any free time, I don't want you drinking or gambling. Go and visit the animals and take them something to eat.' So I did.

"While in Italy, I asked an Italian zookeeper why the eagles were so well fed and the zookeeper told me: 'This sturmbannführer [lieutenant] claiming to represent the SS commander in Italy, General Wolff, had come to see me in 1943, just as the Germans were pulling out of Rome and he said, "Don't keep anything that looks like a German eagle in a half-starved condition. Feed them properly or don't show them at all. When the eagle gets hungry, my trigger finger gets itchy. Make sure the eagle gets the best. To cage a half-starved eagle is an insult to Germany. You'll never know when we'll be back. If we come back and find the eagle starving, you and all your staff will be shot." The same German came back the next day and gave me gold coins. The funny thing is they had been stolen from a robbery in Yugoslavia during the German invasion in 1941, two years before I met him.'"

During WWII Orwell was a member of the Home Guard and in 1941 began work for the BBC Eastern Service, mostly working on programmes to gain Indian and East Asian support for Britain's war efforts. He was well aware that he was shaping propaganda and wrote that he felt like "an orange that's been trodden on by a very dirty boot" – just like the orangutan. Despite the good pay, he resigned in 1943 to become literary editor of *Tribune,* the left-wing weekly where he wrote a regular column, "As I Please".

Orwell opposed the war with Germany and declared that the British Empire was worse than Hitler. He finished his anti-Stalinist allegory *Animal Farm* in February 1944 and presented it for publication, which brought him to the attention of the Soviet Secret Police, complete with file.

Orwell adopted a three-week-old boy in June 1944 and used a cigarette to burn the birth date and natural parents' names off the birth certificate. His son became Richard Horatio Blair, born May 1944.

Nine months later, his wife and MI-6 support died in a routine operation at Newcastle upon Tyne on 29 March 1945. She was 39. They'd been planning to leave London and move to the Scottish island of Jura so he could concentrate on his next book. Upon her death, George Orwell was simultaneously diagnosed with terminal tuberculosis.

WWII ended on 8 May 1945 and *Animal Farm* was published on 17 August 1945 to immediate critical acclaim and worldwide success.

"All animals are equal, but some animals are more equal than others." Soon after, he coined the phrase "Cold War".[2]

George Orwell was a close friend of *The Observer*'s editor and owner, David Astor, and from 1945 he was its war correspondent and influenced Astor's editorial policies. Later he contributed regularly to the *Manchester Evening News*.

The royalties from *Animal Farm* provided Orwell with a comfortable income for the first time in his adult life. He had literary friends over to his apartment, pretty much as cover for his MI-6 information gathering, and the beautiful and intelligent fag-hags that came with them. Marriage proposals were not infrequent and he applied the same technique to the very beautiful Sonia Brownell, editorial assistant for *Horizon* magazine, which belonged to Cyril Connolly, his prep school and Eton buddy.

Sonia Brownell refused and Orwell moved to the remote Scottish island of Jura, two days' journey from London by train, bus and ferry followed by an eight-mile walk to a large house at the very end of Barnhill. Although a solitary man, he dreaded being alone and asked her to visit, but she refused this as well.

While in a state of loneliness in one of Britain's most remote locations, he wrote *Nineteen Eighty-Four* and changed the way the world thinks about itself. He left Jura for the last time in January 1949 and published on 8 June 1949 – "the destruction of language is essential to oppression".

In 1949 Celia Kirwan started working for the Information Research Department, in the Foreign Office unit. This had been set up by the Labour government to publish pro-democratic and anti-communist propaganda.

As a friend of Orwell's, Celia Kirwan approached him for names of pro-communist writers and artists. As a competent MI-6 agent Orwell gave her 37 names which have proved accurate through time. These were not published until 2003 and consisted of many journalists including Kingsley Martin (editor of the *New Statesman*) and the actors Michael Redgrave and Charlie Chaplin – a double agent.

Cyril Connolly came from a wealthy Anglo-Irish family and was 11 weeks younger than George Orwell and his exact comtemporary through school, but continued on to Balliol College in Oxford afterwards.

---

[2] *Tribune*, 'You and the Atomic Bomb', 19 October 1945.

A regular contributor to the leftist *New Statesman* in the 1930s, he wrote one satirical novel, *The Rock Pool* (1935) and the autobiography, *Enemies of Promise* (1938), where he attempted to explain away his failure to produce the literary masterpiece of which he and others thought him capable.

Connolly went on to co-edit the influential literary magazine *Horizon* (1939–50) and was the literary editor for *The Observer*. After Orwell's death in 1950, Cyril Connolly was promoted to the position of chief book reviewer for the London *Sunday Times* – highly paid to read other's works while in control of public perception. He was a fully educated well-funded contemporary of Orwell's, but the literary inferior. Connolly lived to 1974.

Orwell left Jura for the last time in January 1949 and was hospitalised in the Cranham sanatorium near Gloucester, in the Cotswold Hills, near Wales. With easier access, many of his friends started visiting, including Sonia Brownell (1918–80), the Calcutta-born daughter of a British colonial official, reluctantly educated at a British convent school.

"It was well known at the time, though forgotten now, that people in the last stages of tuberculosis frequently formed very strong emotional attachments, indeed those visiting patients were warned against the danger of taking such relationships at their face value."[3]

A relationship ensued and Orwell moved to the closest hospital to where Sonia lived. He moved to the University College Hospital in Gower Street, London and she lived two minutes' walk away at 18 Percy Street. The move happened on 3/4 September 1949, into a bed in Room 65.

Two days later he wrote to his friend David Astor (editor and owner of *The Observer*) mentioning his fever, that he was required to limit his visitors, would marry Sonia, and that his doctor, Morland, was very much in favour. Morland wanted Orwell to travel to a high-altitude clinic in France or Switzerland where there would be less pressure on his lungs – the sanatorium in Haute Savoi seemed to be the favourite.

Orwell had been in and out of hospitals for the last three years of his life, and the tuberculosis was probably contracted during his immersion period (1928–33) as described in *Down and Out in Paris and London*. Hospitals were also one of the favourite listening grounds of MI-6 and people had a tendency to talk to those famous.

[3] W. J. West, *The Larger Evils: Nineteen Eighty-Four: The Truth Behind the Satire*, 1992.

The very beautiful Sonia Brownell began to take over his routine burdens and Orwell lost control of his life from the moment he entered the University College Hospital. It was a bed from which he was never to leave. The battle for his soul had begun. He had lost the use of his typewriter.

"Opinions among his visitors varied as to whether he was dying. Some took it for granted . . . Other visitors were impressed that he was not so much struggling, but resting quietly to live."[4] "It was fairly clear that he was not going to recover; only the length of time that remained to him in doubt."[5]

Some commentators have argued that Sonia Brownell helped George Orwell through the painful last months of his life and gave him a hitherto unknown sense of joy. Others saw her as a mercenary, only interested in becoming his literary widow. After his death, she edited the four volumes of his collected essays and was fiercely protective of his estate.

". . . His marriage took place on 13 October [1949]. Marrying in a hospital involved obtaining a 'special licence'. But David Astor, his Best Man, handled all the necessary correspondence with the Archbishop of Canterbury . . . He looked unexpectedly grand and military in a smoking-jacket . . . David Astor entertained Sonia and a small party of mutual friends to a wedding luncheon at the Ritz. The signed menu was brought to Orwell. He was 46 years old, the certificate noted, and she was 31.

"After the wedding, Orwell at first rallied appreciably, then had some bad days, then good, then bad again; his temperature chart undulated greatly. He wrote only two or three letters in November, and in December they ceased entirely . . . he was reading . . . Dante's *The Divine Comedy* . . . What Morland knew could happen before they got him to a high altitude did happen. Orwell's lung haemorrhaged on the night of 21 January 1950 and he died at once and alone before Sonia could be found . . . The world heard the news on the BBC that morning. As the first sentence of his last book had said, the radios had 'all struck thirteen'."[6]

[4] Bernard Crick, *George Orwell: A Life*, 1992.

[5] Anthony Powell married the daughter of an Earl and was a liaison officer to London for various foreign military missions. He kept himself sane by writing *A Dance to the Music of Time*, 12 volumes characterising all the people he had ever met. Others were not so keen.

[6] Bernard Crick, *George Orwell: A Life*, 1992. In Golden Dawn coven language 21.01.1950 translates '∞1∞' or "infinite one forever" suggesting that his final death throes may have been assisted, not unlike those of his namesake, King George V.

Having requested burial in accordance with the Anglican rite (the religion of MI-6), he was interred in All Saints' Churchyard, Sutton Courtenay, Oxfordshire with the simple epitaph: Here lies Eric Arthur Blair, born June 25th 1903, died January 21st 1950.

Orwell is known for his insights about the political implications of the use of language. In the essay 'Politics and the English Language', he abhorred the effects of cliché, bureaucratic euphemism, academic jargon on literary styles and ultimately on thought itself – a lot like Chaplin. Both were coalface boys.

George Orwell wrote: "The government would have the power to keep its citizens under constant surveillance" . . . "Where freedom dies, slavery thrives" . . . and coined the phrases, "memory hole" . . . "Big Brother" . . . "Room 101" . . . "doublethink" . . . "thought police" . . . "unperson". . . "newspeak" . . . "Cold War" . . . "One cannot really be a Catholic and grown up" . . . and . . .

"If liberty means anything at all it means the right to tell people what they don't want to hear."[7]

[7] George Orwell, *Animal Farm*, published thirteen days after Hiroshima on 17 August 1945; *Nineteen Eighty-Four*, 1949; and *Manuscript Notebook*, 1949.

Appendix 13
Was Wallis Simpson a Man

Wallis Simpson was born a man, but then so are a lot of women. She was in the range of AIS Grade 4/5, commonly known as fag-hags. These women tend to surround themselves with sexually fringe men and women. They often look manly and often cannot reproduce.

AIS is 'Androgen Insensitivity Syndrome'. It is the new PC name for 'Testicular Feminization Syndrome'. It is a biological intersex condition where the reproductive organs/genitalia are partly at variance with the genetic sex.[1]

Androgen Insensitivity Syndrome ranges from Partial AIS (PAIS) to Complete AIS (CAIS). PAIS is the partial rejection of what makes a man. CAIS is the total rejection of what makes a man.

AIS explains the condition where men have small penises and testicles and increased female characteristics and women have increased male characteristics sometimes with testicles and a full dangling penis.

In all of these cases, the child began as XY male fetus with varying degrees of feminization. Here's how it works.

Androgen Rejection

Up to eight weeks gestation every fetus (male or female) has the capacity to develop either reproductive system and all fetus' begin as female. To create an XY male, androgens (male hormones) are required and full acceptance of androgens creates an XY male, complete with fully functioning twig and giggle berries.

At any time during the gestation of an XY male baby (from 8 to 40 weeks) if the androgen is rejected, then feminization occurs. Androgen rejection can continue on until the end of puberty. This creates varying degrees of fertility from a fully functioning man to a fully functioning woman and feminization occurs at varying degrees from a feminized male to a masculinized female.

[1] This is different from transsexuality (Gender Dysphoria) which identifies as belonging to the other sex; and is different from transvestitism, which is dressing as a woman, as was the case with the Duke of Kent.

The Gender Circle

An XX female is born a female and grows up to be a female. An XY male is born a male and grows up to be a male. Males with Androgen Insensitivity Grade 1 have normal sized genitalia with some feminine characteristics and some infertility, but generally reproduce as men. Grade 2 have smaller penises. Grade 3 have penises that don't function sexually. Grade 4 is intersexed. Grade 5 looks like a female with masculinized genitalia and may be able to give birth. Grade 6 is more feminine and can generally reproduce. Grade 7 is the super feminine woman, but was an XY male at some point in the womb.

Grade 1 is the male phenotype and Grade 7 is the female phenotype.

There are two methods of grading intersexed states. The first is by grading it from Partial AIS (PAIS) to Complete AIS (CAIS). The butch feminists (XY males with Partial AIS) use this method. They go on and on about how their enlarged genitalia causes male rejection and isolates them, so they start up pink bannered websites in a bleating search of other XY males who look like women but have male bits. The second method is the AIS Clinical Grading Scheme for the phenotypic features (external appearance) modelled on the Prader Classification for Congenital Adrenal Hyperplasia (CAH).

Grading the Look and the Feel

PAIS ranges from the feminized male to the masculinized female with CAIS as the feminine female stemming from an XY chromosome (male). With AIS the outward genital appearance can lie anywhere along a continuum from Grade 1 (masculine and obviously male when dressed) to Grade 7 (feminine and obviously female when dressed). The AIS grades are as follows:

Grade 1: Normal sized male genitalia but with reduced virility at puberty and occasionally infertile. The penis, testicles and anus are separate.

Grade 2: Slightly smaller penis and/or testicles, one or both. Not so masculine.

Grade 3: Small penis and undescended testicles (cryptochidism) and Reifenstein syndrome. Hitler had this. It was not uncommon to the Rothschilds and illegitimate Rothschilds.

Grade 4: Ambiguous gender, mixed gender genitalia. Hard to tell whether it's a clitoris or a penis. This masculinized vagina looks like two testicles wrapped around a hole with a penis the size of a large clitoris and huge labia often drooping down to the anus – the party surprise only a select few want. The laybia looks like testicles on ice and a common response is "She's a man".

Some say "the penis has been reduced to a urogenital sinus and the testicles have become labioscrotal folds". The two holes can get pretty close together and occasionally become one. The fanny and the pisser are fused and the anus is knocking on the door for a drink.

Grade 5: It's a female with separate urethral and vaginal orifices with a mildly enlarged clitoris (penis on ice) and only a small degree of fusion between the clitoris and anus.

Grade 6: Normal female who has developed dark coarse pubic and armpit hair at puberty.

Grade 7: Complete AIS female (CAIS) fail to develop armpit or pubic hair (downy hair only) and breasts range in size from normal to huge Tanner stage V breast. Many of these AIS Grade 7 females have no pubic or underarm hair, small pale nipples and short vaginas which need to be lengthened by masturbation, sometimes for years before intercourse.

Very sexy women can be Androgen Insensitive so don't give them any. As an added bonus they can still be lactating when their youngest is five. This is the super-female and many AIS Grade 7 have been photographer's models [AIS 007].

An XY male child Grades 1–3 is raised as a boy and an XY child Grades 5–7 is raised as a girl. An XY child Grade 4 is quite intersexed and the parents generally decide how the child will be dressed.

Fertility

The AIS child is conceived with male (XY) chromosomes. The embryonic testes develop inside the body and start to produce androgens, but due to androgen rejection, the external genitalia develop along female lines with the development of internal female organs suppressed by a hormone from the testes. This is known as the Mullerian Inhibitory Factor (MIF) and results in females with small male genitalia and males with small male genitalia.

Dressed males are perceived as feminine around AIS Grade 3. The problem with gender perception around dressed females occurs around AIS Grade 4 and 5. AIS Grade 4 may have a penis. AIS Grade 4 & 5 are generally raised as a female, but their genitalia are quite masculine.

Androids

A lot of these AIS Grade 4 and 5 were popping up all over the States during the 1920s and 30s and they were actually called "Androids". Their main trait was lack of menstruation and inability to have children. The CIA became very interested in these androids and they recruited Adolf Eichmann and John Money.

In 1947 John Money was recruited from New Zealand to the Psychiatric Institute of the University of Pittsburgh and then onto Harvard University (CIA) where he got a Ph.D. Money was used for AIS research amongst twins and he became known for a controversial gender-change case. After a botched circumcision he had David Reimer's parents raise their son David as a girl. This resulted in David Reimer's suicide on 5 May 2004.

Adolf Eichmann escaped Germany in 1947 and spent a year in a Catholic monastery where he was given a new identity and passport as Ricardo Klement. In 1948 he escaped to Argentina and worked for the CIA (1948–60) until he was kidnapped by the Mossad in Buenos Aires on 11 May 1960 and taken to Israel for trial.

Money was a CIA operative and Medical Advisor. Eichmann had become a CIA operative and did experiments on twins, but he wasn't a paedophile, Money was. The CIA were renown for employing and promoting sexually sick academics from post-WWII to the end of the millennium, and especially paedophiles. John Money was no exception and defended paedophilia for the CIA.

Money, with his CIA backed Ph.D., publicly and in writing, put forth the notion, which he backed as an academic (and the CIA backed him as an academic) that paedophilia was the result of "a surplus of parental love". Money also viewed heterosexuality as "societal, superficial and ideological". Because Money was backed by the CIA, his academic views held more weight than other academics.

Money's public paedophile notions were backed by the CIA because those at the top of the CIA were homosexual and paedophiles having been backed into the top ranks of the CIA by communists who ran their intelligence agencies from *their* record of CIA recruit sexual practices. Those with clean sexual records were never promoted.

Money filmed himself sexually molesting the male of one of the AIS twins. When his paedophilia became too obvious the CIA hastened his death by MAD. He got Parkinson's disease and this was rapidly advanced. John William Money (8 July 1921–7 July 2006), a Kiwi arsehole.

Wallis Simpson

At eight weeks gestation Baby Wallis (an XY chromosome fetus) began to exhibit an insensitivity to androgens (male hormones including testosterone) and did not fully develop male genitalia. Thus she was born an XY male with female outer genitalia and partially developed male internal genitalia.

She had a female body shape, reduced female characteristics, her breasts, although small, developed at puberty. She had underarm and pubic hair, did not menstruate, had no ovaries, no fallopian tubes, no uterus, could not conceive children and had a small short vagina with internal testicles.

The AIS vagina is at best two-thirds the normal length, and may be no more than a centimetre or two in length, or even just a dimple. This is called Vaginal Hypoplasia or Short Vagina. Vaginal hypoplasia can be treated by the non-surgical method of masturbation from puberty, which actually lengthens the vagina to something approximating normal, depending on the initial vaginal hypoplasia. Wallis enlarged her vagina through masturbation and a prolific sexual appetite.

In Wallis Simpson's case, she was known as the 'Shanghai Squeeze' and was said to have had "the ability to make a matchstick fell like a Havana cigar".[2] Wallis Simpson was AIS Grade 4/5. Wallis Simpson was born a man.

Edward, Prince of Wales/King Edward VIII

Some PAIS babies may be raised as males as was the case with King Edward VIII who had a small penis and was rampantly homosexual prior to his weeklong engagement to the Queen Mother, and his subsequent arranged meeting with Wallis Simpson. She was the only person who seemed able to satisfy Prince Edward and she used to skite about it.

Edward, Prince of Wales was AIS Grade 3 and had a small penis and undescended testicles. Wallis Simpson was AIS Grade 4/5 with a small vagina and internalised male sexual organs. Both men and women with AIS have problems with fertility. Even slight AIS can contribute to infertility in otherwise normal men and both Edward and Wallis were infertile.

An AIS Grade 4/5 and Grade 5 trait is to destroy the sexuality and direction of drive of the live-in male partner. AIS Grade 3 men tend to travel diligently in the direction they're given, until another direction is given and they bounce in that new direction. Hence Wallis Simpson could treat King Edward VIII as her lapdog – birds of a feather flock together.

AIS Grade 3 men tend to be taxi drivers, whether political or physical. Hitler was AIS Grade 3 and was a political taxi driver. His High Command often complained about his constant change of direction.

[2] Source: w w w.medhelp.org, AIS website and *AIlaS* newsletter.

Treatment

XY females with testes (AIS Grade 4) have lower oestrogen levels than XX females with ovaries (normal) and XY CAIS females (AIS Grade 7), who are immune to being masculinized due to their complete insensitivity to androgens. The CAIS Grade 7 are known for their huge Tanner stage V breasts, model looks and masculine drive.

However at puberty XY females with testes' can spontaneously feminize. If this does not occur, their gonads can be removed aged 20. This is called a Gonadectomy or Orchidectomy. A Gonadectomy can bring about osteoporosis (bone thinning), menopause and cardiovascular disease and hormone replacement therapy (HRT) is recommended. HRT also helps initiate puberty in 10-11-year-old AIS females.

Skin grafts and sections from the intestine can be used to lengthen the vagina, but vaginoplasty should be avoided in early childhood.

With today's technology, "it might be possible for primitive sperm material extracted from intact AIS testes to be used to fertilise a donor egg."[3] That is, Wallis Simpson may have been able to conceive a child as the male and use an egg donor and rent-a-womb – thus giving her the possibility of half the King's ransom.[4]

In 50% of the AIS Grade 4/5 females, the undescended testes can result in a groin hernia during infancy. In the remaining 50% undescended testes may not be discovered until a failure to menstruate at puberty. The AIS Grade 4/5 adult will look like a girl and can lean towards any sexuality. AIS adult females with their testes removed say their testes never bothered them.

Androids in New Zealand

The condition of females being perceived as men is common in New Zealand, especially in politics, and especially in the Labour Party (New Communist) where many of the females have few female characteristics, have not reproduced and have married homosexuals and child-sex abusers as a form of mutual cover. (The Moneys in the Bag.)

When these Grade 4 & 5 women are heard on the radio they sound like men. Some of these masculine females (who actually feminized males) resort to hormone replacement therapy, but it doesn't seem to work for

[3] Source: w w w.medhelp.org, AIS website and *AIlaS* newsletter.

[4] "Half the King's ransom" meant that if a man gave birth he was entiled to half the King's possessions. This was removed from the law books during the 1950s as the result of chromosome research.

long, and certainly not between election photos and election speeches. Thus, in mid-term politics, New Zealanders are treated to masculine sounding AIS Grade 4 & 5 females who have enlarged their vaginas through masturbation, often helping each other in the process. This has resulted in the Labour Party being correctly diagnosed as "Fabian Fisters" and "Butch Lesbians". The Androgenous fist fight is a long journey to the middle.

New Zealand's Prime Minister Helen Clark is a case in point. She has the dressed appearance of AIS Grade 4/5 and looks a lot like the AIS Grade 3 Adolf Hitler. Both were 56 years old when last photographed.

Amongst the tea ladys of the civil service, Helen Clark is known as "Mrs Bull" and there is some truth to the statement "She's a man".

Baby Helen was conceived an XY male and at some later date she rejected the androgen but retained a lot of the male characteristics.

Medically it can be said that Helen Clark was born male.

What is so scary is that this SheMan, with her voluntary radical hysterectamy in December 1976/January 1977, is touted as being the next Secretary General of the United Nations. That would make her a SheDevil.

> AIS has previously been known as Androgen Resistance Syndrome, Feminizing Testes Syndrome, Male Pseudo-hermaphroditism, Goldberg-Maxwell Syndrome (CAIS), Morris's Syndrome (CAIS), Lub's Syndrome (PAIS), Gilbert-Dreyfus Syndrome (PAIS), Reifenstein Syndrome (PAIS) and Rosewater Syndrome (PAIS). Either a lot of sex doctors were Jews or a lot of Jews were inter-sexed. Other XX female conditions with some AIS-like features include: Mayer Rokitansky Kuster Hauser (MRKH) Syndrome and Mullerian dysgenesis. Other XY male conditions with some AIS-like features include: 5 alpha-reductase deficiency, 17 keto-steroid reductase deficiency, Denys-Drash Syndrome, Leydig cell hypoplasia, Smith-Lemli-Opitz Syndrome and Swyer Syndrome (XY gonadal dysgenesis).
>
> The Danish patient register, 1992 "suggesting an incidence of 1 in 20,400 XY births (hospitalized cases only, so true incidence probably higher). PAIS may be only about 1/10 as common as CAIS."
>
> Source, AIS website and AlIaS newsletter, w w w.medhelp.org.

Wallis Simpson
AIS Grade 4/5

King Edward VIII
AIS Grade 3

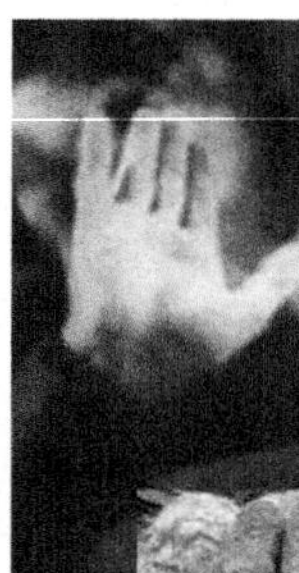

Adolf Hitler
AIS Grade 3

Helen Clark
AIS Grade 5

Bibliography

(Current first)

Politics Politics Politics

Louis Bűlow, The Dwight D. Eisenhower Library, 2002.

Tony McCarthy, 'IRISH–AMERICAN HITLERS', ***Irish Roots Magazine***, 2002.

Ronald Hayman, ***HITLER AND GELI***, published by Bloomsbury, 1998.

Roland Perry, ***THE FIFTH MAN***, Pan Books, London, 1994.

Dmitri Volkogonov, ***LENIN***, A New Biography, The Free Press, 1994.

Webster Griffin Tarpley and Anton Chaitkin, ***GEORGE BUSH, The Unauthorised Biography***, Executive Intelligence Review, 1992, PO Box 17390, Washington DC, 20041-0390.

DOPE INC., written by the editors of Executive Intelligence Review magazine, 1992, 3rd Edition, Ben Franklin Booksellers, 107 South King St, Leesburg, Virginia 20075, phone (703) 777 361, Fax, (703) 777 8287.

Paula (Hitler) Wolf, ***HE WAS STILL MY BROTHER***, VWB, Berlin, 1992.

John Pilger, ***A SECRET COUNTRY***, Vintage, 1992.

Alan Bullock, ***HITLER AND STALIN, Parallel Lives***, Harper Collins, 1991.

Ronald W. Clark, ***LENIN***, A Biography, Harper & Row Publishers, 1988.

Charles Higham, ***WALLIS, SECRET LIVES OF THE DUCHESS OF WINDSOR, The Scandalous Truth about the Century's Most Infamous Woman***, Sidgwick & Jackson Ltd, 1988.

Valdamar Valerian, ***THE MATRIX***, Arcturus Book Service, GA, 1988.

Adolf Hitler, ***HITLER'S SECRET BOOK***, Introduction by Telford Taylor, Grove Press, Inc., N.Y., 1961, 1983.

Bridget (Brigid Elisabeth) Dowling, ***THE MEMOIRS OF BRIDGET HITLER***, edited by Michael Unger, Duckworth and Co Ltd, 1979.

John Barron, ***KGB, The Secret Work of the Soviet Secret Agents***, Hodder and Stoughton, The Readers Digest Press, 1974, 1975.

Richard Hanser, ***PRELUDE TO TERROR, The Rise of Hitler***, Rupert Harris-Davis, London, 1971.

N. K. Krupskaya, ***REMINISCENCES OF LENIN***, International Publishers, 1960.

William Guy Carr, R.D., Commander R.C.N., ***PAWNS IN THE GAME***, USA, 1958, 1959, 1960, 1961, 1962, 1978 etc.

Alois Hitler (William Patrick Hitler), ***ADOLF HITLER***, 1946.

THE HITLER SOURCE BOOK, New York American, Nov. 1940.

Pauline Kohler, ***I WAS HITLER'S MAID***, J. Long, France, 1940.

Werner Sombart, ***THE JEWS AND MODERN CAPITALISM***, T. Fisherunwin, London, 1913, also 1916, 1951, 1962, 1967.

War War War

Nigel Cawthorne, ***WWII, Battles of the Second World War***, Selectabook Ltd, Wiltshire, 2004.

Nigel Cawthorne, ***TYRANTS, History's Most Evil Despots & Dictators***, Bookmart Limited, Leicester, 2004 on license from Arcturus Publishing Limited, London.

Brian Cassidy, ***FLYING EMPIRES, Short 'C' class Empire Flying Boats***, Queen's Parade Press, 2004.

Nigel Cawthorne, ***D-DAY, Dawn of Heroes, 6 June 1944, 60th Anniversary Special Edition***, Selectabook Ltd, Wiltshire, 2004. Originally published as ***FIGHTING THEM ON THE BEACHES, The D-Day Landings***, June 6, 1944, Arcturus Publishing Limited, London, 2002.

Lynn Picknet, Clive Prince and Stephen Prior, ***DOUBLE STANDARDS: The Rudolf Hess Cover-up***, Warner Books, First Books Library, Little Brown, UK, September 2002.

John Harris and M. J. Trow, ***HESS: THE BRITISH CONSPIRACY***, Carlton Books, 2000.

J. C. Masterman, ***DOUBLE CROSS SYSTEM, The Incredible True Story of How Nazi Spies were turned into Double Agents***, Lions Press, New York, 2000.

Jon E. Lewis, ***TRUE WAR STORIES, Eyewitness Accounts of Life on the Front Line in the Words of the Ordinary Soldier***, Constable & Robinson Ltd, London, 2004, 1998.

BRITISH WARPLANES OF WORLD WAR II, edited by Daniel J. March, Airtime Publishing, 1998.

Christopher Creighton (James Bond) ***OPJB, The Last Great Secret of the Second World War***, Simon & Schuster, 1996.

Hugh Thomas, ***DOPPELGÄNGERS, The Truth about the Bodies in the Berlin Bunker***, published by BCA by arrangement with Fourth Estate Limited, 1995.

Kevin Abrams & Scott Lively, ***THE PINK SWASTIKA, Homosexuality in the Nazi Party***, Founders Publishing Company, Oregon, 1995.

William B. Breuer, ***FEUDING ALLIES, The Private Wars of the High Command***, John Wiley & Sons, Inc., 1995.

Donald McCormick, ***THE LIFE OF IAN FLEMING***, published by Peter Owen, London, 1993.

William H. Honan, ***VISIONS OF INFAMY, The Untold Story of How Journalist Hector C. Bywater Devised the Plans that led to Pearl Harbor***, St. Martin's Press, New York, 1991.

F. W. Winterbotham, ***THE ULTRA SPY; An Autobiography***, Papermac, 1991.

Robert L. Gandt, ***CHINA CLIPPER***, Naval Institute Press, 1991.

James Follett, ***A CAGE OF EAGLES***, pub. Wallington, Severn House, 1990.

Robin Mackness, ***ORADOUR: MASSACRE AND AFTERMATH***, Ulverscroft Large Print, 1988.

Geoffry Rice, ***BLACK NOVEMBER, The 1918 Influenza Epidemic in New Zealand***, Allen & Unwin, Historical Branch, Department of Internal Affairs, 1988.

Peter Padfield, ***HESS: FLIGHT OF THE FÜHRER***, Orion, 1988, 1991.

Anthony Cave Brown, ***THE SECRET SERVANT, The Life of Sir Stewart Menzies, Churchill's Spymaster***, A Sphere Book, 1988.

Vladimir Karpov, ***RUSSIA AT WAR, 1941–45***, Stanley Paul & Co Ltd, London, 1987.

David Irving, ***CHURCHILL'S WAR, Volume One, The Struggle for Power***, Veritas Publishing, 1987.

Kenneth Macksey, ***MILITARY ERRORS OF WORLD WAR TWO***, Arms and Armour Press, 1987.

Arnold Kramish, ***THE GRIFFIN, The Greatest Untold Espionage Story of World War II***, Houghton Mifflin Company, 1986.

Christopher Andrew, ***SECRET SERVICE, The Making of the British Intelligence Community***, Heinemann, London, 1985.

Ben E. Swearingen, ***THE MYSTERY OF HERMANN GOERING'S SUICIDE***, Robert Hale Limited, 1984, 1985, 1990.

Wolfgang Paul, ***HERMANN GÖRING, Hitler Paladin or Puppet?***, translated by Helmut Bögler, Arms and Armour Press, 1983 in German and 1998 in English.

David Fisher, ***THE WAR MAGICIAN***, pub. Coward-McCann, NY, 1983.

Peter Allen, ***THE CROWN AND THE SWASTIKA***, pub. R. Hale, London, 1983.

David Irving, ***THE SECRET DIARIES OF HITLER'S DOCTOR***, Sidgwick and Jackson, 1983.

Ellic Howe, ***THE BLACK GAME***, pub. Joseph, London, 1982.

Decie Denholm (Editor), ***BEHIND THE LINES, One Woman's War 1914–18***, Collins, 1982.

Donald M. McKale, ***HITLER, The Survival Myth***, Briarcliff Manor, New York, 1981, updated 3rd edition, Cooper Square Press, 2001.

Peter Vansittart, ***VOICES FROM THE GREAT WAR***, Pimlico, 2003; first published by Johnathan Cape in 1981.

Brian Garfield, ***THE PALADIN***, MacMillian London Limited, 1980.

Harry Patterson, ***TO CATCH A KING***, Hutchinson & Co Ltd, 1980.

Hugh Thomas, ***THE MURDER OF RUDOLF HESS***, 1979; also as ***HESS: A TALE OF TWO MURDERS***, 1988, Hodder & Stoughton.

P. W. Stahl, ***KG 200***, James Publishing, 1979. Originally titled ***Geheimgeschwader*** [**Secret Squadron**] KG-200 die Wharacitnach über 30 jahren.

Hugh Verity DSO & Bar DFC, ***PILOT BIOGRAPHY***, Crécy, 2001; and Hugh Verity, ***WE LANDED BY MOONLIGHT***, pub. Ian Allan, 1978.

Martin Streetly, ***CONFOUND & DESTROY, 100 Group and the Bomber Support Campaign***, Jane's Publishing Company Limited, 1978, 1985.

F. W. Winterbotham, ***THE NAZI CONNECTION***, Weidenfeld & Nicholson, London, 1978.

Tony Wood and Bill Gunston, ***HITLER'S LUFTWAFFE, A Pictorial History and Technical Encyclopaedia of Hitler's Air Power in World War II***, Salamander Books, London, 1978.

W. Averell Harriman and Elie Abel, ***SPECIAL ENVOY to Churchill and Stalin, 1941–1946***, Hutchinson & Co Ltd, London, 1976.

Albert Speer, ***SPANDAU, The Secret Diaries***, translated by Richard and Clara Winston, Collins, London, 1976.

John Toland, ***ADOLF HITLER***, Doubleday & Company Inc., NY, 1976.

Anthony Cave Brown, ***BODYGUARD OF LIES***, Harper & Row, NY, 1975.

F.W. Winterbotham, ***THE ULTRA SECRET***, Weidenfeld & Nicholson, 1975.

Joachim C. Fest, ***HITLER***, translated from the German by Richard and Clara Winston, Weidenfeld and Nicholson, London, 1974.

Ladislas Farago, ***AFTERMATH***, Hodder and Stoughton, 1974.

Ladislas Farago, ***THE GAME OF THE FOXES, British and German Intelligence Operations and Personalities which Changed the Course of the Second World War***, Hodder and Stoughton, 1972.

Harry Elmer Barnes, ***PEARL HARBOR AFTER A QUARTER OF A CENTURY***, published in the journal Left and Right, 1968. Barnes 'died' less than a week after finishing the final draft on 25 August 1968.

George Martelli, ***AGENT EXTRAORDINARY***, George Martelli & Michel Hollard, 1960; reprinted as ***THE MAN WHO SAVED LONDON***, Collins, London and Glasgow, 1967.

Geoffrey Norris, ***THE SHORT SUNDERLAND***, Profile Publications, 1967.

James Leasor, ***THE UNINVITED ENVOY***, House of Stratus, 1962, 2001.

Sefton Delmer, ***WORLD WAR 2 BLACK PROPAGANDA***, *The Viking Press*, 1962.

William Green, ***WAR PLANES OF THE SECOND WORLD WAR, Vol. 5***, **'Flying Boats'**, Doubleday and Company, 1962.

Adolf Hitler, ***HITLER'S SECRET BOOK, The Long-Hidden Papers of Hitler's Confidential Aims for World Conquest***. Introduction by Telford Taylor, transl. by Salvator Attanasio, Grove Press, Inc, NY, 1961.

Heinz Conradis, ***DESIGN FOR FLIGHT, The Kurt Tank Story***, translated from the German by Kenneth Kettle, Macdonald & Co (Publishers) Ltd, London, 1960.

Charles Drage, ***THE AMIABLE PRUSSIAN***, pub. Anthony Blond, 1958.

Lt.Col. A.P. Scotland OBE, ***THE LONDON CAGE***, William Clowes and Sons, Limited, London and Beccles, 1957.

Robert Merle, ***DEATH IS MY TRADE***, Derek Verschoyle, London, 1954.

August Kubizek, ***THE YOUNG HITLER I KNEW***, Tower Book, 1954; also ***ADOLF HITLER, MEIN JUGENDFREUND*** (*My Youth Friend*).

Adolf Galland, ***THE FIRST AND THE LAST, The German Fighter Force in World War II***, 1953, translated by Mervin Savill, Methuen, London, 1955.

Hugh Trevor-Roper, ***THE LAST DAYS OF HITLER***, MacMillan, London, 1947, sixth edition 1987.

Ernst Carl, ***ONE AGAINST ENGLAND***, Jarrolds, London Ltd, 1935.

Fritz Joubert Duquesne, ***THE MAN WHO KILLED KITCHENER: The Life of Fritz Joubert Duquesne***, Williams Faro Inc, New York, 1932. This was also published under the alias Clement Wood.

Hector C. Bywater, ***THE SECRET PURPOSES***, Constable & Co, London, 1932.

Hector C. Bywater, ***THE GREAT PACIFIC WAR***, 1925, St. Martin's Press, New York, 1991.

Hector C. Bywater, ***SEA POWER IN THE PACIFIC: A Study of the American-Japanese Naval Problem***, London, 1921.

Christof Friedrich (a pseudonym for Ernst Zündel), ***GERMANY'S ANTARCTIC CLAIM, Secret Nazi Polar Expeditions***.

Psychology Psychology Psychology

Mel Gordon, ***HITLER'S JEWISH CLAIRVOYANT***, Feral House, 2002; reviewed by The Linking Ring, The Official Publication of the International Brotherhood of Magicians, September 2002.

L. Sterpellone, ***VERY ILLUSTRIOUS PATIENTS***, Antonio Delfino Editore, 1987.

Walter Langer, ***THE MIND OF ADOLF HITLER***, Pan Books, 1972.

THE OSS [CIA] ***PSYCHOLOGICAL PROFILE OF HITLER, Part Four***.

Adolf Hitler, ***MEIN KAMPF*** (*My Struggle*), written in 1925, Hurst & Blackett Ltd, London, 1933.

Documentaries Documentaries Documentaries

Alex Turner (researcher), ***HITLER OF THE ANDES***, a film by David Howards and Madoc Roberts for Channel Four Television Corporation, 2002, as screened on Discovery Channel, 29/30 October 2004, 11.30 pm–0.30 am.

CAMBRIDGE SPIES, 3 September 2003, TV1.

David Gardner, ***LAST OF THE HITLERS***, a film by David Howards and Madoc Roberts, made for Channel 5 Television, screened on Prime TV, 29 July 2003.

WAS HITLER GAY? Directed by Fenton Bailey, Executive Producers Rand Barbato and Jacquie Lawrence, Producer Gabriel Rotello, Narrator Dennis Lawson, World of Wonder Production, Channel 5, 2002, as screened on TV3, 5 February 2004, 9.30 pm.

DESTINATION DISASTER, directed by Cheryl Cameron, Ninox Films Limited, 2002, screened on TV1, 1 November 2003.

THE NAZIS, A Warning from History, BBC, screened on TV1, August 1998.

Films Films Films

Guillermo DelToro, ***HELLBOY***, Columbia Pictures, 2004.

John Cork and Antonia de Barton-Watson, ***INSIDE DR. NO***, MGM Home Entertainment, 2000.

Harry Saltzman and Albert R. (Cubby) Broccoli (producers), Ian Fleming (author), ***DR. NO***, United Artists, 1962.

THE GREAT DICTATOR, produced, written, directed and scored by Charles Chaplin, 1940. The Chaplin Collection, mk2, directed by Kevin Brownlow and Michael Kroft, produced by Patrick Stanbury. Produced for Turner Classic Movies in association with BBC TV. ***The Tramp and the Dictator***, A photoplay and Spiegel TV Production, 2001.

David O. Selznick/Margaret Mitchell, ***GONE WITH THE WIND***, Metro-Goldwyn-Mayer, 1939.

FBI Files FBI Files FBI Files

Charlie Chaplin, ***FBI File Number 100-127090***, 1910–1952, 2063 pages.

Affidavits Affidavits Affidavits

Affidavit of Abdallah Melaouhi, 17 February 1994.

Affidavit of Professor Spann of the Institute of Forensic Medicine, 21 August 1987.

Affidavit of Professor Eisenmenger, Director of the Institute of Forensic Medicine, Munich, 21 August 1987.

Newspapers, Magazines and Articles . . .

NEW ZEALAND WEEKEND HERALD, 29 July 2006.

David Gollust, ***VOICE OF AMERICA NEWS***, Washington, 30 July, 2003.

Reuben Black, 'History', ***THE WIND, New Zealand Russian Monthly, Issue 81***, June 2003, p. 3.

John Maynard, ***AEROPLANE magazine***, December 2001.

Terry Gwynn-Jones, *The Flying Porcupine Earns Its Name*, ***AVIATION HISTORY***, March 1999.

Rob Nesbit, *A Travesty of the Truth*, ***AEROPLANE monthly***.

OTAGO DAILY TIMES, 30 April 1990.

THE ILLUSTRATED LONDON NEWS, January to December, 1947.

Reference & Cross-checks . . .

REFERENCE ATLAS OF THE WORLD, 2003.

David Crystal, ***THE CAMBRIDGE BIOGRAPHICAL ENCYCLOPEDIA***, Second Edition, 1998.

Alain Boureau, ***THE LORD'S FIRST NIGHT: The Myth of the Droit de Cuissage***, translated by Lydia G. Cochrane, University of Chicago Press, 1998.

NEW ETHICALS CATALOGUE, The Basis of a System of Complete Drug Information, Vol. 34, No. 2, Adia International, A Wolters Kluwer Company, November 1997.

Judy Pearsall and Bill Trumble, ***OXFORD ENGLISH REFERENCE DICTIONARY***, Second Edition, 1996.

PEARS CYCLOPAEDIA, 86th Edition, Anniversary Edition, 1897–1977, Pelham Books, 1977.

UNIVERSITY OF MICHIGAN DICTIONARY OF MIDDLE ENGLISH.

ENCYCLOPAEDIA BRITANNICA, 15th Edition, Volume 10.

Claude Jordan, ***VOYAGES HISTORIQUES DE L'EUROPE,*** Volume IV, 1694.

World Wide Web . . .

The 4 July 2003 was '***World Anti-Independence Day***' after which any government department could track anyone's computer.

Henry Makow PhD, ***The 'Ugly' Cause Of World War Two, The Murder Of Lord Erroll*** . . . (*White Mischief*) 30 April 2006.

FINANCIAL WIZARDS & WEALTHY CULTS: The Rothschild Bloodline, May 2005.

Chris Jones, ***BBC New Profiles Unit,*** 29 January 2003 and several other related websites.

Rob Evans and David Hencke, ***WALLIS SIMPSON, The Nazi Minister, the Telltale Monk and an FBI Plot,*** London Guardian, 29 June 2002.

Leonard Ingrams, ***THE BRITISH CONSPIRACY, Secret Agents, The Real 007s,*** 2002.

AIS website and ***AIIaS newsletter,*** www.medhelp.org,

US SECRET SERVICE

THE CIA WORLD FACTBOOK

The signature of Intelligence understanding used to be
"I understand Red Mercury."

Now its
"I understand how **RA**bbits **F**ornicate."

. . . **Fucking RAbbits** . . .

INDEX

Symbols

A

C

D

I

J

K

L

M

N

Q

R

S

T

X

Y

Z

Biographies

Greg Hallett trained in various psychological models in parallel with his architecture degree and training. He travelled widely behind the Iron Curtain during the Cold War, hitchhiking on planes and making bunks out of airmail bags to party and report between cities. His contacts in Eastern Europe led to deep penetration of the Soviet State, how it functioned and how it was to colonise the West. It was these qualifications that led him to buy buildings in Moscow immediately after the Berlin Wall fell. This led to interviews with the KGB and their revelations about the planned sex-communism and deconstruction of Westerners. What the Soviets planned for the West happened in the West. Equally all modern history can be dated back to 1945. What Hitler planned for the world happened to the world over the next sixty years.

"Before and after this meeting intelligence had a pattern of attaching themselves to me and the first person to do so was the King's doctor in 1967, quickly followed by the Queen's brother. In the build up to the Soviet meetings, those with intelligence backgrounds provided me with whatever training and cover they saw fit. Those with CIA backgrounds briefed me heavily from America to Greece and joined me in one operation prior. No operation was ever official, nor were they written up. Cover included haircuts, clothing, relationships, travel arrangements, concise and pertinent history briefings, word of mouth . . . and denial.

"I interviewed the KGB in Moscow on 9 December 1989 at a point when they were open, due to lack of pay. At the time you could buy information for the price of a meal. This led to some psychological information being supplied which led to international contacts, further training and meetings with James Bond III and the Spymaster. The Spymaster and other intelligence operatives have been briefing me for the past four years, resulting in ten books – four in this immediate series."

The Spymaster says that he will often go on operations and end up in entirely the wrong place with the wrong people at the wrong time, but always much wiser. Greg Hallett's attitude to history has been similar and the best information is uncovered by accident and without intention . . . "Perhaps the best intelligence gathering method is good table manners, good mental health, no fear, a small amount of wit, and the most ridiculous levels of courage that border on sheer stupidity to those who calculate such risk-and-rewards."

"One of the best intelligence gathering exercises I ever did was to stand in Moscow's Red Square at 1.23 pm on 5 December 1989 and yell out 'Mokrie Dela' [Wet Liquidations] at the top of my voice. This attracted spies to me like shit to a blanket. It also attracted sympathisers and sympathetic spies."

When the Spymaster teamed up with Greg Hallett they found they shared insights and historical answers to many of the controversies of Europe from WWII to the Cold War and the present . . . not disregarding aspects of the future. In listening to each other's stories they noted a lot of common ground and have attempted to lay this bare.

Through such coincidences, history is often more explicable to the ordinary man than a lot of complicated analysis. After embedded historians, we found 'filling-in-the-gaps analysis' to be a primary cause of ill-informed history. "Field experience is everything. Independent field experience is even better and accidental independent field experience is history altering."

The Spymaster has worked in a background of undeclared hostilities in many countries over many decades. He has done undercover amongst Nazis, Communists, Marxists and some of the most vicious gangs of criminals in New Zealand. Several times other people have been killed in his place in cases of mistaken identity. The Spymaster has been arrested more times than he can remember and by more outfits than he can remember and has been on both sides of enforcement operations.

The Spymaster has an in-depth knowledge of offenders in New Zealand and overseas and is often sought out by people in high places.

Former Prime Minister Rob Muldoon: "If St Peter ever made a mistake and let you into heaven, there'd be a fistfight in five minutes".

Many intelligence officers have been interviewed for this book and they have given the low-down on the many wars from 1936. In some cases, they, or their fathers, were the main players in the vignettes. These personal histories date back to the Spanish Civil War with George Orwell and redefine the origins of *Animal Farm*.

Greg Hallett and the Spymaster have teamed up to give you this insight into how the enemies of war are created and how enemies secretly join forces behind the veil of war. This book is not a dream within a dream, but a reality within a reality and the authors wake up each morning content they're still alive.

Above: The Spymaster shows his face.
Opposite: The author on his way to The Wall, Central Park, 4th July 1988.

As goes Hitler, so goes the moon . . . if you can't make it . . . fake it.

Printed in Great Britain
by Amazon

84435311R00323